A STUDY OF PALMISTRY SCIENCE

A STUDY
OF
PALMISTRY SCIENCE

A PRACTICAL TREATIES ON THE ART COMMONLY CALLED PALMISTRY

By

WILLIAM G. BENHAN

BKP

BHARATIYA KALA PRAKASHAN
DELHI (INDIA)

First Edition : 1937 London
Revised Edition : 2004

Published by **C.P. Gautam**
BHARATIYA KALA PRAKASHAN
3421-A, IInd Floor, Narang Colony, Tri Nagar,
Delhi-110035. Phone : 27393083, 30967505 (O) , 27522129 (R)

ISBN : 81-8090-058-4

Laser Type Setting by
A-ONE GRAPHICS
JD-18C, IInd Floor, Pitampura, Delhi-110053
Phone : 55640278, Mob. : 9811167357

Printed by :
BDH Printer at Salasar Imaging Systems
Delhi-35, Ph. 31045804, 30930620

PREFACE TO NEW EDITION

AS this is written, it is more than forty-five years since "THE LAWS OF SCIENTIFIC HAND READING" was first published. During the intervening years it has found its way into libraries in all parts of the world and into the hands of thousands of students. It is the book of reference for ninety-five per cent of all who are practicing Hand Analysis as a profession. I have received a constantly increasing number of letters from those who have, and are, using it as the basis of their work in Hand Analysis. I have been in personal contact with many thousands of owners since its first appearance. In no instance, either by correspondence or personal contact, has an indication been reported which was found unreliable. On the other hand I am constantly told of verifications, and of results accomplished by adhering to indications as presented herein. My universal experience has been when I meet a reader, I meet a friend.

From my own experience and that of others I have found no reason to change or correct any statement or indication contained in the book as originally published. Before considering an indication fully verified and ready for use, it was tested over many years of research and found reliable. This care in excluding every indication whose accuracy had not been fully demonstrated accounts for the fact that, during the past forty-five years, it has been found a reliable guide for those who have used it.

The TYPES of people who are the basis of this work have been identified in thousands of hands and proved to be the correct foundation upon which SCIENTIFIC HAND ANALYSIS must rest. From a proper use of these types as outlined in the following chapters has grown the science of Vocational Guidance which is producing such astonishing results at this time.

Attempts to solve the lines in the hands have for ages presented the stumbling block which has baffled authors and practitioners alike. The working hypothesis of an electric life current I introduced in the original publication in 1900 (Page 354 et seq.) removed this difficulty. It was offered as a working hypothesis in 1900: to-day it is a fact, proved by the discovery of scientific men that each brain cell is an electric dynamo, and energy generated by thought has been recorded on graphs. This book, therefore, contained the first workable method of reading any line in the hand, enabling the student to follow each line with its detail of events from beginning to end correctly, a result never obtained before, and possible in no other way now.

The scientific explanation of the reason why lines record the events covering the entire life, contained in Chapter I, part 2, in 1900, is the only one of the many theories advanced which has stood the test and been made certain by the greatly enlarged knowledge concerning the duality of the mind accumulated since that time by students of mental sciences. In other words, time has demonstrated and increased certainty in every department contained in "THE LAWS OF SCIENTIFIC HAND READING" as originally published in 1900.

My confidence in the hands as revealing the pattern of every life has constantly increased since the first publication. I am as firmly opposed to the use of the hand as a means of amusement and entertainment as I was at the time this volume was published forty-five years ago. My belief that hands furnish a means of guidance has, by experience, been made even more positive. Thousands of cases have demonstrated this to be true since the appearance of this volume in 1900. That the application of Hand Analysis to individual cases at the present time can assist in solving most of the problems of human life, I firmly believe to be true.

I, therefore, feel that a system of Hand Analysis which has stood the test in so many corners of the earth, for such a period of years, with the test being made by so many thousands of people, of so many nationalities, who comprise people with every point of view, has proved itself worthy of confidence. You, who own the book, can use it with renewed confidence. New owners may regard it as a safe guide which will not lead them astray.

Introducing an Appendix

With this, the 18th edition, there appears an Appendix. For the first time in its history there is an addition to the original text.

Thirteen years ago I felt it my duty to start the preparation of someone capable of succeeding me in carrying on my work. From a class of about one hundred students I was instructing at the time, I selected FLORENS MESCHTER who for the past thirteen years I have had under constant observation as she progressed in an earnest and serious manner, developing a rare talent for the work. She has taught and lectured to classes in my studio where I have had the opportunity to observe her in daily action and coach her when necessary.

The result has been that she has developed, in my opinion, into the most competent Hand Analyst in the world. This is said from personal acquaintance with the best in all the different countries. It is with full confidence in her ability that I asked her to prepare an appendix to the present edition which I heartily endorse as a valuable addition to the literature on the subject. The great and constantly increasing interest in Vocational Guidance now shown by scientific and medical men, personnel directors, business executives and heads of widely known educational institutions make such a text book as this new edition, with the newly added appendix, an event of moment for students, and those who wish to know themselves better, and to help others to know the truth about themselves and thus find their proper place in life.

WM. G. BENHAM
162 W. 56th Street
New York, N. Y.

INTRODUCTION

THERE has never been conceived or made by man any instrument, machine, or contrivance, capable of such a diversity of usefulness as the human hand. Nothing has ever existed with such infinite adaptability to various needs, or capable of being trained to such degrees of dexterity and versatility. Nor is it likely that as perfect a machine will ever be produced by human skill, for the only thing the human hand cannot do is to create an instrument as perfect as itself. There is no possible question but that the fineness or coarseness of a human hand indicates whether it can better do fine or coarse work, nor is there a doubt but that other markings on it show for what lines of work it is best adapted. The delicate hand of a lady cannot perform the same hard labor as the large, strong hand of a blacksmith, nor can the blacksmith do the fine embroidery so deftly wrought by the lady's hand. Neither has the blacksmith's brain the little embroideries of the mind. His brain is of heavier construction, hers more delicately built. His hand, like his brain, is heavy: her hand is fine like her brain. Never was there a hand that did not exactly reflect the brain that directs it, and this is the basis from which a scientific study of the hand must begin. To get at the secrets of the mind embodies the effort toward which scientific hand-reading aspires, for mind is the guiding force in life. Upon that hypothesis are based the teachings of this book.

PERSONALITIES

My special interest in the hand began at thirteen years of age, when by chance I fell in with an old gypsy who taught me what she knew of Gypsy chiromancy. This was not much, it is true, but enough to give direction to my thoughts. Hampered by the entire absence of any literature on the subject, my first efforts were very laborious. In the beginning it was necessary to take a mere tradition and apply it to hundreds of hands, noting the result. This was the first system adopted. Thus the investigation of a single indication often consumed a year, and in the end might be found unreliable and have to be thrown away. No help was found from professionals, for nearly all proved to be ignorant, unlettered, and trying solely to gain money, without any effort in the direction of scientific investigation. During most of this time the word *Palmistry* was so buried under a mass of public disapproval, that a self-respecting person dared not say that he was even interested in it. Fully persuaded that it had a scientific foundation, I set about to discover it. All my investigations led more and more to the belief that it was a subject well worthy of deep study, in search of the key, as yet undiscovered.

I soon found that Physiology played a most prominent part, and then that health as affecting temperament and character, was a leading factor. In order to prepare myself for a proper consideration of these matters, I studied medicine, so that I might be familiar with the entire anatomical construction of the body, and having gained entree to several hospitals, the State institutions for the imbecile, insane, blind, and deaf, the almshouse, jails, and a penitentiary, I used the inmates of these institutions as object lessons, by which means I gained much valuable information on health indications, criminology, and character. I secured all of the available literature on the subject, but it was of a fragmentary nature, only a small portion of it being reliable. I consulted palmists of every nationality, and learned what I could from them, which was practically nothing, for most professionals had frankly acknowledged to me that they knew very little about the hand, but relied entirely upon their natural shrewdness. I then began the study of separate classes and professions of men and women, taking the leaders of each class and studying them. Thus I examined the most prominent doctors, lawyers, ministers, speakers, actors, singers, musicians, literary people, hypnotists, spiritualists, murderers, forgers, and so on through the scale of human life. This investigation bore much fruit, and, combined with my previous work, gave me the foundation and confirmations from which I have built up the structure which this book contains.

That there is so much information in the hand will be a surprise to many, and when it is seen how logical, rational, and even commonplace, hand-reading is, perhaps it will then be taken out of the occult class to which it distinctly *does not* belong, and placed among the other rational means at the service of mankind, whereby they may be enabled to gain a better knowledge of themselves. In the preparation of this book, my ambition has been so to present this matter to the public, that they would see it from a novel point of view, and by disclosing the logical basis on which it rests, presented without a vestige of mysticism or occult halo, lift it from its position as an effete superstition, and place it among the modern sciences. My ambition has been to make Palmistry not an amusement, nor a centre around which cranks might congregate, but a study worthy of the best efforts of the best minds.

When we can tell our sons and daughters what sphere in life they are best fitted to occupy, and what studies they can best master, we shall have largely reduced the failures of young men and women. When we can prevent the marriage of people whose temperaments make it absolutely impossible that they should live together harmoniously, then we shall have largely decreased the number of divorces and wrecked lives. To do these things manifestly requires that we should have a correct estimate of the person with whom we are dealing. In the following pages the manner in which this may be done is outlined and explained. If this book, which is the essence of my labors, should bear the fruit I have desired and believed it would, if the intelligence of the reading public can find in these pages a crystallization of such facts as shall lead them to thoroughly investigate, I shall be satisfied to abide by the results, fearing not the issue.

ILLUSTRIOUS ILLUSTRATORS

The illustrations in the following pages are made from the hands of people located in all parts of the United States. The collection comprises hands of the most famous men and women of the age — those who have made history and ruled nations. The leaders of every profession and walk in life, politics, war, business, art, society, letters, or crime, are gathered here. As the subjects from whose hands these photographs, prints, or casts were taken, live in every part of this country, it has been the work of many years to collect them. Their value lies in the fact that they represent typical lives of typical people, with typical hands. Several reasons make it unwise to give names of the persons from whose hands illustrations have been secured, even though their well-known qualities would make the illustrations more convincing. In the first place, the largest number could not have been obtained except upon the pledge that no undue prominence would be given the original. Second, some hands illustrate markings which indicate undesirable qualities, with which it would not be wise or proper to identify living subjects.

REQUESTS AND ADVICE

The first thing that I wish you to do in approaching the study of Palmistry is to fix in your minds the definite plan on which it is based, as outlined in Chapter I., and to realize that it will require study and practice for you to become a proficient palmist. I make the request that you will constantly examine hands, but that you will not do so, posing as an expert, but with the explanation that you are a student gaining practice. I ask that you will never predict the death of anyone nor its date, that you will use great care and tact never to alarm a nervous subject, and that you will never read hands in a crowd for the amusement of the bystanders. I ask you to feel, with every hand you examine, that you wish to benefit the subject by pointing out ways to strengthen weak places, and I hope you will never be willing to humiliate or discourage anyone. Always remember that if you fail to verify indications, you have not judged the case correctly. The fault is not with the science but with your application of it. For this reason use great care in expressing your opinion; never do so without careful thought, and after a minute examination of the hand in its entirety. Remember that the whole worth of Palmistry will be judged from your standard of proficiency by the subject whose hand you are reading, and that if your work is careless, and you speak without a full knowledge of what you are saying, it will be damaging. In answer to the question often asked, "Am I adapted to the study?" there is but one answer. The more intellect, refinement, tact, and facility of expression you have, the more you can accomplish. The greater your knowledge of life in all its phases, the more skilful you will be. All can acquire by study a certain degree of proficiency; those who are best endowed mentally, and are also the best reasoners, will become the best practitioners.

No index has been prepared for this book. Hand reading as treated here is so entirely a matter of combination that no index which would be of value could be compiled. It is for this reason that it is omitted.

W. G. B.

CONTENTS

PART FIRST

PART SECOND

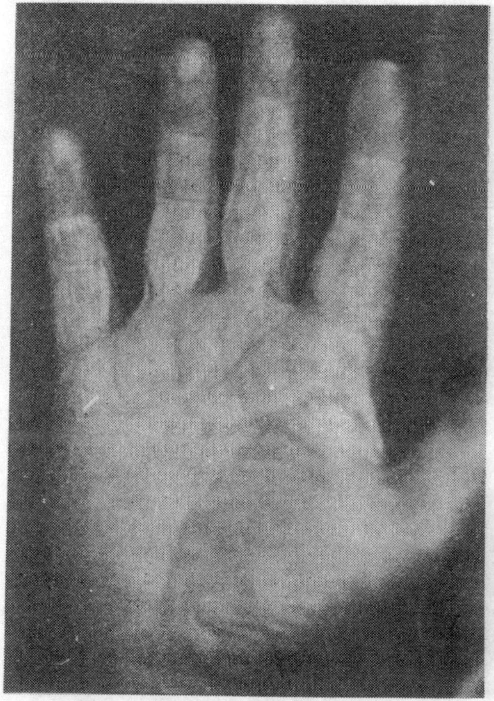

WM. DEAN HOWELLS, AMERICAN AUTHOR

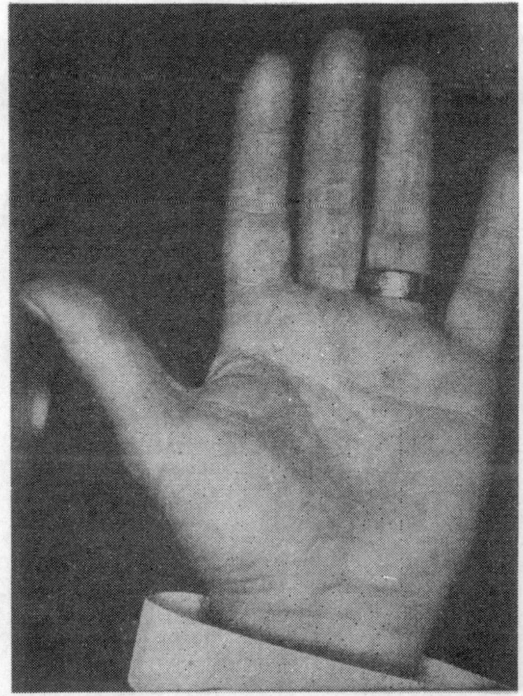

FREDERICK WARDE, AMERICAN TRAGEDIAN

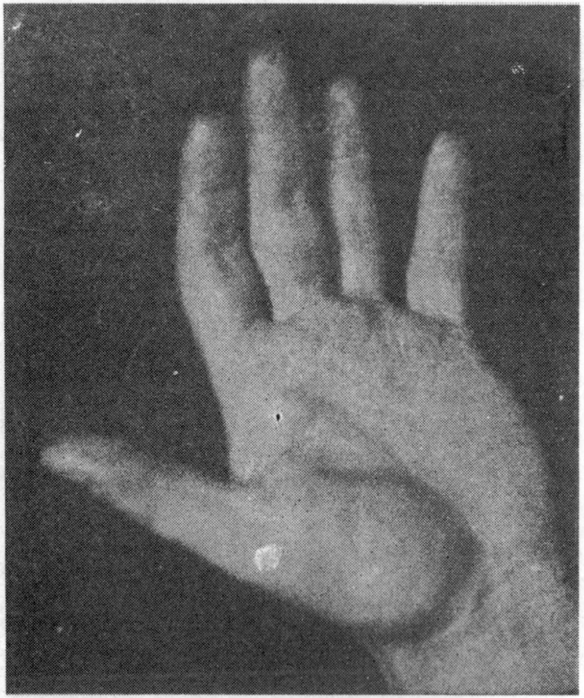

HERR MORIZ ROSENTHAL, THE HUNGARIAN PIANO VIRTUOSO

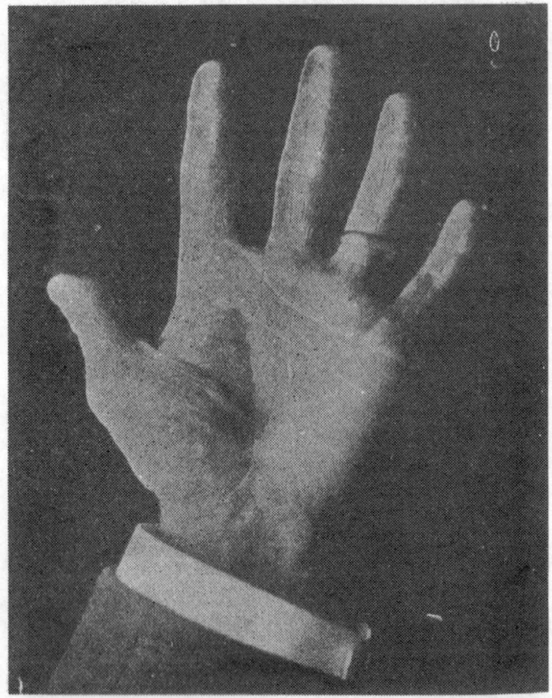

ROBERT FITZSIMMONS, WELL-KNOWN PUGILIST

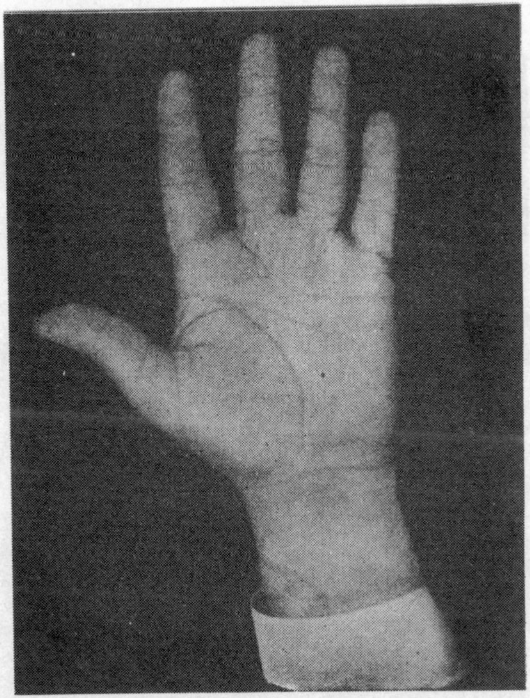

PROF. R. L. GARNER

Who built a steel cage, transported it to the African jungles, and lived there for four months, studying the language of the Apes.

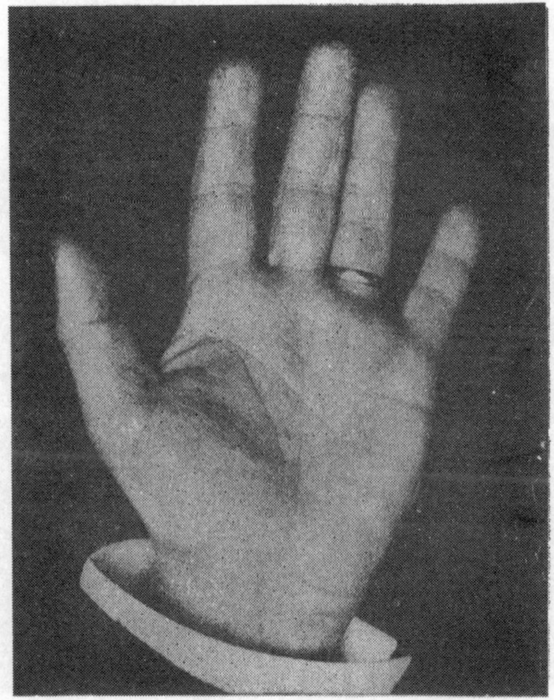

LOUIS JAMES, THE AMERICAN ACTOR

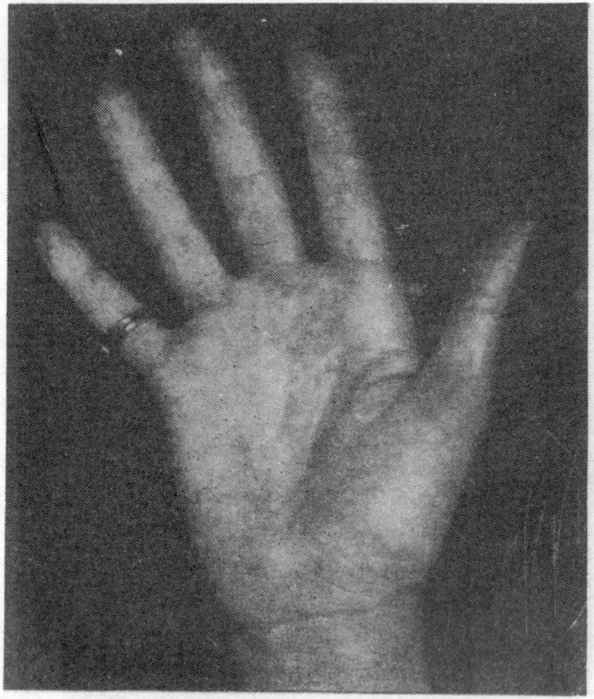

KATHRYN KIDDER, AMERICAN ACTRESS

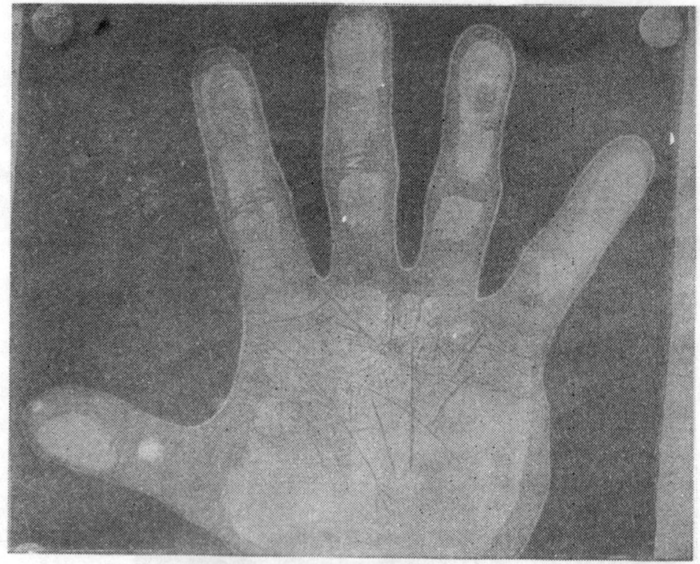

MARTINUS SIEVEKING, THE HOLLAND PIANIST

The largest hand since Liszt

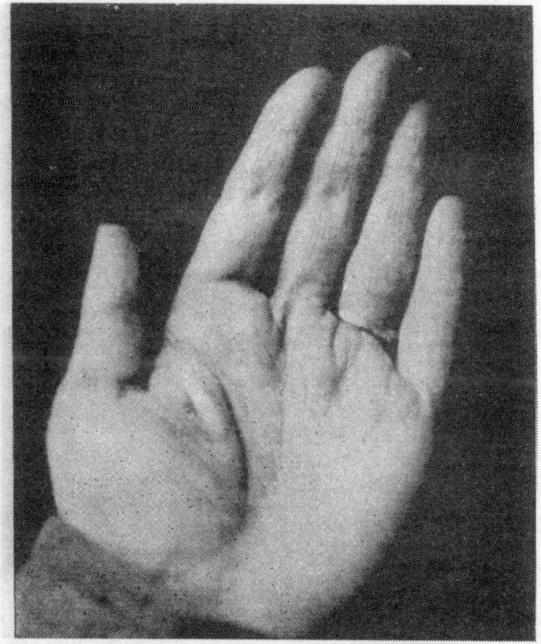

NAT. C. GOODWIN, AMERICAN COMEDIAN

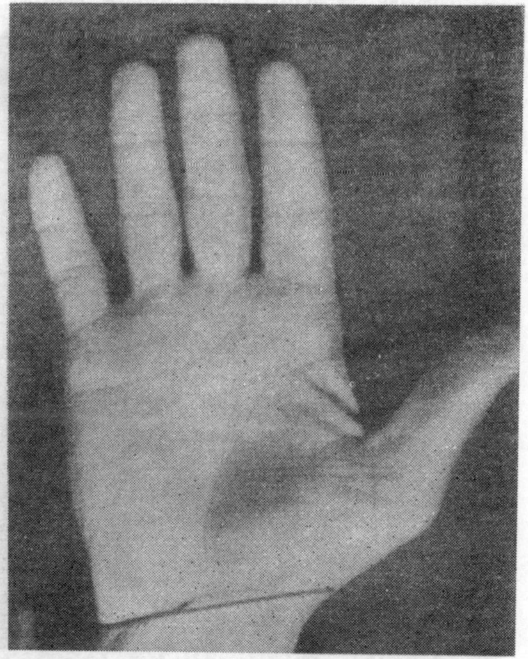

WILLIAM JENNINGS BRYAN, PRESIDENTIAL CANDIDATE, 1896-1900

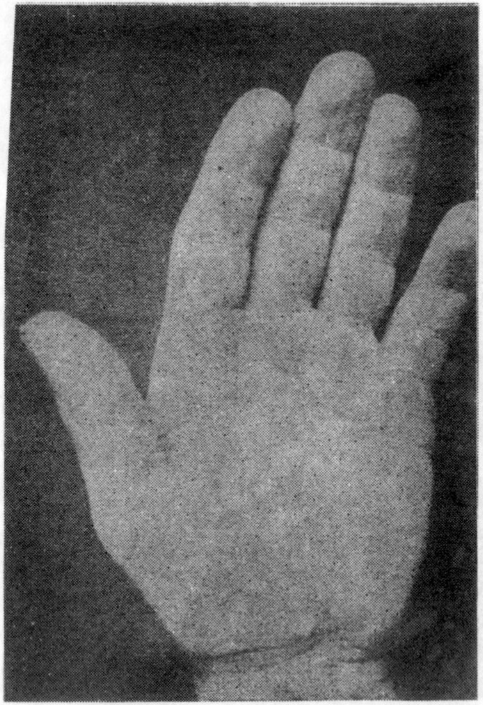

DAVID BISPHAM, OPERATIC BARITONE

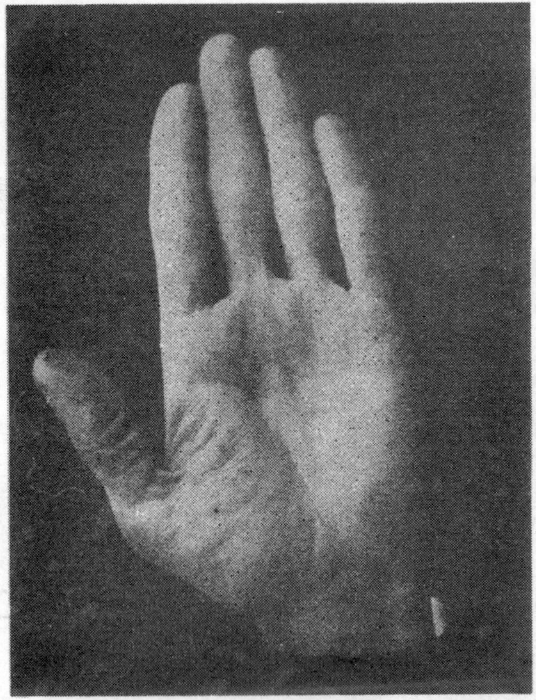

SAMUEL HARDEN CHURCH, AMERICAN HISTORIAN AND NOVELIST

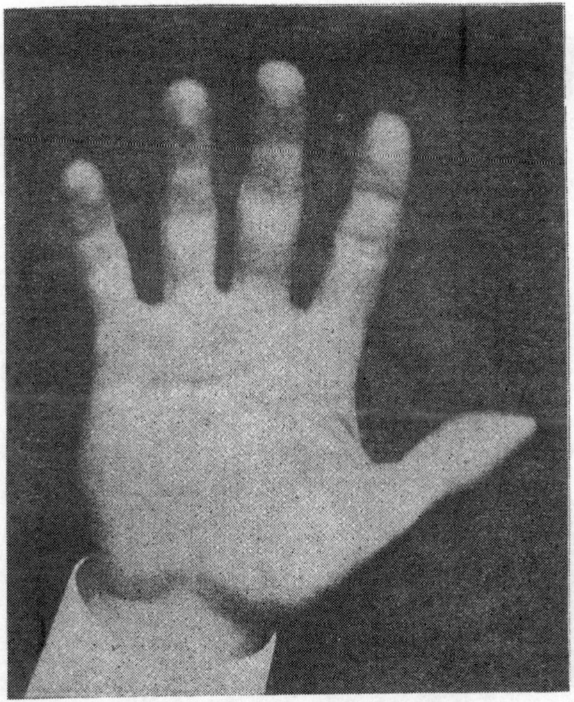

MARK HAMBOURG, THE RUSSIAN PIANIST

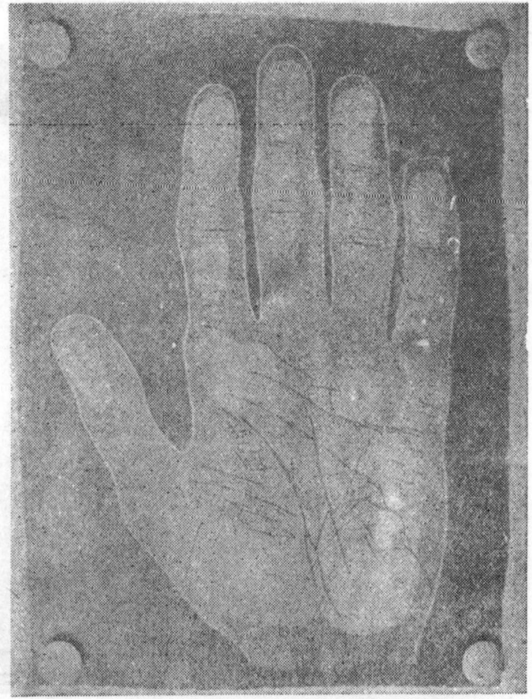

DR. X. LAMOTTE SAGE, A.M., LL.D., HYPNOTIST

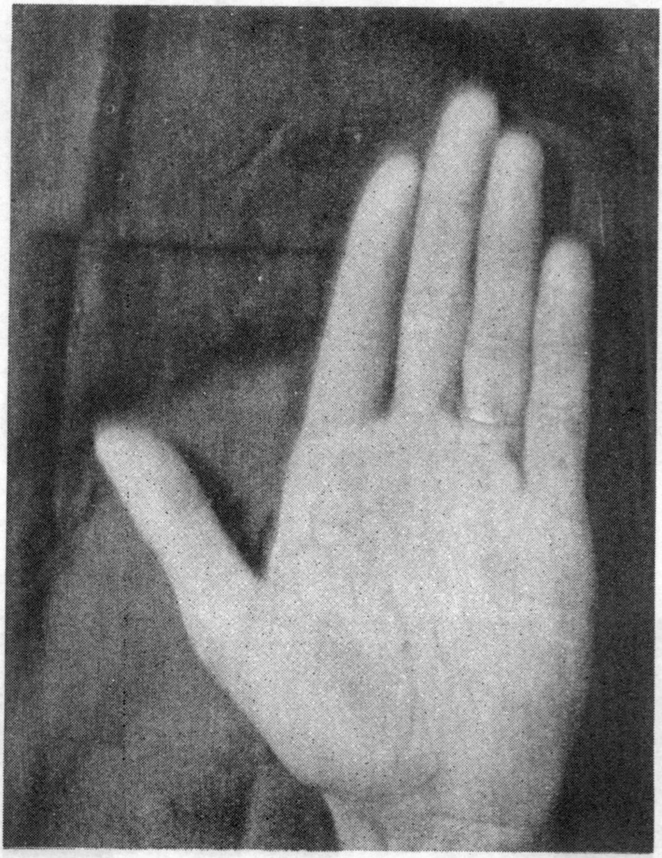

HENRY G. STARR

This noted outlaw, desperado, and murderer, was the terror of the border for about four years. He was leader of the Starr gang, who were contemporaries of the James, Dalton, and Cherokee Bill gangs. With four companions Starr rode into Bentonville, Ark., robbed the bank of $11,000, killed a United States Marshall and departed. He held up trains and terrorized the neighborhood of Fort Smith for four years. It is said that he has committed innumerable murders. Twenty seven indictments are now pending against him. Starr is a model prisoner, and says he is through "sowing his wild oats."

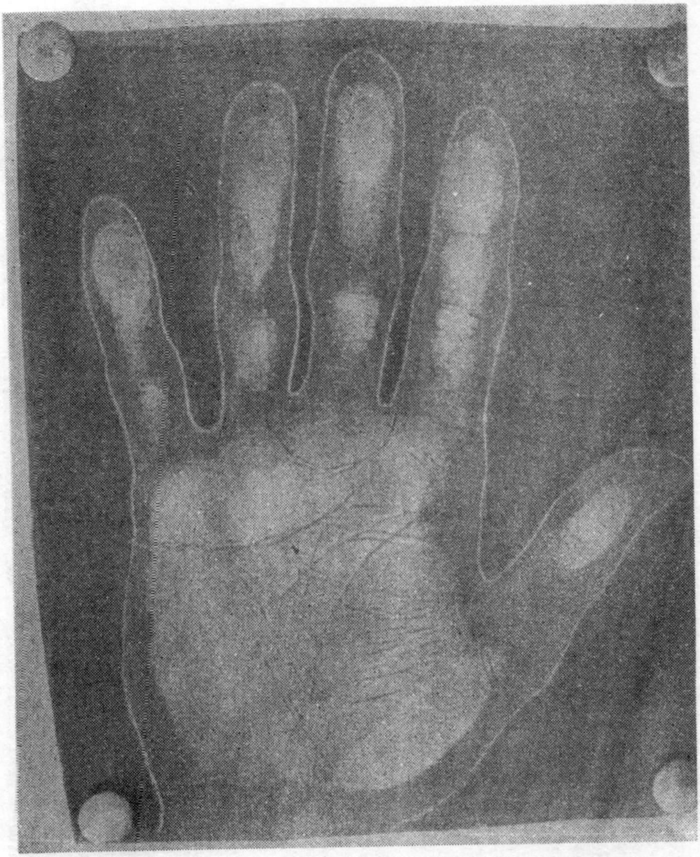

IRA MARLATT

The "Prison Demon," serving a life sentence for murder. He is very cunning, and, soon after his incarceration, procured weapons of various sorts with which he attacked and nearly succeeded in killing a number of guards. Nothing could be done to tame him, and finally a steel cage was built with no opening but a small door, in front of which a guard was constantly stationed. He seemed able in some mysterious way to procure wire, which he sharpened on the sides of his steel cell, with which terrible weapons he assaulted all who came near him. Kindness, and every conceivable means or punishment, has failed to subdue him. He has been fitly named the "Prison Demon." Marlatt has been the subject of great investigation by experts on insanity, who pronounce him sane. The day I secured this impression he came out of his cage, said he would do no violence, and kept his word. The guard with his gun stood near, however.

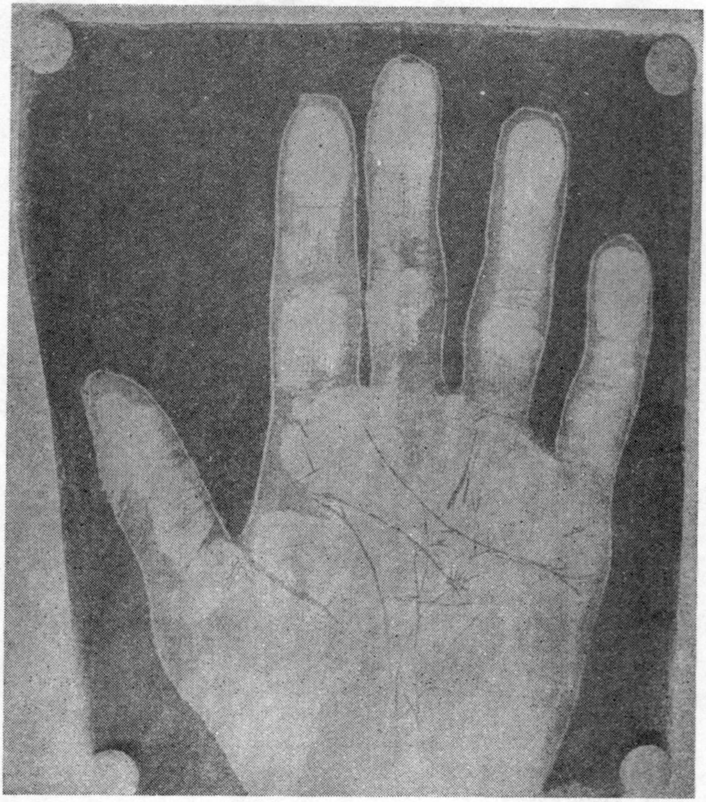

ALBERT J. FRANTZ

The murderer of Bessie Little of Dayton. This case was a celebrated murder mystery. Frantz was convicted on circumstantial evidence, and electrocuted November 19, 1898. His death is indicated on his Head Line.

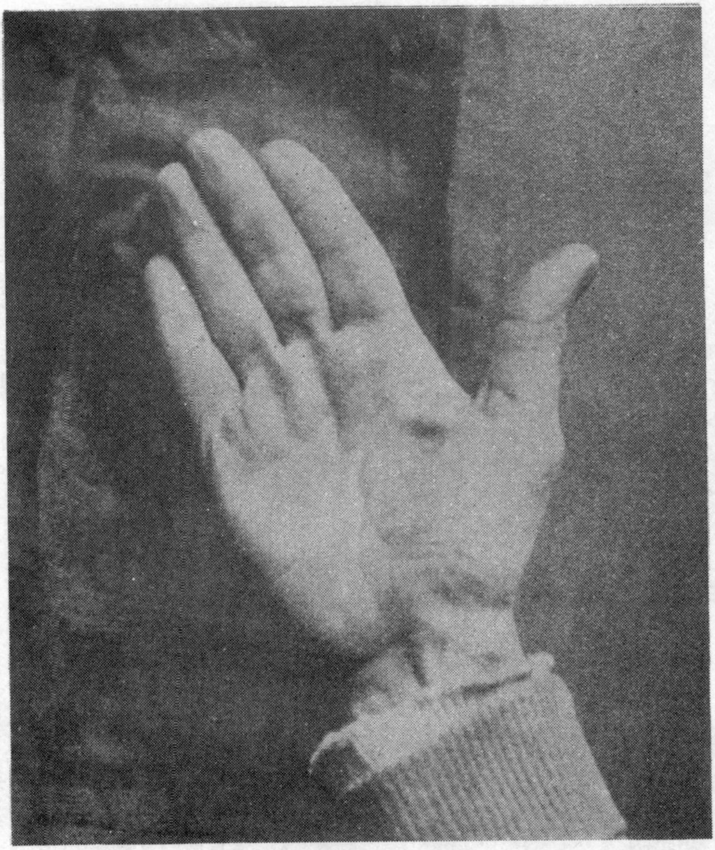

"FRENCHY" WING

One of the most noted pickpockets in the annals of criminal history. He is fifty years old, and has spent thirty-four years in penitentiaries all over the United States. He is very intelligent, writes well, speaks every known language, and has travelled much. His profession is picking pockets; he makes no denial of the fact, calls it "taking up a collection," and says he does not do half the harm nor steal as much as thousands of high-toned thieves who are called "able financiers." Says he only steals enough to support him, that his wants are few, he has no desire to be rich, and does not think that he taxes the community heavily. He thinks it time he was let alone, as he has been punished a great deal, and thinks the police should go after some of the big thieves instead of him. He says they have only to hand him into court, when he will be sentenced on his reputation. The following is his record in the United States: Blackwell's Island, N. Y., two sentences of six months each; Kings County, N. Y., penitentiary, one year; New Orleans Parish Prison, one year; Baton Rouge, Miss., one year; Joliet, Ill., four years; Sing Sing, N. Y., two and a half years; Albany, N. Y., two years; Auburn, N. Y., four years; Havana, Cuba, two years and four months; Ohio Penitentiary, three years and seven years; Hudson City, N. J., six months; Bridewell Jail, Chicago, one year. This latter sentence was served in 1893, "Frenchy" having been caught at the opening of the big show and kept locked up during its continuance. Besides these he has served terms in Alexandria, (Egypt), Constantinople (Turkey), Trieste (Austria), and Havana (Cuba). The displacement of his Head Line is the typical criminal marking.

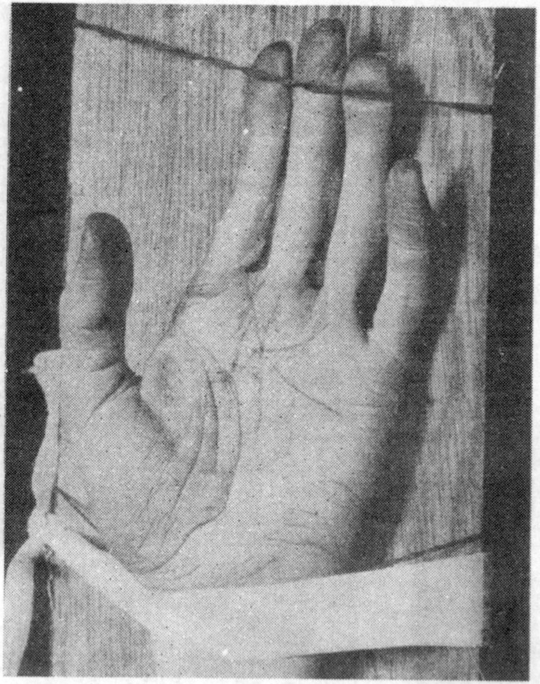 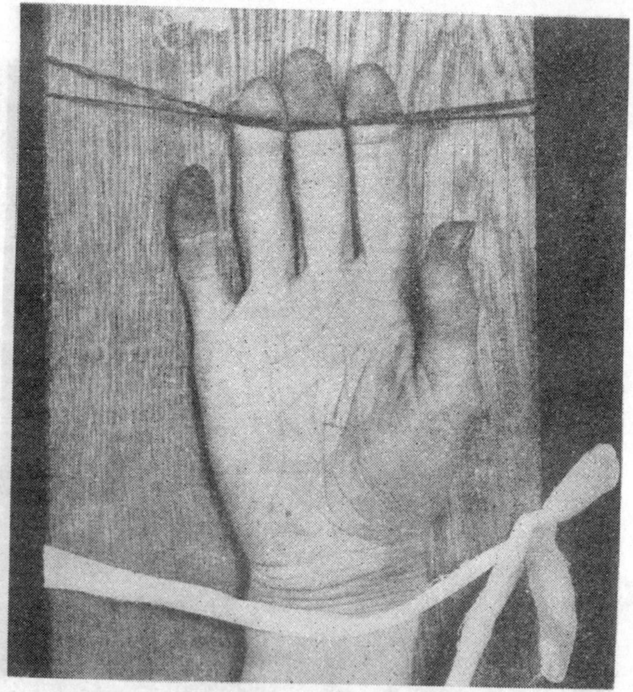

CHITTENDEN HOTEL SUICIDE

In November, 1898, a well-dressed, fine-looking woman came to the Chittenden Hotel, engaged a room for a few days, absolutely destroyed every clue to her identity, and killed herself. She took an enormous dose of morphine, supposedly to deaden the pain of the carbolic acid with which she completed her destruction. Her only request was for a respectable burial, to pay for which she left $150 in her purse. She lay for ten days at the morgue, her picture was printed all over the United States, but she was never identified. The pictures of her hands were taken the day before her burial. The Life Line shows a most remarkable confirmation of her death. The hand also shows the diseases which produce the mental condition necessary for the act.

PART FIRST

CHAPTER I

THE BASIS OF OUR WORK—THE PLAN OF CREATION—THE MOUNT TYPES

"Wisdom hath builded her house. She hath hewn out her seven pillars."—Proverbs ix., 1.

THE science of Palmistry is founded upon the shape of the hand. It is by the development of what are known as the Mounts, seven in number, which lie at the base of the fingers, and along the sides of the hand, by estimating properly their various combinations, that we are able accurately to delineate the character of any subject presented to us. There are other separated elements which enter into and add to a proper understanding of the science, viz.: the manner in which the hand is naturally carried and held when walking, the texture of the skin, consistency of the hand, color of the hand, the nails, hair on the hands, the hands divided into three sections called the three worlds, the shape of the fingers, and their individual phalanges, the shape of the finger-tips, knotty fingers, smooth fingers, long fingers, short fingers, and the thumb. All of these will receive separate and minute attention in subsequent chapters, and a thorough knowledge of them all is absolutely necessary.

Chapters on the above-enumerated subjects comprise the first half of the science of Chirosophy, and collectively form the science of Chirognomy. To this branch has always been allotted merely a study of the *character* of your subject, but it is capable of much greater usefulness, and a far greater scope than has hitherto been given it. There has been from the beginning of the world a perfectly well-defined plan under which the human species is brought into existence, and while by using the currently accepted types of Chirognomy many *attributes* and *qualities* belonging to humanity have been up to now possible of delineation from the hand, the limitations of a really scientific hand-reading from these types have been very quickly reached. This has led practitioners, in response to a demand from the public, to resort to much guessing, where a thorough knowledge of the plan of creation would have made guessing give place to reason; and as no scientific study can depend for its successful application upon guesswork, the whole fabric of Palmistry has of its own weight fallen to the ground. The plan of creation is exceedingly simple, easily understood, and can be verified in every person you meet. You do not have to take anything for granted, nor believe in anything you cannot see or touch or hold in your hand, consequently in this very practical and realistic age, the most advanced materialist can embrace the new science of Palmistry without offending in any way his sense of propriety. A knowledge of the plan of creation is gained from the Mounts in the hand, the exact locations and boundaries of which are correctly shown in the accompanying illustration "A."

The names which appear on the Mounts are not used in any astrological sense, but because they have been so long in use that the mention of each name instinctively brings to mind certain attributes. I use these names for I have found them a great help to the memory of the student, though any other names would do as well. They are not used because it is considered that planetary influences are necessary, or play any part, in our science.

The ancient theory of the seven distinct types of people

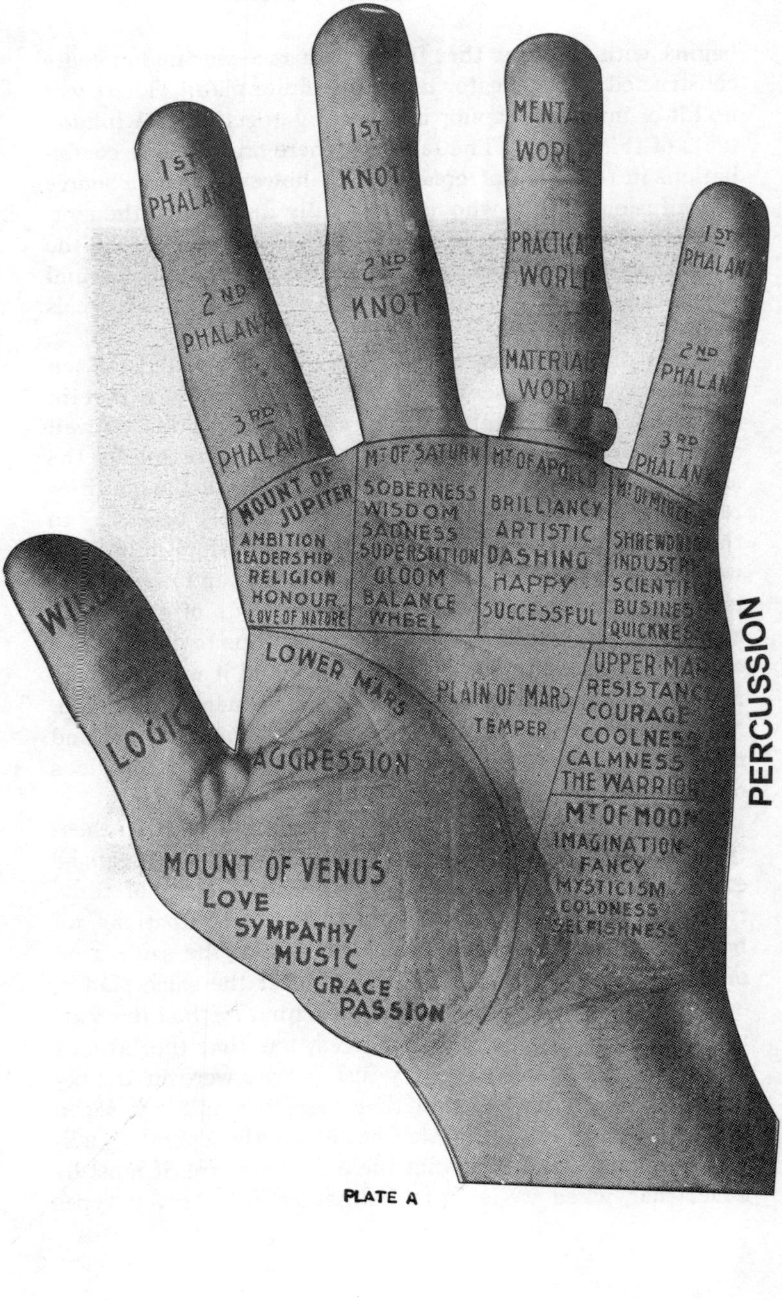
1ST
KNOT
2ND
KNOT
2ND
3RD
MOUNT OF JUPITER
AMBITION
LEADERSHIP
RELIGION
HONOUR
LOVE OF NATURE
MT OF SATURN
SOBERNESS
WISDOM
SADNESS
SUPERSTITION
GLOOM
BALANCE
WHEEL
BRILLIANCY
ARTISTIC
DASHING
HAPPY
SUCCESSFUL
QUICKNESS
LOWER MARS
PLAIN OF MARS
TEMPER
AGGRESSION
LOGIC
COURAGE
CALMNESS
THE WARRIOR
MT OF MOON
IMAGINATION
FANCY
MYSTICISM
COLDNESS
SELFISHNESS
MOUNT OF VENUS
LOVE
SYMPATHY
MUSIC
GRACE
PASSION
PERCUSSION

PLATE A

begins with the idea that the human race was undoubtedly constructed by its Creator under a definite plan. There was no hit-or-miss in shaping and putting together the inhabitants of this globe. The fact that there are so many combinations in this plan of creation has, however, been a source of confusion to those who have not fully understood the matter, but everything in this plan has been worked out by the Creator under the operation of specific laws and rules, and when these laws are understood, the whole plan reveals itself.

Seven distinct types of people were first created. Each of these types represented certain strong qualities, certain strong aptitudes, certain virtues, and certain faults, as well as peculiarities of health and character. The reason for the adoption of this plan was that a combination of the qualities represented in these seven types was absolutely necessary to the harmonious operation of the universe. If all humanity was of one type, progress would be stopped, and diversity of talent and thought, with its various methods of expression and operation, would not be present with us to-day. Take out of existence any one of these types, and it would be like removing one wheel in a watch,—the movement would stop. Each type was thus created for a specific sphere in life, and represents some element indispensable to the harmonious operation of the world as a whole.

The fact that there are well-defined specimens of all these types on the streets of our cities to-day, that they can be easily recognized, and that eighty-five per cent. of these typical people are at their best in the same occupations, all have the same faults, the same virtues, like the same kind of surroundings, live, think, and act after the same plan in everything they do, proves that the original method in creating humanity has not been changed, but that the laws of creation are in operation to-day just as they were in the beginning. If we can feel sure that there are, as I say, seven types of people, each of which has distinctly separate qualities, and if we can know what these qualities are, it must be a fact that, when we learn to distinguish these seven types from each other as we meet them, we shall at once know their characteristics, what people of their type have done through ages past, and what the outcome of their life is likely to be, judged by those of the same type who have gone before. From this point of view we can include a knowledge of the past, for we know what ancestors of the same type have always done; the present, for we know what the typical people always do; and the possible future, for we know what the outcome generally is. And here I say that the correct reading of the past, present, and possible future is based absolutely upon your recognition of the Mount type to which your client belongs, after which recognition you can apply to him what you know is common to the type which he represents. For example, the Jupiterian is always ambitious and a leader of men in whatever sphere of life he occupies; the same knowledge would apply to his health, his food, his home life, his religion, his business, his natural proficiency for certain employments, his vices, his passions, manner of living, thoughts, liability to marry or remain single, the kind of person he always marries, and everything else about him. This type has always the same ideas on all of these matters. Every other type has its own peculiarities. Thus, if your client is a pure specimen, you know he has them all, as have his predecessors of the same type. One type marries young, another marries people older than themselves, another avoids marriage entirely. If you have recognized the type to which your client belongs, you can tell him what he will be likely to do in these matters. Some types are long-lived, some die earlier, and, recognizing your type, you can handle this most delicate subject properly. Length of life, however, is a field that should seldom be approached at all, certainly not unless you are absolutely proficient, careful, and tactful, and no system but that of the types which I am outlining here will enable you to handle this most delicate question without harm to your subject. In fact, all that there is to destiny or fate is this matter of the seven types. Humanity is cast in certain moulds, and unless the course of a type is changed it acts, thinks, lives, and dies in a certain way ; the ancestors of this type have so lived, acted, and died, and it will do the same. If all the people in the world were *pure specimens* of one or the other of these types, then we might be fatalists in the extreme, but the deeper you go into a study of Palmistry the less will you accept an absolutely fatalistic doctrine. In every case, one type or the other will be predominant, its qualities will be the strong controlling element in the life of your client, and in his course through the world the qualities of his type will largely guide and shape his destiny. But there is nearly always present an alloy of some other type, something that may soften the severe lines of his natural mould. If he strongly *wishes* to change his course in life, is fully conscious of what he wants to accomplish and has determination enough, he may modify the qualities of his type to a large degree. A knowledge of his shortcomings, coupled with desire and determination, will enable him largely to overcome them. Since they all emanate from the brain, these faults, these desires, these changes, will all be written on the hands.

People do not change their typical qualities until they have a strong desire to change, and are armed with a firm resolution to do it. Thus it will seem that there is no greater truth than that we are indeed free agents, planned for a prearranged destiny, but always able to change it if we determinedly desire to do so. There is, then, no such thing as absolute fatalism, even though we have so strong an indication in that direction from the seven types. The statement, " The Lord helps him who helps himself," applies.

Thus, instead of rebelling at what might seem a cruel predestination on the part of our Creator in adopting the plan of the seven types, we can see that there is nothing unkind in the operation of this plan. You see the Esquimaux living always in the same way. One generation succeeds the other, lives the same way, eats the same food, reaches the same age, and dies. There is nothing cruel in that; you have never thought that fate was unkind to the Esquimaux. He would laugh at you if you told him so. He enjoys life in *his* way, just as well as you do in *yours*. Each of our seven types reasons in the same fashion. They are best pleased with *their* way of living, thinking, and acting, *they* prefer it to your way. They think you odd that you do not see it as they do. You think it strange that they can be satisfied at all with their ways. Thus the world moves on, seemingly a heterogeneous mass, yet in reality possible of subdivision into seven well-classified types of people.

There is another fact about these types: they look alike, and in my future treatment of the subject I shall give you mental illustrations of their appearance. Thus, knowing each type well, what they look like, how they reason, live, think, work, play, treat their fellows, or marry, as well as their natural occupations and peculiarities, you can, when you meet one of a certain type, dissect him with ease, knowing him better than he knows himself.

The Mount of Jupiter is the place from which you locate the Jupiterian type, the Mount of Saturn identifies the Saturnian, the Mount of Apollo the Apollonian, the Mount of Mercury the Mercurian, the two Mounts of Mars the Martian, one of whom is filled with aggression, the other full of resistance, the Mount of Moon the Lunarian, and the Mount of Venus the Venusian. The Plain of Mars is a part of the Martian type. It may be asked with some reason, Why do the Mounts identify these types? To this question the answer must be given, that at this time we have not fully solved the mystery, but there are some facts leading in that direction which will doubtless in time give us a full explanation of the matter; for we know that the human hand, which is the servant of the brain and which *executes* all of the work we do, only operates in response to the commands of the brain. Sever the connection between hand and brain by cutting the complex system of nerve telegraph uniting the two (as in paralysis), and the hand becomes like a lump of putty, dead and useless. The hand, which is the most wonderful instrument ever created, cannot perform one act *by itself*, for there is no brain or intelligence located *in* the hand to direct it, but all that it does is *by command* of the brain, the seat of mind and intelligence, which is located a considerable distance from the hand itself. This shows that the hand is entirely dependent on the brain for its intelligence, and that, being the servant, it reflects the kind of brain behind it by the manner and intelligence with which it performs its duties. It is a well-accepted fact that the centre of the brain, which is in connection with the hand, has been located, and dissections show that different formations of this brain centre are found accompanied by differently shaped hands. This proves that the hand physically shows what kind of a brain is directing it. If the brain centre which controls the hand is of one shape, the Mount of Jupiter will be largest, and we shall have a Jupiterian brain centre creating Jupiterian thoughts, ways and peculiarities, and the result will be that we have a Jupiterian subject. If this brain centre changes its form the subject develops peculiarities of character, aptitude, and disease, and we shall find other Mounts most developed, for the hand reflects all the changes of the brain, and the subject will belong to the type as shown by the best-marked Mount in the hand. This is unquestionably the idea from which future scientific research will gain a full explanation of the Mounts. In the Chapter, "Mounts and Fingers: How to Judge Them," I have given minute directions for classifying your subject, and when this is done you have solved *the secret of his creation*, and there is nothing about him which you cannot know. This is the *inner secret of Palmistry*, which professionals and amateurs, to whom I have taught it, declare has made them able to attain a proficiency they never hoped for nor believed possible.

The good types are the Jupiterian, Apollonian, and Venusian. These types have good health, happy dispositions, and do not easily become evil. The Saturnian and Mercurian easily cross the boundary and produce bad people. They are both bilious and become warped in their views and manner of life. The Martian easily becomes an ardent, intense type, not necessarily bad, but often violent. The Lunar subject is imaginative, cold, and selfish, easily producing a restless, disagreeable person. Thus you have three good types, two that *may* be bad, one violent, and one which may be disagreeable.

It will be apparent to those who have studied other authorities on Palmistry, that this work, with the Mounts for a basis, opens a rich field for investigation. Many realize how superficial their work has been, and have longed to know *why* they could go only so far and no farther. Without wishing to be captious, I must say that it is because, so far as I have been able to ascertain, no other work begins upon the proper foundation. The elementary hand (dulness), the square hand (regularity), the spatulate hand (activity and originality), the philosophic hand (analysis), the conic hand (artistic sense), the psychic hand (ideality), and the mixed hand (versatility) are the accepted types of all other modern works. These formations show only a certain *quality* of the subject; they do not reveal *him* in his entirety. They show only certain *traits*: they will not tell you of his health, how he marries, loves, hates, eats, lives, dies, whether he is good, bad, cross, or cheerful; they do not thus open the hidden recesses of his heart, as they are revealed by the Mount types, nor can you make that subtle distinction between *disease* and *character* except through the Mount types. The works of other recent authors start from certain *qualities* of the subject (regularity, activity, etc.); *this* work starts from *the man himself*, *created to fill a particular place*, and endowed with all the qualities necessary to enable him to do it. Is it any wonder that greater revelations should come from such a beginning?

The success of hand-reading is a matter of combination. The type of a subject must be combined with his energy, brain power, good intentions, vices, health condition, and many other important factors, before a balance can be struck. Herein lies the difficulty in preparing a treatise on hand-reading. If the types are treated first, the beginner has no knowledge of the important underlying forces which must be combined with them. If the underlying forces are first discussed, the student is not familiar with the types. In the present work the leading attributes of the types are laid down in this chapter and shown in illustration "A." With this illustration and these attributes in mind, a sufficient knowledge of the types to *begin with* is obtained, and we pass to a thorough consideration of the underlying forces. When these have been fully mastered, we will take up a thorough discussion of the types, and will then have in our possession all the knowledge to combine with them. Thus the final chapters on the Mount types unfold the entire panorama, the difficulties in arranging the sequence of treatment of the various matters is reduced to a minimum, and put in the best form for the student's use.

CHAPTER II

THE HUMAN ENGINE — BIRTH OF THE CHILD — THE LIFE CURRENT—A TALK TO PARENTS—GENERAL ATTRIBUTES OF THE LINES

"Mankind are earthen jugs with spirits in them."—HAWTHORNE.

THE human body, the earthly tenement of the mind or soul, is, in construction and operation, very like the mechanical contrivance we call an engine ; with this difference, that the human engine is constructed of bone and sinew, the mechanical engine of wood, iron, and steel, but each is made up of an infinite number of parts. Every mechanical engine is built upon the plan that will best enable it to do the *kind* of work it is intended to perform ; some are so small that their mission is to become the interior works of a watch; some are built to propel a locomotive at high speed, and others to furnish power to some gigantic manufacturing establishment. In each case the plan of construction and size varies in accordance with the work to be done. The engine, no matter what may be its magnitude or power, is only a shell, a thing of great possibilities, but entirely useless and inoperative until the driving or propelling force which is to set it in motion is applied. This driving force is in some cases steam, in others water-power, compressed air, electricity, or, as in the case of the watch, the mainspring. In whatever way the compressed energy or driving power is generated, it is made available only by combining a large number of primary elements and forces. Thus with steam, water is necessary, a boiler to hold it, fire to heat the water, a place in which to burn the fire, and fuel with which to build it. All other driving forces are in the same way made up from distinct and separate elements which, combined, will produce their *particular* kind of power. The engine, we have said, is useless without the driving force, which operates it, and it may be added that the driving force, if it has no engine to operate, only wastes itself in the air. The human body is the human engine ; it is built and especially adapted for specific purposes, it is the most complex of all machines, but it is entirely useless until the proper driving force is behind it. In its first stages of growth, the human body is a mere piece of protoplasm ; it is not until the dawn of mind and the awakening of intelligence manifest themselves that the human embryo becomes a human being. We all know that life, the vital spark which enters our body and sets in motion the organs of mind and sense and makes us *live*, comes into us from a source outside of ourselves. The child before it is born is truly a human being, but it is alive only as any other organ of the mother's body is alive, viz.: it acts in a mechanical way and has motion. This unborn child while in the process of formation, is *getting ready* to live, to think, and act, but until the vital spark of intelligence is projected into it, it does not *really* live. Just as the nose *will become* the future organ of the sense of smell, the ear of hearing, the eye of sight, so the lines in the hand are prepared and *in* the hand, ready to receive the spark that will set the *entire machinery* in motion. And when the vital spark of life has entered the body, as we believe through the ends of the fingers, and causes the nose, eyes, and ears to perform their functions, it at the same moment causes the hand to do its part. The unborn child has not life in the fullest sense: the corpse has not life,—life has departed. You or I cannot impart life to either, neither can they impart life to themselves. Argue as men will against the existence of God, they cannot deny that there is *some omnipotent force outside of us all* that *gives life* and *takes it* without consulting our wishes. Some have called this force Buddha, some Ether, some Electricity, some God, some the influence of the Planets. Whatever the name, the result is the same. But for the *purposes of Palmistry* you must at least imagine that a life current runs through the human body, and that it comes from an outside source. I have observed in the birth of many children the moment at which the awakening takes place, and I have asked physicians to observe for me the same thing in the patients coming under their practice. The results have always been the same. At the moment the child is born, and before it has given the first cry, or taken air into the lungs, the fingers extend with a quick, spasmodic jerk, stand perfectly straight and rigid, and, following this involuntary motion of the hands, the lungs take in air, and a cry escapes from the lips. *Life* has begun. Shortly after, the child feels hunger, and the hand goes at once to the mouth. The brain is acting, and directing her servant, the hand, which seeks to carry food to the mouth, the proper place to receive it. Thus from the first moment of life, the hand takes its place as the servant of the brain, and I believe that *at the moment* the fingers of the child extend, and become straight and rigid, that *life*, the *vital spark* which sets the human machinery in motion, awakens the mind, and habilitates the senses, is projected into the child through the ends of the rigid fingers, and thus becomes the gift of God to His creature. But I do not ask you to believe in any name for this outside force. Call it what you please, but if you will picture to yourself that life comes into the body as above described, this conception will greatly aid you in reasoning out many combinations that you will encounter in your future studies.

Now after life has begun and the child is in the world, a human engine with its driving force, it has a career before it. For the first few months it is little more than an animal, as all of its time is spent in sleeping, eating, and growing. During this period, its hands, by the thick development of the third phalanges of the fingers, show it to be a mere sensualist whose sole desire is to satisfy its hunger. As months roll into the first year, less sleep and less feeding are necessary, and as years increase and mind develops, the trend of its thought begins to manifest itself. During all this time the brain is unfolding, and the hand is changing from the fat little sensual hand of the baby, and taking whatever shape is distinctive to the type to which the child belongs. Up to the age of twelve to fourteen years, the hand is as unformed as the character of the child; but as this age marks the transition from the child to the adult, soon after it is passed the character and hands will begin to assume the proportions which are to guide it in the future. This is the time when a scientific estimate of the character of the child —its type, whether good, bad, or weak in development, together with a knowledge of all the forces back of it—would be of inestimable value to a parent. It is much easier "to correct a fault before it occurs," than to obliterate a habit thoroughly established. It is much easier for a child to learn what it loves and can understand, than for it to master studies for which its mind is not adapted. The child is an engine, and while you may by shifting belts, cogs, and wheels make a locomotive run a saw-mill, you have spoiled the twenty-thousand-dollar locomotive, which was a much finer machine when devoted to its proper uses than it is in its changed condition, and it does not run the saw-mill as well as a little upright engine would, which was built for the purpose at a cost of only about five hundred dollars. Thus, from a lack of knowledge about the human engine, millions of failures are seen of people who could successfully have done the things they were intended to do, but who have grown sour, discouraged, and unsuccessful when forced into vocations for which they were never created. Is this the fault of the Creator? Truly not, for the more one studies His handiwork the more comes the conviction that everthing has been provided for. He made the human hand a reflector of the brain, and He wrote in it a language plain, simple, and easy to understand, which He intended that we should use for our benefit, for He put in human brains the key by which this language could be read. But *man*, all-important in his own wisdom, yet with ignorance as dense as night, has been blind to his own advantages and refused to decipher the story plainly written for his guidance. Some well-meaning folk have laughed and sneered at those investigations having for their object the solving of this great problem, the knowledge of character and aptitudes, and in addition have asked, "Is it not wrong to pry into the secrets of the Almighty?" Such a question, well-meaning in its intentions, is equal to the ignorance of the dark ages, and in no sense is it in touch with the progress of science in this century, when the secrets of the Almighty have been unfolded by those who have discovered and harnessed electricity, and liquid air, and who have made many useful additions to the sum-total of those gifts for which humanity should be grateful to its Creator. No one will say it is "prying into the secrets of the Almighty" for the botanist to study flowers; he sees lines in the leaves which tell him a story and his work is scientific. No one will say that it is prying "into the secrets of the Almighty" for the physician to study disease; he looks at your tongue and tells you that your liver is torpid. The liver and tongue are connected through the alimentary canal, and the tongue reflects the liver. Why is it "prying into the secrets of the Almighty" for the palmist to look at your thumb, and tell you that your will-power is deficient? The centre of the brain is in direct connection with the thumb, and *Will* being a mental quality, why is it so ridiculous that the thumb should reflect this quality of the brain? It is not; *scientific* Palmistry is perfectly logical, and all its deductions are reached from an estimate of the mental and physical condition of the subject. The time has arrived when the intelligence of the world should no longer permit the lives of children to be hampered, impeded, and ruined by the fact that they are forced into vocations in which they can never be successful, when by the conscientious use of our science they can be guided to their proper sphere in life. Many who have reached adult years as failures have asked the question, "What right has the Creator to plunge me into this world without my consent, leave me ignorant of myself, give me no knowledge of the future, allow me to become wicked, careless, or corrupt, and then visit a judgment or punishment upon me?" The Creator has not done this; He has written what you want to know in your hand, but human ignorance and folly have refused either to read it or to allow it to be read. Many have heard when it was too late what they *might have been*. *The time to prevent the failure is before it occurs*, by starting with the child.

Let us approach this study with minds filled with its seriousness, for in no other way can we fully receive its benefits ; and let us put aside forever the idea that its whole object is to tell a gushing maiden of her lovers. The human being, then, is the human engine. The type will tell us for what purpose the engine was created. If this engine is to operate to the best advantage, it must be balanced in all its parts, no one portion so heavy that it overweighs the others. If such a state exists, the machine runs sideways or twisted, and the human being is out of proportion, narrow and warped. A perfect balance is what we seek, and when we find a perfectly balanced hand we find a balanced character and a person who succeeds by steadiness of manner and movement, and not through efforts put forth by fits and starts. It is very certain that brains and health are absolutely necessary to success. Health may sometimes be absent, but brains never. So, in our study of man, we are constantly trying to see how well balanced, how healthy, and how brainy he is. The first portion of our study will be given to Chirognomy, which does not relate to the lines in the hand ; and this section must be thoroughly mastered before the lines can have any meaning for you. For this reason, I ask that you will take each of the following chapters in succession, as this will lead you gradually to a thorough understanding of the fundamental matters which will enable you to appreciate the finishing chapters which treat exhaustively of the Mount types. As we shall refer at times to the lines in the hand before reaching their full consideration, I insert a map at this point showing the seven main lines (Plate B); the location, character, and general attributes of which should now be learned.

The Line of Heart will show the strength or weakness of the affections, and the physical strength of the heart. The clearer, more even, and better-colored the line is,

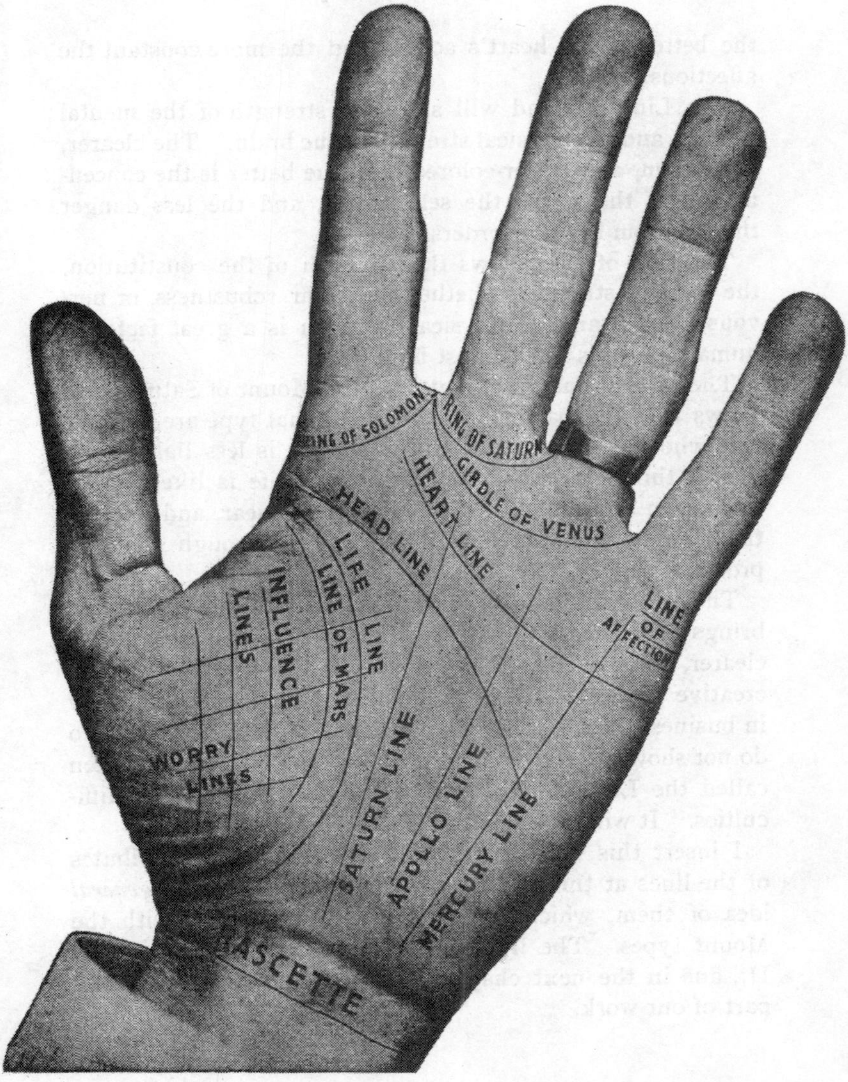

RING OF SOLOMON
RING OF SATURN
GIRDLE OF VENUS
HEAD LINE
HEART LINE
LIFE LINE
LINE OF MARS
INFLUENCE LINES
LINE OF AFFECTION
WORRY LINES
SATURN LINE
APOLLO LINE
MERCURY LINE
RASCETTE

PLATE B

the better is the heart's action, and the more constant the affections.

The Line of Head will show the strength of the mental powers, and the physical strength of the brain. The clearer, more even, and better-colored it is, the better is the concentration of the mind, the self-control, and the less danger there is from brain disorders.

The Line of Life shows the strength of the constitution, the kind of strength, whether muscular robustness, or nervous energy, and, as physical strength is a great factor in human life, this line is most important.

The Line of Saturn accentuates the Mount of Saturn, and shows that the balancing qualities of that type are present. One who has these restraining elements is less liable to do foolish things, and the course through life is likely to be more even and smooth. The more even, clear, and straight this line is, the more even the course through life will probably be.

The Line of Apollo accentuates the Mount of Apollo, and brings out strongly the brilliant qualities of that type. The clearer, more even, and better-colored this line is, the more creative power in art, or productive money-making quality in business the subject has. The Lines of Saturn and Apollo do not show defects of health. The Line of Mercury, often called the Line of Health, shows distinctively health difficulties. It will be treated fully hereafter.

I insert this illustration, and these few general attributes of the lines at this point, only that you may have a *general* idea of them, which knowledge will be helpful with the Mount types. The lines will be minutely treated in Part II., and in the next chapter we shall take up the technical part of our work.

CHAPTER III

POSE AND CARRIAGE OF THE HANDS

WE shall now begin at the first step in hand-reading, and proceed, by successive stages, to consider everything necessary to a thorough comprehension of the science. The space given to the consideration of each subject is in proportion to its importance. It will help you greatly to adopt a method in your examinations similar to that followed in succeeding chapters, and follow it with each pair of hands you read. First, pose, then texture, flexibility, consistency, color, nails, etc., in the regular order given here. By adopting a definite method of examination, such as the above, you will never be at a loss where to begin or how to proceed. The first thing you should consider in reading a pair of hands is the manner in which they are naturally carried. To place yourself in the best position to do this, you should locate your chair on the farther side of the room, opposite the door through which your client will enter. From this point you may observe certain indications given by his hands before he reaches you. It is necessary, in order to arrive at correct conclusions in this matter, that the hands should be held *naturally*, and that your subject should not feel under any restraint or embarrassment. If the mind is at all disturbed, it will reflect itself in an unnatural carriage of the hands, and you will fail to catch the *unconscious gleam* of the *real inner self*. To further this end, your assistant should have the visitor remove hat, coat, and gloves (it will aid materially if this assistant have also the tact to say a pleasant word), so that as the client crosses the floor, he or she may do so carrying the hands in a natural manner, mind at ease, and unconscious that the reading has already begun. It may be stated here that the hand whose owner has little or nothing to conceal opens itself freely to the gaze, and that the hand of one whose deeds and thoughts will not bear inspection wishes to hide itself, or to close the fingers over the palm, studiously concealing it from sight. The mind feels the necessity for hiding its workings, and the

NO. 1

NO. 2

fingers, obeying the suggestion, close over the palm. Thus to you will come the knowledge that if your client seems bent on hiding his hands from sight as he crosses your room (1), or if he seems anxious to keep the hand closed as much as possible, which he may try to do even while you are examining it, he has ideas which he does not like to have exposed ; he has a dark side to his character, and is probably deceitful, hypocritical, or untruthful. You must always give these clients the plain truth ; do not fear to wound them. Be sure you are right, of course, and do not judge by any one indication, but look for other indications bearing on the same line of investigation, then tell them all you know, and do not be disappointed when they say that you have entirely misjudged them.

You may next be visited by the man who is merely *careful* about telling all he knows. He is one who can keep a confidence, or closely hold a business secret. He is not, in gently closing his fingers, hiding a bad thought or a bad trait, but he does not make a confidant of every one he meets. This man will cross your room without any effort to hide his hand from sight (2), and without the studied and evident attempt at secretiveness and the lack of openness which characterizes our hypocritical friend. His hands will be held at his side, the fingers partially closed, and while the hand shows life, and does not hang limp and logy, nevertheless it is *not wide open*. In this case, the greater part of what the man knows is kept to himself; he is self-contained, cautious, trustworthy; one in whom you may confide ; who meets you half way in confidences, and with nothing frivolous in his character. You must, in studying all hands, learn to distinguish a hand that is *full of life*, is springy, and elastic in its outward look, telling you, even before you have touched it, of the vital energy stored in its owner. By pursuing such a " study of observation " of the hands of *all* the people you meet, not trying to individualize in the analysis of their qualities, not mentally trying to class them into types, but merely seeking to get impressions of strength or weakness, attraction or repulsion, that develop under such a study, you will find that every pair of hands has eyes; that they seem to look at you, asking pity, maybe, for their owners, or, that they have mouths, and beseech you to hear their story. This study of the *impression* created by the mere sight of hands must be practised continually. By following this line of observation, and observing the other directions as to method of practice suggested at the beginning of this chapter, you will know the kind of person with whom you have to deal before he takes his seat in the chair, and you will thus know better how to handle his case. It has seemed necessary to say this here, for, in hands carried as described by the latter type, it is the life, the spring, the elasticity looking out from them that will say to you, "This is the self-contained, prudent man ; I must be direct in my statements, say nothing that can imply that I am asking him a question, but tell *him* the story, not let him tell me."

The next client is one who carries the hands at the side, the

NO. 3 NO. 4 NO. 5

fingers nearly open, and the hand dangling in a limp and lifeless manner (3). The whole impression of this hand is that of indecision, and a lack of fixedness of purpose ; it indicates one that it would be exceedingly dangerous to entrust with any secret, unless you want it revealed to the first adroit individual who happens along. In this case the mind is lacking in definiteness of purpose; it is ready to receive suggestions, no matter whether they are correct or not, and the subject, being mentally lazy, will not take the trouble to think for himself. The mind is without a fixed purpose, consequently the hand is one which, by its lifelessness and dangling look, shows that it is the servant of a mind that is ready to be lazily directed by some other mind stronger in purpose than itself. Its fault is in being like a sieve, through which all that is told pours readily, and it is coupled with a lack of ability to be self-contained. Number 2 and number 3 are respectively the "close-fisted" and open-handed people in money matters: the first thinks before he spends; the second is the one of whom it is said, "A fool and his money are soon parted." These undecided hands, in coming toward you, will tell you that you may easily impress their owner, and the only trouble will be to keep him from instantly telling you all he knows.

The next subject for our consideration is the one who crosses your room with his hands hanging at his sides, but with the fists firmly closed (4). This does not indicate the bruiser or the bully, for you will find those qualities in another type, but it indicates one who is laboring under great *determination*. The very act of clenching the fist will indicate plainly that the mind is made up, the determination fixed. The clenching of the fist shows the shutting in of the vital energy, the shutting out of all idea of further parley, and the arrival of the time to *act*. Thus the degree of clenching of the fist shows the *quantity* of determination as well as the *quality*, for if it is merely a *gentle closing of the hand*, it will show you the firm, determined person; if it is the clenched fist with the ends of the fingers pressing hard into the palms, the person is laboring under some pressing excitement, which has brought with it determination. It will thus portray to your mind very strong resolution, either the habitual strength of that quality in the subject, or its temporary occupancy of his mind at the time.

The next person who crosses the room may carry the left hand gracefully at the side, the right forearm vertical and resting against the biceps, the wrist curving gracefully, the fingers of Saturn and Apollo close together, and gracefully curved, fingers of Jupiter and Mercury apart and showing a space between them and the other fingers (5). This will show you one who is dominated by the artistic qualities. You will seldom find this pose of the hand in men, but plentifully among women. It is chiefly useful in distinguishing the really artistic nature from the commonplace one carrying the hands in a dead, lifeless way at the side, and it will give you the inkling of a *love of the beautiful* and tasteful things of life, as possessed by your client. It shows more of the psychic qualities than those belonging to the matter-of-

NO. 6 NO. 7

fact housewife. You can please this subject at once by speaking of grace and beauty as her mainspring, and it will not be hard to find the way to her heart through these channels. As this pose will be most frequently met among the people of refined society, you will have to inform yourself on all subjects pertaining to "proper form," "etiquette," etc. Thus equipped you will be able better to depict their character and probable outcome than if you were not conversant with the rules of those in the "blue book." Then there is the "Miss Nancy" who crosses with a mincing gait, the left hand and forearm held across the abdomen, the hand drooping at the wrist, and held loosely, the right arm carried vertically, the forearm doubling back on the biceps, the right hand drooping at the wrist and held loosely, with a pair of eye-glasses, a lorgnette, or a smelling-bottle held listlessly in the fingers, and either whirled or swayed gently as he walks (6). This person is "finicky" in the extreme, hypersensitive, and shows an excess of femininity in either man or woman. It is odd to say that a woman can be excessively feminine, and yet this is true, for many lack the elastic, firm femininity that does not mean boldness, but does mean *strength*. It is the kind which does not give way under discouragement, but with fine womanliness rises to the occasion, and becomes the support and stimulator of husband or family in times when her strength and encouraging words are needed. The excessively feminine woman sinks collapsed when her help is most necessary, and becomes, for the time, an added burden in place of a tower of strength. In a man it means the "Miss Nancy," caring more for the appearance of dress than for the strength of masculinity. Then there will be the person who seems to find no place for his hands to rest (7); he carries them first up, then down, then in the pocket, then fingering the watch-chain. This person is uncertain in purpose; emotions are passing rapidly through him, and these emotions are not under the control either of mind or will. These people are very often strong characters but need directing.

Then there will come the person who holds the hands in front of the body, or slightly at the side, waving them about as though trying to keep from touching anything (8). If an object should be brought close to these hands, they would instinctively shrink away from it and avoid contact. It looks as though the ends of the fingers contained eyes which were roaming from one place to the other. This person is suspicious, is "sizing up" everything about him, making mental notes of the appearance of yourself, the settings of the room, and is looking for trap-doors and concealed things that are to help you to read him. This action of the mind, showing watchfulness, alertness, and investigation, is reflected in the hands, which roam around evidently searching for information, and in reading this subject it will be well to point out the places in the hand from which you get your information, give him your reasoning frankly, and conceal nothing from him. Handled in this way, these people become your best advocates.

There will be some who will cross the room with the fingers

NO. 8 NO. 9

toying with the handkerchief, a button on the clothes, the watch-chain, or some other trinket or trifle (9). This subject is nervous, and is momentarily under excitement. It is not the calm, placid, even temper shown by the one who crosses in a stately manner with the hands easily clasped together in front of her, the palm of one hand up, the palm of the other hand resting in it (10). This is a most eloquent indicator of repose and evenness of temper, one which will present an unruffled front to all exciting circumstances and events. You must not be hurried with this calm person.

Her mind acts with dignity, and more slowly than the average. If you should talk fast and not give time for what you said to be *absorbed*, you would find her saying to her friends in describing your reading, "I suppose it was good, but really he talked so fast I could not catch all of it."

Then you will be consulted by the bullying person, his fists tightly clenched, his elbows bent, with his arms carried in what I have called the "bow-legged" fashion (11). This

NO. 10 NO. 11 NO. 12

is typical of a bruiser and fighter, and you must be exceedingly firm in what you say. You will also have the person who crosses the room rubbing his hands together, as is the fashion in washing them; he rubs one hand against the other in a most sly, oily manner (12). This will tell you of "Uriah Heep," slippery, adroit, hypocritical, untruthful. You cannot depend on him at all, and you must bring out all his qualities, for he is the personification of insincerity.

Then will come the haughty and proud, very much impressed with his own importance. He will cross your room with a stately mien, the left hand held at the side, the fingers loosely closing, the right arm bent at the elbow, held horizontally across the abdomen, the palm held upward with the fingers closing loosely over it (13). This person is full of self-importance, impressed with his own dignity, and will quickly resent anything like an attempt at familiarity, or anything tending to show that you do not fully agree with him in his estimate of himself.

And next you may be visited by a pair of hands hanging

NO. 13

NO. 14

NO. 15

limp, heavy in shape, thick and fat, which will seem to belong to a dead person, and mentally they do (14). All is heaviness, density, coarseness, no chance for flights of fancy on your part, no chance for rhapsody. If you attempt a keen analysis, he will blankly stare at you. No use trying to lift him out of his trough of materialism. It can't be done. He wants to know his brother's name, whether he is married, how many children, how long he will live, whether he will be rich, and you cannot lift him above this plane.

Finally, we meet the person who will cross with an investigating air, the hands clasped behind his back (15). He is extremely cautious, does not know exactly what is going to be done, does not want to fall into any trap, is looking over the ground before he "shows his hand." Deal gently with him ; he is timid, he means well, but is suspicious.

From the foregoing illustrations, it is apparent how great an assistance it will be to make a careful study of this chapter. Assume the poses described, and learn to recognize them at a glance. Do not try to commit this chapter to memory, it will do no good unless the mental picture of all these people is in your mind, so that the moment they are seen, that moment they are recognized. Thus before your client is seated, you have much to aid you in your method of handling him.

CHAPTER IV

PRELIMINARY ARRANGEMENTS—WHAT HAND TO USE—TEXTURE OF THE SKIN

HAVING carefully noted the indications given in the previous chapter, you are now ready to begin the examination of the hand itself. In order to secure the best results from this investigation, it will be of material help if you have arranged your surroundings so that the client will be comfortable when he seats himself. One of the matters to which you should give most careful attention is the proper arrangement of light. No rule can be fixed in this matter, as the sight of all palmists is not equally strong. It is, however, indispensable that you have the clearest, whitest light possible, and for this purpose nothing is so good as a strong northern exposure of pure daylight. To find the apex of each Mount will require a keen eye and good light, especially if the texture of the skin be very fine. Nothing short of daylight will suffice, and even with this help you will often have to resort to a magnifying-glass. I should advise that you be provided with a strong, clear reading-glass, about six inches in diameter, large enough to cover the palm of the hand; this will bring out any markings which may be only faintly indicated. If your eyes be strong, you will not have to use this glass for the larger and more prominent details, but with a highly strung, excessively lined hand, it is advisable to use the glass. In this way you will often discover faint lines just beginning to form in outline, and these will show you emotions *just starting* to develop. If you intend to go deeply into your client's life, this minute inspection is necessary. Daylight is indispensable to you also in judging the color of the hand. Many palmists absolutely refuse to read by gaslight, and this is a safe rule to adopt, as daylight is an absolute essential in readings covering great attempts at detail.

Now, having comfortable seats, good light, a glass, to use if needed, the temperature at the proper point, say 70° F., you take the hands of your client. In all examinations you should consult *both hands*, and should never attempt specific statements, unless they are based upon a thorough knowledge of the information which can be gleaned only from the hands considered separately, and then together. Many failures are recorded in palm-readings when one hand only has been used, due to the fact that men change as they grow older, and these changes are recorded in the right hand. If you have read from the left hand, you have looked at the man only as he was originally constructed, not as he has developed. To gain a knowledge of him as he *is*, and thus better to tell whether he is progressing or retrograding, you must read from both hands. This is a matter to which I have given most careful study, and in the course of many investigations have often read in the separate hands how weak people have grown strong, and strong people deteriorated. The left hand is the infallible index to the *natural being*, the right hand records unmistakably *what has been done with the talents*. All that has been said about using the left hand because it is nearest the heart or because it has more lines, grows from a false conception of the matter. The heart no more controls nor feeds the left than the right hand, and it is not for this reason that both hands are used. The left hand is the passive hand, the right the active. There are instances in which the subject is left-handed. In this case reverse the order and consider the right as passive, the left as active. Invariably the hand *which does the work* is the one which records the present, the hand which is passive shows the natural endowments. Thus, if you see the passive hand showing one condition, the active hand an improved state, you know that the course has been upward, and *vice versa*.

The first matter that should receive your attention in examining the hand itself, is the texture of the skin. We sometimes forget that the human skin is not merely the thin cuticle that peels off when one is sun-burned, but is as thick as the leather from which a pair of calf-skin shoes are made, that it is capable of much coarseness or fineness, and will be covered either with large capillaries, or with capillaries so fine they can hardly be seen. This coarseness or fineness is what we call texture. In considering it you should largely confine yourself to the back of the hand. The matter of *consistency* of the hand, a wholly different quality, and one which will be discussed in the next chapter, is to be determined by an examination of the palm; in this way you will not get the two qualities confused.

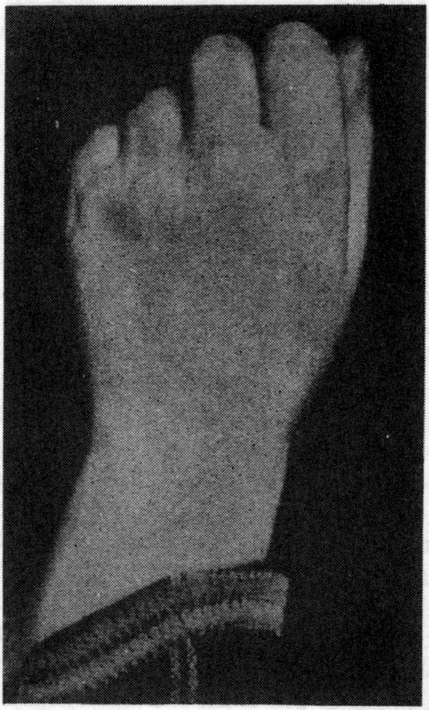

NO. 16. FINE-TEXTURED SKIN

Texture is the key to a knowledge of your client's natural refinement. If the texture be fine, soft, and delicate (16), the greatest fineness being seen in a baby's hand, you have a refined sensitive person, who is influenced by these qualities in everything he does. He is one to whom coarseness and commonness give actual pain, and it will not be possible for the person with this fine texture of skin to do things in a coarse, common, brutish way. This quality of texture will aid you in estimating character, for it is a softening influence on all the coarser qualities seen in any subject ; it makes a Saturnian less morose, melancholy, moody, and less inclined to shun society ; it will make his cynicism less cutting : it will make a Jupiterian less of an overeater, less domineering, less tyrannical, for it will refine him. It will add to an Apollonian a new and quieter love of beauty and harmony, and will make his nature more elevated : it will refine a Mercurian, taking away much of the dishonest side of his character : it will subdue a Martian, refining his brusqueness, his fighting qualities, his warlike spirit, and making him less pugnacious: it will lead the imagination of a Lunar subject into higher channels, and will refine a Venusian, so that base, low passions will not dominate him. In this as in all other matters there are different degrees of development, and this question of degree is said to be one of the things that students cannot easily acquire. Palmistry is frequently met by the criticism that "everything modifies everything else"; there is not the slightest need of any confusion or difficulty on this score.

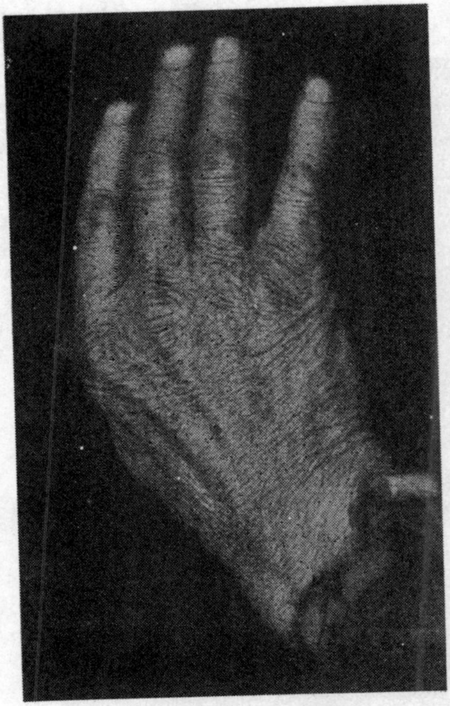

NO. 17. COARSE-TEXTURED SKIN

With a picture in your mind of a baby's delicate skin—one extreme of texture—let us look for a moment at the opposite extreme. There is the skin which feels rough, coarse, and common, as you rub your fingers over the back of the hand. It has big capillaries, and is hard,

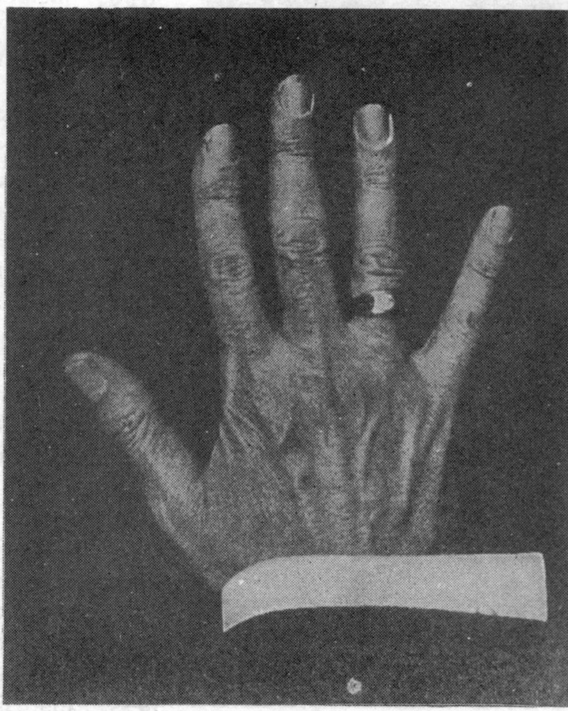

NO. 18. ELASTIC-TEXTURED SKIN

rough, and unsympathetic to the touch. It is like sole-leather as compared to soft flexible kid, and shows by the coarseness of its grain that refinement and delicacy are unknown to its owner (17). This hand you will often find in the gas trenches, shovelling dirt. There is no knowledge in the mind of its owner, that the employment in which he is engaged is not of the most elevating character. To put this hand in the same surroundings as the hand with delicately soft texture, would make it as miserable as to consign the delicate texture to the gas trenches. This coarse skin you will not so often meet, but you should hunt a subject who has it, so that you will be able to have in your mind the

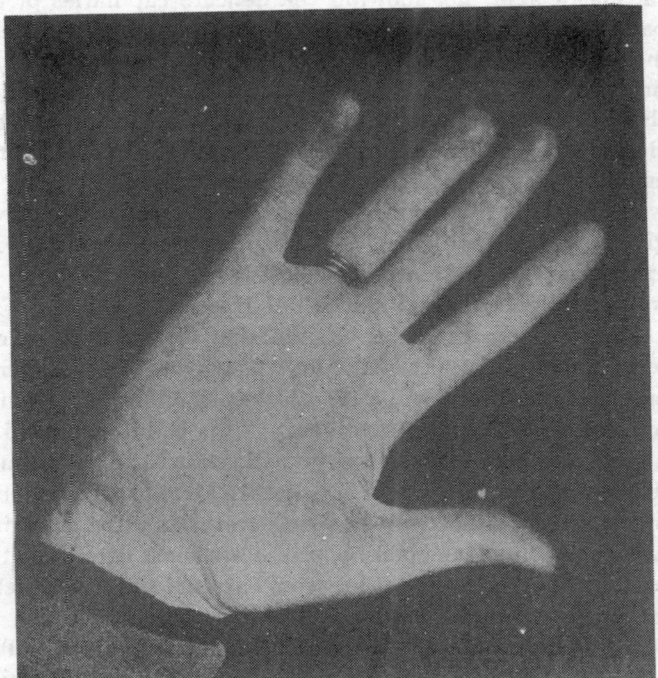

NO. 19. SENSITIVE PADS ON FINGER TIPS

opposite of the baby's hand. The coarse texture will show the lack of refinement, delicate sensibility, or fine quality of nature, and will modify all things in the hand by coarsening them. Coarseness will add the tyrannical spirit to Jupiter, will make Saturn dirty, stingy, superstitious, and a pessimist: it will make Apollo the vulgar blatherskite, and Mercury only a low schemer: it will make Mars insufferable in its aggressiveness, and the Moon will give forth low imaginations: Venus, instead of dealing in love, grace, and sympathy, will stand only for the gratification of vulgar passions. Refined texture softens everything; coarse texture animalizes it.

The medium development will be most often met. It is the elastic skin, not showing the delicate capillaries of the baby's hand, nor the coarseness of the trench-digger's, but a medium between them. The skin will feel elastic, not soft, firm, not hard (18). It is the texture found on the hand of the active business man, the lawyer, the doctor, or the clergyman. It is a texture which shows refinement, yet not effeminacy in men; it shows fineness without idealism in women. It is the balance between two extremes, and will give to all the qualities of the mounts normal support. By examining the extremes I have given, you will have no trouble in recognizing the medium grade.

Before concluding your examination of skin texture, observe the inside aspect of the first phalanges of the fingers; on many hands you will note a little pad of flesh (19) which in some cases is quite prominent. This pad is composed of a large number of nerve filaments and shows the great sensitiveness of the subject. He is keenly alive to all surroundings, easily wounded by slighting treatment, and knowing how such things jar upon himself, he is most careful of the feelings of other people. He would himself suffer intensely, rather than wound another. These sensitive pads are, in a word, indicative of an extremely fine organism. The degree of their development will gauge the degree to which the subject is possessed of this quality.

CHAPTER V

CONSISTENCY OF THE HAND

IN making up your mind about the client under examination, it is essential, that you know at the start the amount of energy possessed, for it must be apparent that no matter how brilliant he may be, if he is lazy, the brilliancy will be wasted in idle dreaming, instead of being turned into active channels. It is to the consistency of the hands, by which we mean their hardness or softness under pressure, that you must look for information on the above subjects. Take hold of the hands firmly, allow your fingers to close all around them if they are small hands, and gently squeeze, until you have found out the amount of resistance opposed to your pressure. You should then quietly loosen your grasp, and press your fingers firmly against the palms, being careful to do it in spots where there are no callous places. What you wish to discover, by this examination, is the hardness, softness, flabbiness, or resisting power of the muscles of the hand. First of all, you must not regard a hand which has callous places as necessarily hard, though I grant you that it requires some energy to do the amount of work necessary to produce this callousness. For example, the bicycle has developed callousness in many hands where it was never known before, and all sports, such as golf, bowling, or rowing, may make these hardened spots in the hands where the pursuit of pleasure, and not real energy, has been the underlying incentive. Evidences of energy thus generated are only temporary, and must not be considered as indicating a force that is inherent in the subject, for these same people might never have labored hard enough at any useful toil, to produce callousness in their hands. I am explicit in this matter because I want you to be careful not to accept a surface indication as denoting real energy, for you can readily see into how much error this would lead you. The consistency of the hands may be separated into four classes, the first of which is the flabby hand. In the grasp which I have described in the opening of this chapter you will find, when the fingers are closed around a flabby hand, that it offers no resistance to your pressure. If you squeeze the hand very firmly the flesh and bone seem to crush together, producing the impression on your mind that if you pressed much harder, the flesh would be squeezed out through your fingers. This is the softest hand you can find, and in the matter of physical energy is absolutely deficient. It is the hand of one who dreams, but does not act, who loves, but whose love finds expression only in words, not deeds. It is the hand of one that desires ease, mental and physical, luxury, and beautiful surroundings, but will not work to gain them. It is the hand of him who prefers to live in squalor, so long as there is plenty of rest and no exertion, rather than to enjoy better living, if labor is the price of the improved condition. In plain words, its owner is the idle, luxurious, sensitive dreamer, who will not work, will not exert, but, like a ship at sea without a wind, is content to drift. Such a person is often highly gifted, possessing fine mounts of Apollo strongly lined, and every indication of creative power, yet, as you close your fingers over the flabby hand, you know that the vital requisite to the development of these talents, *energy*, is absent, and a negative life is ahead. This laziness will naturally modify all other qualities, will bring to naught the ambition of a Jupiterian, increase the sadness of a Saturnian, diminish the brilliancy and achievement of the Apollonian, spoil the energy of the Mercurian, make the Martian a fighter with his tongue instead of his sword, add laziness to the imaginings of the Lunar subject, and even the Venusian will feel the blight of inertia, sapping the vital energy of his nature.

Next in grade to the flabby comes the soft hand. In this

case, the hand will not have the boneless, flabby feeling under your touch, yet will be distinctly soft. You wiil find more difficulty among women in distinguishing the flabby hands from the soft, for women's hands are naturally softer than men's. But by observing the lack of bony feeling in the hand under pressure, and following closely the description of the flabby hand, you cannot fail to attain a clear idea of how to distinguish between the two. The best way to gain practice in this matter is to press the hands of all the people with whom you shake hands, accustoming yourself to distinguish the sensation they give to your touch, by which practice you can quickly learn to differentiate soft from flabby consistency. The soft hand is one which, while by no means approaching the laziness indicated by flabby hands, is still deficient in energy. There is this important difference between the two. The flabby hand will *always* be lazy while the faculty of energy can be *developed* and increased in the subject whose hands are merely soft. This is most important to note, for you may induce the possessor of a soft hand to build up his energy and develop his talents, while you cannot, to any extent, induce the man of flabby hand to improve.

Next to soft consistency comes the elastic. This is a hand which you cannot crush in your grasp. It has, as you close your fingers on it, a feeling of springiness, of life, and resistance. It seems, when you press it with the tips of your fingers, as though the flesh rebounded like rubber would under similar pressure. It lacks entirely the spongy quality of flabby or soft hands, and no word can more adequately convey the idea of its feeling under pressure than elasticity. You find it best exemplified among *active* men and women, those who not only talk, but who also act. If you will pick out one of this class for example, one whom you know to be a hustling business man, which means one who has everything about his place full of life and action, you will find he has the elastic consistency ; ask to examine his hands, and thus make yourself familiar with the sensation they produce when grasping them. When you

B*

find this elastic consistency, it shows that the person has life, energy, push, vim, and vigor, and that in all walks of life he is up and doing. He does no more work than is necessary, but he does enough. He does not overexert, but he occupies the plane of a happy medium, and his life, action, and energy is the moving force in the world to-day. He is trustworthy if of a good type, takes responsibility well, and in the battle of life is the victor. The elastic hand puts vitality into all human qualities. It adds exactness to the square tip and finger, activity to the spatulate, makes the conic do some real thing with their genius of impulse, and (though not often seen in this subject), even adds life and vigor to psychic fingers. It makes the ambition of the Jupiterian a lever to force him upward, brings out the best side of the moody Saturnian, makes the Apollonian a money-maker, the Mercurian more active, shrewd, and successful. The Martian becomes a calm leader, a balanced fighter, but one who accomplishes great deeds. It makes the Lunar mount give forth music and poetry, and Venus stands for active love and the energy of grace. You must, in handling this elastic consistency, realize that it is the embodiment of healthful energy, evenly distributed, and that the subject will surely make his way through the world. It may be summed up fully, I think, by saying that an elastic hand shows the activity of *intelligent* energy and force, in other words, *well-directed* energy, the kind that occupies itself with being "sensibly energetic."

Hard hands follow next, and play their part in the matter of consistency. They will not be so often encountered as soft or elastic hands for extreme types are much rarer than might be thought possible. Hard hands, as a rule, are those which belong to less intelligent people, and the skin will be found coarser in texture. The hard hand will give no sign of yielding under your pressure, will have no spring, no elasticity, but a hardness that resists any effort to dent it. When you encounter such a hand, you will know at once that the subject is of the most active kind, that manual labor is not a burden to him, but is what he expects. You may ally, in your mind, this hand with the mind behind it, and in doing so you will picture a brain that is somewhat dense, that does not receive and assimilate impressions and ideas quickly and readily. The "elastic" brain which guides the elastic hand can change itself, can adapt itself to new conditions, the "hard" brain which guides the hard hand cannot easily take in a new idea. It is difficult for such a "hard" brain to advance with the progress of modern ideas, it is difficult for the possessor to get out of the rut of routine and custom, and to be original. Thus, when you find the hard hand, it will show you the kind of energy that exerts, labors, and toils from a knowledge that labor must be done, but without great brain activity behind this toil. It is energy, indeed, but not the most "intelligent energy."

Thus between this hard hand and the flabby hand you find many degrees of consistency, and in order to get the correct idea search until you find the extreme types, after which the medium developments will be easily determined. The hard hand modifies all the types, as it renders them less elevated and intelligent. As laziness spoils brilliant people, so excess of ill-directed energy will also spoil them. And while you want to find that people are willing to work, to exert, to act, you want also to find intelligence directing effort, which unfortunately is not always the case with the hard hand. When examining for consistency carefully note both hands. If the left is soft and the right elastic you know energy has been increased. If the left is hard and the right soft you know that the subject has grown lazy. In this way you can judge whether the subject is increasing or decreasing in energy. If increasing he is more likely to have success and *vice versa.*

CHAPTER VI

FLEXIBILITY OF THE HANDS

1. *Any object which is flexible can adapt itself to a greater variety of conditions than could the same object if it were stiff.*
2. *A flexible object bends under pressure; a stiff object under the same amount of pressure breaks or remains immovable.*
3. *As the hands reflect the condition and quality of the mind, flexible hands show a flexible mind, and stiff hands a stiff mind.*

IN the present examination, which seeks to determine the degree of flexibility possessed by the hands, you are beginning to judge the mental powers of your client and will aid yourself materially by gaining a thorough understanding of the three statements introducing this chapter.

The flexibility of a hand is shown by the ease with which it bends itself backward, and to test this quality lay the hand of your client, with the palm upward, in the palm of your left hand, and with your right hand exert pressure downward on it until you have bent it as far backward as you can.

Having made a test of both your client's hands as above described, notice whether the whole hand is flexible, or whether the bending occurs only at the knuckle joints, for in the flexibility which means the most, you will find that the whole hand bends, fingers and all, and does not merely give way at the knuckles. In the examination for flexibility there will be great degrees of variation, running all the way from hands in which the fingers bend back at an angle of nearly forty-five degrees to others where the fingers cannot be even straightened. The extreme degrees of flexibility you will find in the hands of women, while pronounced flexibility in the hands of men is a rarity. The flexibility of the hand shows the degree of flexibility of the mind and nature, and the readiness with which this mind has power to unfold itself, and " see around the corner " of things.

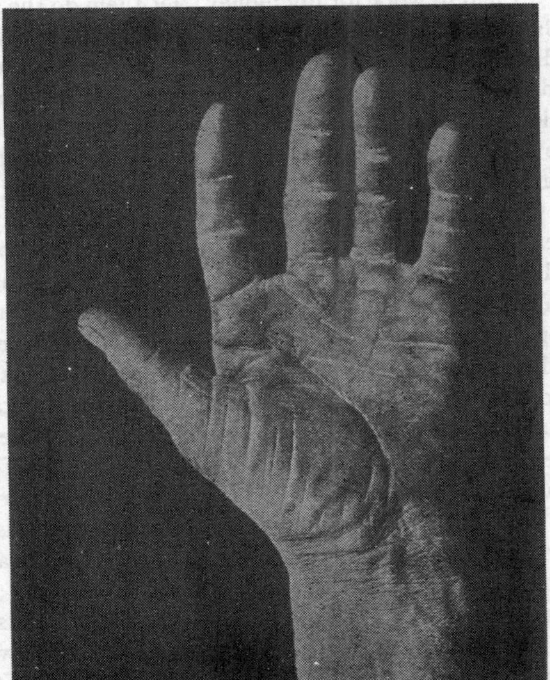

NO. 20. A STIFF HAND

In treating this matter, we shall speak first of the hand which is stiff and hard to open, where the fingers form a curve inward (20). This hand indicates the mind that is cautious, immobile, close, inclined to narrowness and stinginess, and which, in every way, lacks pliability or adaptability. Such a person is afraid of new ventures, afraid of new ideas ; the method of dress and mode of living of his ancestors satisfy him; he has the *political and religious* faith of his fathers, and there is absolutely no use in trying to argue him out of it. When he views the methods and manners of the present generation, he longs for the open fireplace, the stage-coach, and, as he calls them, the " good old days." He is one whose narrowness makes him ungenerous. Appealed to for help, he replies, " I had to work for my money: let them do the same." He thinks that failure comes because the old-time ways have been discarded, and that " new-fangled notions " are ruining everybody. He is the man who succeeds by hard work, deprivation, and saving, and he cannot conceive how success can be achieved in any other way. He is, in short, cramped and narrow in his ideas, stingy in his ways, unprogressive in his views, and lacks flexibility, or elasticity, in mind and manner, as well as flexibility of hands. He is, however, exceedingly close-mouthed, and you can safely trust him with a secret, not from any desire on his part of doing you a favor, but nothing that he can keep gets away from him, so he holds your secret as avariciously as he clings to his own dollars. This is the stiff hand, and under the kaleidoscopic changes during the past age, he breaks on the wheel of time, because he does not bend, and adapt himself to the inevitable march of events. This hand is usually hard.

You will find hands which, when pressed backwards, open readily until the fingers straighten themselves naturally, so that the hand opens with ease to its full extent (21) ; there will be cases where it bends back *just a trifle.* This hand is the medium or normal development, and its owner is balanced, even in action, up to date, and has control of himself. It is the hand of one who does not go to extremes, is self-contained, listens readily, and understands what he hears. He is not held back by old-fogyism, nor impelled into rashness or overenthusiasm. He can use money properly, will help those in need, but does not throw away either sympathy or charity. To him life is a problem, it is serious, and he thoughtfully uses his mind trying to understand it. He looks over the world from a bird's-eye point of view, can appreciate the difficulties that surround humanity, and will not try to find the remedy by crying that we are departing from old ways, neither will he want to turn everything upside down with the advancement of new ideas. He is thoughtful, broad, earnest, sympathetic, yet all within bounds. He is, in plain words, well balanced, and not an extremist. This hand is generally elastic in consistency, and impresses you as possessing *vital force.*

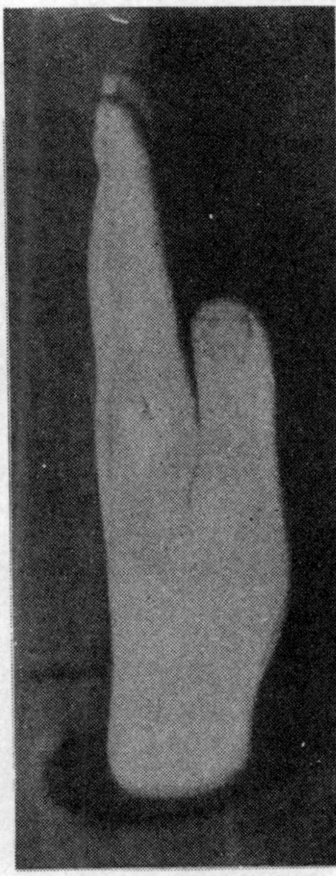

NO. 21. A STRAIGHT HAND

There is another hand that is flexible in the extreme (22). The fingers bend back, without giving their owner any pain, until a graceful arch is formed. The fingers seem mobile, and the bones cartilaginous. This hand, as you bend it back and forth, impresses you with its great pliability, and shows readily what a fine machine it is, and how easily it can adapt and shape itself to circumstances. This flexible hand shows an elastic mind, a brain susceptible of receiving keen impressions, and of understanding them quickly. It is the hand of the person who readily adapts himself to his surroundings, is versatile, and does not require a diagram with every statement. Its elasticity is its danger, for it is a brilliant hand, directed by a brilliant mind. Its owner possesses in the highest degree versatility, and, being able to do *many* things, is liable to diversify his talents and lack concentration in any one direction, thus becoming a Jack-of-all-trades. The possessor of the flexible hand is extremely sympathetic, generous, and money to him is only the means of securing what he wants, not a thing to be hoarded for itself alone. The possession of riches gives pleasure to these persons only in that it allows them luxury, and extravagance is a prevailing tendency of the type. They are emotional, easily moved by a pitiful story, and readily give to any one. Their minds work rapidly, they absorb ideas quickly, and their tendency

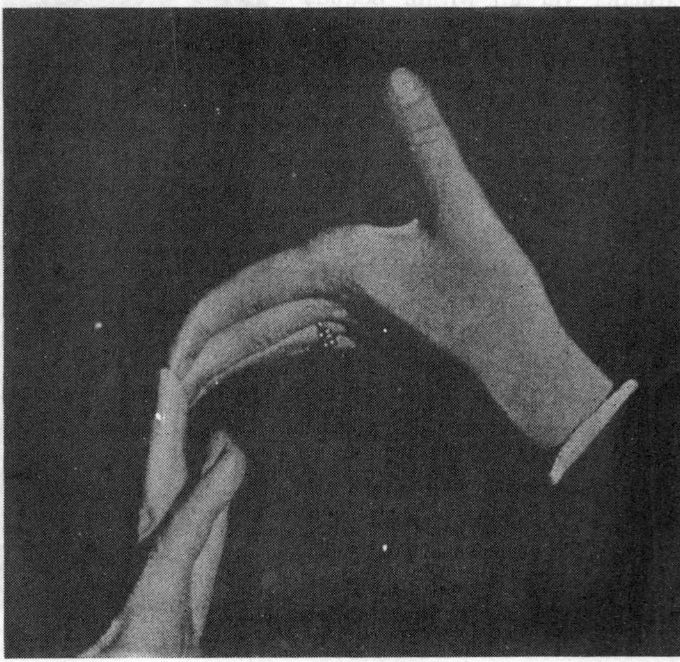

NO. 22. A FLEXIBLE HAND

is to go too fast. These brilliant hands are capable of the most wonderful achievements; they are not the hands of dreamers, but are full of life and action, though too versatile often for their own good. They can do *too many* things, turn their minds in too many directions, and unless restrained they come to naught from too much talent. They are as extreme in prodigality as the stiff hand is in economy, and yet they have this wonderful factor in their favor, viz.:

they are so sensible that they can see their own failings when properly pointed out, and with good head lines, and good thumbs, they turn their brilliancy to fine account by applying determination and self-control to their natural versatility, which qualities give them the highest degree of success.

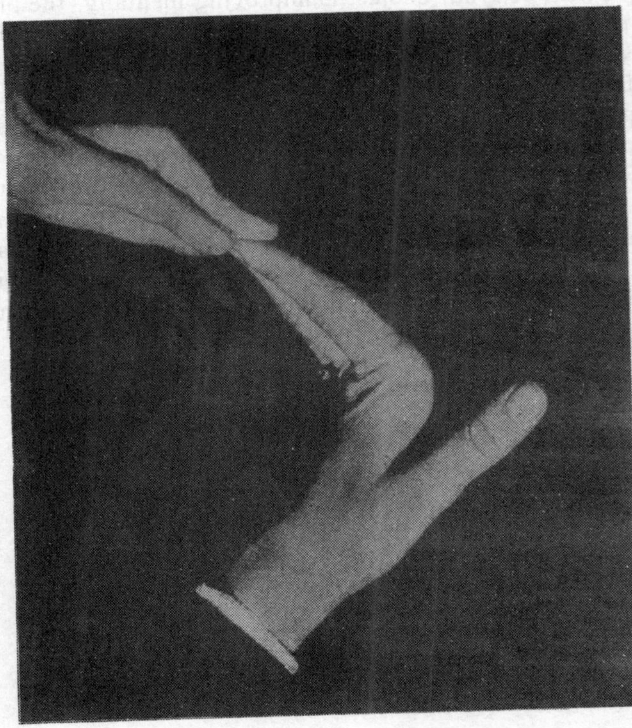

NO. 23. EXTREME FLEXIBILITY

Hands where only the first phalanges of the fingers are flexible, the rest of the hand normal, give one third of the degree of flexibility shown when the whole of the fingers are flexible, indicating flexibility in the mental qualities of the fingers on which this condition is found. Where the fingers bend back at the knuckles (23), you will find, in a musical hand, fine ability in *execution*. It also shows the extravagance of the extremely flexible type. It will not be hard to find good specimens of the hands dealt with in this chapter: the first you will find oftenest among middle-aged farmers; the latter types you will find everywhere. You should always carefully compare the two hands. If the left is stiff and the right flexible, your subject is improving mentally, the brain is becoming more elastic, the subject passing from stiff to flexible qualities. If the left hand is flexible and the right stiff, he has become more stingy, careful, less versatile, and is passing from the qualities of the elastic to those of the stiff hand. In this way you will often be able to do some excellent work by describing how a subject used to throw money away, and how stingy he has grown. Having learned fully the *qualities* of the two hands, you can carry your simile as to the changing condition as far as you like, and in whatever direction the flexible or stiff hand may show it to be drifting.

CHAPTER VII

COLOR OF THE HANDS

There is but one direct means by which man's physical being is developed, by which it is maintained in normal condition, and, when broken down, by which it is restored to a condition of health. Hence there is one chief thing to which the various measures employed for the relief of bodily ills should be directed. It matters not what the measures may be; whether they consist of the administration of drugs, the application of massage, electricity, bathing, mental influences, or any other mode of treatment, all are directed to this one thing, viz.: the circulation of the blood.

If the blood current is strong and free, health is assured; if, on the other hand, the general circulation is sluggish, or local congestions occur, morbid processes are of necessity initiated.

There is not a pathological lesion that does not have its beginning in blood stasis. To re-establish and to maintain a normal circulation, local and general, is, therefore, the great problem that demands solution in the successful treatment of chronic diseases, both medical and surgical.—PRATT.

UP to the present time we have been engaged largely in estimating the *quality* of our subject, and now we naturally consider his *quantity*. By this I mean his temperament, and the indications of health or disease as shown by the color of his hands. This is so important a matter that you must absorb every word this chapter contains, not memorizing, but *catching the idea* and fixing it in your mind, so that when you note a certain color it brings to you all the *qualities* which belong to that color and the physiological conditions that produce it. When we realize that ill-health, which is vital force in excessive degree as in fevers, or diminished quantity as in chills, will have much to do in shaping the course of our lives, we can realize that color, which shows the strength of this vital force, must be mastered before we can scientifically apply the principles of Palmistry. The lack of knowledge on this subject is one of the causes which has made Palmistry so unsatisfactory to many, and it will always be so until a full understanding of color has been absorbed.

Physiologically considered, blood which produces color performs two most important functions. It swiftly courses through our veins and arteries, absorbs and carries away impurities, and at the same time renews and sustains life. These impurities which the blood absorbs carbonize it (which is only another word for devitalization), and unless this life current flowing through us is *itself* renewed, it will turn to poison. Nature has provided for this emergency a most wonderful machine, called the lungs, whose function it is to take into their cells fresh air, and to throw off the poisonous carbonic gas. This respiratory action of the lungs is the influx of new life into us with the inspiration, the outgo of exhausted life with the expiration ; all of the blood in the body *must* flow through the lungs, leaving with them this poisonous matter, and receiving in its stead oxygen, or new life. Thus renewed it returns through the veins to the heart, which receives it and pumps it out again to all parts of the system. In this manner blood is propelled to the outermost part of the body, the skin, and gives to it its color ; it is the *amount* and *quality* of the blood that changes the color of the skin. It is well said, that " blood is the renewer and sustainer of life," and therefore the color of the skin becomes, to the palmist, an all-important subject. Now, suppose this blood throws off only a *part* of its carbonic poison when it passes through the lungs to be renewed, and is only *partially* revitalized. Manifestly it will then return through the arteries, carrying not a *full measure* of renewed life, but only *partially* able to perform its highest degree of revivification. Suppose blood thus *continues* to pass through us only *partially* pure, it will not be long before the health will suffer and, as the health conditions alter or are impaired, the *temperament* will be affected, the *character* will become less strong as vital force diminishes, or will be changed in different ways, as different changes in the blood take place. This physiological side of Palmistry is one of which the public knows little. Few have realized the scientific exactitude of indications given by color, nor why they are so exact. White, pink, yellow, blue, red,—each shows a different condition of the subject's health. You must, of course, have the temperature of the room just right, say 70° F., to correctly judge color, for anything that accelerates or retards the flow of blood will affect the color of the hands, and what you are trying to find is the natural *strength* and *quality* of the blood stream.

In examining the hand for color, be guided largely by the palm, not the back of the hand, and look at the lines and the nails as well, from which combined point of view you can very accurately estimate the *normal* color of the hand under consideration. You must take into account the season of the year, for marked differences will be shown by some hands on this account. In winter the tendency is toward whiter color, and in summer you find sunburn or tan temporarily changing the appearance. These must be taken fully into account, and it is to avoid being misled by such matters that I advise using the palm, which is less susceptible to change from exposure than the back of the hand. Some people burn in summer, and their skin turns red. Others tan, and these hands turn brown. Often between the time when hands have been badly tanned, and the time when they become bleached out again, there is a period when they have a most decidedly yellow appearance. This might, if you did not keep all these matters in mind, lead you to ascribe the qualities of yellow color to hands which were only undergoing the process of regaining their normal appearance. It is the back of the hand, however, that is thus most often artificially colored, and by using the palm as indicated, you will not be led astray.

Remembering the causes of color we will first consider the white hand and its qualities. By white I mean a *dead-white*, one which gives you an impression of *pallor* and lack of blood supply, and not a white hand which is white merely by reason of its fineness. A very coarse, heavy hand may have the pallid whiteness which means lack of red corpuscles in the blood, but it will never have the whiteness which belongs to a woman's hand which is fine in texture, and to which some whiteness is natural. Thus first learn to recognize the watery, pallid look of a dead-white hand, the *corpse-like* whiteness that means the dearth of heat, and that gives the clew to the predominating quality of the white hand—*coldness.* With this color, the nature lacks ardor, heat, warmth, life, and attractiveness; it does not belong to one whose society is sought, whose genial qualities light up with a glow of warmth any company of associates, or one who so radiates good-fellowship that others enjoy his society. These people, instead, are distant, repellent in manner, cold in their views, and not anxious to make exertions to please others. They are cold by nature, and cold physically, for the blood current is reaching the outside skin only in a feeble and insufficient quantity. It is not pounding against it by virtue of the strong action of a strong heart, but comes in lifeless force from a flabby heart that is muscularly weak. Thus you will see that the white color is produced by a lack of force and strength in the life-renewing current,— the blood,—and this white color indicates a corresponding lack of force and strength in the nature of the subject. White-handed people are dreamy, mystical, not enthusiastic, unemotional, selfish, imaginary. They are not sensual, for the vital force of strong health, which gives force to passion, is absent; they are cold in love, and while often very clever they do not seek the society of others. They make good *littérateurs* both as poets and prose writers, and do not find their greatest enjoyment in the gratification of the senses. The mind may be active and at work, though it is not spurred on by martial fire or love. While cold white hands have written some of the most beautiful of all of our literature, their work has the glitter of the frost, the sparkle of the iceberg, lacking the warmth which reaches the heart. In religion these people are mystical; in the business world they make few friends; they do not enter the social world when they can avoid it. So you must feel, when one of these pallid white hands comes into your grasp, the lack of life, heat, energy, generosity, sympathy, and enthusiasm of its owner. Remember that the life-renewing current is weak, blood thin, heart action deficient, maybe from inactive kidneys, and you will recognize that this coldness greatly affects every other quality. A Mount of Jupiter may give ambition, pride, religion, but it will be tinged with coldness, cynicism, and superstition. If Jupiter is in excess, it will make a cold-blooded tyrant. If Saturn is strong, imparting wisdom, melancholy, or gravity, it will be made more cold by the white hand, though yellow color belongs to a strong Saturnian Mount, and the white color will not often be found by itself. The art, brilliancy, and versatility of Apollo will be pulled to the ground by a white hand, while Mercury is made more crafty, scheming, and less the good fellow he might otherwise be. The white hand gives resignation to a Martian, and in exaggerated developments adds to the destructiveness of his aggressive qualities, by making him cold-hearted. Venus is ruined by white color, for love cannot live without heat. White is the normal color of the Mount of Moon, and will be expected in a Lunar type of hand. If you find it with the other Mounts, it is always an abnormal condition.

After white color, we next consider pink. As whiteness shows deficiency of blood supply, pink color shows that a normal amount of blood is coursing through the body, consequently pinkness will be the health color. In this case the force-pump of the body, the heart, is acting with normal strength, is forcing through the arteries a good quality of blood, rich in red corpuscles, full of life-renewing power, and this rich blood is being sent in sufficient supply to the surface of the skin. Blood is what gives skin its color, and as there is, in this case, a normal condition of quantity, quality, and propelling force, the result is the healthy pink glow of the hands that speaks of a well-conditioned subject, full of life, energy, and vitality. A healthy person, whose body is not racked with pain, is necessarily nearer normal in all his qualities than one who is urging himself through life, weighed down by bodily ills. Thus pink color, meaning a good, healthful blood supply, means the nearest approach to normal conditions in temperament. The pink hand belongs to the bright, cheerful, vivacious person, full of the sparkle of a brain unclouded by too much blood or weakened by too little. It indicates one who is attractive, bright, and witty, one who can appreciate the power of love, who has sympathy, tenderness, and a gentle spirit toward all less-favored brethren. It indicates one who finds life pleasant, bright, and attractive, who finds his greatest pleasure in the society of people of his acquaintance, one to whom others are attracted, and whose society is sought wherever he may be. Life to many is full of tragedy, and to such the pink-handed people are a boon. They feel that life is worth living and can be made pleasanter, thus they are willing to make the necessary effort, being healthy, in order to enjoy these pleasures. They are optimists, not pessimists, and it is a blessing there are such people, who may galvanize their white-handed brethren into life. Warmth of love, the fire of enthusiasm, the tenderness of sympathy, belong to pink hands. They suffer when their friends suffer, but they try to cheer those in trouble; they give off magnetism, or heat as it is more properly called, for magnetic people must have warmth or they could not attract others. This is the physical reason why Venusians and Apollonians gather so many around them, why they are so much sought after. They radiate warmth, which is life; not coldness, which is death. The presence of pink color in a hand should bring to your mind a picture of the attraction, warmth, brightness, sparkle, vivacity, life, energy, generosity, and tenderness, which belong to a normal and healthy condition of mind and body. Pink is the happy medium with the mounts, and does not, with two exceptions, intensify or decrease their normal operation, consequently you can apply it favorably to all your types. With the Lunar and Saturnian subjects, reserved above, white and yellow color is normal, pink color will light up their coldness and sadness, and make them less pessimistic in their views of life. Thus pink color is a benefit from every point of view.

In considering, next, the red color we must, to a certain degree, take account of the type of hand. Intensity, which is shown by redness, belongs to the Martian type, and is, in that case, not such a defect as it may be with the Jupiterians, Apollonians, or Venusians. Excess of anything may be as fatal as deficiency, and as the redness of the hands shows the great force with which the blood is being propelled, it is typical of excess in quantity, quality, and force of the blood stream. By redness I mean a clear, full red, not a pink or dark pink, but a deep color. In this case we find the blood full of red corpuscles, consequently teeming with life, with vitality, and the subject correspondingly strong. We find the physical strength of the subject good, and the nature an ardent and intense one. He is a person who cannot do things by halves, who has so much vitality that it may be called an excess of health and strength. Thus, instead of nursing a physical pain or delicacy, he is impelled to great exertions in order to work off or use up the superabundance of vital energy with which he is charged. These people are intense in everything—love, war, business, art, religion; in fact, no place or walk in life in which they may be placed but will feel the impetus of their wonderful vitality and energy. They do not mince matters in speech, but use strong, short sentences. If they love, it is with no feeble flame, but a withering blast of strength. If angry, they are violent, and the red-hand finds the greatest difficulty in exercising self-control. As eaters these subjects are voracious, for the reason that it takes great quantities to feed the intense fires that inflame them. Their difficulty lies in being so much stronger than most people that they overshadow and wear out others by their intensity. Thus we see how it is possible to have even too much of the greatest of all blessings, health and strength. The person with the red hand does not think with the same ease and activity as the pink-handed subject, for the brain is somewhat clogged in its action by too much strong blood. The mind is heavier, coarser, denser, and not susceptible of the keenness which goes with a well-nourished condition and which is lacking when there is an overcrowding of blood to the brain cells. In these persons things are overdone, consequently they are extremists. By this time you have seen the great desirability of the normal condition in life, and can see that excess is nearly, if not quite, as bad as deficiency. The cold white hand freezes all qualities, the red hand burns them up; it is questionable which is the lesser of the two evils. So, when you encounter the red hand, think of the excess of blood, its strength, force, and rich quality. Picture the fires of extreme health and strength that are burning within. Think how ardent, firm, intense is the nature of your client. If strongly Jupiterian, he will have fierce ardor added to his ambition, to pride, and love of rule. If an Apollonian, he will be heated and intense in his brilliancy, excessive in all things, fond of show, and redness will destroy much of Apollo's refinement. If Venusian qualities of love and passion are his possession, he fairly consumes with ardor and heat of passion, and is alike dangerous to himself and to others. To the Martian type it gives ardor, fierceness, and coarseness. He fights, eats, and burns with fierce love. He is liable to strain his stomach by overeating, produce vertigo or apoplexy, and thus in health matters you must consider redness very carefully. If you find heart difficulties in nails or heart line, and also redness of the hands, it is a very serious matter. With throat, bronchial, or intestinal difficulties shown, if you find redness of the hands it is also a very bad indication. Thus through everything this fiery intensity of red hands will add heat and force. In a low, brutal hand, big Mount of Venus, short, thick fingers, hard palm, and clubbed thumb, if redness be added, there is one chance in ten that the possessor will not commit murder,—certainly he will if his affections are trifled with. He who spoke of "the red-handed murderer" may not have meant that his hands were dipped in blood, but he must have spoken of the red hand above described. With such a tremendous force to deal with as the red hand shows, you can understand how far short of proficiency you will be unless able to recognize and understand it.

Yellow color next claims our attention. The Saturnian is the type to which this color really belongs, but the Mercurian claims a share, while in all other types yellow is abnormal.

The reason some hands show this color is because their owners are bilious. The bile, whose function is to assist in the digestion of the food, was never intended to get into the blood. It should be carried away through the intestines and, having performed its natural function, disappear. But cases arise where the liver secretes too much bile, and a portion finds its way into the blood. Bile then becomes an irritant, a poisonous foreign substance, which vitiates the blood stream. Bile is yellowish in color, and as the blood in its course is constantly anxious to rid itself of the irritant, it embraces every opportunity to deposit the bile pigment whenever it can do so. When blood containing too much bile reaches the surface of the skin some of the bile pigment is left, and gradually the skin assumes a yellow color, more or less intense according to the amount of the bilious overflow into the blood. Thus the blood stream, which should carry on its course nothing but renewed strength, is transfusing an irritating foreign substance, and consequently fails to enliven, and build up the health and strength as it should. It is rather like a polluted miasmatic stream, producing weakened vitality, and lessening the vigor and energy. This bile in the blood is a constant irritant in its course, and in addition to poisoning the blood and tissues, it produces its corresponding irritating influence on the nerves, brain, and temper. It gradually lessens the strength of a muscular heart, and in time we find our pump becoming weak and irregular, while the force of the blood stream itself diminishes. Thus is added in chronic cases a paleness to the yellow skin, and we have the cold-blooded, bilious person, a most distressing combination. The person plagued with bile cannot be joyous, bright, and happy as our pink-skinned subject. He is held down by a weight that seems about to crush him ; he is moody, melancholy, takes a dark view of life, and has "the blues." He constantly crosses the bridges before he gets to them. He becomes morose, silent, and forms the habit of shunning society and gayety in every form. His brain is clogged by bilious poisoning, and its views become poisoned. He sees no bright side to anything, but revels in gloom, mystery, and superstition. He takes, in other words, a sickly, distorted point of view, and soon inclines to seek seclusion, and gives way to gloom and despondency. The bile irritates the nerves, so the yellow-skinned subject is cross, irritable, and consequently not a pleasant companion. His is, indeed, an unhappy lot, and you should be full of tender pity and humor his moods, for he is in reality a sick man. These facts cannot fail to impress your mind with the yellow color, its cause and qualities. Now when you detect it in the palm, the nails, and lines you have an aggravated case. If the yellow is *not pronounced*, yet still slightly visible, things are working in that direction, and while you may not be able, at the time of the reading, to say that yellow qualities have reached their *full control*, you know they are *started*, and should, if possible, be stopped at once.

Thus in hands the yellow color will distort all the Mounts. Jupiter becomes saddened and depressed. Saturn is the yellow Mount naturally; pronounced yellow color will bring this Mount to excess; Apollo is shorn of his brilliancy, Mercury is nervously bilious, Mars becomes an unbearable fellow, the Moon becomes cold and gloomy, and Venus has her physical powers destroyed. Remember always what I have said about the tanned color of hands, for you must not ascribe yellow qualities to a person who has merely been on a summer vacation and has not yet "bleached out"; also be watchful for natives of foreign climates whose hands are yellow by nature, but when you do find the color shown on a hand that should be pink it will warn you to look out for one whose view of life is, to say the least, abnormal.

We next consider the blue or purple color found in some hands. Going back to our source of information on the question of color, we find that blueness or purple color is caused by improper circulation of the blood, not necessarily a poor quality, however. We find it chiefly useful to consider this blue color from its health side, as it is a fact that beyond showing physical weakness the poor circulation does not in any marked degree affect the temperament. So you will regard blue color as a health indication, showing an impairment of the strength of the circulation. The white hand showing coldness, pink the normal condition, red excessive blood supply, and yellow poisoned blood, is followed by blue color, showing a sluggish condition of the circulation, indicating that the heart's pulsation is weak, and insufficient to move the blood rapidly, and that it is consequently travelling through its proper channels too slowly, so slowly in fact that it is producing a clogging of the stream, called in medical parlance *congestion*. This is the physiological action which causes blueness of the skin, and it is a most important matter to note, because, when the sluggishness of the flow in the blood stream is sufficiently pronounced to show in the blueness of the hand, the feebleness of the heart action has already reached a dangerous stage. When we study the nails we shall find much to add to this question on the subject of heart trouble, but in merely considering the color of the hand, you must in discovering blue color be at once on your guard for a weak heart. Sometimes you will find blue spots in the palm. These show temporary derangement of the circulation, but it has not reached the chronic state shown by blueness all over the palm. These blue spots can be scattered by brisk rubbing of the hands: the settled blue color cannot. Your handling of a subject with this blue color must be very judicious. It will not do to blurt out, "You have heart disease." I know of one case in which the subject nearly died on receiving such a statement, and only prompt medical attention prevented a fatality. Handle gently, don't excite; recognize that you are dealing with a very delicate person, and if you must touch on the heart at all, say, "Your blood is not circulating very freely this morning." Your client will then tell you he has a weak heart, and all danger of shock will be avoided. Here again we find tact and refined sensibilities necessary to good practice.

After our study of color it must be plain that I have not overstated the great importance of its mastery, and only by a proper understanding of the great part blood circulation plays in human life can you ever read the *fine print* of Palmistry.

CHAPTER VIII

THE NAILS

IN the examination of hands, a careful investigation of the finger nails should be made, and all possible information gained as to their texture, shape, and color. In order to lay the foundation for a good understanding of these matters, we will for a moment consider their structure and uses. Microscopically examined, nails are composed of minute hair-like fibres, so closely knit together that they adhere to each other, and form a compact horn-like substance. The nails grow out of the skin at the ends of the fingers, and do not grow from the muscle or bones. This is proven by the fact that when the skin has been stripped from the fingers, the nails have also been removed, and are found to be imbedded in it. The nail of the human hand corresponds to the claw of the carnivora, and in low types of humanity, like the Digger Indians, grows very long and strong, and is used as a weapon of offense and defense. The lion or tiger depends upon claws and muscular strength to win his battles, consequently his claws are very long, sharp, and strong. The higher intelligence of the human species, and the fact that they have hands to carry out their ideas, enable man to *make* weapons of defense for his use, even though these weapons be only primitive spears or arrows. Thus advanced humanity does not consider the nails in the light of a weapon, and we must seek their usefulness from some other standpoint.

There are located at the ends of the fingers a great number of nerve cells which make possible the sense of touch possessed by this part of the hand, and it is evident that one use for the nails is to protect and shield from harm this concentration of delicate nerve filaments. In order that the sense of touch may be extremely acute, the nerves must be as near the surface of the skin as possible. If there was no protection afforded by the nails, this could not be, and with the nerves of touch deeply imbedded under the skin, the sense of touch would be a blunted one. During a study of the hands, my conviction has constantly increased that the Creator intended us to read from them for the benefit of the human race, so it has appeared to me that there were yet other uses for the nails which have not been enumerated. I have conceived them to be windows, through which the palmist might look virtually into the interior organization of the human being, since the part which lies under the nail, and which is commonly called the "quick," is intensely delicate and sensitive, and has conveyed to its surface in the most accurate manner all the secrets of the circulation. This ebb and flow of the blood seen through the nails, which I have likened to glass in the window, makes wonderful revelations as to health and temperament. All the wealth of information revealed by color in the hands is accentuated by looking through this glass, not at the color *of* the nails as it is most improperly called, but at the color *under* the nails, which is reflected from a part of the hand so delicately organized that in some cases it shows almost the pulsations of the heart. In this way you will see that we have come still nearer to solving the mysteries of the blood current which are so important. Thus also the great nerve centres under the nails, when they are operating in a healthy manner, allow you to see this fact by the *texture* of the nails, and, on the contrary, when the nerve centre in the quick is impaired, it leaves its impression on the nail texture, by changing the *quality* of the nail itself. Here we again encounter very common-sense reasons why the nails are only one more physiological link in the perfect science of Palmistry. Nails show quality, just as does the skin. In fine-grained, fine-textured hands you will generally find fine, smooth texture of the nail. In some hands the skin texture is fine, and the nails tending to coarseness. In this case you know that something is out of proportion and that the normal balance has been disturbed. The coarse nail found on a fine texture of skin may be a short, heavy nail showing great critical qualities, and this nail belongs more naturally to large hands, coarse skin, with hard or at least elastic consistency. It may be that the coarser texture of the nail will show the advanced state of nerve disorder, indicated by the *fluted nail.* In any event, if you find a fine-textured hand and coarse nails, it should cause you to search for the meaning; so in the first part of an examination of nails, compare the texture of the nails with the texture of the skin, and see if they both belong to the same grade of fineness. If they do, so far as texture goes, you have a normal condition ; if they do not, seek to find what is out of balance.

Under the head of texture of the nail, remember that the horn of the nail should be even and smooth in surface, the grain of the nail which runs from top to base must be smooth, and not composed of ridges, or flutings as we call them. Where the nail texture is smooth it is because the filaments that form the nail substance are all of one size, while fluted nails are made up of fibres of different sizes growing together. The nail must also be pliable, not brittle ; it must look alive and elastic. The fluting, or ridging, of the nail from the top to base is an indication of nervous disorder. Accompanying this fluted appearance, if the case be serious, will be found a brittle condition of the nail, causing it to break easily, and instead of growing over the end of the finger in a protecting way, it is growing *away* from the flesh, seemingly not adhering firmly to the quick. In my practice, I regard the white spots which appear on the nails as the first warning of delicate nerves, though there may be no knowledge, on the part of the subject, that his nerves are not perfectly sound. The white spots indicate a *beginning* of the loss of vitality of the nail from deficient nerve force, and are nature's first warning of trouble ahead. As the disorder increases, the white flecks first grow larger, then grow together, then cover the whole nail, taking away the transparency and clearness. The window glass, as I have called the nail, has become clouded. Following this condition, ridges begin to appear, these grow more and more pronounced and frequent, and soon the *fluted nail* manifests itself (24). By this time the subject is painfully aware of his nerves. As the fluting grows more pronounced, the nail

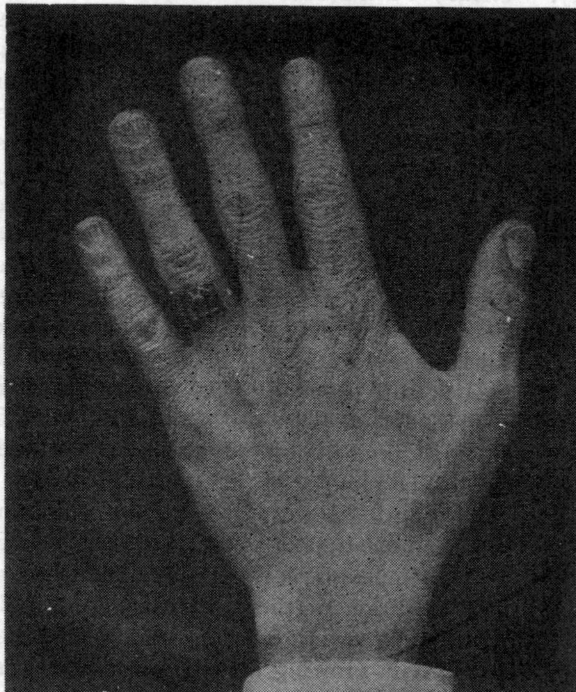

NO. 24. FLUTED NAILS

grows brittle, begins to turn back from the end, loses its graceful shape, and becomes high on one side of the finger and low on the other, or is very short because the nail is bitten down into the quick. At this stage there is great delicacy of nerves or grave danger of paralysis. The nerves under the nail are thus reflecting by means of the nail the disorder which has occurred in the greatest of our nerve centres, the brain, and the vitality of the nail is being *burned up*, the oil dried out of it; the filaments, instead of binding themselves together in a homogeneous mass, are piling on top of each other, and the nervous confusion of the system is producing a confusion of the nail structure and life. Thus

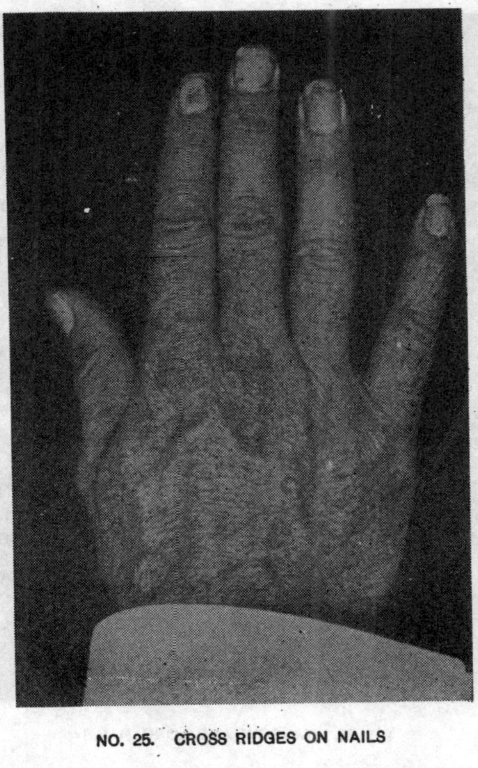

NO. 25. CROSS RIDGES ON NAILS

in this progression, from the mere warning conveyed by the white flecks, through the stage of fluting, to the brittle, turning-back nail, you can trace the *degree* of danger from nerve destruction or disorder in your subject. I have seen cases where smooth, even-textured nails, after a sudden attack of nervous prostration, grew out white and cloudy in color, and strongly fluted. I have seen these same nails, as health returned, gradually resume their normal texture and lose the fluted appearance.

There is another indication which I have often verified, where the nail shows a ridge crosswise. Seemingly the nail has stopped growing, its vitality has been interrupted (25).

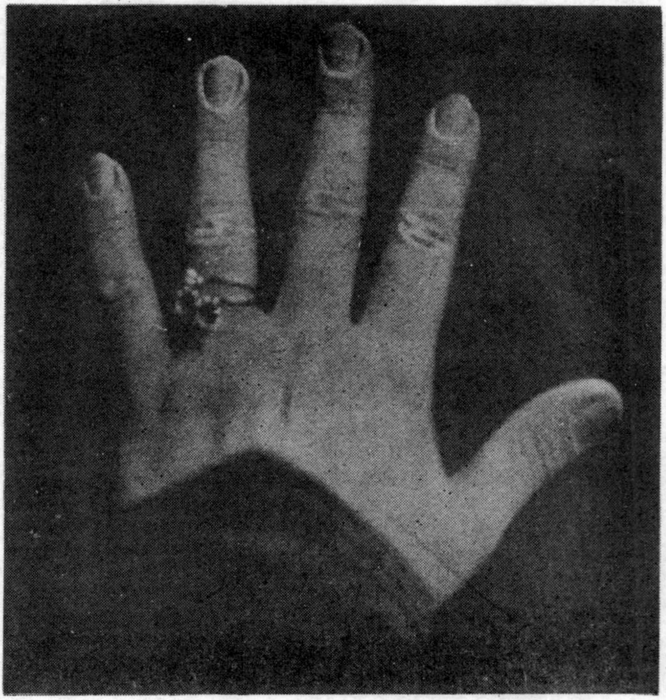

NO. 26. NARROW AND LONG NAILS

It is as if one nail had died, and another had grown on to the finger to replace it. This cross-ridged nail shows that a serious illness has interrupted the health of the subject, and that the illness was attended with grave danger. When you encounter this nail, it will give splendid material with which to work, for you can almost always tell what the nature of the sickness was, and how long previously it occurred.

This nail always records a *past event*, and is not, as has been incorrectly stated, a source of information as to the future. It requires about six months to grow a new nail, so that in handling this indication you can tell how long since the illness occurred by noting how far the ridge has grown: if one

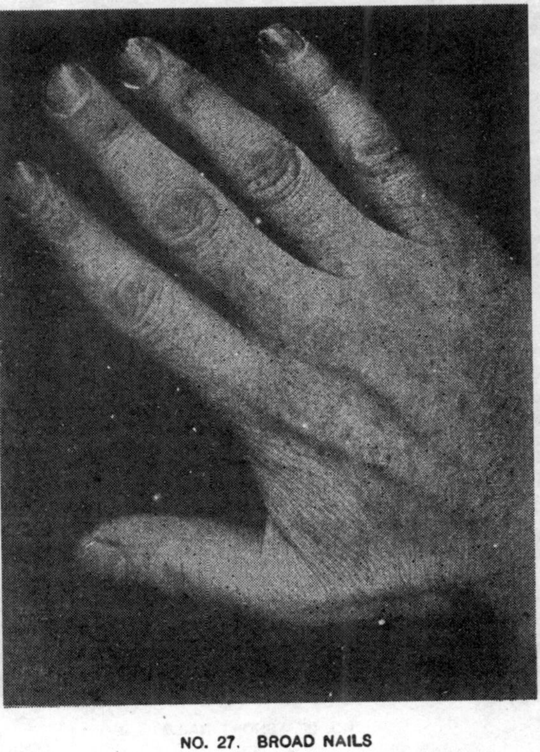

NO. 27. BROAD NAILS

quarter of the length of the nail, about one and one half months; one third, two months; one half, three months; and this can be continued until the nail has completely grown off the end of the finger. With this cross-ridge you will often see a firm-textured nail replaced by a fluted nail. In this case, it shows that nervous trouble has been the cause, and by judging how far out the new nail has grown, you can tell that at some time between one and six months past the subject has been dangerously ill from a nervous disorder. The exact date can be told by the distance the ridge has grown out. If the *new nail* is badly fluted, you can say, "This trouble has not entirely disappeared," and in this case you should

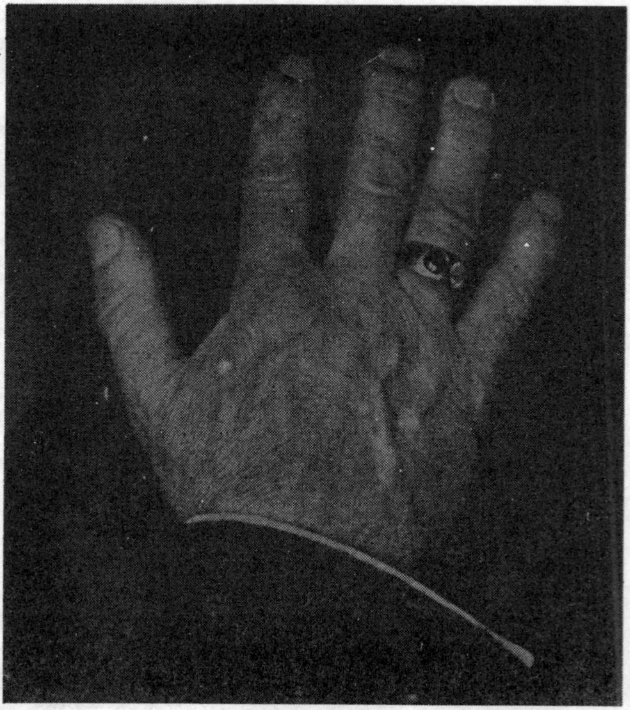

NO. 28. SHORT NAILS

advise rest and freedom from all excitement. In the progress of this chapter, we shall find other nail formations showing disease. If any of these show in the new nail, *that* will be the disease that has caused the trouble. Whenever you find the cross-ridged nail, handle it as above outlined, and it will give you excellent results. Remember that it always shows a grave health indication.

As an indicator of *general* health and robustness of constitution, the nails are also valuable. In this regard it has been my observation that a narrow nail shows a person who has not robust muscular strength, but is carried by nervous energy (26). It is a psychic nail, and the delicacy of the psychic character is present, rather than muscular strength as shown by a broad nail (27). The narrow nail will be either white, yellow, blue, or pink, never red, and it will be often found with the blue color at the base, denoting poor circulation. Neither the broad nor the narrow nails are indicative of *special* diseases, but, as I have said, of *general* health and strength. When you find the delicate, narrow nail, read a delicate constitution, with a broad nail a robust one, especially if the nail be, as it often is, red in color. Of course, if in the handling of these two nails you see abnormal developments, such as yellow or blue color, use these to indicate *special* trouble as is indicated by *color*, and if you also find changes of texture, such as fluting or brittleness, read it as showing nervous trouble. The *general* indications of robustness or delicacy are to be used *only* when found *without* complications of color or texture.

There is a nail which has many degrees of development, and which is to be read as indicating its peculiar qualities in *proportion* to the pronouncedness in which it is seen. This is the short nail (28). All short nails show a critical turn of mind, but if the nail is not *very* short, it will only be a quizzical or investigating disposition. This must be taken as the mildest type, while the extremely short, flat nail with the skin growing down on it, is its opposite, showing pugnacity and a person who does not argue with you because he believes he is always right, but because he loves contention. You will find this latter type, which is the one from which you start in grading the *degree* of shortness, often not a quarter of an inch long and very broad, covering the entire visible end of the finger, and giving the tip an exceedingly flat, blunt appearance (29). This nail gives almost a clubbed appearance to the fingers. The skin seems to cling to the nail, and loves to grow down on it until it can stretch no farther and breaks. This generally results in leaving a ragged appearance where the skin joins the nail. This nail goes with a vigorous constitution, an active mind, and a very critical, pugnacious, argumentative disposition. It shows a person who would rather argue than eat. He disagrees with

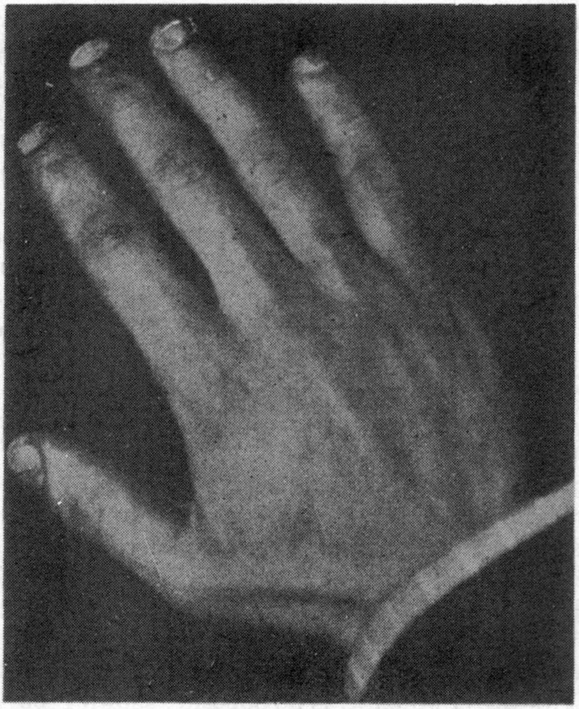

NO. 29. VERY SHORT, CRITICAL NAILS

you on subjects when he knows perfectly well you are right, simply for the delight it gives him to argue. He criticises everything, for in this way he can best provoke contention, and while he does not want to fight with you physically, he loves the battle of the mind, and will bring to bear on the argument all his physical energy, until he tires out an ordinary mortal, and wins a victory not always of right, but of a hang-on, pugnacious, critical disposition. In dealing with these people you are sure of only one thing, and that is that they will be on the other side of the question as soon as they know which side you take. Manifestly the way to handle them is to be entirely negative, giving no inkling as to what

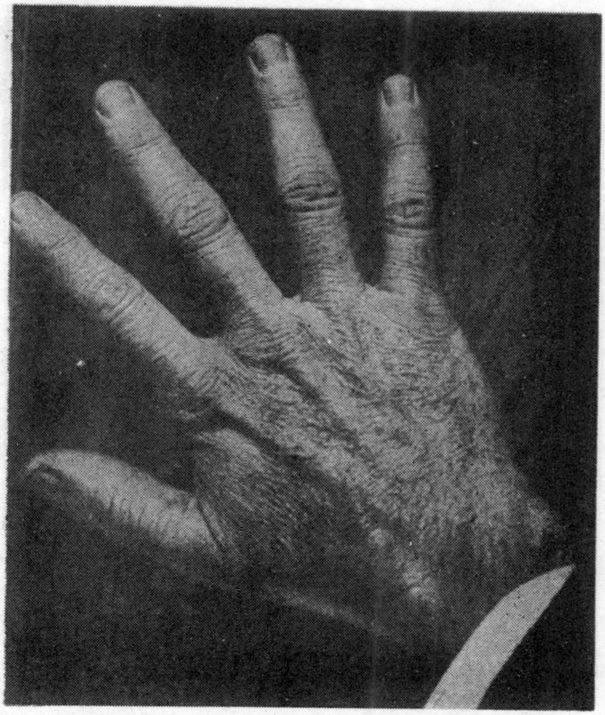

NO. 30. OPEN AND FRANK NAILS

you think. The extreme development of this nail you will not often encounter, but you will meet daily very strong examples of the short critical type. The influence of this nail will be strong on any hand on which it appears. Add to it knotty fingers, a big thumb, a hard hand, big Mounts of Mars, and a most pugnacious, disagreeable creature will result. The critical mind is a factor in everything,—love, business, art, eloquence, war, literature, or music,—so you must look for short nails in every examination, and give them, when found, their full meaning. Remember they always show a *degree* of the critical turn of mind, greater or less as the nails are more or less short.

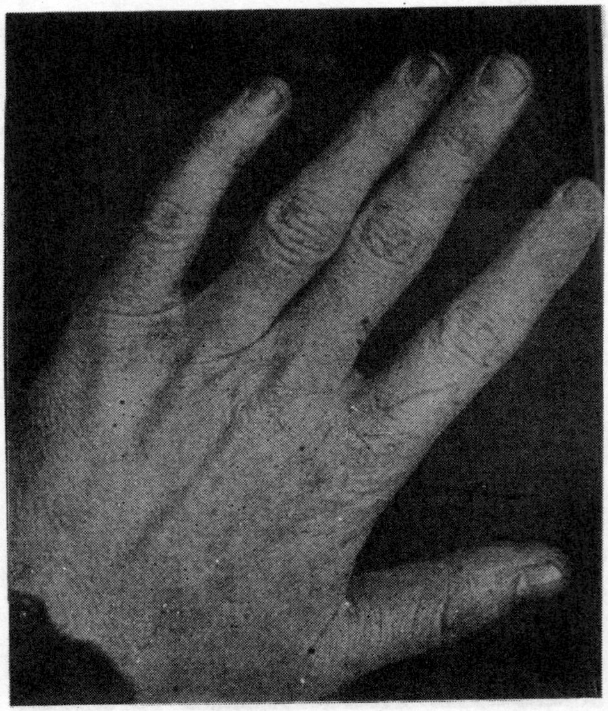

NO. 31. HEART DISEASE NAILS

There are nails that are broad at the tip, curving around the fingers, broadening at the base, pink in color, and fine in texture (30). These nails show the open, frank nature, to whom honesty of thought is natural, and to whose owner genuineness is the mainspring. They are broad, open-looking nails, and in their breadth show the broad ideas of their owners. In this nail, pinkness of color is always to be looked for, before giving the full value to this reading.

There is a nail which is small in size though regular in form, with the end *quite square*, and tapering toward the base, or the base may be the same width as the outer end (31). This nail is often found on long fingers, or otherwise large hands, though it may be seen on small ones. It does not belong to any one type of hand, but is found on all-shaped fingers and hands. It is a nail which shows heart trouble, and more of an organic difficulty than a lack of circulation. This nail is quite distinctive in appearance, and once seen can always be recognized. The nail is a small one, though it does not have the appearance of a critical nail, nor is it at all like the narrow nail described showing delicate constitution. So it is not a narrow nail, nor a short one, but is most properly a *small* nail, yet well-proportioned. With this nail is often found a deep blue color, which is most pronounced at the base, and if the nail has a moon, the blue color may even extend past its top. With the shape of nail above described you know that the heart structurally is not all right, and with the additional blueness you have an unfailing confirmation of the trouble. When you see the deep-set blue at the base of *any* nail, you will at once recognize poor circulation and a weak heart; when seen with the above *shape*, it means pronounced heart difficulty. You must be very careful to note the age of women who have the blue color of the nails, to see if they are near the ages of twelve to fourteen, at which time they are passing from childhood to womanhood, and always have some disturbance of circulation. This trouble terminates when the menses become well established and regular. A blueness found at such an age shows only a *temporary* obstruction of circulation, and you must not treat it so seriously as if found between the years of sixteen and forty-two. Blueness found during these years, when the age of puberty is passed, and before change of life has come, means serious difficulty, not often of a temporary character. Between the years of forty-two and forty-six the change of life occurs, and then again blueness is found, as the circulation is once more temporarily interrupted, and again you must consider the difficulty as of probably short duration. In all of these cases note whether the color is a *general* blue all over the nail, which must be read as nervousness or carbonized blood, or whether it is a deep, angry, purplish blue low at the base of the nail. In the latter case it is a thunder-cloud which threatens destruction

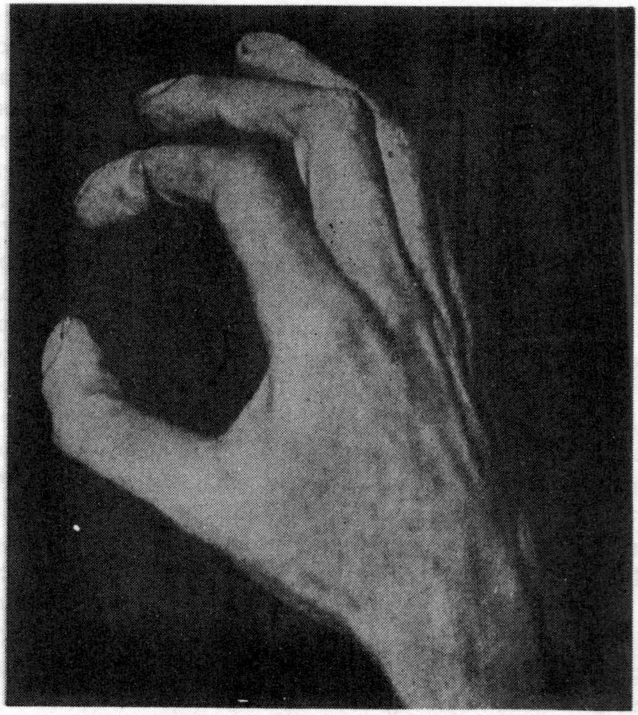

NO. 32. BULBOUS OR TUBERCULOUS NAILS

when the storm bursts, but in all cases watch carefully the ages indicated above, and gauge your opinion by applying the rules given. A *faint* blue tinge covering the whole nail will show you a nervous person with *some* heart weakness, not, however, of as pronounced character as that found by blueness at the *base* of the nail.

There is a nail which you will meet, that is so pronounced

in its formation that, once seen, it will never be forgotten or mistaken for any other. The end of the finger as well as the nail plays a part in the formation of it, and the advanced type is described in order that you may use it as a basis on which to rest your gradings of this nail. It is a *bulbous* nail and grows on a bulbous finger-tip (32). It may have had any shape originally, as you will find it on the narrow, broad, square, or any other tip. Nothing as to squareness or tip formation plays any part with this nail; it is the *bulbousness alone* which is its distinctive feature. This is the nail which shows an advanced stage of consumption or tubercular trouble. Medical authorities say it is a lack of nourishment that produces it, and among physicians it is a well-known and recognized indication of tubercular trouble located somewhere in the subject. In appearance the end of the finger thickens underneath until it forms a distinct bulb or pad, which is sometimes as round as a marble. Over this bulbous tip the nail is curved, forming a complete clubbed, blunt end, the top curved with the nail, the under part fleshy. This formation makes the end of the finger a complete knob, and the appearance is most striking and disagreeable. This nail shows the advanced stage of tuberculosis, sometimes of the spine, most often of the lungs. Often the color of the nail is quite blue, showing the stoppage of circulation incident to the blood congestion, or, in this case more properly, blood contamination. The lungs, which should be removing carbonic acid gas from the blood and filling it with oxygen, are so obstructed or destroyed that the blood is not renewed as it goes through them, but carries many of its poisonous qualities back through the circulation. Thus blood obstruction and impurity give these bulbous nails a marked blue appearance. I always regard them as a most serious indication. I have seen cases, however, and have in mind one now, of a subject who has had a degree of bulbous nail for several years and is still alive. A sudden cold would be apt to produce a fatal case of pneumonia, however, at any time, so that life at the best is held by only a slender thread.

There is a nail which has a curved formation approaching

the bulbous, though in a very slight degree. In this case the end of the finger has not taken on a bulbous formation, but only the nail shows a decided inclination to curve (33). It is not in any sense the bulbous nail mentioned above, and it is in almost all cases found to be a large nail. This nail

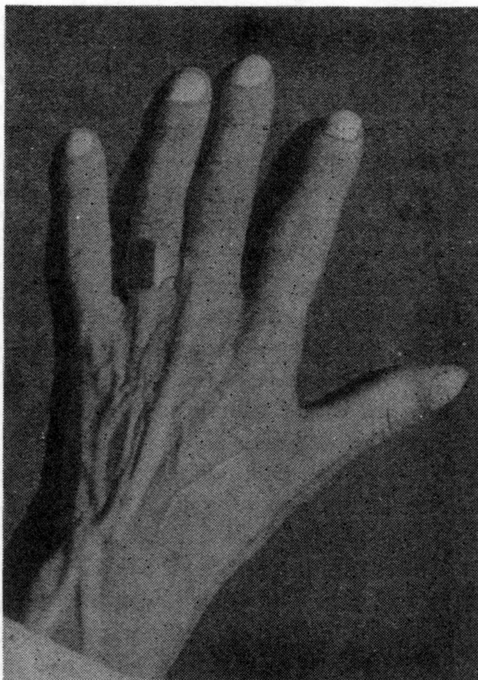

NO. 33. BRONCHIAL OR THROAT DELICACY

may also be on any shaped tip; it is the *curving alone* that distinguishes it. The indications shown by this nail are delicacy of bronchial tubes and throat. Sometimes it may go as far as a *weakness* of the lungs but not of advanced disease. It shows one who is exceedingly liable to colds at least, and for whom sudden changes of temperature produce disturbance of throat and bronchial tubes. It is a delicacy to be guarded against, and the client should always be warned to use care and avoid taking colds. It is a fine confirmation of this delicacy of throat and lungs if you find the Mercury line full of islands, and you need feel no hesitancy in using it. Hundreds of times I have verified this indication. In the readings applied to all nails, you must look carefully to color. Often the color under the nails will be more pronounced and easier of recognition than the color of the palm. The fact is, that the view through the nails gives you an insight of color easier, because the thick skin does not cover the quick and the circulation is more readily exposed to view. The same rules apply to color under the nails as to the palm. The white nail shows the lack of warmth. These must not be confused with the whiteness of a nervous nail, which shows white because the *nail substance* is clouded, but it is the whiteness *under* the nail which relates to coldness. There is a very good way to distinguish the white nail, and that is by putting it beside a pink nail. This is also the way to learn the difference between blue and yellow nails. The pink nails are plentiful — you will see many of them everywhere ; so it will be your best plan to fix the pink nail well in mind, and *from it* judge a nail that is white or of any other color.

In blue nails we must consider the two kinds of blueness. That which tinges the whole nail, and that which settles darkly at the base.

You must note with care if you see redness pronounced under any nail, as it will show you the intense ardor and excess of strength of the person.

In the examination of many nails, you will find them differing in some degree from my descriptions. If you will, however, use your powers of observation until you have located typical nails of types described, you will afterwards, with all ease, be able to grade the other nails you meet, giving them the proper degrees of development.

CHAPTER IX

HAIR ON THE HANDS

HAIR on the hands is deserving of some attention, and while you may not find occasion to use it largely in practice, still it is one of the "little things," and may come to your rescue at a moment when you are having difficulty in unlocking some complex character. The presence of hair on the *head* is natural, for the head was intended to be covered with it. But human beings are not expected to have hairy bodies, and do not, unless they belong to certain types and have certain qualities. The more hairy the body of a human being is, the more physical strength he has, and its presence also indicates the existence of a coarser element. The use of the hands keeps the hair on them worn off to a considerable extent; thus a liberal growth of it on the hand shows that the vitality of the person is very strong indeed. This vigorous nature stands much fatigue, and goes through even severe illnesses without fatal results. In the examination of most hands you will have little to do with hair, especially on the hands of women. When, however, it is seen on a woman's hand, it tells you of an approach to masculinity that you must weigh well in your estimate of her. On the hands of men you will more often encounter hair, because men are more robust than women, but it is not true that the absence of hair on a man's hand in any way shows effeminacy. It shows a finer-strung person,—one not physically so strong, perhaps, but not necessarily weak in character. All hair you examine will be found either coarse or fine. This at once speaks of the nature of the person, for coarse hairs do not grow from the finest-textured people. They grow from *strong* persons, but not necessarily *fine* persons, and no matter how brilliant the glitter of costly jewelry, or how much the clothing may tell of wealth, if you find a woman with coarse hair on her hands, she is, under all of it, by nature common. In all readings, what you are trying to discover is the material from which your subject is made. Thus, to prove fineness or coarseness, or physical vitality by hair on the hands, is well worth the effort. Physically considered, hairs grow out through the pores of the skin, from bulbs or sacs which feed and supply nourishment to them. These sacs, firmly imbedded in the skin, partake of and draw their nourishment from the vitality of the subject. All the hair sacs do not have hairs growing from them ; some never produce any at all. If the vitality of the subject is not very strong, hairs do not start ; if the vitality is impoverished *after* the hairs *have started*, these hairs become dry and stop growing. Thus the heat in severe fevers injures the hair sacs, and the hairs fall out. In severe nervous troubles the nervous fluid burns up the vitality of the hair sacs, and the hair becomes brittle and lifeless. This condition corresponds to the brittle finger nail of nervousness. It is well known that iron in the blood is a source of great strength, therefore various forms of iron are prescribed by physicians when patients lack a sufficient supply of it. The hairs themselves are colorless in their natural state, and the fact that hair is of many shades is due to the amount of iron pigment absorbed from the body by the hair sacs and fed out by them. This is the explanation of white, gray, black, blond, red, or auburn-colored hair.

It is an interesting fact that the prevailing color of the hair of people of northern latitudes is what we call blond (this is the Norse and Saxon color), and the color belonging to the Latin races living in southern climes is black. It is not possible for you to draw the distinction in this way with all the people you meet, because the races have so intermarried that all shades of hair are the result, and we find blond and black hair hopelessly mingling. But you can remember that the hardy Norsemen, Swedes, and

Danes belong to the blond-haired types, and that the French, Italian, Spanish, and Oriental nations are black-haired. When we know how much fatigue, cold, and exposure the Northmen can endure, and remember that iron gives strength, we find it hard to understand why blond hair belongs to them. It is explained, however, by the fact that their bodies are so exposed to cold that they need all the vital force possible, and so consume in their sustenance most of the iron, leaving little to color hair. These Northmen are called cold by nature; they love with frigidity, and have no heat or fire of passion. They do not burn with ardor and consume if their desires are not gratified, as do the black-haired Latins. The men and women live together that they may help each other work; there is little of the softness or ardor of love between them. These people are called phlegmatic. The fact is, that there is so much vitality necessary to *sustain life* with them in their frigid climes, that the heat-producing iron is thus used up, leaving little behind to fire the passions. A passionate nature needs excess of health and vitality. Thus blond hair on the hands shows a person who is even in temper, unexcitable, cool, phlegmatic, not overamorous, constant, less sensual, intensely practical, energetic, common-sense, more frequently honest, and matter-of-fact. This applies to the blond color belonging to the Swede and Norwegian, which is a *straw-colored yellow*. You must not class *all* blond hair as having the above qualities, for if you find it *tinged with a reddish hue* or drifting toward black in shade, you must modify your opinion accordingly. Take the Swede as one side of your blond type, and from it gauge the quality of the person you are examining, as the color of his hair may be modified by an alloy of other colors. In all the hair I speak of here, I of course mean the hair growing on the hands.

Black hair belongs to the Latin and Oriental races. Its owners live in sunny climes and enjoy balmy breezes. Thus they are not the hardy, enduring class that we have just considered. They have plenty of vital energy and strength, the iron in them is abundant, but as it is not needed to sustain and feed their vital fires as in the case of the Northmen, it is absorbed by the hair sacs, enters the hair tubes, and makes them black. The climates of the Latin and Oriental races invite inertia. Theirs are soft, mild atmospheres which possess enervating qualities, and produce love of pleasure and ease rather than a desire for work. Thus filled with vital force, and not having to exert it to keep warm, their strength seeks some avenue of escape, and finds it in the indulgence of the pleasures of sense. In this way do the black-haired people become more ardent, restless, sensuous, volatile, and less evenly balanced than the colder types. Their black hair is the mark of persons who have heat and warmth, vitality enough and to spare, and who love to expend the excess of health on pleasure. Understand now that I am in no wise saying that all the black hair you meet has the temperament and the failings of the French, Spaniards, and Orientals. Black hair will show you strong vitality, and a warm, intense nature, but in our country you will find Saxon qualities behind it, making it more practical, and directing its energy into active channels. Whenever you do find it well marked on the hands, you will not fail, however, to remember the iron, the strength, the way the color is produced, and the people from whom it sprang. With these facts in your mind you will know what black hair means.

You will find gray or white hair on the hands also. White hair is the hair tube without any of the iron pigment in it at all; gray hair still has *some* of the iron present. White hair is produced by the vitality of the subject falling so far below the normal standard that there is not enough iron absorbed by the hair sacs to give even a blond color. That all color is absent, and whiteness present, is because the vital force has gone below the normal point. There are isolated cases where the hair has turned white from fright, and also from much headache. In each of these cases, it will be possible to locate the trouble, however, as indicated later in this chapter. If you find gray hair on the hands look for the color of the tips; if found black or red, and the *texture of the skin youthful*, you at once look at the Mount of Venus, and you will find it flat and flabby, much rayed and lined. With this look for a broad, white Heart-line, filled with chains. A combination like the above will tell you that a worn-out libertine is before you. When gray hair is found which you think is caused by age, look at the skin on the back of the hand and see if it has the wrinkled, satiny-brown color of an old hand or if it bears the aspect of youth. If you see the aged skin, you merely conclude that this is the cause of the color of the hair. If you see youthful skin and gray hair, look for the vitality impaired by excess. Venus will give you the confirmation of this point. Where the hair has been made white by shock, you will find a broken or islanded Head line. If the color is produced by headaches, many small rays cutting the Head line will show it, or many *small* islands and a similar combination on the Life line. The shock will be a single sign on Head and Life lines ; the frequent headaches will show by the continuous cutting of small lines.

Red color of hair is produced by the presence of another chemical combination of iron in excessive quantities in the subject. In examining red hair always look for its fineness or coarseness ; for, a sign of great inflammability at best, it is much more so if the hair be coarse. It is a color that gives heat of temper, excitability of disposition, a certain predisposition to engage in quarrels, and liability to "flare up" on the slightest provocation. If the hair is fine, the fits of temper will be momentary, though violent while they last. If the hair is coarse, it will indicate brutality, violent temper, and the tendency to sullenly nurse a fury and seek revenge. Red hair gives you always excitability, an electric readiness to engage in strife, commonly called temper, and is not a sign of overrefinement. What is called auburn hair, and is so much praised and loved, is a combination of the warmth and passion of black hair with a shade of added fire from the red, which combination tinges the hair with a golden auburn glow, a brilliant combination, but if the possessor happens to have bad qualities, beware ! for a furnace is burning underneath the surface.

As a general rule, you will use hair on the hand to confirm something seen elsewhere, unless you happen to be reading with the hands held through a curtain and do not see the subject. If this is the case hair on the hands will enable you to do work otherwise impossible.

CHAPTER X

THE HAND AS A WHOLE

THE next subject to engage your attention is the appearance of the hand as a whole, and the object of the investigation is to discover whether the hand is evenly balanced, or is heavier or lighter in certain parts than in others.

The best method of proceeding with this examination is to lay the two hands wide open before you with the palms up and the fingers straightened out to their natural length. If the hand is a flexible one, you must not allow it to bend back, showing its flexibility, for that you have already discovered, but merely extend the fingers in a natural manner, until they are held straight. This gives you a full view of the palm, and you first note whether the fingers are seemingly long enough just to balance the palm, whether they are shorter than the palm, or whether they seem to be *much* longer. This is done to see whether the hand seems balanced from top to bottom. In this examination, what we call the Three Worlds of Palmistry first make their appearance. These three worlds are based on the supposition that a person is guided either by mind, by the affairs of every-day life, or by the baser qualities of animal instincts. We now seek, from an examination of the hand as a whole, to discover which of these three worlds our subject inhabits. As far back as we can remember, there have been the three divisions of body, soul, and spirit ; mental, abstract, and material ; air, fire, and water, and many other subdivisions into threes or trinities corresponding to the three worlds of which I have spoken. They all embody the idea of an ethereal element, a material one, and a baser.

In the hand, it is constantly and most aptly used to bring out clearly an idea we wish to convey of the domination of mind, material matters, or baser qualities in the subject. In the hand, taken as a whole, the fingers or upper portion represent *mind;* the middle portion of the hand, from the

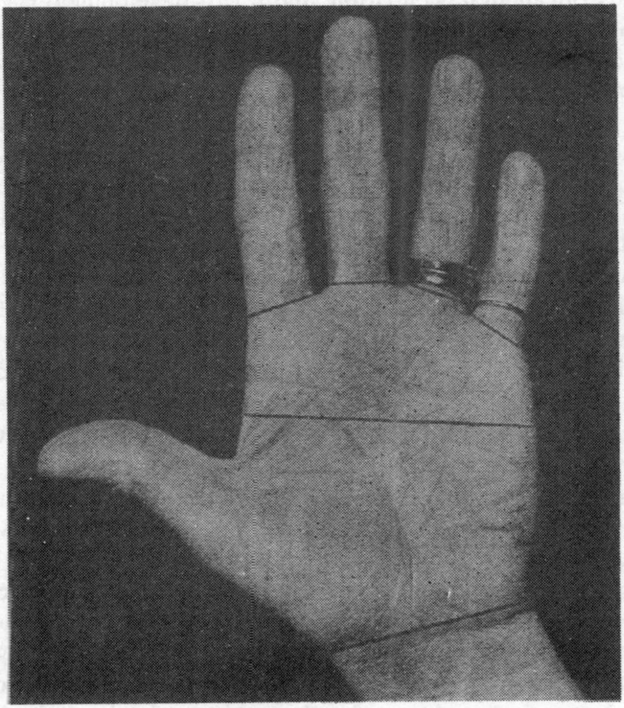

NO. 34. MENTAL, PRACTICAL, AND BASER WORLDS

base of the fingers to a line running across the hand from the top of the Mount of the Moon to Mount of Venus (34), represents the material, and the base of the hand, from the line above described to the wrist, the lower elements. These locate the Three Worlds of Palmistry. In the hand now outstretched before you, if length of finger predominates, mind is the ruling factor. If the middle portion is most developed, the world of business or every-day life is strongly prominent. If the lower part is strongest, the subject lives on a low, earthy plane, and is sensual and animal in his instincts. We of course know that mind is elevating, therefore if the world of mind is strongest, we know the subject is fitted for study, for mental occupation, and if this development is very pronounced, without anything to back it, he will be one who lives in a realm of ideas and exaltation, without sufficient of the practical side present to keep him from following his mental development to the exclusion of necessary and practical matters. This is why so many literary men, teachers, and students are such poor business men that they accumulate nothing. They live entirely in the upper world as Palmistry conceives it, and, while mind is all right, still all mind and nothing practical is a most unfortunate development for one who has to get through this matter-of-fact world. The middle world is the world of practical affairs. This is because we have in the territory covered by this middle portion of the hand the qualities of ambition, soberness, wisdom, art, shrewdness, aggression, and resistance developed. This seems a formidable array of qualities, but to the one who has to battle with worldly affairs in this century, they are none too strong. The middle development, if overshadowing both the upper and lower worlds, will show that business, practical life, every-day ideas, and material success compose the world in which the subject lives. Thus he is better fitted for commercial positions, politics, war, agricultural pursuits, or for anything which is entirely practical. He has a fine contempt for the subject who is all brains. Money-getting is his moving desire, and he lives in the world of material matters.

If you find the hand developed at the base, you will know that your subject lives in the realm of low, base desires, and enjoys himself best when gratifying his sensual pleasures. This is particularly true if the hand be coarse. He can appreciate nothing high or elevating. If he acquires money he does not know how to make a refined use of it. He loves beauty, but it is vulgar, showy kinds that attract him ;

he is fond of eating, but with the gluttony of the gourmand, not the delight of the epicure. He has no mental recreations ; mind is not a guiding force with him. He is sometimes shrewd, but with the instinctive cunning of the fox, not the talent of a high and lofty mind. He loves display, and in his home will have profusion, not taste ; glaring colors, not harmony. He is vulgar and common in all his tastes, and among people of refinement and good breeding is the veritable boor. He does not see how ridiculous he makes himself to men of mind and elevated thought. He sees only from his earthy point of view, and all his tastes, his thoughts, his loves, are coarse, vulgar, and common. This subject lives in the lower world.

You will often find these three developments in the hands you meet, and it is no unlikely nor impossible types that are given here. Very often you will not be able to tell at a glance which world predominates. This is a most fortunate circumstance, for it tells you that the hand is balanced, and in everything pertaining to the human character balance is most to be desired. Thus, to have mind, practical matters, and the lower desires so combined as to give neither one a mastery of the other will show a person who is not one-sided in his view of life. He will be wise, intelligent, practical, prudent, even-tempered, and yet not unsophisticated, for he has enough of the base alloy to give him necessary knowledge. He is thus able to weigh all matters, not from a purely mental standpoint, but can add to his investigations the common-sense needed to make life successful. This balance of the three worlds, as shown by the whole hand, enables a person to become a pronounced success in the world. Consistency must be looked into very carefully, however, for laziness, should it be present, can destroy any amount of genuine ability and any number of good intentions. A soft hand may even break as good a combination as one with the three worlds balanced. When you find that a hand is not balanced, you must note which world is the strongest, and judge whether it is enough more pronounced than the others to lead them in its wake. Sometimes you will see one world only slightly in excess of the others. In this case you can say that the subject *likes* the matters of that particular world best, but it may not be sufficiently in the lead to make him *follow* it. Here, as everywhere else, good sense and practice must guide you in a judgment of how much one of the worlds predominates over the others. Of course, it stands to reason that no success can come in a worldly way unless the middle portion be developed. Mind may win glory, but not money; or the base qualities may be abundantly present and yet not destroy financial success. Link the two upper worlds, and you can obtain financial results from mental strength ; link the two lower and you can gain riches though it may be made in coarse occupations. Take away the middle portion, and you have then the supremacy of the mind and the predominance of the earthy without the leaven of common-sense ; such developments cannot make successful people. Look, therefore, to the balanced hand for your best results, next to the upper or lower in combination with the middle.

CHAPTER XI

THE FINGERS IN GENERAL

AFTER viewing the hand as a whole, and separating it into the three worlds, the next observation should be of the fingers in general. This will lead to a classification of the fingers as either long or short, as belonging to the smooth or knotty class, and will cause you to look at the tips to see whether they are square, spatulate, conic, or pointed.

Do not try to class any set of fingers in a *group*, but consider *each one*, and judge it by itself. Every finger is named for, and partakes of, the qualities of the Mount under it. The first finger is the finger of Jupiter, the second, Saturn, the third, Apollo, the fourth, Mercury. The thumb we do not consider as a finger, but in a class by itself. In examining the fingers first note their length. If they seem unreasonably long, apply the measurements given in a subsequent chapter on long fingers, to determine whether they are long fingers or normal length. If the fingers appear unusually short, apply measurements given in a subsequent chapter, being careful not to class as short fingers those which belong to a normally short hand. Observe the joints to see if they are developed or smooth, using great care in judging the *degree* of development for each joint, and looking to see if the first or second joints alone are prominent. If you find very knotty joints, apply knotty qualities; if entirely smooth, give the subject smooth-finger attributes. Examine the flexibility of each finger by itself; if one finger is more flexible than the others, then the qualities of the Mount type it represents are more pronounced in this subject. See if the fingers are straight or twisted. See if the bending is lateral or if the finger seems to twist around on its own axis. Fingers bent laterally (35) increase the *shrewdness* of the qualities of the Mount on which they are placed, while a twisting on the axis shows a liability to moral or physical defects in the Mount qualities. To determine which, use the nails, the lines on

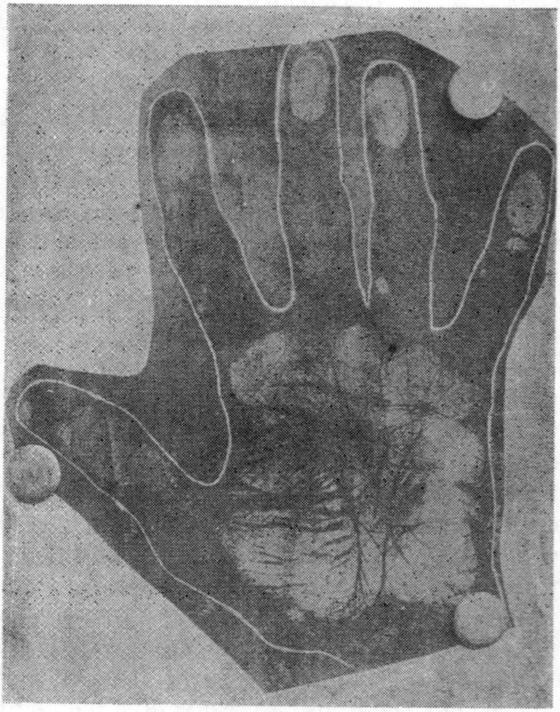

NO. 35. FINGERS BENT LATERALLY

the Mount, the Life line, and the line of the Mount itselt. You can easily separate moral from physical defects in this way.

Note carefully the tip of each finger, and apply the square, spatulate, conic, or pointed qualities to the individual finger and its Mount. Note whether any finger seems to stand more erect than the others, with one or more fingers inclined toward it (36). This will show you the strongest finger on the hand. Every finger leaning toward another gives up some of its strength to the finger toward which it leans. This applies if the leaning finger be only *straight* and merely appears *drawn* toward another. If the leaning finger is *bent* it

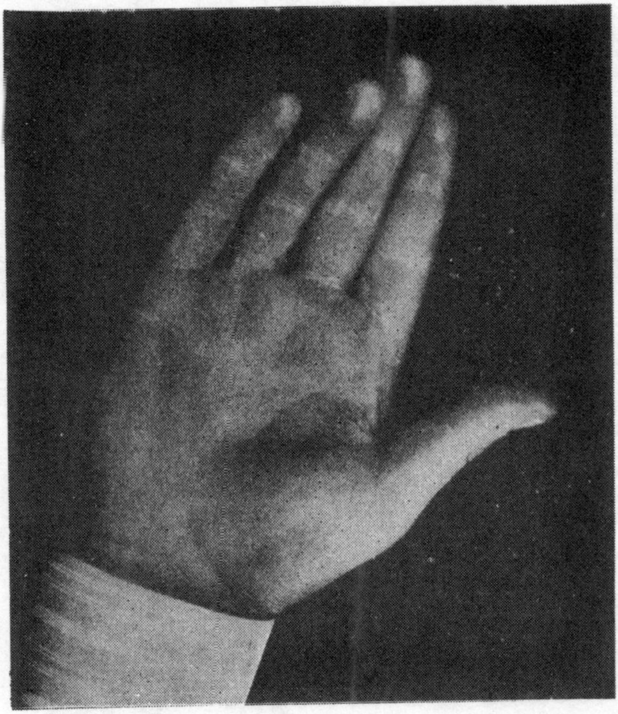

NO. 36. ONE FINGER ERECT, OTHERS LEANING TOWARD IT

accentuates the strength of *its own* Mount and you will generally find other fingers leaning toward *it*. A straight, leaning finger and a bent finger must not be confounded. Fingers to be well balanced should set evenly on the palm (37); one finger should not be placed lower down or higher up than the others. Any finger set lower than the normal line (38, two illustrations) reduces the strength of the Mount under it, and any finger set higher than the normal line (39), increases the force of the Mount under it. The best development is the evenly set, normally placed finger. At some part of your examination get at the normal way in which the subject carries his fingers, in order to find out which are bound

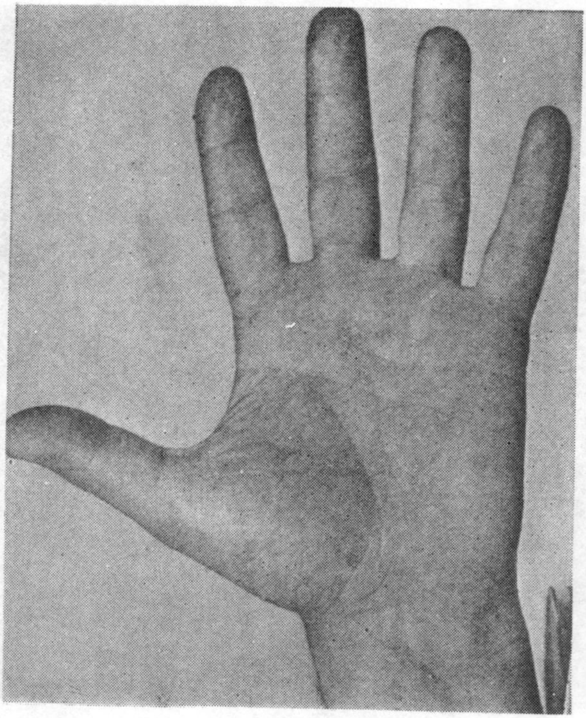

NO. 37. FINGERS SET EVEN

together and which are widely separated. In this examination it is indispensable that the fingers should be held naturally. Any strained position would defeat the object. Various ways can be devised to accomplish this. You can ask that he place his hand in a perfectly natural manner on a piece of white paper as though you were to draw an outline of it. By asking that he lift the hand up and place it on the

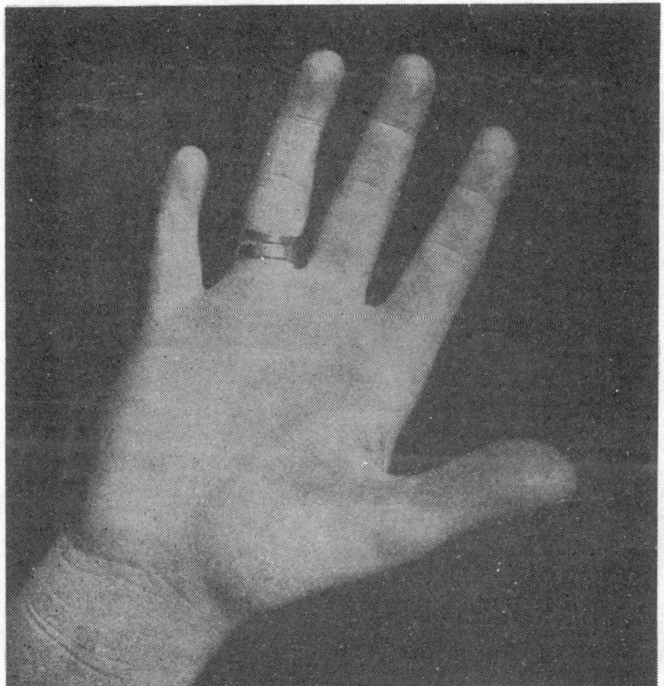

NO. 38. MERCURY LOW SET

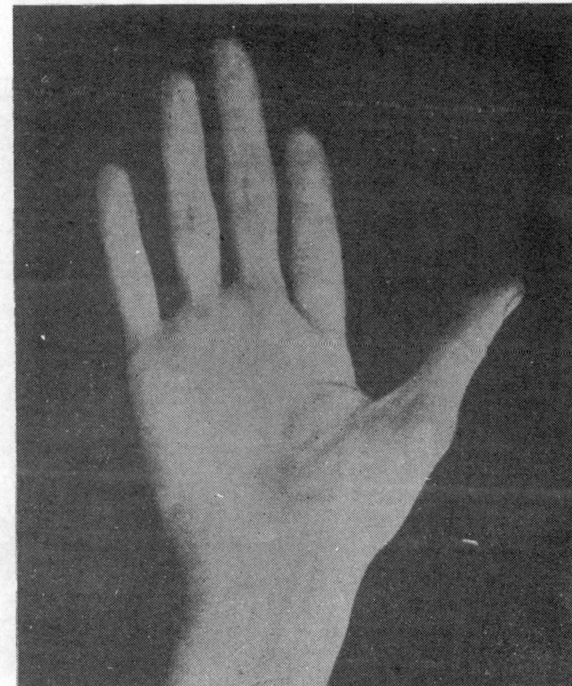

NO. 38. JUPITER LOW SET

paper several times in succession, you will get the natural pose accurately. Another way is to ask him to hold the hand up, clear of every support, and extend the palm toward you. When this is done, the fingers assume their natural pose. When the hand thus held shows the space between

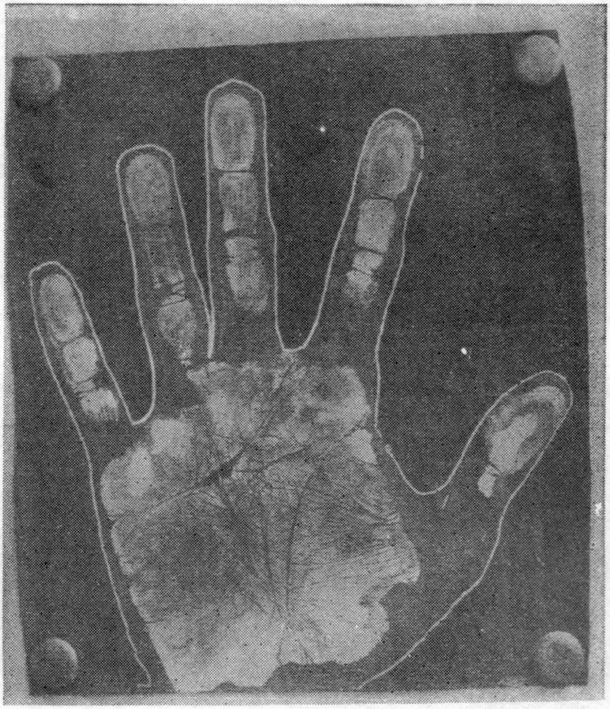

NO. 39. SATURN HIGH SET

the thumb and side of the hand to be very wide (40), your subject is generous, loves freedom and independence, and is intolerant of restraint, these being the qualities belonging to the low-set thumb. If the fingers of Jupiter and Saturn separate widely (41), the subject has great independence in thought, is not bound down by the views of others, but forms his own opinions. When the fingers of Saturn and Apollo

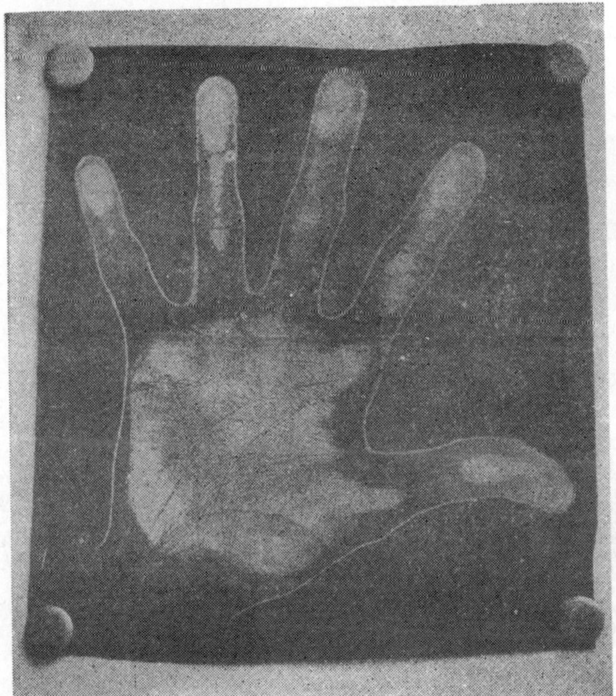

 NO. 40 SPACE BETWEEN THUMB AND JUPITER WIDE

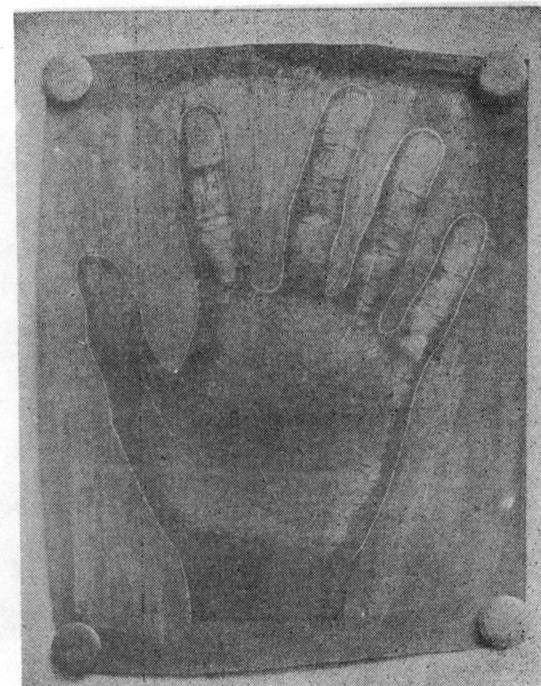

NO. 41. SPACE BETWEEN JUPITER AND SATURN WIDE

widely separate (42), the subject is careless of the future, Bohemian in ideas, and is entirely devoid of stiffness and love of formality. When the fingers of Apollo and Mercury widely separate (43), the subject is independent in action. He does what he wishes without caring what others may

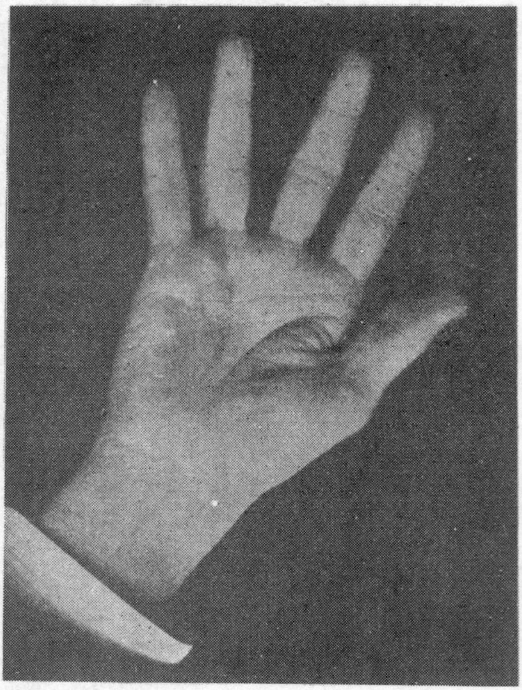

NO. 42. SPACE BETWEEN SATURN AND APOLLO WIDE

think. These separations of the fingers will be very useful and very accurate in their results. You will find the separations variously *combined*. Oftenest you find freedom in thought combined with freedom of action, with Saturn and Apollo close together, showing care for the future. You may find freedom of thought with the other fingers close together. Then your subject is a free thinker, but one careful in actions and of the future. When all the fingers separate widely (44) you have free thought, Bohemianism, and freedom of action. This subject will be easy to get acquainted with, entirely lacking in conventionality, and not tied down to rules of etiquette. If the separa-

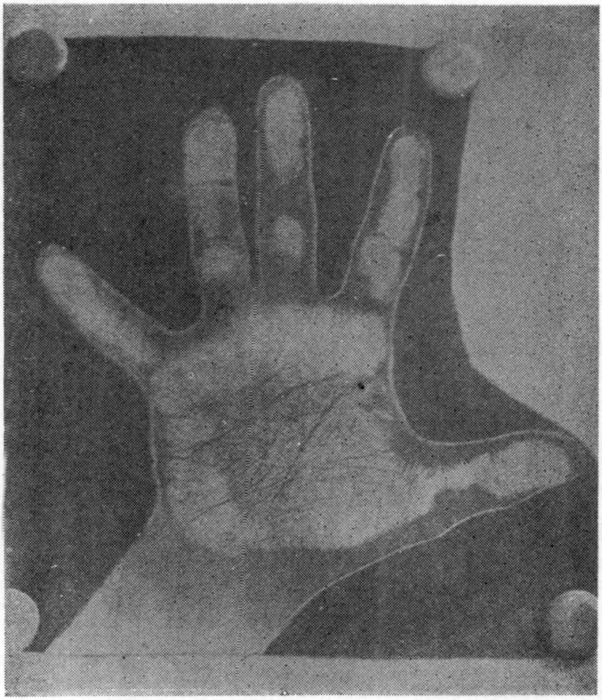

NO. 43. SPACE BETWEEN APOLLO AND MERCURY WIDE

tion is *very wide*, he will be a " hail fellow well met"; if only *moderately* wide, the person will be easy of approach. If all the fingers are held tightly together (45), the subject will be hard to get acquainted with, stiff, and lack independence in either thought or action. He is a slave to formality, and to make his acquaintance one must approach in a respectful manner. He is also stingy, for he is self-centred and constantly looking out for the future. You must compare the fingers with each other as to length, tips, and thickness. Saturn should be the longest finger always, for it is the balance-wheel of the character. The fingers of Jupiter and Apollo should be of equal length to be in balance ; the one which is the longer of the two will have its qualities

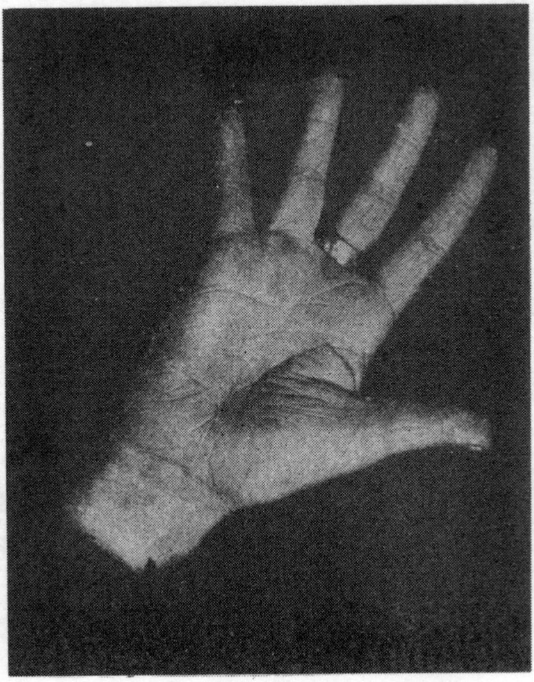

NO. 44. ALL FINGERS SEPARATED WIDELY

dominant over the other. Tips must be considered, for spatulate or square tips are stronger and more practical than conic or pointed. The fingers of Jupiter and Apollo being of equal length, the one having a square or spatulate tip will be stronger in a practical way than the one having a conic or pointed tip, which, however, is likely to indicate greater keenness. Consider carefully both length and tips of the fingers, in estimating which finger is the strongest. Mercury is naturally the smallest finger. The Mercurian is the smallest of the seven types, Saturn is the tallest, the fingers following the respective height of their types. Mercury, normal, should reach the first joint of the finger of Apollo. Shorter than that it is not a leading finger. Longer

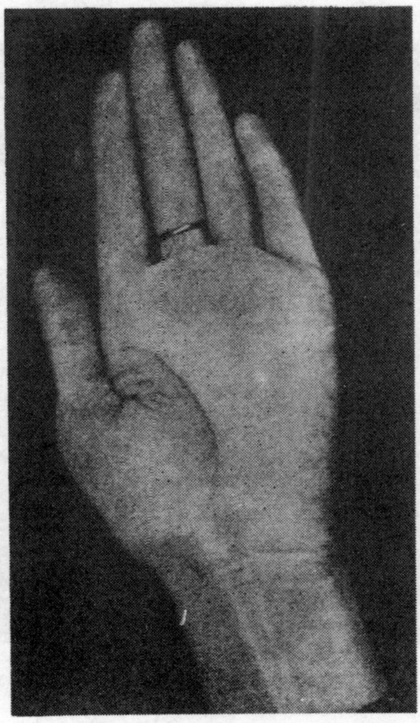

NO. 45. ALL FINGERS CLOSE TOGETHER

than this, the Mercurian type is predominant. If the finger of Jupiter is of *normal* length, normal Jupiterian qualities are shown ; *in excess*, excessive Jupiterian qualities are present; if *deficient*, the Jupiterian qualities will be deficient. This rule must be followed with Saturn, Apollo, and Mercury. The Mounts of Mars, Moon, and Venus have no finger, and all judgment of them must be from the Mounts alone.

Examine the individual phalanges of the fingers, counting first, second, third, from the tip down. Here, again, we find the three worlds of Palmistry, mental, abstract, and material, represented by the first, second, and third phalanges of the fingers. This is a very important matter to understand thoroughly, for it will tell whether the qualities of the Mount types will be expended in the mental, the practical, or the

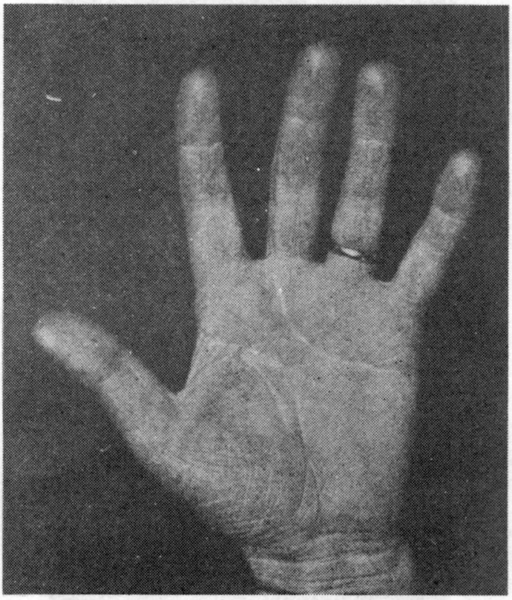

NO. 46. LONG FIRST PHALANGES

baser worlds. If the first phalanx of any finger is the longest and largest, the mental will rule, and the qualities of the type will be expended in that direction. If the second phalanx is longest and largest, the business side of the type will prevail, and the efforts will be expended in pushing the commercial side of the type. If the third phalanx be strongest, the material qualities will prevail, and either coarseness or brutishness in the attributes of the type will be the moving force, in proportion as this phalanx is thick or narrow. The longer the first phalanx (46), the more will mental matters absorb the attention, and if this phalanx is found short (47), it will tell that the enjoyment of mental occupations is lacking, and that qualities more material absorb the attention. If the second phalanx is thick and long (48), the money-mak-

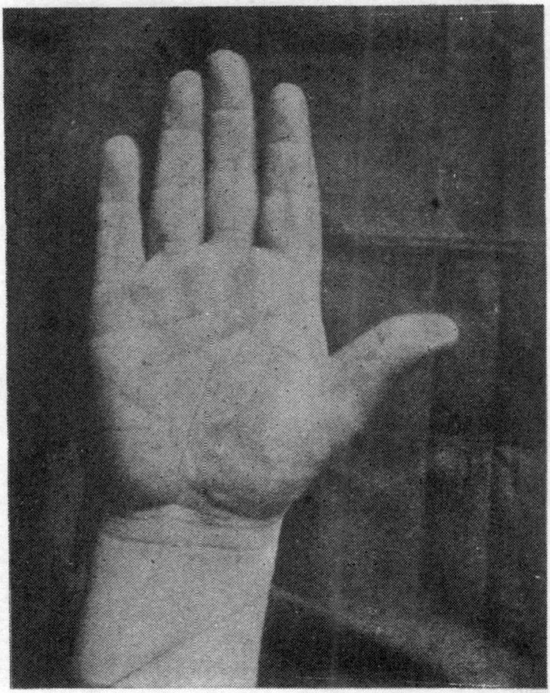

NO. 47. SHORT FIRST PHALANGES

ing side is uppermost. If the third phalanx is very long and very thick, it will show that sensualism and the gratification of appetite and luxury are the pleasures which the subject seeks (49). The extreme thickness of the third phalanx shows a great love for eating and drinking. If with this subject the first phalanx is short, the second normal, and the third very thick, he will not care for mental pursuits at all, but only cares to make money and to have plenty to eat and drink. It is not the sexual sensualism that is shown by the thick third phalanx, but the sensuous gratification of appetite and a love of luxury and comfort. The more pronounced the thickness, the more these traits are strengthened.

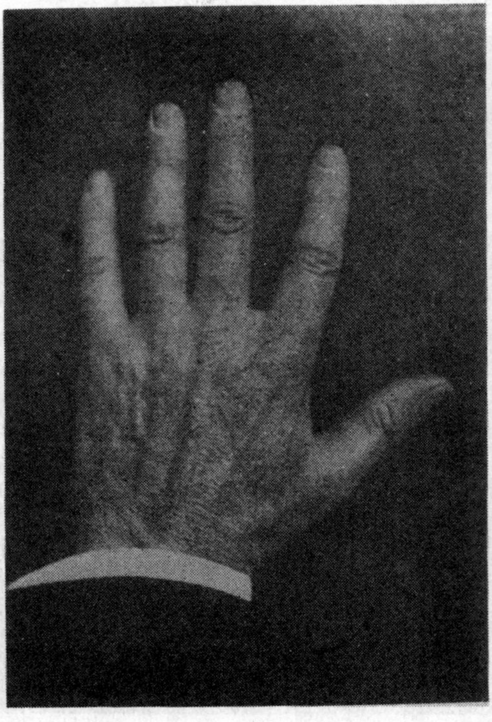

NO. 48. LONG SECOND PHALANGES

If the third phalanx is moderately developed, then there is only a fair degree of these desires. Love of sensual pleasures will always be shown by the thickening of these third phalanges, and the *degree* of strength will be graded by the *degree* of thickness. This indication will have added force in different types, for the Jupiterian, being naturally a large eater (as is also the Martian), will be much more so if the third phalanx be thick. Length of the phalanges shows strength of the qualities, thickness shows coarseness and liability to excess. When the third phalanx, instead of being thick, is narrow and waist-like in shape (50), it shows that the subject eats to live and does not live to eat. He is

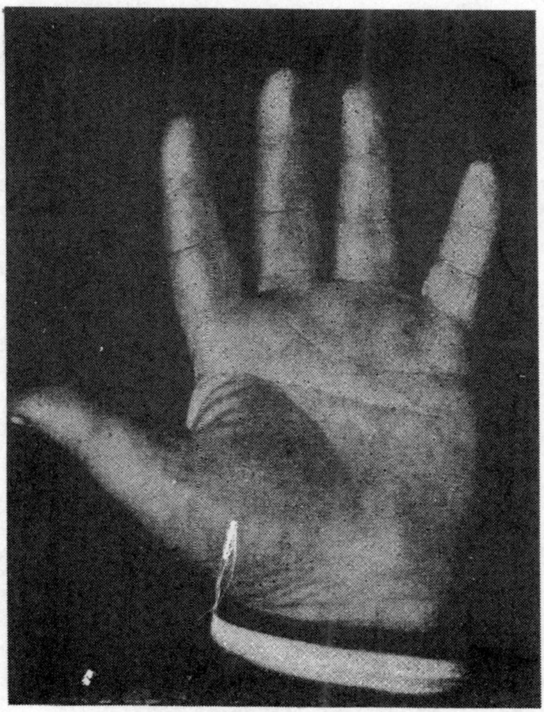

NO. 49 THICK THIRD PHALANGES

one who expends his strength in either the mental or business worlds, not in the sensual. He does not care for money except for what it will buy and the pleasure it can bring. It slips through his fingers for whatever suits his fancy. He has an inquiring mind, as shown by the chinks between the fingers. If the fingers are very long and the chinks very wide, the subject becomes, not an investigator, but one who is merely curious. He pries into the affairs of everyone from innate curiosity. I have reasoned that as this phalanx, when thick, shows gluttony, and as a gorged stomach produces an inactive brain, the subject with a thick third phalanx is too busy digesting to be an investigator. If

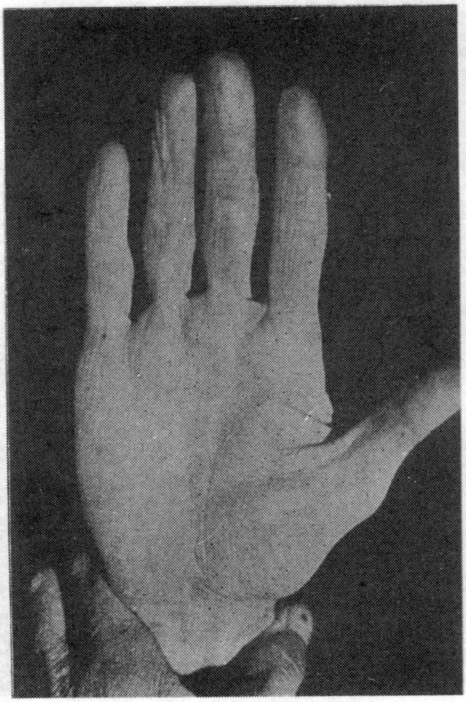

NO. 50. WAIST-LIKE THIRD PHALANGES

the phalanx is waist-like, the subject is only a slight eater, and his brain, instead of being clogged and heavy, has force to expand, and does it through its faculty of investigation. This waist-like indication, so estimated, is very accurate in its results, and may be used freely as showing little care for money, an absence of gluttony, and the inquiring, even curious, mind.

In the study of individual phalanges, take account of the tips. On each finger the long first phalanx represents the mental attribute of the qualities of the finger, which are those of its Mount. Conic or pointed tips will show the idealism of these qualities; square tips will show the practical application; spatulate tips will show active and original mental application. The long second phalanx shows the business side of the type ; conic and pointed tips give an artistic, impulsive turn ; square tips a practical, common-sense application ; spatulate tips an active and original method in business matters. The third phalanges indicate the sensualism of the finger qualities ; conic tips make them more pronounced, square tips less liable to excess, and spatulate tips active and original in devising ways for expending their efforts. With every finger, the phalanx which is in excess shows which is the strongest *side* of its qualities, and the *tips* show whether these qualities are idealized by conic tips, made practical by square tips, or active by spatulate. This system of thoroughly analyzing each finger by its phalanges and tips gives the ability to minutely dissect a subject, and in the attempt to estimate his future success, these things cannot be overlooked.

CHAPTER XII

THE FINGER TIPS

THE finger tips, in Palmistry, are classed as the Spatulate, the Square, the Conic, and the Pointed, and all refer to the impression the tips make on the eye. In this chapter we are considering only the shape of the *tips* of the fingers and not of the *whole hand*, so that fingers with spatulate *tips* are not to be classed as *spatulate hands*, but as *spatulate tips*. My observation has been that students become hopelessly confused by speaking of *spatulate* and *square hands*, owing to the fact that one seldom sees a hand taken as a whole which belongs, pure and simple, to one of these formations. You constantly see spatulate and square or conic *fingers* and tips, maybe a different tip on every finger in the same hand. These have been called mixed hands. Students have constantly told me they could not tell to which class hands belonged, and I have found that this inability to class *whole hands* as square, spatulate, or conic has entirely befogged those who have tried to do so. I have, for this reason, dropped the practice of speaking of square or spatulate *hands* and use, instead, square and spatulate *tips*.

The first tip to be considered is called the Spatulate, named because of its resemblance to a druggist's spatula (51). As an aid to memory, which is sure to be of great assistance in handling *all* the tips, remember the vital life-current entering the body through the tips of the fingers. The more pointed the tip, the easier this current enters, consequently the more direct the connecting link between the subject and its Creator. For this reason it has been found that the more pointed the tip, the more idealistic the subject ; the broader the tip, the more practical and common-sense he will be. When we look at the spatulate tip, we see the broadest tip, as well as the one presenting the greatest amount of resistance to the entrance of the life current, consequently this tip has a very practical side. The man possessing it is the exponent of realism in

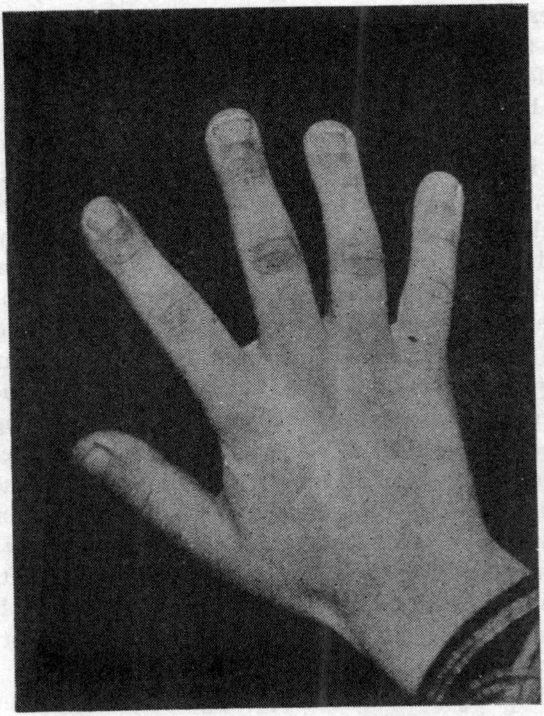

NO. 51. SPATULATE FINGER TIPS

everything. In life he seeks always the practical, common-sense side, and spatulate tips have been called the tips of real life. The moving desire of the spatulate tip is for action, exercise, and movement. There is no walk in life where the spatulate tip is found, that is not made to respond to this marvellous activity. In his daily life its possessor is constantly on the go; he inspires all about him with his wonderful enthusiasm and activity. In books he loves tales of action, hunting, war, or history that is filled with achievement and life. In amusements he seeks the active sports, is fond of the chase, of football, baseball, golf, or anything that gives expression to his great love of activity. In pictures he loves scenes depicting motion and action, and still-life does not appeal to him at all ; battles and hunting scenes are his favorites. He makes a good soldier, for he is filled with life and enthusiasm, and will go to his death for a leader whom he loves. He is fond of horses, dogs, in fact, of all animals. He is a strong lover and is constant and true. There is little that is vacillating about him. He is real, earnest, and practical. The spatulate tip also shows great originality. This man does not do things by any well-ordered system or by established rules. He likes to think of new ways in which to expend his energies, so he invents new methods or new machines, always with something practical in view. He follows no creed, but has his own ideas on religion, and is often called a crank. He loves independence, and pursues his active way through life caring little what people say of him. In whatever he undertakes, you find him skilful, for it is not his intention to be in the rear. For this reason he is among our great discoverers, and has scoured sea and land, hunting for new fields and new countries on which to expend his energy. When he gets to a new country he at once sets to work putting all of his activity and originality into operation: thus he not only discovers, but builds up and develops new lands. He is everywhere a power in activity, originality, and enterprise. Whenever you see this tip, think of these qualities.

The Square tip is one which is distinctly square at the end of the finger, the exact appearance being well shown by the accompanying illustration (52). This tip indicates regularity, order, system, and arrangement in everything. These are the people to whom disorder, whether in the home or in the store or shop, is an abomination. They can be happy only when everything with which they are connected is well ordered, systematically arranged, and done according to rule. "A place for everything and everything in its place," is their motto. They think by rule, eat by rule, are never late to dinner, always on time at the office, and insist that everyone else shall be. They do the same things at the same hour each day, and punctiliously keep every appoint-

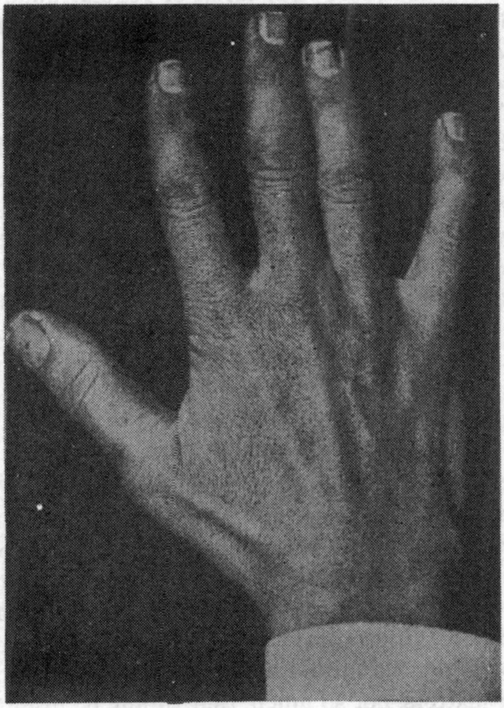

NO. 52. SQUARE FINGER TIPS

ment they make. They have a certain hook for their coats, and they are always hung there, so that in the dark they can put their hands on everything they own, provided conic tips have not been around. They rise and retire at an appointed time, and everything they do is governed by rule and system. They are polite, strict observers of social customs, and resent any breaking away from accustomed forms. In literature, square tips love history, scientific and mathematical works. In art they love paintings of natural scenery, still-life, or buildings. They are also fond of sculpture, and make the best sculptors. They are skilful in games, often good shots, careful in dress, and methodical in everything they think or do. Thus, with square tips, think of regular qualities, system, order, and arrangement in everything. If the tip is *very square* these qualities are most pronounced; if a little conic they will be less tied down by such absolute regularity. The square tip is the useful tip, and is found in all the practical walks of life. It shows the good bookkeeper, clerk, merchant, or librarian, the calculator, mathematician, and exact scientist; in fact, these people will be found useful everywhere that system, order, and good methods are required. Square tips will add square qualities to each individual finger and Mount, and make the Mount types punctual and systematic. Their possessors do not act by impulse but by thought and method. Always, in everything, good or bad, they have order and system.

The Conic tip (53) is found mostly on the hands of women, though it is possessed by many men. In shape it forms a distinct cone on the end of the fingers, and has many degrees of development. Where the cone is not pronounced, it shows less of the conic qualities, tending more to square or spatulate. Conic tips show the artistic, impulsive, quick, intuitive person, one to whom the beautiful and harmonious in all things appeals most strongly, and who is very impressionable. To those having the conic tip with smooth fingers, it matters not so much that things be useful as that they be beautiful, and this side of life is *their* point of view, consequently they care little for system To them the regularity of the square tip is burdensome. They greatly love all that attracts the eye or pleases the ear, and life seems less a matter of labor than of enjoyment. They do not care to deal with figures, nor do they have a place for everything; surely they do not always keep everything in its place. The conic tips being talented, quick of mind, and highly intuitive, this faculty of intuition is one of their greatest possessions, and greatest dangers, for they rely on it much more than on methodical systems of reasoning, which take labor to acquire. They think quickly ; the life current does not take as long to enter the conic tips as through the square or spatulate ; thus it is quick, instinctive intuition that guides

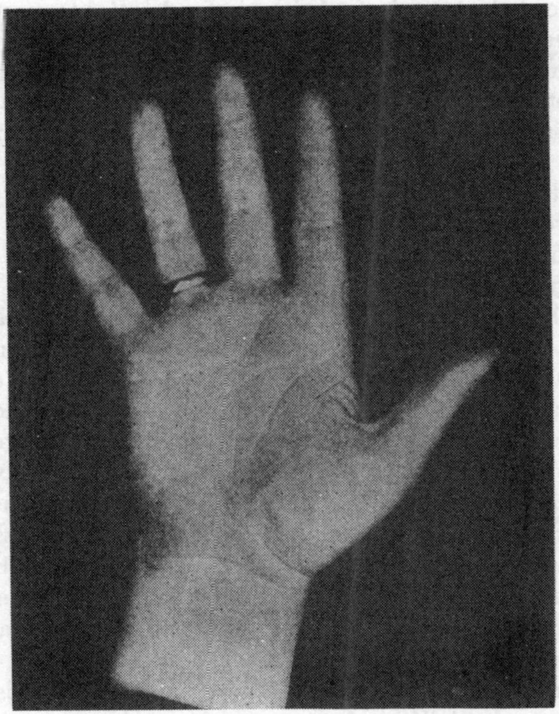

NO. 53. CONIC FINGER TIPS

them, rather than slow methods of thought. They are more inclined to idealism than to the actual and real things of life, and with these artistic tendencies they seek occupations where there is a good field for the operation of their intuitive powers, and where their love of beauty and art can find a fuller expression. In all things these conic qualities are shown. The home will be beautiful and artistic, but not systematically arranged. Their dress will be in harmony, but their bureaus at home are probably in confusion. In art they do not like battle scenes so much as pictures which appeal to the imagination. They want inspiration in their paintings rather than actual landscapes. Art, to them, means freedom from conventionality. In books they prefer romance to history; in food they prefer dainties to roast beef, and everywhere artistic, intuitive qualities are theirs. They are sympathetic, emotional, often easily led, consequently are not such constant lovers. Strongly susceptible to impressions, while beauty lasts they love better than after it fades. The eye, the ear, the senses are all trained to respond to beauty, harmony, and artistic surroundings. Conic tips are a poetic, lovable, attractive class. So when these conic fingers are seen, think of art, beauty, quickness, intuition, grace, harmony, and idealism, and you will find these the ruling forces in the subject, rather than the desire for action, or the common-sense regularity of the square fingers.

Pointed tips (54) are an exaggerated form of the conic. Their appearance is so characteristic that, once seen, they are never mistaken for any other, as their long, narrow, extremely pointed look will not be forgotten. These pointed tips belong to a class whose realm is entirely mental. They have no part or place in the materialistic operations of business, nor can they be held down to any set way of doing things. They are highly inspirational, idealistic in the extreme, and dwell in cloudland, mentally far from the bustle of a practical money-seeking world. To them beauty is all in all— thoughts, dreams, and visions take them through a vista of imaginings, and life is happy or unhappy in proportion to their ability to indulge these beautiful fancies. They are in no sense fitted for hard knocks, but are constructed on a plane too high for usefulness or great happiness on earth. They are beautiful and refining in their influence, but if they fall into coarse and brutal surroundings, or even those which are too practical, they chafe and suffer from the uncongeniality. Life to them is not real; it is poetic, visionary, and dreamy. Earth is not their sphere; they are the spiritual leaven placed among us, for the purpose of giving a view of the higher planes of existence. They are dreamers, too finely constructed to be practical, too much engrossed by mind to care about matter. Thus the more pointed the tip the more pointed the qualities and the less question that life has only

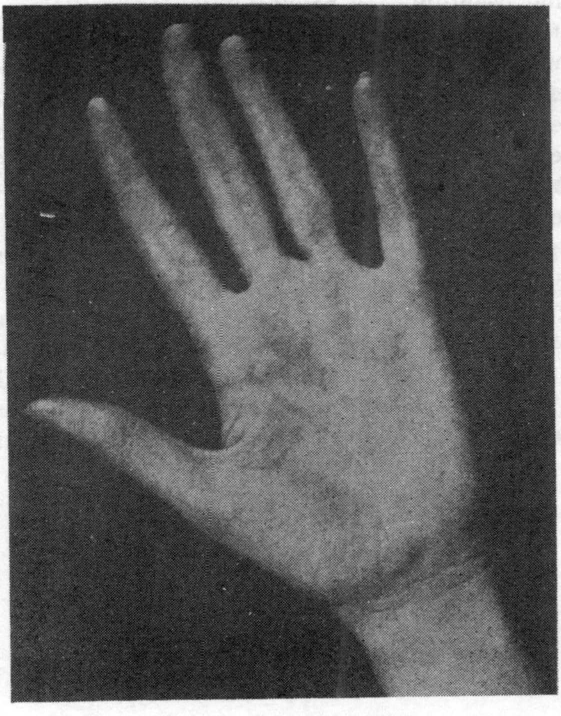

NO. 54. POINTED FINGER TIPS

disappointment for them, unless they can be so placed as to be fully at liberty to indulge all of their fancies. The time was when women loved to own such fingers. They did not know the qualities that belonged to pointed tips, and thought only of the beauty of appearance. As they have come to learn that the hands which are real, practical, and useful, the ones which are making the world move, are large, square, and knotty, this preference for pretty pointed fingers is passing away. The very fact that in order to keep these pointed fingers manicured and in their greatest state of beauty, the owner must not labor or use them in harsh employment, shows their practical uselessness. When you see these pointed tips, think of the visionary dreamer, impractical, but poetical and beautiful. In handling all classes of tips, do not forget to see what is behind their qualities. A soft hand will make the spatulate tip a *lover* of action, not one who indulges in physical action himself. It will lessen the vigor of the square tip, and add to the idealism of the conic and pointed. A big thumb, Mounts of Jupiter, Saturn, Apollo, and Mars, will show whether their respective qualities are back of the tip qualities as a driving force. Ambition (Jupiter), soberness (Saturn), quickness (Mercury), aggression (Mars), and energy (consistency), are necessary to bring out the greatest possibilities of spatulate, square, conic, or pointed tips. Thus the tips show what kind of a machine you have before you, and you must find out whether there is water in the boiler and fire to turn it into steam, before you can say that the machine is *acting* in its intended fashion.

CHAPTER XIII

KNOTTY FINGERS

IN looking at your client's fingers, they will impress you either as being smooth, or as having knotty joints (55). These smooth and knotty developments indicate two exactly opposite kinds of people. The smooth fingers are more often found on young persons, while knotty joints belong to maturer years. This is not an invariable rule, however, for the philosophical qualities shown by knotty joints are often born in a subject, in which case the knots develop early; but as most persons become more analytical as they increase in years, knotty fingers are more often found on older subjects. On some fingers only the first joints are developed. This first joint is what we call the knot of *mental order*, and refers to the symmetrical qualities of the mind. On other hands the second joints are developed, and these are called the knots of *material order*, indicating the love of order that manifests itself in neatness of the home, the office, or, in short, in all material things. A combination of the two knots shows both mental and material system, and consequently one who acts more slowly, thinks over things more carefully, and applies the gauge of mental and material neatness to whatever he does. This way of gauging things by rule, of judging them from the standpoint of a systematic mind and body, leads to a habit of *analyzing everything*, of *reasoning* out all questions, of tracing back the thing as it stands, to the elements which compose it, and thus we find that analysis, reasoning, investigation, and thoughtfulness, are the ever-present qualities of knotty joints. For these people to accept anything as true means that they first hear it, think of it, and digest it. They examine every statement, refer it to their systematic minds, and gauge it from the additional standpoint of common sense and practical reasoning indicated by the second knots. They are not carried away by enthusiasm or impulse, but bring to bear on every-

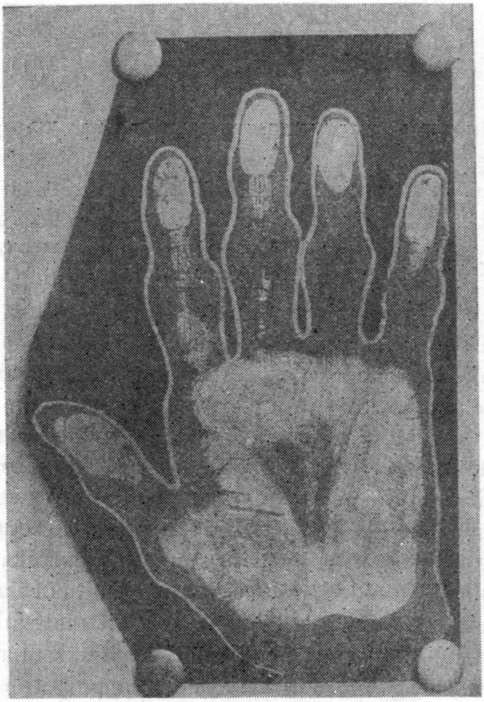

NO. 55. KNOTTY JOINTS
(Not produced by Rheumatism)

thing, the light of thorough investigation and thought. These knotty-fingered people are well named philosophical, as they are hunting for truth. They do not analyze from any frivolous motive, but because they wish to arrive at the facts, so while they do not seem to respond as quickly as smooth-fingered subjects, always remember that they are honestly striving to get at the bottom of the matter, and will be guided by the result of their investigations as the facts may appear to them. With this analytical tendency, it follows that the knotty fingers are seldom emotional, not easily led by sentiment, but that reason (head), not impulse (heart) is their guide. Knotty fingers cannot be suddenly rushed into anything. Give them time to think, something to think about, and abide the results of their investigations. If you have a hobby or a pet plan, do not expect them to adopt it, or at once to fall in with your ideas. Put the case as strongly as possible and give them time to think it over. Knotty-fingered persons are studious ; they do not rely on impulse or inspiration to carry them through life, but depend upon a well-stored brain, in which information is classified and ready to be used when occasion demands. For this reason knotty joints belong to scientists and historians, rather than to romance writers. Knotty fingers always give an impression of energy and common sense. You realize the study and labor necessary to arrive at all their philosophical conclusions. Knotty fingers often make original deductions, but they never swerve, once convinced that they are right. In religion they are as likely to be atheists as Christians, for knotty fingers require much proof before they will believe anything. They are the doubting Thomases, are naturally skeptics, ready to be convinced, but wishing to hold in their *own hands* the evidence. If they cannot do this, they may conclude there *is no evidence*, and as it is often easier to prove that a thing *is not* than that *it is*, they become atheists. Whichever side they are on, however, they honestly believe it is *right*. Philosophical and analytical they are ; reasoners, investigators, seachers for truth ; honest, energetic, hard to change, thinkers, doubters, slow to arrive at conclusions, patient, and systematic. Knotty fingers thus hold the world in check, and prevent its going too fast. If you remember the life current bringing its flash of intelligence into the ends of the fingers, and think of it as stopped by the first, or knots of mental order, until these knots can digest it and let it pass ; and then think of it as stopped by the second, or material knots, until these knots can digest it and let it go by, you will have a mental picture of how hard it is to get an idea through the philosophic knots. Smooth fingers may and do develop knots. I have seen many such cases in people who have developed reasoning faculties as they have grown older. This is why I say, knots are oftener found on the hands of old than of young people, for these persons have passed from a way of acting by impulse to a habit of analyzing and reasoning. You will often have people tell you that the knots on their hands came from labor or baseball. This is not true. It is the habit of analysis that has produced them. Every analytical reasoner may not be a scientist of renown; don't get that into your head. You will find reasoners in the gas trenches, who analyze everything in *their sphere of life* just as carefully as the sage. I have seen the smoothest of fingers, whose owners have done hard manual labor for years. Labor does not produce knots (see 20); mental qualities do (see 55). I have made a thorough investigation of this matter, for it is one of the first questions one hears from those who wish to argue against the accuracy of hand-reading. If only the knot of mental order is found on the hand (56), it will indicate an intelligent mind, a systematic way of thinking, and mental processes that are careful and regular; this, of course, if this knot is of normal size. The good results of mental system can be largely overdone, however, as it is responsible for pronounced cranks and even insanity. I once met a man who had a tremendous development of this knot. As it is my custom to investigate any pronounced formations I led him into conversation, and found him most intelligent and well educated. It was not long before he unfolded a plan by which he hoped to concentrate all the business in the world under one management. He had figured it all out on paper and was sure it could be done. Men called him crazy, but, in view of the organization of trusts during the past few years, he may not have been so insane after all. At any rate, he had immense knots of mental order. He had no sign of the second knot, however, and was careless to an extreme in his personal appearance. The mental development had entirely displaced the material. He was out of balance.

If the second or knot of material order is found well developed (see 55), it will tell of the method in material affairs

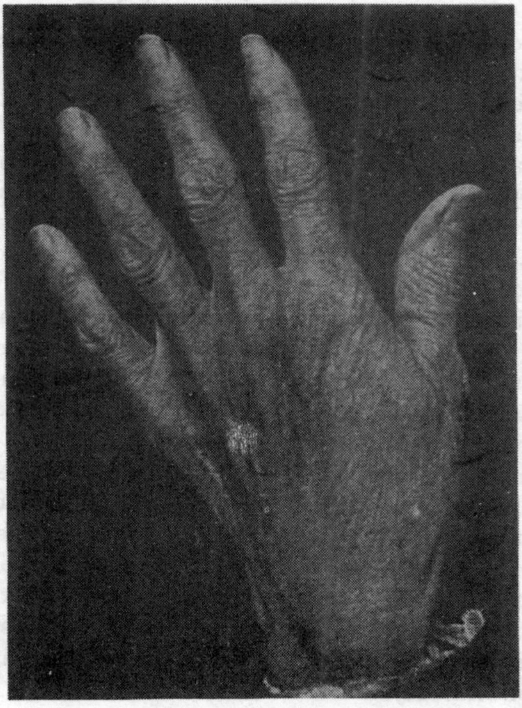

NO. 56. FIRST KNOTS DEVELOPED

possessed by the subject. He will want his home neat and well kept, his place of business clean and orderly, and in all material matters will be careful and systematic. He will be neat in appearance, though his clothing may be old and worn, methodical in his daily life and habits, and with square tips he will be carried away by system. When knotty fingers are seen, look to the tips. If square tips are found, add square to knotty qualities. In this case you will have a severe disciplinarian and taskmaster, who, whether husband, wife, or employer, will be almost fanatical in redtapism. Spatulate tips, with the first knot, will give you the most obstinate kind of a person, one cranky in the extreme. Remember that the vital spark has increased difficulty getting through the tips of these spatulate fingers with the added knot, and realism in the greatest degree will be indicated. Conic or pointed tips lighten the intensity of the knots, and give them the best possible complement. This is the ideal knotty hand, one which lightens the severity of the philosophical disposition by letting in a little idealism. The conic tip and knotty fingers are the hands which are religious, for the conic tips allow the analytical doubting qualities a little idealism, and this formation is the only one willing to take anything for granted. Spatulate and square tips, and knotty joints are so bound down to materialism that they will not believe in what they cannot see and touch. Thus people with these formations are usually skeptics.

Examine the consistency of the knotty hands before pronouncing fully upon them, for softness or flabbiness will make them only lazily analytical. Before you say they really expend time and effort in study and research, be sure that they have hard or elastic consistency. Flexibility is not often found. The knotty minds are not elastic, they achieve results from labor and study, not from elasticity of mind or brilliancy.

In speaking of knots on the fingers understand that these knots must be so pronounced as to be recognized at first glance. Unless they are thus plainly marked do not class fingers as knotty. If they are so bulging that they distort the fingers, consider the knotty qualities very pronounced. If they bulge out at the sides of the fingers, and in addition at the backs, so that it looks as if a ring were around the bone under the skin, it is an excess in development of the knots, which entirely spoils their good effect. In such developments the first phalanx of the fingers is bent inward, and the stiff qualities of the mind predominate. Flexibility is absent, the brain is hard, not elastic, does not take new ideas, but rides hobbies to death.

CHAPTER XIV

SMOOTH FINGERS

YOU will encounter many hands on which the fingers are distinctly smooth in appearance (57). This means that the knotty joints, which are the distinctive feature of knotty fingers, are not seen, and the sides of smooth fingers, where the joints would naturally show a development, are even and without bulges. These smooth fingers may have any shape of tip; it is only the absence of developed joints which leads you to recognize them. As analysis and reasoning are the attributes of knotty fingers, so impulse, inspiration, intuition, and the lack of a disposition to pick everything to pieces, belong to the smooth fingers. This smoothness, or lack of prominent joints, has always been considered in Palmistry as constituting artistic fingers, but in order to have the strongest artistic sense, smooth fingers must also have conic tips. The conic tip, which we suppose to afford less resistance to the entrance of the vital spark, stands for ideality, and this in many minds stands for true art. In the examination of the hands of successful artists, I was surprised and disappointed to find, instead of smooth, conic fingers, the ideal of an artistic hand, large knots, square or spatulate tips, or distinctly mixed tips. This at first seemed an anomaly, for the hand of the artisan had become the hand of the artist. Still another anomaly lay in the fact that small thumbs have always been considered the accompanying indication, with conic tips, of an artistic hand, and I found large square thumbs on the hands of many successful artists. In using the word *successful* artist, I mean not merely a dabbler with color, but one who has made a name. When we analyze the matter, however, this is not at all wonderful. Smooth fingers are artistic in that their owners act by impulse, inspiration, and intuition, not by reason, calculation, and premeditation. To be a genius, brilliant, full of inspiration and talent, means one thing, to put these talents to practical use is another. The one who can dream

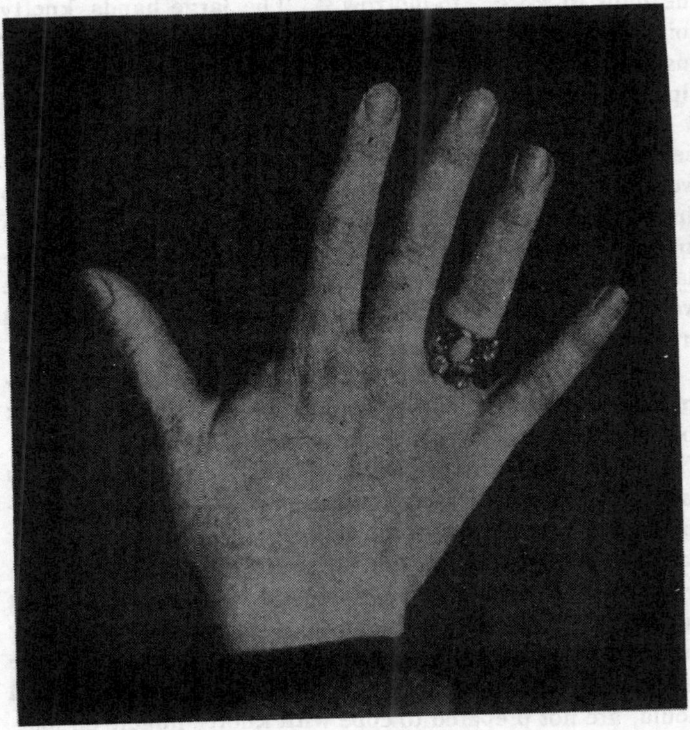

NO. 57. SMOOTH FINGERS

best is the one who has the artistic visions that would be most valued if transferred to canvas. From such visions have come the *inspirational* pictures that have lived through centuries of time. But how many all told are there of these masterpieces? Countless numbers of human beings have lived and died, and yet how few have produced anything immortal? I believe only a few inspired visions out of the countless millions which have floated through human brains have ever been *recorded.* This is because the minds able to dream artistic dreams have had, with their smooth fingers, soft or flabby hands (laziness), and small thumbs (no determination), consequently they have *only* dreamed, always meaning to *work* "to-morrow." The large hands, knotty joints, and square tips, while not possessing the genius or inspiration of smooth fingers, have had common sense (square tips), and determination (big thumbs), so they have worked *to-day;* and while not so gifted, they have copied nature in field and forest, copied humanity by portraying men and women as they saw them, so that while they have had no dreams to paint, they have reproduced material surroundings, and that is what comprises much of the art we see today. It is labor, determination, and common sense that have won the victory over imagination. This is why successful artists are found *without* artistic fingers.

Smooth fingers always speak of the unimpeded current flowing through them. These people are artistic in taste, quick to think, and act always by inspiration, not by reasoning. They do not delve to the bottom of every subject, but rely on the impressions which come to them without stopping to reason out all the "whys and wherefores." They are not by nature reasoners, though they often grow into a habit of analyzing, and as these tendencies increase, knots appear on their fingers. Smooth-fingered subjects are most safely guided by their first impressions and seldom are wrong in their intuitive deductions. Their minds, not being formed in an analytical mould, are not prepared to cope with knotty fingers on matters requiring deep analysis, consequently smooth-fingered folk in dealing with knotty-fingered ones are safer if they rely upon their leading characteristic, *inspiration*, than if they use analysis, which is the Gibraltar of the knotty fingers. In reading smooth fingers, do not fall into a common error in the use of the word *artistic.* That is, do not confuse a *lover of the beautiful* with a *producer* of it. It is true that with their impulsive, quick, intuitive qualities, smooth fingers see more beauty in life, see more of the artistic side, the grace and attractiveness of color and form, and in this sense they are artistic. They think quicker, dispose of any subject with greater rapidity, and consequently cover more ground in a day than their knotty-fingered brethren, but they are not as a rule so thorough. In religion, while seldom skeptics, they vary from profound devotees to those who merely have a respect for religion, but are not often agnostics. They do not doubt, for they take much for granted. They do not *reason* out their religious faith, but take the word of others for much of it. They are not always trying to find flaws as are the knotty fingers, so smooth fingers are more agreeable and pleasant companions. In daily life a love of beauty will be one of their prevailing characteristics. Being less engrossed in mental deductions than knotty-fingered people, they consequently think more of dress, of surroundings, of decoration in the home, of the adornment of their cities, places of business, and of their religion. The smooth-fingered Latin nations love ritual and decoration in their churches rather than simplicity which belongs to the knotty, square-fingered Puritans. Smooth-fingered persons love those things which please the eye or appeal to the sense of beauty, are inclined to love tasteful dress, and this may degenerate into a love of *show* if the fingers are coarse. In dealing with smooth fingers always bear in mind the kind of hand on which they are found. You must not expect that the quick, inspirational, intuitive, impulsive nature will always belong to a high grade of character. Neither must the word artistic be associated with high-born dames alone. You will find smooth fingers on the most unenlightened, and on people far removed from the "four hundred." But be the nature fine or coarse, the station in life high or low, smooth fingers will always tell you of one who does not rely on reason and analysis, but on inspiration, impulse, and intuition, who loves the beautiful according to *his standard*, and who acts generally on the spur of the moment. Smooth-fingered people are more susceptible to emotionalism than knotty-fingered ones, they may be "carried away" easier, thus while they are very successful in business and life, there is always one element of danger and uncertainty about them: their inspirations may be wrong. These people need a good Head line to make them safe, as their desire is to go too fast. To them the plodding and thinking of the knotty-fingered ones is far too laborious. They are willing to take a great deal for granted in order to *get through* with the day's occupations, consequently smooth fingers are quicker in every way than knotty ones. While in the realm of painting, and some kinds of music, we find other fingers making their possessors succeed better than smooth ones, yet in the realm of acting we find the latter winning applause and dollars. Copying may be done with the brush and pencil, and by pursuing certain rules and measurements, but to *act* a part, to *be* some one else, requires the inspiration of smooth fingers. If an actor having knotty fingers has planned just how to impersonate his part in a play, but finds, on his entrance to the stage, that something unforeseen has changed the surroundings, he cannot fall back on analysis and reason in this emergency. Inspiration on the spur of the moment is the only thing that will carry him through such a crisis. This inspiration is only possible to smooth fingers. In my observation of hands among members of the dramatic profession, I have found few if any other kind than smooth fingers. These are the fingers of those who have created parts, whose acting is full of life, true to nature, and lacking in stiffness and conventionality. They are the ones who appeal to the heart by grace, taste, and naturalness. Acting with them is truly art, it is creative power. These smooth fingers make the most of every opportunity, seize the incidents of the day and hour, and apply them with great ingenuity to whatever they are doing. If a baby in the audience cries, instead of being disconcerted, they will turn the incident to account. They are not easily taken off their guard, their minds are more elastic, quick, and ready, and they are able, in a flash, to see an opportunity and turn even a mishap to their advantage.

In music, smooth fingers are a necessity, unless very heavy music is to be produced. Music which sways the soul, does not do so by its rigid conformity to rules, but by its freedom from them. *Melody* cannot flow from the heart, if nothing but *metre* is to be considered. So the inspiration of smooth fingers is a necessity. Stately marches, oratorios, and recitatives may be produced and sung by less artistic souls, but the music to *reach* the heart must come *from* the heart. Knotty fingers are ruled by analysis (head), smooth fingers by impulse (heart), so it is to the latter that music must turn for its greatest exponents. Composers need square palms or square fingers to give them rhythm, they need smooth fingers for inspiration. With square tips they will produce marches, with spatulate, band music, with conic, weird or dreamy compositions, but the fingers must in each case be smooth.

In business, smooth fingers are often successful. The success of to-day is not won, as in days of yore, by saving alone. Some of the most brilliant lights in the business world succeed by rapid modes of thought, spend money recklessly, and rely on the large amount they can make, not the amount they can save. Rapidity has succeeded slow methods, and a transaction that can now be concluded in five minutes, would have taken our forefathers a week, maybe a month. There is this to be said about the operation of smooth-fingered impulse to-day: Men have learned more about life and natural laws, they have found that certain acts produce certain results, and with this knowledge can hear a proposition and tell the probable outcome without long thought. Knotty-fingered people have had to reason out these laws, the smooth-fingered ones use them, which is a great saving of time to the latter. Smooth-fingered people are much fonder of society than knotty-fingered ones. They are not engaged in making deductions and calculations nor in reasoning out intricate problems, but ideas come quickly, and they rely on these. For this reason people with smooth fingers find time to mingle with their fellow men. They have more leisure hours than knotty-fingered ones. To this add that smooth fingers indicate greater readiness of expression, more fluency in thought and speech, so their possessors are better adapted to shine in brilliant social surroundings than the slower, knotty-fingered folk. Altogether we see that quickness of thought, inspiration, impulse, and spontaneity are the guiding forces indicated by smooth fingers, and when seen, always think how these factors swiftly impel such people forward in every sphere. Always examine most carefully the consistency and color of hands with smooth fingers, too much energy (hard), and ardor (red), will cause failure from over impetuosity. It would require a phenomenally straight and strong Head line to keep these people from continual blunders. Examine the tips always. If pointed, you have the most artistic side of smooth fingers. If square, their quickness and inspiration will operate in practical ways, they will be less idealistic. If spatulate, their force will be strongly augmented by the originality, activity, and independence of the spatulate tips. Such a combination will need most careful handling to prevent the subject from becoming a crank, and by excess of good qualities from having ill success. With whatever combination found, always remember that smooth fingers indicate a less critical, careful, analytical way of thinking, that impulse and inspiration are the guides in every way, and by applying these qualities you can always properly estimate their force in the life of your subject.

CHAPTER XV

LONG FINGERS

IN looking at hands, the fingers of some will impress you as unusually long (58). Others will seem about to balance the rest of the hand, and some fingers will appear decidedly short. These are called respectively, long, normal, and short fingers, and to make a test in this matter of length, have the client close his fingers over the palm and note how far toward the wrist they reach. In thus closing the hand, the finger of Jupiter will be shortest, Saturn, even though the longest finger, next, and Apollo, by virtue of its position, will appear to be the longest finger of all. This is due to the way they arrange themselves over the Mount of Venus. It has been generally believed that the fingers closing thus should reach to the wrist or be as long as the palm, yet this is seldom the case. As the prominence of the Mounts under the fingers will make quite a difference in the distance the fingers reach toward the wrist, I consider the plan of relying entirely on the closing of fingers as likely to lead to false deductions. The longest hand I have ever seen was sent me from Little Rock, Arkansas, about five years ago, and measured, from finger-tip to rascette, ten inches. In this hand the finger of Saturn extends nearly to the first rascette (59). This would be classed as of the *extremely* long-fingered type. When the measurement taken extends anywhere between a little below the centre of Venus and the rascette, class the fingers as long.

In this examination you should reason that the longer the fingers the more pronounced the long-fingered qualities, and be careful not to apply a *full measure* of these qualities to fingers only a *little* over normal length. *Long hands* are found in which the palm, as well as the fingers are exceedingly long, though the fingers themselves may be only a trifle over normal length in proportion to the palm. These long hands show the slow-going, slow-talking person, who,

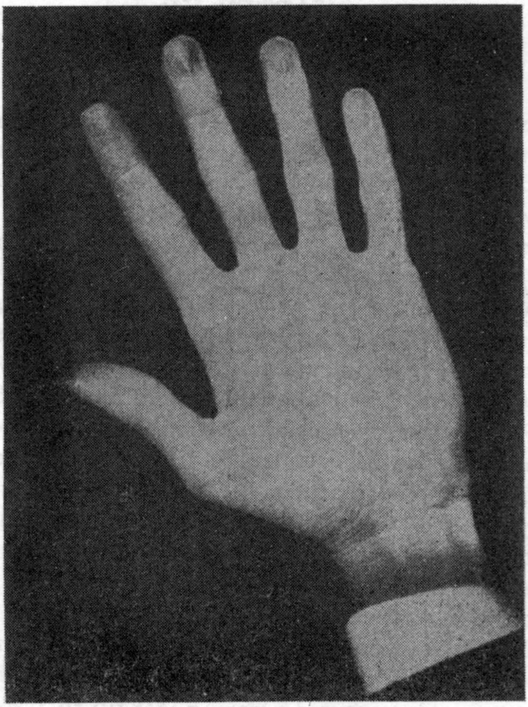

NO. 58. LONG FINGERS

in speaking, enunciates each syllable of every word, and who while he does not drawl, still is slow in forming and speaking his words. Anyone who is quick in thought knows, after the first few words just what he will say, and wishes he would hurry and finish. The long hands indicate slow-acting minds, consequently these people are slow in movement, dignified, and lack the rushing, dashing way of short-handed persons. These *long hands* must always be considered *together* with *long fingers.* It makes a great difference in long fingers whether they are thin or thick. The thin fingers accentuate long-fingered qualities, and lead you perhaps to form a more disagreeable estimate. The animal

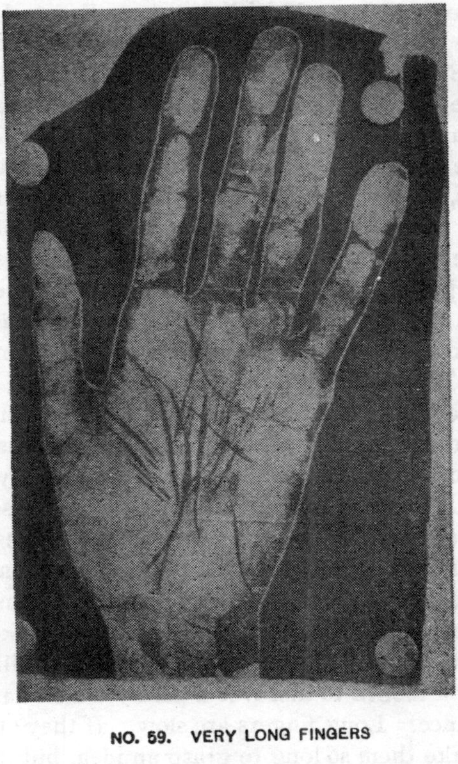

NO. 59. VERY LONG FINGERS

vitality belonging to thick fingers of any kind makes those having *thick, long fingers* less given to pushing long-fingered qualities to excess than to seeking pleasure, so they will indicate fewer of the disagreeable qualities than *thin, long fingers.* To form a correct judgment is not at all difficult if you follow the rule of measurements given above, but be exceedingly careful in making your classifications, relying always on measurements until practice enables you to judge off-hand without error.

The long-fingered person is peculiar. His is the mind which goes into the minutiæ of everything, seeks every detail, and accepts nothing as a whole until first separated into its parts. He is particular, especially about small things. He will engage himself with some small detail and allow a large one to escape him. He is suspicious and does not feel quite sure that seeming friends are true. In dealing with these people be most punctilious in your behavior, as well as in your apparent regard and respect, for they are easily offended, and little things, not thought worthy of any consideration by others, would be construed by them into intended insults. They are careful about everything. In dress they are neat, and while they may not be in fashion, yet there is an evident effort to put the best foot forward. They are exceedingly sensitive, easily wounded, and hold in their breasts smoldering animosities, which have been aroused by fancied or real slights. They see the *little things*, the minutiæ, the details, and, if you have short fingers, your outspoken quickness may embroil you with them. Long fingers must not be set down as of little account, for they are eminently useful and necessary. People having them being possessed of good memory, and fond of looking after details, make good book-keepers or office men, where the performance of accurate and careful work is required. If the fingers are at once long and square-tipped, the regularity and detail will make these people almost infallible as accountants. They will check accounts for a month to discover a penny which has destroyed their balance. Long fingers are slow. If they are smooth it will not take them so long to grasp an idea, but if the fingers are knotty it means love of detail and minutiæ (long fingers), with analysis (knotty joints), and this class will always be very slow. Plodders they always are, not achieving success by brilliancy or quick spurts, but by slowly and carefully laboring to keep abreast of the times. Patient they are, for they see many pass them on the roadway of life, and it requires patience to see oneself outstripped and not get moody.

As musicians they achieve success from carefulness and close observance of detail. They do not depart from the composer's conception, but adhere strictly to every notation and mark of expression. In conversation they are apt to be tiresome, for in telling a story or describing anything, they go into every detail with wearisome accuracy. In literature they are exact, and didactic in style. They tend to give too much attention to detail, and run into long and tiresome descriptions. Their work in literature, as everywhere else, has the stamp of painstaking carefulness. Send them to describe natural scenery and not a tree nor leaf will escape them, and as reporters they will see and describe every little thing. Their love of detail leads them to be "long-winded" writers and the blue pencil is in constant demand.

In art they paint the pictures that show every detail of their study. They are not impressionists but artists who paint the individual hairs of their subjects. They do not paint meadows by drawing at one stroke a broad brush across the canvas, but they paint in every blade of grass. Every leaf on the trees, every feather on the birds, every button on the coat, is depicted with accuracy in their pictures.

In ordinary, every-day life they are the ones who look after all the little comforts of home. They do not forget the slippers, the chair at fireside, the paper, or the thousand and one *little things* that make home bright. They are thoughtful, watchful, careful, patient, and in looking after the minutiæ of life they fill a very useful place. They have, by reason of their care of the details of everything, inquiring minds. They are not, as are those with knotty fingers, trying to analyze, but they are watchful that even the little things shall not be overlooked or forgotten. While the carefulness and the watchfulness indicated by long fingers might make it appear that they were about the same as knotty fingers, still they are not. The motives which actuate each one will show you the difference between the two. They of the knotty fingers are trying to pick things to pieces and to analyze them, they of the long fingers are trying to avoid overlooking even small matters. In one case it is analysis, in the other looking after detail.

Long fingers indicate faults, among which are slowness, and tediousness. These people are often bores, and worse than this they are frequently selfish. This comes from the fact that their suspicious way of looking at things causes them to draw within themselves, and they do not push out among people, nor do they love to mingle with others. In this way they acquire habits of selfishness which grow with years. Thin fingers and critical nails will accentuate this quality, and in dealing with long fingers, always view their possessors as inclined to be a selfish class; if they lack either the Mount of Venus or Apollo, they surely are. If they have the Mount of Moon strong, it is trebly sure. Long fingers are cold-blooded, to a large extent lack sympathy, and when generous it is often because they do not want to *appear* mean, rather than because they have real generosity. They are a class who do not grant favors readily, and incline strongly to stinginess except in matters which give pleasure to themselves.

They are not bold and fearless, but incline to be cowardly and, consequently, servile; this applies particularly to lean, long fingers unless spatulate tips, and a large thumb, added to Mount of Mars, give them strength. They are willing to receive a favor, but do not go out of their way to grant one.

Long-fingered friends are not always true to you. They are suspicious, often nurse feelings of resentment, and become hypocritical. This is especially the case if the fingers be long and lean. They of thick long fingers will be truer. In considering long fingers, the tips must be carefully noted, to learn in what direction the long-fingered love of investigation, minutiæ, and detail will expend itself. If they have square tips; regularity, practical matters, business, or common-sense duties will attract. If spatulate tips, activity and originality are their moving forces, making them most remarkable inventors, careful explorers, and adding spatulate qualities to long-fingered detail and minutiæ. This is the best combination to indicate originality. The square tip is too much bowed down by routine and custom to be original. With conic tips, long fingers will turn to art and love of the beautiful. In this case conic qualities must be added to long-fingered ones. Long fingers will be found on various classes of people, and in all walks of life. They will be seen on ignorant persons, but each will have the faculty of looking after the trifles and the little things in their lives. Ignorant people may have long fingers with conic tips. To these must *not* be ascribed creative artistic talent, but they do love beauty ; perhaps not the things *you* might think beautiful, but that which appeals to *their grade* of intelligence.

Long-fingered hands are the ones which do the finer work in the mechanical world. These long-fingered people often are the fine engravers, and those who can chase the most delicate lines and tracery on jewelry. They can handle little parts of machinery, and in general they do the minute and fine little things in mechanics and mechanical art.

Long fingers will be found on hostler and nobleman, on housemaid and on mistress. In each case they will not stand for the same *grade of fineness*, but *will* tell of the irresistible propensity for detail, of dealing with minutiæ, of observing little and trifling things, of a tinge of suspicion, and, if the shape bears it out, of selfishness and hypocrisy.

CHAPTER XVI

SHORT FINGERS

FINGERS which may be classed as short (60) are found among all types of people, and are equally divided between the sexes. Usually they may be recognized at a glance, and you will never fail to read them aright if you master a knowledge of short-fingered qualities. The fingers which are properly classed as short, will reach hardly to the centre of the Mount of Venus, and will appear short in proportion to the rest of the hand. Having carefully fixed in your mind the appearance of long fingers, there will be no possible trouble ever after in recognizing the short. Of course there will be found varying degrees of shortness. The fingers may reach nearly to the middle of the Mount of Venus, the normal length, or they may fall far short of that. The palm of the hand may be a long one, and the fingers short. In this case they will reach *far* short of the normal line, and their peculiar qualities will be very pronounced. There will be added to the latter combination the strength of the large palm which, if square, will make them practical.

Short-fingered qualities are exactly the reverse of long. Instead of wishing to go into detail, short-fingered people despise it. Instead of dealing in minutiæ, they want everything considered as a whole. To be compelled to think of little things gives them positive pain. They think quickly, if the fingers are normally short, like a flash if they be *very* short, and they also act as quickly as they think. In stating a proposition to such people come right to the point. There is no element of slowness in the operation of their minds nor any desire to go into details; all is quickness and action.

They are highly intuitive and correctly judge whether you are telling the truth or trying to humbug them. Their minds work rapidly, and, while you are still talking, they have formed their opinion, before the last words are fairly spoken. No analysis, no detail, no minutiæ with them.

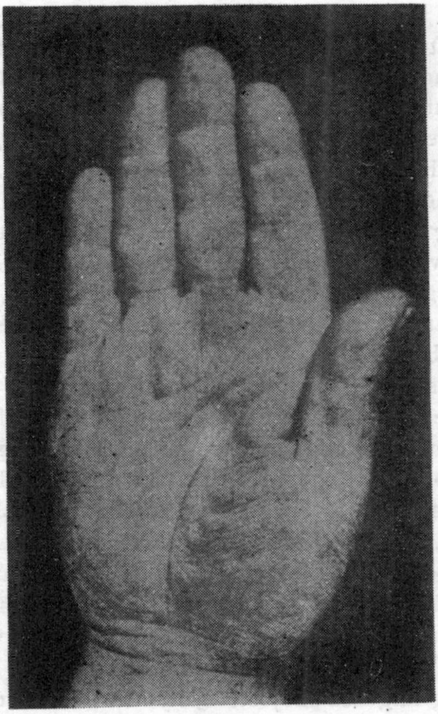

NO. 60. SHORT FINGERS

Things as a whole are what they deal with, and this without any delay. What they of the short fingers want to get at is the meat, the *result* of a thing, not the details of how it was done. If trying to interest them in a new scheme, talk fast and to the point. What they wish to know is whether there is money in it, not the details as to how you are going to get it. They will tell you, "We can leave all the minutiæ to someone else," in which case "someone else" means long-fingered folk. Short fingers are often hard to handle. Their owners think rapidly and make up their minds so quickly that you do not get a chance to tell your story before they say: "I have heard something like this before, and don't believe I want to go into it." They are impulsive, act on the spur of the moment, and do many hasty things for which they are afterward sorry. They are in danger of falling into error through jumping at conclusions. While they possess very brilliant possibilities, they often ruin them by impetuosity. They are hot-headed, and once started, push with extreme diligence any enterprise undertaken.

These short-fingered people are never satisfied to be doing any but *big things*. They plan the gigantic enterprises that move the world, they build enormous buildings, lead armies, and, casting aside detail, control large matters, settle lines of policy, and leave long fingers to attend to the minutiæ in carrying them out. While people with long fingers are plodding, saving, careful, even stingy, those with short fingers are dashing, impetuous, quick, full of big plans, looking down on small matters such as are engrossing the attention of long-fingered ones. Short-fingered people are not always careful of appearance, they are planning big enterprises, so little things, like care for the toilet and clothing, must be for others than themselves. They are too much occupied with large matters to attend to the trifles of etiquette or society. They do not notice a slight which would drive the sensitive soul of a long-fingered subject to despair. While long-fingered subjects eye you with distrust, and feel suspicious of the words you are uttering, short-fingered ones are thinking nothing of the kind, they are quickly digesting what is said in order that they may determine at what you are driving. Short fingers do not indicate hyper-sensitiveness, consequently, as a rule, these people are happy and lively companions. At all times you feel, when in their company, the force of their impulsiveness, quickness, intuition and, with good qualities behind them, their brilliancy.

Of one thing you may be always sure, they are quick witted in the extreme, and are very concise in their method of expression. Their letters are marvels of brevity, as they have a great facility of saying much in little. This makes them excellent newspaper reporters or short-story writers. It stands to reason that such pronounced qualities, as those indicated by short fingers, need great strength behind them in order to give success.

One of the first matters to consider, in this regard, is the finger tip. The pointed tip, with its ideality, fervor, poetry of heart and soul, impressionability, and indifference to worldly interests, is the most dangerous companion for short fingers. The impractical view indicated by the pointed tips will lead short fingers to be much more impulsive, and quick, in which case the subject is in positive danger from excess of his short-fingered qualities. Conic tips will not lead short fingers into quite so great danger, but will still emphasize these qualities.

Square tips, when found, will direct the short-fingered impetuosity into more practical channels, make it less impressionable and less likely to "go off half-cocked." Spatulate tips will add great activity and originality, but are not such good tips for short fingers as the square, which add more calmness and common-sense than any of the others. Flexibility of the hand with short fingers, will add elasticity of mind to short-fingered qualities, showing a great adaptability to a large range and variety of subjects It adds much to the keenness, but is likely, on account of the versatility and predisposition to extreme views, not to be a good combination. You can see how bad for the subject, pointed tips, short fingers, and flexibility would be, for, with this combination the boiler would surely burst. Flabby consistency will make these people lazy and will pull down the force of their qualities. They *think* quickly, but being lazy will not *act* with the same quickness It will be purely the mental attributes of short fingers that will be called into play in this case. Soft hands will be more active than flabby ones, but still not intense. Elastic hands will bring out fully the force of short-fingered qualities, and, as the elastic hand stands for intelligent energy, it will not be a bad combination. Hard hands showing the energy of an unelastic brain, will push short-fingered qualities, but perhaps push them too much. Elastic consistency is thus the best with short fingers. Knotty joints reduce the short-fingered qualities of quick thought, and are in consequence excellent companions. The knotty qualities of analysis, if possessed by the subject, and the faculty of always having a reason for everything, will check the impetuous impulse of short fingers. If only the first knot is developed, the quick thought of short fingers will have mental order and arrangement added to it. If only the second knot be developed, the short-fingered subject will not be so careless in his dress and surroundings.

The thumb plays a most important part, with short fingers, for add to their strong qualities the determination of a large thumb, and if it is not of just the *right sort* you will have a very bad combination. The clubbed thumb with short fingers will add the brutal obstinacy of that thumb, and drive the short-fingered qualities to an intolerable extreme. The flat, nervous thumb will add nervous excitement to a set of forces already too quick, producing bad results. A thumb with a short phalanx of logic will show that reasoning qualities are not behind the already unreasoning short fingers; this is an unfortunate combination. It requires thumbs of intelligent and healthy strength, balanced in all parts, to operate favorably on short fingers.

Short fingers will operate strongly on all the Mounts. With them the ambition, pride, religion, and honor of the Jupiterian will have impulse and quick thought behind them. Saturn will be less taciturn, slow, stingy, and superstitious. Apollo will be more brilliant, will scintillate, as intuition is already one of his strong qualities. Mercury will be quick as a flash, whether he be orator, business man, professional man, scientist, or thief. Mars will be in need of much help from some source, to keep short-fingered impetuosity from running away with him, and causing him to undertake hazardous ventures. The Moon will be quicker, less selfish, and less dreamy. Venus will have an added fire of quick thought and impulse.

Note the individual phalanges of the short fingers to see whether the mental, the abstract, or the material worlds rule, for the direction in which the short-fingered qualities will operate can be determined from them. This will either be in mental projects (first phalanx), business enterprises (second phalanx), or in providing a meal with plenty of wine (third phalanx). You can judge the probable outcome of short fingers by estimating whether ambition is behind them or whether too much Martian aggression will force them into extreme positions. Apply all the Mount qualities as a force *behind*, and see what this driving-power will do.

Then, most important of all, look at the Head line: see if it is strong, clear, and straight; whether drooping, or if it be a line showing, by islands and chains, defects in mental strength and balance. A good clear Head line, showing sound and healthy judgment, will do more to bring short fingers to perfection than any other factor. I regard short fingers as a fine possession if the proper qualities are back of them. There is nothing little or mean about them; they are not cramped or dwarfed in their views. But with their abhorrence of detail, quickness of thought and action, with impulse, hasty conclusions, and the great distaste for doing anything slowly, they are in constant danger of making mistakes as the result of a lack of deliberate and careful thought. Brilliant as they are, they need square tips, elastic consistency, proper thumbs, and fine, straight Head lines. With such companions they are capable of any achievement. Give them the company of pointed or conic tips, hard hands, coarse or nervous thumbs, and poor Head lines, and you know what the result must be—utter failure.

CHAPTER XVII

THE THUMB

"There is no chance, no destiny, no fate
Can circumvent, or hinder, or control
The firm resolve of a determined soul.
Gifts count for nothing; will alone is great;
All things give way before it soon or late.
What obstacle can stay the mighty force
Of the sea-seeking river in its course,
Or cause the ascending orb of day to wait?
Each well-born soul must win what it deserves.
Let the fool prate of luck. The fortunate
Is he whose earnest purpose never swerves,
Whose slightest action or inaction serves
The one great aim.
Why, even Death stands still
And waits an hour sometimes for such a will."

ELLA WHEELER WILCOX.

IN all the study of the hand, no portion is of more importance than that devoted to the thumb. The consideration of this most wonderful member should be undertaken with a full appreciation of its power, and a realization of how much it can mean to you if properly understood. So great a revealer of character is the thumb that many of the Hindus base their entire work upon it; the Chinese have a most minute and intricate system based solely on the capillaries of the first phalanx; and all gypsies use the thumb for a large part of their Chirognomic work, for they have found that a knowledge of the thumb, added to their Mercurian shrewdness, gives them enough data for ordinary purposes. Without consideration of any other parts of the hand, the thumb would furnish a source from which could be given a very good reading, and a thorough understanding of it should be had before going into a discussion of the types with which the qualities of the thumb play so strong a part.

The thumb cannot be called a finger, because it is infinitely more ; it is really four fingers, as it can oppose itself at will to the four others (61), thus doing away with the need of

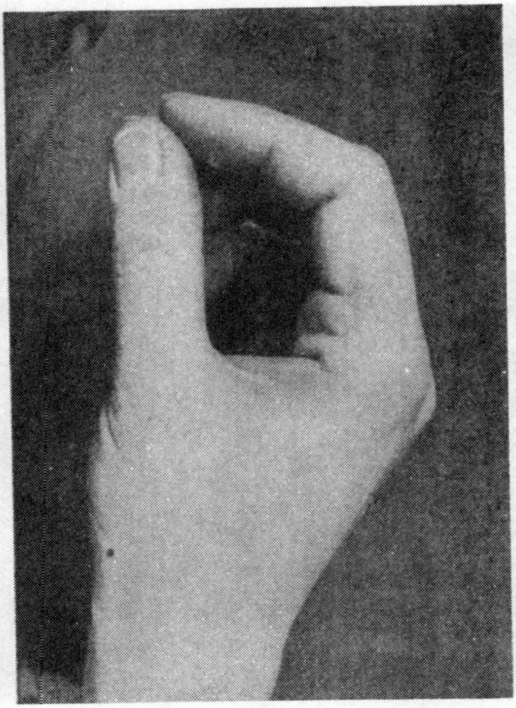

NO. 61. THUMB OPPOSING THE FINGERS

four additional single fingers to perform this necessary function. It is the fulcrum around which all the fingers must revolve, and in proportion to its strength or weakness will it hold up or let down the strength of the subject's character.

Large thumbs (62) denote strength of character, and belong to persons who are guided by the head ; small thumbs,

(63) show weak character, or persons who are guided by the heart. Large thumbs show force of character, small thumbs, lack of force. So in taking hold of a hand and finding a large thumb you will know that strength and head guide the subject, and that something pronounced may be expected. These are the people who naturally rule, and this

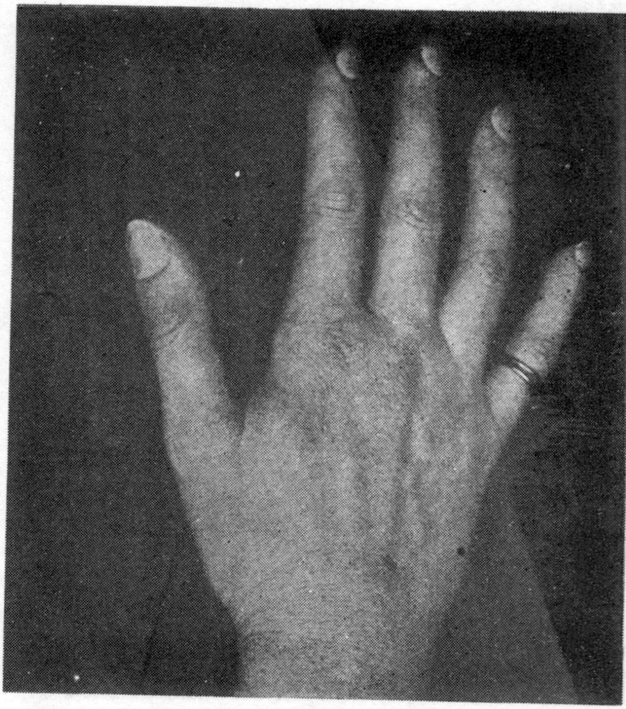

NO. 62. LARGE THUMB

will be more certain if the thumb is at all coarse, in addition to its size. If a small thumb is found, the character is weak; the heart and sentiments rule; these are the persons who are certain to *be* led. Big thumbs show a love of history, small thumbs, of romance. People with big thumbs seek for and enjoy useful, necessary, and practical things in life; those with small thumbs appreciate only the beautiful, poetical, sentimental side, consequently they will not be able to go into the world and hold their own against their big-thumbed brethren.

The thumb as a whole is composed of three phalanges, as are all the other fingers. It is a mistake to divide it into only two phalanges. The Three Worlds of Palmistry apply just as much to the thumb as to any of the fingers, and it is

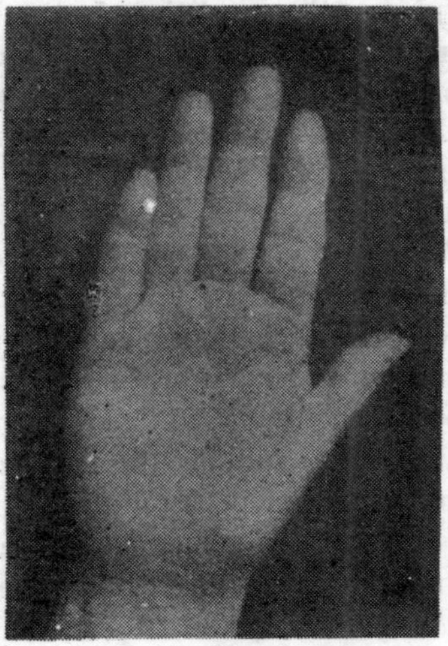

NO. 63. SMALL THUMB

no more complete without three phalanges than would the fingers be with only two. So in your examination of the thumb, divide it into mental and abstract worlds, indicated by the first and second phalanges, and add to these the material world shown by what we call the Mount of Venus, which is really the third phalanx of the thumb. These three worlds of the thumb embody three qualities supremely important to the success of any human being, and they may justly be classed among the greatest *moving forces* in the entire category of human levers. Without them no amount of brilliancy or talent, no amount of scholarly attainment, will enable a subject to achieve great success. These three factors so strongly estimated are *will power* and *determination*, indicated by the first phalanx, *reason* and *logic* by the second, *love* and *sympathy* by the third, or Mount of Venus. Thus it will be seen that in the thumb we have determination backed by reason, and forced on by love, which is a combination so strong that it will overcome any obstacle which may seek to impede its progress, and will often force success when such an outcome seems impossible. Realizing how powerful are the qualities shown by the thumb, you will understand why many palmists are content to centre their efforts upon it alone. When big thumbs are seen you know that determination, reason, and love in large supply are present, and you know the effort to which these qualities will lead. Small thumbs are found best developed in the third phalanx (Mount of Venus), and deficient in the other two, so here are love and sentiment strongest (Mount of Venus), without the accompaniment of will and reason; making a combination certain to bring only weakness to the subject. The special attributes indicated by the first phalanx are will power, decision, and ability to command others; those of the second phalanx, perception, judgment, and reasoning faculties; of the third phalanx, love, sympathy, and passion; a combination of the three phalanges showing you the amount of *moral force* of your subject, without which no character is strong, no brilliancy is of great value. That the thumb is of supreme importance to the usefulness of the hand is shown by the fact that on the hand of Man only is it found. In descending the scale from humanity into the animal kingdom we find that the thumb at once disappears when the break between man and the monkey has been made. Most animals live together as individuals, not as a community governed by one head. Each animal does what it likes, looks out for itself, goes or comes as it pleases, seeks its own food, and protects itself when attacked. One animal has no power to rule or govern another. Even the young remain at the mother's breast and under the mother's control only long enough to gain sufficient strength to enable them to strike out for themselves. This comparatively early age reached, they become *individuals*, each looking after its separate interests, and one has no control over any other. Knowing that *ability to command others* is shown by the thumb, and knowing that the thumb is absent in the animal, we see why it is that they do not gather into communities and are not governed and ruled by some one of their own kind. This will also explain in some degree why man is so immensely superior to the animal in his achievements. He unites with his kind and presents a common front to an enemy. When man plants a settlement in the wilderness he drives out the native animals because a body of human beings united is stronger than a body of animals, each of which is an individual, to whom the qualities of the thumb are lacking. It is thumb quality opposed to a lack of it; it is the triumph of the hand and its thumb over the paw which has it not.

Physiologically the thumb is more abundantly supplied with muscles than the fingers, which have only flexor and extensor muscles that give them the ability to open and close in a vertical way. The strong muscular development of the thumb is so arranged that it can move in a rotary direction, enabling it to oppose itself in turn to each of the fingers. It is this *opposing power* of the thumb that makes the human hand so skilful in large or small things, that makes it able to master arts and sciences, hold tools, operate engines, or grasp pens and pencils ; instruments which have made, developed, and recorded human history. It is the thumb which enables humanity to invent, manufacture, and use all the devices which we have to-day. It is the lack of the thumb that forces the animal to tear food with its teeth, holding it on the ground with its paw, in which case the ground performs the duty of the thumb.

We say the thumb shows will power, and it shows as well the exercise of it. The child when first born has no will ; it is entirely under the control of others. For the first few weeks of life, if healthy, it sleeps about twenty-two out of twenty-four hours. During this time the thumb is closed in the hand, the fingers concealing it ; in other words the will, represented by the thumb, is dormant,—it has not begun to assert itself. Soon the child does not sleep so much; it begins to have some ideas of its own, and often shows that it has a temper. At once the thumb comes from its hiding-place in the palm, the fingers no longer close over it, for will is beginning to exert itself, and when it does, the thumb, its indicator, appears. In examining the hands of idiots — those poor souls whose minds have been destroyed by some shock, or some illness, or who perhaps were born witless,— you will find weak thumbs. These idiots are unable to exert control over themselves or others. If the idiocy is of a congenital nature, the thumb will be very poorly formed, small and weak looking. This formation, which amounts sometimes to a deformity of the hand, will show that the subject was born idiotic, and that the mind and will never existed. If a thumb indicating good strength of will is found on the hand of an idiot, then the thumb is carried in a lifeless, unsteady manner, and when the hand is not in use the thumb is closed into the palm. This shows that the mind and will were once present, but are now weakened or gone. This idiocy is produced by shock or disease, and is not congenital.

Epileptics also show confirmations of thumb quality. Just before a seizure, and before any other warning has been given, the thumb closes in the palm. It is beyond the power of the patient's will to prevent the seizure; disease temporarily displaces the will, and its indicator, the thumb, gives way and hides itself. When persons are very ill it is important to note how their thumbs are held. In battling against disease the will must be strongly called into play, in order that life may remain. If will is holding its own, it is an indication that disease has not gained the mastery. When, however, the thumb folds into the palm, the brain is much disturbed, and the will cannot hold out a great deal longer. This operation of the thumb can be seen even in those who are unconscious or suffering with high fever. I believe this action of the thumb which is often seen on dying people comes from the fact that man alone has a knowledge of death, man alone has the faculty of reason, man by reason of his knowledge of death opposes his will to its operation. So long as he does this, the thumb stands. When the thumb folds into the palm as death approaches both will and reason are in abeyance, the faculties give way, and the dissolution of reasoning power and will takes place.

There are two kinds of will power to be borne in mind: instinctive will, which gives us a faculty of being stubborn without any definite purpose, and the will born of reason. Instinctive will is possessed by animals, and leads them to fight obstinately against others of their kind, through mere inherent stubbornness. Animals have also a sort of instinctive logic and instinctive decision. The kind of will which is represented by the thumb is not this animal instinct, but the will of reason, the logic of reason, the decision of reason. In this case, a human mind is back of the forces, giving them direction. In the development of the hand we find its most primitive formation in the Amœba (Drummond), a small jelly-like water growth which is headless, legless, and armless. Whenever it has use for a hand to grasp its food, it bulges out at some point in its circumference, touches the object it wishes, flows over it and absorbs it. This bulge, or hand, in its side, appears at any point when a need demands it, and disappears whenever the need is satisfied. This is the first and lowest form of hand, belonging to a bit of protoplasm which has neither form nor shape. From this amœbic hand, as intelligence increases, there is a steady development in paws or hands. First a few tendrils operate as fingers, as in the case of sea anemones, then through the carnivora, where toes and claws appear, until we come to the monkey. Here we find the nearest approach to the human hand, and on the monkey's paw the nearest approach to the thumb. It consists of a bit of cartilage covered with skin and sets *very high* on the paw, is loose, and is without great stiffness. It is the kind of thumb which cannot oppose itself firmly to the fingers, has little strength, and serves to impress us that Man only has a real thumb. Two things to remember concerning the monkey's thumb are the fact that it sets very high on the side of the paw, and that it lacks the ability to oppose the fingers. Also bear in mind, that the more intelligent the monkey, the nearer this "finger" approaches to a thumb. Those found in the wild state have little approach to such a member, those bred and reared in zoölogical gardens are developing better thumbs, and

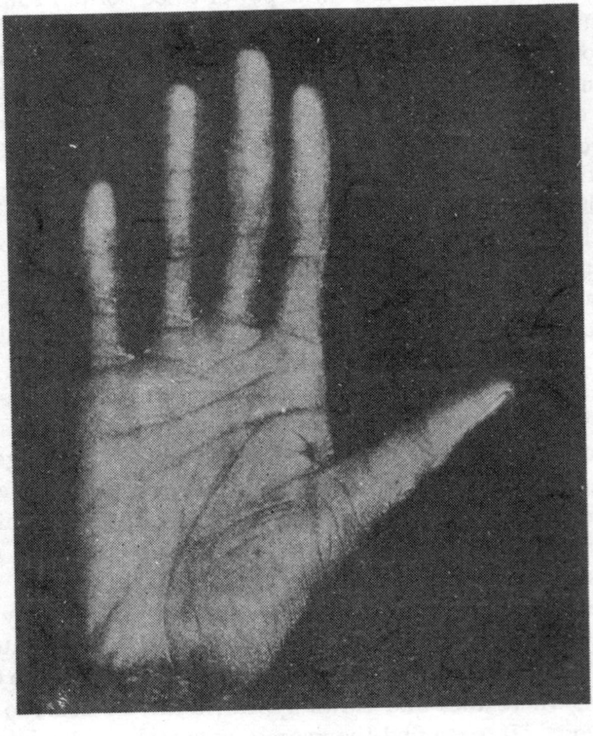

NO. 64. HIGH-SET THUMB

there will be a continued improvement in this regard as the monkey more closely approaches the human species in intelligence.

In noting the thumbs on your client's hand, have him hold the hand up in front of you, palm in your direction, very much as you had him do when examining the carriage of the fingers. This is in order to find whether the thumb sets high at the side of the hand, is low, or in the medium position. Remembering how the monkey's thumb is placed high at the side of its paw, and also that the idiot's thumb is also high, at once reason that the higher the thumb grows out from the side of the hand (64), the lower the grade

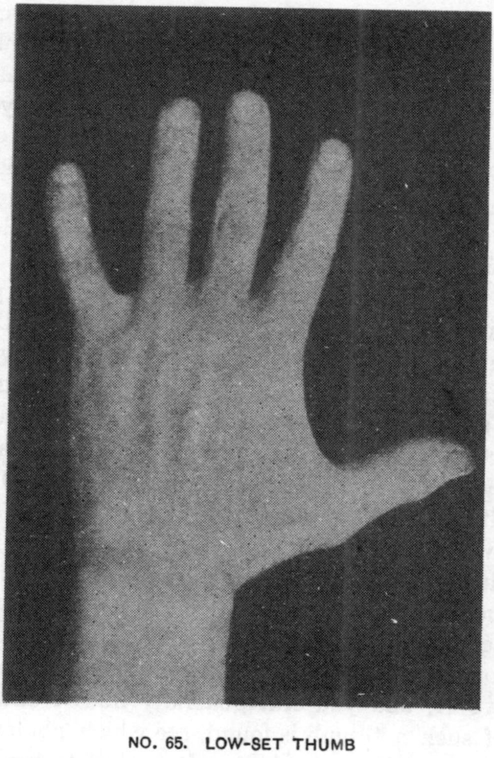

NO. 65. LOW-SET THUMB

of intelligence, and the less adaptability has the subject. The smaller the thumb thus highly placed, the nearer it approaches the monkey thumb, and the nearer the approach of the subject to the qualities of the monkey. Monkeys may be bright and shrewd, but in an animal way, lacking entirely the human quality, *character*. If the thumb sets low it generally follows that it will open wide from, and will not lie close along, the side of the hand. This low-set thumb, leaving a large space between itself and the finger of Jupiter (65), will indicate a nature full of the highest human qualities. It speaks of generosity, independence, love of liberty for itself and others, sympathy for all who are in distress, and a readiness to share with less fortunate brethren. While this low-set thumb does not bear all the qualities of the *supple* thumb, in that the low thumb, while liberal and generous, does not throw money away as do the supple thumbs, still the low thumb is the intensely human thumb. Its possessor is filled with the greatest strength of Venusian qualities, sympathy and generosity (this thumb forming as it does the lower part of Venus), and he is fired with warmth, which, while it may not mean passion, does bespeak one who is not cold-blooded. If you ask a favor, this man with the low-set thumb will grant it if possible. You know in asking that the cold response of a selfish person will not be given you, but that, having a feeling of common humanity, he will do for you all he can. This low-set thumb is generally long, and if so it means power and force of character, which, with determination and reason, will intensify generous and sympathetic qualities. If the thumb is short, it will take away much of the good of its low setting, for, while the position is good, the thumb itself is nearer the smallness of the monkey formation, which will tend to give it monkey will and selfishness. With a low-set small thumb the good quality it has will be independence, and this comes from selfish motives. The low-set small thumb is rare, however, and you will generally find it close to the hand. If such a thumb is found, see which phalanx is deficient, which rules, and whether it is close to the hand or falling wide open. After noting all its landmarks, look at the tip, and with this combination of evidence you will be able to judge it aright.

Before proceeding farther, I must speak of the two phalanges, the first and second. For brevity I shall call these two, respectively, will and logic. In all thumbs, long or short, see whether one or the other phalanx is deficient or in excess. The normal length of the thumb, with a medium setting, is when the end of the first phalanx reaches about to the middle of the third phalanx of the finger of Jupiter, when the thumb is held against the side of the hand (66). If the thumb is much shorter than this it is a short thumb, unless it be set so low that, while the thumb itself is of normal

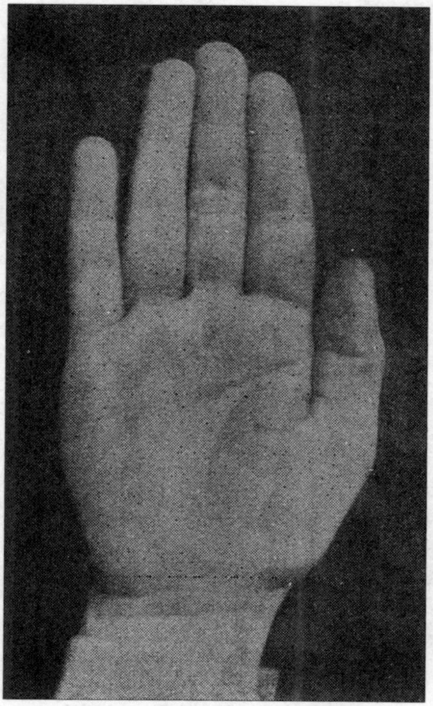

NO. 66. THUMB NORMAL LENGTH

length, the low setting accounts for its shortness. Again, if set very high it might overreach this measurement and still be only of normal length. In judging individual phalanges of the thumb see that the first phalanx is a trifle shorter than the second. This gives normal development. If the will phalanx is longer than logic (67), will is in excess of reason, and the person will act first and think afterward.

He is set and determined in his ways, and makes mistakes because he has allowed these qualities to rule reason. He is stubborn, and cannot see that it is better to acknowledge and correct an error than to suffer the consequences of unreasonable obstinacy. If the second phalanx is much the longer (68),

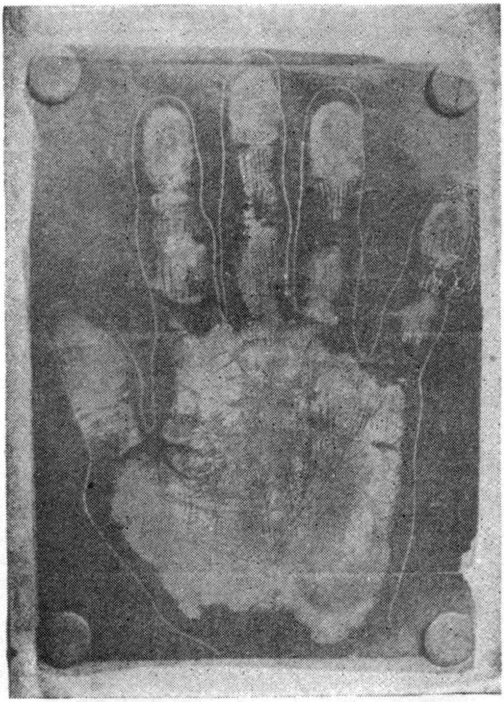

NO. 67. WILL LONGER THAN LOGIC

reason is in excess of will, and this person can reason cleverly, but is not good in carrying the results into execution. He is the reasoner who does not act. He knows how things *should* be done, but does not carry this knowledge into operation. Some time ago, during one of my lectures, I was asked, " Do you believe that a person naturally deficient in will power, and knowing his weakness, can school himself so that he will *develop* strong will?" To this question I answered, "No." Since then I have given this matter most careful observation and study; have taken subjects whom I knew to be deficient in will, found good situations for them, surrounded them with the best influences, and put before them

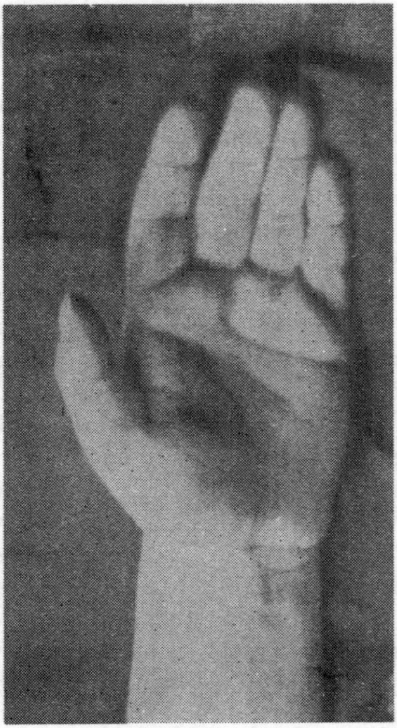

NO. 68. LOGIC LONGER THAN WILL

every incentive for effort. They developed the most tremendous determination for a while; when they thought they were being *watched* or put to a test they were as obstinate and immovable as a rock, but taken off their guard, they succumbed to the first temptation. Deficient will is strong when on guard, stronger than a normal will under similar circumstances, but it is not the *real quality*, and subjects with such a will fall by the way whenever they are not intentionally exerting it. Whenever drunkards have, by sheer force of will, reformed, it was because they had the strong will to begin with; they could not otherwise have succeeded. Many students have come to think that all persons with large will phalanges will be necessarily successful, as they have so much determination to push them forward. This will be true if they have *anything* to push. Determination is only *a force* that can push *something else ;* it is not worth much *by itself.* It can *drive* some other power to achievement, but determination must have *something to drive*, or it is valueless. If your subject is literary, musical, artistic, or practical, determination *behind* these gifts will undoubtedly bring them to good account, but it would be worth little that a man was merely determined, for he must have some *ability* before determination can bring him success. Understanding this, do not say, upon seeing a large thumb, "You are bound to have great success, you have so much determination." The person may be ignorant, heavy, and coarse ; if so the will phalanx would only make him stubborn, and his coarse qualities would be the coarser.

And now go back to the position of the thumb on the hand. We have considered the high-set thumb, which is akin to the monkey's, as well as its opposite, the low-set one ; we will now take up the straight thumb, set close to the hand (69). A thumb placed either high, low, or normally, and which has, as its distinctive mark, the closeness with which it lies by the side of the hand, the straightness of its carriage, and lack of flexibility at the joint, shows a person the opposite of the one whose thumb is low set and opens wide from the fingers. This is not called the stiff thumb ; for it is not always pronouncedly stiff, although it has not the flexible or supple joint. The marked peculiarity in this thumb is its carriage, as a whole, and its disposition to lie close to the side of the hand. This indicates a cautious person, one who will be afraid to say much because he fears you may presume on the acquaintance and ask some favor. These people are close, lack sympathy, and are hard to approach. They surround themselves with a wall which is difficult to scale. They hold you at arm's length, and are entirely lacking in independence, narrow in their views, bigoted and set in their ways, and do not impress you as being open or frank. They are secretive, neither giving nor

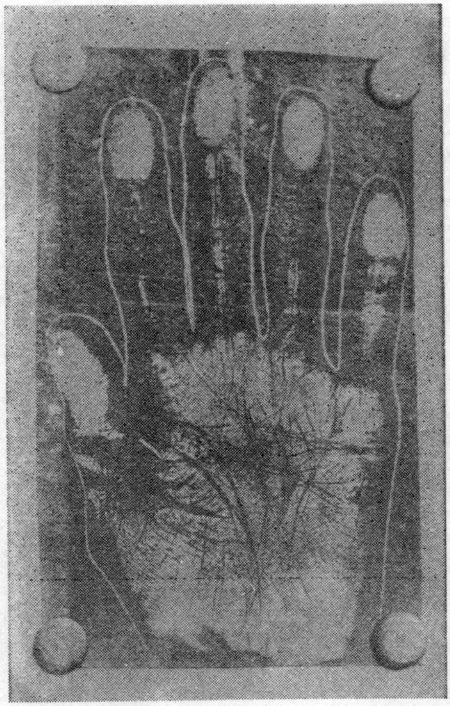

NO. 69. THUMB CARRIED CLOSE TO HAND

inviting confidences, consequently they are persons who do not make many friends, nor do they seek them. If with this thumb you find the fingers stiff and lacking flexibility, it will accentuate all of the peculiarities; and if they have short, critical nails, it will, in addition, make them mean and petty. This thumb shows at a glance the want of warmth and sympathy, the caution, secretiveness, narrowness, and unresponsiveness of its owner.

The medium setting of the thumb (70), neither too high nor too low, not tied closely to the hand, and not lying away from it as if trying to break loose, but seeming to stand upright, bold, fearless, independent, and full of life ; shows a person with well-balanced views, not prodigal, yet not stingy

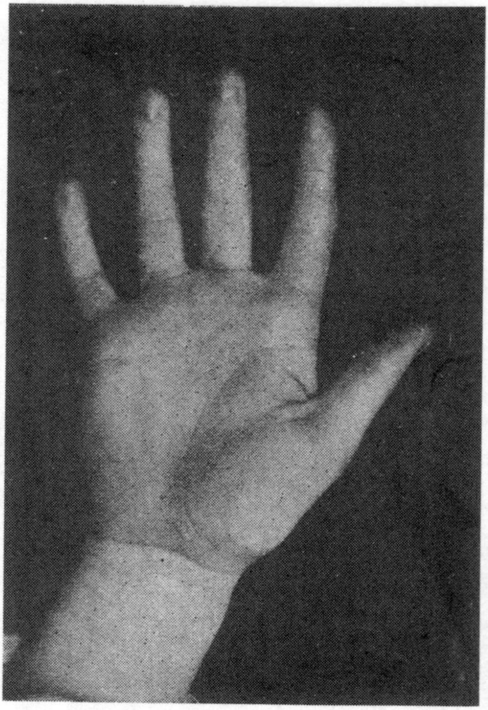

NO. 70. MEDIUM SETTING

and mean. One who always listens to a reasonable appeal, and who responds in a sensible way. He is ruled by neither head nor heart, but by a combination of both. He is balanced, properly cautious, reasonably generous, dignified, and responsive to approaches coming in sensible and reasonable ways. He does not overflow with sentiment, nor does he shut himself off from his fellow-men; but in business, religion, love, home-life, everywhere, he is a balanced, sensible person. You feel, with this thumb, that the owner is not hiding from you either thoughts or actions that he is frank in disposition, true to friends, and that his acquaintance is worth cultivating. It is a thumb that attracts you

NO. 71. ELEMENTARY THUMB

and gives you confidence, shows neither the domineering will, nor the quibbler, speaks of no extreme in anything, but of even temper, good thoughts, and a balancing of qualities.

We now come to a consideration of the *shape* of the thumb as a whole, and it is very important to understand this thoroughly. In this consideration we shall begin at the bottom and go upward in the scale, starting with the heavy, elementary development (71). This thumb is one which is shaped like a banana, is entirely devoid of symmetry; the two joints do not show where they separate, but the whole thumb looks like a wad of flesh stuck on the hand. The

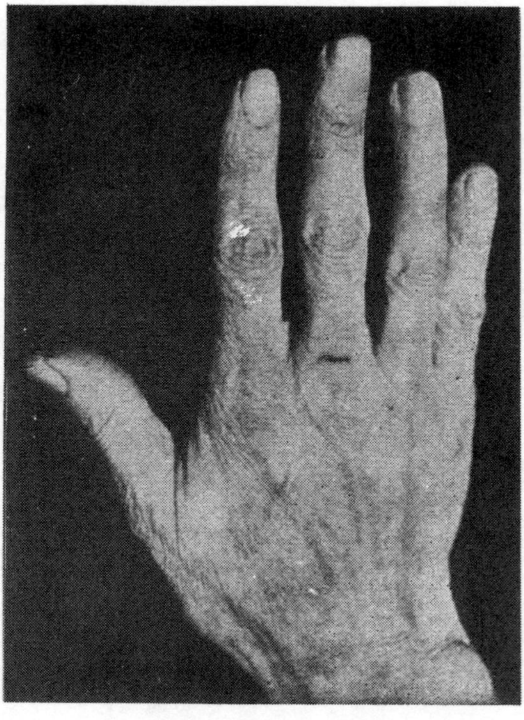

NO. 72. NERVOUS THUMB

illustration shown gives a clear idea of this thumb, and is the best specimen I have ever seen. Everything about this thumb speaks of heaviness, coarseness, animalism. It is brute force in will, brute force in reasoning, and brute passion in love. There is nothing elevating or uplifting about it ; all is heavy, coarse, and common, blunt, tactless, and ignorant. The owner of this thumb walks over everyone he meets, cares nothing for refinement of manner or speech, nor for the feelings of others, and is boorish and clownish even among those as coarse as himself. It is the personification of ignorant obstinacy, operated in an unreasoning way. Any thumb resembling the heavy formation of this one shows an

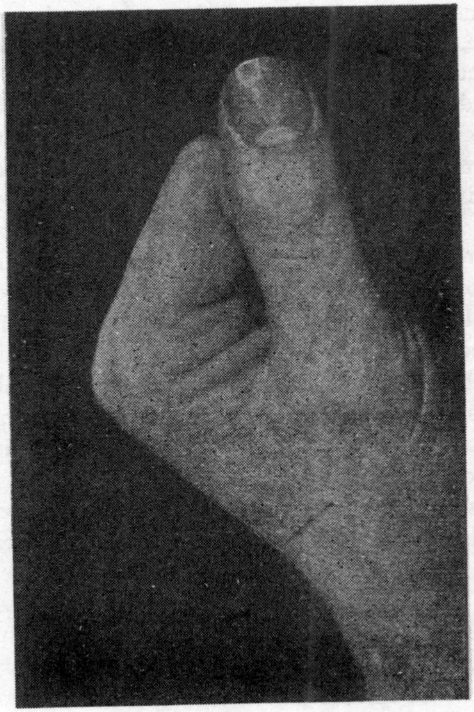

NO. 73. STRONG WILL, WITH MUSCULAR STRENGTH

approach to its common qualities, and while you will not find many as coarse as the illustration, you will find some so near, that they tell tales not hard to understand.

Thumbs will be found which, as you look at them and take hold of them, are seemingly *quite flat*, looking as though they have been pressed until the substance is gone out of them (72). They are found in all textures of skin, all kind-of hands, and with any tips. These thumbs are soft or flabby, and it is the *flatness* that is their distinguishing mark. This is a nervous thumb, and will show you the nervous force and nervous energy that are proving too strong for the owner. When this flat thumb is found you often find the fluted nail, many lines in the hand, and a soft or flabby consistency, all of which is an indication of nervous unbalance. It tells of the nervous excess in the subject, for the *flat* thumb is the *nervous* thumb.

A thumb may be found which is not round and shapeless, as is the elementary, nor flat like the nervous thumb, yet, when viewed from the nail side, it has a broad look (73). It is broad in both phalanges, and has a strong, healthy appearance. This is a formation which will show you a *strong determination* backed by physical strength. It is not the brutish obstinacy, the ignorant unreasonableness of the elementary, but it is a healthy strength, so healthy that it may at times be too strong. It indicates the determination that accomplishes its object and, rising over every obstacle, is pushing and aggressive, but may easily be turned into a violent quality of obstinacy, and often needs guidance and holding down to keep it within bounds.

There is the thumb which appears of one thickness throughout its entire length ; it is delicate and shapely, with square or a conic tip (74). The nail is of smooth texture and pink color, the skin of fine quality and the entire aspect of the thumb full of life, grace, and refinement. This thumb shows strong will, for the first phalanx is good, shows good logical qualities also, for the second phalanx is strong, yet it shows at the same time refinement, taste, and tact in the use of these qualities. Its owner will more certainly reach the end he aims at than will he of the heavy, coarse thumb, but he will not wound feelings, nor will he walk rough shod over anyone. With diplomatic mind, and firm determination, instead of knocking people down that he may pass, he will slip by and between them so easily, that while he "gets there" no one wishes to check him. This beautiful thumb attracts you, tells of the strong character of its owner, and also of the refined, intelligent, kindly nature, filling the lives of all around it with beauty, yet having ample firmness of purpose. It shows the refinement of will, the refinement of intelligent reason, taste, tact, and perseverance.

The four thumbs just described will enable you to judge upon what plane the thumb qualities operate.

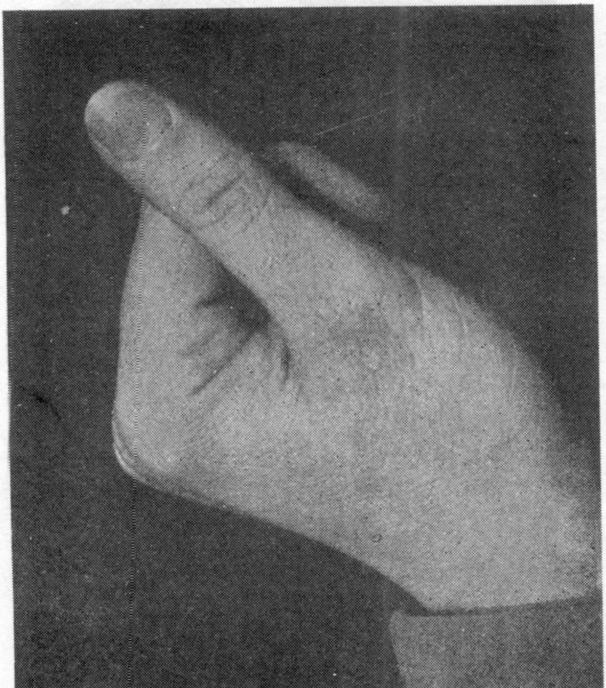

NO. 74. STRONG WILL, TACT AND REFINEMENT

After treating the thumb as a whole, next consider the phalanges, and examine them as to length, shape of tips, and form. Remembering the rule that the first phalanx should be a little shorter than the second, and that with a thumb placed normally on the hand the tip should reach to the middle of the third phalanx of the finger of Jupiter, we will proceed with our examination as to length of phalanges. In estimating the *strength* of any phalanx of the thumb, the *length* is an important consideration at the outset. A thumb with the first phalanx *much* longer than the second will tell you that *will* is much stronger than *reason*. These subjects

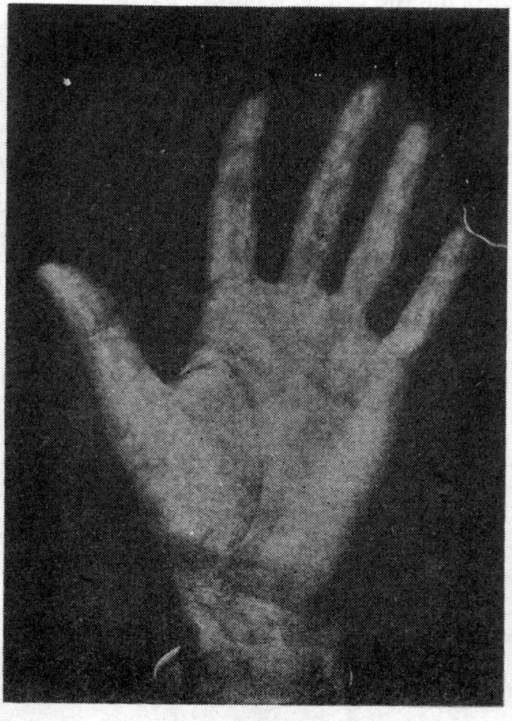

NO. 75. WILL AND LOGIC BALANCED

are obstinate, tyrannical, despotic, and if crossed in the operation of their plans will, with unreasoning stubbornness, fly into a temper. This is another instance where the excess of a good quality may bring evil results, and when *will* is stronger than *reason* it is easy to predict that unreasonable obstinacy will be the result. Where the first phalanx is the same length as the second, the two qualities are balanced

(75). Will is strong, reason is strong, consequently the determination of this subject will be the quiet strength that comes from good judgment, and no bullying, no tyranny, will be shown as in the case of the excessive will phalanx. In the balanced phalanges there will be as much firmness, as much determination, as is necessary, but it will be *controlled* and operated by logic and reason. There will be no weakness, no fickleness, but intelligent strength that marks the natural leader.

The thumb with the second phalanx strong and the first phalanx deficient shows a nature out of balance. In this instance, reason will dominate, will is secondary. The subject will think but not act; these people lack the power of carrying out their ideas, the determination to live up to their intentions. They are the ones who are always telling how the government, business, religion, and everything ought to be run, but are doing nothing to have their ideas carried out. They are planners, not operators, reasoners, not doers. Thumbs in which the will phalanx is *wofully* short, and entirely out of proportion to logic, will tell of the *absolute* weakness of the owner. He may be ruled by any person, no matter how ignorant, and goes through life an easy tool for anyone who chooses to command him. These people are "weaker than water," easily discouraged, and stand no chance to be anything but servers. These subjects sometimes show great stubbornness, especially if on their guard, but this display of will is only spasmodic and puerile, and the inherent weakness of the subject does not permit it to continue long. So from the excess in length of the will phalanx to the absolute deficiency above described are found the various degrees of will power of your subject. Too much is as bad as not enough, and often does more damage to the subject and to the world. It is an unreasoning *force*, which may be more harmful than a passive *weakness*.

The tips of the thumbs must be noted as carefully as those of the fingers, for different tips will increase or diminish strength. A conic tip to the thumb (76) makes the subject impressionable and weakens or softens the strength of the will. The conic qualities of impulse, love of beauty, and idealism take some of its strength away from even an excessive *length* of will phalanx. The subject will be less tyrannical, despotic, and more easily influenced if the tip of will be conic. All through the scale this conic tip will add

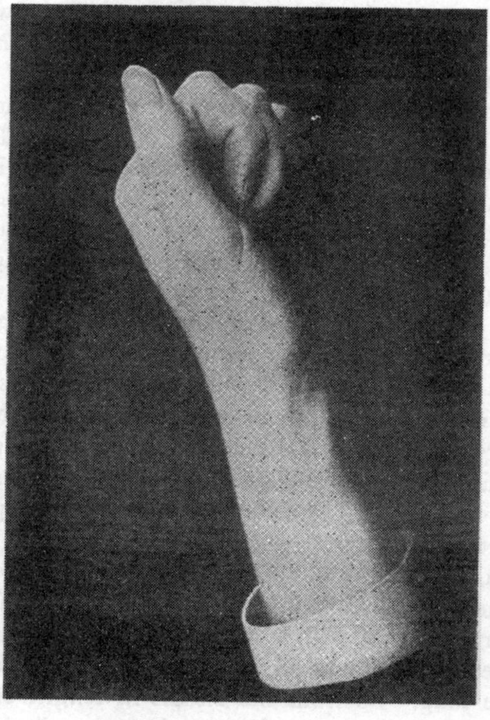

NO. 76. CONIC TIP TO THUMB

its softening and reducing qualities to the various degrees of will shown by the length of the will phalanx. The conic tip on *deficient* will phalanges makes a subject hopelessly weak, shifting with every change of the wind, and instability becomes the leading characteristic. The conic-tipped thumb is the impressionable person, with will power modified and reduced by the qualities of the conic tip. Whatever the *length* of the phalanx, when making your estimate take something off for the conic tip.

The square tip (77) is the practical, common-sense tip. It is the one which adds strength, when found on the deficient will phalanges, adds common-sense to the normal develop-

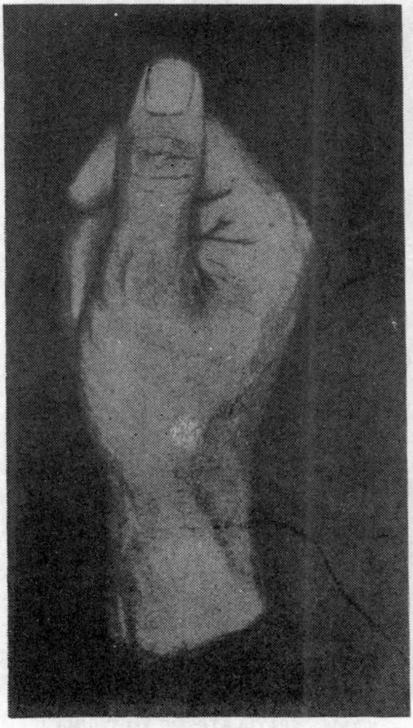

NO. 77. SQUARE TIP TO THUMB

ment, and makes the excessive length more pronounced in its operation. In the latter case it is almost as bad as the spatulate tip, for an excessive length of will phalanx with a square tip makes the subject fanatical in his obstinacy.

The spatulate tip (78) adds all the spatulate qualities to the thumb. It adds action, independence, and originality, and its operation will give a commanding turn to the will. The

F

spatulate tip adds great strength to a deficient will phalanx, gives originality and action to a normal, and fire, action, and ingenuity to an excessive, length. It is a benefit to the weak, and adds to the excess of the strong, both in its active operation and the originality which finds new ways to ex-

NO. 78. SPATULATE TIP TO THUMB

pend force. With the excess in length of will phalanx, the spatulate tip is a positive menace, and always endangers the success of the subject. These three tips all have reference to the shape of the tip, and follow the same formations as the tips of the fingers. We must consider several other shapes of the will phalanx which are often seen and yet which cannot be classed as belonging strictly to any of the above classes.

Many thumbs will be found with the will phalanx broad as viewed from the nail side, but not thick through. This is not the flat, nervous phalanx, for it is not thin enough yet it is not as thick as is the clubbed thumb. It is the extreme breadth, often called "paddle-shaped," that is its dis-

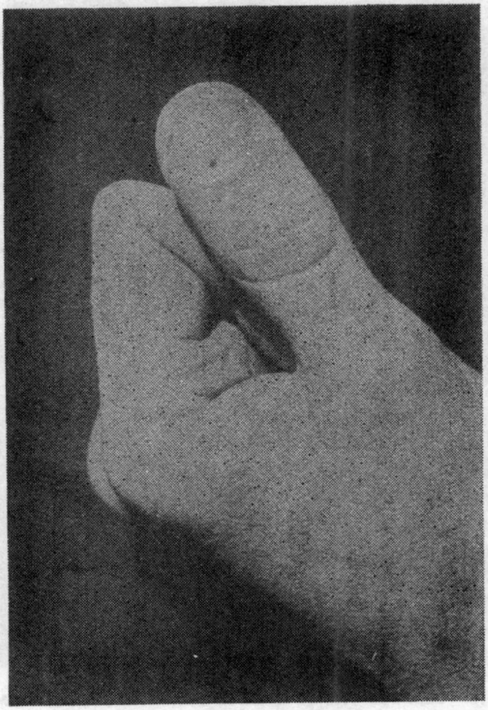

NO. 79. PADDLE-SHAPED THUMB

tinctive feature (79), and this breadth belongs to a long phalanx, giving both length and breadth but not thickness. This shows an exceedingly firm determination, which in excessive developments, degenerates into absolute tyranny and obstinacy. It is always a strong phalanx and must be read so. Even if the length should be somewhat deficient, this "paddle-shaped" phalanx will make it strong. This strength of will is not usually backed by robust health, but is much oftener found with weak physical constitutions. It is an indication of strong *mental* will, which goes boldly through a trying emergency and then collapses after the strain is over.

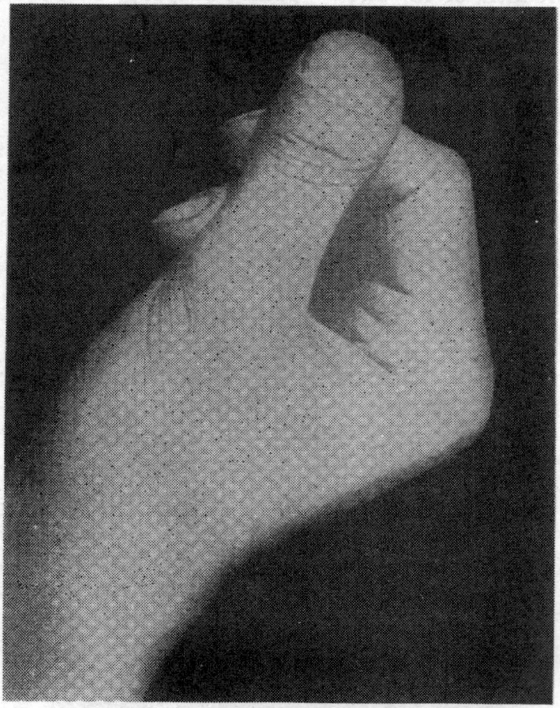

NO. 80. CLUBBED THUMB (CALLED THE MURDERER'S THUMB)

The father of this subject was a sailor. In a fit of drunken rage he attacked a companion, beating him into insensibility. He fled thinking he had killed him, ran home and recited the scene of the fight to his wife, continuing the recital at intervals through the night. In nine months a child was born marked with a clubbed thumb, a deep crimson band surrounding it. That child is the subject of this illustration.

Occasionally a thumb is found with the will phalanx thick and rounded, or broad and thick, with a nail short and very coarse in texture. This is not the consumptive formation of nail and tip, but is found on the hands of healthy persons. Owing to its peculiar club-like formation, it has been called the *Clubbed thumb* (80), and owing to the thickness, coarseness, and brutal obstinacy shown, *has been designated the* "*murderer's* thumb." This clubbed thumb shows terrific obstinacy, and on a bad hand, a common grade of it; which produces a coarse degree of a good quality and is coupled with a violent temper. Whether these coarse and disagreeable qualities have been, or ever will be, brought out is another question. If they have not, if the environments are good, a clubbed thumb will never display its rough and brutal side. We may not, however, ignore the fact that a mine lies underneath, and it will only take a match properly applied to explode it. These clubbed thumbs are largely hereditary, and their presence, on any hand, can be traced back to some parental influence. I have seen cases where they have gone from generation to generation, and yet have never produced harmful results. They are dangerous companions, however, and not to be trifled with at any time. The fact that they are called "murderer's thumbs," should, by no means, lead you to conclude that the owner either has or necessarily will commit murder. They are, as a matter of fact, found on very mild-mannered people, in which case their presence is due to something occurring at conception, or during the gestation of the subject. But put one of these clubbed thumbs on a hand developed all at the base, with a big Mount of Venus, hard consistency, no flexibility, short fingers very thick in third phalanges, and very short in first phalanges, with short nails, and the lines in the hand deep-cut and red, and the first impulse of the subject, on being crossed, is to beat your brains out. Many murderers have had clubbed thumbs; they have also had bestial hands like the one just described. Their brutal instincts being strong, jealousy most often has led them to fits of violent rage, and the terrible qualities of the clubbed thumb have given them passion and determination strong enough to take human life. In this case the clubbed thumb *becomes* the murderer's thumb. This thumb undoubtedly possesses the brutal obstinacy, the violent temper, the low qualities characteristic of a murderer; but it is the balance of the hand that must tell you whether there are not refinements and good traits that will keep the clubbed thumb from doing harm. Always a danger, always showing terrific obstinacy if roused, a brutal temper and furious rage if kindled, the clubbed thumb requires careful study whenever seen ; no hasty judgment

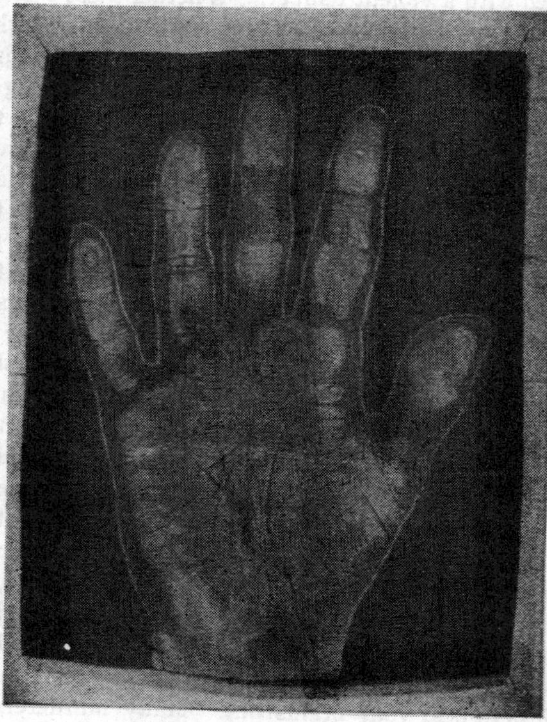

NO. 81. KNOT BETWEEN WILL AND LOGIC

should be passed on it, but every part of the hand estimated and cast in the scales before the balance is struck ; and, above all, it should not be confounded with a spatulate thumb. Texture (for refinement), consistency (for energy), color, especially red, giving intensity and ardor, as well as everything that brutalizes or coarsens the nature, must be taken into account. Flexibility, to see if the elastic mind or the one-idea brain is present, the Mount of Venus to tell of love or sympathy which softens the nature, or of animal passions which may make it unmanageable, — all such things, and everything bearing on them, must be carefully looked at before you are in any position to say what a clubbed thumb means for your client. With all these matters considered and understood, you can properly estimate this most difficult and dangerous indication.

The knot separating the phalanges of will and logic (81) is sometimes present, sometimes absent. It operates exactly as does a knot found anywhere else, — it creates an obstruction to the passage of the vital current, and consequently means deliberation of thought. It adds to the strength of the first phalanx, by making it more analytical and less guided by impulse. Thus it will greatly strengthen a conic tip and will add force to all the other tips. It increases the reasoning of the second phalanx, by reducing the intuition of the first, making a hasty operation of the will unlikely until thought and consideration have had a chance.

Having passed the knot, we reach the second phalanx, indicator of logic and reasoning qualities, perception, judgment, and prudence. In this list of qualities you will notice prudence, which is not generally ascribed to the second phalanx, but as prudent people are those who reason rather than act by impulse, it is evident that caution, or prudence, must belong to this phalanx. I have noted in my study of the second phalanx that this quality applies to it, and is strong in operation, especially if the thumb be carried close to the hand or is stiff. In the latter case the prudence comes from a stingy tendency. In examining the second phalanx, first consider its length. The second phalanx should be estimated as beginning with the joint which connects it to the palm, and as extending to the joint between the first and second phalanges. First look at the thumb held up naturally, and next bend the first phalanx toward the palm, to show the joints plainly and thus give you the exact length of this phalanx (82). This length, to be normal, depends on the length of the hand ; a very long hand will have a long phalanx and *vice versa*, so accustom yourself to noting whether this phalanx is in proportion to the hand, and whether it is longer or shorter than the will phalanx. Normally it should be a *little* longer, but it is still a good development when you find the first and second phalanges of the

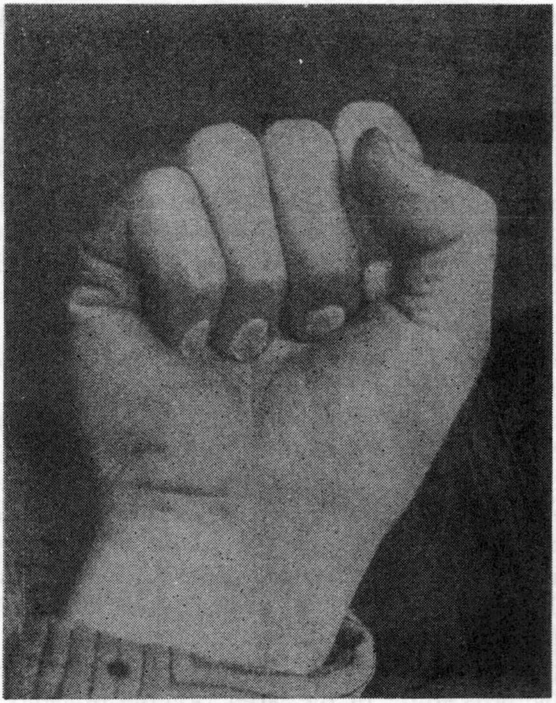

NO. 82. SECOND PHALANX FROM JOINT TO JOINT

same length. The second phalanx shows the reasoning faculties, as well as logic, the science of reasoning. Being the seat of this most important function, it shows by its length and formation how much and *what kind* of reasoning are behind the will, so the second phalanx really occupies a position as director of the will. When the phalanx is found long and in good proportion as regards the will phalanx, it shows strong powers of logic, quick perception, and prudence. With these qualities its possessor will act from well-defined motives, will know what he is doing, be sure of his opinion, and will guide the forces of the first phalanx to expend themselves in beneficial ways. With this long second phalanx you will never find unreasoning obstinacy, but a will power guided by a reasoning brain. The direction, definiteness, and firmness of the will are largely augmented by this long second phalanx, but it is *reasonable strength* that is added, so even with an excessive first phalanx, and the second long also, you may be sure that, however obstinate your subject may be, he will still be amenable to reason.

In noting the tips of the thumbs, the long second phalanx will tell you that strong judgment is behind all of their separate qualities. Reasoning faculties added to conic tips will strengthen their impulsive ways and make them less impressionable; to square tips they will add sound practical judgment; with spatulate tips they will direct the spatulate energy into well-thought-out channels. From every point of view the second phalanx is the balance-wheel. Occupying the position it does between the first and third phalanges (determination and love), it will, if long, be the factor that will hold these strong forces in check, or, if short and deficient, will allow them to run riot. Reason, between will and love, must be the agent to guide them well or ill.

If the second phalanx is found shorter than the first, it will tell you that will is stronger than reason. In this case the subject will have excess of ill-directed will, modified in cases where the second phalanx is exceedingly waist-like. If the second phalanx is short and *thick* the subject will be stubborn, headstrong, acting without careful thought, and making many mistakes which he is too stubborn to correct even though it be to his advantage to do so. The short second phalanx is a sign of weakness that must not be overlooked. If with it the first phalanx be *very* strong, bad results are bound to follow, as obstinate will *must* have logic to direct it properly. If the tip of this thumb be conic, the short second phalanx will add to the weakness of the indication, for an impressionable will with lack of logic behind it produces deficiency of all good thumb qualities. With a square tip it makes the subject a martinet who makes a poor attempt to show strength when there is only weakness. It makes the spatulate qualities fussy without producing any tangible results. If the second phalanx be exceedingly deficient it pulls down the entire structure, and weakens it in every place. Will, if strong, runs riot for want of direction, and with conic tips the subject becomes the plaything of anyone who chooses to lead him. Square-tipped people spend all their force in brushing clothing, dusting the room, or cleaning up the desk. They would rather see things *in order* than to see much accomplished. All the good qualities of square tips are narrowed and dwarfed by the short second phalanx. Spatulate tips are only sputterers, and worry as well as aggravate by their foolish restlessness, for deficient logic has ruined all. The *length* of the second phalanx has shown what *amount* of logic our subject has ; we must now examine the *shape* of the phalanx to discover what *kind* it is.

A phalanx which is not thick and coarse but merely broad shows good muscular strength and robustness in the reasoning faculties. The subject will have healthful views, and, while vigorous and strong, will not be coarse. If the tips be square, he will be practical, and, with a good first phalanx, determined. This development of second phalanx is rarely found on thumbs otherwise weak. If it is, you may be sure that great strength has been added to the deficient thumb. A conic tip with this shaped phalanx is an extreme rarity, but when found the subject is much more healthful in his views with this broad second phalanx.

A flat and flabby second phalanx is the nervous development (see 72). It indicates weakness of constitution and vitality. There may be knowledge, but not physical strength to make logic operative. With this formation, there will be a poor and weakened exhibition of all the tip qualities. Physical strength is needed here. If the second phalanx be coarse, heavy, and thick (see 71) it shows elementary reasoning, the brutal, common point of view, and this will operate on the will phalanx and the tips. It is a part of the elementary thumb shown elsewhere, and partakes of its coarse qualities.

If the second phalanx be slender, round, and the skin of fine texture (see 74), refined logic is possessed by the subject. He

NO. 83. WAIST-LIKE SECOND PHALANX

thinks in a fine, delicate way, but loses no element of strength by the fineness. He reasons and plans how to gain his ends tactfully, and gives the will phalanx and tips refined direction. If the thoughts are evil, this type is much more to be feared than the elementary phalanx, not from a point of physical danger, but from the clever and adroit direction it can give to the will. In this case it shows the crafty, fox-like designing villain. If the thoughts are good it is one of the best shapes to be found.

When the second phalanx is very narrow in the middle, or waist-shaped (83), it is the sign of a brilliant, tactful nature. This subject does everything in an adroit and diplomatic way, and has the faculty of approaching persons in the right manner. He never "rubs you the wrong way," but seems to know how to gain his ends by pleasant means. These people are pleasant to meet because they do not always

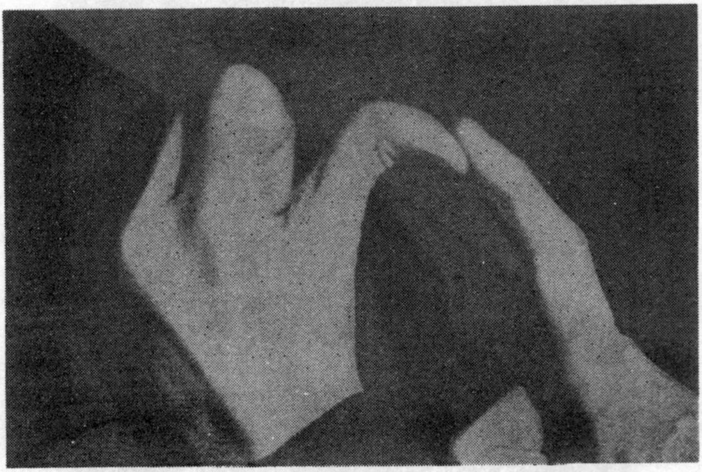

NO. 84. SUPPLE THUMB

step on your toes. Whenever you see this waist-like second phalanx, it should at once speak of tact, taste, brilliancy, diplomacy, and, if long, great mental strength. All these qualities, behind a good will, make a combination from which future success may be expected.

There are two formations of thumbs often met in various degrees of development, each of which possesses strong and opposite qualities; these are what are known as the *supple* and the *stiff* thumb. The first, or supple thumb, must be distinguished by the fact that it bends back at the joint as does the flexible hand, not merely that it opens wide as does the low-set thumb, and for this reason I believe it better to call it the *supple* and *flexible* thumb (84), inasmuch as it possesses flexibility in the highest degree. This supple and flexible thumb personifies extravagance, and those who possess this type are spendthrifts,—brilliant, versatile, easily adapting themselves to changing circumstances. They are at home anywhere, are sentimental, generous, and sympathetic, will give their last cent to a beggar, are improvident, and do not lay up for a "rainy day." They are emotional, consequently extremists, up one day, in the depths the next. This arises from great versatility and from the fact that their brilliant qualities enable them to do so many things. They are never plodders, but by brilliant dashes achieve their successes. Never satisfied to be led, they aspire to surpass their brethren, and as a rule they find no trouble in so doing, as they are both talented and versatile. Theirs is a most brilliant and happy nature, but often ruined by its very brilliancy. When you see these thumbs, look at once for indications that may hold in check the supple thumb qualities. Square tips, a good Head-line, and good Mount of Saturn will do more than any other combination to hold them in balance. Spatulate originality will not help them, neither will conic impulse; it must be sobering qualities.

The stiff thumb is one which is stiff in the joint, and does not bend back as does the supple (85). This thumb inclines to carry itself erect and close to the hand, as well as to be stiff in the joint. You must use the joint as your guide, in determining the stiff thumb and its degree of development. The stiff-thumbed subject is practical, common-sense, economical, stingy, and weighs everything carefully. Those who have it possess a strong will, stubborn determination, and are cautious, reserved, and do not give or invite confidence. They save their money, plod along, and wonder how their supple-thumbed brethren can throw their money away. They cannot make one fourth as much as supple thumbs, but they save what they do make. They are steady, not extremists, do not expect a great deal, and are consequently not disappointed when they do not receive much. They enjoy life in their way, but it is in a quiet fashion. They cannot do many things, but what they do attempt is done well. They are not erratic, but stick to one thing, commanding respect by their strength of purpose. They have a sense of justice and great self-control. Stiff-

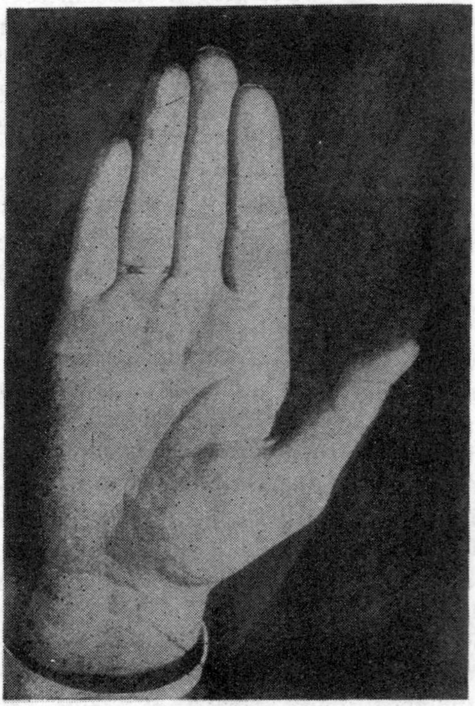

NO. 85. STIFF THUMB
(No amount of pressure will bend this thumb farther back)

thumbed people are a quiet, cautious, economical, practical, reliable set, who do not attract as do more brilliant and versatile natures, yet who possess many qualities which command respect. If the stiff thumb is coarse and common it will lower the quality of all its attributes, and make a mean, stingy, hard-hearted subject. In estimating all stiff thumbs, note most carefully the quality of the subject, so you may not err by placing the stiff-thumb qualities in the wrong class. A fine grade of stiff thumb should be given a fine grade of stiff-thumb qualities; a coarse stiff thumb must be given a coarse grade of stiff-thumb qualities.

In noting all thumbs take full account of consistency. See if energy or laziness is directing will and reason. A weak thumb with energy behind it is better than a strong thumb on a flabby hand. Consistency will make or mar the operation of all thumbs, so always see whether there is energy or laziness back of whatever kind you see. Good thumbs on soft hands would *like* to exert themselves, but are "too tired."

Examine color with the thumb, see if coldness, ardor, normal health, or biliousness is to influence the operation of will and the reasoning qualities of the brain. A healthy subject will do more with a weak will than one who is ill or by nature cold. Biliousness clogs the brain, so yellow color will spoil or impair even a strong second phalanx.

Examine the Mounts with the thumb in order to determine what effect the possession of determination, or lack of it, good reasoning, or lack of it, will have upon the qualities of the Mounts. The ambition, pride, honor, and religion of a Jupiterian will be much more surely brought to some account by a good thumb. Ambition is good, but does not produce its full measure of success unless backed by a reasoning will. The Jupiterian qualities will be correspondingly weakened by a small or pointed thumb. Always think what they stand for in looking at good Mounts, what qualities they indicate, and then by the strong or weak thumb, see whether will and reason in strength or weakness is behind the Mount qualities. The wisdom of Saturn will be made firm and strong by a good thumb, weak and vacillating by a weak one. The brilliant Apollonian with a strong thumb will be the man of business; with a small, pointed one, he will be possessed of pure artistic feeling, which will be more practical if the thumb tip be square. The shrewd and quick Mercurian, if he have a large thumb, will be firm and strong in whichever of his many sides he may be developed, but with a weak thumb, will be weak in the operation of his qualities, especially if the tip be conic, more practical if square. Lower Mars, full of aggression, will be *determined also* with a strong thumb, especially if spatulate or square, but will lose much of his force if possessed of a small thumb, particularly so if pointed or conic. Upper Mars, showing resistance, will be cool and undaunted with a large thumb, and more liable to discouragement with a small one. The Moon will have more practical fancies with a strong thumb, especially if square or spatulate, and will be more imaginative with a small thumb, which quality will be increased if tips be pointed. Venus, with a strong thumb, will be firm and practical in love and sympathy, and inconstant with a small one, especially if pointed. Large thumbs will add determination to critical nails and make them more critical. A strong thumb will make stronger every type of nail, a weak thumb will make them weaker. Large thumbs will add persistence to the analytical propensities of knotty fingers, and make them more painstaking in search for truth. Small thumbs will decrease their operation, and allow many things to be taken for granted.

Large thumbs strengthen smooth fingers, small thumbs make them act more by impulse and lend added artistic conic qualities. Large thumbs push square and spatulate tips to greater activity, and along practical lines. Small thumbs make these tips talkers not doers. Large thumbs decrease the artistic qualities of conic and pointed tips by making them more practical and more likely to accomplish something and to exert themselves. Small thumbs make these tips dreamers and averse to effort. Large thumbs make the short-fingered qualities quicker and more determined ; short thumbs leave the quickness, the inspiration, but take away the force and practical application of these qualities. Large thumbs make long fingers more determined in the application of their peculiar qualities. These subjects, always great lovers of detail, will, with large thumbs, carry out these details A small thumb with long fingers will still love detail, but will not trouble to secure it. Hands with smooth fingers, conic or pointed tips, and a small thumb, indicate artistic and poetic feeling.

Large hands, knotty joints, square or spatulate tips with large thumbs, are scientific, mechanical, and practical hands. The woman with a small thumb marries for love, and does not stop to think whether her lover can support her or not. She will brave poverty, and will marry a drunkard, thinking she can reform him. These women are ruled by heart and sentiment. The woman with a large thumb loves as truly as any, but has regard for the bread-and-butter supply as well. The man she marries must be able to support her; if adversity comes she makes the best of it, will put on a brave front, and help to overcome the difficulty. She is ruled by head and is strong.

In the beginning of this chapter the statement was made that many palmists rely on the thumb for their entire work. You can see that a good reading could be given from the thumb alone, by bringing its qualities to bear on the various forces which make up a human life. I earnestly commend to you a careful and thorough understanding of this chapter before proceeding farther. All the various thumbs are illustrated, and there should be no difficulty in gaining a proper understanding of the subject.

CHAPTER XVIII

MOUNTS AND FINGERS—HOW TO JUDGE THEM

Of the seven Mounts in the hand, four are located at the bases of the fingers, two along the side of the hand which has been called the Percussion, and one at the base of the thumb, being, as before stated, the third phalanx of that member. The Mount of Mars is divided into the upper and lower Mounts, and the Plain of Mars. The plate which accompanies Chapter I. gives the geography of these Mounts. It will be necessary to become familiar with their exact positions and boundaries, in order to tell whether a Mount is in its proper place or is pulled to one side by the greater strength of one of the other Mounts.

As the great difficulty with beginners lies in classifying subjects under their proper types, especially when the type is not markedly prominent, great care has been taken with this chapter to make it very explicit. While, at the first reading, it will seem hard to fully digest, it will grow clearer as you put one after the other of its rulings into practice. It will be a most useful chapter of reference while gaining from experience the ability to classify your subjects under their proper types.

As each Mount represents one of the original types in the plan of creation, it is from the development of a certain one or more of these Mounts, that you can tell to which type the subject belongs. Each finger is named for the Mount to which it is attached, and partakes of the qualities of its Mount. Physiologically these Mounts are the balls or pads of flesh which bulge up from the palm at the base of the fingers, and at other points in the hands. In some hands they form little hills (86), in others they are perfectly flat (87), and, where the Mounts should be, in some cases there are actual holes or depressions (88). Mounts which are very prominent are considered strong Mounts, the flat ones are ordinary, and depressions show weakness and absence of the qualities of the Mount.

In your examination, first try to discover which is the

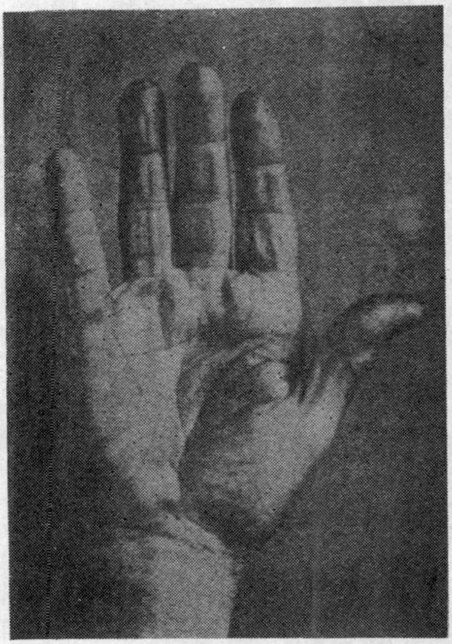

NO. 86. HIGH MOUNTS

strongest Mount. Whichever one it may be, will show that the qualities of that type are leading ones in the subject. If one Mount is found to be very large, and the others normal, it will be a strong indication that the subject belongs to the type of the strong Mount. If on this Mount is found a single deep, vertical line, it will confirm this opinion. If in addition the finger of this Mount is very long and well developed, being appreciably larger than the other fingers, it is certain that the subject represents practically a pure specimen of this Mount type. Highly developed Mounts, that is, those which rise high, are the strongest in operation. A well-marked vertical line on a Mount, deep and uncut by cross-lines, must be considered, even on what appears to be a flat Mount, as giving the Mount almost equal prominence

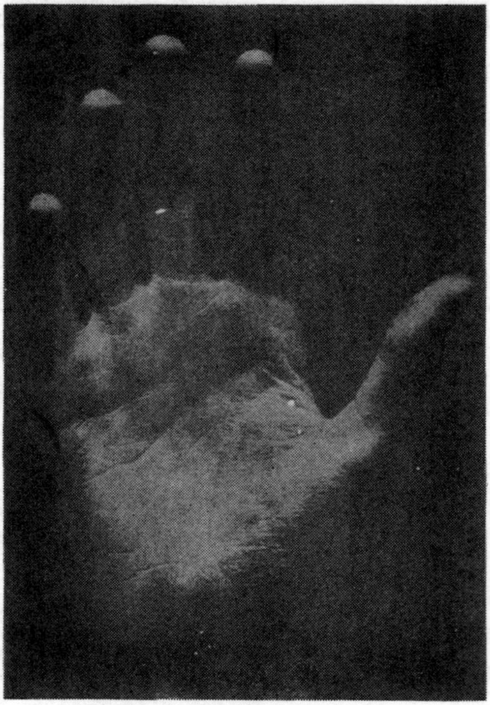

NO. 87. FLAT MOUNTS

with the higher development. Two vertical lines add strength, but not as much as one, three lines less, and so on until you find a Mount full of vertical and cross-lines, so mixed that they form a grille (89), which degenerates into the *defects* belonging to the Mount.

Each Mount type has a good and a bad side, a weak and a strong side. The Mount which is well developed and well placed, shows the good development: grilled and cross-lined, or with cross-bars or crosses, it shows defects of the type. Hard consistency and red color shows strength of the Mount: flabbiness and whiteness, even though the Mount be prominent, show weakness and lack of energy. When a strong Mount is found, with a good line on it and a large finger, next see whether the Mount is hard or flabby, and also

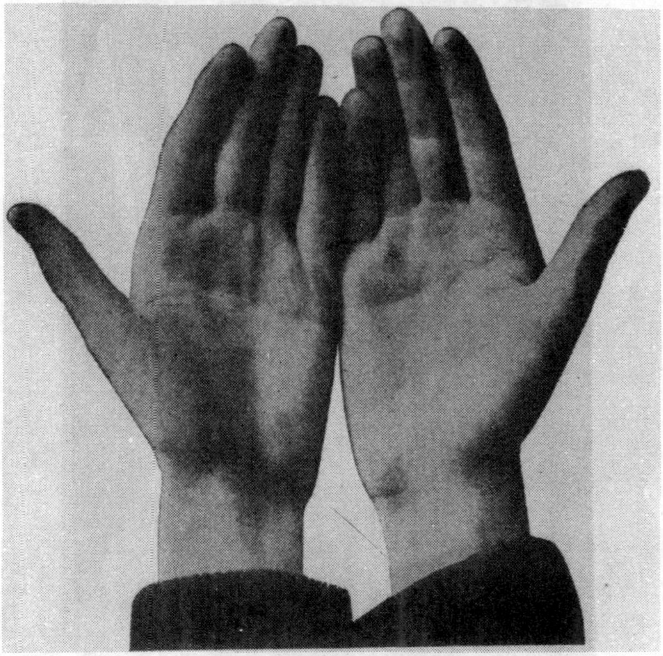

NO. 88. DEFICIENT MOUNTS

note its color. If in addition to the strong signs above enumerated you find hard consistency and red or pink color your subject is surely a specimen of this type. In some hands you will find one Mount *harder* than the others; this, even though the Mount may not be over-well-developed, will add energy and vigor to it. *Color* also plays a strong part, for all the qualities which it indicates will belong to the Mount on which you may see it. In sensitive hands and those with very fine-textured skin you will find some of the Mounts pink, others white. In that case apply pink and white qualities to the Mounts *having them.* In a hand having two Mounts equally developed the subject will be a combination of the two types. If, in this case, one

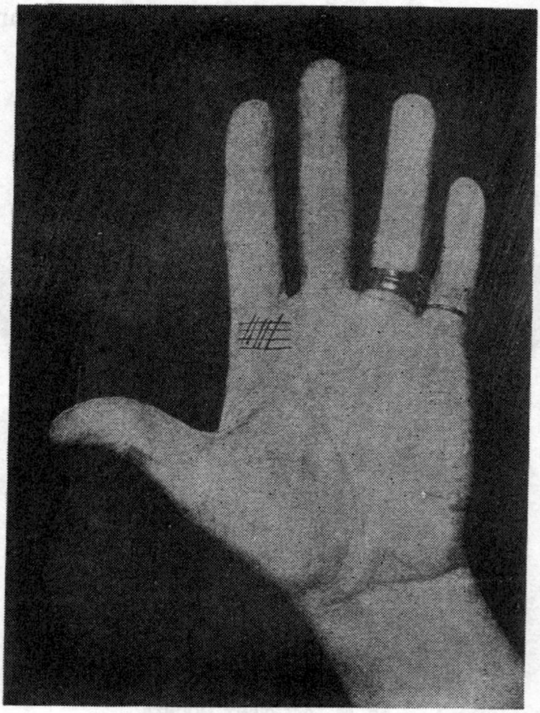

NO. 89. GRILLE ON A MOUNT

Mount has a good vertical line, or if it should be harder or redder in color than the other, you will know that, while your subject is a combination of the two types, the Mount which either has a vertical line, or is harder, or redder, is somewhat stronger than the other. If you cannot tell by these methods which is the leading type, note the finger carefully, for the Mount with the strongest finger will be the leading one.

In judging the ability of fingers to add strength to a Mount, compare their lengths with each other and with the finger of Saturn. A normal finger of Jupiter should reach the middle of the first phalanx of Saturn (90). Saturn should always tower above the other fingers, if the subject is to have a good balance to his character, for Saturn repre-

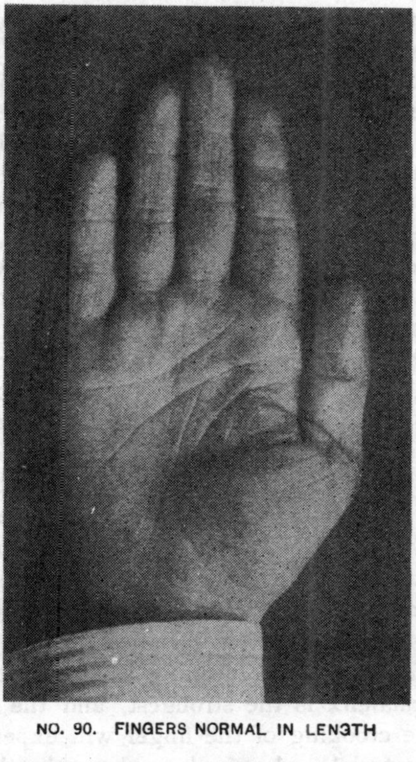

NO. 90. FINGERS NORMAL IN LENGTH

sents wisdom and sobriety. The finger of Apollo should reach the middle of the first phalanx of Saturn (see 90). Longer than this will show strong Apollonian qualities; shorter than this is deficiency. The normal finger of Mercury reaches the first knot on the finger of Apollo (see 90). If it is pronouncedly longer than this, the subject has strong Mercurian qualities; shorter than this is deficiency. In judging the length of fingers, as regards each other, note whether their seeming length is due to *their own* increased size, or to the other fingers being *under size.* By this means you can determine whether the seeming long finger may not be only normal size for the hand, and the other fingers much under-sized. In examining individual fingers note the separate phalanges, for these represent the three worlds — mind, material qualities, and baser — as indicated by the first, second, and third phalanges respectively. The first, you remember, is the nailed phalanx, second the middle, third the lower one. The fingers so considered will tell whether the subject will use the qualities of his type for mental advancement, for practical pursuits, or for more sordid ends. Note also the tips of the fingers to see if the subject will be guided by Spatulate, Square, Conic, or Pointed qualities in carrying out the purposes of his type. Observe whether the fingers are set in regular fashion, or whether one finger is placed lower on the palm than the others. Remember that any finger placed low takes away from its Mount a portion of its strength. If the finger encroaches so that the Mount is one third shorter than the others, you can consider the Mount as having two thirds of the normal strength. Apply this method to every Mount having low-set fingers. Remember if a finger leans toward another Mount, it gives some of its strength to the Mount toward which it leans. If a finger tends to crookedness, this will add to the strength of the Mount to which it belongs, and gives added shrewdness, even dishonesty, to the qualities of the finger. To judge the meaning of this crooked finger, note which phalanx is the strongest, and the shrewdness shown by the crooking of the finger will expend itself on the mental, material, or baser plane shown by the first, second, or third phalanx best developed. Sometimes one finger will be flexible and the others either stiff or normal. In this case the flexible finger will show the elastic mind (as treated in chapter on Flexibility), and the flexible quality will apply to the qualities of the *single finger* only.

Sometimes there will be found a different tip on each

finger, and, this being the case, apply the Spatulate, Square, Conic, and Pointed qualities to each individual finger having them. As each of the seven types is liable to certain diseases which may be told from the Mounts, look carefully at the nail of each finger and see what health indications are given. If all the nails but one are smooth, and that one is fluted, the health qualities of that type are in danger of a nervous complication, to be determined from shape and quality of the nail. For instance, the Apollonian is prone to weak heart; if on one of this type a fluted nail is found on the finger of Apollo, it is certain that the subject has *both* a tendency to weak heart (peculiar to the type) and also extreme nervousness, as shown by the fluted nail. This manner of reasoning will apply to all kinds of nails. A health defect, shown by the shape, texture, or color of the nail on any finger, brings out the health defect of its Mount type. If the subject is prone to more than one disease, the nail will show which one is prominent in his case. For example, the Saturnian is liable to biliousness, paralysis, etc. Yellow nails by themselves will show that biliousness is one of his troubles; fluted and brittle nails will show that there is a nerve disturbance; yellow nails which are *also* fluted and brittle will show that he is troubled with both. By following a system like this, and applying it with your Mount types, you can most accurately estimate what disease the subject has had, or is likely to have. Note whether the fingers belong to the short class. If they do, the quick-thinking, quick-acting traits of short fingers must be added to the estimate of the operation of the Mount. Remember, quickness of thought and action, impulse, impatience at detail, and desire to deal with all subjects in their entirety, also a strong desire to achieve big things, are the characteristics of short fingers. Apply all this in reading the Mounts. If only one finger belongs to this short class, apply the short-fingered qualities to that one Mount, not to all.

If long fingers are seen, remember their love of detail, slowness, suspicion, care in small things, and their instinct for going into the minutiæ in everything. Apply long-fingered qualities to the Mounts. If only one finger is long, apply the long-fingered qualities to its Mount.

On meeting knotty fingers, remember the analytical, reasoning, investigating qualities that belong to them. If only the first knot of mental order is developed, remember these people have stored away much knowledge, all well classified and arranged. These qualities, added to the Mounts, will make the subject an intelligent example of his class. It will make the type operate in a well-ordered way mentally, though these subjects may lack system in material things. At this point consult the tips of the fingers. The mental order and intelligence of the subject will be directed in Spatulate, Square, Conic, or Pointed directions according as these tips are found. If the knot of mental order is only found on one finger, apply its characteristics to the qualities of the finger on which it is found. The presence of the first knot in this case will also identify your subject as belonging to the type indicated by the finger on which the knot is seen. If only the knot of material order is developed, remember the order and system in the household, the store, the dress, which belongs to this knot, and apply it to the Mounts. If found on only one finger, apply it to the qualities of that finger.

If both knots are developed, apply their philosophic tendencies to the Mounts; found only on one finger, apply to that Mount alone.

If smooth fingers are found remember the artistic instincts they indicate, the action by impulse and intuition, rather than by reasoning, and apply these qualities to the Mounts. If only one finger is smooth, apply smooth-fingered qualities to the one Mount.

Bear in mind all the time that short fingers may have knotty joints, as well as any shaped tips. In this case, take quickness of thought (short fingers) added to analytical tendencies (knotty joints), and you get a quick reasoner, more or less practical or visionary according to the tips. Smooth, short fingers show the height of all short-fingered qualities; they are more practical and somewhat slower of operation with the spatulate and square tips, and, with conic or pointed tips, like a flash in their quickness. Apply all of these qualities to the Mounts, or, if only found on one finger, to the individual finger.

Long fingers and knotty joints show a distressing love of detail (long fingers), and analysis (knotty joints), consequently the subject is painfully slow; it is the intensifying of both the long-fingered qualities and the knotty joints. Apply these qualities to the Mounts or to only one if found on one finger alone.

Long fingers and smooth joints love detail (which comes from the long fingers), but think much more quickly (because of the smooth joints). Spatulate or square tips make the detail of long fingers more practical. Conic or pointed tips make their possessors think more quickly and lighten some of the severity of the long fingers. Apply all these to the Mounts, or single fingers if only seen on one finger.

Short, critical nails add their distinctive qualities to both the knotty and long fingers.

Color of the nails gives to all the above fingers the qualities peculiar to color.

Hands will be seen in which all the Mounts seem to be equally developed. This shows a well-balanced character, partaking of a general supply of qualities from all the types. These subjects are always more even-tempered, broader in their general views, more amenable to reason, healthier, and more perfectly balanced than those who are of one strongly marked type. In such a case as this, to get the natural type of the subject, see whether one Mount may not have a good line on it or whether a strong finger will not give the key. On each of the Mounts of Jupiter, Saturn, Apollo, and Mercury, it will be important to note the exact apex or tip of the Mount (see 91, three illustrations). This is of value, in that you may discover whether the apex of the Mount is in the exact centre or whether it leans toward one of the other Mounts. In the hand with every Mount of equal development, this will aid materially in determining which Mount is strong enough not to be influenced by any other. If, in this hand, so nearly equal, you do not find the tip of one Mount higher on the Mount or nearer its centre than are the tips of the other Mounts, or if you cannot find a vertical line on any Mount which gives you the key to the type, or if you do not discover that any finger is abnormally long or large, you will have to note which finger has the squarest or most spatulate tip, or whether the first knot is developed and thus determine the type to which your subject belongs. It is sometimes very hard to handle evenly balanced people; those with pronounced characteristics do not bother you so much. The balanced man is the one who tests your skill. To tell him that he is evenly balanced will not satisfy you have to find out more about him, and to do so you must locate *his type*.

NO. 91A. APEX OF MOUNT (GREATLY MAGNIFIED)

You must learn how to locate the exact tips of the Mounts. I have photographed a portion of the hand which shows the manner in which the capillaries of the skin run (91, first illustration). Note that a little triangle is formed by these capillaries. The centre of this triangle is the exact centre of the Mount. It does not matter that this apex is not on the most prominent or fleshy part of the Mount. Many students have considered the most fleshy part as the top of the Mount; this is incorrect. It is the centre of the capillary triangle which is its apex. To find and use this apex may appear to be insisting on burdensome and unnecessary detail, but if you expect to get below the surface in hand-reading you must be able to recognize at once the slightest displacement of the tips of the Mounts. In coarse skin you can easily locate this apex with the naked eye, but on a skin of fine texture you will have to resort to the glass. By gaslight, even with the glass, it is almost impossible to locate it.

As a general rule, the apex should lie exactly in the centre of the Mount. If it is nearer the top it elevates the qualities, if towards the base of the Mount it pulls them down.

The three worlds apply here as everywhere else. If the apex lies in the centre it shows the Mount to be well placed, and adds great strength to any Mount. In the hand with all Mounts equally developed, if the apex of one Mount is better placed than the others, that one will dominate, and

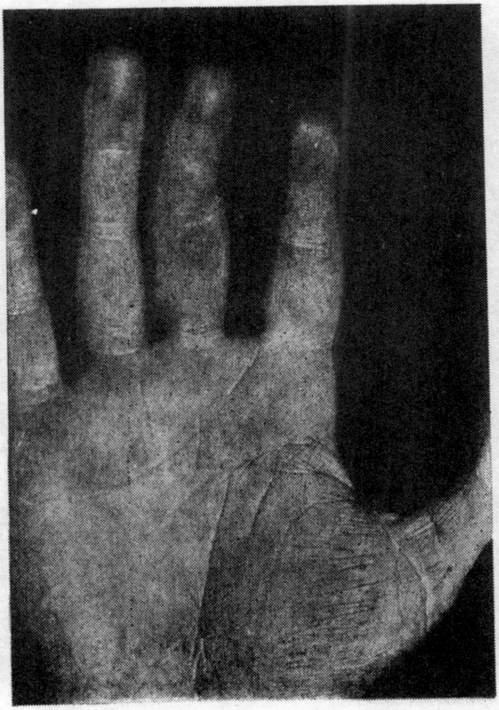

NO. 91B. APEX OF MOUNT

(USE MAGNIFYING GLASS)

in a puzzling case it will often open the way to a location of the type. If the apex is pulled toward another Mount, it shows that the Mount toward which it leans is the stronger, and it gives up part of its type to the stronger Mount. This will be fully discussed in chapters on the different Mounts, but the general rule is given here.

In the seven types of people, all could not have the same degree of perfection, so *defects* in the types, as well as cases of extremely bad and vicious development, are found. In all cases vertical lines are good lines, while horizontal lines which cut and destroy these lines are bad. The general rule

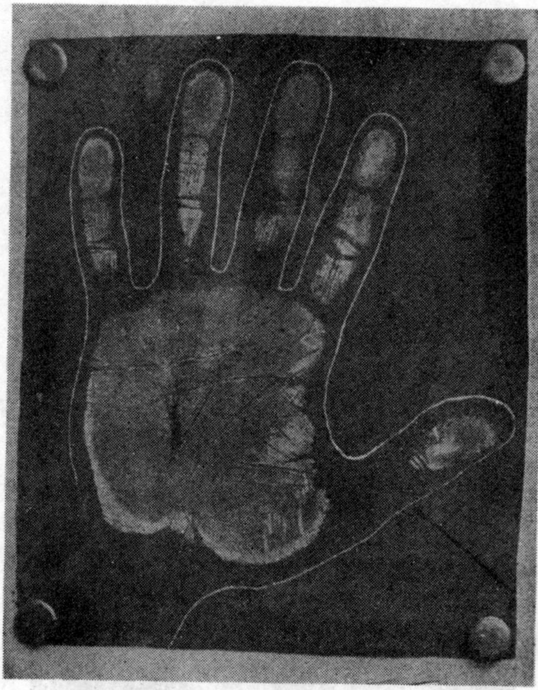

NO. 91c. APEX OF MOUNT

(USE MAGNIFYING GLASS)

is therefore laid down that a grille, which is formed by a combination of the two, is a *defect* of the Mount, and the Mount which has *only* cross-lines is *bad* (92). In cross-lines alone all is obstruction, and there is not even an *attempt* of the vertical lines to counteract the evil. In the case of the grille there is *some* good shown by the vertical lines, even though marred by cross-lines. In the different types some incline more naturally to evil than others; so a grille or cross-lines on a Mount whose natural instincts are bad means more of evil than on a Mount whose type is naturally good. In examining for defects you must note

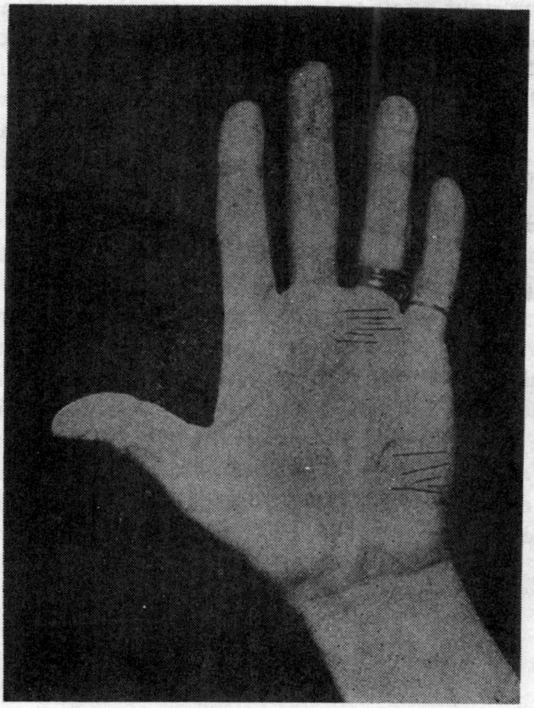

NO. 92. CROSS-BARS ON A MOUNT

color and nails. These will show both health defects and defects of character. There are types who naturally become criminals, others are bad on account of their environment or special temptations. The Mounts will show these facts. In examining Mounts always remember excess is as bad as not enough. Ambition, kept within bounds, is both necessary and useful, but too much of it may make men steal in order to keep up appearances. Lack of ambition is a bad thing, for it usually means little success, but a man who on this account amounts to very little may still be an honest man.

In examining the Mounts, in no case fail to look at both hands. In the left hand you may discover a hard Mount, and in the right a soft one. In this case the vigor natural to the Mount has become weakened. The reverse of this combination will produce reverse results. You may find the color in one hand red, yellow, or white, changing, however, to some different color in the other hand. In this case the qualities indicated by color in the left hand have been changed for the qualities shown by the color in the right hand. This will be useful when you wish to tell a subject what kind of a person he *was* and what he now is. By applying the rules laid down in previous chapters on color, consistency, and development of the left and right hands to the individual Mounts, there will be no trouble in successfully dealing with the Mounts as found in the two hands. The same rules apply to the individual Mounts and fingers as to the whole hand. It is by learning to apply all of the *general rules* to the *individual parts* of the hand that you will be enabled to read the mixed combinations so frequently encountered.

CHAPTER XIX

THE MOUNT OF JUPITER

AS single signs, or in combination with each other, the star, triangle, circle, square, single vertical line, or trident strengthen a Mount (93).

As single signs, or in combination with each other, the grille, cross-bars, cross, island, or dot indicate defects of the Mount either of health or of character, the main lines, chance lines, color, etc., will determine which.

There are a few variations of this rule as applied to some of the Mounts. At the beginning of each chapter on the Mount types will be found an illustration, giving the indications as applied to *it*. Note these carefully for variations.

Entering now upon the consideration of the seven types of humanity, we find the first type is the Jupiterian, identified by a developed Mount and finger of Jupiter. In a previous chapter I have told how to judge Mounts, in order to determine which one is the strongest, as well as how to proceed when several Mounts seem equally well developed. To understand this is, of course, essential to proficiency.

The Jupiterian is ambitious and a leader of men. His commanding presence and the love he has for high positions make him often a politician. He is found also in the army, for here again is the opportunity to hold commanding position and to lead men. In the church he is prominent as well. Religion is one of the strong attributes of Jupiterians, and they will be found holding all shades of opinion, from the most rigidly orthodox to a breadth dangerously near skepticism. The tip of the Jupiter finger will indicate which extreme. Ambition, love of command, pride in position, religion, honor, love of nature, are main forces with the Jupiterian, and these mould his manners and actions in every walk in life. There are many Jupiterians to be found, and in practice you will have much to do with them. They represent a good type and a strong one.

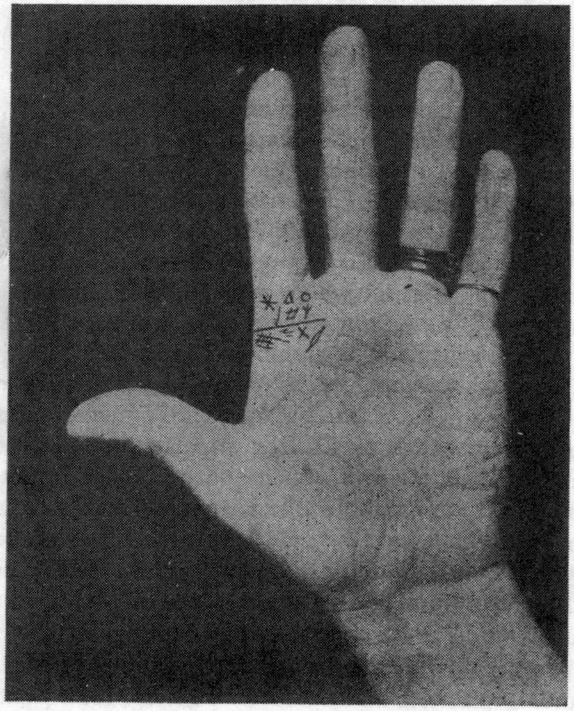

NO. 93. DISTINGUISHING MARKS ON THE MOUNT OF JUPITER

When the Mount of Jupiter is found full and strong, apex centrally located, finger long and strong, with color of hand pink or red (94), you have located a Jupiterian. In this generation you will not often find a *pure specimen of the type;* there is generally an accompanying mixture of other types; but the one I here describe is a *pure* Jupiterian, the leading qualities of the type being always found present where the large Mount of Jupiter is found, although when other Mounts are also well developed it is accompanied by added qualities belonging to other types.

The pure Jupiterian is of medium height. He is not the tallest of the seven types; that distinction belongs to the Saturnian; neither is he the shortest, for this honor belongs

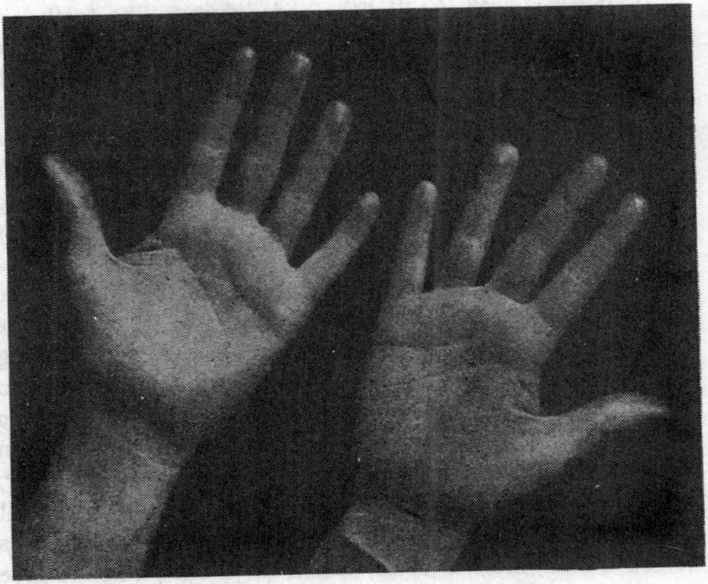

NO. 94. JUPITERIAN HAND

to the Mercurian. He is, however, a large man, very strongly built and inclined to be fleshy. His flesh is solid and not mere fat, nor does it partake of the spongy softness of the Lunar type. His bones are large, strong, and well able to support his weight. He has a smooth, clear skin, which inclines to be fine in texture, pink in color, and healthy looking. His eyes are large and expressive, pupils are clear and dilate under the play of the emotions. There is no fierce look in his eyes,—the expression is mild and almost melting, bespeaking honesty and a kindly spirit.

The upper lids of the eyes are thick, looking as if somewhat swollen, and the lashes are long and curl up gracefully at the ends. The eyebrows are arched and the hairs grow evenly, giving the brows a clearly defined outline. The nose is straight and well formed, tending to be large in size, and often Roman in shape. The mouth is large, the lips full and red, and owing to the position of the teeth the upper lip is slightly prominent. The teeth are strong and white, but grow long and narrow, the two front teeth being longer than is usual. The cheeks are well rounded, so the cheek bones are not to be seen. The chin is long and firm, with a dimple at the point. The ears are well formed, regular, and set close to the head, which rests on a well-shaped, thick neck of medium length and strong looking. The back and shoulders are fleshy and squarely set. The legs and feet are shapely and of medium size, but strong and firm. The walk is stately and dignified. The hair is brown or running into chestnut; in women of the type, grows long, is abundant and fine in quality, inclining to be curly. The Jupiterian perspires freely, especially on top of the head, from ordinary exertion. This often leads to baldness early in life. As he is of a vigorous constitution he has considerable hair on his body, which, you remember, is a sign of strength. The chest of the Jupiterian is well developed, and his large lungs are bellows from which is forced a rich, musical voice, which is just the voice to give words of command, or speak to and influence a multitude; helping to make a Jupiterian the natural leader that he is. It is not hard to see why such a personality as the Jupiterian should command followers, for his strong and robust manhood proves attractive, and confidence in his strength at once moves men to desire an alliance with him. He is designed to command; nature has given him the strength and attractiveness that will enable him to secure and to lead followers.

The Jupiterian, therefore, is classed as belonging to a *good type*. It is not possible to keep out all alloy, however, even in this type, for there are bad Jupiterians who pervert their rich endowments, and these will be considered later. The object in mentioning this now is to avoid conveying the idea that all Jupiterians are good. The type has its faults, but the one above described is the Jupiterian as he was planned and intended to be. The natural build of the type makes these people self-confident. They are conscious of their strength, and this gives them reliance in their ability. They depend upon themselves, work out their own plans, and thus do not have the habit of asking advice. They are inclined to bluster and talk loud, not in a quarrelsome way, it is true, but in a manner full of self-confidence and self-assertion. They are aware of the influence they exert, and it naturally makes them vain. This vanity knows the power of the rich, musical voice in swaying men, and they like to hear the sound of this voice as well as to see it shaping the views of others. Leadership is always uppermost in their minds.

With all his vanity the Jupiterian is warm-hearted. He has a fellow-feeling for humanity that exhibits itself in practical ways. A word of comfort from so strong a person to one in distress does a world of good, and the kindly spirit he shows to all who appeal to him binds closer the following he attracts. Nor is his kindness confined to words, for he *gives* as well, and is generous and charitable. These Jupiterian beneficences are dispensed in a manly, open-hearted way that makes the recipients feel that the donor is glad to give. Here again his nature furnishes him help to carry out the things he was created to do—viz., to attract and lead. The Jupiterian, in his capacity as a leader, would, if unjust, inflict harm in many ways upon his fellows. With his big, manly way of looking at things he is eminently just, and strives to encourage and support fairness and business honesty. He is a dashing fellow, one who has much attraction for the opposite sex, and will always be found gallant and courteous. He is extravagant. To him power and rule mean more than money, and while he obtains large sums from his enterprises, he does not hoard it, and has a contempt for anything resembling small dealing or miserliness. He is inherently religious. Created to lead his fellow-men and to have dominion over them, it is apparent that the Creator gave him instincts which would make him good, and safeguard him against evil. Religion (which must here be understood as no worship of cult or creed, but as embodying a belief in, and reverence for, some omnipotent power which is good and kind) was given the Jupiterian in order that he might be influenced by all the benefits which religion can bestow. Refining, broadening, uplifting influences are given the Jupiterian, so that the natural leader, created under the plan of the seven types, is a good, well-meaning commander. Religion, therefore, is one of his strongest attributes. The Jupiterian is fond of show and ceremony, and in his methods of worship, his system of government, or in whatever sphere he may operate, he will like pageantry and observance of form. He is a believer in and an upholder of law and order; loves and encourages peace; his preference and struggle is not for martial supremacy, but that the populace may clamor for him. He is aristocratic and conservative, believes in ancient lineage and the manifest destiny which has called him to his particular sphere of activity. He is honest, and in all things despises cheating and fraud, honor being one of his leading attributes. He believes in right and independence, and his counsel and support are always with the oppressed. This faculty of insisting that common people have their due makes him, despite his aristocratic tendencies, the idol of the multitude. He is not hard to get along with, is easily pleased, especially with attentions to himself, and has a faculty for keeping friends. Jupiterians are, if any type may claim this distinction, lucky, for they have so many desirable and attractive qualities that they are pushed forward by their friends into successful careers, because they are general favorites. There is another factor in their composition that enables them to rise over every obstacle. They are *ambitious*, and with this tremendous force behind them, urging on the strong qualities they possess, the Jupiterian is one of the most invincible of all the types. Ambition is powerful as a moving force in human success, and the

Jupiterian is the embodiment of ambition. He has pride as well, for no man could possess his aristocratic, dignified, ambitious qualities without also having pride in himself and his achievements. This pride is but natural; it is not a fault, and for its possession he should not be blamed.

To recapitulate: leadership, ambition, religion, honor, pride, dignity, and an intense love of nature are his predominant characteristics, and these, strengthened by the many accessories carried in their train, should come to your mind when you see him. In his marriage relations the Jupiterian is very ambitious. He matures early in life, and marries when young one of whom he believes he can feel proud. His ambitious desire to have the helpmate shine before the world is not always realized, for a Jupiterian, as well as any other person, may be deceived, so is often unhappily wedded. He is *predisposed* to marry, and, knowing this, you will not need as strong confirmations of marriage with this type as are needed with some of the other types. In health matters the Jupiterian is predisposed to certain disorders. He is a great eater, and in this regard is somewhat of a sensualist. He eats highly seasoned, strong food, is fond of wine, and is addicted to smoking. He is a high liver and his danger is from being an *over*-eater. Thus he injures his digestion, has vertigo, or fainting fits, as his first warning, and these attacks increase in violence until apoplexy ends the story. He has gout and stomach trouble, and these produce impure blood which often affects his lungs, making them weak. Disordered stomach, indigestion, vertigo, apoplexy, gout, and sometimes lung trouble are his peculiar health dangers.

In this description I have used the pronoun *he*, and considered the Jupiterian as a masculine type. There are, however, just as many feminine Jupiterians. On recognizing a strong Mount and finger in a woman, leadership, ambition, pride, honor, and all the Jupiterian attributes belong to her. I have used the masculine pronoun with all the Mounts only as a matter of convenience and brevity. With this idea of the Jupiterian character and attributes, it remains to find how they are distributed, and how they will probably be expended. On recognizing strong Jupiterian traits, locate the apex of the Mount. If it is distinctly in the centre of the Mount, the qualities will be evenly distributed. If leaning over toward Saturn, the sobriety, sadness, and wisdom of that Mount will hold down the Jupiterian ambition and make it safer, for Jupiter will be guided by Saturn. If the apex leans or is marked on the outer edge of the hand opposite Saturn, the Jupiterian qualities will be directed to seeking purely selfish, personal advancement. If the apex lies near the Heart line, the ambition and pride will be for those loved, and if near the line of Head, the ambition will be for intellectual success. Note the consistency of the hand, to see if energy will back the ambition, or whether soft or flabby qualities will cause the ambition to be only unfulfilled desire. Examine the texture of the skin to see if the Jupiterian qualities are refined or coarse. Take flexibility into account, to see whether an elastic mind is to help carry the Jupiterian ambition forward, or a hard, unyielding mind, as shown by a stiff hand, is to hamper them. In estimating the outcome of life for a subject, it makes all the difference in the world what strong characteristics, such as the Jupiterian possesses, have behind them, and whether there is coarseness or refinement, a clear or a dense mind. Naturally more would be expected from a fine combination than from a coarse; you will have refined, high-minded leadership in one case, common, selfish ambition in the other. Look carefully at the color of the palm, nails, and lines, for weakness, strength, or disease indicated at these points. With white color and its accompanying coldness, the Jupiterian will be selfish, less attractive to others, less magnetic. He will lose much of his Jupiterian power to attract men and lead them. He will have ambition and desire for power, but will be repellent to his fellows, who will not so readily follow, applaud, and elevate him to positions of command. With white color you cannot predict any such degree of success as with the next grade, pink. Here is the normal flow of the life-renewing current, producing normal conditions of health and temperament. The subject is bright, active, vivacious, attractive — and all of his powers are brought out, making him the magnetic and successful Jupiterian. He is admired by his enemies, loved by his friends, and is the idol of the masses. Red color indicates excessive strength and ardor. To add intensity to an already strong character can easily make it too strong. All the dangers to health are increased. He is an over-eater, has dyspepsia, and tends strongly, on account of the amount of blood rushed to the brain by a strong heart, to have apoplexy. This type of the Jupiterian is the apoplectic subject. In character he is too pronounced, and inclines to the excess of a commanding disposition, which is tyranny or despotism. He becomes the ruler to whom men are attracted not by common sympathy but because he is stronger than they. When a pink-colored type of Jupiterian appears, the crowd flock to him and desert the red-colored type, whose influence becomes more uncertain in that he rules by fear, not love. Red color is too strong; it leads to excess of the type. Yellow color is not often found, for the Jupiterian is seldom troubled by liver disturbance. You may find a combination of Jupiterian and Saturnian or Mercurian, and in that case, yellow color will be found. This will apply to the Saturnian or Mercurian side of the combination, not to the Jupiterian. Blue color is sometimes found, for the excessive action of the heart may weaken that organ and cause some congestion. This is not so often found, and is not a health danger of the Jupiterian that is permanent or typical.

In examining the nails of the Jupiterian, remember what traits they may emphasize or weaken. He is naturally a healthy type, so it is not to be expected that bad-health nails will often be found. But disease sometimes creeps into this type, so be on the lookout for anything that may show it. Nervous or fluted nails will be recognized by texture, shape, or brittleness, and nervousness in the degree the nails indicate must be applied to him. Bilious nails are seldom found; the broad nails of robust constitution are oftenest seen. Temperament and character will be indicated by either the short, critical nail, or the nails of honesty and openness. If the nail be very short, the Jupiterian desire to lead will be more intense and aggressive, and these qualities will be likely to show excess in strength. The open, honest nail will be the best, and adds to this type all of their good qualities. Expect hair on the hands, for the Jupiterian has a strong constitution, and hair shows strength. It should be carefully noted what color it is, and also whether coarse or fine, for these will tell us how the Jupiterian characteristics will be manifested. With light hair this subject is less ardent, less liable to suffer from diseases peculiar to the type, because less sensual ; he is more phlegmatic, colder, and not so likely to attract, but he is not lazy, and is very practical, strong, and determined in the pursuit of his ambitions. Black hair adds sparkle, fire, vigor, and ardor, but shows a liability to Oriental sensualism and love of ease. This will incline the subject to be a greater eater, and thus more likely to injure his health.

The hand, as a whole, will tell you of the plane on which he will operate. If the mental world is most pronounced, his ambition will be for distinction in a literary career. He will be the author who writes of great leaders, politicians, and generals. His trend is toward mental work, but he shows the Jupiterian love of rule and leadership even in the choice of subjects for his writings. If the middle world of the hand is most prominent, he will lead in business and affairs of the commercial world. If the lower third of his hand be most prominent, an already sensual person, from his natural type qualities, will become more so, and bad results will follow. The best combination is of the two upper worlds. Next come the two lower, for in this case he will have the common-sense middle world to hold the lower in check. Take out the middle and leave the two others and a sensual dreamer will be left. The same rules apply to individual fingers, especially the finger of Jupiter. Note whether the mental, the abstract, or material world predominates, by noting which phalanx of the finger is longest, if a long finger of Jupiter is seen, and also notice which is shortest with a short finger. In this way you can tell which world is in excess or deficient, or whether, with a long finger, the worlds are all long, but *equally* developed. If the finger reaches to the middle of the first phalanx of Saturn, the Jupiterian desire for leadership will not be excessive. If the finger is as long as Saturn, the desire for

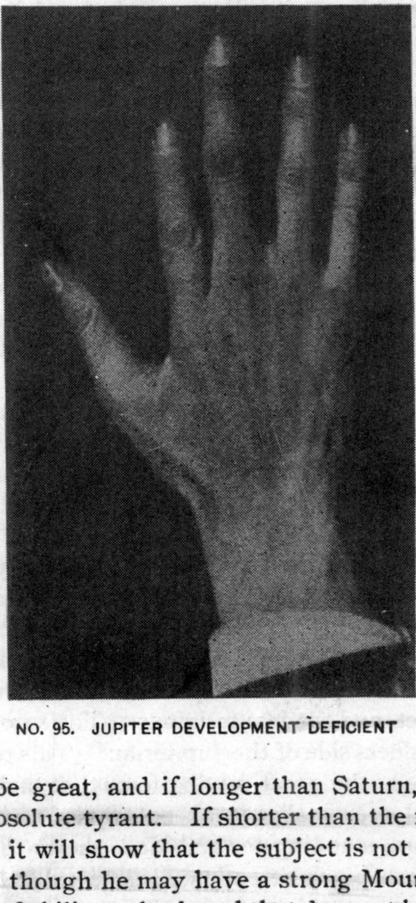

NO. 95. JUPITER DEVELOPMENT DEFICIENT

power will be great, and if longer than Saturn, the subject will be an absolute tyrant. If shorter than the first joint of Saturn (95), it will show that the subject is not a pure Jupiterian, even though he may have a strong Mount, for there will be lack of ability to lead, and that does not belong to this type. In this case, ambition, religion, and honor may remain, but the full strength of Jupiterian ability is not present. A crooked finger of Jupiter adds *shrewdness* to the Jupiterian qualities, and is not necessarily a bad sign, though it strengthens the Mount very much. It shows that the subject will *systematically plan* all his moves, and will lead other men, always knowing how he manages to do it. This curved finger may be combined with a bad Mercurian type, be bilious, and evil, in which case it will make a bad and dishonest subject, but by itself this bent finger which you will often meet only adds *shrewdness* to Jupiterian qualities. In studying the finger by separate phalanges, the tips must be taken into full consideration. If the first phalanx, indicating mental strength, be long, it will show that the mental world rules, and intuition and religion will be strong. If the tips be conic it will show that idealistic, intuitive qualities are added to the mental. The Jupiterian being naturally religious, this *long* first phalanx with conic tip will *prove* that the subject is so. He will have great reverence and idealism in his beliefs, his religion will be an inspiration, and he will be a strong, high-minded person. If the tip be square, he will show more common-sense, will reason and take less for granted. His religion is plainer in form of worship and more practical. If the tip be spatulate, he will more readily be an agnostic, have original views, and follow no creed or church. By carefully noting this first phalanx and tip you can tell, with a good deal of accuracy, to what church, if to any, your subject belongs. The spatulate or excessively square tip on a finger of Jupiter shows a domineering spirit which in family, business, and every walk of life will make the tyrant and the despot. The broader the first phalanx, the more domineering the subject, and the less religious. The second phalanx shows the business side of the Jupiterian. This phalanx will tell of ambition, the great driving force that makes Jupiterians lead, and even makes weak natures advance. A long second phalanx, standing for ambition, shows that practical affairs will have much attention, for the subject will want to lead in money-making ways. Here again tips must be consulted. Conic tips will add conic qualities, square tips with this second phalanx strong are the best business indications, spatulate tips will show an active, ambitious, original subject who is sure to force his way in the world, especially on practical lines.

The third phalanx of this finger is most important. Note

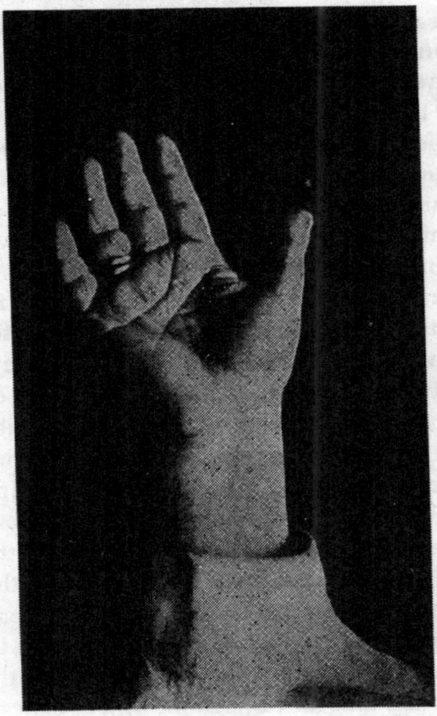

NO. 96. THICK THIRD PHALANX OF JUPITER FINGER

whether it is merely long and not thick, whether it is long and *also* thick, or long and waist-like; or whether short with any of these combinations. When long but not thick, this phalanx shows that the lower world is normal, and lends the support it should to the upper phalanges. If this phalanx should have excessive length over the other two, it would show that the Jupiterian ambitions and desire to rule are sordid and they will operate in a manner not always the most refined. The third phalanx, being the baser world, will be *leading*, while the aspirations and qualities of the upper phalanges will be only *following*. With this development there will be a coarsening of the whole nature; but as the phalanx is not thick, the Jupiterian *sensualism* will not be present, and it will indicate only a common way of exercising the Jupiterian qualities. If the phalanx be long and *also* thick (96), it shows that Jupiterian gluttony is to be added. Thus we will find the subject, if this long and thick phalanx is the most prominent, ruled by the common, sensual side, and the Jupiterian ambitions and desires will be coarsened and made very pronounced. The subject will certainly be a voracious eater, and this will bring on the health troubles peculiar to the Jupiterian in a marked degree. Apoplexy and the sudden end of life will be almost certain. No place so fully shows gluttony as the long, thick third phalanx of Jupiter. It is a menace to health, ambition, and success, for the mind will be more attracted to eating than to anything else. This subject has a desire to rule, not from high ambitions and motives, but rather that he may never fail in his food supply. All his efforts are directed by such motives. In the three phalanges of the finger of Jupiter we have gone from intuition and religion (first phalanx conic and long), to gluttony (long, thick third phalanx), and between these are healthy business desires and ambitions (second phalanx). By separating the phalanges in this way it is possible to determine the kind of motives and ambitions that will guide and rule the subject. There is also the long third phalanx which, instead of being thick, is waist-like (97). Here has entirely disappeared the Jupiterian gluttony, and no matter how strong the finger may be, the subject will contend for higher ideals, not baser gratifications. In this case the Jupiterian health difficulties will not appear. His troubles will come from nervousness, or from throat and lungs. If this waist-like third phalanx shows by its flabbiness that it *was* thick, but has shrivelled, your subject has been an over-eater, has ruined his stomach and become a dyspeptic, suffering from stomach disorders of various kinds. Short phalanges show that the qualities belonging to the particular phalanx which is short are deficient.

In examining a long finger of Jupiter, see if each phalanx is normal, or whether the length comes from excess in a single phalanx, or from two excessive phalanges and one

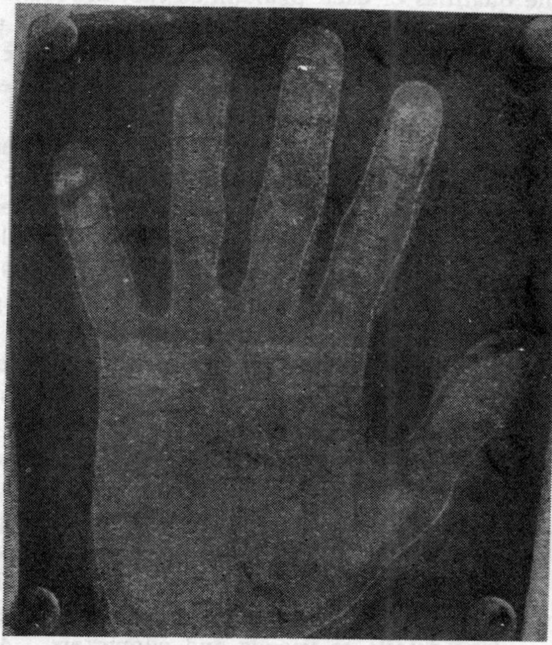

NO. 97. WAIST-LIKE THIRD PHALANX OF JUPITER FINGER

short one. Remember where the tip of the normal-length finger should reach, then note which phalanx is deficient and which excessive. In reading this hand the excessive phalanges show the worlds in which Jupiterian qualities would operate, and you can tell whether the subject wishes to lead in intellectual matters, business, or pleasures, and also which of these are absent by the deficient phalanx. Intuition and religion with the first phalanx, ambition and business with the second, desire to rule and gluttony with the third. If, with the thick third phalanx, you find great redness, gluttony will be still further fired by ardor and strength of blood current, and apoplexy with this subject is doubly certain. Apply color to each phalanx. White will make religion cold, business and ambitions cold, and decrease the ardor and danger of the thick third phalanx. Apply color *qualities* to the qualities of each phalanx as they are found in a greater or less degree, and it will further help in the reading. This ability to separate and read each phalanx will give a complete mastery of the types, for it will enable you to tell *which side* of them will dominate.

Knotty fingers will add knotty qualities to a Jupiterian, and he will be an analyst and reasoner. If only the first knot is developed he will have mental order and system in carrying out his plans. If the second knot is developed he will have order and system in his business affairs and be neat in his personal appearance. With smooth fingers, impulse, inspiration, and artistic ideas will guide him. He will act on first impressions rather than by the slower, analytical methods of thought. With long fingers, he will go into minutiæ, and in planning his Jupiterian campaigns, no details will be omitted. He will be suspicious and distrustful even of his own supporters, will be neat in appearance, and have all the other long-fingered qualities. Finding a Jupiterian has short fingers, you will know that he is quick in thought and action, impulsive, will dislike minutiæ, and will plan the campaigns, but leave the carrying out of details to friends and supporters. Apply short-fingered qualities to the Jupiterian as a type, then to whichever world the Jupiterian qualities will operate in, judged from individual phalanges; in this way you can tell whether mental quickness, business, or common instincts will rule the short fingers. The supreme test is made by the thumb. Are strong determination and reason back of Jupiterian desires and ambitions? Analyze the thumb, see *what kind* of will is present, as shown by the shape of the will phalanx,—whether clubbed, spatulate, square, conic, paddle-shaped, broad, or refined. Then see *how much* will there is by the length of the will phalanx. See if reason and logic are strong by *length* of the second phalanx, see *what kind* of reason by the shape of this phalanx, then see if will is stronger than reason, evenly balanced with it, or deficient. From these examinations you can tell whether good sense and determination will make the Jupiterian ambitions succeed or whether lack of these qualities will ruin them. No matter what the ambitions, there must be will and reason to bring them to anything. No matter how strong the Jupiterian, he must have a good thumb to make him what he was built to be, a commander and leader.

Now by discovering the type of the subject, you know what sphere in life he was created to fill. You can picture what the *pure type* looks like. His characteristics, his health difficulties and dangers, his faults and virtues, have been shown; whether he is refined or coarse (texture), has an elastic or stiff mind (flexibility), energy or laziness (consistency), is cold, warm, bilious, or congested (color), is nervous, has heart disease, consumption, bronchitis, is robust or weak, honest, cranky, or critical (nails), is full of vital energy (hair), lives in the mental, abstract, or material worlds (hand as a whole) what side his peculiar type qualities will take (phalanges of finger), whether artistic, practical, active, or original ideas will govern (tips), whether reason and analysis will rule (knotty fingers), whether inspiration will guide him (smooth fingers), whether minutiæ and detail, or quick thought and action and generalities, will be his modes of procedure (long and short fingers), and whether will and reason will push all these qualities to a successful conclusion (thumb). Intelligent application of this information will enable you to read a subject accurately and thoroughly.

Unfortunately, we cannot have all good Jupiterians, but find the bad type so often that it must be fully considered. In this bad type the appearance is changed, the life, beauty, and strength diminished, and in place there is an undersized man, not commanding in appearance, eyes in which kindliness is lacking, a bad skin without the healthy glow of the good type, straight, stiff hair, a poorly shaped nose, mouth very large, full and sensual, with long, dark teeth. This Jupiterian is forbidding and unattractive, and no crowd follows in his steps. The bad type has all the Jupiterian love of command, but no power of enforcing it except upon those weak and unable to resist him. He is the tyrant and despot at heart, but frequently finds only his family upon whom to exercise these qualities. Thus in his home he is a person of overbearing pettiness. He is grossly extravagant, but in spending his money he furthers only his own pleasure and gratifies only his own appetite. He is a sensualist, selfish in the extreme, and a debauchee. His family are subjected to indignities and forced to submit to a tyrannical will. With no one to rule but these helpless victims whom he should cherish, he forces them to feel his rough Jupiterian despotism and sensualism, producing misery and unhappiness for them. He is unsuccessful in life and miserable, for desire to rule is always thwarted, and realizing this ill-success, he turns to debauchery and makes life a burden to himself and to his family. Weak as he is, mean as he is, the Jupiterian desire for power and rule is in him, but instead of making him successful in the world he is only a producer of woe. The bad type is shown by a full red Mount of Jupiter, deep red lines, a very crooked finger of Jupiter, excessively thick in the third phalanx, coarse skin, a stiff hand, short nails, large thumb with thick will phalanx, and short thick second phalanx. The best hand for a *good* Jupiterian is large with smooth fingers and square tips, broad, pink nails, square or rounding on the end, the finger of Jupiter conic and large, with the phalanges equally developed, a good Mount of Venus and Mercury, elastic consistency, normal flexibility, a large thumb with long, broad, or paddle-shaped will phalanx, and long waist-like second phalanx. Nearly all Jupiterian hands will be thick in the third phalanges, and have deep Head and Life lines, with color very pink or red. There is no trouble in recognizing the good and bad types here described, if found in the pure state, but as other types blend with the Jupiterian, the hands will not show these unmixed Jupiterian qualities, and you may not feel sure to what type the subject belongs. Follow the directions of Chapter XVIII. in locating the Mounts and you will have no trouble in finding the predominating Mount, as well as the second in strength. From these the combination of types to which the subject belongs can be determined. If the Mount of Jupiter is strongest and Venus next, he will be a Jupiterian-Venusian and all the Jupiterian ambition, desires, and qualities will be present, as well as love, sympathy, and the long train of Venusian attributes. Always consider the qualities of the leading type as *predominant*, to which *add* those of the secondary Mounts. Note in the secondary Mounts, by the phalanges of the finger, which world rules, as either the mental strength, business qualities, or the baser elements of the secondary type will be the ones which will support the leading type.

Thus with a Jupiterian-Mercurian, the finger of Mercury having the *second* phalanx longest, the Jupiterian, which is the leading type, will be supported and helped by the *scientific* qualities of the Mercurian, this being the indication of the second phalanx of Mercury. If the *first* phalanx of Mercury, in the above combination, is the longest instead of the second, it will be the Mercurian powers of *oratory* and *eloquence* that will help the Jupiterian. This is a great assistance to one who wishes to influence others. By locating the leading and the attendant Mounts, and by noting which phalanx of the fingers lead, as I have done in the above instances, there is no hand to be found in which you cannot distinguish the leading type, the attendant types, and determine also *what quality* of the leading one is predominant, as well as *what side* of the attendant Mounts will help forward the combination.

This is the way to decide upon occupations. It is absolutely accurate in determining what is the best vocation in life for a client.

The Jupiterian seldom commits suicide. When he does it is the result of disappointed ambition or wounded vanity. As a general rule, when he reaches the stage of discouragement that is supposed to cause men to take life, the Jupiterian takes to drink and drowns his sorrows in the "flowing bowl." Jupiterians who commit suicide have short fingers and act upon impulse. Thus in a sudden disappointment they may on the spur of the moment jump from a high place or use a revolver. Long-fingered or knotty-fingered Jupiterians do not take their own lives. Give a Jupiterian time to think it out and he will never do so. The drink habit is a danger which all Jupiterians have to encounter, and this is especially a danger if the color of the hands, lines, and nails be red. These high-spirited subjects find a great temptation to indulge their appetite for stimulants. If the Life line shows great vigor of constitution by its depth and color this is a positive menace to a Jupiterian.

CHAPTER XX

THE MOUNT OF SATURN

THE Saturnian is the second type to be considered, and the parts of the hand by which he is identified are the Mount and finger of Saturn. The higher the Mount of Saturn is developed, the larger and longer the finger, and the squarer the tip of this finger, the more pronounced is the type of the subject. A highly developed Mount of Saturn is a rarity, and in the greatest number of hands there is instead a depression. A long finger of Saturn is quite common, however, showing the presence of *some* Saturnian qualities, and the Mount, though it may not be prominent, often shows, by the lines upon it, that it is of more than ordinary development. Great care must be used with this Mount, as it shows strong characteristics.

As single signs or in combination, the triangle, circle, trident, single vertical line, or square increase the strength of the Mount of Saturn. The cross-bar, grille, cross, or island indicate defects of the Mount, either of health or character ; nails, color, etc. will determine which (98).

The largest number of Saturnians will be known from the fact that the apex of the Mount of Saturn is central, and the apices of the other Mounts all lean toward it. A more pronounced identification of the type, and also a very common one, is to find the finger of Saturn standing upright, with the other fingers drawn toward it (99). I have chosen such an illustration to accompany this chapter because it is quite typical and much more common than the high Mount. Illustration No. 39 is also a Saturnian subject, identified by apices leaning toward Saturn, Head line deflected toward Saturn, this finger being also highest set.

The Saturnian is a peculiar person, and, while we need a goodly degree of his sober qualities, it is a blessing that the world is not peopled entirely with this type, or it

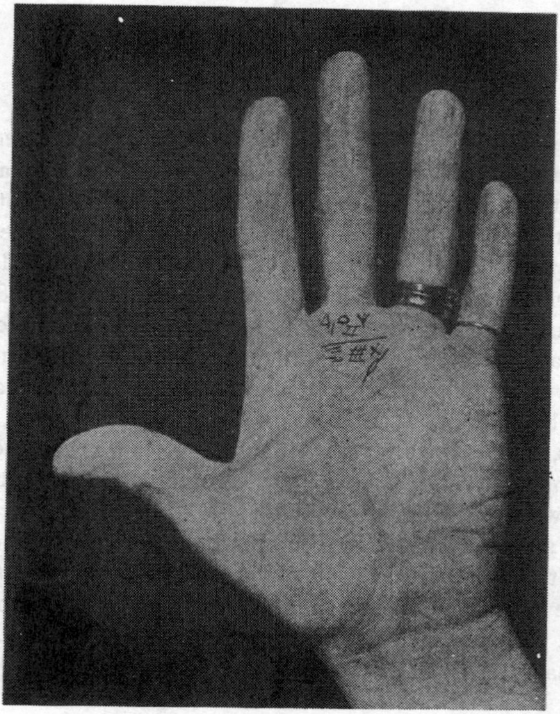

NO. 98. DISTINGUISHING MARKS ON THE MOUNT OF SATURN

would be, in reality, "a vale of tears." I consider the finger of Saturn as the *balance-wheel* to the character, and, as an indicator, of great accuracy concerning the power possessed by the subject to hold undue enthusiasm in check. The Saturnian type keeps the Jupiterian, the Apollonian, the Martian, and the Venusian from going too fast and from being carried away by their excessive spirit. These brighter types, while adding gayety to the world, need the Saturnian to restrain and hold them back. The Saturnian is a prudent, wise, sober necessity, greatly needed among the seven types, but not the one to be chosen if in any excessive degree of development. The Saturnian is the

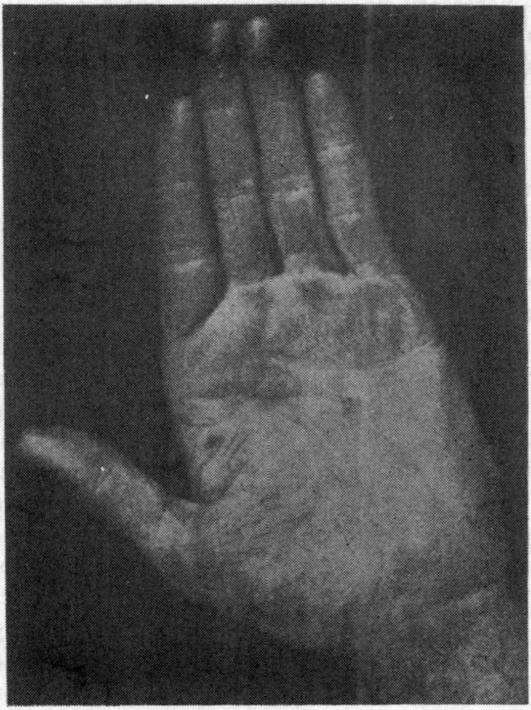

NO. 99. A SATURNIAN HAND
(See also No. 39.)

represser, who lays his hand on the shoulder of enthusiasm and bids it take a view of the dark side before leaping. Other types are so endowed with health and ardor that there seems to be no cautious side to their natures, and they become reckless and careless of results and the cost. The Saturnian's point of view is the gloomy one, consequently it is he who brings that forward, and causes the spontaneous types to pause and think. He is the man who can show you "how the other half lives," and thus makes you appreciate your own blessings. Socially, he lacks the ability to enter into the spirit of the occasion, and, therefore, he is often called a "wet blanket." I consider him the *balance-wheel*, a necessary evil, if you choose, but a type the world could not do without. The Saturnian type, to bring out its better side, should be only slightly developed. It is a bad type, as will appear later, if found in excessive degree, and not the happiest type for the possesser, even when present only in normal quantity.

The typical Saturnian is the tallest of the seven types and his finger is the longest on the hand. He is gaunt, thin, and pale, his skin is yellow, rough, dry, and wrinkled, hanging in flabby folds, or else drawn tightly over the bones. He is the purely bilious type, and yellow is his distinctive color. His hair is thick and dark, often black, straight and harsh. He loses it when quite young, adding baldness to his otherwise unprepossessing appearance. His face is long, commonly called "hatchet-shaped" from its thinness, his cheek bones are high and prominent, with the saffron-hued skin drawn tightly over them. The cheeks are sunken, with skin flabby and wrinkled. The eyebrows are thick and stiff, growing together over the nose and turning up at the outer ends. The eyes are deep set and extremely black, with a sad, subdued expression which changes only when flashes of anger, suspicion, or eagerness stir his mind. Being bilious, the whites of his eyes show yellow color. His ears are large, and stand out from his head, often seeming to be actually heavy. His nose is long, straight, and thin, coming to a sharp point at the end. The nostrils do not dilate as he breathes, but are rigid and stiff. His mouth is large, the lips thin and pale, the lower jaw and lower lip quite prominent and firm. He has good teeth in his youth, but they are soft in texture and decay early. Neither are the gums healthy, having a pale, sickly, bloodless look. If the Saturnian has a beard it is dark, stiff, and straight, growing thickly on the chin and lip, but very sparse on the cheeks. The chin is prominent and large, the neck lean and long, with muscles showing prominently like cords, and the blue veins standing out under the shrunken and flabby skin. His Adam's apple is plainly in evidence. His chest is thin, the lungs seem cramped, as if operating in narrow, contracted quarters, and his voice as it comes through the thin lips is harsh and unpleasant. The shoulders are high and have a decided stoop, and the arms are long and hang in a lifeless manner at his sides. His step has no spring, and his gait is a shambling one, seeming to proclaim a person who is miserable, bilious, and gloomy. The whole appearance of the Saturnian impresses you with its lack of nourishment, lack of healthy blood supply, and its lean gawkiness; the dark, sad eyes, stiff, black hair, narrow chest, stooping shoulders, and shuffling gait all combine to bear this out. He is a man to whom a bright side in life does not often appear, one whose life is lightened by no joy of exuberant spirits, filled with no animal vitality, no heat, warmth, and magnetism, but rather with yellow biliousness, mingled with white coldness. The insufficient blood current, poisoned with bile, is weakly flowing through his body, pumped by a flabby heart, and reaches the outer skin with a diminished force, casting over his spirits the depressing effect of a bilious influence. This is the typical Saturnian. It is small wonder that, when the dashing Apollonians or Venusians, handsome, attractive, and magnetic, filled with the joy of living, meet him and try to fill him with their enthusiasm, the Saturnian cannot feel their joy, or share their enthusiasm, but shakes his head mournfully, and thinks of how much sorrow there is in this world.

As the Saturnian is the represser, you will appreciate the wisdom of constructing him ugly, gloomy, and sad, in order that he might accomplish the purpose of his creation. If he were only wise and formed in the Apollonian mould of physical beauty, the love of gayety would run away with his wisdom. Mere wisdom, if he were beautiful, bright, strong, and healthy, could not hold in check the Apollonian enthusiasm. But the Saturnian is *physically* built so that he cannot be carried away with enthusiastic, joyous, or frivolous amusements. No matter how much he may *want to be*, he *cannot*, with his ugliness, have Venusian power of attraction; he cannot be other than the Saturnian that he is.

In addition to all this, he is cynical, lacks veneration, and is a born doubter. Instead of seeking the society of others he avoids it, and his tendency is to withdraw himself from the social world. He prefers the country to the city, is often a student, and chooses agricultural pursuits, chemistry, and other laboratory occupations, which do not require him to come in contact with people. He is not a "mixer," has not the faculty of attracting and holding friends, so does not succeed well in business where he has to depend upon genial ways or attractive manners. His love of solitude makes farm life peculiarly attractive to him, and his penchant for earthy things makes him by nature a horticulturist, market gardener, florist, or a botanist. By reason of his love for digging and exploring in the earth, he has often found wells of oil, or mines of coal and minerals. This has led people to consider him lucky, and for this reason Saturn has become the Mount and type of Fate. The Saturnian has a love for all occult studies, and is proficient in them. He has a mystical streak that makes him extremely superstitious. He loves chemistry, for the compounding of drugs and elements has an air of mystery about it, and physics is also a congenial study. Higher mathematics and medicine are strong favorites, and in both these fields he is very successful. The Saturnian is no shallow fellow, but is deep and a true scientist. While others are spending their time in gayety he is engrossed in study, has secluded himself from society, and, surrounded by his books, retorts, and figures, is working out difficult problems.

He is eminently cautious and prudent. He is suspicious of both the fidelity and honesty of his fellows, and does not readily go into business enterprises with them. Real estate, farms, and buildings seem to him less risky than stocks, bonds, or mercantile enterprises, consequently these are the investments he chooses. He is, of course, a conservative person, and does not do anything hastily, for prudence and caution are his watchwords. The Saturnian can be led, not driven. He instinctively dislikes to obey, but feels flattered at an attempt to *induce* him to do anything. He rebels if rubbed the wrong way, talks a great deal, what he says has weight because he has the reputation of being profound, so he often makes all kinds of trouble. His caution, however, enables him to get away and not get hurt in the upheavals he causes. In all his surroundings he likes soberness, and gray, black, or brown will be apt to predominate in his apparel, nor will his home have any startling colors in it. His physical heat being under normal, he is not amorous. He shuns society rather than courts it, he repels the opposite sex rather than attracts. Thus the fervor of warm passions does not glow within him, and he does not care to marry. In fact, a pure Saturnian would not marry; the idea would be absolutely repugnant to him. In handling the marriage question, for a subject strongly Saturnian, you will know that marriage is not likely, so *absolutely* plain indications must be found before you commit yourself on the subject. His prudence gives him another quality,—he is saving and even stingy and miserly. The stronger the Saturnian indications, the stronger these avaricious tendencies. He is slow,—one so cautious could not be otherwise,—but is a patient, indefatigable worker. The Saturnian loves music and is often a fine performer and a composer, but his music has a tinge of sadness and melancholy and is severely classical. He is not a great lover of art, though he admires beauty. His favorite pictures will be landscapes and natural scenery, flowers, and the product of field and forest. He writes well, produces histories, fine treatises on scientific and occult subjects, books on chemistry, or short articles on agriculture. He sometimes writes excellent ghost stories or tales, in which morose heroes go into monasteries. For amusement the Saturnian seeks his books and the studies which take him away from the haunts of men. He is opinionated, does not like to be contradicted, is independent, and dislikes restraint. Under the surface the Saturnian dislikes mankind. He is not beautiful or attractive, is less loved than others, and feels his ugliness, knows his ungainliness, and withdraws himself from his fellows, having in his heart jealousy and hatred of them. This feeling is present even with a Saturnian who cannot be classed as belonging to the bad type. Dislike of mankind is a Saturnian quality developed in some degree even when the type is not pronounced. We may say truly this is a dangerous type at its best, and at its worst produces a poisoner and a malevolent wretch. When we see stooping shoulders, a hunched back, and the sapped vitality has produced a cripple, with perhaps crossed eyes added, scant, coarse hair, and leathery skin, you have a creature capable of the deeds of Mr. Hyde. This is the low, mean, jealous, surly, dishonest villain ; a lower state of degradation than any other type can reach, except the Mercurian, but vile enough for all. These malformed Saturnians will stick a dagger into your back, and gloat over your death agonies. No more malevolent creatures live. This, of course, is a picture so exaggerated as to be scarcely conceivable, but it is sometimes found.

We have now followed the Saturnian from the sober "balance-wheel," through a series of developments and characteristics to the wretch just described. You can appreciate the gravity of this type, and the handling of the Mount must be done with great care. With a pronounced Saturnian development, use all your powers to learn *how much* of it is in the subject uncounteracted by other qualities. *Some* Saturnian should be present, for the absence of any makes an unbalanced character, but the subject wants only *just enough* to give the balance needed. Any excess will make a morbid, melancholy, gloomy person, pessimistic and stingy. The very strong Mount and finger, or, which occurs more often, all the fingers and apices leaning toward the finger of Saturn, will show the good type I have described, who is peculiar but not necessarily evil. The excessively grilled or crossed development of the Mount, bad Heart-line and with crooked, gnarled fingers and hard hand, will show the bad type. Everything you know should be brought to bear on the case when a Saturnian is before you, in order to determine how strongly the qualities of the type are developed. In health matters there are certain diseases to which Saturnians are predisposed, and in a strongly Saturnian subject, with bad health showing on the Life line, it is nine chances to one that the trouble will be one of the diseases peculiar to the type; *which one* can be told by the nails, color, or some other health indication.

First of all the Saturnian is the purely bilious type. His is not a temporary trouble of the liver, but a structural disease of the organ, hence the presence of bile poison in the blood. This makes the Saturnian yellow, which color will be found tinging his nails, palm, lines, and Mount. All the troubles which yellow color indicates, both as to health and temperament, are to be attributed to the subject if that color is present. As bile in the blood creates intense nervousness, the Saturnian is troubled with this as one of his health difficulties. If this nervousness goes far it causes danger of paralysis. The degree of nerve trouble is easy to determine from the nails, which should be carefully noted. Rheumatism is another trouble, also hemorrhoids and varicose veins; the tendency toward the two latter can be determined by noting how prominently the veins on the hands stand out, seeming as if filled with hard blood. The paralysis which threatens this type will probably attack his lower limbs, for there is his weak point. His teeth are delicate, and he is liable to ear trouble, which is indicated by dots or small islands on the line of Head under the Mount of Saturn. With every Saturnian subject look for these health difficulties if any disturbance is seen on the line of Life. A grille or cross-bars on the Mount of Saturn will suggest health defects of the type, which can be easily located from nails, etc. In estimating the degree of strength of the type, bring to bear all your knowledge. Texture of the skin will show whether the subject is refined or coarse. The finer the grade the less liability of the development of the evil side. Such a subject may be blue or despondent, but not necessarily a pessimist

The coarse texture of skin will make all the Saturnian qualities coarse. It will emphasize the hatred for mankind, will make an inciter of riot; one who wants complete liberty and rebels against restraint of any kind. Fine or medium texture is best. Flexibility of the hand will greatly modify the severity of the type. The elastic mind will not so readily yield to gloom, despondency, or bad instincts as the unyielding mind, shown by the stiff hand. The Saturnian is naturally stingy, and the stiff hand adds greatly to this tendency, while the flexible hand takes away from it. A flexible hand will make the subject likely to enjoy the society of his fellow-men; a stiff hand will make him shun and hate mankind intensely. With the flexible hand look for a good type; with the stiff hand look out for a mean, unenlightened, selfish exhibition of bad qualities and tendencies.

If his hand has flabby consistency, his laziness will make him useless. He will indulge all his morbid tendencies, for he will not work, and labor might throw off some of his bad side. Being lazy and still possessing the qualities of his type, he will talk a great deal, will rail at capital, trusts, and all things which are successful, and from this class of lazy Saturnians often come the anarchists who throw bombs. Soft hands will be a slight improvement over the flabby. This subject will not be quite so lazy and will have higher ideals. Elastic consistency is the best, for it will show a proper amount of energy, which will keep the liver more active and reduce the gloom and morbidity of the subject. He will have the elastic qualities of mind and method, the intelligent energy which will lift him out of much of his difficulty. Hard hands, again, coarsen the type and emphasize its bad qualities. This over-energy will cause him to push his already unpleasant views to excess; the stubborn brain will oppose progress and invention, and will clamor for a return of the "good old days." This fellow is the chronic opposer of everything. No matter what it is, he is against it. He will be stingy, narrow, ignorant, and superstitious.

The color of the hand is of much importance. Yellow is expected, for there is an excess of bile. The yellower the hand the "yellower" the point of view of the subject. Gloom, melancholy, distorted views, rancor, irritability, intense nervousness, and even criminality will be found if yellow color is pronounced. White color is often found. This makes a subject cold, repellent, and unattractive. He will strongly incline to fly from the society of his fellows, will be shunned wherever he goes, and being sensitive, this will add to his hatred of men, while his cutting remarks will make him more disagreeable. He cannot succeed in anything where he must come in contact with the public. A cold Saturnian is a picture of misery, and this subject is likely to be bad. Pink color will show a better state of health and a more cheerful and better Saturnian. To him all things will not be hopeless. The bright vivacity of pink color will lift and lighten the veil of gloom with which the Saturnian is enveloped, and there will be no such chance for a malevolent creature as with yellow or white color. Red is also good. It shows the increased ardor peculiar to the color, also indicating better health and strength, which reduces the gloom and brightens the subject. Unless there are other things present which red qualities might influence, red is a good color. Blue color will show liability to hemorrhoids and varicose veins, as well as heart disease, and if a grille is on the Mount of Saturn or cross-bars with blue color, you may be sure of piles, possibly of varicose veins. Look to the veins on the back of the hand for further confirmation.

Nails are important to consider for both character and disease. The short, critical nail on a bad Saturnian will be a poor accompaniment. All the mean, critical qualities of this nail will be added to the disagreeable qualities of the type. Critical nails on even a good Saturnian are an unpleasant indication, and will make him cranky and pronounced in his views. The best nail is the broad healthy one, which will tend to give better health and consequently better temper. The narrow nail of delicate constitution does not help his condition, nor does it make him any more agreeable. Consumption and heart-disease nails will show these diseases present, though not being difficulties peculiar to the type, their presence would not be expected. If seen, use them as denoting their *peculiar trouble.* Fluted and brittle nails are expected, as nervousness and paralysis are health defects of the type. Judge the degree which the trouble has reached by the extent of change in the nail. Beginning at the white spots, through all the various stages to the brittle turned-back nail, you can tell how far the difficulty has progressed. In all nails first determine what the nail indicates, its degree of development, and then apply it to the Saturnian qualities which will give the correct reading. If it is a health indication, think whether the trouble is peculiar to the type; if it is, the danger is greater than if it is not.

Hair on the hands will tell by its presence and color how hardy the subject is. Black hair will add tricky tendencies to a Saturnian, blond color will make him more likely to be frank and trustworthy. Gauge the amount of hair found, its color and fineness, and use these hair qualities in judging those of the type.

The hand as a whole must be considered, for if the fingers be in excess of the palm it will show that the mental world is in excess. This will make the subject a student and scholar, but he will not be much of a business person. He will write learned books, make a good teacher, but will not be a money-maker. If the middle portion of the hand is most pronounced the abstract world rules, and he will find success in business. If the lower third of the hand is developed grosser qualities will be added to the Saturnian and make him a very bad person. If one of the three worlds is absent and the other two developed, work out the combination. If it is mental and baser worlds with the middle absent, you know that a visionary Saturnian, who is ruled by bad, earthy qualities, is present, without the good influence of the middle world. Use this same reasoning with the other worlds which are present or absent.

Note also the phalanges of the finger. If the first is longest the mental world is the strongest. The subject will be a student and a thinker inclined to superstition and fond of occult sciences. The second phalanx of the finger longest will show that farming, agriculture, scientific investigations, chemistry, physics, history, and mathematics are the things most to his taste. This is the medium world and the business side of the Saturnian is shown here. With this second phalanx longest he will be able to gain a livelihood from the pursuit of the vocations peculiar to the type, and should be advised to go into such occupations and pursue these studies. If the third phalanx is longest, the baser attributes will be in the ascendency. As the Saturnian is not sensual we cannot attribute sensualism to him from the long third phalanx. The baser quality which belongs to the type is money-worship. If the type is *good* and the third phalanx long you can say he is only economical. If the type is *coarse* or bad and third phalanx long it means *miserliness.* If this third phalanx is *thick* it will make him less studious, if it is *waist-like* he will pursue with great eagerness the investigation of the studies for which he has peculiar aptitude. If the finger is bent it adds shrewdness to the Mount and the Saturnian qualities. If the finger is very short he is not a Saturnian, and entirely lacks seriousness and balance. Note whether the apex of the Mount leans toward Jupiter; if it does the wisdom of Saturn will be added to the Jupiterian ambitions, pride and love of command. If the apex lies toward Apollo it will lend soberness and wisdom to the Apollonian qualities. In either of these cases the severity of the morbidness of Saturn is diminished, for he gives himself over to the other Mounts. If the apex is in the centre of the Mount all his interest is centred in himself and is uninfluenced by the qualities of the other Mounts. If the finger leans toward Jupiter it will give off some of the strength of Saturn to Jupiter. Thus Jupiter will become wise and cautious as a leader. If the finger leans toward Apollo some of the Saturnian soberness will be drawn toward Apollo and he will become more quiet and careful.

You must note the finger tips. If all the tips are of one shape and Saturn's tip is different, it means that Saturn will have the qualities of his tip, the other fingers those of the tips they have. This is very useful if the fingers be conic.

for a conic tip to *Saturn alone* with all other tips square or spatulate, would make the *balance wheel* weaker than the rest of the fingers. If the other fingers are conic and Saturn conic also, it does not throw him out of balance. The more pointed the tip of Saturn, the more idealism enters into the subject. Superstition is rampant, and he is ruled by dreams, signs, and omens. This is especially true if the first phalanx be long as well as pointed. The character is more erratic,

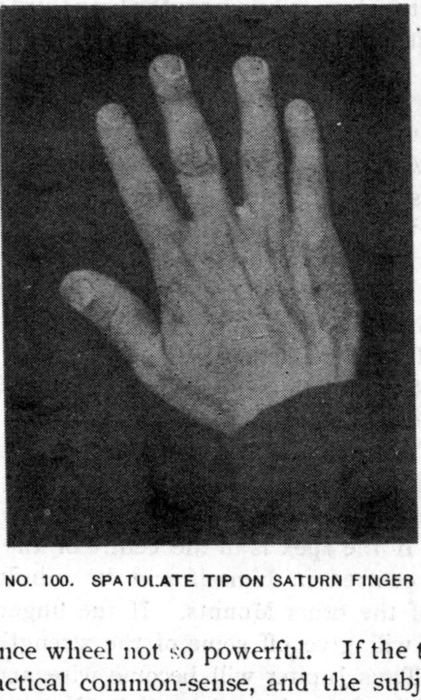

NO. 100. SPATULATE TIP ON SATURN FINGER

and the balance wheel not so powerful. If the tip be square you find practical common-sense, and the subject becomes quiet, less superstitious, and inclines to soberness and even melancholy if very square. Note which phalanx is the longest. A conic tip and long second phalanx will give *idealism* to the attributes of the *second phalanx* and affect their operation. In like manner it will affect both the first and third phalanges if they are longest. Square tips will make the farming, chemistry, medicine, physics, or mathematics of the second phalanx very practical, useful, and likely to be productive of money results. It will add greatly to the economy or miserliness of the third phalanx, and take away from the superstition of the first. Spatulate tips will add activity and originality to the Saturnian wisdom and soberness, will

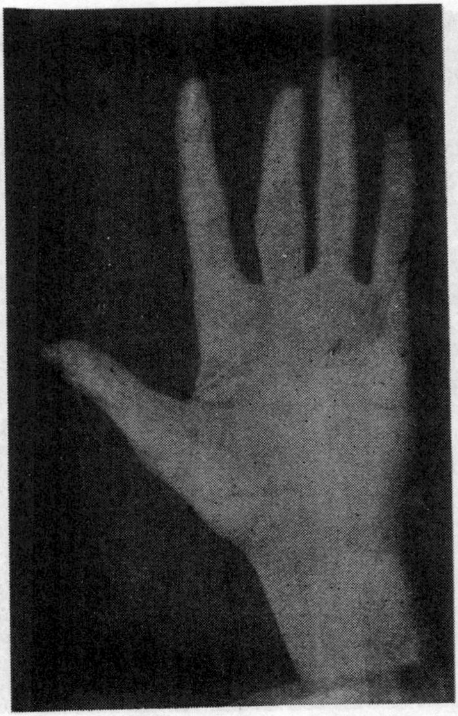

NO. 101A. MOUNT AND FINGER OF SATURN DEFICIENT

impel the subject to mingle with his fellows, be more active, and will make him a great worker, if he is a farmer. If a chemist, it will lead him to seek new compounds, if a doctor, new treatments, if a mathematician, new systems for figuring, and it will give great activity in all these operations. The individual phalanges must be judged, and spatulate qualities added to them as found developed. The spatulate tip is the broadest of all ; it will thus give the greatest seriousness to the finger. The spatulate balance wheel will be the strongest balance of all. If the Saturnian type be very pronounced with this spatulate tip (100), the subject will be gloomy, morose, sullen, and hard to get along with, for he

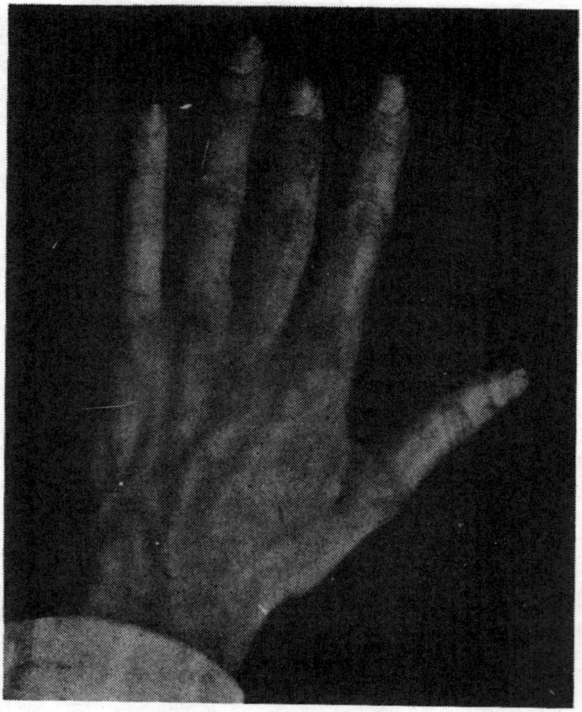

NO. 101B. FINGER OF SATURN DEFICIENT

will push his disagreeable qualities with spatulate activity and originality. If the finger be very deficient with a conic tip, the subject will be led by everyone and will have no stamina whatever (101 two illustrations). The balance wheel is entirely lacking, and even a good thumb will not help this subject, for he is flighty and entirely untrustworthy.

If the fingers are knotty, the qualities of analysis and

reasoning will be present. They will make Saturnian qualities more pronounced and add to the seriousness of the subject. Always a careful type, knotty fingers will make them more careful and slow and with knots, there will be no such thing as impulse or sentiment. A natural doubter, the Saturnian with knotty fingers will be an absolute skeptic, he will be analytical in his agricultural and scientific pursuits, and a methodical person. The knotty-fingered Saturnian makes a good judge, for he is wise, not governed by sentiment, and analytical. Conic tips lessen the intensity of knotty fingers. Square tips make them practical, spatulate tips, active and original. All these combinations of tips will be seen on knotty-fingered Saturnians, and life to this subject is serious and real. Smooth fingers make a Saturnian impulsive, a lover of the beautiful, and his musical nature becomes prominent. If the tips be conic this is most pronounced, if the tips be square the artistic side becomes practical, and with spatulate tips spatulate qualities are present. The smooth-fingered Saturnian is a decidedly happier type, and not so liable to despondency. He tends strongly toward superstition and becomes proficient in occult sciences. Long fingers give him detail and minutiæ. If the first phalanx be long, he goes into the depths of mysticism and superstition. With the second phalanx long, he will not omit a detail in the scientific studies or the agricultural pursuits which he follows. Short fingers will give the quick thought and action peculiar to them. The Saturnian qualities will be present but will be operated with short-fingered quickness. If the tips be conic, the short-fingered impulse will be very great, if square it will decrease in degree, and spatulate tips will add the fiery impetuosity belonging to these tips. Short fingers will make the Saturnian less careful in dress but also less repellent and more approachable. Long fingers make him tidier, but the suspicion of long fingers leads him to distrust and dislike mankind, and he is hard to get acquainted with. The thumb tells what support will and reason are to give to the subject. A short thumb will show a weak character and will make the Saturnian vacillating. A large thumb will add to the gravity and determination of the type. With the thumb thoroughly understood it will not be hard to apply whatever thumb is found to the Saturnian qualities of the subject. The *amount* of determination, gauge by length of the will phalanx, what *kind*, by the shape of the phalanx, *how much* reason is present, by the length of the second phalanx, and *what kind* by the shape of this phalanx. Whether will or reason are balanced, is determined by the comparative lengths of the phalanges. These will all tell the amount and kind of force pushing the Saturnian qualities forward. Pointed thumbs take away from the strength of the type, square or spatulate add greatly to it. Note carefully which Mount type is secondary and which world guides it from the phalanges of its finger. In this way having found in which world the Saturnian subject is most prominent, you will be able to judge what side of the secondary Mount will operate to aid him.

The Saturnian is predisposed to suicide as an end to his woes. Always more or less gloomy by nature, ill-success, sickness, or slighting treatment often casts him into depths of despair from which he sees no relief but death. If he be a high type he may, by mental force, hold himself level. If he be ill or weak in character, a dose of poison will relieve him from suffering. (See hands of the Chittenden Hotel suicide.)

In considering the matter of criminology in connection with the types, we find more real criminals come from the Saturnians and Mercurians than from any of the others. There is in these two types an instinct of dislike toward mankind, even if the subjects have only a slightly excessive development. This leads the bad specimens to constantly invade the rights of others. The prisons are occupied by a majority of Saturnians and Mercurians. In examining the crimes for which law-breakers are incarcerated, it becomes apparent that the other types have fallen, often from bad environments or from sudden temptations to do wrong, which have overcome the subject before he has had time to think it over. In these cases the subjects are heartily sorry they transgressed the law, and very infrequently become chronic law-breakers. They are the so-called criminals who can be reclaimed. The fact is, they were never real criminals. The professional crooks who commit crime at every opportunity, and serve two and three sentences, becoming under the law "habitual criminals," are almost all Saturnians or Mercurians. They are real criminals at heart—mean to do wrong; their hands are against every man, and they live and die planning how to best their fellows. These subjects do not reform in reality—all pretences in this direction are merely to deceive and gain an advantage over the unsuspecting. An interesting fact to note in this matter of criminality is that the two types from which criminals come are the *two bilious ones*, the Saturnian and Mercurian. Bile seems capable of perverting everything and making it evil; certainly its two types are those from which the most desperate criminals spring. Keep this well in mind in estimating the Saturnian. Do not fall into the error of thinking there are no good Saturnians. Some of the grandest of men, noble, high-minded, and successful, belong to this type. Abraham Lincoln was one. Always do your Saturnian subjects justice; they may be Lincolns; but at the same time do not forget the large number of "Burglar Jims" who belong to the same type.

CHAPTER XXI

THE MOUNT OF APOLLO

THE third Mount type is the Apollonian, and the parts of the hand which identify him are the Mount and finger of Apollo. This is a pleasant type to handle, because it is a good type, and, while the Apollonian sometimes becomes mercenary and shoddy, he does not often become bad or criminal. As has been already noticed in the study of the types, the two which become bad and vicious are the bilious types (Saturn and Mercury) and, while the others are sometimes coarse, they do not often descend to criminality. When they do, we have seen, it is the result of sudden emotions or circumstances, and not as a result of inherent badness.

As single signs, or in combination, the star, triangle, circle, single vertical line, square, or trident, strengthen a Mount of Apollo.

The cross-bar, grille, cross, island, or dot, show defects of the Mount, either of health or character. Nails, color, etc., will determine which (102).

The normal Apollonian is a healthy, vigorous person, consequently happy, genial, and attractive. He is a spontaneous type, and versatility, brilliancy, love of the beautiful and artistic in everything, are his attributes. Standing alongside the Saturnian, he is the direct opposite of that gloomy fellow. The dark side of life is in the background with him and, as the Saturnian was needed as a check to over-enthusiasm, so the Apollonian is needed in order that darkness and gloom may not dominate. Play and diversion must follow work if we are to keep ourselves healthy and vigorous, and someone must provide these recreative things, these rests from seriousness. We must have comedians, for laughter is a tonic to the tired brain. The Jupiterian is engrossed in his schemes for aggrandizement; the Saturnian is absorbed in wisdom, sobriety, or gloom; who then shall provide the

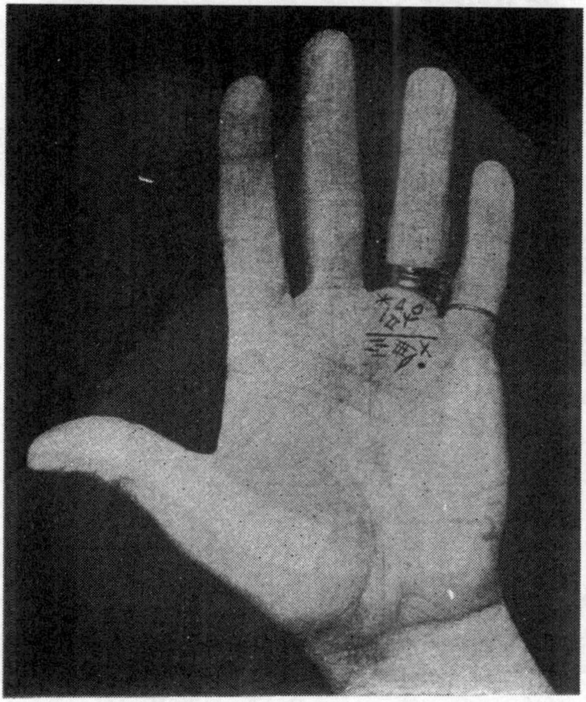

NO. 102. DISTINGUISHING MARKS ON THE MOUNT OF APOLLO

bright things which shall make life worth living? That task is the Apollonian's. This type has been completely misunderstood. It has always stood for art and brilliancy, and the temptation has been to ascribe to every hand which has a good Mount of Apollo great artistic talent, frequently far in excess of that really possessed by the subject. All Apollonians are not artists or actors, and never can be. But all Apollonians love beauty in dress, home, business surroundings, and every walk in life in which they are found. They enjoy life by the force of their spontaneous natures, and cause those around them to enjoy it. All things beautiful and artistic appeal to them. It by no means follows that

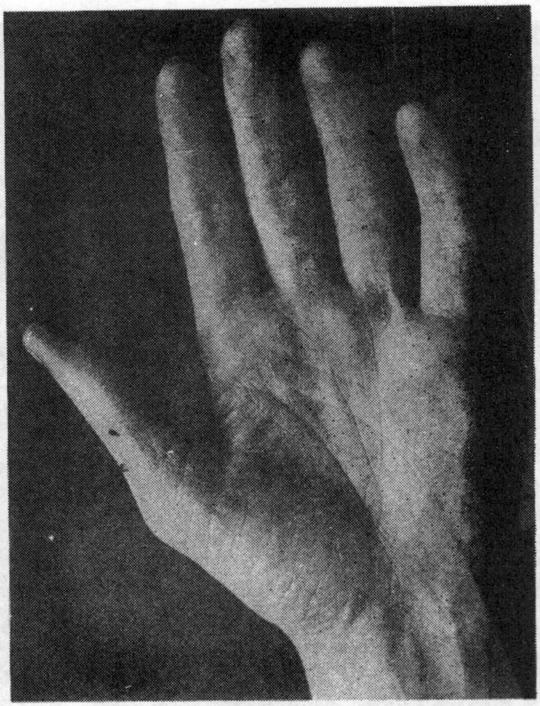

NO. 103. APOLLONIAN HAND

they will ever be *producers* or *creators* of art, but it is certain they always *love* it. Between a person with creative power and a mere lover of the beautiful there is a wide difference, never lose sight of this fact in the Apollonian type. Do not ascribe great artistic talent to one who is merely fond of beauty in dress and surroundings. To be sure, the Apollonian is a lover of art, but unless he has a finely developed

Mount, apex in the centre, finger long, first phalanx long, and a fine, deep-cut *Line of Apollo* (103), often with stars on it, do not ascribe *creative* artistic power to him. With the above strong markings he will *have* creative power and will not be merely a lover of the beautiful (104).

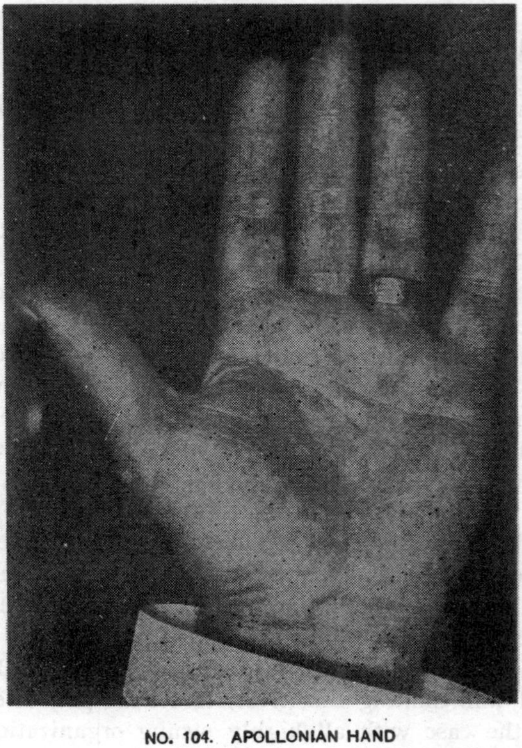

NO. 104. APOLLONIAN HAND

The Apollonian has another side. He is highly successful in business, and he carries his love of beauty here as everywhere else. He is richly endowed with graces which draw people to him, and with his natural brilliancy and versatility he adapts himself to the conditions of the times, the demands of the public, chooses his goods with a tasteful eye, and makes money thereby. This subject is found strongly marked with a high Mount, apex in the centre, but not necessarily cut with deep lines; if there are any such, you will find *several* vertical ones on the Mount, showing diversity of talent, but not the creative power of the artist. Generally you find a secondary, Mercurian development to accentuate the business shrewdness. With the Apollonian it is necessary, above all, to distinguish these two classes, — those capable of creative power in art, and those who are mere lovers of the beautiful and tasteful things of life.

The Apollonian is a handsome and a manly type. He is of medium height, between the Jupiterian and Saturnian, is not fleshy like the Jupiterian nor lean and lanky like the Saturnian, but is shapely, muscular, and athletic. The lines of the body run in graceful curves, and he is light and supple. His complexion is clear, his skin white, fine and firm in texture, and cheeks rosy. This pinkness of color gives the clue to a healthy condition and consequent attractiveness. The hair is thick, wavy, and black or auburn in color, fine and silky in quality, and when he has a beard it partakes of the same fineness and abundance, growing over the chin, lip, and high on the cheeks. His forehead is broad and full, but not high, the eyes are large, almond-shaped, brown or blue in color, with long lashes curling up at the ends. The eyes have a frank, honest expression, which changes to sweetness and sympathy when the emotions are in play, and they sparkle with the brilliancy and life of the brain behind them. His cheeks are firm and rounded, showing no hollows. The nose is straight and finely shaped, the nostrils beautifully proportioned, and dilating sensitively under the play of emotions; as is the case with all highly strung organizations. The mouth is graceful in outline, the lips curved and set evenly, neither thin nor large and thick. The teeth are finely shaped, strong, even, and white, firmly set in healthy red gums. The chin is shapely and rounded, neither retreating nor protruding, showing evenly balanced firmness. The ears are of medium size, well formed, and pink, setting close to the head. The neck is long, muscular, and well shaped, but showing neither cord-like muscles, nor a prominent

"Adam's apple." This shapely neck connects the well-shaped head with strong shoulders, which are muscular and graceful. The chest is full and capacious, expands well under the inspiration, which fact undoubtedly contributes much to purifying the blood, pink color with healthy conditions following. The voice is musical, but not full or resonant. The lower limbs are graceful, muscular, finely proportioned, and are never fat. The feet are of medium size, the insteps arching and high, which gives spring and elasticity to the walk. This is a particularly distinguishing feature of the Apollonian. In this type is a picture of healthy conditions, beautiful proportions, grace and symmetry of body, and to these must be linked a mind full of similar charms and attributes. From every point of view the Apollonian is brilliant, full of the love of beauty, art, color, and form. The Mount, from its brilliancy, has also been called the Mount of the Sun, and the Line of Apollo, when strongly marked in the hand, has been called the Line of the Sun, or of Brilliancy, and to it has been ascribed a fortunate career, with wealth and fame as the reward. As this line shows the strength of development of the Apollonian qualities in a subject, making the Mount stronger, thus the type also, it is not unreasonable that wealth and fame should be secured by so brilliant a subject as is the Apollonian.

The Apollonian is highly intuitive. He sees through things more quickly than other people and especially is this perceptive faculty strong in art and literature. He does not labor to learn, as does his companion, the Saturnian, neither is he as profound and deep. But the Apollonian, no matter how little he may really know, will make a brilliant show of it, and in any company, from the seeming depth of his knowledge and research, is a surprise. This arises from the wonderful versatility of his nature, and the quick way he has of grasping a small idea and making a great deal out of it. He is inventive as well as an imitator, and can put old things in new ways. Thus he often gets credit for knowing a great deal more than he really does. He is always the centre of attraction in whatever company he may be found, and will adapt himself to circumstances and people. He can be thrown with scientists and will cope with them in whatever field of research they are working. He will, with equal facility and without thought or preparation, join a body of socialists, artists, anarchists, doctors, lawyers, or any profession or class, and will astonish those present with his seeming mastery of the particular subject. His adaptability and versatility are astonishing, and "brilliant" is the only word that fitly describes him.

He fairly sparkles with intuition, and seems to learn without study. This makes him sought by all classes of people. He is the life of the drawing-room, the hero of the athletic field, the daring and successful plunger either in the stock market or at the gaming table. In any and all walks of life he is found, full of dash, brilliancy, versatility. For him the beautiful in nature, women, home decorations, and dress, have always a fascination. Anything that lacks beauty is repulsive. With this strong passion in him he is the artist always and in everything. He may not be the great painter, but if he have short nails, surely he is the critic. He adores art in every form, and owing to his versatility, he is always a dabbler in it. He loves fine clothes, luxurious home surroundings, and jewels. If he is the refined type with first phalanx the longest, he will have excellent taste in all these. If he belongs to the class who have the world of the third phalanx longest, he will be loud and shoddy in displaying his love of such matters. He is a good fellow. Health is good with him, so he feels kindly toward mankind, especially as he manages to cope with them so easily. He is a warm friend, but being somewhat changeable is not always constant. Being brilliant, he makes enemies among those less so than himself, and these enemies often become bitter and envious rivals. His brain is clear, and in all matters of business, religion, art, or literature he sees things from a logical point of view He has a great facility of expression, and while not always deep is easy to understand. To him success is natural, it comes by the very force of circumstance. Friends and the world like him and gladly do much to forward his interests, and he is thus pushed by his admirers into many advantageous enterprises. He attains high positions and is a great money-maker. He is never economical and does not rely on putting away a part of his earnings, but by brilliant and successful spurts forges ahead. His tastes are luxurious and his expenditures follow them, but he makes so much that the expenses seem little. He is always figuring in the thousands, and looks down upon the single dollars.

The Apollonian is never afraid to air his views, or to speak his mind freely, and he loves to hear himself talk. He is religious in his instincts, and seemingly understands religion as he does every other subject and problem of the universe. He is not a fanatic, nor superstitious, nor is he a doubter; but he embraces religious faith with the eagerness characteristic of him. Among his other accomplishments, he is proficient in occult sciences, and does some wonderful things. He cannot explain how, but knows it is not from deep study. It is in reality his highly intuitive faculties that make him proficient here. He is cheerful, happy, and bright, and though he is subject to bursts of quick temper which are fierce while they last, it is only a momentary flash, and he holds no resentment. He does not harbor grudges and has the ability to win over his worst enemy to at least a seeming friendship. He does not make lasting friends, but by his brilliancy temporarily attracts and enslaves. He himself is not a lasting friend, consequently he does not inspire true friendship in others.

As much as he loves pleasure and gayety he is neither amorous nor sensual,— that is, in the high type. He loves a banquet as much for the after-dinner wit, the music, the decorations, the beauty of dress, as for the viands which grace the table. He loves women who are beautiful, finely or tastefully dressed, and passions of the baser sort do not inflame him. He does not fall a prey to dissipation as easily as might be thought, though he will not refuse pleasure in any form when it has the proper accompaniments. He is a great traveller and fond of seeing the world. He is honest, and acknowledges his faults, fully appreciates his own brilliancy and does not deny it. He does not need to steal for he can make money too easily. He honestly desires celebrity and gains it. If he relied more on effort and less on brilliancy, he would reach fame more frequently and in greater degree. If he could chain his talents, his brilliancy of mind, body, and endowment, down to a definite line of work, he would dominate the world. As it is, he moves among us a brilliant possibility, a magnificent specimen physically and mentally, a joy, a pleasure, a benefit, but too often, through his versatility, a "Jack-of-all-trades." In his marriage relations the Apollonian is often unhappy. He is predisposed to marry, does not, like the Saturnian, withdraw from and hate mankind, but his ideal is very high; he is brilliant himself and he wants a mate who can shine with him. Humanity is frail, and those most brilliant often choose much less-favored helpmates. When this is the case the Apollonian finds himself disappointed and his marriage a failure. With a large percentage of the type this is true and should be so treated in your readings.

There is a bad type of Apollonian. In it you find the markings of Mount and finger strong enough to show you that the subject is of this type, but you find a thick third phalanx, short first, crooked finger with short nails, hard consistency, no flexibility, or with other indications showing a decrease of the mentality and fineness of the type. Then the subject will be undersized, with common features, none of the beauty of the best type. The hair will be stiff, crisp, and a dingy yellow. The complexion will be either red or sallow, the eyes sometimes crossed, and instead of a clean, tidy, artistic being, you have a common person not giving any indication of the brilliancy of the type. This specimen will be vain and boastful, and have a good opinion of himself and his ability. He is fond of show and display (the material world rules) and, with the extravagance of the type present without his brilliant way of money-making, he will be improvident and poor. He craves notoriety, will tell how talented he is, seeks to be an actor, and greatly overestimates himself. When repulsed he becomes bitter and revengeful and thinks himself badly used. He imagines that his want of success comes from the fact that others are conspiring against him. He will stop at nothing to make himself conspicuous, and will commit any folly to produce this result. Altogether he is an unhappy, unsuccessful creature. Note, however, that he is seldom criminal. The two extremes of this type have many degrees of development between them, and the Apollonian type is often combined with other types that modify it.

With the mental picture of the two extreme types, I do not believe there will be any trouble after practice in estimating the degree of Apollonian quality possessed by any subject. All Apollonians have health difficulties peculiar to them. The type is naturally a healthy one and to this fact may be attributed much of their success. They are entirely wanting in that most baneful influence, biliousness, so none of its irritating, depressing effect is present. This shows on health, temper, and character, for the Apollonian, free from bile, is usually healthy, happy, and good, and even on his worst side not a criminal. He does not over-eat and his stomach is healthy, but his heart is often irregular in its movement. Heart trouble is the principal health defect of the type. When examining an Apollonian for health, look for blue nails, the heart-disease nail, look at the Heart-line for islands, dots, cross bars, cuts in the line, chains, stars, or anything that is a defect of the line, and then at the Life line for some sign of delicacy there. Look for a grille on the Mount, and if found *with* any of the above indications, it will tell you that it is a *health defect* of the type and not a check to his prosperity. Look for cross-bars cutting the Mount; these are worse than a grille. By this method you can locate heart trouble, the leading health difficulty of the type. The Apollonian is subject to weak eyes. If you find a health defect in your subject, see if a small dot or small island is found on the Head line under the Mount. This will locate the trouble in the eyes. He is also liable to sunstroke and should avoid danger from this source. Fevers are also likely but they are acute attacks, and, unless the Life line shows great disturbance and other indications are found, you will have trouble in locating them. This matter will be fully treated later as it does not properly belong here. It is essential to know the health defects of the type, as necessity to use them will frequently arise.

Note carefully the apex of the Mount, see if it is directly in the centre or whether it leans to one or the other Mounts. If Apollo leans toward Saturn it will *give off* some of its brightness and gayety to the melancholy Mount. Thus Saturn will be less sombre, sad, and severe. If Saturn leans toward Apollo it will make Apollo more grave, serious, and less spontaneous. If Apollo leans towards Mercury it will tinge that Mount with the love of beauty and the artistic sense and brilliancy of Apollo. If Mercury leans toward Apollo it will make Apollo partake of the business shrewdness and scientific qualities of Mercury. By understanding each Mount thoroughly and remembering that when one Mount leans toward another, it *gives off* some of its force to the Mount toward which it leans, you can reason out all displacements of the Mounts. This is a great advantage gained by thoroughly understanding the Mount types.

Having now a thorough understanding of the Apollonian type, we will apply to him the qualities which underlie his character and find out what they will do for him. Texture of the skin will tell us whether the subject is refined or coarse. Here, as everywhere else, we do not find the type exclusively in any one station or grade in life. Common as well as refined people have Apollonian qualities. Texture will help to locate the grade. If fine, the mental world (first phalanx) is probably predominant, and the love of refined beauty and art the result. Coarse texture will make the tastes coarse, and with it we expect the lower world to rule, (third phalanx). In this case a love of loud colors and display will be present. The medium texture will follow the middle world (second phalanx) and the business side will be strong. Consistency will show whether energy or laziness is to make or mar the success of the subject. The flabby hand will produce the hyper-refined idler, full of beautiful visions, with the most luxurious and fastidious tastes, but too lazy to do any work to gratify them. In this case someone else will be the support, as no more impractical subjects exist than the flabby-handed Apollonians. They are attractive, however, and have many friends for they do not have energy enough to make enemies. Soft hands are better, for these show the subject will put forth some effort. These subjects are as artistic and refined as the flabby hands, but will do something occasionally, and can cultivate energy if they wish to. The elastic consistency belongs to the Apollonian who makes money out of his brilliancy. If he is an artist he produces something marketable and has the faculty of finding a buyer. If he is an actor he finds a good salary in return for his talents. As a writer he gets pay for his efforts. He is successful in business for he brings intelligent energy to bear on these pursuits and turns his brilliancy to account. The hard hand belongs to a coarse Apollonian, who talks much and lacks the refinement belonging to the higher development of the type. Flexibility will show elasticity added to an already brilliant mind. If the flexibility is great and the Apollonian type strongly marked, it will show the most versatile, brilliant person imaginable. Too much so in fact, for he will fly to extremes and will constantly shoot over the heads of the inhabitants of earth. Every impression and emotion find quick expression with him, and he enjoys and suffers much, so delicately is he organized. This is the brilliant artist who works by fits and starts producing only a few things in a lifetime but each of them a gem. This subject is very extravagant. The medium flexibility will be best for the subject, for no additional mental elasticity is needed by a pure Apollonian. This will make a subject well balanced, even tempered, and self contained; one who will not easily fly off at a tangent, and in both the worlds of art and business, he will, by being more conservative, be more successful. The stiff hand will show that the stiff-brain qualities have taken away some of the versatility of the subject. He will be less likely to scatter his energies, and more inclined to confine himself to a definite occupation. He will be less brilliant, as the typical Apollonian qualities are much reduced.

Pink or red color we expect to find in the Apollonian for the healthy type must have one of the healthy colors. Pink will lend vivacity and cheer to the already happy subject, and is the color *par excellence*. Red will show strong, healthy blood supply, but it should not be too pronounced for heart trouble is a difficulty of the type. If found, look at nails and Heart line to see how much pressure the heart is sustaining. White color is not expected, for Apollonians are not cold, if present it will pull down the attractiveness and health of the subject, showing a weak heart, and this is dangerous, for it is the health defect of the type. Here again look well to nails and Heart line. With white color, there will be no such success as belongs to the natural type, and when found, it will tell of the probable spoiling of the best qualities of the subject. Yellow color is rare with the pure type of Apollonian. Saturnian or Mercurian types may be found to be secondary, in which case yellow color may be present, but it is not expected with the Apollonian type, and is a great defect when found. It will, to a large degree, spoil the subject and make his success harder to accomplish and much less certain. One source of beauty in this type is his freedom from excess of bile, but when he has this, he is no better than other types which have it. If yellow color is found, examine carefully to see if it is merely temporary, if not, give yellow color qualities to the subject in whatever degree of pronouncedness you find it. Blue color will be seen if heart difficulty is present. It will be seen in temporary blue blotches in the hand, or, if severe, in the coloring of the whole palm. The nails will also have the deep blue settled at their bases which will tell of serious heart trouble. This is augmented if the heart-disease nail is found. Be careful what you say to this subject, so as not to alarm him, for that would be dangerous It is well to look carefully to the Heart line, and note whether an island or dot appears on it under the Mount of Apollo. If so, this case is very serious. The Life line should then be examined to judge to what extent the difficulty has undermined the constitution, or is likely to. The nails will tell by their size, whether the general health is strong or delicate. This will have much to do in estimating the subject. The color under the nail will show whether pink health, white coldness, yellow biliousness, red ardor, or blue heart trouble is present. The latter is most important with this type. Pink nails are what we expect; others are abnormal and when found give their quality to the subject.

The texture of nail will show whether nervous trouble is present. This is sometimes produced by the manner in which the subject takes chances and rushes into speculation. Through all the nervous formations it can be judged what degree of trouble is present. Bulbous nails add tubercular trouble, either of lungs or spine. Short, critical nails will give argumentative force to a person already fond of talking, and he will push his view with vigor. Heart-disease nails will show structural defect in the Apollonian's weak spot. A finely textured, pink-colored, smooth, open nail is what we expect to find, which will tell of brightness, spontaneity, and honesty. Hair on the hands tells of the vigor of the constitution. Blond hair is expected and must be distinguished from yellow or silver color; and to be the typical Apollonian blond must be of a brilliant golden hue. There is more fire and snap to this hair, which approaches black than when it is a dull, straw color. Black hair makes the subject quicker and more vivacious, adding to the sparkle of an already sparkling character. It also lends to the subject a dash of the fire belonging to black color, and makes him unusually sharp and keen. The more hair found on the hand the more vitality the subject has.

The hand as a whole, will tell in which world the subject moves. If the fingers predominate in length over the palm, then mind will rule, and either in literature, art, poetry, drawing, architecture, or kindred subjects will he find his proper vocation. If the middle world is best developed he will be the man for business. He will organize syndicates, indulge in large speculations, head great companies, and be a brilliant figure in the commercial world. If the lower third of the hand be strongest he will be ruled by baser instincts, commoner in his tastes, and fond of show. This is especially marked if the third phalanx of the finger of Apollo is thick. Note carefully if the three worlds are in balance or if one is deficient. Whatever the combination, reason out the result by noting which worlds are present, which absent, and combining the attributes of those found.

The fingers must be closely studied. If the fingers of Apollo and Jupiter are of the same length, then we have a balance between ambition and brilliancy which will produce good results. If Apollo is longer than Jupiter, then artistic or business tastes will be in the ascendancy. If Apollo is as long as Saturn, or nearly so, the subject will take great chances in everything,—will risk life, money, reputation, in carrying out his enterprises. He is the plunger, speculator, or gambler. If Apollo is longer than Saturn, he will be the foolhardy gambler, unable to restrain his propensities. If the finger is bent laterally it will add shrewdness to his character, and with the finger extremely long and crooked also, will show the tricky gambler. If the first phalanx is flexible, bending back easily, it will show flexibility in the mental qualities of the type. If the first phalanx is longest, it will show that artistic mental qualities are the strongest, and here is the place you must separate the artistic from the business side of the subject. The first phalanx longest indicates the artist, the writer, the poet, and the subject who will be given to these pursuits. With the second phalanx longest the business side prevails. When the third phalanx is longest, the subject is not destined for art; he will be fond of display and will have common tastes and love flashy colors. If the first and second phalanges are equal in length, then the artistic talents can be made to yield money, as the business and artistic worlds are combined. If the business world is short, the Apollonian may achieve a reputation, but will make little money. If the second and third phalanges are equally long, and the first short, there will only be a desire for money-making, and no artistic quality. This subject will wear flashy clothing and incline to be "shoddy." In judging the phalanges, see which is shortest, and which has gained length at its expense. Estimate what has been taken out of the subject, and what has been furnished in increased supply.

The finger tips will add their qualities to the finger and the character. Conic tips will make the subject more artistic and, with the first phalanx longest, add to its qualities the artistic conic qualities. Square tips make them practical and regular in habits, spatulate tips very active and original. With a long first phalanx the square tip will almost equal the presence of a long second phalanx. With the second phalanx longest and conic tip, the subject will add the artistic qualities of the conic tip to the business side of his nature. He will dress well, keep his place of business attractive, and wherever he goes will have artistic things around him. He will be fond of pleasure, and may not keep down to business as closely as he might. If the tip be square it will add common-sense, practical ideas, to an already good business person, and there will be every chance of success. With a spatulate tip he will be very original and make a natural entertainer. All his Apollonian qualities of pleasure-giving have originality and activity added to them, producing a clever after-dinner speaker and a mimic. Pointed tips idealize everything and make him visionary and impractical. When the third phalanx is longest, with conic finger tips, he will be fond of color and form, but with no taste for higher art. With square tips he will desire to be rich, and when so will make a show of his wealth. With spatulate tips he will be fond of games, and will be skilful in them and full of dash.

Knotty fingers will check some of his enthusiasm and spontaneity, and are not common to the type. He is not given to analyzing, his mental processes are quicker and more intuitive. Knotty fingers are really a defect, for they make him operate in a manner which is not best for him. Smooth fingers are his natural kind, for artistic feeling, impulsive ways, and great intuition are the main sources of the Apollonian strength. Note the phalanges and see if knotty or smooth-finger qualities are to rule in the world best developed. Long fingers show that minutiæ and detail will be strong with the subject. If he is an artist, he will give every detail of the scene he is painting. If a portrait painter, he will reproduce every button, every hair, and every eyelash. If a sculptor, nothing will escape him. If an author, he will describe minutely every character and incident. In business he will be accurate, but more careful than usual for the type; will be a good accountant and office man. Short fingers will make him quick as a flash. He will have added to his already intuitive nature the short-fingered quickness of thought and action, and it will be surprising how quickly he makes a decision. His first impressions are his best. He is in danger of "plunging," however, especially if the Apollo finger be nearly the length of Saturn. The short-fingered Apollonian is always a strong factor in speculation or at the gaming table. The thumb will tell whether strong determination is present to bring out the best side of the type. A large thumb will strengthen the character, and the subject will be more of a "doer" than he would be with a short thumb. The small thumb takes away much of the practical, and leaves the artistic in full sway, but without the will-power necessary to develop it. The short-thumbed Apollonians are geniuses, but never accomplish much. The length of the will phalanx shows the strength of this element, and its shape tells whether the will is coarse, refined, tactful, nervous, or brutal. The second phalanx will show whether good reasoning powers are present, and, by its length, whether there is a balance with the will phalanx greater strength or deficiency. You will thus know whether the subject is ruled by will or reason. A strong second phalanx of the thumb will be a fine addition to any Apollonian, as it adds to his character caution and prudence, which he often sadly needs. A good, clear Head line is necessary to achieve the best results, adding self-control, judgment, and a clear brain.

There are many people who have much Apollonian quality in them, but pure specimens of the type are rare. The Apollonian leaven that is mixed with humanity does much to brighten life, and is a constant benefit, not only to the subjects themselves, but to all around them who share in and enjoy their cheerful moods and charming manners.

CHAPTER XXII

THE MOUNT OF MERCURY

THE fourth Mount type is the Mercurian, who is identified by the Mount and Finger of Mercury. He is always pronounced in his characteristics, and has great power as an orator, a scientist, a physician, or a lawyer, and is also very successful in business. The first aim, with every subject of this type, should be to discover which of his several phases is strongest, and whether the good or bad side is dominant, for of all the types, none gives way to dishonesty with more ease than the Mercurian. On its good side, it is one of the best and most successful of all of the types, but no greater liars, swindlers, or cheats can be found than bad Mercurians. For this reason the fourth type requires careful consideration, for in this type are combined more different elements than in any of the others. The Mercurian is generally successful, primarily because of his shrewdness and the fact that he is a wonderful judge of human nature, and secondarily on account of skill with his hands and his tireless energy. In the professions of law and medicine he is in his element, since, in the former especially, natural shrewdness and facility of expression help him greatly. The Mercurians are fine writers and shrewd business men, achieving the greatest success in both lines.

As single signs, or in combination, the star, triangle, circle, single vertical line, trident or square strengthen a Mount of Mercury. The cross-bar, grille, cross, island or dot, show defects of the Mount, either of health or character, nails, color, etc., will determine which (105).

When the Mount of Mercury is well developed, finger long

and large, and apex of the Mount centrally located, you have a Mercurian subject (106).

In stature the Mercurian is small, averaging about five feet six inches, compactly built, trim in appearance, tidy looking and with a strong, forceful expression of countenance. His

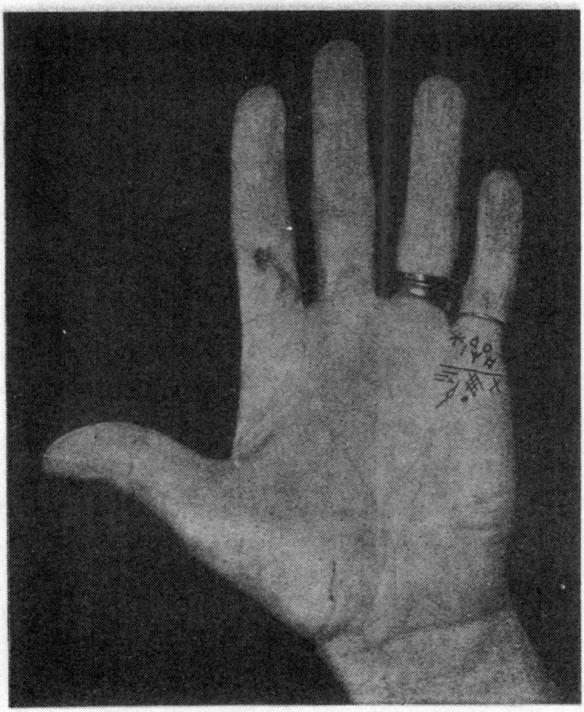

NO. 105. DISTINGUISHING MARKS ON THE MOUNT OF MERCURY

face is oval in shape, features inclined to be regular, and the expression changes rapidly, showing the quick play of his mind. The skin is smooth, fine, and transparent, tending to be olive in color, and shows the passing of the blood current underneath, by easily turning alternately red or white when excited, embarrassed, or in fear. The forehead is high and bulging, the hair is chestnut or black and inclined to be curly on the ends. The Mercurian grows a beard easily, which covers the face well, and is generally a little darker than the hair, if it be any color other than black. He likes to wear his beard trimmed closely and running to a point on the chin, Vandyke fashion. The eye-

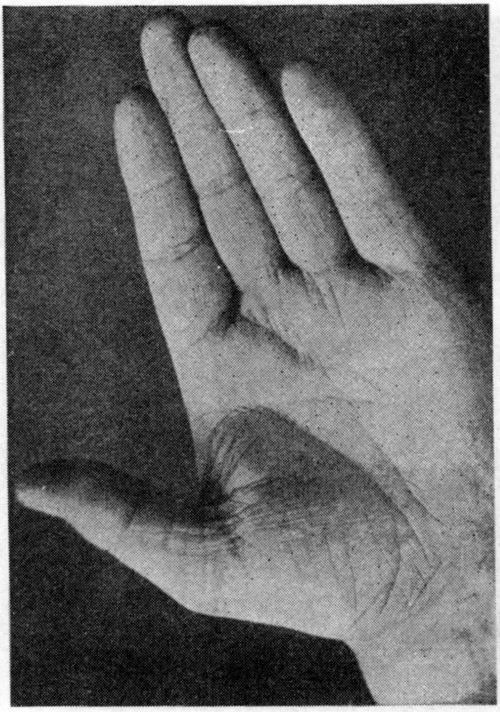

NO. 106. MERCURIAN MOUNT AND FINGER

brows are not thick but are regular in outline, running to fine points at the ends, and sometimes meeting over the nose. The latter growth is rare, however, belonging more distinctively to the Saturnian. The eyes are dark or quite black, restless and sharp in expression. They look right at and seemingly through you, and sometimes produce the disagreeable but correct conviction that you are being estimated by one well able to do it. The nose is thin and straight, somewhat fleshy on the end ; the lips are thin, evenly set and often a trifle pale or bluish in color. The whites of the eye frequently have a trace of yellow, as the Mercurian is of a nervous and slightly bilious type. His nervousness makes him breathe quickly and often through his mouth. The chin is long and sharp, sometimes turning up slightly at the end, completing the oval contour of his face. The neck is strong and muscular, connecting the head with shapely shoulders, lithe and sinewy and graceful in outline. The chest is large for the stature, well muscled and containing big lungs. The voice of the Mercurian is not full and loud, nor weak and thin, but is of medium timbre and possesses good "carrying" quality. The limbs are graceful, giving him agility and the quickness of movement for which he is noted, as well as a power of endurance coming from muscular strength. His teeth are white, small in size, and set evenly in the gums which are medium pink in color. Altogether the Mercurian impresses you as well knit, agile, and strong, not always beautiful, but shapely and well proportioned.

The Mercurian is the quickest and most active of all the types, and this activity is not confined to his physical agility but applies to the mental as well. He is like a flash in his intuitive faculty, and enjoys everything which puts his quickness to either a mental or physical test. He is the personification of grace in his movements and is skilful in everything he undertakes. In all games he is proficient, and he plays with his head as well as his hands, winning because he plans his plays, and shrewdly estimates the ability of his opponent. In all athletic sports where dexterity and skill, rather than brute strength are needed, he is the victor. In argument he is at home, for no one has greater facility of expression than he. This, added to the quickness with which he can grasp and turn an opportunity to his account, brings him out ahead, if his side of the question has even a semblance of probability. He is especially fond of oratory, and eloquence in any line strongly moves him. With his keenness and the power of expressing himself well, he is very tactful and adroit, thus making many friends by saying the right thing at the right time. As an after-dinner speaker he is a success, and in a battle of words or badinage is an opponent hard to overcome.

One of the chief elements of the Mercurian's success, is his ability to judge human nature and character. He mentally estimates everyone whom he meets, and uses his quick mind and tactful way to make a friend and accomplish what he wishes. He is adroit, crafty, and a constant schemer, using all his powers of shrewdness, intuition, and oratory to get himself through the world. He is a dangerous person, you say. Verily he is, for not one of all the other types is for a moment his equal in diplomacy, craftiness, tact, persuasiveness shrewdness, or adroit methods of approach. This power makes him influential and if he is bad, much to be feared. He is a clever manager and well knows how to keep in the background and push forward some puppet to do his bidding. His power over men comes largely from the shrewdness with which he lays his plans, and the clever way in which he gets someone else to carry them out if necessary. He understands humanity thoroughly, and uses this knowledge to his own advantage. He is not lazy ; one of his prime elements is industry, consequently he loses no opportunities through napping but turns every hour to account.

He has a love for study, especially along lines of scientific investigation. He is a born mathematician, and no problem is so intricate that he cannot solve it. He is, of all the types, the most successful as a physician, and in my observation of the medical profession, the men who have succeeded in attaining fame, and with it a lucrative practice, are Mercurian in their leading type, with the Jupiterian type second. The reverse is also a good combination, provided the Mercurian qualities are very strong. Numerous small vertical lines on the Mount of Mercury, with the Mercury finger longer than normal, or with the second phalanx long, will be a strong indication of talent for medical studies. This marking is to be found on the hands of prominent and successful doctors—It is called the "Medical Stigmata" (107). On the hand of a woman it shows great ability as a nurse. Energy, studiousness, scientific aptitude, combined with keenness in judging human nature, make the Mercurian an excellent diagnostician and practitioner. He is also talented as an occult scientist, being able, with his shrewdness and keenness of perception, to master all the intricacies of the intangible sciences. Thus the Mercurian is well adapted to these occult studies, but, as he is fond of money-making, and

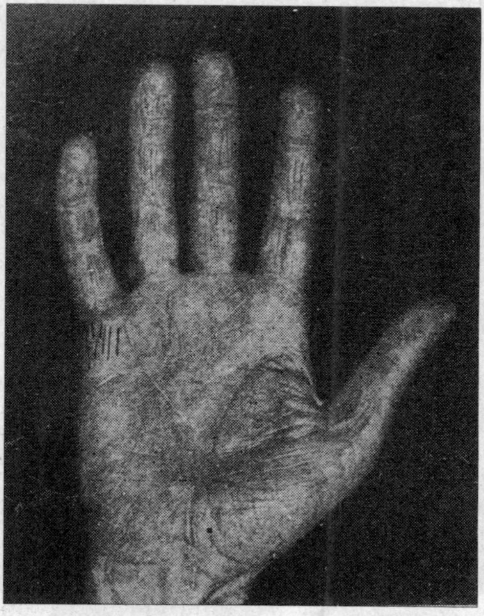

NO. 107. MERCURIAN DOCTORS' HAND

bad Mercurians are conscienceless, we find the humbug clairvoyants and fortune-tellers all belonging to this type. Having met a number of alleged palmists who claim to tell your name from the hand, and the names of friends, I have found them all specimens of the bad Mercurian type, and they have often admitted to me that they knew little about Palmistry, but resorted to sleight-of-hand tricks, together with their ability to judge human nature, in order to fool the public and get money from them. These bad Mercurians, *and the superficial knowledge of amateur palmists* are responsible for the disfavor which in the minds of some people rests to-day on Palmistry.

The Mercurian is a lover of that which is near to nature,

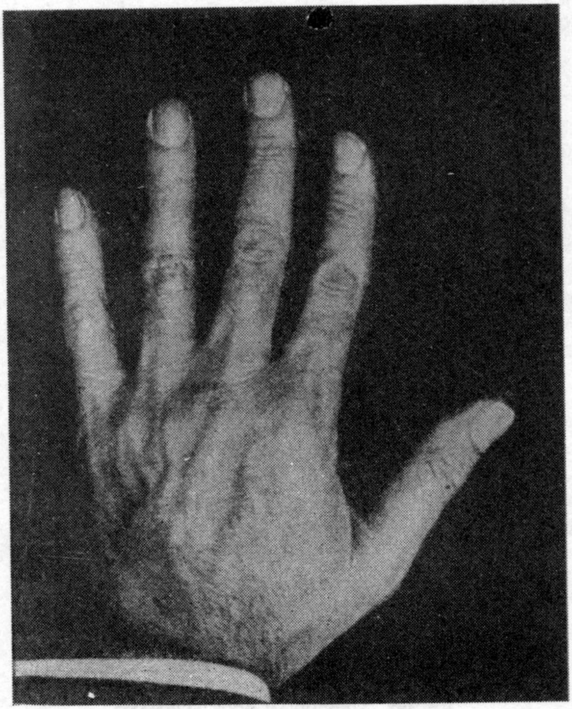

NO. 108. MERCURIAN BUSINESS MAN

consequently he admires horses, dogs, pictures of real life, natural scenery, or portraits. He is fond of reading, but it is not romance that attracts him so much as books which are true to life, nature, and humanity. Dickens and, as a latter-day author, Kipling, are favorites with Mercurians.

Of all the types none is stronger in the business world than the Mercurian (108). He has shrewdness, diplomacy, tact, management, influence over people, judgment of human nature, energy, and power of expressing himself, all of which are the very strongest elements one could have for a successful business career. No better illustration of the success of the Mercurian in the business world can be given than to point to the standing of the Hebrew race in mercantile circles to-day, and to state that a very large percentage of this people are Mercurians. They are ingenious in their ways of planning new schemes to make money, and original in their manner of putting them into operation. Mercurians are great imitators, and so clever that they can steal some other man's idea and pass it as their own. They make good actors and their powers of mimicry and study of nature enable them to create on the stage lifelike and realistic characters. They make excellent lawyers, having the keenness, the faculty of seeing a question from its many sides, as well as a knowledge of the failings of humanity. To this add oratory, and it completes an excellent combination for a lawyer. They are excellent teachers, for their grasp of scientific knowledge, backed by an ability to say what they mean gives them a mastery in this field, and being judges of human nature, they know how best to reach each and every pupil.

The Mercurian, on his good side, is not vicious and criminal, he is only shrewd and keen. He is even tempered, loves children dearly, is devoted to his family and makes a constant friend. He is not in any degree a sensualist. His pleasures are largely mental and, while he is fond of beauty and women, he is not an amorous type. He is nervous and restless, his mind is active and he likes to travel, for changing scenery gives him the recreation and diversity that he needs. He is fond of nature, which appeals to him more strongly than anything artificial.

In the marriage relation the Mercurian is a match-maker. He enjoys the society of his fellows, marries early in life, chooses one of his own age, and very often one of his type. He loves trim, neat, stylish women, full of fire and life, and no type furnishes these elements so well as his own. He is proud of his wife, likes to see her well dressed, and makes a good husband, provided he represents the good side of the type.

In health the Mercurian is nervous; his quickness and energy speak in unmistakable terms of the electric current which is coursing through his nervous system, stimulating it to great activity. This nervous energy prevents his being lazy, makes him love to travel, and this energy sometimes becomes excessive, so that you will find many Mercurian hands with fluted nails more or less pronounced in development. Be on the lookout with this type for nervous trouble, which interferes with his liver so that he becomes bilious. His liver trouble differs from that of the Saturnian, for it disappears when the nervous trouble is relieved, as it is not structural difficulty as with the Saturnian. His olive complexion shows a tinge of bile; and stomach trouble, dyspepsia, and kindred disorders are often met. His activity tends to drive away these difficulties, and his system quickly responds to treatment for them. If he has paralytic trouble it most often attacks his arms and upper extremities. It is often helpful to note the Line of Mercury with this type, for by its wavy or broken course it shows the extent of bilious and stomach trouble. The Mercurian is a healthy type, so we do not look first for *illness* with them, but for peculiar mental characteristics. They have their disorders, however, so be always on your guard that you do not overlook them.

I wish it were possible to say that all Mercurians were good, but unfortunately this cannot be done. This second bilious type (Saturn being the first) produces members of the criminal fraternity which will be found in many penitentiaries and penal institutions, condemned for all manner of crimes. It also produces a class who have not yet reached the prisons, but who deserve to, even more than many of those who have been convicted. There is very often an almost imperceptible line which marks the place where shrewdness in business ends and actual dishonesty begins, and the Mercurian seems ever near the line. His natural shrewdness makes it easy for him to outwit his fellowmen, and the temptation for him to do so is great, often so great that he cannot resist it. The invisible line once crossed and the conscience being quieted, a second slip is easily made. Thus inch by inch even a good Mercurian often degenerates from a sharp business man to a criminal, a liar, and a thief (109). When this class is engaged in bond speculations, or stock-jobbing enterprises, they are not often

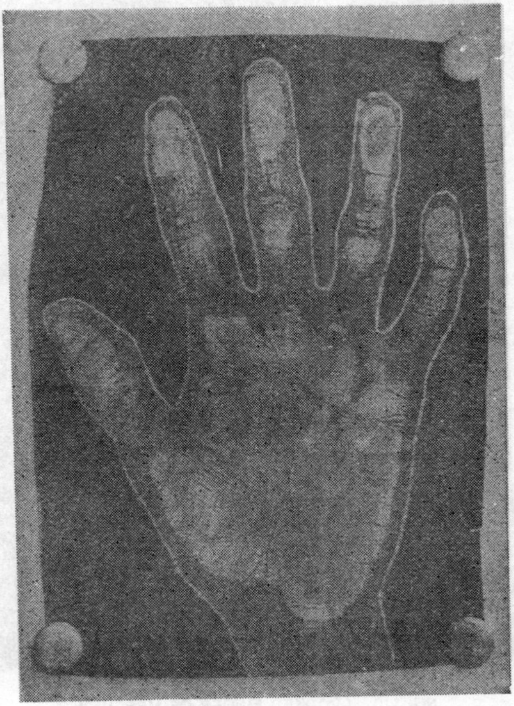

NO. 109. MERCURIAN THIEF

made to pay for their knavery by imprisonment; for they are keen enough always to have a loophole ready through which to crawl. When they are merchants, they simply cheat their customers with ease and facility, and talk so glibly that the customer does not realize it. These high-toned thieves have fine hands, but crooked fingers of Mercury, grilled Mount, or bars on the Mount, cold Head lines, narrow quadrangles, and will often hide the hands from view, or will rub them in the Uriah Heep fashion. When a crooked finger of Mercury is seen on any hand (110) the thought of *unusual shrewdness* should at once come to the mind, and you

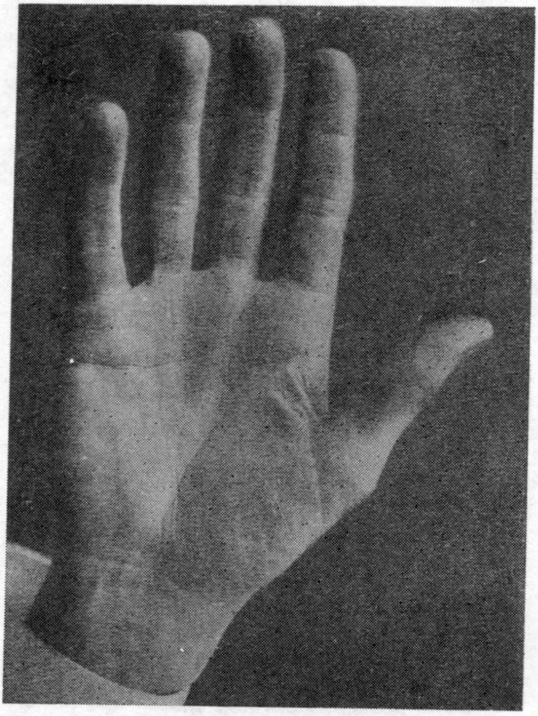

NO. 110. CROOKED FINGER OF MERCURY

should be on your guard and search for everything that will tell whether actual dishonesty exists or not. Having located a Mercurian subject, and finding a crooked finger of Mercury, be on your guard to investigate at once for actual dishonesty. This applies to whatever station in life your subject may occupy. If his position be high, you know that the temptation to overstep the line of honesty has often been great even though it has been resisted. With this crooked finger *and other bad signs*, feel sure that he will not resist very stubbornly.

The criminal type of Mercurians are quick, sharp fellows, small in stature with dark complexion, shifting, restless eyes that either cannot face you squarely, or else look at you with a forced, brazen stare. The hair is straight and stiff, seeming to lack vitality. They are vile and criminal wretches. Gypsies are Mercurians, and usually of the dishonest class who stop at nothing. These bad types have crooked, warped fingers, twisted and bent inward, crooked, claw-like nails, grilled Mount, twisted finger of Mercury, bad or absent Heart line, cold Head line, narrow quadrangle, high, stiff thumb, and often the first knot of the Mercury finger developed. These are the bank robbers, pickpockets (see 109), sneak thieves, confidence sharps, and dishonest gamblers, who run to all kinds of crime and are criminals pure and simple. These people are intensely superstitious.

Thus you will see the great diversity of the Mercurian type,—how good or how intensely evil he may be. The first thing to do on finding a Mercurian subject is to decide to which class or grade he belongs, and what underlying forces he has. Then apply this knowledge to the side of type present, whether it be the oratorical, the scientific, the professional, business, or the criminal.

With this type note especially the pose of the hands ; if he hides them, deceitfulness is indicated. The texture of the skin tells of refinement or coarseness. If you see bad signs do not be misled by a fine texture of skin, for you must remember that there are villains who wear fine clothing as well as rags. It will tell that, if villainy be present, it will be consummate in its skill, and so keen and fine in operation that a subject can go for a lifetime and never be found out. If it is the scientist, the lawyer, the physician, or the business man that is before you, fine texture of skin will tell of a refined nature that will operate in its special vocation with refinement back of it. Coarse-textured skin tells that coarseness will operate, and no such perfection is possible as with fine texture. Expect coarse-textured skin in low criminals.

The consistency of the hand will show the amount of energy, whether laziness and inertia or elastic vigor and intelligence are present. Flabby hands will ruin all hope of brilliant attainments, and fortunately these are not often found. Soft hands will indicate that there is something abnormal about your subject, for energy is a leading characteristic of the Mercurian type. To find any degree of laziness is unusual, and must be given full weight, as it will ruin the chances of success, whether the subject be lawyer, doctor, scientist, business man, or thief. Elastic consistency shows the normal condition and that the qualities of the subject will be highly developed in whatever direction they may lead him. Hard hands will show a tendency toward coarsening the type, and the keenness natural to it will be lessened, as the brain back of the hard hand does not work so rapidly.

Flexibility of the hands must be noted, for it shows an additional elasticity of the mind which makes these people brilliant subjects. Flexibility will make the doctor keener in his power of diagnosis, more ready to keep up with new remedies, and gives the intuitive faculty which aids so powerfully in estimating his patient. Flexible hands on a lawyer make him unusually shrewd, brilliant, and able to devise many avenues of escape for his clients; and to discover loopholes that a hard-handed lawyer could not see. The flexible hand on a business man makes him brilliant and keen, but likely to be an extremist and extravagant in conducting his business. The stiff hand will take away much of the dash and brilliancy of the type, and is not often found on the best developed specimens. Old-fashioned ways and notions and stingy habits are present when you find the stiff hand.

The color of the hands will tell much about health and temperament. White is not often seen, for the Mercurian is not by nature cold. When whiteness is found, coldness added to his keenness and shrewd tendencies makes him very likely to be bad and cold hearted whatever his business. Pink color gives health, warmth, and vigor, which added to his keenness makes him a brilliant person. Red color when present will add its pushing qualities to his already quick nature, making him a great worker and a strong force in the community. Yellow color is often seen, for the Mercurian inclines to be bilious. When found it will show a spoiled temper and that the subject will more easily become bad and dishonest, his stomach will likely be out of order, and he will be at cross purposes with his fellows.

The nails must be examined, for if fluted they show that the nervousness which belongs to the type is making rapid headway. If brittle and bending back, the subject must be warned to use his vital energy sparingly. Blue nails will tell of defective circulation, and yellow that the irritating bile is poisoning his blood. Pink nails will tell of a sharp and healthy subject who is a match for most men, and who acts with great quickness and shrewdness. Short nails will show a critical turn of mind, and in argument or debate no point will be overlooked by this subject in his effort to advance his side of the case. Broad nails will show a strong constitution, narrow nails delicacy, the medium being most often found.

Hair on the hands will tell of the iron in his constitution. Black hair is most often to be seen, and is plentifully found on the hands of many Mercurians. It tells of the fire and vigor of health and the strong tendencies of the type. With black hair there is the suspicion that these subjects have the keenness of the type in full measure, and the crooked finger is often seen. Light hair is not so often met with on this type, though sometimes seen. When found it makes them more phlegmatic and less volatile than with the black. Red hair gives added electric force to the already great quickness, and would lead to excess. Chestnut hair, which is a medium color, is often found, and tells of an evenly distributed set of Mercurian qualities.

The hand as a whole will tell in which world the subject is strongest, and with this type you nearly always find the middle or business world fully developed, for he is always a good money-getter whether he be orator, doctor, lawyer, or business man. Note carefully if the apex of the Mount lies in the centre or is displaced. If it is at the outside of the hand, toward the percussion, the subject will employ his aptitudes for his own advantage and be selfishly inclined. If the apex lies in the centre of the Mount you

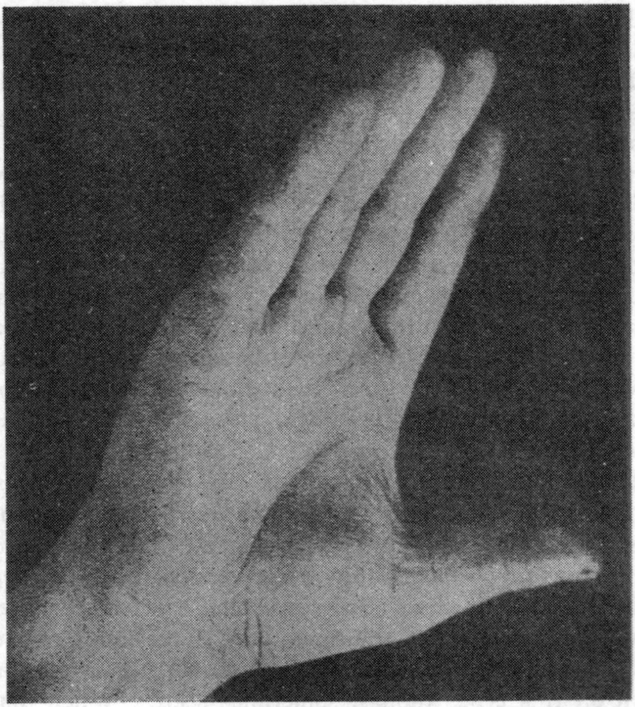

NO. 111. LONG FINGER OF MERCURY

have the normal development, and the subject will have true Mercurian ideas in whatever sphere in life he is placed. If the Mount leans toward Apollo, the love of art and beauty will be great, and he will give up part of his Mercurian qualities in order to enjoy them. His life will be less dominated by the shrewdness of the type, and more given over to the Apollonian instincts. If the apex is in the centre and the apices of the other Mounts are pulled toward Mercury, you will have a very strong Mercurian, a "dyed in the wool" kind, who will be typical in whatever he does.

The finger must be carefully noted. First, is it longer than the first knot of the finger of Apollo (111)? If so, the subject is strongly Mercurian; shorter than this is deficiency,

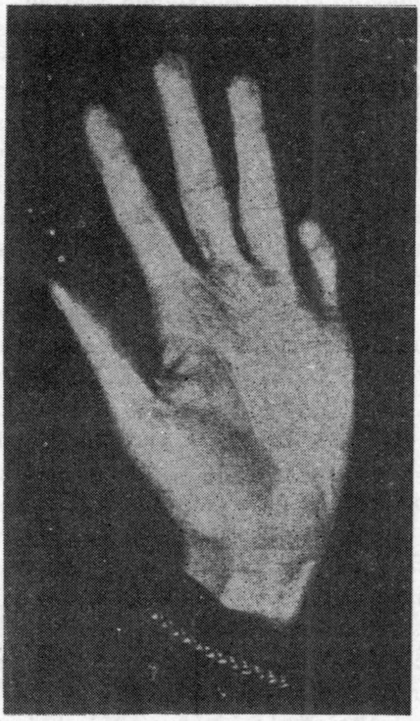

NO. 112. DEFICIENT MOUNT AND FINGER OF MERCURY

in whatever degree the Mount and finger is lacking (112); if it should be crooked in addition to being long, the type becomes more pronounced, and you must look to grilles, Head line, Heart line, and quadrangle, and see if dishonesty has taken hold of the subject. If the finger is long, note which phalanx is the longest, for the three worlds are most marked in the Mercurian finger. If the first phalanx is very long the subject will have great powers of expression, amounting even to eloquence and oratorical ability. This will enable him to give expression to his ideas in writing, and thus it becomes a fine indication for a public speaker or writer. If the second phalanx is long it shows that the scientific side is strong, and he will make a good doctor, lawyer, or scientist. If the third phalanx is long the commercial side is prominent, and he will be an excellent merchant or business man in any capacity. In judging the field of labor in which the subject will best succeed, these phalanges must be your guide.

Note which world of the *secondary* type is strongest, as this shows the backing the Mercurian aptitudes will have. If the finger of Mercury is long, it may be found that two phalanges will be long and one short. This will show which worlds are strongest and which are deficient. As the Mercurian is a complex type, it will be only by this careful estimate of the finger that you can properly estimate your subject.

The tips must be carefully noted. If the first phalanx of the Mercury finger be long, ability as a speaker is shown. If the tip be pointed, he will be able to draw on his imagination, will indulge flights of fancy, and charm by his oratorical idealism. If the tip be conic he will be artistic and eloquent, with plenty of word painting and mental pictures. If the tip be square he will talk on practical subjects ; common sense and reason, facts and figures will be the forces he employs, and logic is his talisman, especially if the second phalanx of the thumb bears this out. If the tip be spatulate he will be the magnetic speaker whose fiery oratory moves the masses with its vigor, originality, and strength, and he fairly carries his audience off their feet. If the second phalanx be longest and the tip pointed, the idealism of this tip will permeate his scientific researches. If with the long second phalanx the tip be square, common sense and practical ideas will rule him, and if spatulate he will be active in his search for fresh discoveries in old sciences, and not satisfied to follow in the ruts made by others. If the third phalanx be longest and the tip conic or pointed, the idealism and love of the artistic belonging to this tip will be linked with Mercurian business ability. If the tip be square, then common sense and practical ideas alone will operate, and the subject will be a true Mercurian business man who makes every dollar tell in his expense account, and who does not brook any foolishness in business matters If the tip be spatulate, then great activity and energy will cause him to push business ventures without tiring, and the spatulate originality will enable him to devise new ways for making money. This is a very strong combination.

Knotty fingers will show that analysis and reason are strong in the subject. If the first knot alone be developed, it will show order and system in his ideas. If the second alone be developed, he will be neat in personal appearance and in everything about him. With both knots he will have the analysis of the philosopher added to the Mercurian quickness and shrewdness. If this subject be an orator he will write his speeches and commit them; if he be a lawyer he reasons out every case for his client. If a doctor he does not diagnose by intuition but by reasoning from cause to effect and *per contra*. If a business man he does everything by a system, and after careful thought.

Smooth fingers will add impulse and intuition to an already very quick subject, and with his ability to read human nature he is unusually keen and intuitive. His estimates of those he meets are seldom wrong, and he should always trust to first impressions. He loves beauty and is artistic in all of his ideas. The tips must be considered with all these fingers, adding conic, square, or spatulate qualities to the knotty or smooth, and making the philosophical or impulsive tendencies more or less pronounced according to the degree of development in which they are found.

Long fingers show that the subject will go into the minutiæ of everything. If he be a speaker he will describe every detail of any subject on which he is talking. If he be a lawyer he will hunt every bit of testimony that can bear on his case, and will prepare his petitions and papers with the greatest care ; will have the records in his cases exact, every exception noted so that he can appeal if beaten. If he be a doctor he does not neglect a detail in the treatment of his patients, attends to diet, hygiene, air in the room, and is in everything most careful. As a business man he is constantly going over everything in his place of business. Not a thing escapes him, and no detail is omitted that can add to the result he wishes to accomplish, viz., money-making. He adds the suspicion of long fingers to Mercurian suspicion, and the long-fingered neatness to Mercurian tidiness; thus he is a most pronounced specimen. If he be a talker he is very tiresome.

Short fingers add their quickness and action to a subject already remarkably quick, consequently knots are needed on these fingers to reduce the quickness if it is not to be a positive menace. Impulse, inspiration, intuition, and a train of kindred qualities encompass the short-fingered Mercurian, and he is volatile and spontaneous in the highest degree. The orator relies on the spur of the moment for his material, the lawyer acts by inspiration and shrewdness, the doctor seems to diagnose by intuition, and does not always know why. They are correct in all these estimates, however, for which they must thank the Mercurian type. The short-fingered business man at once makes up his mind as to the credit of a customer, the honesty of an employee, or whether his business cannot be improved by some change in methods. All of these quick ideas which flash into his mind he puts into immediate execution. With short fingers note the tips. Added quickness will be given by conic tips, and reduced, by square or spatulate. The tips will also tell whether conic, square, or spatulate qualities will operate.

The thumb if low set, will tell of advanced mentality, if high set a decrease. By its size, whether head or heart will dominate, and by its shape whether a fine or coarse nature is present. The thumb of the Mercurian has a tendency to be stiff, for he loves money, and while generous to his family and free to spend money for things that he enjoys, he does not do it with a lavish hand. The first phalanx, by its length, tells of the power of will in the subject, whether he will carry out his schemes or merely plan and let them drop. The conic first phalanx will show how impressionable he is, the square or spatulate that he is practical, original, and firm. The clubbed thumb on a Mercurian is a doubly bad indication. The second phalanx of the thumb will tell of the logic and reasoning faculty back of your subject, and whether it is stronger or weaker than the will which should carry it into operation. By its shape it will show whether commonness or refinement is present. This latter formation with a Mercurian is usually expected. In the largest number of cases the thumb will be found with a large first phalanx, square or paddle-shaped, a long second phalanx with a waist-like formation. This combination will tell of strong will and refined reason back of a very shrewd specimen of humanity.

It must now be apparent that the Mercurian is a many-sided fellow, and can be either the best or the worst of all. He is the type to which we look for shrewdness, keenness, diplomacy and skill, energy and success. But this type contains the polished villain, the bank wrecker, the hypocrite, the burglar, or the petty liar and thief. Use great care when you find one, that he may be put into the proper class. He is up to all possible tricks and schemes to fool the unwary, and will tax your skill as fully as any type you may have to handle. Take time in the examination of this type, do not be hurried, bring to bear everything upon him from the texture of his skin to his thumb, and you can accurately classify him, and determine his grade in the class. Some of the most honest men I have ever seen are Mercurians, and the reverse is also true. The low thieves you will easily discover, the polished, hypocritical villain is harder to unmask.

CHAPTER XXIII

THE MOUNT OF MARS

THE fifth Mount type is the Martian, and the portions of the hand which identify him are the two Mounts of Mars, the Upper Mount located on the percussion and above the Line of Head, and the Lower Mount under the Line of Life and above the Mount of Venus. There is also the Plain of Mars, located in the centre of the palm, which bears some relation to the Martian type. For the exact boundaries of these Martian developments consult the map of the Mounts, where they are clearly shown, and note carefully that on the map the lower boundary of Lower Mars is the word "aggression," and all under that word belongs to the Mount of Venus.

As single signs or in combination the star, triangle, circle, single vertical line, trident and square, strengthen the Upper Mount of Mars. The cross-bar, cross, island, dot or grille, show defects of the Mount, either of health or character. Nails, color, etc. will determine which.

All cross lines, stars, crosses or grilles in the Plain of Mars, increase the inflammability and temper of the subject.

Signs on the Lower Mount of Mars must be read on the Influence lines inside of the Life line (113). In the earlier history of Palmistry the Plain of Mars was considered to be the principal part of the Martian development. The Upper Mount was afterwards located and found to be a strong factor, and in later years the Mount of Venus was subdivided so as to give the upper portion to what is now called the Lower Mount of Mars because it is *below* the Line of Life. Any attempt to use only one of these Martian developments to the exclusion of the other, will lead to error, and it is only by the combined use of the two Mounts and the Plain of Mars that you will be able properly to estimate the Martian, a type constantly encountered in very pure development, and which you will find in combination with most of the other

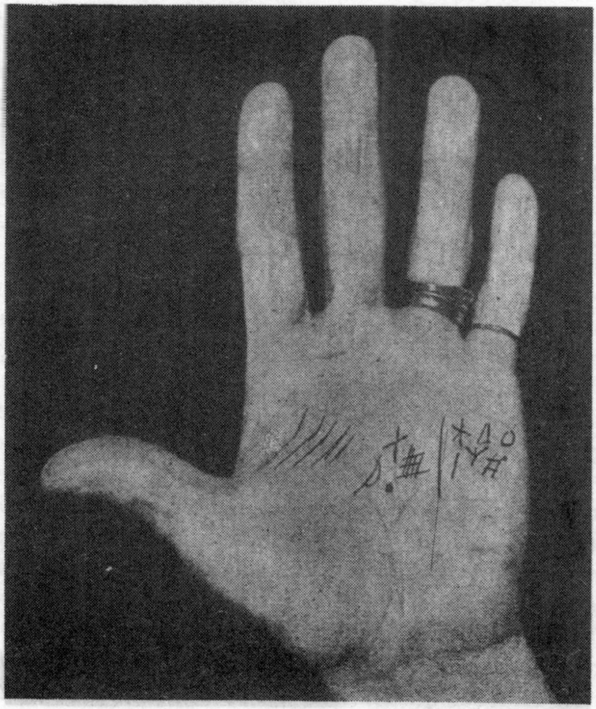

NO. 113. DISTINGUISHING MARKS ON THE MOUNT OF MARS

types. In gaining the material for this chapter I have taken the most pronounced Martians, and alongside of them, subjects who have been entirely deficient in Martian development, and from these pronounced cases, several thousand in number, I have tabulated what I believe to be an accurate and trustworthy system of handling the type. This statement is made here because there has been of late such a diversity of opinion on the subject even among the very best students, that I feel sure all will welcome an elucidation of the Martian question based upon an experience covering many thousand verifications from among the best known Martians in the world. This type embodies the elements of aggression and resistance, and the Martian is consequently a fighter. Do not by any means infer that the Martian always fights with the sword and pistol, or engages in fistic combats, for he is more often found fighting his way against adverse elements and circumstances in the *mental* or *business* world. It must not be understood that all Martians will be soldiers (though all true Martians would quickly enlist to fight for a beloved country), but they will always push with vigor anything with which they may be connected, and will more stoutly resist the efforts of those who seek to force them, than will the other types. Thus wherever they are found, Martians are those who fight, and the Martian disposition is an aggressive one. In almost all hands we find some Martian development. If we fail to find it, the subject is easily discouraged and overcome in the struggle for existence. The Martian qualities of aggression or resistance are necessary to the completion of any character, for without them the subject will be run over and trampled under foot, and no matter how brilliant or talented he may be, without the Martian fighting qualities, his brilliancy will never be brought before the eyes of the world. There are two kinds of fighters: those who are the aggressors and force the issue, and those who act in self-defense or resist the pressure brought to bear upon them. This separation of Martian qualities is shown in the Upper Mount of Mars, which indicates *resistance* (114), and the Lower Mount of Mars, which shows *aggressive* spirit (115). Often you find one of these Mounts largely developed and the other small, in which case the subject will have either great aggression, or great resistance, according as it is the Lower or the Upper Mount which is the larger. Often you find both Mounts very largely developed. In this case you have a large supply of *both* aggression and resistance, and the subject will push himself forward with great persistence, and will also *resist* vigorously the attempt of anyone to impose upon him. These subjects with *both* Mounts large, simply shove themselves over every obstacle and stubbornly resist any attempt to force them down. They never know when they are beaten, and permit no one to think that defeat is a possibility

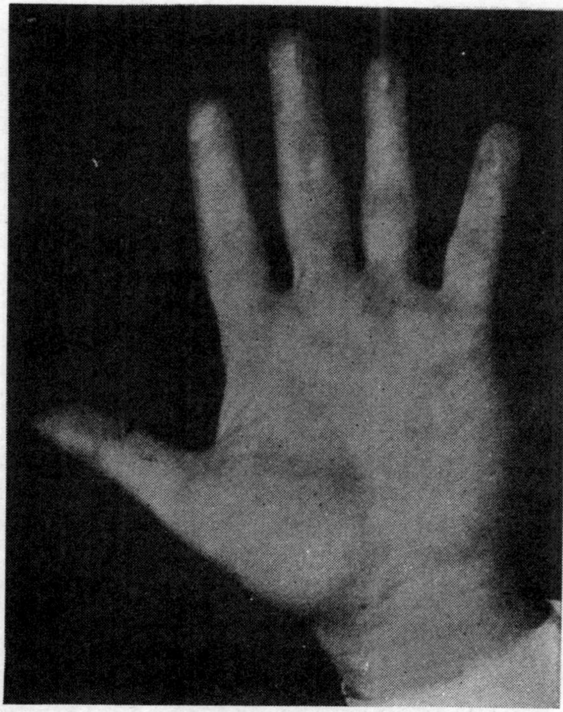

NO. 114. UPPER MOUNT OF MARS DEVELOPED

with them. The strong double Mount is a most advanced Martian development, and when seen, the subject must be classed as a Martian at once. This type is unmistakable. The Plain of Mars, if largely developed, or if much crossed by fine or red lines, will show sudden temper to be present. This development with the other two Mounts large will make a dangerous combination, for it will add inflammability to the already great aggression and resistance. To the Plain of Mars used to be attributed the aggressive qualities which we now ascribe to the Lower Mount of Mars, for it was observed by the old palmists that sudden tempers which were present with a strong Plain of Mars made the subject

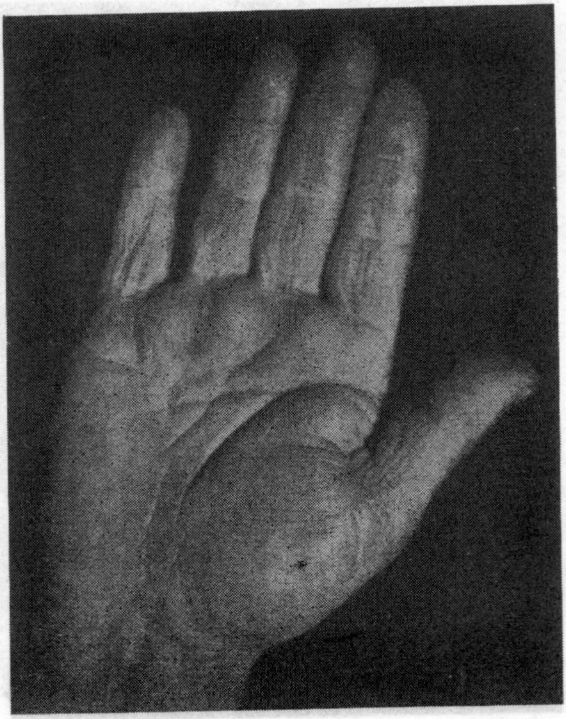

NO. 115. LOWER MOUNT OF MARS DEVELOPED

flare up and become very aggressive. But this temper soon died, and it has been observed that there is a vast difference between one who steadily and coolly *pushes* his way over all opposition, and one who simply *gets mad* and for the time being makes " Rome howl." The ancients fully appreciated the value in human success of this aggressive quality which would force men to overcome opposition at any cost, and when they put forth the rule that "A hollow palm indicates misery, loss of money, and failure in all enterprises," it was because they thought that the hollow palm showed lack of aggression and that its absence would produce these results. In this case the hollow palm *did not* locate the seat of aggression, and its absence only showed a *lack*

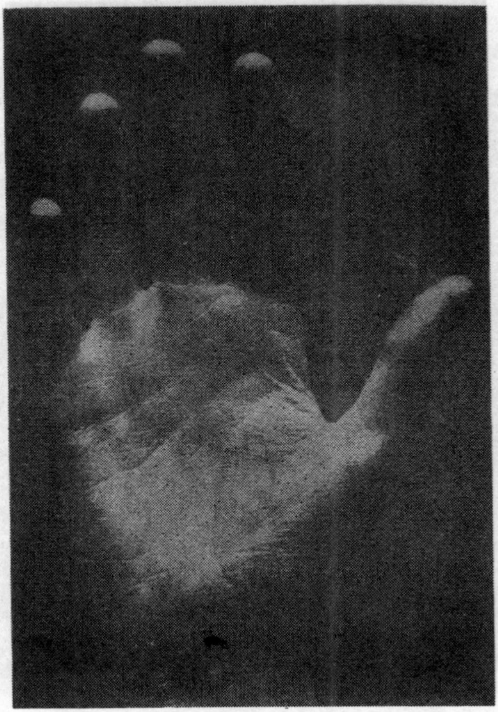

NO. 116. LOWER MOUNT OF MARS DEFICIENT

of temper, which had been confused with *real* aggression; so the hollow palm is now shorn of its terrors, and is to be found in the hands of very successful people. The absence of the Lower Mount of Mars (116) is much more likely to produce the resulting failure attributed by older palmists to a hollow palm, for without the Lower Mount developed, a subject will allow someone much inferior in attainments to push past him by the sheer force of aggression. The three subdivisions of the Martian are resistance (Upper Mars), aggression (Lower Mars), and temper (Plain of Mars). The Martian according to this division becomes a three-sided fellow and you will have no trouble in estimating him

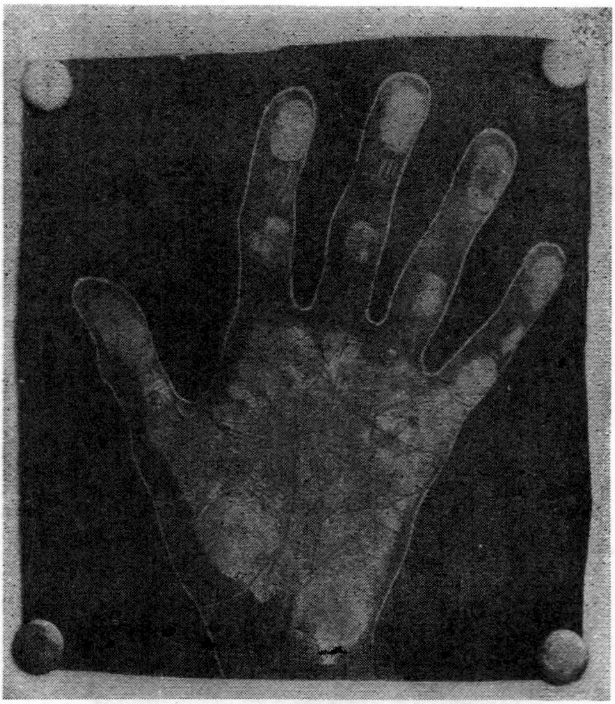

NO. 117. UPPER MOUNT OF MARS DEFICIENT

properly if you carefully note which formation he has, and in what degree of development. When the Upper Mount of Mars is developed so as to make a curve *outwardly* at the percussion of the hand (see 114), it is a strong Mount ; when, in addition, it is so full that it forms a perceptible pad on the *inside* of the palm, it is unusually strong. When the side of the hand at the percussion is straight, or with a depression where the Mount ought to be, the qualities of the Mount are absent (117). This absence of Martian development is to be noted carefully, for dire results often follow such a deficiency. The Upper Mount of Mars gives to a subject the power of resistance, that is, under all circumstances he is cool, collected, calm, does not lose his head, is equal to emergencies, and does not get discouraged if things go against him. He does not give up fighting even when the chances seem slim, and when knocked down he rises again seemingly unaware of the possibility of defeat. This power of resistance, this faculty of never giving up, often makes the Martian successful over all obstacles. When, on the contrary, this Upper Mount is absent, and the side of the hand flat or hollow, you know that the subject is easily discouraged, gives up quickly when hard pressed, and lacks resistance. In moments of danger he becomes excited, and when knocked down he *does not* rise, for he thinks that it is no use to try any more. Thus you can see what a wonderful power this Upper Mount gives through this faculty of resisting, and what a loss the lack of it is. In the reading of every hand it must be thoroughly taken into account, for even dull or ordinary persons will push themselves through the world if they do not get discouraged. This deficient Mount is found on the hands of almost all suicides. The subject with only the Upper Mount developed will not force the fighting, will not hunt strife, but will be content to resist opposition, and to overcome oppression when it appears. The Lower Mount of Mars (see 115) will show the subject who pushes his plans to the fullest extent, does not stop to consider other people, but with "hammer and tongs," if necessary, forces himself over and through all opposition. He seeks strife, loves it, and is always the pusher who is full of aggression. *Note this point carefully*, if you find a hand with the Lower Mount strong and the Upper one lacking, the subject will be a great bluffer, but not having resistance will back down easily if pressed. Having fixed the distinction between *aggression*, *resistance*, and *temper*, we will consider the typical Martian, and judge him as being the aggressor, the resister, or a combination of both, according as the respective Mounts are developed.

The Martian is of medium height, very strongly built, muscular looking, carries himself erect, shoulders back, and has the appearance of one ever ready to defend himself. His head is small, bullet shaped, with an unusually large development at the base of the brain. The back of the neck is broad and, in a pronounced specimen, developed much above the average. The face is round, the skin thick and strong, red in color, and often presenting a mottled appearance. The hair is short, stiff, sometimes curly and of an auburn or red color. The beard is short and harsh. The eyes are large and bold looking, with a bright expression, dark in color, and with the whites often bloodshot, showing the great strength of his blood supply. The mouth is large and firm, the lips thin with the under one slightly the thicker. The teeth are small, regular, strong, and yellowish in color. The brows grow thick, straight, and low over the eyes, giving often the appearance of a scowl. The nose is long, straight, or of the Roman type, the chin firm and strong, often turning up slightly at the end. The ears are small and set close to the head, the red color of skin being quite prominent around them, this red often turning to a purple, congested appearance with strongly marked subjects. The neck is short and thick, connecting the head with a finely developed pair of shoulders, broad and muscular, with large muscles running down the back and a big expansive chest. In this chest is a pair of large, strong lungs which send forth a big commanding voice full of resonance and power. The legs are short but stout and muscular, the bones of the body are big and strong, the feet are broad and the instep inclined to be flat, making the subject walk in a proud, determined manner. Altogether he shows himself one well able to force his way through the world, mentally if he can, physically if he must. The Martian by his very appearance shows his true character, full of fight, either aggressively or in self-defence, mentally or physically, a strong, robust constitution, and one ardent in all things. The Martian is first of all brave, to him the conflict brings no thought of danger. Consequently the Martian makes an excellent soldier. If an army could be marshalled which should be composed of typical Martians, there would be no such thing as defeat possible to them, it would be victory or death. (Leonidas at the pass of Thermopylæ undoubtedly had such a band and their work was tinged with the true Martian spirit.) The Martian has also robust health, consequently is naturally energetic, and with good health is not so likely to have his vital forces sapped by inertia. This gives him an added power, which pushes forward his aggressive side and makes him able more readily to resist discouragements. As a soldier it also makes him able to endure the fatigue of any campaign, and to push forward by rapid marches to seek and smite his opponent. His vigorous constitution fills him with the desire to accomplish whatever he sets out to do, and his energy makes him put forward the utmost effort to gain success. He is exceedingly generous in the use of his money, caring for wealth only for what it will buy for him. He is one who loves to have friends and admirers, and generally succeeds in gaining them. He is exceedingly devoted to these friends and will fight for them, as well as spend his money freely with them and in their behalf. He is not always refined and delicate in his ways, but is often brusque and lacking in tact. He is well-meaning, however, and while he sometimes accomplishes his purposes in a vigorous manner, his typical characteristics must be taken into account and you must not expect him to be always a Chesterfield. He is determined, and the stronger the type the more this is accentuated. Do not think you can oppose a Martian with impunity, and be sure that if you do oppose him there will be a fight on your hands. The Martian can be reasoned with and coaxed, but never driven, and he is exceedingly amorous. His strong blood current and big muscular development speak of an exuberance of health, and fill him with the fire of passion, and the opposite sex becomes very attractive. When he falls in love it is with all the intensity of his strong nature, and he simply proceeds to storm the heart of his charmer, as he does the works of an enemy, and this Martian fire and dash so astound the object of his love that she is apt to surrender to the assault. No sickly sentimentality takes part in his wooing, it is audacity and vigor from start to finish. The Martian is domineering, especially if the Lower Mount is developed. Remember opposition rouses all of his fighting qualities, and this is his strong side; so all other types do well to mollify him, leading him by tact and diplomacy, rather than trying to force him. The Martian is a heavy eater. It takes plenty of fuel to feed the fires of his strong body, so it takes a great deal of food and the heartiest kind at that. He wants plenty of rare beef, potatoes, eggs, cabbage, turnips, and all of the more solid kinds of food. Salads and dainties that attract the epicurean taste do not suffice for him. He is very fond of games that require physical strength and power. Wrestling, boxing, football, baseball, and all kindred sports strongly appeal to him. The rougher the sport and the greater the strife, the better he likes it, and the better he succeeds. His is a big nature, he is not narrow in his views, and in all games or sports he wants absolute fairness to rule and the best man to win. He is primarily an active type, so those things which are accomplished by daring and energy seem to him the real things. The student and the philosopher appear to him small and insignificant. The achievements accomplished before the eyes of the world are what appeal to him. The Martian is found in every walk in life. His strong characteristics are daily felt in the mental world, the business community, the army, the church, the state—everywhere. He must be put into occupations and surroundings where he can work off his surplus energy either in pushing his affairs or fighting in the field. To put a Martian where he must be under restraint would be like stopping the safety-valve on a boiler and crowding on steam. Outdoor active occupations best suit him, and one confined to office routine should have a gymnasium near at hand. Wherever he may be, in whatever walk in life, he is always the same ardent, strong fellow, proud to a degree, fond of show, an imposing figure and the hero of the masses who bow down to his superior strength and daring. As a painter the Martian will choose battle scenes, hunting scenes, or games of sport. As a reader he chooses tales of war or strife, and never tires of the heroes who have come down through the traditions of the ages. As a musician he loves music full of fire and pronounced rhythm, and not the plaintive love song. A brass band most strongly appeals to him. As a speaker he deals in strong sentences, and loves to tell of battles and physical prowess. In everything he is the same, and his Martian ideas tinge his horizon with their ardent strength.

The Martian has a bad side, which becomes so, not from the fact that he is inherently a criminal, but from the intensity and ardor of his nature. In order that a Martian may develop his best side, it is essential that he be refined in every way possible. Everything that tends to coarsen him makes him more brutal, and with his strong tendencies, brutality makes him bad. On his bad side he becomes lascivious, a drunkard, and, as the worst development, a murderer; and this common type is not at all hard to distinguish. The hand is hard, stiff, skin coarse, color very red, capillaries big and coarse, fingers short, with the third phalanges thick, nails short and brittle, and the Mounts of Mars very large. The Plain of Mars will be either high or badly crossed. In some cases a large single cross is seen in the Plain of Mars indicating uncontrollable temper. On this hand you will find a big first phalanx of the thumb, often the clubbed formation, and quite frequently the spatulate thumb. This Martian will be short in stature, the face very red, eyes blood-shot, the skin spotted and with a purplish tinge, mouth twisted, hair a dirty red, and ears long. Such a Martian is the kind who lives only to gratify his low passions, and to him there is nothing but brutality. When he is crossed in love he murders, and either by using an ax, a club, or a knife—even the act of murder he brutalizes as much as possible. When he steals it is to gratify his passions, so while he is bad it is the wickedness of animalism.

He does not steal because he is a thief and the act of stealing is a pleasure to him, but merely because he wants to use the proceeds of his felony to appease his appetites. Surround a crooked Mercurian with everything he wants, and he will steal because he loves to. Give a bad Martian all he wants to eat and drink and he will not steal. The Martian is always predisposed to marry. He makes a devoted husband, though an ardent one, and is particular to choose a good-looking wife. The Venusian women please him best, as he wants a purely feminine type as a wife. He himself possesses enough masculinity for the whole family. The health difficulties of the Martian are a predisposition to fevers, blood disorders owing to the richness and abundance of his blood supply, throat trouble, bronchitis, laryngitis, and kindred difficulties with the bronchial tubes. These troubles are shown by grilles or cross-bars on the Upper Mount of Mars, emphasized by color, nails, and other health indications. Health difficulties are not shown on the Lower Mount. Health difficulties marked on the lower third of the Upper Mount of Mars and the upper third of the Mount of the Moon indicate intestinal troubles even going as far as tuberculosis of the intestines. This I have many times confirmed.

The various qualities of the hand play their part with this type as with all the others. The texture of the skin is important for the reason that refinement elevates the Martian. If you find fine texture of skin, you know that coarseness and brutality are not so likely, and that while the subject will be intense he will be more delicate in his methods than if he is unrefined. Very fine texture is not common to the Martian, although it is found. I once saw a typical Martian with very fine textured skin and found that he was a minister and very intellectual ; another Martian with the same fineness I found to be a celebrated wrestler, very cool and level-headed, and not at all brutal (118). The medium texture is often found on the Martian who moves in good society, and it shows him to be a thoroughly manly man. With this texture is most often found the Upper Mount leading and only a moderate Lower Mount. This combination shows the power of intellectual and refined resistance under discouragement, with just enough aggression to keep up the necessary balance. Coarse texture will, by taking away refinement, make a loud and disagreeable fellow, so intense that his society is not sought.

Flexibility of the hand will show the elastic mind back

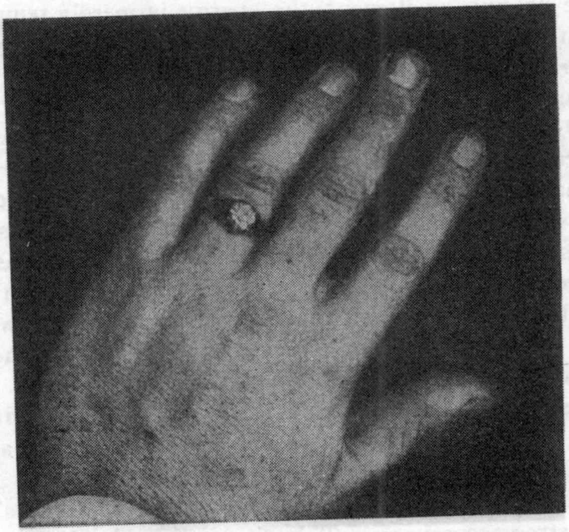

NO. 118. WRESTLER'S HAND

of Martian qualities. A very flexible hand will refine and elevate the mentality of the type, and make the subject more versatile. It will also make him less intense, not likely to be disagreeable, but more apt to fly to extremes, especially of temper. Great flexibility is not often found with this type, for while they are clever they do not think as quickly as other types. The medium flexibility is often seen and shows a balance between the elastic mind and its opposite. This subject is calm, clear-headed, evenly balanced, and not so likely to fly into a temper, especially if the Upper Mount is strong. If the Lower Mount is large he has greater aggression. The stiff hand will make him dense and inelastic in mind, and being naturally slow, he becomes with this stiff hand very set in his ways. The stiff hand will be found on an obstinate, unintelligent, quarrelsome fellow.

The consistency of the hand will show you whether the Martian fighting qualities will be put into operation, or remain inoperative. The flabby hand will show that sheer laziness is present, and while the subject may flare up under some passing excitement, the energy is merely temporary. With the Lower Mount strong he will be a very aggressive *talker*, but will push his way spasmodically. Flabby consistency is not often found with Martian hands. Soft hands show that inertia is present, but that it may be overcome by determination. Elastic hands show the best consistency for a Martian, for he will have intelligent energy back of him, and will only push his strong qualities within reasonable limits. He will never be lazy, is a thoroughly masculine subject, and will have developed one of the Martian's best qualities, energy. Hard hands will coarsen and lower the type. The hard brain indicated by the hard hand cannot adapt itself to new conditions, and gets into ruts. This consistency makes a terrible fellow of a subject with the Lower Mount developed, as it adds intense energy to aggression, which is a most formidable combination.

Color in the hands is important. Red is the normal color in a strong specimen. This shows rich blood, the strong heart, and the greatest amount of vitality. If it is very pronounced it is dangerous, for it will make the subject so intense that he knows no bounds. As a sensualist he will be extreme, and if he belongs to the bad type, he will commit any excess, and even crime to further his ends. These are the men who murder from jealousy. Pink color tones down these qualities, and reduces the danger greatly. The normal strength of the pink color will not lead to physical excesses, nor to the inflammable temper shown by red color. The subject will be milder, less likely to fight, more evenly balanced, and in every way a better Martian. White color with this type is abnormal. When found the Martian is much reduced in strength. Even a strong Mount will be diminished in its operation by white color. Coldness is the opposite of the red qualities, and these belong typically to the Martian. When white color is found it indicates such a reduction of the blood current that it must come from ill-health. In this case tone down your estimate of the degree of intensity of the subject. Do not give him even the full measure of resistance or aggression that the size of his Mounts would seem to justify. Yellow color is sometimes found and tells of the crossness, the nervousness, the fits of blues that come from excess of bile. This will make a strong specimen of the type very mean, and from this bilious combination alone do we get the really *criminal* Martian. With a strong Lower Mount, a high or rayed Plain of Mars, the bilious subject will be a quarrelsome person, one always declaring himself to be misused and abused by the world. With the Martian's rich blood supply and strong heart, if the blood current becomes poisoned with bile it will make him vicious.

The nails must be closely examined. The broad nail of a strong constitution is expected, and will be most often found. The narrow nail is not common, and tells of a more delicate person. Short, critical nails will add materially to the fighting qualities, and if very short make the subject pugnacious in the extreme. With a large Lower Mount and very short nails you have a person who fights everybody and all the time. He cannot keep away from strife, and is either in it himself or has everybody around him fighting. Color must be observed in the nails; red, pink, white, yellow, and blue each telling the story of color qualities present. The nails must be examined for health to see if fluted or brittle, which formations make the subject a nervous Martian, and pretty hard to get along with. With this type look for the nail showing throat and bronchial delicacy, for these are difficulties which beset the Martian. When these nails are seen on this type it means danger, and must be used to warn the subject against colds and exposure from carelessness.

The hair on the hands will be most often red, auburn, or blond. In all of these colors judge the degree of strength added to the type by the depth of color. Red hair will make an inflammable subject, liable to sudden violent temper, and one who will lose control of himself under excitement. If the Lower Mount be strong, red hair will be as bad as short nails, and if both these should be found, then it will be absolutely no use trying to get along with this subject. Auburn color decreases the intensity and makes the subject less likely to "fly off the handle." Blond hair will again reduce the ardor of the type and make it more phlegmatic, calm, and less excitable. Blond hair reduces the intensity of Martian qualities more than any other color, while black shows the vivacity and spontaneity of its qualities, and to a degree lights up the Martian fires in a subject.

The hand as a whole will tell you of the mental, practical, or baser worlds which rule the subject. This observation of the whole hand is important with the Martian, for the reason that this is the first Mount type which has not a finger to guide us. The Head line, together with the length of fingers and the general balance of the hand, must be used in connection with the individual phalanges of all four fingers. If the hand as a whole shows the mental world to rule, you will find that the first phalanx of the four fingers will correspond. Then note the Head line to see whether it is clear, well marked, and colored, and by this combination class your subject as a Martian ruled by the mental world. He will then develop his peculiar traits in the world of mind, and will be good as a lawyer, minister, debater, politician, and in kindred occupations. If the middle portion of the hand is best developed, it will show that the practical world is strong, and the subject will be a Martian business man, full of fight, push, and energy, not subject to discouragement, and consequently not likely to give up when hard pressed. These subjects are most successful in the business world, and more pronouncedly so if they are refined. If the lower third of the hand be best developed, then the animal desires, already strong in the subject, will take their lowest form and he will become vulgar in the extreme. Such an one commits crime to gratify his appetites. He may be successful in business, but he will be low in his tastes.

Note the secondary Mounts, and which side of them is best developed, for this will tell what forces are behind the subject to drive his already strong qualities into action. These matters consider from the other Mounts, and the phalanges of the individual fingers.

Pointed finger-tips with this type will tell you that idealism will rule, in which case your Martian will be much less practical and reliable, and apt to rush into ill-conceived ventures. Pointed tips are, however, not often found on strong Martians. Conic tips are often found, for the Martian is fond of beauty and of artistic things. He likes dress and home decorations, and notwithstanding his strong nature there is a tinge of conic quality often found. Square tips are frequent, for the Martian is eminently practical. If he be a soldier these tips will show common-sense, and his commissary department will be well equipped. In any vocation square tips will make him practical, and even if he has great aggression he will use and guide it sensibly. Spatulate tips will give great activity, and everything that adds this to a Martian puts him in danger of excess. Link great aggression (Lower Mars) and great activity (spatulate tips) with the other quality of these tips, originality, and you have an active and aggressive fellow who is hunting original ways to expend his force. He is trying new ways to do old things and becomes a person that wears out everybody around him. Spatulate tips will make the Martian a great explorer, a brilliant and forceful general, and a successful business man, *if a good clear Head line is present to give self-control and good judgment.*

Knotty fingers will show that reason and analysis will guide the subject. If only the first knots are developed he will be unusually intelligent, the mind will be well ordered, and his information systematized. If the second knot is developed he will be neat in his dress, tidy in his surroundings, and in whatever vocation he is found you may be sure he will be regular and methodical, especially so if the fingers be square throughout their length. If both knots be developed it will make him an analyzer who does nothing from impulse, but reasons always. Smooth fingers will add to his love of beauty, and make him impulsive and quick. He will not stop to reason out everything, but will rely on first impressions and his intuitions. He will be fond of dress, of flowers, paintings that depict war scenes, and will love stirring music. Smooth fingers are a danger to this type, for, already very spontaneous, he needs only thoughtlessness to make him wild, so in a subject who has smooth fingers and a strong Martian development, see if a clear Head line is present to give self-control. It is a good thing to find knotty fingers on a Martian, as they make him careful, but you find more subjects with smooth fingers, as the type is naturally impulsive. Long fingers will show that the subject is fond of minutiæ and detail. If he be a soldier he will plan his campaigns with the utmost care, he will look after the equipment of his men, and will see that they are amply provided with proper food. Not a detail that can add to the efficiency of the service will be overlooked. He will be neat in his dress and require his soldiers to keep their equipments constantly bright; he will be suspicious of those with whom he deals, and does not implicitly trust anyone, therefore he *himself* sees that his instructions are carried out. The long-fingered Martian becomes a slower subject, one not moved to act under impulse, and who does not make rapid and impetuous dashes, but proceeds always with care and caution. His aggressiveness will not be so strong, for he will be particular that all the little things are attended to, and will thus lose part of the pushing qualities contributed by a strong Lower Mount, which does not generally stop to consider minutiæ. Short fingers make the Martian a fiery, impetuous fellow, who dashes ahead without stopping to consider where he will come out, and with the short-fingered quickness in both thought and action he rushes pell-mell through the world, either achieving great success or constantly committing blunders. With a big Lower Mount and very short fingers, he will see only the object he wishes to reach, and not the things which stand between. Impulse and quick thought are his guides, and a very aggressive person who is also thoughtless and careless of the feelings of others can do endless damage. The dash and push of such a Martian strike terror to more timid brethren, and thus he accomplishes his ends by very audacity. But there is always the danger that an opponent may be cool, calculating, and strong, and this combination can resist a daring charge and bring to grief the short-fingered Martian. The thumb will show what determination is back of the Martian. If he be a refined type, we need a refined thumb, which will make him rely more on tact than on brute force. There is generally found the thumb which shows muscular strength and robust energy. You do not often find the delicate, refined thumb, but will often see a broad first phalanx, or a paddle-shaped phalanx, with a waist-like second phalanx. These will be seen on high-grade Martians and will show great determination, coupled with tactful reasoning qualities, which will reduce the brutality of a big Lower Mount, but will not lessen the aggression, for it will operate with just as great strength of will, but governed by good reasoning power and tact. Big long thumbs will give strength to the subject; small thumbs will make them sputter and "bluff," but they will back down if vigorously attacked. Pointed thumbs make the subject impressionable and weaken the type materially. Even a strong Lower Mount will be spoiled by a pointed thumb. Square or spatulate tips to the thumb give great common-sense, or great activity and originality to the will. They produce most determined subjects, and add great strength to the type. These subjects must always be coaxed; they can never be driven. The clubbed thumb belongs to the brutal Martian hand. Denominated the "murderer's thumb," and showing the brutal obstinacy that will kill from blind fury, we see that it is on the fighting type this thumb properly belongs. Always feel that the clubbed thumb, on a strongly Martian hand, hard and red, with short fingers and short first phalanges, will make the subject likely to give way to the first sudden fury that may seize him. Clubbed thumbs are found on all kinds of hands, telling their story of obstinacy and strong tendency to brutality, either hereditary or acquired, but in the Martian type they reach the highest danger-point, and must be given the most careful consideration. The Head line, by its clearness, straightness, and even color, will be a great factor with the Martian type. With a subject who is likely to be inflammable, there is great need of self-control and good judgment. These qualities are abundantly supplied by a good Head line, and in the final summing up of your Martian type this test must be applied to see if they are present, and if in such degree that their full benefit will be assured. In handling this strong type always remember that he is a fighter, that he may fight physically or mentally, and that you must distinguish between aggression and resistance. With these ideas in mind, and the material in his hand to judge by, apply all the tests to him, in order to determine the degree of his Martian development and the forces back of him that will either add to or take away from his strength. After a careful study of this chapter I am sure no mistakes will be made with the Martian type.

CHAPTER XXIV

THE MOUNT OF THE MOON

THE sixth Mount type is the Lunarian, so named from the fact that the portion of the hand by which he is identified is the Mount of Luna or, as it is more commonly designated, the Mount of the Moon. As single signs or in combination, the star, triangle, circle, single vertical line, square, or trident strengthen the Mount of the Moon.

Grilles, crosses, cross-bars, islands, dots, or badly formed stars indicate defects of the Mount, either of health or character. Color, nails, and other matters detailed in the course of this chapter will determine which (119). The Mount of the Moon must be judged both by the strength of its curve outwardly on the percussion of the hand and by the size of the pad it forms on the inside of the palm. If it is seen forming a decided bulge outwardly, call it a *well-developed* Mount (120); if in addition it is exceedingly thick, forming a large pad on the inside of the hand, it must be regarded as a *very strong* Mount (121); and if the outward protuberance and the thick pad are both unusually large, you have an *excessive* Lunarian subject (122). In this type vertical lines on the Mount add strength to it and cross lines show defects. If you see a strong vertical line extending the length or nearly so of the Mount, it will indicate an added strength, and a number of vertical lines if lying close together will also increase its power. These lines on a Mount developed at the side, but flat in the palm, will be nearly as powerful as if the Mount showed a medium development inside the palm. If the outward development and the large pad in the palm is seen, which has *also* a deep, well-cut vertical line or lines, it will show an *excessively* developed Lunarian reaching to the danger-point of the type. The Mount must be divided into three sections, the upper, the middle, and the lower, corresponding to the three worlds of the fingers in their qualities, each section enabling one also to locate *health difficulties* peculiar

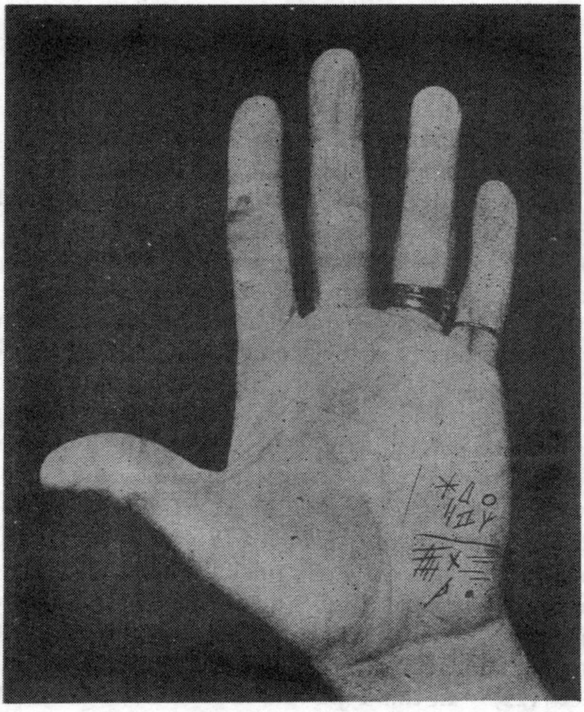

NO. 119. DISTINGUISHING MARKS ON THE MOUNT OF MOON

to the type. Grilles, cross-bars, or crosses on the Mount, badly formed stars, islands, dots, chained or wavy lines will locate health defects, and when seen, the health indications of color, nails, Life line, and line of Mercury must be examined in connection with the Mount to aid in confirming the indications. The health defects of the Mount of the Moon are important, especially with women, as they bear directly on diseases peculiar to them, affecting life, temper, maternity, and future happiness. The upper, middle, and lower thirds of this Mount each show separate health difficulties, and when defects are seen on any particular third, you are at once warned that the health troubles

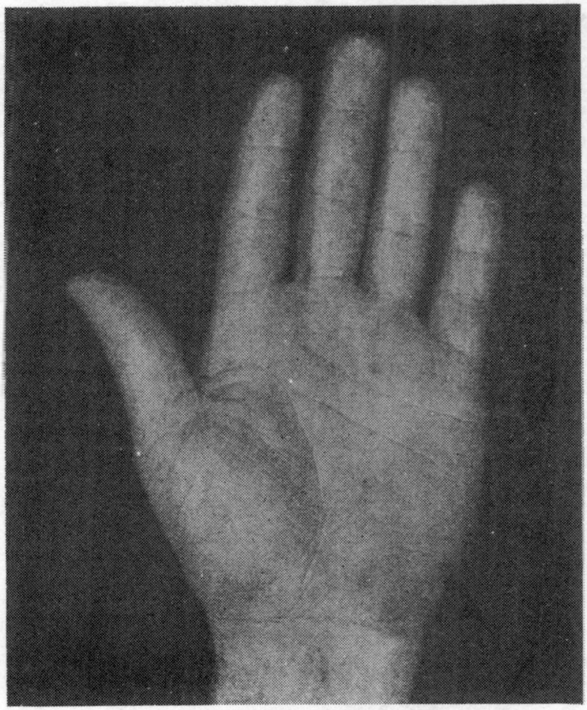

NO. 120. NORMAL MOUNT OF MOON

peculiar to that third of the Mount are present. In this manner you can not only tell that your subject has a health defect, but as well what this defect is. Cross lines at the side of the hand have been erroneously called travel lines, and were supposed to show journeys. Vertical lines have been used to indicate voyages by water, cross lines journeys by land, and these interpretations given by the older palmists have come from the fact that the Lunarian has a penchant for water, is naturally nervous, restless, loves change or travelling, and when strong lines have been found on the Mount, his restlessness has been accentuated, making him *want* to travel, which he *will* do if such a thing is at all possible. Vertical lines, strengthening as they do his typical love of travel and also his typical love of water, make him

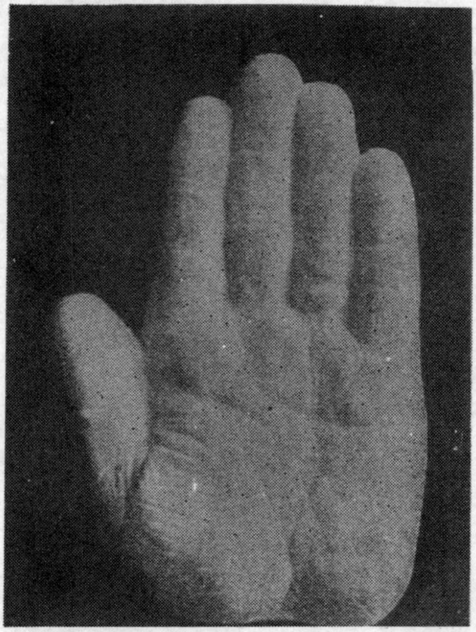

NO. 121. STRONG MOUNT OF MOON

the more likely to choose journeys by water rather than by land. This is the method of reasoning from which the use of vertical lines to indicate voyages arose. I mention these supposed travel lines at this point because, in our study of the Lunarian type, *health defects* must be constantly watched for, and if you should be led, by any previous knowledge, to consider cross lines or vertical lines as indicating journeys, you would not be in a position to diagnose the health defects of this type, especially among women, for you would be likely to read as a journey what really indicates illness. The entire percussion of the hand is often found covered with cross lines. This shows that the subject is delicate in more ways than one, even if no sign of it has appeared to make him conscious of any health delicacy. They are

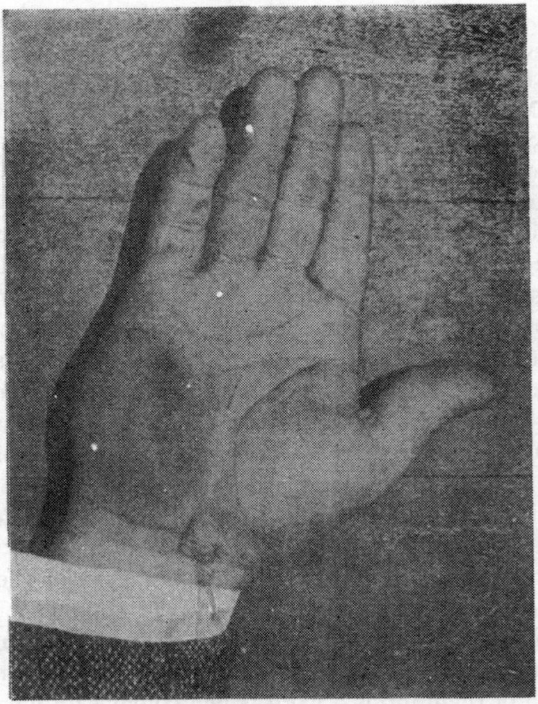

NO. 122. EXCESSIVE MOUNT OF MOON

always hyper-nervous, which precedes actual disease. These cross lines are also seen on the hands of old persons, often those who did not have them when young. They have appeared as age has weakened the constitution. The health defects of Upper Mars, which are throat and bronchial difficulty, intestinal inflammations, and blood disorders, are all shown by these cross lines on that Mount, which lies on the percussion. Those of the Mount of the Moon, which will be enumerated later, are also shown by cross lines on the Mount, and thus a crossing of the *whole side*, or percussion of the hand, would show delicacy of the entire structure from throat to kidneys and bladder. If any portion of the percussion is more thoroughly cross-lined than the others, or lines run across from it to the Life line, with health defects of nails, color, etc., shown, you can tell *which one* of the delicate parts will first give way, by the portion of the Mounts at the side of the hand on which these markings occur most strongly, or from which a line runs to a delicate Life line. This will be more fully treated in the study of the lines.

While the Lunarian is not often seen in pure development, still he is to be found, and a *part* of his typical qualities will be present in nearly all of the subjects met. His realm is the world of imagination ; he keeps humanity from becoming too material, and enables us to see with the "mind's eye." It is entirely because of the possession of imagination, a quality of mind which does not belong to the lower animals, and which gives to man the ability to form mental pictures, that certain words, sounds, or signs convey meanings—in short, that we have the power of speaking and communicating with each other. These methods of communication may be either by word of mouth in various languages; by telegraph, where each combination of dots on the sounder means a different letter, by combining which, words conveying ideas are produced; by writing, where each letter and every combination of them forms a word which conveys an idea to the mind; or by the sign language of the hand as employed by mutes, where each different manner of placing the fingers either means a letter, a word, or, with advanced users of this method, a whole statement. But none of these methods of communication would be possible if we lacked the imaginative power to link these lines, words, or gestures with the idea which they are intended to convey, and the understanding of these varied forms of communication would be impossible if we had not the ability to form a mental picture of the thing to which they refer. If I write the word *house*, it brings to mind a building and you mentally picture some sort of a structure. If I add, " A white frame house with low roof and red chimneys," you mentally see the house in your " mind's eye." This is the power of imagination, and if we did not have it we would be unable to communicate with each other, would have no ability to express ourselves. Thus the Lunarian was necessary, as he represents imagination, which makes possible communication, and he was made one of the seven types. Manifestly the more refined and greater the power of well-balanced imagination a subject possesses, the larger will be his vocabulary ; the power of description will be greater and the ability to evolve new ideas increased. The more dense the subject, the more material are his imaginings, the more restricted his vocabulary, and, instead of catching an idea quickly, you have figuratively "to beat it into his head." This faculty of imagination and speech is what makes a high type of Lunarian brilliant; the lack of it makes the clodhopper, who can never say just what he wants to, who never mentally rises above the earth. Those subjects who can believe in nothing that they cannot touch, and who cannot carry in their minds mental pictures, lose much enjoyment and have little expansiveness of mind to help them through the world. When we find a subject with a well-developed Mount of the Moon, we have one who expresses himself well and can enjoy the pleasures of imagination ; when we find it absent (123) we have one who can picture nothing to himself ; when we find it excessive (see 122), we have a subject who easily becomes flighty, imaginative to a dangerous degree, and who even loses control of the mind entirely, becoming insane. Manifestly we care to find no excess nor deficiency with this Mount, but a good medium development, showing the presence of a healthy imagination, one that lifts the world above the plane of materialism into the realm of fancy. In the hands of the greatest linguists, musicians, composers, fiction or romance writers, we find this Mount strong. They are able to see their characters in the " mind's eye," clothe them with proper attributes, and make them living realities in the minds of their readers. It is the power of imagining how scenes described look, and how characters portrayed appear, that makes it a delight to read. If the power of imagination were gone from us, we could conceive nothing but the bare

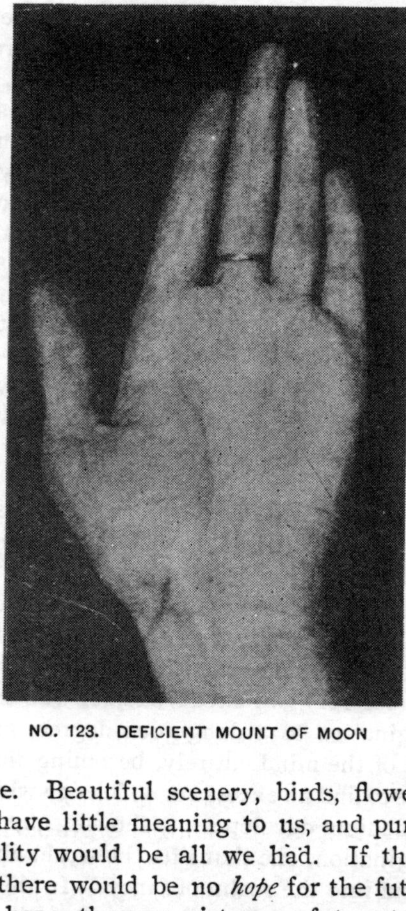

NO. 123. DEFICIENT MOUNT OF MOON

things we see. Beautiful scenery, birds, flowers, color, or form would have little meaning to us, and pure, dull, monotonous reality would be all we had. If there were no imagination there would be no *hope* for the future. Many have no such hope; they can picture no future toward which to press. These subjects are deficient in Lunarian qualities, and spend their lives arguing that nothing is true, and that life is a vain struggle. Granting that imagination may sometimes lead to false conclusions, it is better to have some of them than to be unable to see beyond a limited horizon.

The Lunarian is tall in stature, fleshy in build, with the lower limbs thick and the feet large. He is often quite stout, but his flesh is not firm and his muscles are not strong. He is soft and flabby and instead of muscular vitality, his flesh has a spongy feeling. His complexion is dead white, giving him a decided pallor and marking him as the victim of a weak heart's action, anæmia, kidney trouble, and often of dropsy. His head is round, thick through the temples, bulging over the eyes, and with a low forehead. The hair is not thick, but straggly and fine in quality, blond or chestnut in color, and quite straight. His eyebrows are scanty, uneven in contour, and often grow together over the nose. The eyes are round and starey in appearance, often bulging, and frequently watery. The color is gray or light blue, the whites are clear, and the pupil has a luminous appearance, seeming to refract light and showing a prismatic gleam. The lids are thick and flabby, giving them a swollen look. The nose is short and small, quite often turning up at the end, and sometimes showing the nostrils very plainly. Frequently it is what we call a "pug" nose. The mouth is small and puckers, giving the appearance of being drawn together. The teeth are large and long, yellow in color, and irregularly placed in the gums, which are prominent and bloodless-looking. The teeth are soft and decay early. The chin is heavy, hanging in flabby folds and receding. The neck is fleshy, flabby, and wrinkled, connecting this peculiar-looking head with the fleshy-looking chest, which is again flabby and spongy in consistency The voice is thin and pitched often in a high key. The ears are small and set close to his head. The abdomen is large and bulges forward, giving an awkward look, and the legs are not graceful, but thick and heavy, having a dropsical appearance. The feet are flat and large and the gait is a shuffle or is shambling, very much like the gait of a sailor when he walks on land. The hand of a Lunarian is often found puffy in appearance, flabby in consistency, white in color, fingers short and smooth, with tips conic or pointed; the thumb small in size, with the first phalanx pointed or deficient in length. The Lunarian is controlled by imagination, consequently he is dreamy, fanciful, and idealistic. He is one who builds air castles, plans great enterprises, which are never put into operation because they generally have no practical value. From the flabby, spongy character of his hand and muscular development, he is lazy in the extreme, preferring to live in cloudland rather than to dwell in an abode upon earth. He is constantly a prey to his imaginings, thinks he is ill, and has divers ailments, is fickle, restless, and changeable. It is hard for him to settle down to humdrum life, for he is always yearning for things beyond his reach. Therefore he is never satisfied long in one place, but desires a constant change of location and scene. This restless disposition leads him to spend his last dollar for travel, and often the Lunarian becomes a great traveller. The more lines there are on the Mount the more restless he becomes and the greater is his desire to go from place to place. So while the lines on the Mount of the Moon do not *per se* especially indicate journeys, they *do* strengthen the Lunar qualities of the subject, and this Lunar restlessness makes him a traveller if he has money to gratify this desire. If the hand is firm and the wealth equal to it, you may be sure that a subject with these lines will gratify his love of travel by taking long voyages. If the circumstances do not permit the subject to gratify his love for change you will find that these lines produce in him a yearning for travel. The Lunarian, by his physical construction, has white color and white coldness of temperament. To him " self" is a great word. He is lazy physically and lazy mentally. He loves to dream dreams, and work, which means either mental or physical exertion, is extremely distasteful to him. He is dreamy in look, his eyes have an uncanny expression, and their light blue or gray color speaks of coldness and dreaminess. Thus he becomes mystical, often melancholy, and grows superstitious. He believes in signs and omens, and has wonderful visions and hallucinations which grow to be real to him and influence him greatly. He is slow in his movements, phlegmatic in disposition, and extremely sensitive. He imagines slights when none are intended, and shrinks into himself and away from company. He does not love nor seek society. He realizes that he is different from other people, so retires to the woods or secluded places where he can enjoy himself by himself. He loves nature, birds, flowers, and all things which elevate the senses and excite the imagination, and to such surroundings he goes when out of touch with the world and its inhabitants. He is fond of poetry, but it is the epic kind or verses which bring to mind a chain of new material to dream about. He loves music, but of the deep classic kind, not the gay, sparkling melody that attracts the Venusian. He is a composer, and in seclusion and retirement produces profound classics. The Lunarian is very fond of water. He loves the murmur of the waves and the roar and thunder of the tempest. As far as he is able he lives near water, and is *on* it as much as possible. The Lunarian makes a good sailor. He is never generous; to him selfishness is innate. He is a big eater, though not sensual nor amorous. In his case the sexual appetites are excited by imagination, and not by physical heat. The Lunarian is lacking in self-confidence, and feels his unfitness for the active pursuits of life. He also lacks energy and perseverance, consequently is unsuccessful in the business world. If he is of a common type he has a hard time to get along. If of a high type he becomes a good writer of romance or fiction, and even of history. This type will be much assisted if he has a long finger of Mercury with the first phalanx long. With this latter combination, conic tips will add to the imaginative tendencies of his writings ; they will become more practical if the tips are square, and active and original if spatulate. Thus we see in the Lunarian a peculiar subject, in whom imagination and fancy are always the dominating motives. It is a blessing that the pure type is not more common, but it is necessary to have *some* of the imagination common to it. If all the people in the world were pure Lunarians it would not be long before there would not be insane asylums enough to hold them. But the possession of a healthy imagination is the farthest possible step from insanity, and the development of the Mount must be very bad and very strong before you begin to think of attributing such an outcome to your subject. Imagination must mean a good quality until it is spoiled by being found in excess. The Lunarian, while not as strongly impelled toward matrimony as some of the other types, still does not avoid it entirely. He is cold by nature and incapable of strong affection. He has not great physical strength, so the fires of passion do not inflame him. He is as fickle and capricious here as everywhere else, and makes strange alliances. Sometimes he marries one much older than himself, sometimes one a great deal younger — you cannot tell much about what he will do except that he will make a peculiar match. These subjects have not the faculty of being constant, and as they are naturally fickle, restless, and selfish they make poor husbands or wives; this is pronounced with conic or pointed tips, less a fact with square or spatulate. No type appears in greater abundance among those having marital unhappiness than the Lunarian. The health difficulties of the type are many, for he has poor circulation, thin blood, white color, and spongy muscles, and therefore readily falls a prey to disease. Note in the description of the type that he has a paunchy abdomen, which in all pure specimens is largely distended. This shows that the same flabby condition is present in the intestines as with the muscles, and this condition, which may properly be called a weakening of these tissues, makes them a fertile place for bacilli to propagate, and we find the Lunarian a victim of peritonitis, inflammation of the bowels, appendicitis, and all other inflammations that are liable to attack the intestinal tract. In epidemics of Asiatic cholera, Lunarians are the first victims, as the bacilli which produce cholera propagate readily under such conditions as they present. This liability to intestinal disorder is shown on the *upper third* of the Mount by cross-bars, grilles, badly formed stars, dots, islands, crosses, or similar defective markings. When such are seen on this part of the Mount, bowel delicacy exists, and the Life line should be at once examined to determine how serious it is. If the Life line

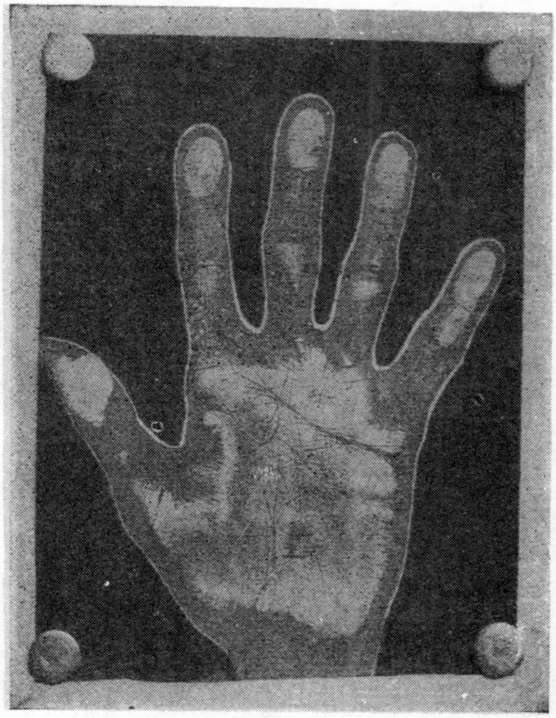

NO. 124. RHEUMATIC MARKING FROM SATURN

is broken, crossed, islanded, has a star on it, forks, or any of the innumerable defects peculiar to it, feel safe in saying that the subject has bowel difficulties of a serious nature. The Lunarian is also predisposed to gout and rheumatism. These are shown by the defects, such as crosses, grilles, etc., mentioned above, appearing on the *middle third* of the Mount. Other indications often confirm this ; for instance, you will sometimes see a line running from the Mount of Saturn to the line of Life, either cutting it or stopping on it. This line has in addition frequently an island (124). I follow the practice with this indication of always looking for health defects of Saturn, one of which is

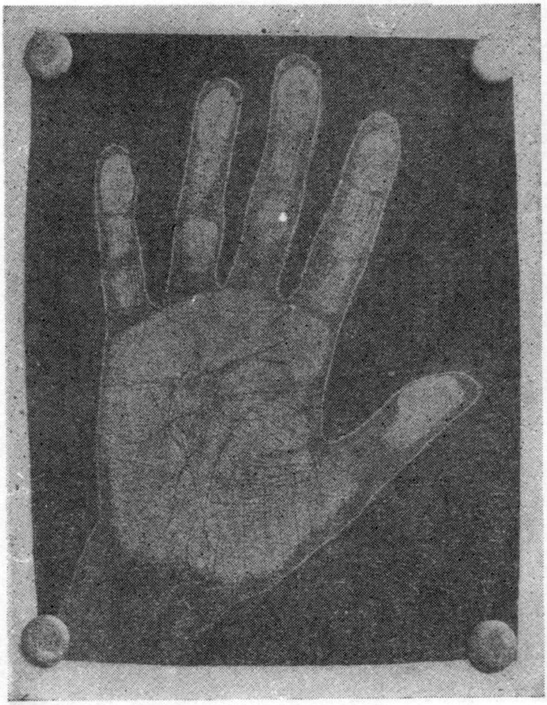

NO. 125. FEMALE DISEASE ON MERCURY LINE

rheumatism. I have many times seen a line running from the middle portion of the Mount of the Moon, another seat of rheumatism, and joining the line from Saturn either where it cuts the line of Life or somewhere in its course (124). This has shown invariably that the subject is either at the time a victim to severe rheumatism, has had it, or will have it, for when this double marking is seen, the rheumatic tendency is hereditary. The lower third of the Mount with defective markings found will indicate kidney and bladder trouble in men, and on a woman's hand, in addition, very pronounced female weakness (see Chittenden Hotel suicide). If you find the defective markings on this portion of the Mount, and the hand and nails very white, swollen and flabby in consistency, it will indicate kidney and bladder difficulty as well as tendency to dropsy. This dropsy will attack the feet and legs of this type, which are already swollen in appearance. I have noted also that kidney trouble is most often shown by cross-bars on the Mount. Often a line from such a bad marking on the Mount will be found running to the Life line, which will be forked or defective in some way, and this will show that these diseases threaten the life of the subject. Female trouble is also shown by this lower third of the Mount when defectively marked. When female weakness is present, there is often a star on the line of Mercury, usually near the line of Head or at a point where the Mercury line crosses the line of Head (125). When this star is seen, it is an unmistakable indication of serious female weakness. This I have verified hundreds of times. Remembering that these organs make possible the reproduction of the species, and that their diseased condition makes maternity either impossible or hazardous, the importance of this indication is very great, for it may tell why women seemingly healthy never have had children. It is also valuable as a pre-marriage indication, tending to show whether a union is likely to be fruitful. This is the place on the hand you must examine if consulted as to why no children have blessed a woman — a question that is often eagerly asked. You can thus readily detect proof of diseased conditions of the reproductive organs, and the subject cannot have children while they are in such a state. Subjects so afflicted are frequently unaware of trouble of this character, consequently do not consult a physician and get the relief which is possible to them This is one instance where a good practice of Palmistic knowledge can transform a barren, joyless home into one of fruition and happiness. These health indications shown by the three sections of the Mount of the Moon are so often encountered and so reliable that I commend them to most careful attention. It does not follow that when these markings and health defects are seen the subject is a Lunarian, but it does show that he has a health defect peculiar to this type. Which one it is will be indicated by whatever portion of the Mount shows the defective markings: bowel trouble, upper third; gout and rheumatism, middle third; kidney, bladder, and female trouble, lower third.

The Lunarian is found, as are all the other types, with his bad side developed. In this case he is shorter in stature, the hair stiff and brittle, the skin dead white and spotted, the eyes watery and gray, and the pores of the skin exuding disagreeable perspiration. This subject is talkative, is apt to be untruthful, often allowing the imagination to run rampant, and thus he deceives not only others but himself as well. These subjects are mean and selfish, cowardly, and, while they have no physical passion, they constantly seek amorous pleasures in order to gratify their imagination. In this low class of Lunarians are found nymphomaniacs. They are deceitful, hypocritical, and slander everyone who incurs their displeasure. They are insolent, unchaste, and most disagreeable creatures, and are shunned and abhorred by mankind. There is an important matter always to consider in connection with the Mount of the Moon, viz.: its excessive development and consequent liability to produce insanity. If it is very large, both bulging at the percussion and thick in the palm, having strong vertical lines, or with a well-marked star, it is a Mount liable to lead to the excess of imagination, and, consequently, insanity. This may be a mild species of hallucination if the hand is fine and the indications not pronounced, or it may be dangerous and brutal mania with a coarse brutal type of Lunarian. Excess of the Mount will make excess of the imagination, which, *per se*, means an unbalanced condition of mind; so with every excessive Mount look for this unhinging of the mental faculties commonly called insanity, whose presence is indicated in several ways, the excessive Mount of the Moon being one of them. In seeking the cause which has produced insanity in any subject, that arising from the excess of the Mount of the Moon shows it has not been shock or disease, but that it is excessive imagination inherent in the subject. This form of mania is difficult to treat, for the nature of the subject, which is inherently crazy, cannot be changed. There is another matter bearing on the subject which this Mount shows. With women suffering from female trouble there is always more or less disturbance of the mind. They grow gloomy and despondent when their trouble is intense, and especially at the time of the monthly periods. During some such periods the mind of an otherwise strong and healthy subject becomes temporarily clouded, and she imagines all sorts of things, frequently that her husband is growing less affectionate, and kindred ideas. During all such periods these subjects should have the greatest care and kindness, and nothing should ever be allowed which will annoy them. I have seen the hands of a number of suicides with this lower third of the Mount of the Moon showing female weakness, and who were undoubtedly temporarily unbalanced when they committed the act (see Chittenden Hotel suicide). In the insane asylums are many cases from this cause, all showing this marking on the hand. It is natural that the Lunarian type will be much influenced by various qualities indicated by the several parts of the hand. Texture of the skin will bring to bear refining or coarsening influences. If the texture is soft and fine, it will undoubtedly be found with flabby consistency, consequently while the imaginings will be on a high plane of refinement these subjects will be lazy and accomplish little. Their ideals will be high, tastes refined, the dreams that come to them will be of beautiful and refined things. Coarseness will be abhorrent and æstheticism extreme. Oscar Wilde is an example of this class. The medium texture is best with a well-developed Lunar Mount, for it will speak of more energy and more practical ideas. This is the subject who will not be bound down by materialism, but who has a reasonable play of the mind. Coarse texture will mean an accompaniment of the hard consistency. This subject will have an inelastic mind, coarse and unrefined ideas, low ideals, with superstition extremely marked, or intense mysticism, and often the bad development of the type is accompanied by this coarse texture of skin. The less the intelligence and the coarser the nature, the more superstitious is a subject. Consistency will tell how much the natural Lunar laziness is increased or how much energy from some of the other types has been infused. Flabby consistency is expected in a pure type, and accentuates all the qualities of the type — idealism, fancy, dreaminess, and laziness. Such subjects are idle dreamers, and the world seldom knows that they have lived. Elastic consistency shows that intelligent energy will put to some use the ideas of the mind, and the subject will be clever, not bound down by rule, versatile, ingenious, a good talker, and will have original ideas, for healthy imagination produces these things. In addition, he will not sit idly and make nothing of his ideas, but will work, for he has energy. If a business man, the subject will devise new schemes to push his business. If a writer, he will be happy in his efforts, for he will have both the mind to produce and energy to do the work. Some of the best authors belong to this class. As a musician and composer he will have the natural ability for his work and the energy to do it. Hard consistency is abnormal. It will give great activity and will make the subject restless, superstitious, selfish, and mystical. These people are not contented with their lot in life, but are growlers and trouble breeders. Their imagination is active but not directed toward elevated matters, and, being constantly dissatisfied themselves, they create dissatisfaction among others. The hard-handed Lunarian has distorted views on religion and all matters of life. He is often uneducated, though he assumes to talk like a professor, but reaches after an idea which he never succeeds in expressing. He is superstitious, and often seeks all of the lower manifestations of Spiritism which appeal to his love of the supernatural. These subjects are the greatest travellers, always discontented, out of tune with the world, and seeking change or excitement. Flexibility shows the elastic mind, and consequently adds to the Lunarian imagination. If marked, the subject will be flighty, will be extreme in views and moods, one moment exalted, the next depressed. These people are brilliant, for with the flexible mind added to imagination they could not be otherwise, but they hate effort and do not make much of their talent. They are good conversationalists, and versatile mentally. Normal flexibility will reduce the danger of extremes. The mind will not so readily become a prey to imagination, but will be held in check and directed into practical channels. There will be no lessening of the ability to form mental pictures, but there will be less tendency to be dominated by them. Thus medium flexibility is best for a Lunarian to possess. The stiff hand will indicate lack of intelligence in the subject. He will have the lower qualities of the type, will be miserly, will lack sympathy, and his imagination will satisfy itself in hunting mysterious manifestations rather than in developing any product of a highly original mind. He will shudder when the door creaks, will be terrified when a dog howls, and being cold, selfish, and fanciful, is a hard subject with whom to deal. The color of the hands claims attention with this type. White is the color typical of the strong Lunarian. It will aid greatly in judging the degree of type. If very pronounced, the coldness of the type will be strongly marked, and health defects must be carefully studied. If the hand is pink, it will show that the type is warmed up, and the heart is stronger, the blood richer and is reaching the skin in good supply. With this condition there will be less mysticism, less idealism, more practical ideas, more warmth of nature, less selfishness, and less restlessness. The subject will be even tempered, less fickle, and less liable to health defects of the type. Red color will show a great increase of these improvements. Ardor and warmth will be marked, and often, when you cannot understand why a Lunar subject shows so little coldness, it will be found that the hand, lines, and nails are quite red. This warms him up in every way, and makes health troubles of the lower third less likely, but renders him more liable to the bowel inflammations of the upper third. It also makes him amorous and easily excited by anything that is suggestive or appeals to his imagination. Yellow color will add a disagreeable indication, for it will make him cross and ugly. These qualities added to coldness and selfishness, which are always present with yellow color, form a combination that leads the subject easily to become bad and vicious. He has distorted (yellow) views of life people, and things, and, with a brain affected by poisoned blood, and being already highly imaginative, he sees everything from a bad standpoint, and easily becomes insane. With yellow color we find gouty and rheumatic troubles preliable, as shown on the middle third of the Mount. These must be looked after, for they will greatly influence the life of a subject. Blue color is often found, for with poor blood sluggishly pumped we find indications of a weak heart and consequent blue color. This is often an accompaniment of the diseases of the lower third of the Mount, and especially with women. When found, the age must be carefully noted, in order to tell whether the disturbance is permanent, or incidental to puberty, or change of life. The nails must be considered, for if we find a broad nail indicating strong general health, it will show that the subject is less liable to health defects and has a better temperament. This broad nail, if of good texture and pink, will add to the subject's chances, for with good general health, lack of nervous excitement, and normal circulation, the temper, mind, and disposition will all improve. If the nail is narrow, it will show delicate constitution, and the Mount must be carefully examined for health indications. Color must be carefully noted under the nails, for here we see a reflection of the white, pink, red, yellow, or blue disturbances of health and temperament. The texture of the nail must be considered. A badly crossed Mount with fluted or brittle nails shows a highly sensitive, discontented, irritable, nervous person. Such an one will be a victim to many hallucinations. Heart-disease nails will be a bad indication, for they will add organic disturbance to a subject already predisposed to heart trouble, which is almost always complicated with kidney trouble. Short, critical nails will make a pronounced subject pugnacious and more irritable, constantly criticising and fault-finding. Black hair on the hands will strengthen the subject and tend to show that there is sufficient iron in the blood and system to largely counteract the flabby condition of the tissues. It will add fire, vigor, and force to the character. This subject is liable to be capricious, not always trustworthy, and generally given to stretching the truth, as Oriental instability is added to vivid imagination. Blond hair will make these subjects more phlegmatic, less volatile, and less strong. It will make them slower, but more trustworthy and less likely to indulge in falsehood. They are not so easily carried off their feet by excessive imagination, and are consequently more practical, having a tinge of Teutonic-Saxon quality to restrain them. The hand as a whole, when taken in connection with the Mount, will indicate which of the three worlds will rule. With excess in the fingers the mental will dominate, and the imaginative faculties will be devoted to language, for which these subjects have great aptness, easily becoming expert linguists, or it will expend itself in scientific or literary studies. This subject would make a good college professor. If the middle portion of the hand is well developed, business qualities will be present. This subject will, if a writer, professor, or business man, bring good business ideas to his assistance. With this combination he may become celebrated and rich at the same time. If the lower portion of the hand is largest we have the dominion of the baser world. The imaginings will be low, not elevating. If the appetites are base, this low imagination will make suggestive what to other minds would convey no such meaning. The Mount itself must be subdivided into three sections and the same general rules applied as to the fingers and their individual phalanges. If the upper part of the Mount is developed most fully, all of the imaginings will be of a high order, and the same rules will apply as with the hand as a whole. From this formation we get linguists, professors of language, literature, and music of a classic kind, and authors. With the upper and middle third both developed, these subjects will make money through their efforts, for the mental and business worlds are joined. When the upper two worlds are deficient and the

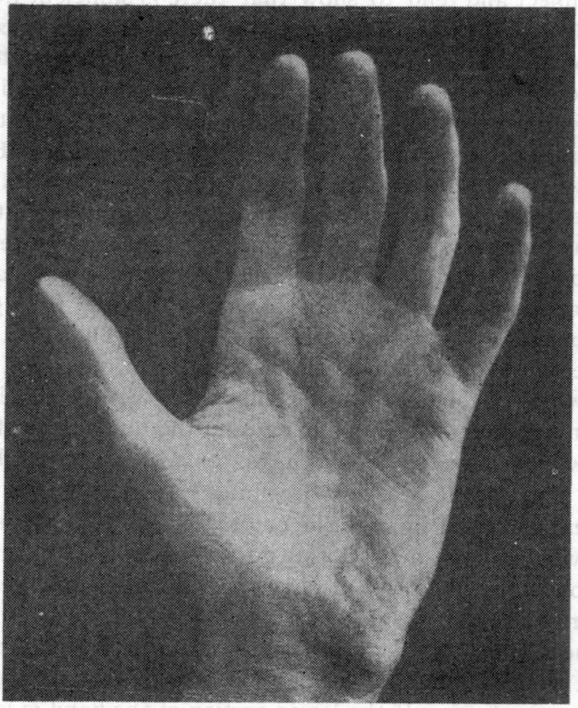

NO. 126. DEVELOPMENT OF LOWER THIRD OF MOUNT

lower is like a knob on the base of the hand it shows the domination of the lower side of the type, and the thoughts and imaginings are all low. With this development of the lower third of the Mount, together with a deficient Mount of Venus which is grilled, a double or triple Girdle of Venus, a chained white Heart line, and an oozy palm, you have those who practise secret vices (126), bringing on nervous disorders, the mildest form of which is hysteria. The finger-tips must be applied to whichever world of the Mount is in the lead. Pointed tips make the subject a prey to great idealism, religious exaltation, and he is utterly unpractical. Superstition, mysticism, and etherialism will make the life of this subject miserable and useless. He yearns continually for the impossible and unrealizable. Conic tips are normal to the type, and add their intuitive qualities, tinging the subject with romance and fancy. These subjects hate to work and belong to the lazy class. Square tips make the subject more practical. They pull down the idealism to a common-sense plane, make the subject more regular in habit and thought, and we get the best results of the type. Historians, composers. musicians who regard all the rules of metre and rhythm, are found with such combinations. Here we find a healthy imagination, which, coupled with practical ideas and common-sense, produces successful Lunarians. Spatulate tips add activity to an already restless person, especially if the Mount is grilled and cross-lined. They are original in ideas, entirely unconventional, and their danger is that they may constantly chase some will-o'-the-wisp of the fancy, until they become rovers indeed. If they have a smooth Mount, good Head line, and some square formation of the sides of the fingers, they become brilliant essayists, deep students or musicians, in which lines they excel as executionists. Knotty fingers reduce the fanciful condition to a marked degree, as they make a subject reason. They are in fact one of the greatest reducing factors for a Lunarian, and these subjects produce practical writers, teachers, and deep thinkers. They can throw over the most abstruse question a shimmer of imagination which makes it interesting, and wherever they are, or whatever the subject of their efforts, good reasons are given for everything they say, while at the same time they are not tied down to the earth by severe materialism. Smooth fingers, with their impulse and intuition, their artistic sense and distaste for analysis, form an accompaniment which brings out the Lunarian qualities strongly.

In this case imagination is heightened, usefulness becomes subservient to beauty, and the result is a highly artistic nature full of poetic ideals. These subjects love romance, poetry, and fiction, and, if writers, they produce such works. They love art, painting, and sculpture that is the product of some artist's imagination. They are quick in forming opinions, not always practical, and add the artistic intuitive qualities of smooth fingers to the imaginative ideals of the Lunarian. Such subjects are likely to be continually changing in their ideas and occupations, winding up their lives without having put their naturally brilliant qualifications to good account. Long fingers add minutiæ and detail to the Lunarian qualities. Such subjects when describing some creation of their fancy will not omit an iota that can make the picture complete. These long fingers with this naturally slow type add to the slowness; and to the selfishness belonging to the type, the distrust and suspicion of long fingers. The subject is apt to be orderly in dress and surroundings, and extremely likely to be sensitive and ready to take offense at trifles. If writers, they are prone to sacrifice strength to detail, and as teachers will prolong their dissertations to unwise lengths. As painters, they can create an imaginative scene, and not omit a detail in their treatment of the subject. In conversation they are fanciful and tiresome. Short fingers make the subject quick, impulsive, and likely to "fly off the handle." They also make him slovenly in appearance, careless about everything he does, and apt to rely entirely on inspiration. These subjects plan the greatest schemes, which are usually entirely unpractical. They are continually in danger of making mistakes from going too fast and attempting too much, and they are the persons who always have a new idea which is "sure to be successful," and this leads them into continually fooling themselves. The thumb will either calm the subject or make him more visionary. A large thumb will show strong will and reason, which materially strengthen the subject. A short thumb reduces both will and reason and makes him visionary, vacillating, and weak. This is especially true if the thumb be pointed

Remember that a square, spatulate, or paddle-shaped *short thumb* is more stable and strengthening than a pointed or conic short thumb, and that pointed or conic tips will reduce the strength of a large thumb. Examine the individual phalanges of the thumb to see if will is in excess of reason, or *vice versa*, then apply your information to the Lunar qualities. See if a thick, coarse thumb is to brutalize the imagination, or whether a delicate, refined thumb will make the ideals high. Then note the Head line. If it goes straight across the hand it makes the ideas more practical ; if it droops to the Mount of the Moon it tinges them with imagination. If it is clear, well marked, and of good color, you have a strong mind, self-control, and healthy imagination. This gives all the benefits of the type without its dangers. If the Head line is broken, wavy, islanded, chained, poorly marked, or badly colored, containing perhaps in its course a star, you must ascribe poor faculty of mental concentration, lack of firmness, a weakened brain, and vivid imagination ; and from such subjects come those who are continually changing their mind, are restless, never satisfied, and vacillating, and, if actual insanity is escaped, are continually verging on an unbalanced condition of mind. Thus the Lunarian ranges from a highly gifted subject to one who is insane, all indicated by the size, character, and markings of the Mount. Wherever no Mount is found, you find dense materialism ; when you find too much Mount, there is too much imagination, which may mean insanity. So, again, we seek to find the happy medium which will show the healthy operation of the mind. Do not expect to find many typical Lunarians, but *do* expect to find with nearly every subject, imagination in some degree developed. You need have no trouble whatever in grading its extent, the plane on which it operates, nor the combinations that accompany it if you have thoughtfully digested this chapter and what precedes it.

CHAPTER XXV

THE MOUNT OF VENUS

THE seventh Mount type is the Venusian, and the portion of the hand which locates him is the Mount of Venus, situated at the base of the thumb. As single signs or in combination, the triangle, circle, square, or single vertical lines strengthen the Mount of Venus.

The cross, grille, island or dot show defects of the Mount (127). This Mount rises into the palm, has the largest prominence shown by any of the Mounts, and by its size and markings you must estimate the amount and kind of Venusian qualities possessed by the subject. If the Mount is very prominent, highly colored, and deeply grilled with long lines, it is an *excessive* development, and the Venusian characteristics will be strong in the subject (128). If it is not out of proportion with the rest of the hand, it is a *normal* Mount, and Venusian characteristics will be present in normal degree. If there is an absence of any development and the Mount has a flat and flabby appearance (129), it is a *deficient* Mount, and the Venusian qualities are entirely lacking. Between these extremes are many degrees of development. The Venusian type is a pleasant one to meet, healthy, happy, joyous, and though it descends the scale of morality at times, it is always agreeable and attractive. It is a type which must be carefully handled, for to estimate it incorrectly is a serious matter. Dealing as it does with love and the sexual passions, there is needed much perception and a lofty attitude of mind in the practitioner, for the temptation is to be influenced by the known proclivities of the type, and thus inexperienced or low-minded palmists attribute base desires to many subjects who are instead filled with the magnificent qualities that belong to the elevated Venusian type. In the Plan of Creation, as we have conceived it, there was needed that great bond of sympathy and attraction which brings together the human

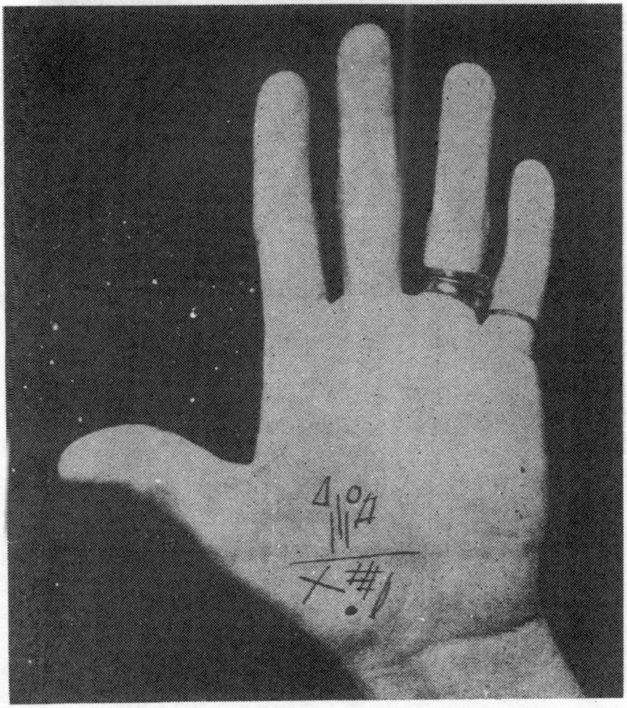

NO. 127. DISTINGUISHING MARKS ON THE MOUNT OF VENUS

family, drives away soullessness, coldness, and selfishness, and substitutes for these generosity, warmth, and love. To supply these necessary factors and to accomplish these purposes, the Venusian type was created. Standing as it does for love, sympathy, and generosity, the Venusian type is a good one, and, as one of its greatest qualifications is attraction for its fellows, it necessarily needs warmth and heat, for heat attracts and cold repels. This Venusian heat means a plentiful supply of good-quality blood, and a strong heart to pump it, consequently the Venusian is a healthy type and a handsome one, for good health begets good looks, producing not always rounded, doll-like beauty, but freshness and at-

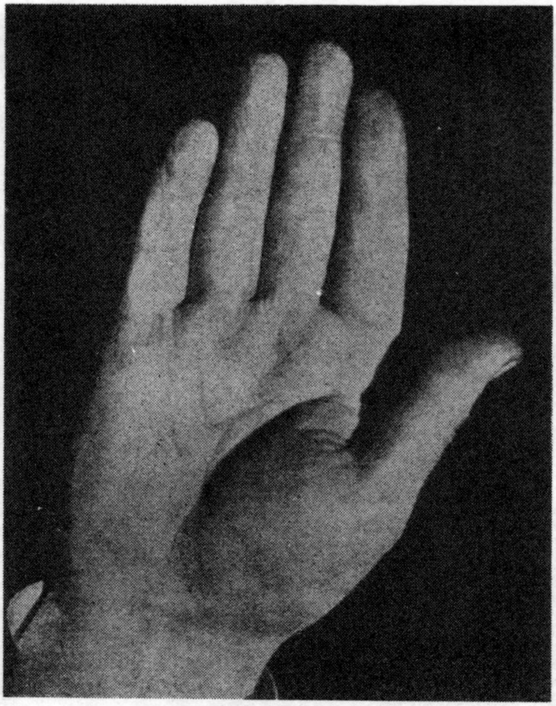

NO. 128. LARGE MOUNT OF VENUS

tractiveness. We find each type endowed with whatever accompaniments of health and characteristics are necessary to best fit it to bring forward the elementary forces which it represents, so the Venusian, being created to emphasize love, is given health, warmth, and physical attractiveness, that, wherever he appears, love may be inspired. There is about the Venusian no hint of gloom, biliousness, coldness, or selfishness—all is warmth, life, beauty, and attraction; consequently the Venusian is beset with many temptations, is constantly attracted to the opposite sex, has strong physical passion, and needs a fine Head line (self-control and judgment) and a large thumb (determination) to keep him

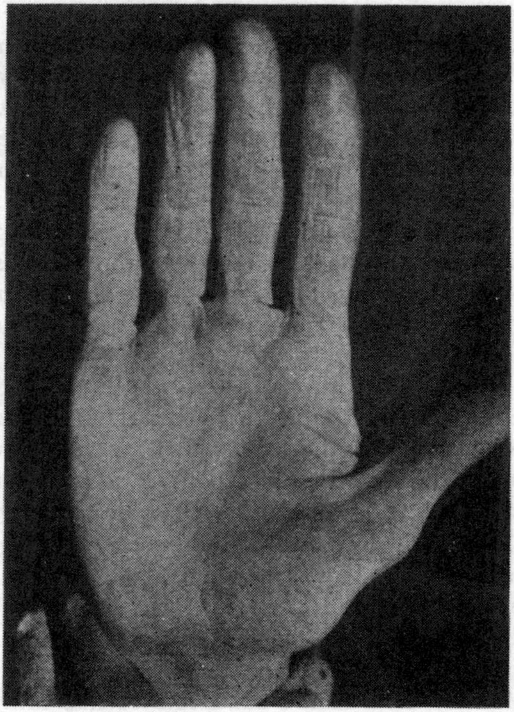

NO. 129. FLAT MOUNT OF VENUS

in the straight and narrow path. Although I treat this type in the masculine gender, it is a feminine type, for we all know that such attraction as belongs to it is more the province of the weaker than the sterner sex. Man is battling with the world, while woman is filled with love, sympathy, and all the finer qualities which refine and elevate, and the tender passion grows more tender and refined in her character than in his. Man may love, but not with the same degree of delicacy possible to woman, who embodies the ideal of the highest form of this God-given quality. So the Venusian type, representing the greatest perfection in human love, is necessarily a feminine type. Woman also represents a higher grade of morality than man, consequently Venusian attractiveness to the opposite sex is much safer in her charge than his. When a Venusian development is found strong in a woman's hand, it will not speak of such profligacy as the same development would in the hand of a man. In a man a strong Venusian Mount either makes him somewhat feminine in his characteristics, especially if smooth fingers, conic tips, and soft consistency are present; or else it makes him fiery and heated in his passions, and if the hand be hard this subject will indulge these desires, not restraining them as will a woman with the same development. In some hands the Mount is very full and seems as if it would burst through the skin (see 128). If this kind of Mount is smooth the subject will love all Venusian things powerfully, but will not be as excessive as will one with the same sized Mount *grilled* (130). In the latter case the grilling shows that the electric currents running over the Mount will excite the Venusian passion to an increased degree. Smooth Mounts, if not large, will indicate love of flowers, music, form, color, paintings, etc., but not strong sexual passion. The same Mount grilled will have added sexual attraction. If the Mount is full and grilled in a woman's hand, she will be most strongly attracted to the opposite sex, even as much as would a man with a similar Mount. In a man's hand this Mount brings him to a grade of femininity equal to woman in the Venusian directions, and he becomes dangerous in his tendencies, for he has the power to attract without the seeming necessity for resisting that the woman has. If on the Mount of Venus the grilled lines are very deep, strong, and red, it will add greatly to the fire and danger of the Mount. Often a Mount will be seen which is full of grilled lines, and the Mount shows, by the loose skin, that it *has been* very full. The Mount has the appearance of a sucked orange in its flabbiness, and tells of one who *has had* strong Venusian desires, which have been indulged freely until vitality is gone and the subject is worn out. It is a pity that human depravity should make it necessary to write of the Mount of Venus anything but the beautiful qualities that properly be-

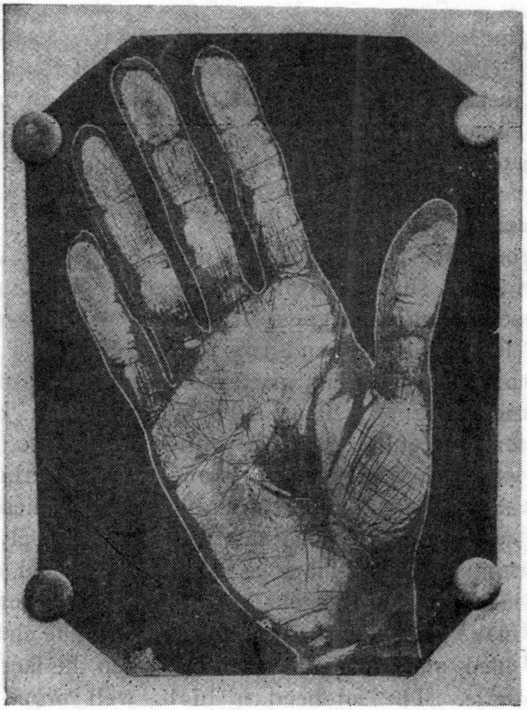

NO. 130. GRILLED MOUNT OF VENUS

long to the Venusian. These same sexual desires that we find debased by the profligate and the libertine were put into human beings so that they might be attracted by each other, and by this constant attraction the marriage state perpetuated and the human family increased through the continued birth of children. The *attraction* to marriage was necessary in order that the pain of child-bearing might not prevent reproduction, and Venusian qualities of love and attraction were intended only for high purposes. That the depravity of man has abused these faculties we all know, and this knowledge may grieve us, but as palmists we are bound to study humanity as we find it, and not as we might wish it. So with the Venusian type we stand in the presence of one of God's greatest creations, which we must examine to see if the functions are being used for the proper purposes, or debased to feed the flames of sensuality. The Venusian type, then, stands for love, sympathy, tenderness, generosity, beauty, melody in music, gayety, joy, health, and passion, an array of forces which place it on the pinnacle of attractiveness, and render it liable to many temptations and dangers.

In appearance the Venusian is attractive and beautiful. He is graceful, shapely, well balanced and easy in his manner, presenting more a type of feminine beauty than masculine. The Apollonian and Jupiterian are types of manly beauty, the male Venusian partakes of the soft voluptuousness of female beauty. These subjects are of medium height, and present graceful curves of form from head to foot. The skin is white, fine in texture, soft and velvety to the touch, transparent in its fineness, through which a delicate pink color glows, showing normal health and blood supply. The face is round or oval in shape, is finely proportioned, with no high cheek bones, thin cheeks, prominent temples, or square jaws to make it angular or mar its beauty. The cheeks are well rounded, and often show dimples when the face breaks into a smile. The forehead is high, well proportioned, gracefully rounding in front, perfect in contour The skin on the forehead is tightly drawn, and does not wrinkle, nor do crows'-feet appear at the corners of the eyes in young subjects. These come later in life and after Venusian fires have fiercely burned. There is a Venusian mark on the forehead which is seen in young Venusians, which consists of three vertical wrinkles over the bridge of the nose between the eyes. The hair is abundant, long, silky, fine, and wavy. The Venusian does not grow bald naturally;

when so found it is from some unnatural cause. The eyebrows are well marked, abundant, and form graceful curves on the forehead, well pointed at the ends, sharply outlined, and seldom growing over the nose; when they do, it indicates a tendency toward coarsening the type. The eyes are round or almond-shaped, brown or dark blue in color, and have a tender expression of human sympathy. When the passions are aroused they have a voluptuous expression which it is impossible to mistake. The Venusian is a fine subject—in his whole physical make-up this fineness of texture shows constantly; his eyelids are smooth in quality, with delicately traced blue veins showing through, and with long silky lashes curling upward on the ends. The nose is shapely, full sized, but with fine curves. The nostrils are broad, and show varying moods by their rapid contraction or expansion when the subject is excited.

The mouth is beautifully shaped, with bow-like curves and full, red lips, the lower one slightly more prominent. The teeth are white, medium in size, strong, and set in beautifully colored, healthy-looking gums; so when the Venusian smiles — the dimpled cheeks, the expressive eyes, the white teeth showing through full red lips, and set in pink gums — make a most attractive picture. The chin is round and full, often dimpled on the end, and completes the graceful contour of the face. The neck is long, full, and shapely, connecting the well-shaped head with gracefully drooping shoulders, which, while they do not speak of muscular strength, show breadth and health. The chest is large, full, round, and expansive, thus giving the lungs full play. The voice is full, musical, and attractive. It shows no weakness in tone, and yet has not the Martian strength. The legs are graceful in shape, the hips high and round, even in male Venusians, and the thigh proportionately long. The feet are small and shapely, with a high-arched instep, which gives him grace and elasticity in his walk. Altogether, the Venusian is refined, graceful, lovable, and attractive, the most apt figure to fill the very sphere in life for which he was intended, by adding brightness, joy, gay spirits, and love to a world without which selfishness and monotony would surely rule. The hand of the Venusian is white, soft, fine in texture, pink in color, fingers of medium length or short, tips conic, slightly square or of a small, spatulate shape, nails filbert and pink, thumb medium or small, and a large Mount of Venus either smooth or grilled.

The Venusian is essentially an affectionate subject. He is instinctively drawn toward his fellow-man by feelings of kinship and human sympathy, and these feelings easily ripen into love, which is his primary and typical attribute. With the Venusian there is no such feeling of repellence, or a desire to retire from the haunts of mankind, as we find with the Saturnian. Neither has he the Saturnian's instinctive hatred of his fellows. He is rather attracted toward them, seeks their society, is agreeable, kind, sympathetic, lovable, and popular. Never will you find a Venusian who turns a deaf ear to the sufferings or appeals of any human being, and never will you find a Venusian with a stiff thumb. Supple thumbs are always present, and their generosity and liberality extends to all who appeal for help. Thus the Venusian is besieged by those who have a tale of woe, for all are sure to find heartfelt sympathy in their misfortunes, and they know that whatever aid is possible will be given. In hours of affliction or despair the Venusian never deserts a friend, but with open hand and all the tenderness of his warm heart he relieves distress and suffering wherever found. Thus the Venusian attracts all who know him by the bond of humanity, which seems to link him to mankind in general. He is often the victim of rogues, who, knowing his sympathetic nature and generosity, impose upon him with ease. But this does not discourage or cause him to withdraw his sympathy or benefactions from others, for he would rather be imposed upon several times than fail to relieve one worthy case.

The Venusian is not fickle; even though there is a platonic love in his heart for all humanity, still, when the one true love has taken possession of him he is steadfast.

He is always gay. To him living is a joy. He has no bile poisoning his blood, no rancor fills his heart, no malice actuates him toward anyone. Good health brings in its train a good disposition, the world looks bright, and its beauty brings to him a feeling of restfulness, joy, and gratitude. On the same day, and amid exactly the same surroundings, the Saturnian will be in gloom, melancholy, pessimism, and sadness, while the heart of the Venusian will bubble with gladness, happiness, and thanksgiving for his blessings. Everything is bright to him, and this brightness he sheds upon his more serious-minded fellows, attracting and helping them through the world. This is why he is popular and loved, and from the exuberance of goodness in his heart he returns this love in abundant measure. He is fond of all amusements, dancing, society, gallantry, and all forms of gayety. His lack of seriousness is often carried too far, for he will pursue pleasure to the exclusion of business, and therefore does not grow wealthy. He does not value riches nor assume responsibility, yet such an one as he always gets along in some way, so he is careless and improvident — but happy. He is entirely unselfish. When distress is present he sinks self entirely, and his first thought and effort are for others. He is bright, sparkling, vivacious, spontaneous, and genial, and the life of every company in which he may be. He is not profoundly studious, nor very ambitious, but is content to enjoy life. He is a great lover of the beautiful. Dress, home, surroundings, flowers, pictures, and art in every form attract, and in all of these he loves harmony, taste, and beauty. To him it is more essential that things should be beautiful and enjoyable than that they should be useful. He is passionate, so when his eye is pleased and a responsive echo is awakened in some other breast, he will gratify his passions. If such a thing as harmlessness were possible in a matter of this kind, it would have to be accorded to the Venusian, for to him heat, ardor, and love are inherent and a part of his very existence. But always remember that all Venusians do not give way to their desires, and no matter how strong these may be, they are often curbed for a lifetime, and the world knows nothing of the struggles such a subject undergoes.

Venusians are honest and truthful. They are not schemers for money-making, or ambitious for high positions or distinction, consequently the temptation to cheat or lie does not come to them. They are constant friends, and readily forgive and forget an injury or injustice. Their human feeling causes them to see matters from "the other fellow's" point of view, often to their own disadvantage. They hate quarrels or strife, and would rather suffer an injustice than engage in them. The Venusian loves to give pleasure to others, and will put forth all his powers of amusement and fun-making, exerting himself to the utmost as long as he sees that those in his audience are enjoying themselves. But he loves to have his efforts appreciated, and likes to be told that he is agreeable and pleasant.

Music appeals most strongly to the Venusian, and the Mount of Venus is often called the Mount of Melody. You will never find a strong Mount of Venus without the accompanying passion for music. In examining hands for musical ability, fully note this Mount. When prominent, musical *love* is always present, and *some* ability to become proficient. With a hand fine in texture, a good line of Apollo, a good line of Mercury and line of Head, smooth fingers, square at the sides, with either conic, square, or spatulate tips, and a good Mount of Moon, you have a musician, and some of the greatest the world has ever known have had such formations. Remember, all do not have the opportunity to develop their talents, so do not be discouraged if you find all these things on hands not belonging to musical people. If they had been trained properly, they would have been musical. The music that appeals most to the Venusian is melody. To him, classics savor too much of seriousness, but Strauss waltzes, Sousa marches, and kindred compositions will set Venusian feet to going and Venusian hearts to throbbing. The Mount of the Moon adds additional musical taste to a subject. Harmony, fugue, and counterpoint will be present with a developed Mount of the Moon. Love of color, form, and art, while present in a Venusian, will remain *only a love* of these things if unaccompanied by a good line and Mount of Apollo, with the Apollo finger longest in the first phalanx, and a Mount of Jupiter well developed to back them up. The Venusian will always love bright colors natural scenery, dress, and art, but other things are necessary to transform mere love into creative power. The Venusian often writes well, and although his nature is gay his writings are tinged with sadness. He also acts well, and many of these subjects are found on the stage. I have been interested to note that Venusians excel in tragedy or serious parts which move the audience to tears; and some of our greatest comedians are Saturnians (Sol Smith Russell is an example). In whatever way the Venusian talents are expended, we find that he touches the heart, and his music, writing, art, or acting speaks to the soul, appeals to the human interest of his hearers, and it is this fidelity and closeness to nature and nature's heart that brings tears of sympathy. A comedy rôle enacted by a Saturnian is the irony in his nature cropping out.

Venusians always marry, and generally at an early age. They mature rapidly as children, and, being exceedingly healthy, attain their growth when comparatively young. To them love and attraction for the opposite sex are natural, and thus they look upon marriage as a desirable state, which they do not put off longer than necessary. They are attracted by strong characters and by persons in good health. While they feel sympathy for those who are in distress, it is not weak persons who gain their love. The Martian is strongly attracted to the Venusian type, and the Martian strength and vigor attract the Venusian. Whatever the type they choose, it will be a robust, strong specimen of it. As much as Venusians love sexual pleasures, abandoned *demi-monde* Venusians are rare. Of course, this class of society has some Venusian quality, but it is not the pure type with all its good qualities. The sexual predisposition of the Venusian type makes them doubly liable to bear children. Their cheery nature and joyous ways fill their homes with brightness, and seldom do they appear among the marital unfortunates.

The Venusian never commits suicide. To him life is too bright, there is too much to be thankful for and too little to be discouraged about. Of all the types these are the real philosophers, who, though not so deep as some, still are happy, and self-destruction is abhorrent to them. Good health is the normal condition of the type, so with the Venusian we do not look for diseases. They are often nervous, and may have any of the acute disorders which attack mankind in general, but they have no chronic ailments peculiar to them, and diseases which a Venusian has will be found marked on some other Mount, and not on the Mount of Venus. With low Venusians, whose good qualities are overshadowed by their evil desires, we find often venereal diseases, and such will be shown by black dots or brown patches appearing on the Mount or back of the hand. Physiologically, these are produced by impaired and poisoned blood which has contaminated these portions of the hand.

Unfortunately, we must record that there are bad Venusians. Even this good type does not escape that blight. These subjects have only a vestige of good, and the lower instincts and desires rule. They are short in stature, stout in figure, with prominent abdomens, and all the grace and beauty eliminated from them. No finely curved lines are left, no elastic step, no bright eye. The hair becomes red, the nose upturned, and the eyes bloodshot. Excess is stamped in every place, and bad desires and appetites have the upper hand. The lips are thick, red, and sensual ; the face has a coarse skin, and the neck, body, and hands are marked as belonging to the lower world of base desires. The bad Venusian hand is very thick, especially the third phalanges of the fingers, the base of the hand, and the Mount of Venus, which is very prominent, hard, and red. The fingers are short and smooth, with the first phalanges deficient. The skin is coarse in texture, red in color, and the hand inelastic. The thumb is small, especially the first phalanx, which is often pointed. This subject is low in his tastes, warped in his ideas, and inordinate in his appetites. He enjoys life in a coarse fashion, but is dominated by low desires and low pleasures. Not having fineness of nature, nor strength of will, these subjects do not distinguish between a refined pleasure and one which is low, so they debauch themselves, do not consider how much harm they may do, and are unscrupulous and bad. Everything takes on a tinge of vulgarity, and obscene literature and pictures or ribald talk give them pleasure. They are animals merely, and know as pleasure only the gratification of animal appetites. The bad Venusian is a reprobate, a conscienceless libertine, and disgusting to decent people. Between this creature and the high type there are innumerable grades of Venusian development. It must be your task properly to estimate it by a careful examination of every part of the hand. Do not debase this splendid type by overestimating its sensual side, nor elevate a bad set of Venusian qualities by underestimating their grossness. Care and thought must be used and a complete study made of everything in the hand.

The texture of the skin will show refinement or coarseness of the subject. Everything that refines elevates the type; everything that coarsens degrades it. Thus, with fine texture the higher side of the subject may be looked for. The tenderness and sympathy will be increased, and the sensualism decreased. Beauty of form or color will be a delight, and evil thoughts will not be in the ascendant. With a large, or even an excessive Mount, or one fully grilled, the fine texture will show the passions to be refined and love to be more ideal and purer. This subject, while strongly attracted sexually, will be attracted only to those mentally equal to him or those of the same degree of refinement. His pleasure from these things will come largely from knowing that they are operating in a refined way. Coarse texture, showing coarseness of nature, acts in an opposite way. When found with a large grilled Mount of Venus, the subject will not care what is the grade of the opposite sex in mental or moral fineness, or the color of the skin; his enjoyment comes from the mere physical pleasure he derives from them. With fine texture, passion and love is refined ; in coarse texture, it is brutalized, and made animal. The coarse-textured Venusian is the nearest approach to selfishness that we find in this type, for he indulges his pleasures without regard to others, especially if his thumb be at all stiff.

Consistency will show what amount of energy your subject has. If it be flabby, he will be a mere pleasure hunter, and no thought of usefulness or advancement in life will actuate him. The only exertion this subject will think of making is in pursuit of enjoyment, and inertia even in this respect will be marked, for he will be best satisfied when pleasures come to him and he does not have to seek them. Soft hands will show more energy than the flabby, and will be more useful in life. They still show laziness, but that which can be overcome, and must not be read as showing the hopeless inertia belonging to a flabby-handed Venusian. Elastic consistency is a fine combination. Here we have the excellent Venusian qualities, directed by an intelligent energy, which bring to perfection the best side of the type. It does not grow any less attractive, lovable, or sympathetic, but it becomes more practical, real, and less sensual. The idleness of flabby hands gives too much time for thoughts of mere pleasure-seeking. The elastic consistency pushes the subject to action, and this does not allow the baser side to develop. " Satan finds some mischief for idle hands to do " applies to the flabby-handed Venusian and not to the elastic. No better, happier, brighter, healthier type exists than the elastic-handed Venusian, for, while full of fire, the energy works out these fires in better ways than in the indulgence of low appetites. Hard hands show unintelligent energy directing the Venusian qualities, consequently this subject will be common, less refined, and ignorantly ardent. He will have strong desires, and will gratify them in an unintelligent way with the energy of hard hands, and these subjects are found as heads of families among the poor, where there are many children. With this subject, love, sympathy, and generosity are subjugated to desire.

Flexible hands show the elastic mind. This makes a very

intelligent, highly strung, gifted subject, but he is preliable to be an extremist, versatile, and too fond of admiration and pleasure. Flexible-handed Venusians need good balance-wheels to hold them in check. They are attractive, have many admirers and temptations, and often have their "heads turned." In such subjects look for clear, deep, well-marked and colored Head lines and good thumbs. These will be needed to keep them from wasting their lives and energies in a round of pleasure. The normally flexible hand is better balanced, more inclined to self-control, and to be self-contained. These subjects may have as strong Venusian traits, but will not be so frequently carried away by them, nor so liable to be mere pleasure hunters. These are the subjects, especially if they have elastic consistency, who accomplish a great deal in the battle of life, which, by reason of their attractive personality, is not to them so severe a struggle. First judge whether the Mount be a sensual one, an excessive one, or merely a smooth and normal development. Behind whatever kind you see, the normal balancing qualities of the normally flexible hand must be placed, and the result estimated. The stiff hand will show a stiff mind and the lack of elasticity of the nature. This subject is immeasurably more apt to be sensual and low in ideas and appetites, which he will indulge freely. He has no such sympathy or generosity, no such love of music, flowers, or the beauties of nature, as has his flexible-handed brother. He is full of lower desires, coarse in every way, unprogressive, and borders closely on stinginess and selfishness. In this subject there is a failure to complete the type; he has its low side and narrow views, minus the elevating qualities of a higher specimen of the same type.

The color of the hands is important. Pink is normal to the Venusian, and all other colors show an abnormal condition of health and consequent temperament. White color, showing a reduced strength of the current, pulls down the Venusian warmth and adds coldness. It will never be found that white color destroys the Venusian warmth and attraction, but it will reduce them. The subject will be less sympathetic and less ardent. The love of beauty will be present, but the fire of passion will burn with decreased force. Thus the white-colored Venusian will be less attractive to the opposite sex, less liable to the follies of the type, even though the Mount be strong or grilled. Pink color will show the normal condition. Here health is present in the blood and its operation, which brightens life ; and vivacity, gayety, and all the pleasant Venusian qualities will be in normal operation. This subject is perfection, so far as color goes, and will be more refined, will tend to the higher side of the type qualities, and will be attractive, lovable, and tender, without the presence of vulgar sensualism. These subjects are full of generosity and sympathy, and win their way by love and gentleness. Red color shows excess. If the color be deep, it adds fuel to the already inflammable subject. Therefore he will be easily excited by the opposite sex, will be greatly attracted by them, full of burning ardor and passion, and, while not criminal in thought or disposition, is dangerous, for the sexual attraction is so great that, when aroused, all thought of consequences is lost. If the Mount be full and deeply grilled, the color very red, be on your guard for excess in all of the Venusian directions. If the fingers be thick in the third phalanges and the palm be developed at the base, this excess will be extreme, and will stop at nothing to accomplish its desires. About eighty per cent. of murderers whose crimes have been committed upon husbands, wives, or lovers have such Venusian developments, and in sudden fits of jealousy or passion have committed their deeds. Yellow color is not common in a Venusian. The type is not predisposed to biliousness, so when yellow color is seen it means a most abnormal condition. The blood poisoned by bile destroys all the good qualities of the subject, who becomes cross and fretful. Already a highly strung type, the bilious irritation increases the nervous tension and destroys its sympathy and attractiveness, replacing these qualities with bad temper. The sexual attraction is at the same time destroyed, for bile acts most disastrously in this direction, producing a nervousness which makes it impossible. Blue color is often seen, for the Venusian frequently has heart trouble. When seen in palm or nails, it must be used to indicate the degree of trouble present.

The nails must be carefully considered. Broad nails, pink in color and fine in texture, will show good general health and a frank, honest disposition. They are likely to be flecked with white spots, for the subject is ultra-nervous. Narrower nails will show a less rugged constitution, and color and texture must be noted. In any reduction or change the normal condition of the subject is reduced or changed by whatever has changed the color. If the nail be very thin and narrow, it shows a very delicate constitution, and the normal healthy expectation of the type must be reduced accordingly. Critical nails are seldom seen on this type, for the Venusian is easy-going, and seeks pleasure instead of strife. If this formation be seen, estimate the subject as a critical or pugnacious Venusian according to the degree of development. Fluted nails will indicate that nervousness plays a prominent part. If very marked, the subject will be excitable and flighty, especially if the hand be flexible, the fingers long and smooth, and the tips pointed. The brittle nail, turning sharply back, is sometimes seen, and the danger of extreme nerve trouble, even paralysis, is present. These nervous nails will take away from the good nature and attractiveness of the subject. Bulbous nails, in whatever degree found, will tell that throat, bronchial, or pulmonary trouble is present, and must be considered in estimating the subject. Note this peculiar fact in these cases, that the consumptive Venusian has his sexual desires increased tremendously. This seems to be a symptom of this disease, especially in the middle stages.

Hair on the hands, if black, will show the increased vitality peculiar to that color. If it be plentiful, it also shows increased muscular strength. Black color, showing plentiful supplies of iron, adds to the ardor of the type, and the subject is vigorous, energetic, and volatile. If the Mount be a strong one, black hair must be considered as an addition to its strength. Red hair adds its flashing excitability to the subject, making him preliable to quick temper and sudden changes of mood. In both these colors I suppose the hair to be fine in quality. If coarse, it will show all the indications of color, but in a coarse degree. This coarse black or red hair with a large Mount, grilled, will make the subject very susceptible to sexual attraction, where physical instead of mental charms are the moving power. Red or black hair, fine in quality, shows volatility in refined degrees. Gray or white hair is often seen on Venusians even when young. In these cases if the depleted vitality shown by this color comes from exhausted powers due to excess, the flabby much-grilled Mount will be seen. Blond color is normal, and gives its typical qualities. If straw color, it is not the Venusian blond, which must have a tinge of auburn or red to be normal. The more silver the blond color, the more it shows Teutonic phlegmatism, and the more it is tinged with the auburn shade, the more ardor is present.

The hand as a whole will show the three worlds, and these must be more largely depended upon with this type than with any of the others except the Martian. With the fingers long, and especially the first phalanges of them, the mental world will govern the subject. The love will be ideal, the sympathy lofty, and the generosity intelligent. He will love music, poetry, romance, all of which will be viewed from a high plane and away from base thoughts and ideas. The middle portion of the hands and fingers strongly developed will add practical ideas, and make the subject less idealistic. The feeling of fellowship with all mankind will be very marked, and a full operation of generosity is expected, especially if the thumb be supple. This subject will love warmly, but will be sensible, not carried away by the idealism of the upper world nor the sensualism of the lower. These people are strong in the Venusian qualities, but regulate them. If the base of the palm be full and large, and stronger than the upper developments, the subject will be dominated by the low desires of the type. Fierce passion will inflame him, and he will regard all persons simply from the standpoint of ability to satisfy his desires. The pure, ideal side of love is unknown, and the bond of attraction to his fellows is physical desire. If this development of the base of the palm be very great, the third phalanges of the fingers thick, the first short, the Mount of Venus red and deeply grilled, and the thumb weak, the subject will murder if necessary to gratify his desires. These are the markings found on ravishers.

The fingers and other Mounts must be examined to see what types are secondary, or which side of these types. If the Venusian has no Jupiterian ambition, Saturnian wisdom or soberness, or Mercurian shrewdness in his make-up, he will not achieve success in worldly or business affairs. While a lovable, attractive type, the Venusian needs some other types in combination to develop him. Whatever the secondary or tertiary types may be, they must be considered as *back* of the Venusian qualities as *driving forces.* The Apollonian is too closely akin to the Venusian to make a good combination; he has too many similar qualities. The Lunarian is not a good secondary combination, for imagination in too great degree will inflame the passions and make an already inert subject more lazy. It needs some side of the Jupiterian, Saturnian, Mercurian, or Martian type to perfect the Venusian.

The finger-tips will tell their story. Marked ideality is present with pointed tips, in which case the dreamy qualities will render these subjects impractical, but lovable and fascinating. They are hot-house plants, "human china," fit to love and play with, but unequal to a struggle against the roughness of the world. Conic tips show artistic tastes and give conic qualities to the subject. Square tips make him practical, regular in habits, tidy in dress, and methodical in his ways. Delicately square tips are often seen, but not those which are broad, or pronouncedly square. Spatulate tips add energy, fire, and originality to the subject. He is ready, seldom taken off his guard, and in ideas or speech is always equal to the occasion. The spatulate tip is a fine combination for the Venusian, for it makes him human in sympathy and love. These subjects are intensely fond of pets,—horses, dogs, or all animals; they are constant in their affections, original in ideas, active in games, skilful, graceful, and charming. They are passionately fond of children, and tender and gentle with everyone.

Knotty fingers will greatly reduce the impulse of the subject. Though knots are unexpected still they are found, and must be considered. The first knot alone will make the subject intelligent, systematic in his mental operations, and less frivolous. The second knot will make him tidy, unusually careful of his appearance, and orderly in everyday life. Both knots will make him analytical, but, as the subject is dominated by enthusiasm and impulse, they are seldom seen well marked.

Smooth fingers are expected. The artistic ideas, impulsive ways, and spontaneous methods in thought and action which are peculiar to the Venusian are all emphasized by smooth fingers; there may, however, be seen a slight development of the second knot, and still the fingers may be considered as smooth. These subjects love dress and good appearance, and are nearly always tidy.

Long fingers are not expected, for the Venusian does not love detail. He loves pleasure, and to have someone else see that everything is planned and systematized. After all these details have been attended to, the Venusian likes to be called in to enjoy the things prepared. He will then be full of praise, and the long-fingered subject who has done all the work will say, "What an agreeable fellow he is, and how appreciative." Thus the Venusian by a few kind words often compensates for hours of labor, and his fellow-men will crowd each other in an effort to serve him. He lacks long-fingered detail, and also the suspicion and sensitiveness that belong to long fingers. When long fingers are seen, add their propensities to the subject, always remembering that they are not normal to the type. Short fingers, with their quickness of thought and impulsiveness of action, are normal with the type. Note carefully whether they are too short, for the impulsiveness of this type needs nothing to increase it. The natural distaste of the Venusian for detail emphasizes his short-fingered qualities, and increases the impulsiveness and desire for quickness in thought and execution. Thus, when short fingers are seen, place short-fingered quickness and liability to carelessness back of the Venusian qualities and you will get the proper result. The thumb will be largely the key to your subject. If small or pointed, or both, you know the character is weak and vacillating. The desires will rule and be gratified, the subject will be easily led by others, and, with his natural pleasure-loving proclivities, will be led away by whoever obtains an influence over him. The natural laziness of the type will be increased, and determination lacking. You must compare the two phalanges to see if will or reason is greater. If will be stronger, determination will be exercised without good judgment, and this subject is determined by fits and starts. If the will phalanx be pointed, the impressionability is increased and the will weakened. If it be square, the will is stronger, common-sense, and practical. If it be spatulate, the will becomes very strong *per se*, but if unsupported by a good second phalanx and a good Head line will not be brought into operation. The clubbed formation is not often seen on this type, and is not normal. There is no fierceness nor bloodthirsty desire for murder in the good Venusian. When he kills, it is in a fit of jealousy or thwarted passion, and it is a low specimen of the type who does it. Refined, high-class Venusians never commit murder—there is too much kindness and sympathy in them. On low type Venusians you will always find a strong secondary type present, nearly as strong as the Venusian, and it is from this secondary type that they get the nerve and brutality to commit murder. The Venusian type supplies the passion and jealousy, the secondary type the instinct to kill. If the clubbed thumb be seen on a refined Venusian subject, you will find that the brutal tendencies are inherited, sometimes from generations back, and often never display themselves. The paddle-shaped will phalanx is an excellent one to find on this type, for the tendencies of the type are so strong that it needs all the restraints possible to hold them in check, and strong, evenly balanced will power is one of the best possible restraining elements. The second phalanx must be long and well balanced to get the best results, for reason and good judgment are needed to keep the subject level. If this is deficient, he becomes a prey to his emotions, impulses, and desires, and lacks the good sense and judgment to restrain them, even if he has a will strong enough to do it. In this case, *will* is in operation, but is not backed by judgment. The best formation of the second phalanx is the waist-like, for tact is then indicated, and the subject does not offend by brusqueness. Thus, on a Venusian, the large thumb, giving good judgment and determination, will hold in check any amount of strong desires. In the chapter on the Thumb we said that this digit shows will, reason, and love, the three great moral forces of the universe. Thus the Venusian, in a perfect state, combines all these. The Head line must be clear, well cut, well colored, and unbroken, to give the best results, for the Venusian needs self-control and clear judgment to steer him from pitfalls. These elements he gets from such a Head line, which is a fine adjunct to a good thumb. Of the seven types the one which lightens the world with love, charms with beauty, attracts with health, sympathizes in sorrow, and relieves distress is the Venusian, and while we can by no means say that he is faultless, we must recognize that his good qualities are so predominant that his faults are forgotten.

PART SECOND

CHAPTER I

INTRODUCTORY WORDS—WHAT LINES ARE FOR—THE LIFE MAP—SOME GENERAL SUGGESTIONS

"The soul contains in itself the event that shall presently befall it. The event is only the actualizing of its thought."—EMERSON.

BY continued study and observation of the lines in the hand, and by carefully tabulating the results of innumerable experiments with them, it has been shown that lines found in *certain places* always indicate the *same thing*, and that certain formations of these lines invariably show the good, bad, or weak operation of the things they indicate. It has also been proven in like manner that lines show *details* of the *life*, and that, when events have strongly impressed themselves upon the brain of a subject, lines have appeared in certain parts of the hand, have disappeared, broken, or changed in various ways as these events have produced good or bad results for the subject. By observing thousands of results, it has been possible to locate *where* in the hand these various emotions or influences appear, and *what kind* of lines indicate their good or bad effect. Lines are seen in the hands of newborn babes as well as of adults; they cross in various directions, often make their appearance where the skin has formerly been smooth, and in many cases strong lines fade and disappear, leaving a smooth surface of skin, that shows no sign that any line has ever been there. Lines increase in depth and grow in length, often clearly cutting their way across the hand. They also vanish entirely, beginning at the end and gradually diminishing until the whole line has disappeared. *These changes follow profound impressions made on the mind of a subject.*

Many believe that every detail in the anatomy of the human being is constructed for a specific purpose, and that nothing was created without a reason. Thus we are either forced to declare that the lines in the hand are an exception to all the rest, and that the Creator did a vain and useless thing when these lines were put in the hand, or else we must acknowledge that the lines are there for a purpose.

Not so very long ago the medical profession knew comparatively little about the human organism. There are organs whose functions anatomists have not yet discovered, but these students of the human body do not, for this reason, claim that such organs have no usefulness. One by one the mysteries of our construction are being discovered, and it is the belief of progressive students that in time the function of every part will be revealed, and nothing found that is not necessary to the operation of the human machinery. As long as every physician undertook to master the entire range of medicine and to treat every form of disease, we had the *general practitioner*, who possessed only a *general* knowledge of anatomy, disease, and treatment. During this period the real information about the several parts of the body possessed by any one man was necessarily limited, the practice of medicine and surgery was crude, and the results obtained were comparatively unsatisfactory. But when one man began devoting his entire life to a study of the eye, another of the ear, another of the skin, and so on through every organ of the body, we had the evolution of the specialist, and at once great progress was made and wonderful results were achieved. The *whole body* was too complex and *too big* a subject for one man to master, but the specialist, by giving a life study to one organ, began to understand that organ thoroughly, and in each was found such an infinite number of details that it has taken more than a lifetime to accumulate the present stock of information about them all. Strange as it may seem, the hand has been neglected in this separating of specialties, and this, most important and wonderful part of the whole body, the organ which bears the stamp of the type to which each subject belongs, and which contains the map of his natural course through life, is only beginning to receive the attention it deserves.

As palmists, we are specialists with the hand, and in reaching the point where we are to study the purpose for which *lines* are in the hand, we claim to have found and proved this purpose. There is a natural course through life that every subject *would* follow if nothing took place to change it, and no effort was made to improve. In other words, we believe that there is a general outline of the course and limitations of the life of each subject, which exists at the beginning of that life. This general course is what the subject would *naturally* do through life, *because* of the combination of type qualities which he possesses. This natural life plan comprises those things which the *possession* of these type qualities would naturally *lead* him to do, the kind of health his type qualities would *cause* him to have, and the result is stamped upon him by the lines in his hand, which thus form a *map of his natural life's* course. If no change takes place in his mental or physical attitude, and no accidents occur, this course will be followed. Thus the lines in the hand are the writing placed there by Him who created the subject, and when the key to their meaning is used, it enables us to interpret the life map and to judge what the natural course of that life will be. Many earnest thinkers, having followed the study of the hand through Chirognomy, have halted when the lines were reached, and, while admitting that lines do enable us to read the events in a life, and being forced to acknowledge from what has been seen of actual cases that the future is often outlined, they pause for the explanation as to how this is accomplished.

There are now two well established facts, which when brought into combination explain these functions of lines in the hand. First, it has been positively proven that *lines change in unison with changes in the mental attitude of a subject, when these changes are great enough to alter his temperament and characteristics.* It is also proven that the *lines respond to changes in health and constitution,* that they indicate mental strength, and reveal details in the life, when certain events have produced a powerful impression on the mind of a subject. *Therefore we may say with positiveness that the lines in a hand are the direct reflex of the subject's mind, and that his mind produces, controls, or alters them.* This statement completely explains the accuracy of lines in outlining *past* events, for things which *have impressed* the brain are a part of the past, and it has proven a satisfactory explanation of *this part* of their usefulness. It is the accuracy of lines in outlining *future* events which has been difficult to explain. Recent experiments by scientists have demonstrated that the human being is possessed of a double consciousness or mind. One part operates in our material existence and makes us conscious only of those things which we can see or handle, and the other part operates on the plane of our spiritual existence, and gives us SPIRITUAL consciousness of things which we cannot see, touch, nor fully explain. This second mind rarely manifests itself in an objective way, and this is why it was not sooner discovered. The first, or worldly mind, has limitations. It is conscious only of things which *have* happened, or *are* happening before our very eyes. This side of our consciousness cannot pierce the veil of the future, or rise above our material existence; it only knows the things of to-day, which soon become the things of yesterday. Our inner consciousness, or spiritual mind, has no such limitations as has the objective. It knows not only what *has* happened, but what *will* happen. It is not confined within the prison of our earthly body, but it can rise above earth, and peer into the future. If it be true that mind produces, controls, or alters the lines in the hand, these lines must be subject *not only* to the influence of the worldly or objective consciousness or mind, but also of the subjective or spiritual. *If one consciousness has dominion of the past and present, and the other of the future, manifestly our past, present,* AND *future are in the possession of the* TWO MINDS, *and through their influence this past, present, and future is stamped upon us by means of the lines in the hand which we know reflect the mind.*

The accuracy of this hypothesis rests upon the two statements:

First, that mind produces, controls, or changes the lines in the hand; and,

Second, that there are two minds, the worldly or objective and the spiritual or subjective, with the functions ascribed to them.

If these two statements *are* true, the logic of our reasoning is unassailable, our hypothesis correct, and this will give the much-sought answer to the question, "How is it possible that lines in the hand can presage the future?" In support of the first basis of our hypothesis, I offer my own experience and that of many students of the hand, who have watched the formation of new lines and the change or disappearance of old ones, in perfect accord with the established rules of line reading. This fact can be proven by anyone who will take the trouble to observe. During the past five years I have made a special study of this subject, and have many recorded cases where these changes have occurred. It would be impossible, owing to their length, to present individual cases in this work, but the fact that lines *are* thus formed and changed is so well known to thousands of students of the hand, that I do not believe this point will be gainsaid by anyone. As to the correctness of our second basis, that the dual mind exists and operates as has been stated, I refer to the many scientific works now in existence on this subject, which have fully proven the fact. Many of the greatest scientists and scholars of the day and age have recorded the results of their investigations in such clear and concise form, that no room is left for doubt that the mind is dual in its nature, that it operates in illimitable space, is unhampered by material surroundings, and that it has in many cases looked into the future. It is not my purpose here to present the individual cases which have demonstrated these facts. It is not the place, and the literature on the subject is so voluminous and easy of access that all who wish may read it. I only state facts that *have* been proven, so that we may use them in support of our hypothesis. To sum up the matter: we have started from a given basis, contained in two statements which, if true, make our hypothesis correct, and explain the function of the lines. These two basic statements we have found *are* true, therefore our hypothesis *is* correct, the lines *are* produced, controlled, and changed by the mind, the dual mind has knowledge of *past, present, and future*, and, reflecting itself through the lines, forms the life map of a subject, easily read by one who understands it.

No one will claim that the map of any life may not be altered. Our life plan may be changed by many circumstances. These may be the influence of other people, accident, strong desire to change backed by determination, or perhaps failing health. Thus when these changes do or are to occur, new lines appear, and cross, obliterate, weaken, or strengthen, as the case may be, the Main lines, which are the *original map* of the life, and strong lines fade and disappear as the mind changes upon the matters these lines indicate. There has been a popular teaching that in paralysis the lines in the hand disappear, and the obliteration of lines occurring when this death of nerve force takes place has been cited to prove that lines are formed and controlled by the brain. The lines do not disappear with *all* paralytics. The course of the life in some cases goes on uninterrupted by the paralysis, though *impeded* by it, for though the body may often be helpless the mind may remain keen. In such cases the lines only become dulled and dimmed, but not obliterated. When the brain softens, as in paresis, the lines do fade and vanish, in the same proportion as the mind is destroyed, for as mind disappears there is nothing that will sustain vitality in the lines and preserve them as they were. Thus though there may be a brain, it will not control the lines unless it has a *mind* behind it, and though motion of the body may be lost by paralysis, the mind may still be bright and in operation, in which case the lines will be retained. In the hands of insane whose lunacy comes from a lack of mental balance but not from cellular brain destruction, we find strong lines. In this case mind is present, but in an unbalanced condition, for the possession of mind does not always mean mental balance. In every case where mind is *obliterated*, the lines in the hand disappear.

The Main lines indicate what the natural course of the life is, new lines just beginning to form show emotions and ideas just starting within the subject. Man is an enigma; you do not know the workings of his mind as you talk to him, often he does not fully understand them himself. If you looked at his brain you could not learn his thoughts. Patient students are, and have been, giving years of life to the search for a key with which they can unlock the secrets of the human mind. They have been working from many different directions, but the objective point has always been the same. One key is the Hand, the servant of the brain, plainly in sight; and with this key you can unlock the secret chambers of any mind. And, while I do not say that there are no other keys, I *do* say that this is the most reliable of which I know, for while men may be dissemblers, they cannot change the expression of the hand as they can the face. By the hand is revealed the man as *he is*, not as he may pretend to be, and you can learn from it his mental attributes and their probable outcome. One thing you must never forget. You cannot find the same events marked in every hand. And if your subjects are closely examined, it will be found that they are not all profoundly impressed by the same things. Therefore never claim you can read a certain series of events before examining your client's hands. Only the matters which are hereditary or are natural tendencies with him, or those things which have developed in him, and have created a profound impression upon his mind, will be shown in his hand. Manifestly, as all subjects are not impressed alike, and not knowing in advance what has most forced itself upon any mind, you cannot, until you have examined the hand itself, tell what it is possible to read from it. So the claim of any palmist that he will tell everyone who consults him all about love, marriage, wealth, or any certain set of events, is based either upon his ignorance or his dishonesty. Every hand tells only its own story, and it is impossible to tell what that story is until you have looked into the hand. Reading from lines is the delicate part of Palmistry. It is where consummate skill is required, and where an absolute mastery of the science is needed. There is one great danger in the work of the amateur, and that is, that he attempts too much in the beginning — he is apt to be too daring. The best method to pursue is to confine your work at first to the Main lines, and gradually as you find your skill increasing begin to use chance lines and combinations. By proceeding cautiously, confidence in the science and in yourself will be gained, and your proficiency rapidly increased.

Every palmist finds his investigations leading him into channels corresponding to his trend of mind. Some will see every hand from its business side, some from its artistic, others from its scientific or health sides, and in this way palmists become specialists in certain directions. As their numbers increase this will be more marked, and it will add much to the value of the practice, just as it has done in medicine. My advice is, to note the trend of your greatest interest, and equip yourself for this specialty. In the beginning be satisfied to locate two or three prominent events in the life of a subject, and increase that number as skill increases, and the life map becomes easier for you to read.

CHAPTER II

A WORKING HYPOTHESIS—MAIN, MINOR, AND CHANCE LINES—PROPORTION—THE TWO HANDS

IF the hands of a thousand people are examined, in each one will be found a different combination of lines. If the number of examinations is carried into tens of thousands, you will still find the lines in every hand different from every other one. No matter how many hands are seen, you will find new lines in all of them. An offer of $1000 was once made for any two hands found marked exactly alike. There was no risk incurred in this offer, for no two hands will ever be found which do not differ in some respects. This universal difference cannot be attributed wholly to accident, for if that were the cause we should sometimes have the "accident" occur of finding two hands exactly alike. As such a thing never happens, we must look elsewhere for an explanation. This explanation is afforded by the knowledge that no two people are exactly alike in character, temperament, or in any other way, and thousands of experiments have proven that in whatever way these persons differ, a corresponding change *is found* in the hand. This is no theory; it is well proven, actual experience, and until we find two persons exactly alike in every way, without even a shade of variation in any direction, we shall never find two hands lined exactly alike. It is, however, a well established fact that the nearer people are like each other, the nearer alike are the lines in their hands. Thus we often find in the hands of children strange cases of similarity to those of the parents, but there is always a difference in some particular. With such a wide variation existing in the lines of the hand manifestly no one could ever tabulate *all* of the possible differences. It became apparent to me many years ago that unless a *working hypothesis* could be established, and a set of general principles laid down, which could be applied to *any line* and which would never vary, reading from the lines in the hand would always be uncertain. That there was a reliable working hypothesis I felt sure, if only it could be discovered. This I have found to be true, for bit by bit the one herein laid down has been gathered together, until to-day it is possible of application to every hand, and will never fail if properly applied. Even though you do not at first accept this hypothesis as being true, nevertheless give it a trial, and apply it faithfully and carefully to your line reading. If this is done you will find that, whether you believe it true or not, you are able, through its application, to correctly read the lines in the hand, and after you have acquired the ability to do this, it matters little to you whether the theory be false or true.

Of all the fingers of the hand, that of Jupiter is the only one which can stand erect by itself. The other three are so bound together that they cannot be straightened out independently of each other. Thus the finger of Jupiter is the magnet which attracts the life Current that passes through it into the body. There is no doubt in the mind of any thinker, but that we are surrounded on all sides by an atmosphere, and that this atmosphere is charged with some imponderable force, which, if not actually electricity, is still very like it in action and results. This force is widely diffused, intangible, and possesses great power. It is by the concentration of this force that the life Current is formed, which is a connecting link between the human being and the Unknown. This force we can neither see nor feel, and can only judge of its presence by its results. That at the moment of birth it enters our body through the finger of Jupiter, forms a magnetic Current which ceaselessly travels through us during life, is continually passing out of us again, and that it stops at death, I have no doubt. And this is the same life Current spoken of in Chapter II., Part I. I have no desire now, nor is it necessary, to enter into any lengthy discussion to prove the existence of this life Current, but as it forms a good working hypothesis, I desire that you use it, *at least theoretically*, as I have found that through its application to the lines in the hand, it becomes a key with which we can easily unlock their meaning. The finger of Jupiter we will then conceive to be the attractor, which, standing erect, draws together the diffused force surrounding us and concentrates it into a steadily flowing Current. The more we study this body of ours, the more we find it to be like an electric dynamo, and this life Current which we have conceived is a good deal like the Electric Current which keeps the dynamo moving. As everyone is more or less familiar with the operation of an Electric Current, I have found in teaching Palmistry that this simile is the best I have ever used, and that it conveys a mental picture which is easily applied to the lines. So I shall call this Current hereafter the Electric Current, and we will conceive it to be flowing steadily into us through the finger of Jupiter, reaching first the Heart line and setting in motion the circulation, passing next to the Head line and awakening the mind; and when circulation and mind start to operate, life begins, so this Current passes on to the Life line and courses through it. In the study of the lines we consider the whole sphere of their operation to be in the hand itself, so when the Current has passed through the Life line, we think of it as passing out again, travelling over the lines of Saturn, Apollo, and Mercury, and finding its egress through these fingers.

You will thus see that the beginning of the line of Heart is under the finger of Jupiter, and it is read from this beginning across the hand to the percussion. The line of the Head is read in the same direction, and the line of Life is read from its start, under the finger of Jupiter, downward. The beginning of these three lines covers the earlier years of life, and the ends of the lines cover the latter years, while the central portion records the middle part of life. It is not until the Current *reaches* a line that it begins to operate, so since the line of Saturn receives the Current from the end of the Life line, we begin to read it from the bottom upward; the lower part of the line of Saturn covering the first years of life, the topmost portion the latter days, and the central portion the middle part of life. The lines of Apollo and Mercury both are read in the same direction. The Main lines in the hand are six in number, and are called the Heart line, the Head line, the Life line, the Saturn line, the Apollo line, and the Mercury line, each one of which indicates different qualities. The Mercury line has also been designated Hepatica, Liver line, and line of Health, but it is in reality the line of Mercury, and I shall call it so. In addition to the Main lines there are seven Minor lines. These are the Ring of Solomon, the Ring of Saturn, the Girdle of Venus, the lines of Affection, the line of Mars, the line of Intuition, and the Bracelets, three in number, but of which only the upper one is worthy of consideration. There is another Minor line, called the Via Lascivia, and supposed to be a sister line to the Mercury line. I do not consider it as any more than a chance line, and consequently not entitled to be given a fixed place among the Minor lines. These thirteen lines when found in any hand are always in the same relative location, though their start and course through the hand vary infinitely. With a little practice, you will have no trouble in locating them or in noting their absence. We do not find all the Main lines in every hand, but always some of them. The Heart line is seldom absent, though more often so than the lines of Head and Life. The Head line is present in ninety-nine per cent. of hands, though sometimes very short. The Life line is seldom entirely absent, though I have seen cases where it was, in subjects who had no robustness of constitution whatever, but existed entirely on their nervous force. The line of Saturn is frequently absent, and the lines of Apollo and Mercury more frequently so. The Minor lines are found in varying degrees of frequency, and as they indicate peculiar qualities, are more often present in some types than others.

On examining a pair of hands do not be disconcerted at not finding all, or a majority, of the Main lines, but read what are there and estimate how much those which are absent have taken away from the subject. In some hands you will find hundreds of lines crossing the palm in every direction. This multitude is made up of chance lines, worry lines, and lines showing various emotions, and every line not a Main or Minor line belongs to this class. This multiplicity of lines shows an intensely nervous person who is a prey to innumerable conflicting emotions, and through whose hand the Electric Current is zigzagging in every direction, producing electric nervousness. Your first task, in such a case, should be to pick out the Main lines, see how much they are injured by the confusion of chance lines, and for the first part of your apprenticeship in line-reading this much-rayed hand should be read simply as denoting intense nervousness. Every one of these many chance lines is an emotion. Some begin in no definite location, and end the same way ; these are fugitive impulses, which have started the subject vigorously in some direction, but the enthusiasm has died and the effort has been abandoned. While such an emotion lasted it was strong enough to burn its mark in the hand, but in the end it came to naught. These lines are not worth reading. Other chance lines begin on one Mount and end on another Mount ; such lines will show the connection of the qualities of these two Mounts and have some valuable meaning. Some chance lines begin in a Main or Minor line, and end either on a Mount or on another Main or Minor line. These lines are all important. It will not be long before you will learn to distinguish between the lines of fugitive emotions and those that are really valuable. By all means do not puzzle and worry trying to read chance lines until the Main and Minor lines are plain to you, for the ability to read chance lines develops as the Main lines become easy to understand.

First learn to observe whether the lines are in proportion to the hand. If you find a very large hand, you expect deep, large lines, and a small, fine hand should be delicately traced. The amount of Electric Current that is attracted into the body by a large finger of Jupiter, on a large hand, will be considerable, and the lines through which this Current is to flow must be large enough to carry it, just as electricians need large wires to carry a large Electric Current. If in a large hand the lines be very delicate and thin and of the size that would properly carry the Current attracted by a small subject, the Current attracted by the big hand will be too great for small lines, and disaster in some form will ensue. I remember a doctor who once consulted me, in whose big hands I saw lines totally inadequate to carry the Current they were attracting. I advised him to use great care in his mental labors, not to overdo, for the Head line was most noticeably thin. He did not give the advice serious consideration, and in little less than a year he was sent to an insane asylum a hopeless wreck. The Head line could not carry the strong Current attracted, and destruction followed. As a contrary proposition, if the hand be small and the lines very large and deep there is too much channel for a small subject to own with safety.

It is necessary to analyze each line minutely, beginning at its starting point and following its course to the end. It will not do to judge a line in its entirety without regarding every variation in its direction, depth, size, color, and noting whether it runs clear and even, or whether it breaks, is crossed, or has other defects peculiar to lines. The changes and events in our lives are read with more ease and greater accuracy from this minute examination of the lines themselves *along their entire length*, than from chance lines.

It is advisable to have a method in the examination. Begin with the Heart line, study next the Head line, the Life line, and so on. This will accustom you to be systematic in work, and less likely to overlook important matters. If the Main lines in the hand are clear and strong and the chance lines few, the subject is even-tempered, and is largely following the natural course of his life. If the chance lines are many and cross the Main lines in various ways, the subject is impressionable, drawn in many directions, and will change his natural life's map.

Pay greater attention to the two hands when reading the lines than in your Chirognomic examinations. People do not so readily change their type construction as they do the course of their lives. A Jupiterian subject will always be a Jupiterian, but *events* may change and alter the natural course of his life. He may ruin a strong physique by excess, or he may allow his ambitions to undo him, but he will always be a Jupiterian, though the course of his life has been diverted. The type, Chirognomy will tell you; the outcome of his career must be read from the map of the lines. Thus the left hand is most accurate in showing you the naturally designed map of his life, and the right hand will tell you how the subject has altered it. In the examination of innumerable cases I have seen naturally fine lives outlined in the left hand, while ruin showed in the right; and I have seen naturally nervous, weak, vacillating lives, shown in the left hand, changed to strong, well directed lives in the right. Poorly marked, badly traced, and defective lines in one hand, changed to strong, clear, well marked lines in the other, will show the change in the life of the subject, either from good to bad or bad to good, as the case may be.

With all the lines, note where they begin, the course over which they travel, and the place they end. From the source of a line the origin of a trait may be determined, and by the bends in a line we may learn what things have drawn it out of its course, and the final outcome is indicated by the place at which it ends.

Note every defect in the line, see whether these defects destroy the line, weaken it, or what change they effect. Note all added lines, sister lines, or individual signs which strengthen or repair the lines. Before beginning a separate consideration of each line it is necessary to learn to distinguish a good line from a defective one, and to tell what the defects are, and how they may be repaired. The next chapter will accomplish this, and in it we will also consider the individual signs, some of which are produced by defective lines and should be considered as such, and all of which should be thoroughly understood before starting with the

separate lines. In these first chapters I desire to make clear the general principles governing the lines, and to start you to applying the Current theory to them, after which there will be no difficulty in reading the separate lines.

CHAPTER III

CHARACTER OF THE LINES—DEFECTS AND REPAIR—INDIVIDUAL SIGNS—STRENGTHENING LINES

IN examining lines, note first the *character* of the lines themselves. By this I mean their clearness, depth, evenness, and whether they are perfect or defective. If the latter is the case, what is the defect, does it cover the entire line or only a part of it, is the line repaired after the defect, does it regain its original depth and clearness, or does it show diminishing strength until it gradually fades away? The first general principle governing lines is, that the more evenly they run, the clearer they are, the less they are crossed, broken, islanded, or chained, and the nearer pink in color, the better is the line, and the more vigorous and clear the operation of its attributes. These clear, even lines furnish better channels through which the Electric Current can flow, offering as they do less obstruction and fewer impediments to free circulation. Conceiving the Electric Current to be flowing in and out through the finger ends, you can readily see that all vertical lines facilitate its passage and all horizontal lines check and impede its progress. Thus vertical lines are favorable, and horizontal lines crossing them are defects. This is why vertical lines on a Mount are good indications and increase the force of its type, and likewise the reason why grilles and cross-bars on the Mount are bad indications and obstructions, bringing out the bad side of the type or its health defects. The study of the lines makes clear the general law that lines operate best when the Current has the least obstruction to its free passage, and defects and bad effects are produced on a subject when it is impeded.

The slighter the defects and obstructions seen, the less marked are the bad results, and, conversely, the greater the obstruction the worse the effects. Clear, cleanly cut, even, pink lines show the best operation of any line; and every break, cross, island, or obstruction of any kind which may cause the Current to be impeded and to scatter or overflow its banks, will produce a defective operation of the qualities indicated by a line. Note whether any one line is deeper or shallower, is more defective, or has a different character in any way from other lines in the hand. If lines in general are of the same size and character, but some one line is much deeper, clearer, better colored than the others, the thing which this deep line indicates will be the strongest thing told by the lines in that subject's hands. If all the lines are deep, well colored, and clearly cut, and some one line is found much less clearly cut and deep than the rest, then the quality which that line indicates is the weakest point. Look for proportion constantly, and anything which disturbs it must be used for or against the chances of the subject. If the lines in the hand are broad and shallow, instead of deep and clear, there is an imperfect channel for the Current to pass through, and instead of being a deep stream full of strength and power, it is a shallow brook, and the Current spreads over too wide a surface to make it strong. This broad and shallow line is a feeble and weak one, and is generally full of defects and obstructions. When you see that lines are clearly cut, deep, well colored, uncrossed, or unspoiled by other defects, these lines show vigor and strength in the operation of their several qualities, steadiness of purpose, evenness of temper, and these are the subjects who, while they may have many difficulties to encounter, overcome them. Broad, shallow, poorly colored lines show weakness, vacillation, and discouragement, and generally these subjects achieve few results, and those are gained only after great effort and with strong outside influences to spur them. All of the changes, obstructions, and defects that occur in the lines themselves have special names, and these we will consider separately.

One of the first defective lines to notice is the *uneven line* (1). This is a line which, to a superficial observer, may seem to be a good one, but, upon a close examination, it will be seen that it cuts much deeper in certain parts, becoming thin afterwards, sometimes becoming broad and shallow, and often fading away entirely. Sometimes this uneven line may start broad and shallow, become deep and clear, and then grow thin again. The uneven line is one which does not run the same in depth and clearness during its entire length, and yet does not break, island, or show other similar defects. It is its *unevenness* of character that distinguishes it. This line must be read from its beginning, and if the line starts thin it shows the Current flowing in a thin stream during the length covered by this thinness of the line. If it then grows deep, it shows that a great intensity of purpose has been expended during the time covered by this depth, and that the Current was flowing strong and cutting too deeply during this revival, and consequently producing a defect in the line. If, after this depth, the line grows thin again, it shows that the great pressure of Current has been followed by a reaction, and the thin place following the deep one indicates a period when the Current was flowing in a weak manner. By following the course of an uneven line from its beginning, and by applying to it the measurements which indicate the ages of life upon the lines, you can locate the periods of strength, weakness, intensity, and all the consequent changes in the life of the subject. The uneven line shows the unequal, spasmodic operation of the qualities of the particular line which is found uneven. Please remember that, in this chapter, we are applying our statements to lines *in general* and not to *particular lines*, and the illustrations show *in general* different formations of uneven lines, all of which may be found on *any line*.

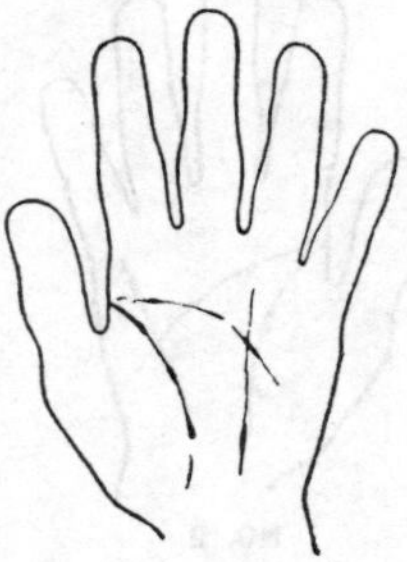

NO. 1

Next to the uneven lines we have those which split (2).

These splits are splinters which have broken the lines and produced defects in any line by reducing its clearness and strength, also impairing its usefulness by crippling its ability to carry the Current within the boundaries of the line. These splits must not be mistaken for sister lines, nor for islands, as they do not join the line again after splitting away from it, but must be read as simply split lines, which show a weakened quality of the line during the period of life covered by its continuance on the line. Splits are sometimes very small and fine, and if any doubt exists as to whether a line is split or not, make a careful examination with your glass. The true split line leaves the Main line, and does not come back and attach itself to it again. This split line allows a portion of the Current to be diverted from the Main line and changed to some new direction. It is a leak in the line. This divides the strength of the Main line by taking away from it part of its ability to carry the Current in the original direction. These split lines are often the beginning of a new course in the life of the subject. They show that the natural life map may have been altered at the time they occur. If this is true, the new line will continue to grow in length and pull the Current from its original channel into the new one which is cutting through the hand. If split lines run only a short distance and stop, and the Main line continues strong, these split lines will show that the attempts to change the natural course of the life have failed, and while they show by the splits the attempts to change, they also show by their shortness that they did not succeed. The closer these splits lie to the Main line the less likely they are to divert much of the Current. The wider they open away from the line and the deeper and clearer they are, the more importance must be placed upon them, and the more likely they are to produce a change in the course of the life. If a split line pulls away from a line and runs clear and strong to a Mount, it shows

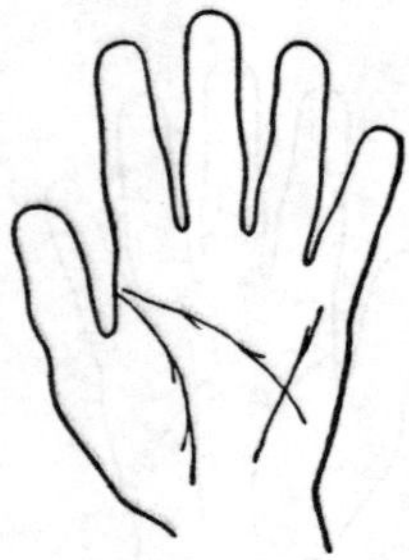

NO. 2

the great attraction that Mount has for the subject, and such subjects will either strongly partake of the qualities of that Mount or will seek the companionship of subjects of that type. This is why older palmists read such lines breaking away from the Heart line as showing that the subject would marry some one of the type represented by the Mount to which this line ran.

When the seven types were less often combined than they are now, and pure specimens of the types were plentiful, it was often easy to describe the color of hair, eyes, etc., of the person a subject would likely marry. This was possible by following the description of the appearance of the types indicated by the Mount to which the split line ran. Such feats are still possible when the split lines are strong and the types pure specimens, and while in my own readings I have never said that any subject *would* marry someone of a particular appearance, I have often described in this way the appearance of the person who would be most attractive to the subject as one who would be his ideal, and whom he would *prefer* to any other for a life partner. The split line will tell of many events, ranging from a mere trivial defect of the line, shown by a small short split, up to an entire change in the life of a subject. There must always be a distinct separation of a line, showing that it plainly divides, before you should read it as a split. With care and practice you can learn properly to judge such defects. During the study of this chapter examine as many hands as possible, looking for each of the signs and lines as treated here, and accustom yourself to recognize at once the different formations, not trying to interpret them fully at first, but learning to distinguish them quickly when seen. Remember that a divided line is not as strong by one half as if the split had not occurred, and this will give you the proper *general theory* to apply to split lines.

The next defect is the island (3). This sign is one which has been misunderstood and improperly handled by many palmists. In the first place the island is not a single sign, but is produced by the splitting of a line and the return to the original line of the lower end of the part which has broken away. Chance lines which merely cross each other in such a way as to make the same shaped figure as an island (see 3 B) do not form a *true island.* The fact that the ends of these chance lines overlap each other, constituting defects for each other, may spoil the operation of both the chance lines, but it does not form a true island. One fact I wish to strongly impress,— that a *true island* is produced by a splitting of the Main line, and a return of the split to the Main line, and that islands are formed in no other way. Islands of all sizes are found, ranging from those which are mere dots and distinguished only under the glass, to those which sweep wide circles in the hand and instantly attract your attention. Whenever you find a figure in the shape of an island, make yourself sure that it is produced by a splitting of the line before pronouncing it an island. If it is formed by two chance lines crossing each other, or by a chance line crossing a Main or Minor line at both ends, read the chance lines separately and not as an island. The only reason why palmists have been at all successful in handling the island according to the present acceptation of what constitutes an island, is that the effect of chance lines crossing each other is similar to some of the bad effects of the island, and it has not been because the island itself has been thoroughly understood. The island is always a defect, always a disturber, a warning to look out for something, and must never be disregarded. The operation of an island is to divide the Current flowing along a line. One half of the Current passes around one side of the island, the other half going around the other side. These divided currents reunite on the lower side of the island and resume their course. The word "island" is taken from its geographical namesake, and the true island in the hand is literally what its name implies, an isolated surface of skin surrounded by the divided line. Thus the island is an impeding object in

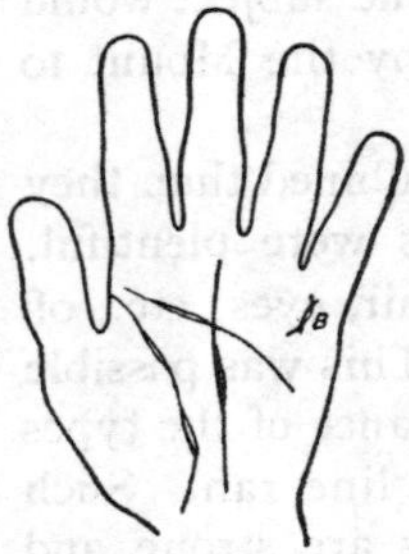

NO. 3

the course of a line, which divides the strength of the Current, producing a consequent division of strength and force. The size and length of the island shows the extent of obstruction and its duration, and from the point at which it is seen on a line you can read the age at which this weakening of the force occurs. It is not the intention here to do more than to impress upon you the general meaning of the island. Its specific application will be made to each line as we study it. When an island is seen remember the divided stream, the impeding, obstructing island, and the consequent weakness and impairment of the line during its presence, and you will always think of a menace to the subject from some direction.

Breaks in the lines (4) are frequently encountered, and always indicate a defective condition. In this case the Current is interrupted and stopped in exactly the same manner as when a telegraph wire is cut. The kind of a break will make a great difference in the outcome of the defect, and it is only by the Electric Current theory that you will be able to judge correctly and quickly what the seriousness of any break in the line is. The theory is this: when the Current reaches the break it is checked, and some repair process is needed at once, else the Current will flow out of all regular channels, producing the same condition as the overflow of a river which is not properly confined within its banks, that of spreading destruction. If the break in a line is small, and the line continues clearly after the break and in a direct course, the Current may skip over the small break and continue in its regular path. In this case the danger is serious, but not insurmountable. In such an instance the two ends of the line will probably grow together eventually. The wider the break, the more serious it becomes and the less likelihood there is of the Current's passing over the space between the broken ends. Everything tending to make it

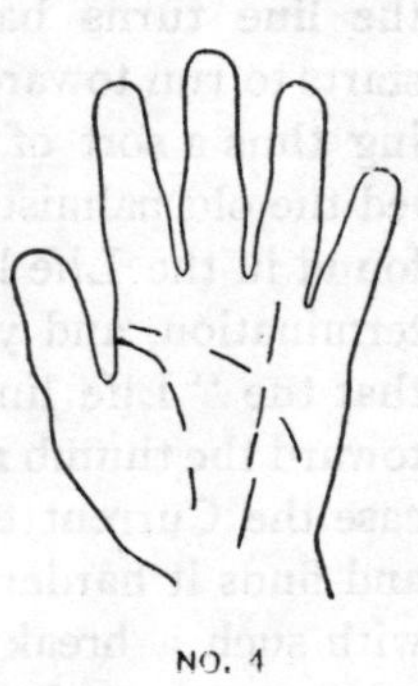

NO. 4

easier to hold the Current in its proper course, or enabling it to get back to it after a break occurs, lessens the serious results of the broken line, and everything that makes it harder for the Current to continue its course without interruption adds to the complication. Thus broken lines may be repaired when the broken ends overlap each other, or by a small cross-line uniting the ends of the two lines, by sister lines running alongside of the line and break, or by squares (5); all of which means help transmit the Current from the broken end of the line to its regular channel, and while during this break and its repair there is a decided check to the best operation of the line, still it is possible of repair, and not so serious as if unaccompanied by any sign of repair. Always a danger, breaks must be regarded seriously, and from their size, or the repair signs present, you can accurately estimate their outcome.

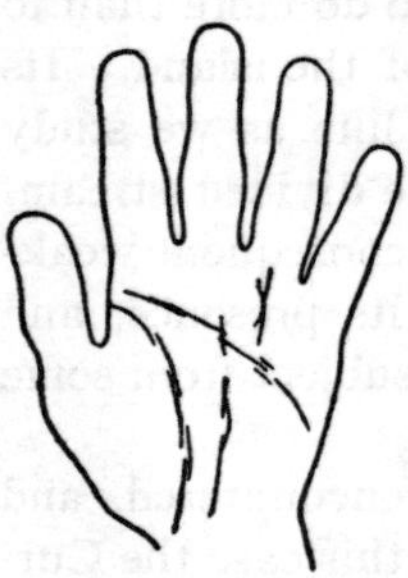

NO. 5

One of the worst forms to encounter is when the end of the line turns back after a break and starts to run towards its source (6), forming thus a sort of hook. This probably led the old palmists to use this indication found in the Life line as denoting a fatal termination, and you have read perhaps that the "Life line broken and turning toward the thumb means death." In this case the Current turns back upon itself, and finds it harder to continue its course with such a break than in any other formation; it overflows where there is no channel to carry it forward. If there is no means by which this Current can be carried back to its original course, it produces disaster. There are various methods of repair, some by lines joining the turned-back end of the Main line, by sister lines, squares, or various lines which will attract the Current and take it back

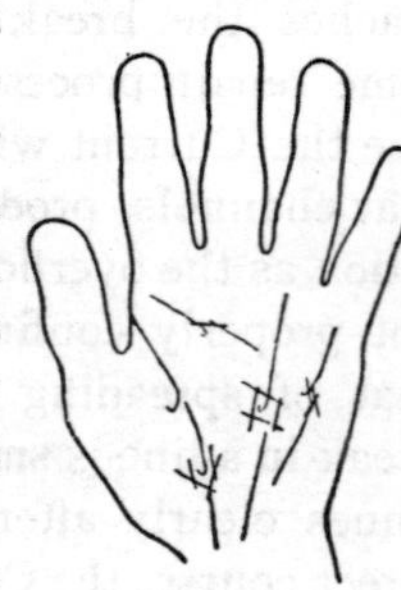

NO. 6

to its regular channel. These methods of repair are shown in Fig. 6. Every turned-back line is a *most serious* check to the subject, either as to life, health, or career; the line on which it is found will tell in which direction this check leads. If unrepaired it is well-nigh fatal, even worse than when the line ends abruptly, for in the latter case the Current may be forced *through new paths*, and may dig itself a new channel; but when it is deliberately turned back to its source there is little hope that it will ever go on in its original direction. Of all repair signs the best and most certain is the square, shown in Fig. 7.

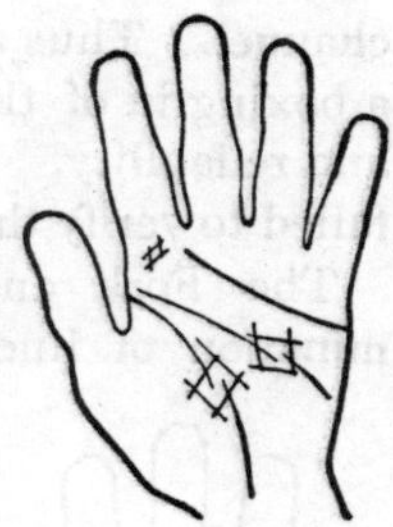

NO. 7

The Square (7) is an individual sign, and has been used by the old palmists as an indication of protection from some impending danger. It is always a good sign, wherever found. No matter what the break in a line, or what its menace to the subject, a square surrounding it will partially repair and mitigate the danger. The square I conceive to be a box which forms itself around the break or danger point, and concentrates and boxes in the Current, making escape impossible, holding the overflow in check, and forcing the Current to find and discharge itself again through the regular channel, no matter how great the turmoil inside of the square may be. Sometimes a square is found on a Mount, where it does not surround a defect in a line. Such squares will indicate that the defects of the Mount will not predominate with this subject.

My conception is that lines are channels for the transmission of the Electric Current, and that our effort is to find out how well they can and will perform this function. If the Life Current has an unobstructed channel across the hand, the life will be unobstructed. But if the channel shows defects at a certain point we know trouble is going to occur there, and that if the Current is kept *in* the channel and from breaking its bounds and overflowing, the danger will be overcome. When the defective place is *boxed in* by the square, we feel that the Current cannot get out of the *box*, but *must* find and discharge itself through its regular channel. Thus a square is always a protection from danger, a boxing in of the Current, and a repair agent of certainty and reliability. In thousands of examinations I have never failed to verify this estimate of the square.

The Fork and the Tassel (8) are found at the termination of lines, and by applying the general theory to them they are easy to understand. The termination of a line shows the end of the operation of its peculiar qualities, and must be noted to see in what manner the end will be accomplished. Some lines gradually fade away until the line is lost in the capillary lines of the skin; in other cases the line ends abruptly, sometimes with a cross, a star, a dot, or an island, and often it terminates in a fork or tassel. These tassels may be found on the end of a short Life, Head, or Heart line, and, whenever found, indicate the dissipation and diffusion of the strength of the line and the end of its usefulness. The Current, instead of continuing, is scattered and diffused, and spreads itself like a tassel or fan, dissipating its force, and ending the strong operation of the qualities indicated by the line. If a fork composed of two lines occur in the end of a line, it amounts only to a split, and is not so bad as a tassel, for this split may form itself into an island and continue the line; but the tassel, composed of *many* lines, is the distribution of the Current over so wide a space there is no hope that it will be gathered together again in a single strong line, though, if it occur early in the line and not at its end, you may sometimes find a single thin line continuing after a tassel. In some cases you find the tassel protected by a square.

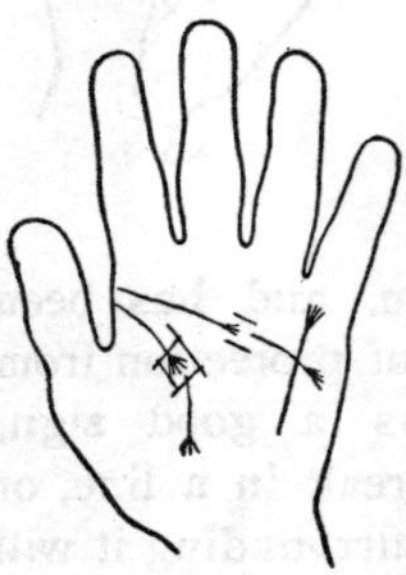

NO. 8

The tassel is always a defect, sometimes overcome, but producing while it lasts great disturbance of the Current. By following the theory of the Current over the line, you can accurately estimate the extent of seriousness, the possible repair, and the outcome, though a tassel generally marks the end of the usefulness of a line.

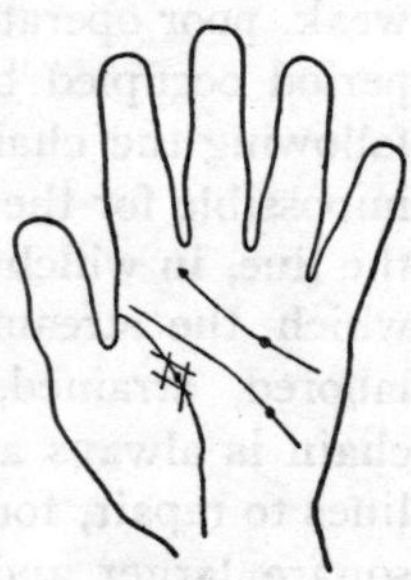
NO. 9

The Dot (9) is a sign which is not frequently seen, but is worthy of note. It varies in size and depth, some being mere specks, and others large enough to put in the point of a pencil. Dots are always a defect, either of a line, when seen on one, or they may be found independent of the lines. On a line the dot forms an obstruction to the flow of the Current, and if it is a large one it produces destruction of the line by interposing so deep a cavity that the Current cannot pass. Very small dots are not serious, but often come after severe illness, generally of a febrile character. I have seen dots on the Life line marking the spot when a severe attack of scarlet or typhoid fever had occurred, on the Head line under the Mount of Saturn in deaf and dumb subjects, under the Mount of Apollo in heart-disease subjects, on the line of Mercury showing when severe intestinal disturbances had occurred, and in other parts of the hand indicating the occurrence of difficulties peculiar to the parts of the hand on which they were seen. Dots may be red, blue, white, or yellow, and will indicate by their color the disturbances peculiar to the locality or line on which they appear. They are subject to repair by a good square.

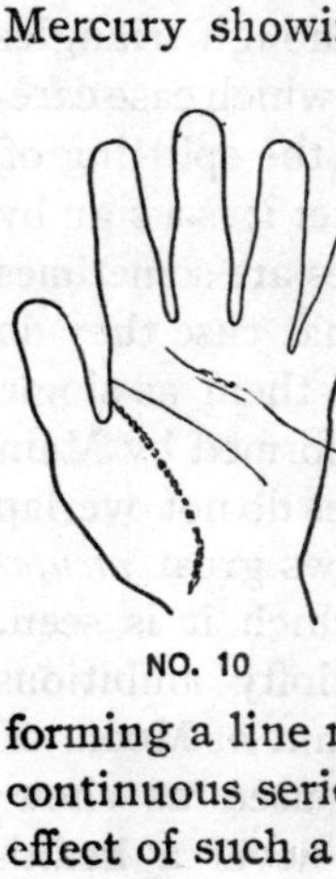
NO. 10

The Chained line (10) is formed by the joining together of a number of links, forming a line not clear, even, and deep, but one which has a continuous series of obstructions from the beginning. The effect of such a line is the weak operation of the qualities of the line. If it is the Head line, it makes a vacillating subject, lacking in self-control, and liable to headaches and other brain disturbances. If chains are seen in only part of a line, the weak, poor operation of the line will occur only during the period occupied by the chained condition, though the line following the chain is apt to be thin. The chains make it impossible for the Current to flow freely and evenly through the line, in which case the channel is full of shallows over which the stream makes its way with difficulty. It is a labored, strained, obstructed condition, consequently the chain is always a serious defect. It is one of the hardest lines to repair, for, unless the chain is very short, it takes a square larger and more regularly placed than is usual in order to enclose the chain. In almost all hands the chain is repaired by a sister line, or lines, and in no other way. The chain is seen on nervous Life lines, and on sentimental and deficient Heart lines, sometimes on Head lines, but not often on the other Main or Minor lines or chance lines. Remember in reading it, that it is a shallow, obstructed channel, and form your estimate from this basis, applying the weak operation of the Current to that part of the line covered by the chained condition, and estimating how much it is repaired by any sister lines which may be present.

The Triangle (11) is often a single sign, though triangles are frequently found in the course of a line, in which case carefully note whether the triangle is formed by the splitting of the line, as in the case of an island, or whether it is a sign by itself and has formed *over* the line. Triangles are sometimes formed by crossing of the Main lines. In that case they do not have all of the power which belongs to them as single signs. When a well-marked triangle is not formed by Main or Minor lines, and when the lines at the angles do not overlap each other, but make well-cut points, it shows great *mental* brilliancy of the *line*, *Mount*, or *finger* on which it is seen. On the Mount of Jupiter it will tell of lofty ambitions and Jupiterian *mental* qualities ; on the Mount of Moon, of brilliant imagination. It must always be used as showing brilliancy of mental attributes, and is never a health indication. If the triangle is formed by crossing chance lines it is not as powerful in its operation as when it is a single sign, still it adds greatly to the subject in whatever direction its location indicates. On all of the Mounts a triangle applies only to the upper world of that Mount. It is not intended here to apply the single signs to the Mounts, fingers, lines, and individual phalanges, giving their meaning in each location, but to outline the *general* principles governing them, and in a subsequent chapter to apply them. Remember the strongest triangle is the single sign, that it is always a favorable indication, never applies to health, but

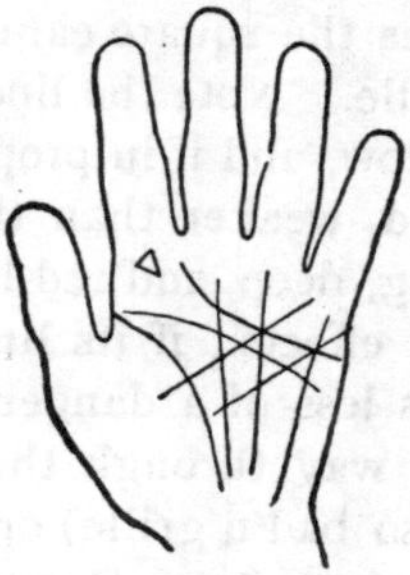

NO. 11

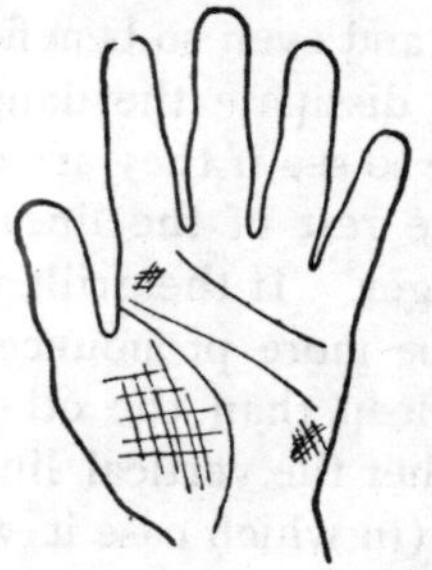

NO. 12

adds brilliancy to the mental side of the location where it is found.

The Grille (12) is a formation where lines are found crossing each other in such a manner as to form a network or dam through which it is almost impossible for the Current to pass ; as, for example, if an Electric Current were turned into a wire netting, when we know it would zigzag in every direction, be obstructed so it could not continue its passage, and would be forced to escape through the ends of each wire in the net. This would diffuse and dissipate the Current. It would also intensely electrify the point where the diffusion occurred. In the lines of the hand we must keep the Current free from obstruction, so when the grille is found in any hand, we feel at once that if a deep line shows that much Current is flowing in its direction, we have in the grille obstruction and overflow. Whenever seen, the grilling of lines is a serious defect and a menace. If it is very pronounced, and composed of deep red lines, the menace is great; if only a confusing and interlacing of several small thin lines, it is not as serious. On the Mounts the grille is a bad sign, bringing out the bad side of the Mount types, since by causing the exciting Electric Current to overflow into them it produces an abnormal condition. It also brings out prominently their health defects. When a grille is seen on any Mount, look for a bad or spoiled specimen of the type, or one who has the health defects peculiar to his type. A square may repair a grille if it boxes the defect entirely, but such markings are rare, and even so beneficial a sign as the square cannot entirely dissipate the danger of a grille. Note the lines in a grille to see if they are deep or shallow, and if in proportion to the rest of the lines in the hand, weaker than they or stronger. If the grille is very strong, deep, and red-lined it will be more pronounced in its bad effects; if its lines are less deep than the other lines, it is less of a danger. See whether the vertical lines cut their way through the cross lines (in which case it will not be so bad a grille) or if the cross lines cut the vertical lines cleanly. Some Current can pass if the vertical lines cut their way through; none can get through if the cross-lines cut the deepest. A grille with lines not running exactly vertical and horizontal is not as bad as one which is found composed of vertical and horizontal lines running at right angles. Thus with all grilles gauge with judgment your estimate of their destructive force, and do not apply the worst effect of a bad grille to a less dangerous one. Carefully estimate the good of your subject by Chirognomy in order to get the true effect of the grille as applied to him, and always use great care with this sign.

Cross-bars (13), or horizontal lines closely grouped together without the vertical lines of the grille, I consider a worse indication than the grille itself, for in this case the Current is *entirely blocked* and has no chance to escape except by overflowing the obstruction, and to do this it must first overflow the surrounding parts. I have given the name of *Cross-bars* to this marking, as I have often encountered it as a single sign and verified its bad effects. The cross-bars will bring out the bad side of a Mount, such as health defects, and fortunately are not often found. When you encounter this sign, see how strong and deep are the cross-lines, also how they compare with the rest of the lines in the hand. The deeper they are, the worse the indication, and *vice versa.* The Current theory will always unlock their seriousness.

The Circle (14) is quite a rare sign, and is chiefly valuable when found on the line of Life, or on the Mount of Apollo

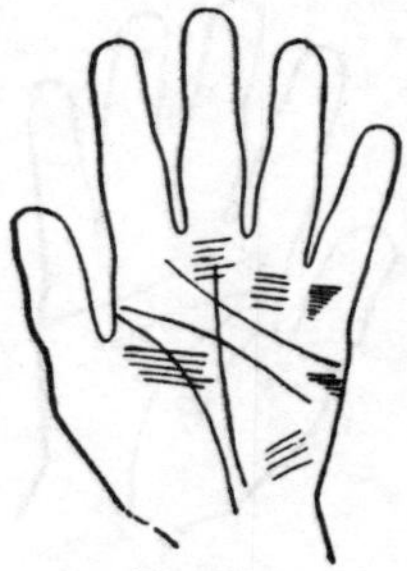

NO. 13

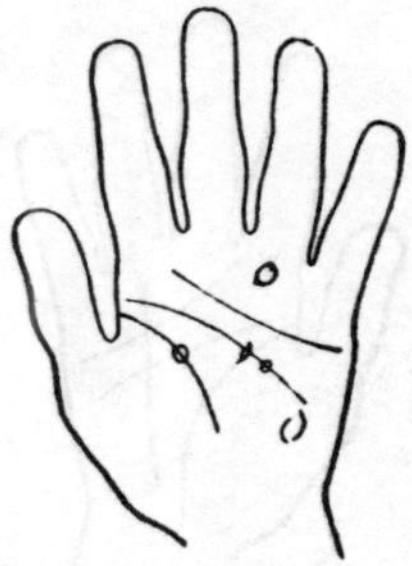

NO. 14

or line of Head under the Mount of Apollo. Such markings emphasize the Apollonian tendency to trouble with the eyes. This indication I have verified in a few instances. When seen it will be accurate as indicating delicacy of the eyes, but is not seen on the hands of all who are either blind, have poor vision, or weak eyes. It is not usually perfectly marked. Imperfect circles sometimes close their edges, however, and become perfect in shape as the difficulties with the eyes increase.

The Trident (15) is found at the upper end of a line, is sometimes a single sign, and sometimes is connected with either the lines of Saturn, Apollo, or Mercury, or with a chance line that runs in a vertical direction. It is a favorable indication when found on the upper end of a line, as it allows a good escape of the Current through proper channels. It adds strength to the line of Apollo, increasing its brilliancy and the chances of success for the subject. The trident is a rare marking and always a good one. It must be perfectly marked to give its full meaning.

The Star (16) is an important and valuable sign. It is found in many hands, in all possible locations, and is sometimes a good indication, sometimes a bad one, depending entirely upon its location. As the Current flows along the lines it is ready at any moment to burst into a flame and illuminate its surroundings. Just as the Electric Current produces the electric light, so the Life Current also produces periods or points of illumination. The star is the electric

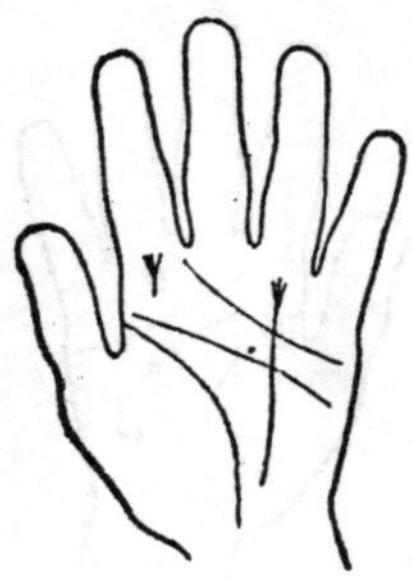

NO. 15

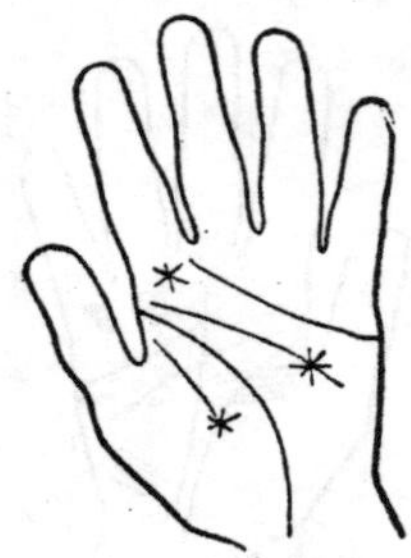

NO. 16

light of Palmistry, the place at which the Current sends out its points of light from a common centre; and thus the star, if small and even in proportion, means *illumination*, and if large and diffused, *explosion*. It is always a *lighting up* and *intensifying* indication wherever seen. Be careful in handling stars to note their formation, size, depth of lines, location, and relative proportion to the rest of the lines. You will see stars perfectly formed, with each ray of the same length and coming from a common centre, forming a perfectly proportioned marking. These are the best stars, and give the even illumination that lights up a Mount or line without destroying it. When the star is imperfectly formed and the lines do not proceed from a common centre it is a poor star, partaking of the defects of a grille and producing feeble light, and is in no sense so brilliant a marking as the perfect star. If the star is large, with deep, red lines, and a deep dot for the centre, it is the explosion which destroys, as does the boiler which bursts. On the Life line it means sudden death, on the Head line it means an explosion in the mental faculties, or insanity, and wherever found this large, deep star is excess, which means danger. Instead of having to memorize the meaning of a star in all of its locations, fix in your mind the Current theory and the fact that the star is the light or the explosion, according to its formation. Whenever seen, instead of trying to *remember* what it means in each location, simply say : " What will this kind of a star do for the subject when located in the position in

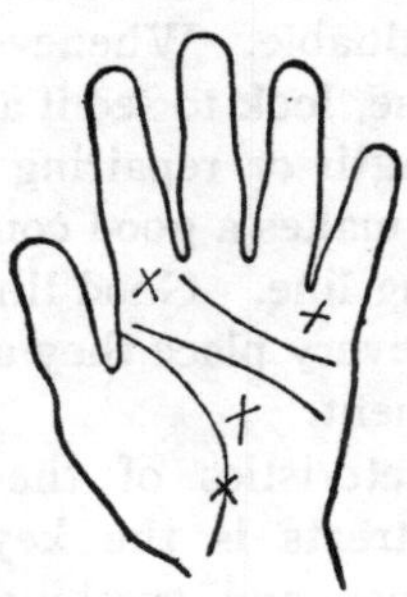

NO. 17

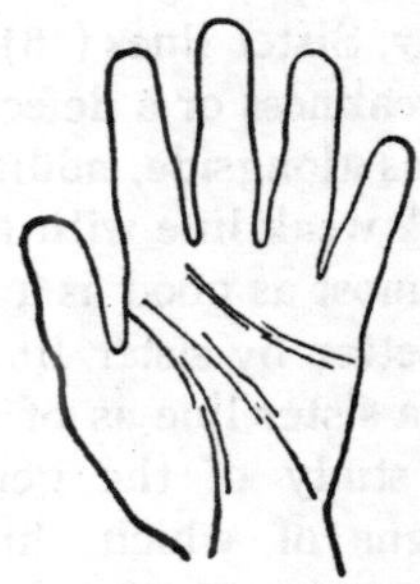

NO. 18

which I find it ? Will it light up and make more brilliant, or will it explode and destroy ? " If you have correctly judged the kind of a star, you can apply either its brilliancy or its explosive force to the location or line on which you find it. This is the only correct and at the same time simple way to read stars. It is such an important sign, and so often found, that you must be able to read it quickly and correctly whenever it is met. Only the *general theory* of the star is intended to be made plain here : the application will be made to different lines and Mounts later. The star is the illumination, the electric light, making brilliant if a good one, but the danger signal or explosion if too large, deep cut, and red.

The Cross (17) is a common sign. It is sometimes a well-marked single sign, and sometimes is formed by lines crossing other lines. Always note how deep the lines forming it are, and how they are in proportion to the other lines. A deep-cut cross is a sign of grave import, especially if highly colored. The cross is an obstacle or a defect, and generally produces either a bad quality, a health defect, or a change in the course of the subject's life. The Current running along the line on reaching the cross "burns out the fuse," to use electrical parlance, and a stoppage for repair is necessary, often with the result of changing the course of the subject's life. In any location it must be regarded as unfavorable, and as indicating a defect.

In the repair of any line, weak, broken, or defective in any way, Sister lines (18) are most valuable. Whenever you see a weakness or a defect in any line, look to see if a sister line runs alongside, adding its strength or repairing qualities. A weak line with a sister line makes a good combination, almost as good as a single strong line. Good lines are made better by sister lines, and in every place they appear regard a sister line as of decided benefit.

The study of the general characteristics of the lines and signs of which this chapter treats is the keystone to the study of the individual lines and combinations. I have been explicit concerning each change in the lines, all defects, and the way individual signs are produced, as I wish to get the general theory of the *Current* well fixed in your mind. The application of this hypothesis to the individual lines makes it easy to read their innumerable variations, and it is only this conception of the Electric Current which will make it possible to reason out all of the possible combinations of lines you will be called upon to read.

CHAPTER IV

THE AGE OF THE SUBJECT — AGE AS INDICATED ON THE LINES

UP to this time, there has not been discovered any way of positively telling from the hand the present age of a subject. There is no marking in the hand or on the lines which will, independent of everything else, indicate this. But by close observation of the general appearance, color, and skin, you can approximate the correct age within a few years. Youthful skin is fresh looking, elastic, generally well colored, and has the appearance of vitality. As age comes on the skin grows less fresh looking, takes on a satiny, glossy appearance, and gets darker, often becoming brown in spots. This satiny appearance begins at about fifty years of age, and grows more pronounced from that time on. There is not much trouble to distinguish the hands of youth by size and appearance, neither is it hard to judge the hands of middle-aged or old persons. But from the years of twenty to fifty there is greater difficulty in reaching accuracy, though proficiency can be acquired by a close observation of skin, consistency, color, and general appearance. It is desirable to acquire skill in this matter, for knowledge of the present age of a subject will enable you to tell what events seen in his hand have *passed*, and about what point the subject has reached in the life map of the hand at the time your reading takes place. Until you have gained some proficiency in this respect, it is much better to ask the subject what age he has attained, and use his answer as a basis. I do not mean that you should rely absolutely upon it, for all persons will not be truthful; but they will be within reasonable distance of the correct age, and you will have to use your own judgment, based upon the appearance of the hand, as to how much they are misleading you. I believe there *is* a way to tell the age of a subject from the lines, and have been experimenting with it for some time, but the results do not as yet warrant me in giving the method as an absolutely correct one. If the temperature of your room is exactly right, and the subject in perfect health, you will often find by pressing the Life line *quite hard* from the top downward so that you force all of the blood out of it, repeating, if necessary, this pressure several times, that there will sometimes appear, only for a second, a white spot in the line. In about half of the cases on which I have tried this experiment, this white spot has shown itself at the correct age of the subject. It has been successful so often that I believe if the conditions of health in the subject, and temperature of the room were *always* just right, that the results would be astonishing in their accuracy, but we encounter such varying conditions that I do not feel justified in making the positive statement that age can always be discovered in this way. It will be valuable to Palmistry if this possibility can be fully established.

If our hypothesis that the lines in the hand are a map of the natural course of the life is correct, then the different portions of the lines must show to which parts of the life they refer. Experiments have clearly shown that the beginning of a line (remembering always from which end the line in question is read) records the first years, and that, as the line continues, it records the advancing years of that life.

The degree of proficiency possible to attain in reading the age at which events occur depends entirely upon the keenness and good judgment of the practitioner. There are some who can tell of an event and fix the time within a year, but those who have reached such skill are few. Others are successful within two, three, or five years. No one can do more than fix *the year* in which an event occurs if he relies entirely upon the rules of Palmistry. To fix scientifically a month or specific day for any event is impossible. Neither is it possible, relying solely on the hand, to tell the name of a subject, the initial of his name, or that of a friend or relative. In every case when you are asked to write these things on a paper, no matter what is apparently done with the paper, you may be absolutely certain that the practitioner is relying upon sleight of hand to enable him to read what you have written. There is no possible method either of locating "lucky days," and nothing should more quickly give the stamp of fraud than such a statement from a practitioner. Neither does a scientific palmist confine himself entirely to the *future*, telling of wonderful things that will happen after he is gone. Such practitioners succeed because there is just enough credulity in our human nature to make us *hope* these things—which are always made to be pleasant—will come to pass. Any palmist who understands his art can tell *past events*, and if he cannot deal correctly with your character, health, temperament, and a good deal of your past life, do not put faith in his skill.

Trifling events are not shown in the hand. The mere routine of living does not appear in the life map, so any claim to trace your life from day to day is a false one, intended merely to deceive. Only important events, serious illnesses, changes of condition, severe trials, great joys or dangers, will be seen, or those things or persons who have greatly influenced and have produced strong brain impressions upon you, or have made marked changes in the course of the life.

To be correct in reading age on the lines, we must consider how long the average human being lives. Those age measurements of the Life line which continue the life up to one hundred years and over are manifestly incorrect, for people do not often reach such ages. The tables of expectancy used by insurance companies are certainly near the facts, for they are the result of large experience, and are considered sufficiently reliable to form a basis from which the companies are willing to assume great financial risks. These tables place the length of the average insurable life at sixty-five years, but, for the purpose of allowing extra time to our subjects, it is better to assume that the human life, except in rare cases, will not greatly exceed seventy years. Thus we start a line at zero and end it at seventy. The intervening space we divide into sections mathematically exact, which point out the intervening years of the life.

The division of the Life line (19) begins at the starting of the line under the finger of Jupiter and ends at the *rascette*; the intervening sections recording all the various years of the life. For convenience and to facilitate quickness in reading the line, I divide it in the centre, fixing that point as the age 36, which is approximately one half of 70. The space above this central point I divide into the ages 4, 6, 12, 18, 24, 30, and the portion of the line after the central point to read as ages 43, 51, 60, and 70. To reach a date as close as a year, it is necessary to subdivide the line between ages 4 and 70 into periods, each representing one year, and *mark* the space on the line, as few can so accurately gauge it with the eye.

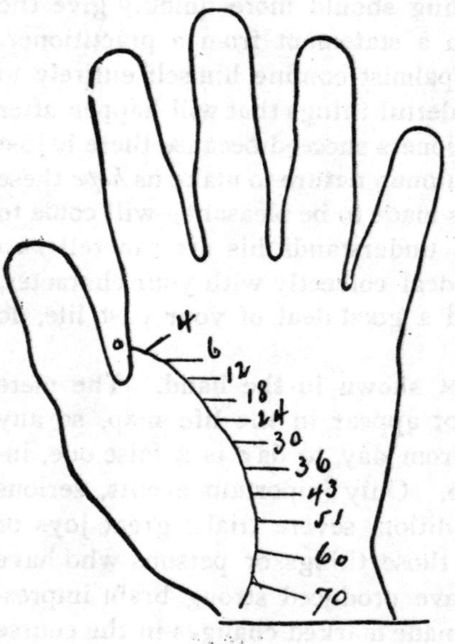

NO. 19

With a little practice you can recognize where the ages 4, 6, 12, 18, 24, 30, 36, 43, 51, 60, and 70 are marked on the line, and learn to read these ages quickly and accurately. In a case where the indication you are reading does not come at one of these ages, you may, if you wish to be *very* accurate, mark off the line into years and arrive at the exact date as indicated above. In reading *offhand*, without marking the line with a pencil, always consider whether the hand is long or short, and, after first noting the central point on the line, which indicates the 36-year division, mentally mark off the several spaces *in proportion* to the *length* of the hand. A long hand will have wider spacing between each 6-year period, and in a short one they will come closer together. The above division of the Life line I have found more accurate than any I have ever used, and, while the results obtained depend entirely upon the correct judgment of the practitioner, they can be made very accurate if sufficient pains is taken.

Reading periods of time on the lines of the Heart and Head is often useful in order to see whether events marked on them fit into conditions seen on the Life line. To estimate time on these lines the same rules must be observed, and the same remarks and reasoning apply to these lines as to the Life line. They begin under the finger of Jupiter and their course is *across* the hand. As these two lines have many variations in the direction they pursue, I have found it best to use an imaginary line beginning in the middle of the Mount of Jupiter and running across the hand to the percussion as a guide to measure by. On this imaginary line (20) I lay out the periods of 6, 12, 18, 24, 30, 36, 43, 51, 60, and 70, and when anything is to be read on the Heart or Head line, note under which of these periods it lies, and this is found to be the proper age. If closer dates are desired, mark the Heart or Head line into spaces representing single years, and proceed as directed in the use of the Life line. The above tables of measurements I have used with much success, and believe them to be correct if properly applied.

Age on the line of Saturn is read from the bottom upward (21), the space from the rascette to Head line covering the years from 0 to 30, from line of Head (normally placed) to line of Heart 30 to 45, and from line of Heart to finger of Saturn 45 to 70 years. By remembering these three general subdivisions, you will soon accustom yourself to quickly read the principal periods. If you wish to read within a year, mark off the line and proceed as with the Life line. The different directions in which the lines of Head and Heart often run across the hand make the location where the line

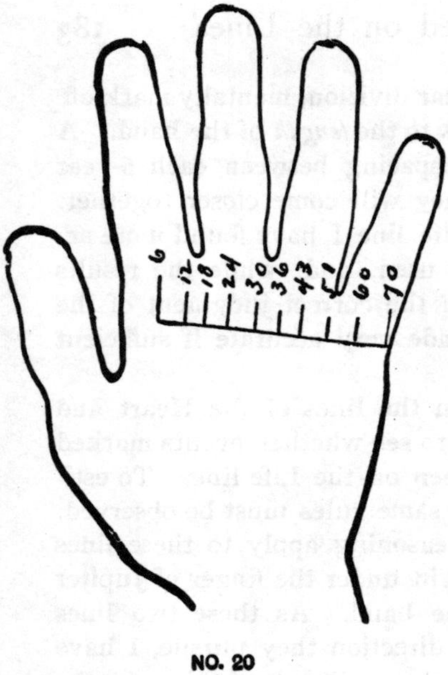

NO. 20

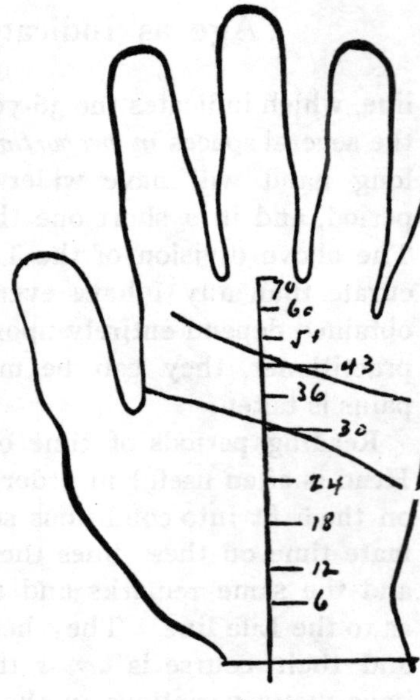

NO. 21

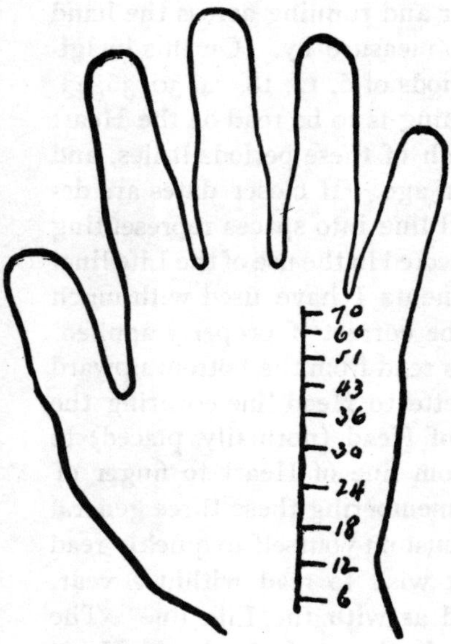

NO. 22

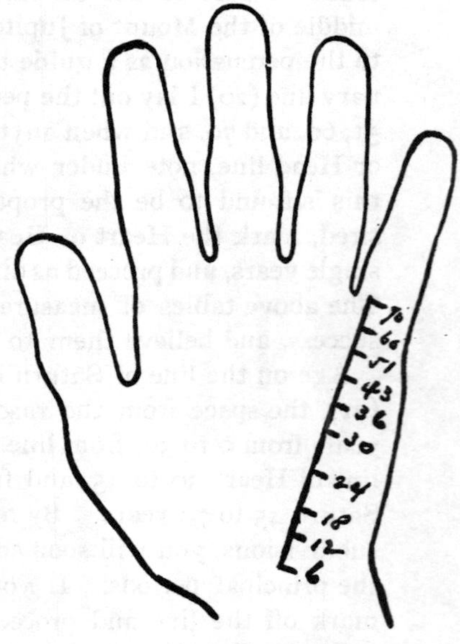

NO. 23

of Saturn crosses them not always the same. If they are misplaced, producing a wide or a narrow quadrangle, do not rely on the space between them as covering the ages from 30 to 45, but at once measure the entire line of Saturn for correct dates.

The line of Apollo (22) is read from the bottom upward as is the line of Saturn, and the same rules and measurements apply to it as to the line of Saturn, and also the same methods of arriving at exact dates. The line of Mercury (23) is read from the bottom upward, the same scale and rules applying to it as to the other lines, except that the spaces on this line are closer together, inasmuch as the line is shorter. It is often desirable to read age on this line, as it is such a valuable line in connection with the line of Life. It is not necessary to read age on chance lines. These lines will either cross the Main lines, start from them, or so near, that age on the chance line can be read *from* the Main line. These chance lines, which are the changes or possibilities in the natural map of the life, run in so many directions, and start from such unexpected places, that no rule can be made for reading age on them. You will, however, never have trouble in arriving at the proper dates with these lines by computing from the Main lines. No part of Palmistry requires more practice than the reading of dates, and time can be valuably employed in gaining this practice. At first you will record many failures, but it is your judgment and not the rules that is at fault. This you will prove for yourself as you become careful and deliberate in making up your mind before you speak. No one reads dates so fluently as the beginner. The older in experience he becomes, the more carefully he works and the better results he achieves. Some disappointment in line-reading comes to beginners from the fact that they do not look in the right places for events. At present few look for illness anywhere but on the Life line, while the Head, Heart, and Mercury lines and the Mounts all record health afflictions, their date to be read from these lines.

CHAPTER V

THE LINE OF HEART

UPON entering our bodies through the finger of Jupiter the first line reached by the Electric Current is the line of Heart, so named because it has been found to reflect accurately the condition and operation of this organ. It is a very important line, as it deals with that central life-sustaining mechanism which pumps and controls the blood stream, which, by its quantity and quality, we have found so largely affects our health and temperament. The line of Heart rises from some point under or near the finger of Jupiter, and traces its way across the hand under the Mounts, ending on the percussion. It is not proper to say that this line has any *normal* starting place, or any *normal* stopping place, for what might be normal with one subject would not be with another, so the line of Heart must always be considered in relation to the individual on which it is seen. The old saying, that a person has a " warm heart," or a " great deal of heart," has become synonymous with the idea that these persons are affectionate and sympathetic. This is largely true, for we have already seen that the action of a strong heart is followed by pink color, indicating warmth and health, and this we know produces genial, sympathetic people. Plenty of blood, pumped by a strong heart, means the antithesis of whiteness and coldness. So a " warm heart" really refers to the physical health of that organ, and the warmth that follows good blood supply, which condition produces the consequent attraction towards its fellow-men peculiar to such natures. Thus we find that a strong physical heart means not only health, but a strong attraction for and to others. And, conversely, a weak, flabby heart, pumping the blood current with lifeless force, produces white color, which indicates a lack of warmth, and consequent weak or less magnetic or energetic quality of affections. Those to whom the reading of variations in the affections from the Heart line has seemed impossible have not recognized the direct connection existing between the strength of the physical organ and the emotions, for every variation in the strength of the heart's action produces more or less health and a corresponding variation in the kind and strength of the affections. Thus the Heart line is, in truth, a revealer not only of the muscular, vital strength and action of the heart itself, but, as a result of these conditions, also of the strength and character of the affections.

You will not find the line of Heart absent in many hands, and yet it sometimes is. You will occasionally see only one line crossing the hand below the Mounts, and will be at a loss to tell whether it is the Head or Heart line. I have but once seen the Head line entirely absent, though I have seen many hands lacking the Heart line. (I had intended at this point to show this hand with Head line absent, but upon going to secure a print, found that a Head line had appeared in the hand since I last saw it, a period of about a year.) If we consider that the lines are controlled by the brain, and not by the heart, we can understand that the Head line will nearly always be present, being the indicator of that organ which controls and produces all lines. It is often seen, however, in a very elementary state of development. When a single line is seen occupying a position which is, relatively, where the Head line ought to be, it should be classed as a Head line and the Heart line considered to be absent. In order that this single line may be considered the Heart line and not the Head line, it must rise high on the Mount of Jupiter (24), or in that vicinity, and must trace its way across the hand just under the Mounts, and not by any means low enough to be in the location of the Head line. When the Heart line is absent, its absence speaks of a lack of sympathy and the affectionate side of the disposition, and warns us of one who is cold-blooded, selfish, and who desires personal success even at the expense and detriment of others. It is a bad marking, which easily leads from mere selfishness into hypocrisy, deceit, lack of candor, and positive dishonesty.

If this marking is seen in the hand of a bad Mercurian, or

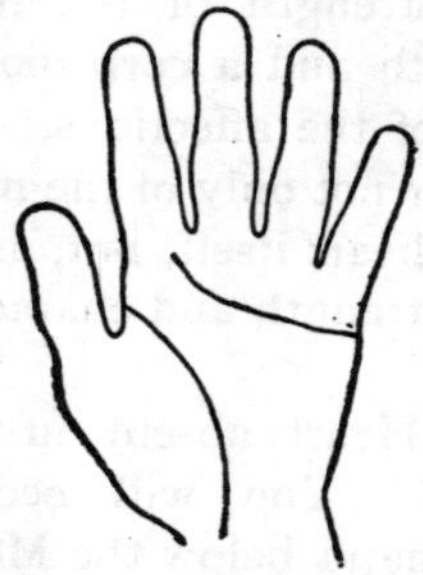

NO. 24

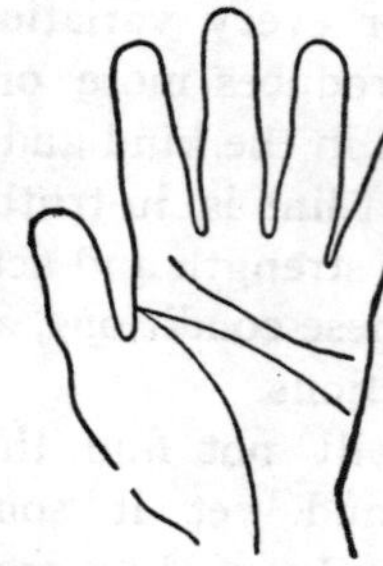

NO. 25

even of an unusually shrewd specimen of this type, it will at once mean natural temptation toward dishonesty. If the finger of Mercury is crooked and twisted, and the nails are narrow or short, you may be sure that the subject cannot be trusted. He will lie, swindle, cheat, steal, or do anything to get money; this is the hand of typical cold-blooded dishonesty. On a Martian the absence of the Heart line would show him to be unscrupulous, cold-blooded, and even on provocation bloodthirsty and dangerous. He will burn with physical ardor, and will gratify his lusts with no thought of the consequences to his victim. On a Saturnian it is a distressing indication, for it will add to his natural hatred of mankind, his desire to get even with them, his avarice; and, consequently, his chances of being dishonest will be increased. The Jupiterian will rarely be found with such an indication; when he is, some one of the three types just mentioned will be strong also, and the traits indicated by the absent Heart line will come from their side of the house. The Apollonian may have a defective Heart line, but it will not be found entirely absent with him; neither will it be with the Venusian, as these two types have too much sympathy and feeling ever to be absolutely deficient in heart. The Lunarian may be found with the line absent, or badly deficient, as he is naturally cold and selfish. Fortunately, you are not likely to meet many Lunarians. So the absent line of Heart will tell you that the subject lacks heart in a moral way, is cold and selfish, and that he will also be cowardly and sneaking in his disposition, though sometimes a great "bluffer." The line of Heart generally rises from some point on or near the Mount of Jupiter, sometimes extending over and rising on the Mount of Saturn. Sometimes the line has forks at its beginning, all of which may start from Jupiter, and sometimes these forks spread like a fan, extending over as far as Saturn.

There are three well-verified readings attached to three starting points, and these should be used as a basis for your work, modifying and changing them in accordance as you see the starting points vary. 1. Rising from Mount of Jupiter (25) we read the development of the sentimental side to the

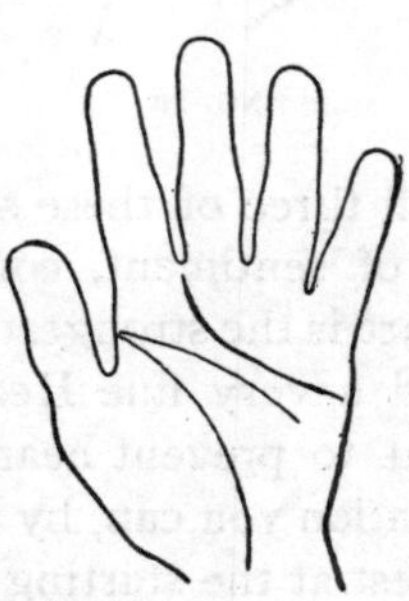

NO. 26

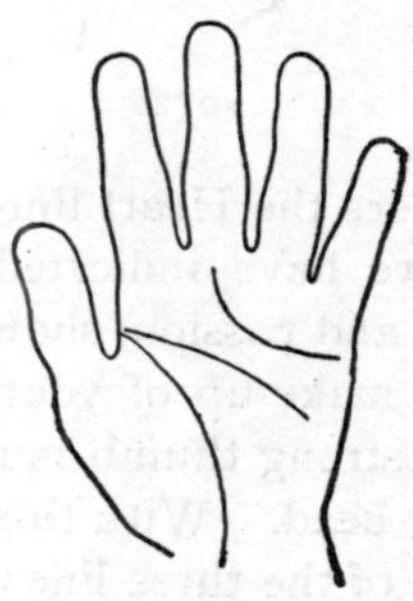

NO. 27

affections. The subject is one whose love is ideal, to whom love is an adoration, and to whom love, even with poverty attached, is attractive. 2. Rising between Jupiter and Saturn (26) the line shows the common-sense, practical, "middle ground" with the affections, indicating one who is not carried away with sentiment, but who views love from a practical standpoint; is not "soft" or "spoony," but who is inclined to think that love in a cottage without plenty of bread and butter is a myth. This person is never carried away by sentiment, and while strong in affection is sensible and not foolish. 3. Rising from the Mount of Saturn (27) the marking shows the sensualism in the affections of one whose love is tinged with the idea of pleasures from sexual relations. This is infallible if with it is seen a large Mount of Venus of pink or red color. and with strong Life and Mercury lines. These will tell of physical desire by the point at which the Heart line starts, and of physical strength sufficient to carry out these desires by the other indications.

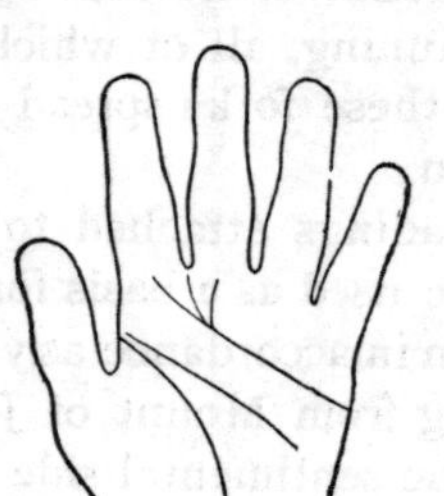

NO. 28

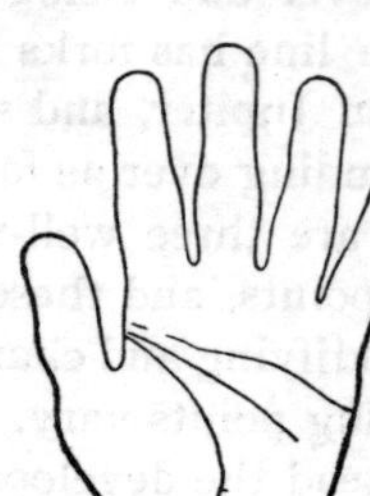

NO. 29

Where the Heart line rises from all three of these sources (28) we have indicated the union of sentiment, common-sense, and passion, showing that heart is the strongest factor in the make-up of your subject, and a very fine Head line and a strong thumb must be present to prevent heart from ruling head. With this strong formation you can, by noting which of the three lines is the deepest at the starting point, tell whether sentiment, common-sense, or passion is the strongest force. This always produces an affectionate person, who has a warm heart, a great deal of it, and loves friend, relation, and mankind in general. His danger is too much heart, and he does not always look after his own interests when considering those of others. This will be increased if the fork from Jupiter is strongest, and decreased if the middle branch is strongest, because the practical side will then be prominent. The fork of the Heart line will not always be so pronounced as that shown in the illustration, but every variation of it can be read *based* upon the full indication here given. Sometimes the line will start in several forks on Jupiter alone, in which case it increases the sentimentality of a single line starting from that point. The same rule applies to the other starting points. The general rule applies that a single line tends to make the affections more self-contained, and the subject loves family and friends strongly, but does not reach out to everybody as does the one whose Heart line forks at the start. The deeper and

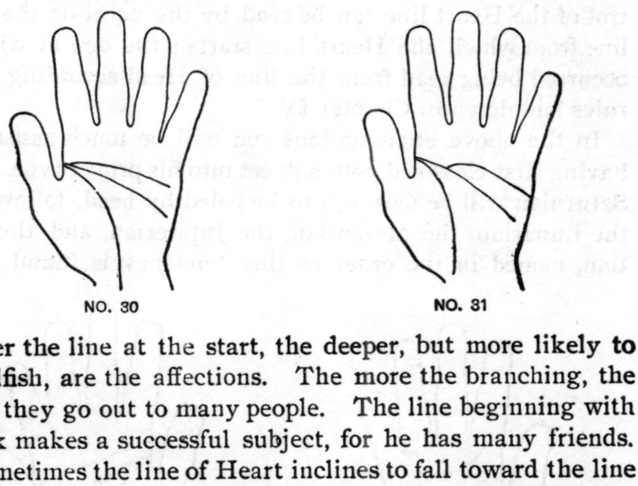

NO. 30 NO. 31

clearer the line at the start, the deeper, but more likely to be selfish, are the affections. The more the branching, the more they go out to many people. The line beginning with a fork makes a successful subject, for he has many friends.

Sometimes the line of Heart inclines to fall toward the line of Head at its start (29). This shows the head to be powerfully in the lead, and that when it comes to a choice between sentiment and utility the heart will be second best. Sometimes the line starts *from* the line of Head (30), in which case it will show that head has control of heart and completely dominates it. This is especially true if the *Head line* be *deeper* and clearer than the Heart line. If it is so marked, read with confidence that the head completely rules. If the lines of Head and Heart are marked as in the above two cases, there will be a continual struggle between them for supremacy, with the chances in favor of the head as the

Heart line droops or takes its source from it. The constant effort in our study of the hand is to discover what forces are strongest in the subject, and what ones will most influence him. In this battle between head and heart, reason and sentiment, minutely inspect the *source* of the Heart line and with it the *comparative strength* of the two lines, Head and Heart, in order to tell which will rule. Note in practice that the Heart line when rising from the Head line does not *always* do so just at the start, as in the illustration, but may rise farther along in the course of the Head line (31). In this case the time at which the Head line obtained control of the Heart line can be read by the point on the Head line from which the Heart line starts; the *age* at which it occurred being read from the line of Head according to the rules laid down in Chapter IV.

In the above examinations you will be much assisted by having first classified your subject into his proper type. The Saturnian will be most apt to be ruled by head, followed by the Lunarian, the Mercurian, the Jupiterian, and the Martian, named in the order as this tendency is found. The

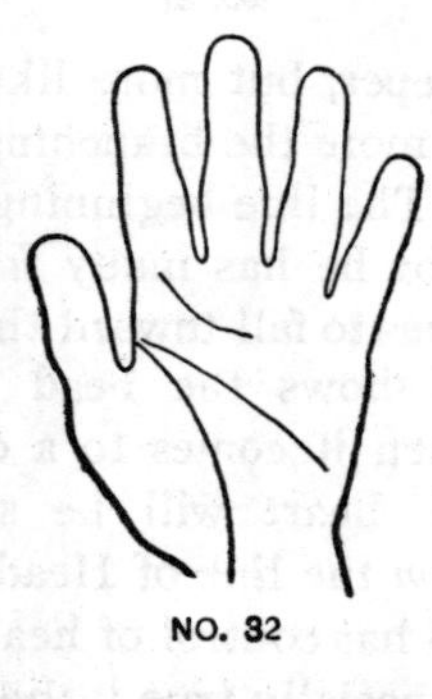

NO. 32

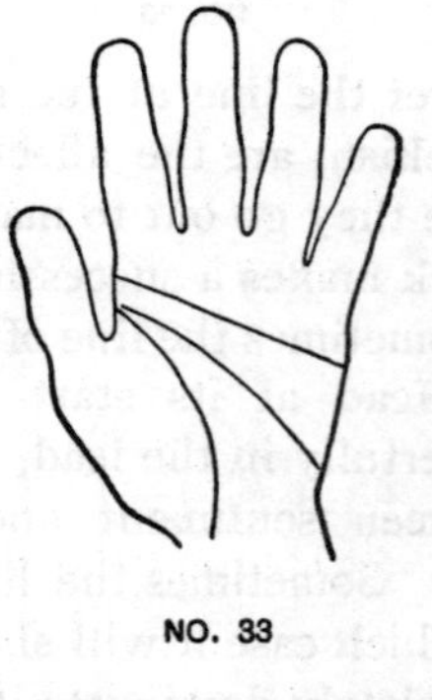

NO. 33

Apollonian and Venusian incline to have heart lead them. With the above markings base the strength of your statements of the indications upon the type as well as the indications of the line itself, and you will arrive at absolute accuracy. The length of the line should next be noted, for it will tell of *much* or *little* heart. If the line rises normally but runs only a short distance and stops (32), it indicates that the subject will have serious difficulty at the time at which it ends, even if all the other lines go on to their normal length. This abrupt termination of the Heart line means either that the heart will stop beating, or else that the subject has little heart or affection for others. You can judge which by the directions given later in this chapter. It is, in either case, a poor sign. If the Heart line crosses the entire hand (33) it shows that the subject has too much heart and will allow sentiment to guide him in everything. In business he will not choose employees because they are best fitted to do his work, but because they "need a job," and in all the walks of life he will be guided by sentiment. He will become easily jealous, and will love much and suffer if he does not get much in return. The older palmists read a line rising well up into the finger of Jupiter and running clear across the hand, "failure in all enterprises." This reading was probably based upon the fact that one who is in everything ruled by sentiment can seldom cope successfully with cold schemers. You can see that such a subject will not *necessarily* "fail in all enterprises," though he is not likely to get along so well as one more practical in matters of heart. So our reading, "too much heart," is the best.

After satisfying yourself as to the length of the line, next note its course through the hand. By this I do not mean to take a sweeping glance at the whole line, but that you note its every variation in direction. See in what directions the line is deflected, how long it runs in this course, the character of the line during the change in course, the age at which it occurs, and, if many of these changes take place, note each one, its duration, and all that happens to the line during the various changes in direction. It is this minute analysis of a line that gives its complete history as applied to the subject, the events that go with it, as well as the ages at which they occur. By noting the course of the line, I do not refer to defects in it, which we will consider later, but to the direction it takes in crossing the hand. With the exception of Jupiter, where it starts, the normal line of Heart marks the lower boundary of the Mounts of Saturn, Apollo, and Mercury, so that if its course is even and smooth and runs along at the base of these Mounts, ending just under the Mount of Mercury on the percussion, we do not consider that it is deflected from its usual channel. If in its course it rises to one of the Mounts (34), it shows that the attraction of that Mount is very strong, and that the subject will love the qualities and the persons belonging to this Mount type. The Current in its passage through the hand is constantly drawn and influenced in various directions, and in this case it is one of the Mounts which deflects the line. You will not often see

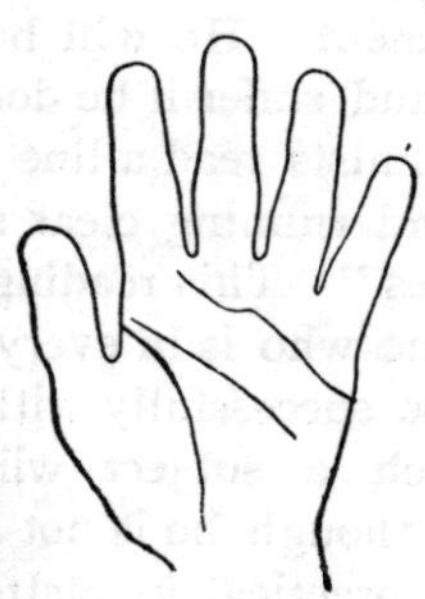

NO. 34

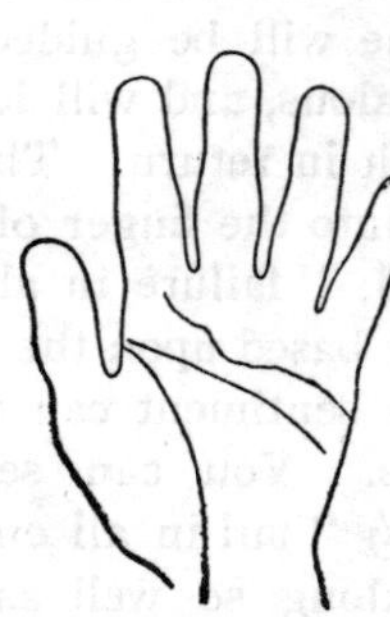

NO. 35

the line rise to more than one Mount, and if it so rises under a Mount it indicates *the age* at which the strongest attraction did or will occur in this direction. If the subject has attractions at other ages, they will be shown by a chance line leaving the Heart line, or some other line, *at the age* at which the attraction occurs, and running to the Mount *to which* it is attracted.

The Heart line *itself*, deflected to any Mount, shows by this deflection the source of attraction and the age at which it occurs. If the line in so rising *loses itself* in the Mount to which it deflects and ends there instead of at its usual stopping place, it shows that the attraction has overcome the affections and that the heart has surrendered completely. If it merely rises and then resumes its usual course again, it shows that the attraction occurs but does not master the subject. You can, by noting how long the line is deflected from its course, tell, by reading the age on the line, what period of years was covered by it. By noting how much the line is pulled out of its course, you can tell *how serious* the attraction has been. You will not often see a line pulled wide of its course, for, generally, before such a great *deflection* can occur, a chance line will *split* away from the Main line and rise to the point of attraction. But you will often encounter slight variations of the line, and these are important, for any attraction great enough to pull a Main line out of its course is a strong one. If the Heart line is deflected

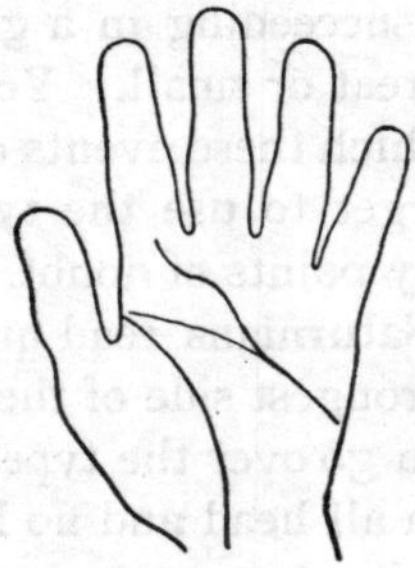

NO. 36

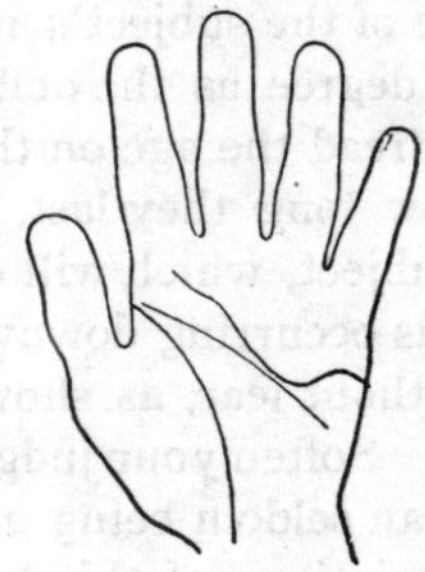

NO. 37

toward any Mount, the people of that Mount type attract the subject greatly and exert a strong influence over him. They form his ideal as to qualities and appearance, and you can describe the kind of a person your subject likes best, and often how they look, by describing the appearance of the type of the Mount to which the line is deflected. If the line dips downward in its course (35) it shows that at the time of this deflection the *head* has exerted a powerful influence over the heart; and reason and head dominate sentiment and heart. During such a period the subject will be indifferent to others, avaricious, selfish, and cold-hearted. This deflection of the Heart line may occur at any period in its course. The point at which it begins will tell the age at which this tendency begins. If it is lost in the Head line (36), it shows that these qualities have swallowed all further independent action of the affections. These subjects are henceforth dominated by head. If the line of Heart after such a serious deflection regains its former course (37), it shows there is still left a portion of the former affectionate disposition, and that head and worldly interests have not entirely overcome heart and sentiment. Such a character will always be tinged strongly with much head and little heart.

These deflections toward the Head line are very frequent, but in an infinite variety of degrees. They vary from slight curvings of the line which are scarcely perceptible, to great swoops downward. In whatever degree seen, it shows the pulling force of the head, striving to overcome the sentimental side of the subject's nature, and succeeding in a greater or less degree as the deflection is great or small. You can always read the age on the line at which these events occur, and how long they last. Do not forget to use the type of your subject, which will clear up any points of doubt. Deflections occurring downward with Saturnians read quickly and without fear, as showing the strongest side of the indication. Soften your judgment as you go over the types, the Venusian seldom being afflicted with all head and no heart. The variations of this line are infinite, but you can accurately read each one of them if you understand the *general principles* governing, and use good judgment in estimating the degree of disturbance or difference. There are cases where the line of Heart, in deflecting downward from its course, cuts the Head line in two instead of merging with it or going back to its original course (38). In this case serious injury and damage to the Head line are indicated, and at the time at which such a cut takes place the subject will have either an unbalancing of the mental faculties, serious brain fever, or death. Such a marking cannot take place without disaster. The two strong Currents in the Head and Heart lines crossing each other will, to use electric parlance, burn out the fuse, or cause an explosion, and as the affair occurs on the Head line, the explosion will be in the brain. Apoplexy is most to be feared, followed by an impairment of brain or paresis if the acute attack be survived. In such a case look well to the Mount type. Jupiterians are predisposed to apoplexy, and with such a marking in this type your diagnosis will be plain. Saturnians are predisposed to paralysis, and with such a type this will be his trouble. Apollonians are predisposed to blindness and heart disease, so heart failure is the strong presumption here, with blindness (a defect in the head) second. Mercurians, predisposed

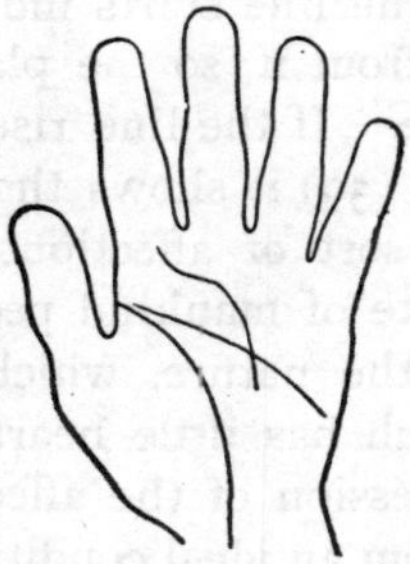
NO. 38

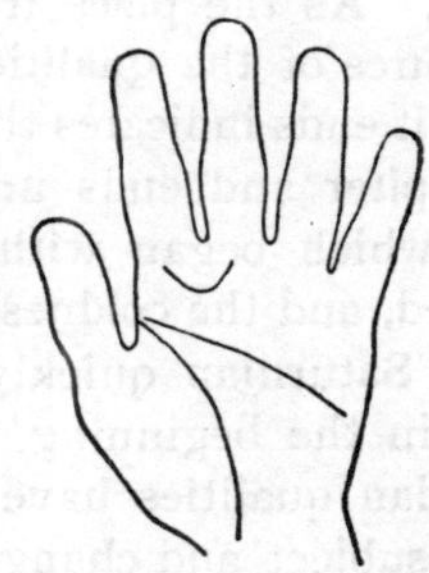
NO. 39

to nervous, bilious trouble, will point you to paralysis. Martians, with excess of blood supply already greatly marked, will likely have apoplexy. Lunarians and Venusians are not likely to have this marking. Though the acute attack of apoplexy probable in the above cases may not be fatal, it leaves an impairment and injury to the brain. In any event this marking, when the Heart line cuts the Head line, must be considered very serious. Note both the lines of Life and Saturn to see whether they stop or are deflected at the same age at which this cutting occurs. If so, the indication is more serious. This deflection of the Heart line and cutting of the Head line may occur at any point in its journey across the hand. The age at which it occurs reads from the line. If at the point where the two lines cut they are deep and red, the consequences are more serious. Examine nails to see if by color or flutings they show predisposition to heart trouble or paralysis : if so the danger is greater.

We may sum up the rules for the course of the Heart line by saying that every variation in its course means a change in the qualities for which it stands, that the age and period covered by these changes may be read from the line, that they are more or less pronounced in their effect and consequences, as these changes are slightly or definitely marked. Practice will enable you to properly estimate all these variations.

We have already considered the Heart line as to its source and course through the hand, and must now note its termination. As the place from which the line starts indicates the source of the qualities we read from it, so the place at which it ends indicates their outcome. If the line rises under Jupiter and ends under Saturn (39) it shows that the heart which began with the right sort of affections soon changed, and the coldness and dislike of mankind peculiar to the Saturnian quickly changed the nature, which was warm in the beginning, to one which has little heart left. Saturnian qualities have taken possession of the affections of the subject and changed them from an ideal condition to one of indifference. If this marking be seen, look at nails for paralysis and heart disease, at the Life line to see if a dis-

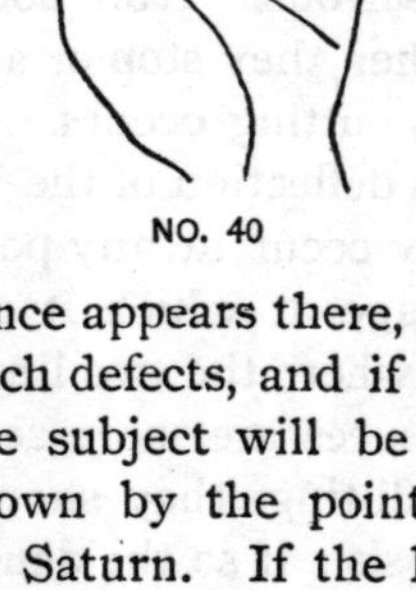

NO. 40

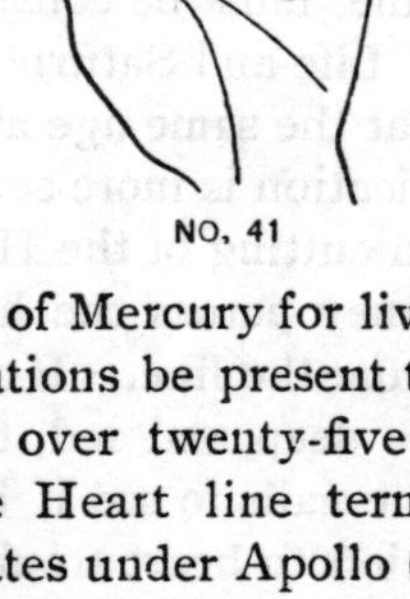

NO. 41

turbance appears there, at the Line of Mercury for liver and stomach defects, and if these indications be present the life of the subject will be short—not over twenty-five years, as shown by the point where the Heart line terminates under Saturn. If the line terminates under Apollo (40), it shows that Apollonian ideas of beauty and art strongly attract the subject, who will be unsatisfied in marriage except with an Apollonian or one approaching that type. If with this termination the line rises on Jupiter it will give ideal love, which, added to that for the Apollonian character, makes one indeed fond of beauty, love, and grace. As one of the health defects of the Apollonian is heart disease, if the Heart line ends on this Mount, examine nails, character of the Heart line, Life line, and Mercury line, to find whether the marking does not indicate heart disease. By remembering the health defects peculiar to the types, and the manner in which nails, color, etc., show them, you will never have any trouble in separating a *character* indication from a *health* defect. With the Heart line ending on Apollo, look out for everything bearing on heart disease, to confirm

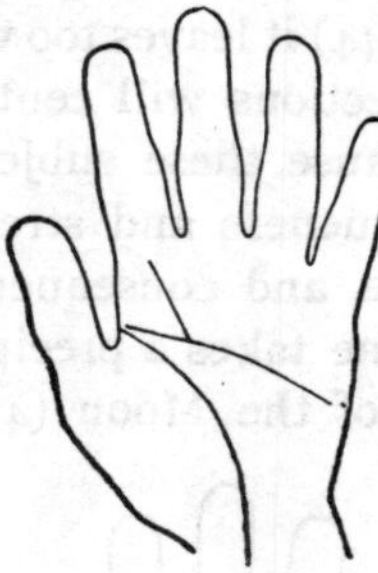

NO. 42

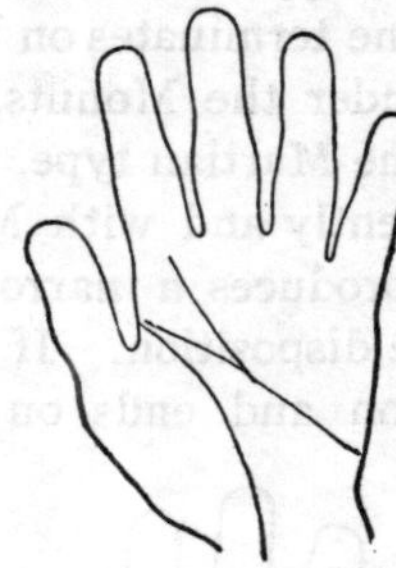

NO. 43

it. If health defects are not present, it indicates, not disease, but the trend of the affections.

If the line ends high on the Mount of Mercury (41), it shows that the affections are largely influenced by finances. The Mercurian shrewdness guides this Heart line, and it must always have money in sight before love is recognized. The line so terminating does not, *per se*, lead us to look for a health defect, as heart trouble is not a defect of the Mercurian. It is well, however, never to omit a search in health directions, even in places where we do not expect to find them, for they sometimes take us unawares.

At all times bear in mind the course a Heart line ought to travel, and remember that the Electric Current is flowing through it. Every change in its course takes this Current out of its proper channel and turns it loose at some point that was not designed to receive it. A line like Fig. 42 shows that the Heart line has never run over its proper channel, but pours a double Current into the Head line It operates to make the subject cold and heartless, and should be read like an absent Heart line. These people are very ambitious, as the line leads down from Jupiter, but will consider the welfare of no one when furthering their ambitions. The line may run into the Head line farther along in its course (43). In this case the indication points in the same direction as Fig. 42, but in a modified degree, as the line of Heart runs longer before being absorbed. In 43 it is practically a Head line beginning with a fork, with the Heart line absent. In 43 there is more of the Heart line present, which produces a better effect. If the Heart line terminates on Upper Mars (44) it leaves too wide a space under the Mounts, and the affections will centre on one of the Martian type. This will cause these subjects to love ardently and with Martian brusqueness and strength. It also produces a narrow quadrangle, and consequently a secretive disposition. If the Heart line takes a precipitous depression and ends on the Mount of the Moon (45), it

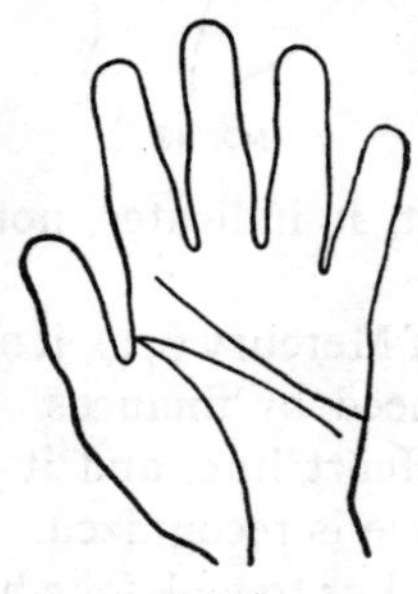

NO. 44

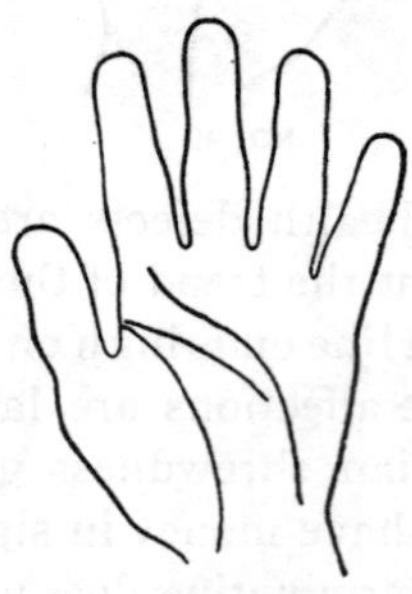

NO. 45

makes the subject extremely jealous, for there will be too much Heart line, backed by the imagination of the Lunarian, which will magnify every act of one he loves into some form of unfaithfulness. This formation is a most unhappy one. This does not necessarily indicate a danger to life, for the Heart line may not cross the Head line. If the Heart line forms a curve and ends on the Plain of Mars (46), it will be a serious menace, for it will cut the Head line squarely, will pour its Current into the Plain of Mars (the seat of temper and excitability), and will consequently endanger life by cutting the Head line, and will also show the subject to be exceedingly irritable, changeable in affections, constantly seeking excitement, and hard to get along with. Carefully note the Life, Head, and Mercury lines if this indi-

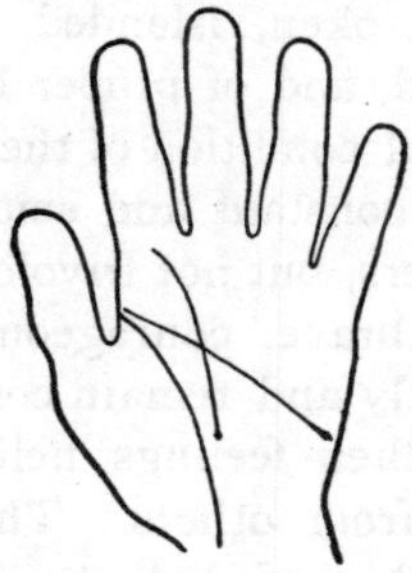

NO. 46

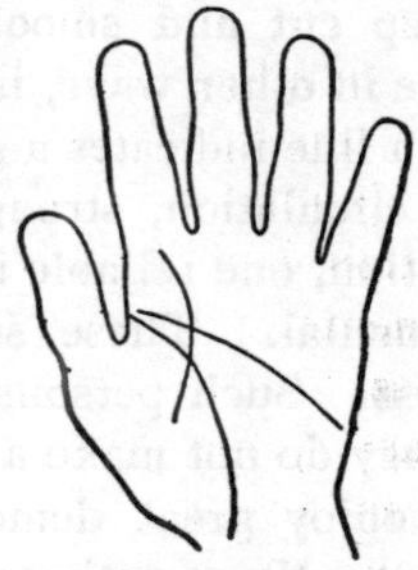

NO. 47

cation is seen, to determine whether the outcome is serious. Bad defects in these lines at the age at which the Head line is cut would confirm this reading. Be careful not to confuse this marking with a Saturn line rising in the Plain of Mars. If the line goes well up into Jupiter, read it as the Heart line; if it goes into Saturn, or only to the edge of Jupiter, read it as a Saturn line with the Heart line absent. If the line curves around and ends on the Mount of Venus (47), it is a serious indication, for it cuts both the lines of Head and Life. In this rare marking, note carefully the condition of lines where the cutting takes place, and the condition of Head and Life lines afterwards. If defects appear in either, you know damage has been done to the head and that life is in danger. If the Life line ends or fades away soon after, you know that the life terminates.

It is not my intention to give every possible variation of the Heart line here, but it is my desire to indicate constantly the general principles governing it, and the methods of reasoning out its combinations, which will start you in the way of using your own reasoning faculties rather than of memorizing a set of illustrations. It is to teach the *way* and *habit* of reasoning that I aspire, and this is the only kind of work that possesses any value. When you have acquired the habit and way of thinking combinations out, you can throw books away.

The *character* of the Heart line, which we will next consider, is most important, and must be carefully noted, not in its entirety, as I have said before, but bit by bit from source to ending place. The perfect line is one which is deep cut and smooth, is not broken, islanded, or defective in other ways, is well colored, and of proper length. Such a line indicates a good physical condition of the heart, good circulation, strong affections constant and smooth in operation, one reliable in love matters, but not frivolous nor sentimental. These subjects are brave, courageous, and fearless. Such persons love ardently and remain constant, but they do not make a display of their feelings, neither do they enjoy great demonstrations from others. They are consequently sometimes thought cold and distant. This is incorrect; they love devotedly and constantly, but they do not "wear the heart on the sleeve." With deep Heart lines there is little fear of heart disease from a weak condition of the organ itself, and there is little use to look for health defects of the line. With this Heart line the subject will have fewer love affairs, but what he has will be strong. He will have confidence in those he loves, and a disappointment will affect him severely, for, while quiet and undemonstrative, the Current runs deeply. Such subjects do not pick up any and everyone and make a great demonstration over them, but they love their dear ones and friends with a steady devotedness. With such a clear line there is the best kind of a channel for the Current to run through, no obstructions, and, consequently, the best kind of heart action and the strongest and most reliable affections.

If the line is small and thin, the person has little care for others, is narrow-minded, cowardly, timid, unsympathetic, and has no real affection for anyone. All display of love which he might make is from a desire to further selfish ends.

Do not make the mistake of calling a Heart line thin and giving it the above reading unless it *is* thin, while the other lines are well marked, in which case it has its full meaning and puts the heart out of proportion to the rest of the lines. With all kinds of Heart lines, apply them to the type of the subject. A Jupiterian and Venusian will be expected to have the best kind of Heart lines. The Apollonian may have his health defect, heart disease, show on the line, but will have outside of this a good line and strong affections. The Martian will be expected to have a good Heart line, but it may be excessive in strength. A good specimen of the Mercurian type will have a good Heart line, but a bad specimen will have the thin line showing the selfish disregard for others and the furthering of selfish ends. The Saturnian, if good, will have a good line, if bad, a thin line. The Lunarian, naturally cold and selfish, will be expected to have a thin or chained, shallow white line. If you should find the thin line on a subject belonging to a type on which it is abnormal, read the line properly, but do not give it *all the force* you would on a type where it is expected. For example, the thin line found on a Venusian will not be read so strongly as the same line on a Lunarian.

If the line be broad and shallow, the heart action will be physically weak, the affections will correspond, and the subject is fickle if the hand be weak ; sentimental and loving a display of affection if the rest of the hand be good. These subjects fall violently in love, but quickly change their affections to the next attractive person who comes along. Their Heart line is broad and shallow; the affections are the same. They like to be told how much you love them every time they meet you, and they are often the people who love you during prosperity, but turn their backs in times of trial. There is in their nature no true ring of deep, strong affection ; they are incapable of a lasting attachment. This is what we call a sentimental Heart line. It is of great value in the estimate of the probable outcome of a marriage to know these facts, for on the Heart line can be told who is to be counted on when the clouds of adversity lower. Do not forget to apply the broad and shallow line to the subject's type, and estimate the effect of such a line on such a type. If found on an Apollonian it will point to one of his health defects, and you should look carefully at color, nails, and for defects on the Life line to judge the degree of its seriousness. Note whether this line *alone* has this broad and shallow formation ; if so, it must be read in a most pronounced manner. If all the lines are of the same character the subject has the same defects all around. If the Heart line is chained, it presents a continual series of obstructions to the Current, and the heart's action is irregular, the circulation poor, and there is in general a poor physical condition of the heart. Note well the type of subject ; if there is much Apollonian in him, either in the primary, secondary, or tertiary type, be on your guard for severe heart disease. A Life line that is thin, islanded, broken, or defective in any way, combined with a chained Heart line, will show the serious menace of the heart to the life. If the Life line runs too deeply in any one place it will be most serious, and if a star be seen in it, sudden death from heart disease is certain, *absolutely so* if found in both hands under the Mount of Apollo.

The chained Heart line shows a constant uncertainty in the affections. The subject thinks one day that he is in love and changes his mind the next. He will rush up to you and smother you with a great demonstration of affection, and the next time you meet he will hardly speak to you. He vacillates and changes, is cowardly, uncertain, and weak. The constantly interrupted Current has no deep permanent channel, and the result is no permanent health or affections. Note whether this chained condition applies only to the Heart line, and whether all the other lines are deep and well cut, in which case read the Heart line in a pronounced manner ; if all the lines are chained, the Heart line is not more defective than everything else. Proportion must be in mind constantly.

All of the above kinds of lines have been treated in general, —that is, as if they were deep and well cut, narrow and thin, broad and shallow, or chained during their entire length ; but such is the exception. You will find the Heart line generally deep and well cut at the beginning, and changing to other formations as the line runs its course across the hand. The qualities of the lines just described apply to the line *only during the time the line shows these formations*, and when the character of the line changes the qualities of the subject change. For every change in the character of the line there will be a change in the subject. By noting on the line the age at which these changes take place, and their duration on the line, you can read at what age the modifications they indicate took place, and how long each condition lasted. If the line begins deep and well cut (48) and continues so until it reaches under the Saturn finger, then becomes broad and shallow, continuing thus until under the finger of Apollo, then becomes thin until under Mercury, and chained to the end, it would read: deep and well-cut qualities up to age twenty-four, changed to broad and shallow up to age forty-three, changed to thin up to age sixty, and chained for balance of life. Interpret as follows: The subject during the early portion of his life was very warm-hearted, constant, trustworthy, and strong in affections; at the age of twenty-four he changed in these respects, and became weak, changeable, and inconstant; at forty-three he grew very selfish, cold-hearted, and sought only to further his own ends, which condition lasted until sixty, when he grew weak, had poor circulation, became vacillating, cowardly, and unreliable in his affections, and these conditions lasted until the end of his life. This example shows the method of applying general rules and indications to each part of the line on which different formations are seen. The manner in which these combinations occur on a line varies infinitely, but you will have no trouble in reading each case if you remember what deep, shallow, thin, or chained lines indicate, and apply these qualities to the line for the period of years they occupy. In any reading make the

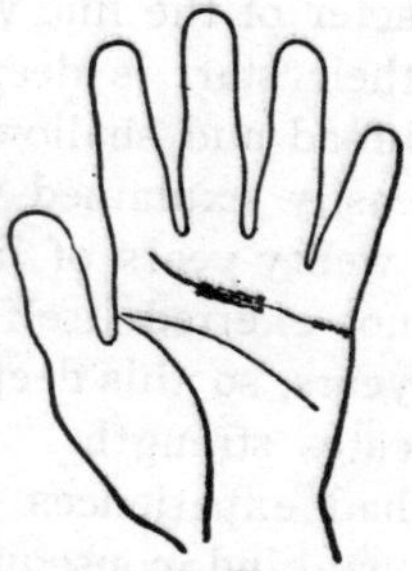

NO. 48

application as past events to those parts of the line before the present age, and future events to all parts of the line ahead of the present age. If you have judged the line correctly the past events will be recognized by the subject, and my experience with future events has been so accurate that you need have no hesitation in boldly reading them as shown by changes on the line. Before attempting such detailed reading, however, learn to diagnose the character of the line very accurately. In nearly all Heart lines their start is deep and well cut, while they are generally broad and shallow, chained or tasselled at the end. This is easily explained when we remember that during the first twenty years of life the heart is strongest in action ; it has not exerted itself and become worn as is the fact in later years, so this deep and well-cut beginning of the line indicates strength. At this time of life the subject has not had experiences which make him doubt the sincerity of mankind, consequently the line is more perfectly marked. As old age comes on the action of the heart grows weaker, and the line becomes defective, the subject loves petting and display of affection from others, and the line, instead of the self-contained depth which shows at the beginning when such things are not sought so much, becomes shallow and sentimental.

With every Heart line, color plays an important part. When beginning the examination of this line, it is useful to press the line from source to termination with the finger, and note the facility with which the blood flows under this pressure. This will indicate the strength of the blood stream and will help to distinguish the color of the line. In some lines the blood flows freely, and in others the whiteness under pressure shows the weak blood supply. In the Heart line color is important, for it tells whether a subject is warm- or cold-hearted. If with the deep, well-cut Heart line we find white color, it will not be so strong an indication of a good physical heart as if the color were pink. We know by the deep line that, while the heart was intended to be of full development, something has taken place, as shown by white color, by which it has been weakened. In such a case look at both hands; if the line colors well in the left and shows white in the right, it will indicate plainly that the naturally strong heart has been impaired and weakened. White color in the line of Heart, even if the line is otherwise good, shows the heart's action to be weaker than normal, and the affections colder. With color, always apply it to the type of the subject. Coldness belongs to the Lunarian primarily, the Saturnian second, Mercurian third, while Martians, Apollonians, Venusians, and Jupiterians are warm-hearted. So, with a white-colored Heart line, apply its coldness to the type of subject, and estimate the result. It will much reduce the strength of the four warmer types, and will make the cold types colder. With the thin and narrow, broad and shallow, and chained lines, white color exaggerates their cold qualities, and selfishness, vacillation, and fickleness will be exceedingly pronounced, according to which characteristic the line has. Here, again, look at both hands to see if matters are growing better or worse.

Pink color will make a deep line operate properly, and all the warmth, steadfastness, and reliability of this good line will be accentuated. If found on the warm types, it will make them strong in the natural directions. If found on the cold types, it will warm them up. Pink color will make a thin line less selfish and narrow; it will make a broad and shallow or a chained line less fickle, and often with these formations pink color is the thing which saves the subject from being entirely inconstant. Red color is the intensity of rich, warm blood, and in the Heart line makes intense all the fires of affection. It shows a heart so strong that it may be dangerous. On the Martian type we expect it, but it is too strong to be good for any of the others. It is seen on Jupiterians, but is not good on this type. Naturally overeaters, they tend to apoplexy and heart failure. So a deep red line on a pronounced Jupiterian is indeed a danger signal. Red color in a Martian Heart line will make the affections of the subject intense and his passions great. It will warm up the cold heart of a Lunarian, and make him less selfish. The Saturnian yields some of his hate of mankind to red color, while Venusians and Apollonians become too intense. Red color in the deep Heart line will make a strong combination, too intense to be good in many cases. It tends toward excess of this good line, and excess is not desirable. You rarely see red color in thin and narrow, broad and shallow, or chained Heart lines, but when you do, always considerably reduce the estimate of their qualities. Yellow color in the Heart line will tinge the affections with morbidness and will make even the subject with the good, deep line suspicious of those he loves. Bile spoils everything, even a good Heart line, and adds its pessimistic view even to love. A yellow Heart line, though it may be deep, is less to be depended upon and is more incline to double dealing than even a white one. Whiteness indicates simply indifference, while yellow color leads to distortion in the manner of looking at things. A yellow Heart line on a strong Saturnian will make as mean a subject as could be found, and it would take very little inducement to make such an one a criminal. A yellow Heart line on a Mercurian, especially if a bad or an unusually shrewd specimen of the type, would easily make a swindler, and with little encouragement a villain. Yellow Heart lines mean a poisoned, bad heart, so they pull down every type. Blue color in a Heart line tells of the congestion, the sluggish movement of this organ, and the type must at once be located, for if the Apollonian it is serious. Nails must be looked at to see if the trouble is a structural one, or only a defective circulation, the Life line must be examined for any defects which indicate an end to the career, and from this combined point of view, you will be able to estimate how serious the blue Heart line is.

You will constantly be called upon to judge whether some marking seen on a Heart line is a health defect, an event in the life, or an indication of character, and this is a point which has puzzled many excellent practitioners. The difficulty is not hard to overcome. The line of Heart indicates, first, the physical state of that organ, and, second, as a result of that physical state, the mental characteristics and qualities of the affections; and, third, it often shows when this mental attitude has taken such hold as to powerfully draw the subject in different directions, causing decided preferences which have led to certain events in his life. All of these matters are not shown in every hand. The first and second always are, but the third only at times. As strong brain impressions alone produce changes in the lines, manifestly the third will be seen only in those hands where the brain has been so profoundly impressed that the effect has been transmitted to the lines. If you encounter an unusual formation of the line, or any change from the normal, you wonder whether it is health or character that is indicated. Your first thought should be that it is a health indication, for the line shows, first, the physical condition of the heart. Note the type of your subject, and whether heart disease is a natural defect of this type. If it is, the presumption is strong that the marking is a health defect. Next examine the nails, and see if the structural heart-disease formation or blue color at the base be present, and if both or either of these indications are seen, you should be still more strongly convinced that it is a health defect. Note the Life line to see if there is any unevenness, whether it breaks, splits, islands, is crossed, and especially if a line runs from the defect on the Heart line to the Life line. If the Life line shows such defects be sure the indication on the Heart line is one which refers to the physical heart. The Saturn line will often show confirmations of a check to the career seen in the Life line by breaking in two or by other defects. The Mercury line, either by stopping at the same age indicated by the defect on the Life line, or by showing some defect, often gives an added confirmation. Not finding any of these health defects, it is evident the mark on the Heart line is one showing some characteristic of the affections and not disease. This method must be adopted with every line on which you encounter a change from the normal condition. Review everything bearing on disease, first beginning with the health defects of the type to which your subject belongs, and noting in succession nails, color, and all lines that bear any relation to the defect under consideration.

Careful practice will in this manner enable you to make a distinction between character and disease. Begin at the starting point of the Heart line, and examine the line along its entire length for defects. These may be splits, cross-bars, islands, dots, or breaks. Wherever one of these defects appears, it is either a health indication, or one showing some event connected with the affections. The first thing is to examine in the manner above outlined, in order to determine whether ill health is indicated, and if it is, draw your conclusions as to the effect the condition found will have on the affections of the subject. Finding no confirmatory indications of heart difficulty, you turn naturally to other matters. The first defect to consider is the split, which you already know how to diagnose. If you find it to be a health defect, it is serious in proportion as it splits the Main line in two and divides the Current, directing part away from its proper channel. Split lines as health defects show a weakened condition of heart with impaired circulation, and the date of the trouble can be read from the line. As character indications, the place they occur, size of split, and the place to which they run must be guides in reading them. Splits will occur upward or downward according as the split lines rise above or fall below the line. All lines which rise from a Main line are more favorable than lines which fall from it, so split lines rising from the Heart line are better indications than those which fall below it. These lines which split from the Heart line will rise to or near a Mount, and will indicate that either the characteristics of the Mount, or someone belonging to that type, so strongly attract the heart as to split off part of the line and draw it up toward the Mount. Thus a split rising from the Heart line under Jupiter (49) will show that ambition will guide love, and the person who will attract this subject will be someone on the Jupiterian order. He does not necessarily have to have money, but he must be prominent, or one who gives promise of rising. A split line rising under Saturn (50) will indicate that the subject is attracted by some of the Saturnian qualities. If the subject, on whose hand you find this line, is developed in his mental world, it will be this side of the Saturnian that will attract him, and he will love one who has scholarly attainments. If your client's middle world is strongest, he will love one who has farming, mining, or horticultural aptitudes, or scientific talents. If his lower world is strongest, he will love one who has the saving disposition of the Saturnian. In every case this subject will like best one who has the soberness, caution, and wisdom that belong to the Saturnian type. The subject himself may not belong to the Saturnian type, but he will admire these qualities. I have seen the most giddy persons with this marking, and believe they realize

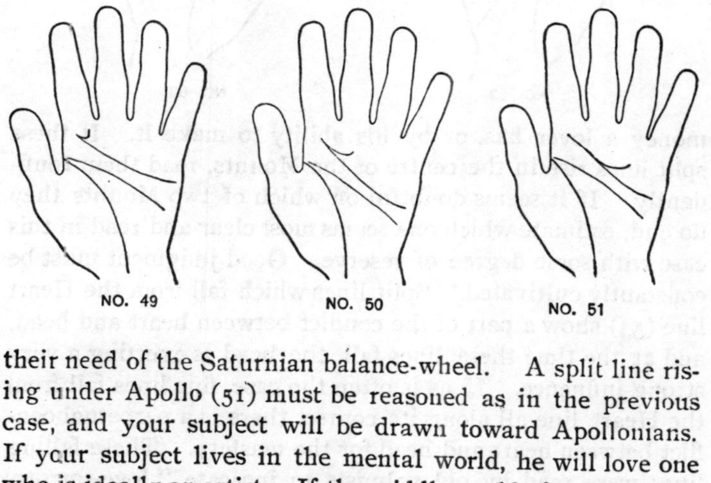

NO. 49 NO. 50 NO. 51

their need of the Saturnian balance-wheel. A split line rising under Apollo (51) must be reasoned as in the previous case, and your subject will be drawn toward Apollonians. If your subject lives in the mental world, he will love one who is ideally an artist. If the middle world of your subject is strongest, he will love one who is an artist, but he wants this artist able to make money from his art. If the lower world is strongest your subject will love one who dresses in a showy fashion and who knows how to make a display. Remember the Apollonian, and that this split line from the line of Heart makes the subject love the qualities of that type; you can carry your explanation as far as you please by describing all that Apollonians are, and saying that this is what your client will love. If the split line rises to Mercury (52) your subject will love Mercurian qualities; *which side* will be shown by the world which rules in his hand—the oratory and eloquence of the upper world of Mercury, the scientific side shown by the middle, or the money-making side shown by the lower world. In the latter case the subject will suffer love to be influenced by the amount of

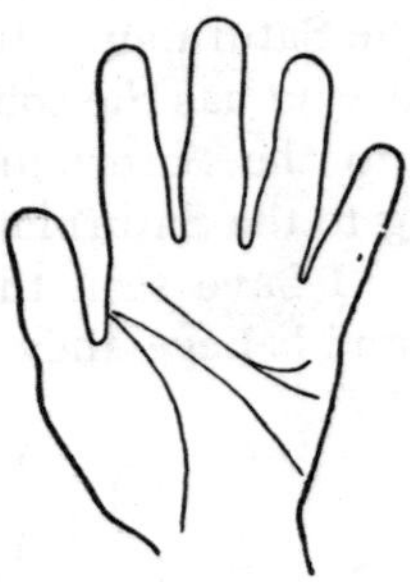

NO. 52

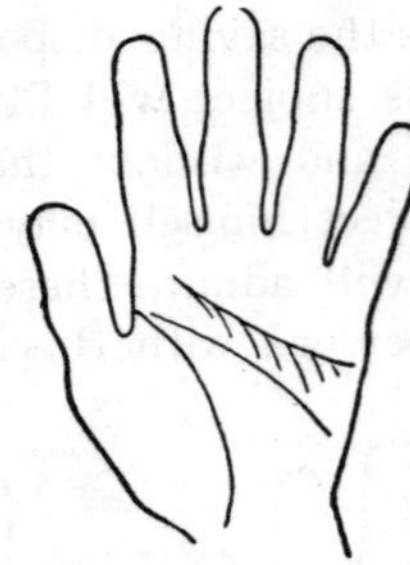

NO. 53

money a lover has, or by his ability to make it. If these split lines rise in the centre of the Mounts, read them confidently. If it seems doubtful on which of two Mounts they do end, estimate which one seems most clear and read in this case with some degree of reserve. Good judgment must be constantly cultivated. Split lines which fall from the Heart line (53) show a part of the conflict between heart and head, and at the time these lines fall, the head is exerting a very strong influence. If, as is often the case, fine lines fall from the Heart line all along its course, there is a perpetual conflict between heart and head for the mastery. These falling lines were read by old palmists to indicate "love-sorrows and disappointments." When we think that they do indicate an effort of the head to control sentiment or heart, we can understand how it was reasoned out, for if one loves but allows the head to say that the loved one is not so good a match as someone else, he will have "love-sorrows and disappointments," for calculation (head) has stifled sentiment (heart).

Sometimes a large line will split away from the Heart line

and gradually fall to the Head line, merging itself in it (54); this will show that heart has surrendered to head and is thereafter ruled by it. The age at which it begins is shown by the point at which the line splits away, and the complete surrender by the point at which the line loses itself in the line of Head. Cross-bars cutting the line (55) are constant heart irritations, either illness, or worries in the affections. On noting them make a search to locate whether they are health defects or whether they apply to the affections. If health defects note how deeply they cut. If only little lines they show temporary heart disturbance of a functional character, if very deep they are more serious; so note all these lines carefully, to see how disastrous they will be in their effect. If these cross-bars cut the line in many places, it shows that the trouble is continuous. If heart disease, it will show palpitation and valvular difficulties, and generally with such bars present the Heart line grows dim and more defective toward its latter end, and the cross-bars become deeper cut. If these bars do not relate to disease, then constant jars to

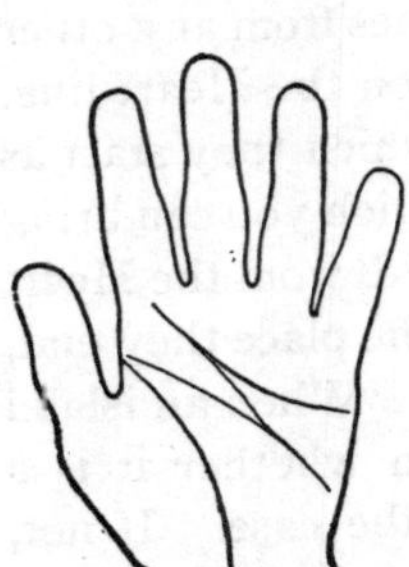

NO. 54

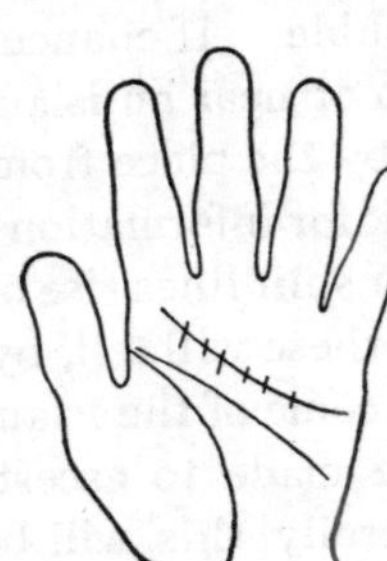

NO. 55

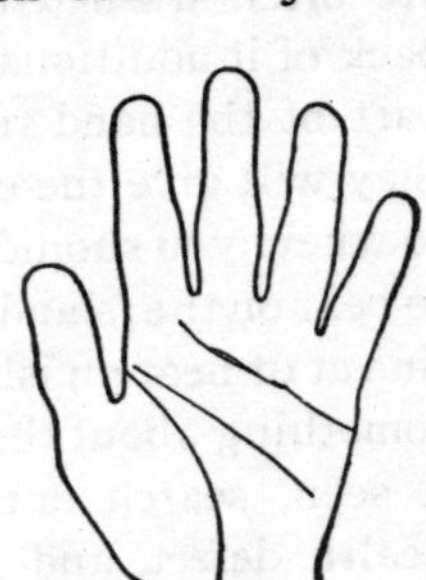

NO. 56

the affections will be indicated at the age at which these bars show on the line.

All defects on the Heart line are more serious if they appear under the Mount of Apollo. Islands in the Heart line (56) are always defects. They obstruct the Current, weaken it, and most often indicate weak physical action of the heart. The size of the island will show how serious the difficulty is, mere dots being not more than temporary disturbances, while those which are large and deep cut are menaces to life. Islands found in the Heart line under the Mounts will generally add a heart complication to some health defect of that Mount type. When seen always locate the type of the subject and hunt for a health defect peculiar to him, which if found must have heart weakness added. In this way you

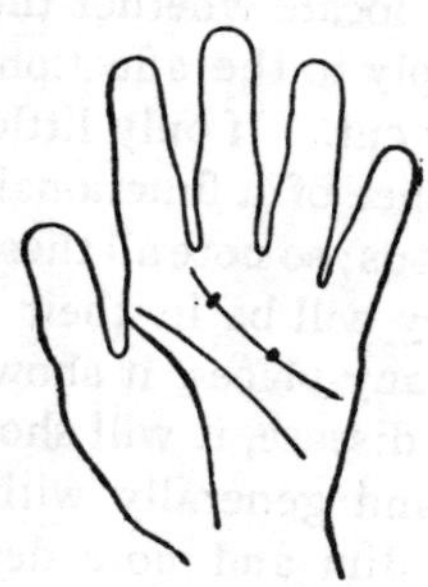

NO. 57

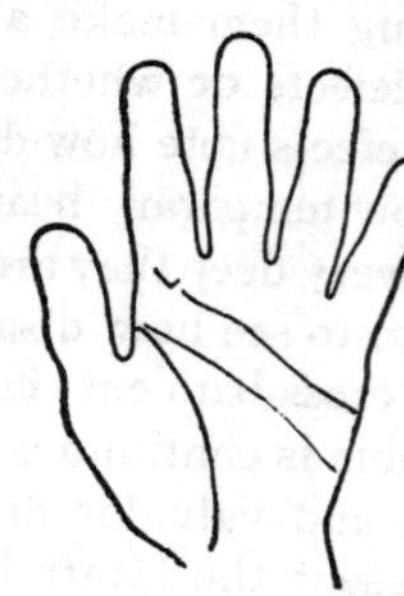

NO. 58

are often warned by an island on the Heart line and find back of it additional trouble. If chance lines from any other part of the hand run to or near an island on the Heart line, they will give the clue by the place from which they start as to where you should look for information which you can bring to bear on the island. If split lines rise or fall from the Heart line at or near an island these will tell, by the place they end, something about the outcome of the island. When an island is seen, search must be made to ascertain whether it is a health defect, and generally this will be the case. If not, look to location, chance, and other lines for information bearing on some disappointment to the affections. An island on the Heart line under Apollo is always a health indication, and you will seldom fail to get the complete confirmation from nails, etc.

Dots on the Heart line (57) are generally health defects, and their degree of seriousness is gauged by their size. When seen, always examine for heart disease. If no indication is seen anywhere else, and the dot is small, the case is not serious. The more pronounced the signs of heart trouble which are seen elsewhere, and the larger the dot, the more serious the difficulty. Breaks of all degrees of size are often seen in the line. With nearly every break, one end of the broken line will go wide of its course and will show what has influenced the line sufficiently to break it. Breaks must always be considered as serious even though small, and when wide or when the ends of the broken line are far apart and unrepaired, they become serious enough in their meaning to warrant the reading of probable fatality. When breaks of any size are seen look for repair signs. If the ends of the line lap, or have sister lines joining them, squares surrounding, or anything which will help retain the Current in its course, read it as serious heart difficulty which is prevented from coming to a fatal conclusion by the repair signs. With breaks examine in the usual manner to see if they are health defects, and if found to be so, read the break as denoting illness; if it is not a health indication read it as an interruption in the affections. If the line breaks and runs up to Jupiter (58) it will be read the same as the line deflected to that Mount, or as a split line running to Jupiter, showing that Jupiterian qualities attract the client and that the break in the line, if a health defect, is due to a disturbance of heart brought about by the Jupiterian disposition to overeat. This will produce functional heart disturbance, which can be overcome by removing the cause. If the break be not a health indication, it will show that one of the Jupiterian type has caused the break, or that it has been caused by too much ambition or pride (Jupiterian qualities). Always examine the character of the line after the break, noting the changes in it which tell the outcome of this break. If the line afterward continues deep, it will be overcome, if it grows thin, or chained, or defective in other ways it will be a continuance of difficulties and the age at which each one of these changes occurs can be read from the line. If the line breaks under Saturn and rises to the Mount (59) first look for health defects. In this case gout and rheumatism are the Saturnian health defects that will probably complicate trouble with the heart's action, and rheumatism of the heart is often diagnosed from this marking. You can tell from the Life line about how serious the results will be. If this break is not a health indication it will show that either a Saturnian subject, or that Saturnian qualities have caused the break in the line. The greatest care should be used in making an estimate in all of these cases. The type of your subject will show how much he would likely be influenced by the several types either in a health way or in his affections. If the Heart line breaks under Apollo (60) it will be nearly conclusive proof that the difficulty is a health defect. Examine closely all other indications bearing on heart disease, for while this defect is natural to Apollonians, all of this type do not necessarily have heart disease. See if the broken line, as it goes up into the Mount, grows deep and red, if so it will add to the certainty of disease. If it is not a health indication it will tell of the affections having been influenced by Apollonian qualities, or by one of this type. This break occurring in the line *under* Apollo is at age forty-three. If an Apollonian subject has caused strong attraction at an earlier age it will be shown by a chance line coming from the Heart line at an earlier age

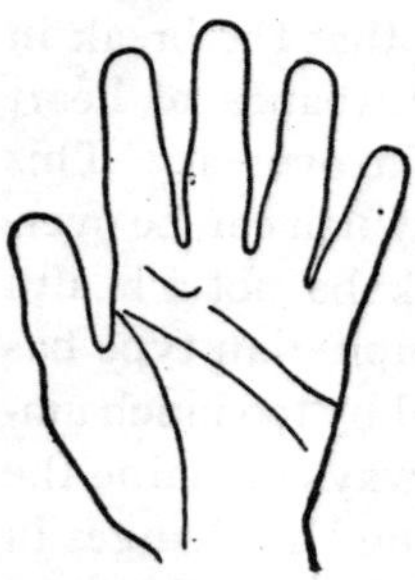

NO. 59

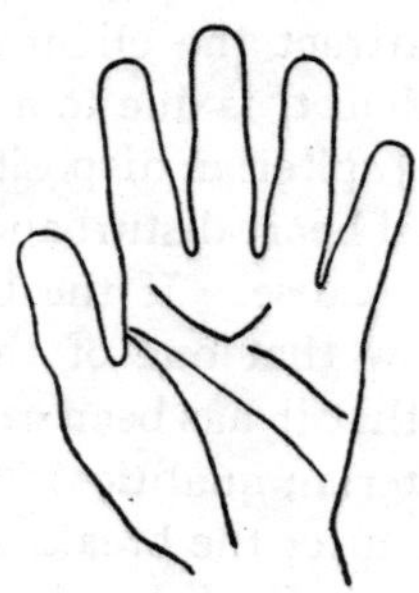

NO. 60

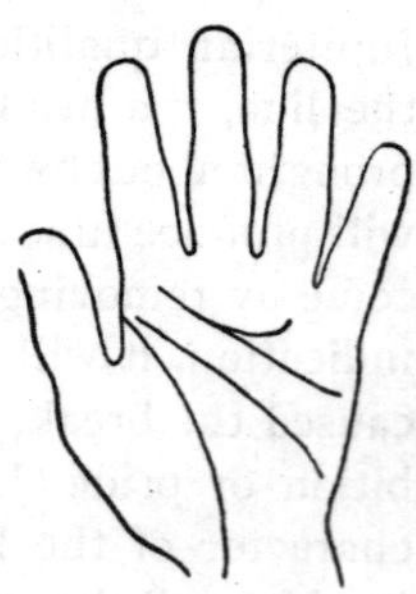

NO 61

on that line, and running to the Mount of Apollo (61). If the line breaks under Mercury (62) it will not likely be a health defect coming from any type qualities of Mercury; from the fact that the position of Mercury registers sixty years on the Heart line, and the heart's action generally gets weaker at this age, and is likely to become disturbed. In seeking to discover if this break is a health indication, bear in mind the age and consequent liability to heart weakness. At this age it is not likely that an affection will cause the break, for the age of youthful love is passed. If affection toward a Mercurian has influenced your client it will much more likely be shown by a chance line similar to (61), than by this break under Mercury. The usual investigation will probably disclose a health defect; if

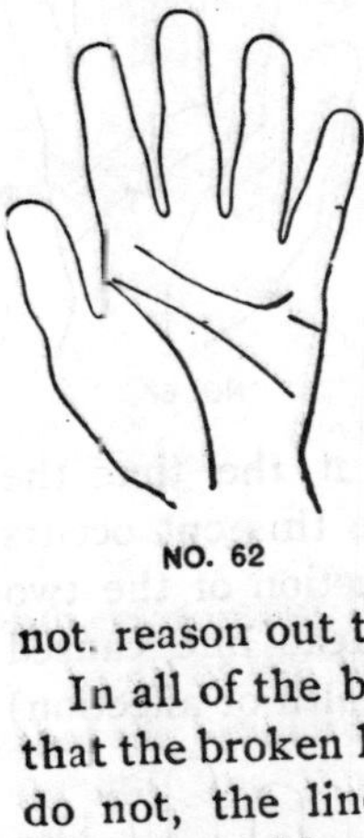

NO. 62

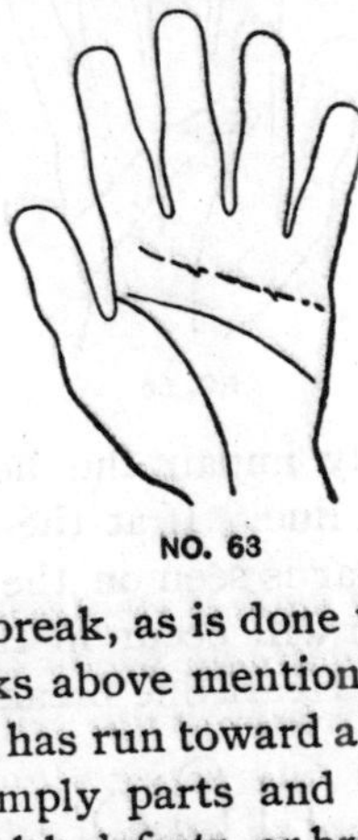

NO. 63

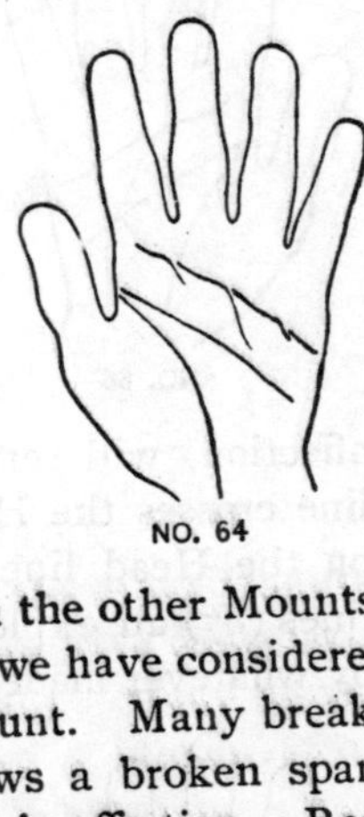

NO. 64

not reason out the break, as is done with the other Mounts.

In all of the breaks above mentioned, we have considered that the broken line has run toward a Mount. Many breaks do not, the line simply parts and shows a broken span. These are either health defects, or breaks in affection. Reason them all out according to their size by following the general plan outlined. If many breaks are seen in the line (63) your client has either had a constant recurrence of weakness in the heart's action or of broken love affairs. If the breaks come close together he is likely to have heart failure. If the ends of these broken lines turn down instead of rising to the Mounts (64) then the head strongly influences the subject at the times the breaks occur, and cold reason fights against warm sentiment. If the broken ends are short, head does not rule completely, but if the line merges into the Head line, reason obtains the mastery over sentiment (65). If the break is wide at this time, the subject never entirely gets over it; if it is narrow he does, though unhappy at the time. By noting each break it can be told at what age these events occur, and by noting where the ends of the broken line go you can tell what has caused them. The variations are infinite, but by applying the general principles you can correctly reason out each one. If the end of the broken line drops and cuts the Head line sharply (66), the thing which caused the break, be it health or

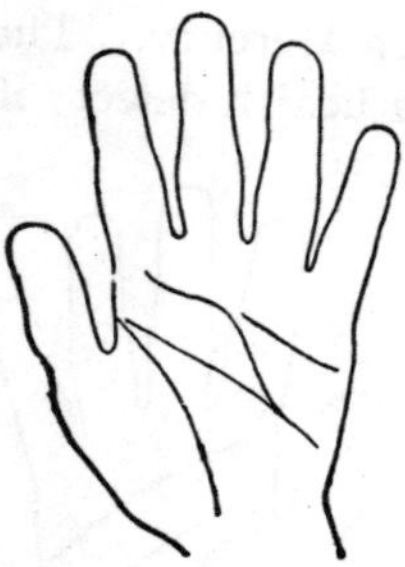

NO. 65

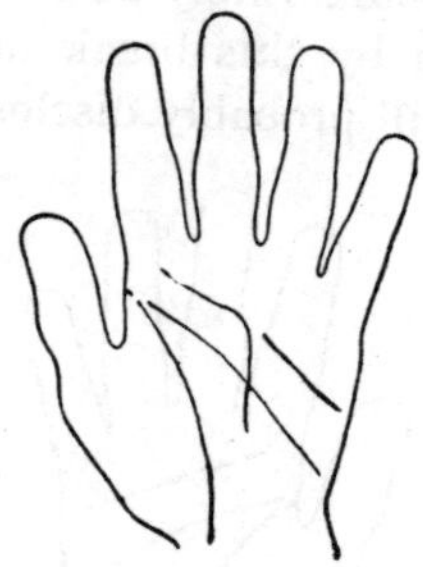

NO. 66

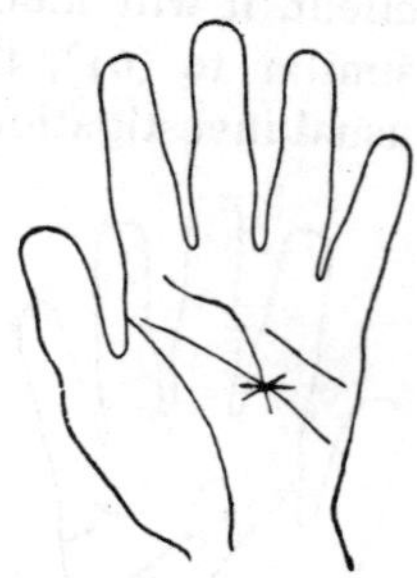

NO. 67

affection, will seriously impair the head at the time the line crosses the Head line. If at the time this cut occurs on the Head line a star is seen on the junction of the two lines (67) an explosion will occur in the Head line, caused by whatever made the Heart line break (health or affection)

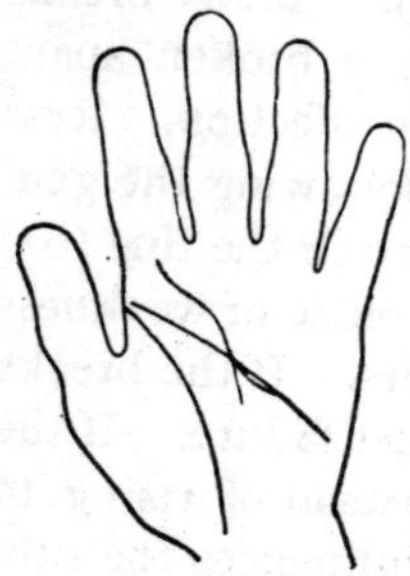

NO. 68

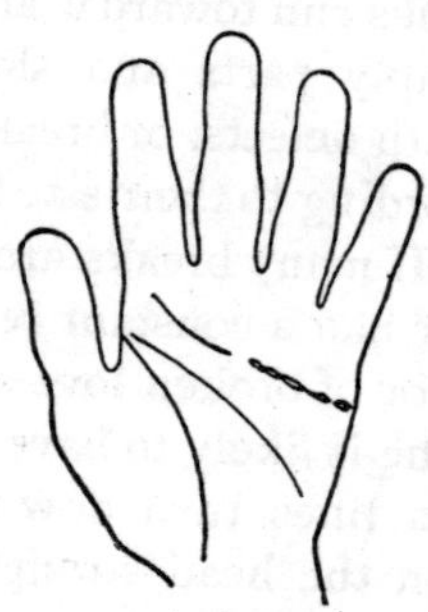

NO. 69

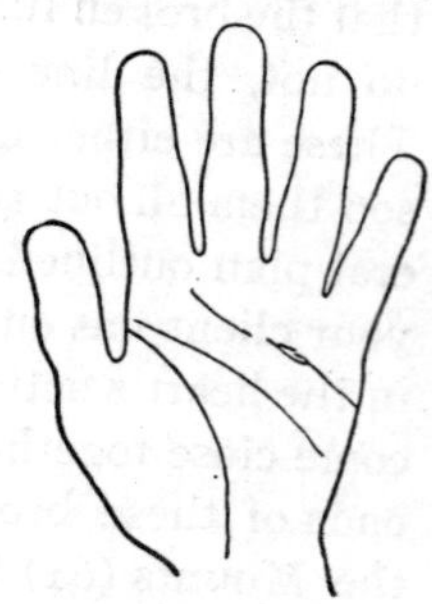

NO. 70

and brain fever or even death may ensue. The latter must be judged from the Life line, and the condition of the Head line after the cut occurs.

If an island be seen in the Head line, following the cut by the Heart line (68), the head will be left in a delicate condition afterwards, this delicacy lasting as long as the island is present, the age to be read on the Head line. If after a break in a Heart line, the line is chained (69), it shows that the heart never fully recovers from whatever caused the break. If after a break the line has an island or islands (70) it will be delicate during the time occupied by these islands.

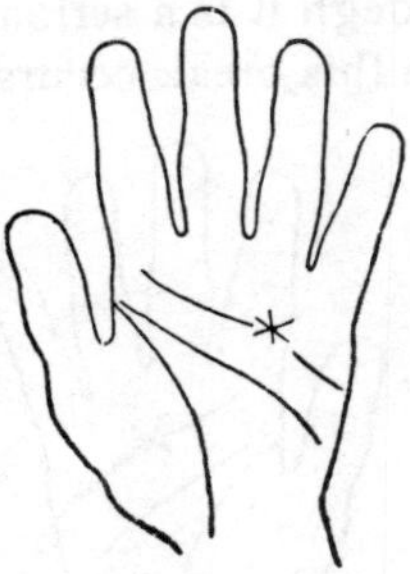
NO. 71

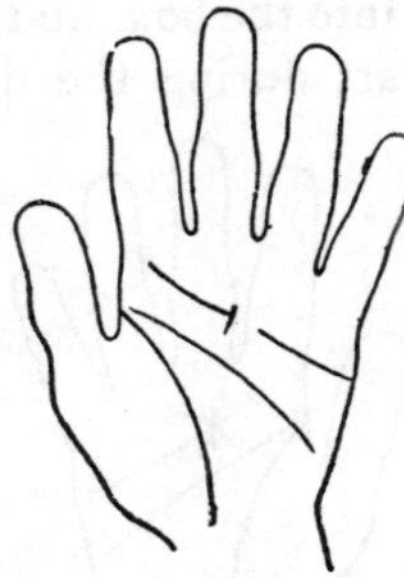
NO. 72

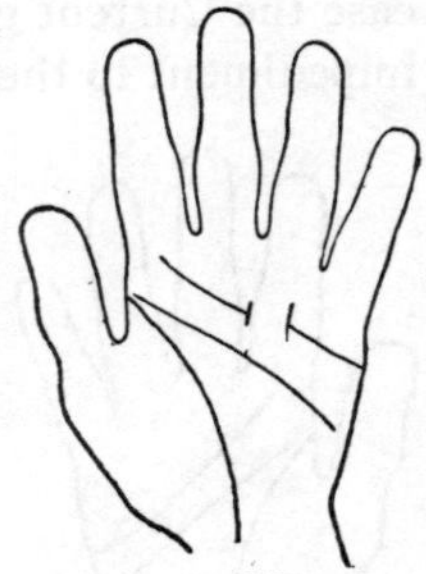
NO. 73

If after a break a well-marked star is seen filling the break (71) the subject will die suddenly or have a very serious attack of heart disease at the age the star comes on the line. This is more certain if seen under Apollo. If the line breaks and is cut by a cross-bar (72), the Current can hardly get by at

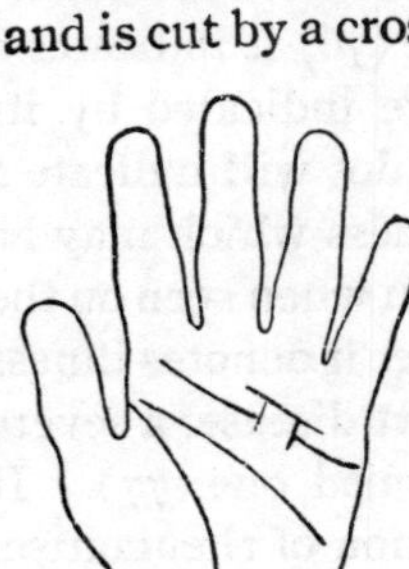
NO. 74

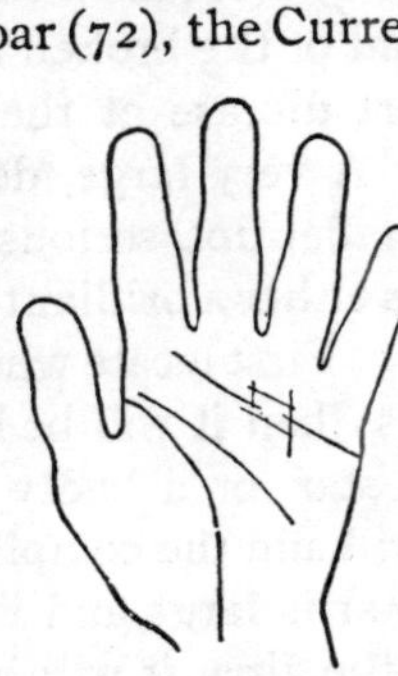
NO. 75

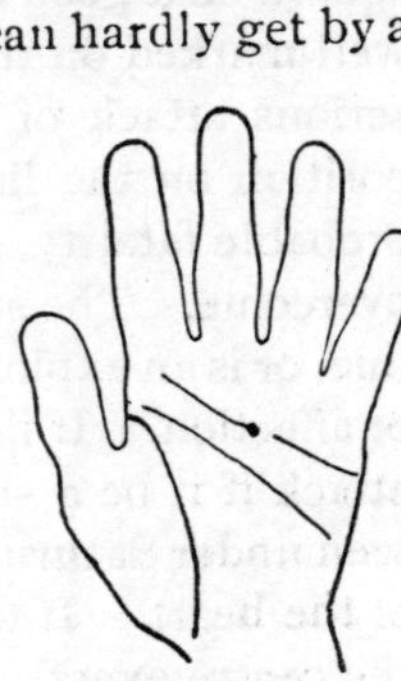
NO. 76

all, and sudden death, by heart failure, will occur in ninety-five per cent. of cases. If a break has a cross-bar on both ends of the line (73), death from heart disease will occur in ninety-nine per cent. of cases. How serious every case is, judge by the difficulty there will be to repair the damage and get the Current into its proper channel again. In the latter case the best repair would be a sister line joining the ends of the cross-bars (74). In this case there would be great danger at the time of the break, but the Current could be led back by the sister line to its channel again. This serious defect is also well repaired by a square (75) in which case the Current gets into the box, and though it is a serious impediment to the heart during the time this break occurs,

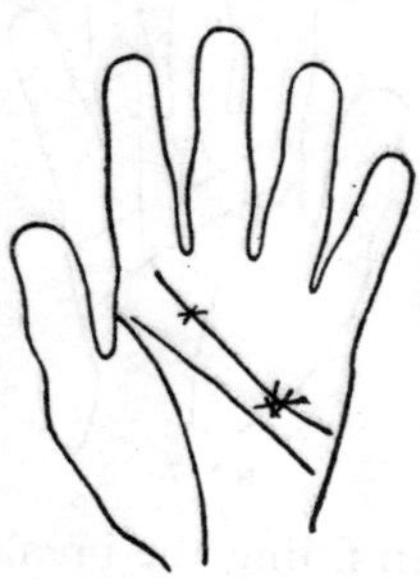

NO. 77

NO. 78

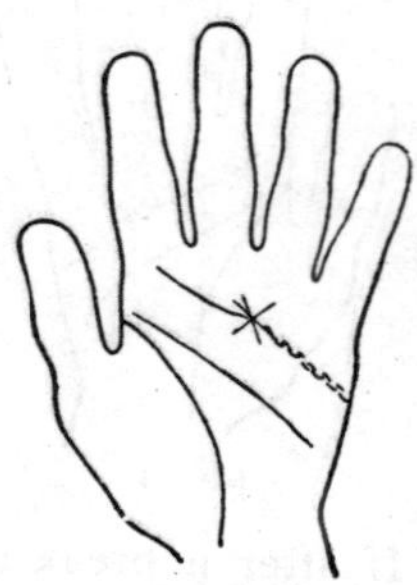

NO. 79

it will likely find its way into the Heart line again if the square be a good one. If a break in the Heart line has a dot well marked on the end of the broken line (76) it indicates a serious attack of heart disease at the age indicated by its position on the line. A very large, deep dot will indicate a probable fatality, a smaller dot, serious illness which may be overcome. The star is either a brilliant sign when seen on the line, or is an explosion. First locate whether it denotes illness or affection. If illness, then it will be heart disease, a severe attack if it be a small star, or a badly formed one (77). If seen under Saturn it will add the complication of rheumatism of the heart. If the star is large and well formed (78), with the centre exactly on the line, it will indicate the excessive formation, or, as we call it, the explosion. This means sudden heart failure at the age on the line at which the star appears. If after a star the line shows chains (79) the subject will have a serious attack of heart disease from which he will never entirely recover. If after a star there are islands (80) the subject will have a severe attack of heart disease with delicacy afterwards, most pronounced and severe during the periods covered by the islands. The age at which each event occurs can be read from the line of Heart. If after a star the line becomes thin and narrow (81) it tells that the illness shown by the star destroys the vigor of the heart, which is always weak afterwards, and the affections become cold and views selfish and narrow.

The combinations of defects, and the character of the line in its different parts are possible of infinite variation. All along the line every variation of character means a different operation of the line during the period it lasts. The characteristics of each formation of the line have been previously explained ; so in practice apply to each part of the line the characteristics which belong to that kind of a line, reading the age at which these events occur by their position on the line. Use color to strengthen all these matters. Remember big red stars indicate greater intensity than big white ones, and that yellow ones show more nervous, morbid, and ugly qualities. Every defect on the line means an event either of health or affection. Make this distinction by rules already

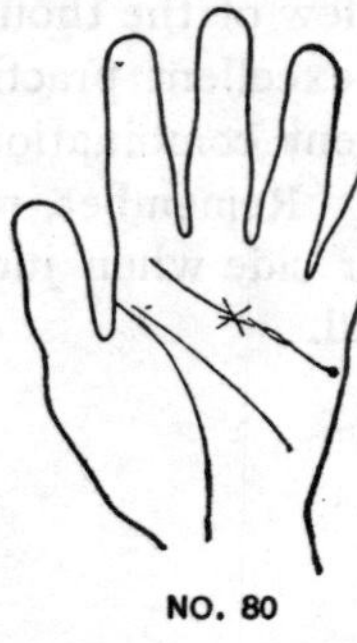

NO. 80

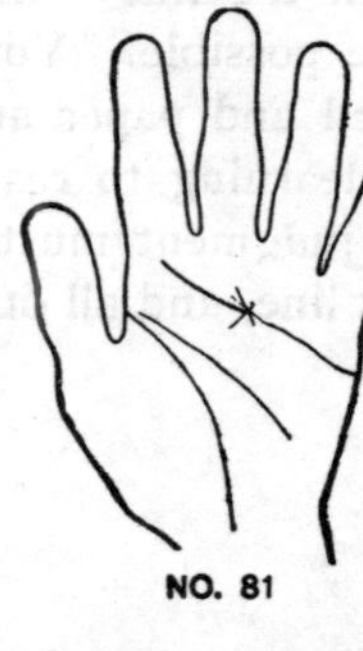

NO. 81

laid down, and then tell what the defect means and how serious it is.

Keep always in mind the theory of the Current, what it is trying to do, and how well the line will enable it to perform its functions. Think of the stream as flowing smoothly or impeded by defects. You have the types as a basis for the whole work, and it is by using and combining this knowledge, and adapting it to each particular case, that you will be enabled to reason out what each event shown on the line means, how it will affect the subject, and whether it is repaired or produces destruction. Go slowly in reading the line; don't expect the meaning to come the first time you look into a hand. Do not become confused because it does not, but think it over carefully. Above all, never allow yourself to be rushed. Don't begin to read because you feel you must "say something." Don't say *anything* until you have it clearly in mind. Practice will increase the rapidity with which you can work, just as the child grows from the primer to his higher readers. Get the theory in mind first, then practise until you can apply it. All my effort in this chapter has been expended to teach *how* to read a line by using the general rules and indications and applying them to that line. I have dealt only with changes in the Heart line itself. Understand each separate Main line thoroughly, and when you have learned them all you will be able to understand all the combinations. The illustrations in this chapter serve only to put you in the *way* of reasoning out the possible changes in the line — they are only a few of the thousands which are possible. You will find it excellent practise to take pencil and paper and draw different combinations for yourself, learning to reason them out. Remember, reason and good judgment must stand at your side when judging the Heart line, and all other lines as well.

CHAPTER VI

THE LINE OF HEAD

THE second line, which, according to our hypothesis, receives the Electric Current when it enters our bodies through the finger of Jupiter, is the line which may be seen tracing its way across the hand below the line of Heart, and this has been named the line of the Head (82). It is an important line, and innumerable experiments have shown that it absolutely indicates the amount of mentality possessed by the subject, the kind of mentality, the power of mental concentration, and the ability to exert self-control. The importance of this line will be recognized when we consider what a tremendous part *mind* plays in the shaping of our destiny. No matter how fine the rest of the human machine may be, it can never operate perfectly unless there is a proper mental attitude The mental attitude cannot be what it should be unless the brain is physically healthy and the subject possesses the ability to concentrate his mind and thus go through life with definiteness of purpose. Mind is the force that enables us to alter our natural life map, makes us able to modify our type qualities, and, more powerfully than any other factor, influences the life of every human being. The *kind* of mind that each subject possesses will be largely the key to his future, for it makes him whatever he is, improves or mars his natural self, builds up or tears down the strong places in his character, and acts correspondingly with the weak ones. Thus the

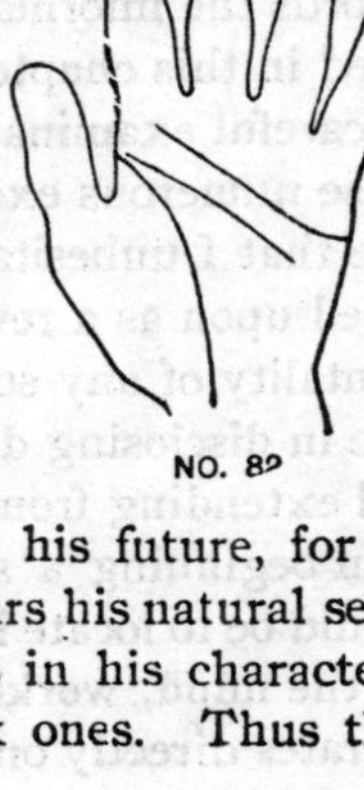

NO. 82

Head line will demand the closest study, in order to correctly determine the quality and quantity of brain power present.

The organ called the brain is the centre from which emanates the vital force that throbs along every nerve in the body, and, manifestly, whatever reflects it is also a wonderful revealer of disease, especially of those disorders termed nervous. As the human brain is locked within the skull and is so extremely delicate and sensitive that physical examination of it cannot be made with safety, it is only when accident has laid bare certain portions that its workings can be studied. Even the closest microscopical examination fails to reveal any essential difference in structure between the brain of a man of high intellectual endowments and blameless moral life and that of a criminal of the most brutal type. This fact I have seen verified in post-mortem examinations before a body of scientific experts. It is because the brain is so carefully protected that it cannot be studied and examined minutely during life that we have not yet learned to locate in *it* the seats of good and evil. But the *hand is always present* to be studied, and in the Head line it has been found that the inner workings of the mind are disclosed. Therefore, for the present we must be satisfied to use the Head line rather than the brain itself to discover the workings of the mind, and we can feel satisfied that it accurately records the information. All of the data which is incorporated in this chapter concerning the Head line is the record of careful examinations and verifications, and it is because these numerous examinations have been so universally accurate that I unhesitatingly state that the line of Head may be relied upon as a revealer of the amount and condition of the mentality of any subject. In the same way it is most accurate in disclosing diseases due to an impairment of the brain, and extending from it to the nervous system.

In beginning a study of the line of Head, your first care should be to locate it, and if it be absent, to discover that fact. As the mind, working through the brain, is the force which operates directly on all lines, the Head line is seldom absent, for it is the indicator of that which produces lines. However, there will often be only a single line crossing the hand, and you may be at a loss to tell whether it is the Head or the Heart line. In ninety-nine per cent. of cases such a single line is the former, and it is the Heart line which is absent. I think it best to read such single lines invariably as lines of Head. The length of the Head line should next have

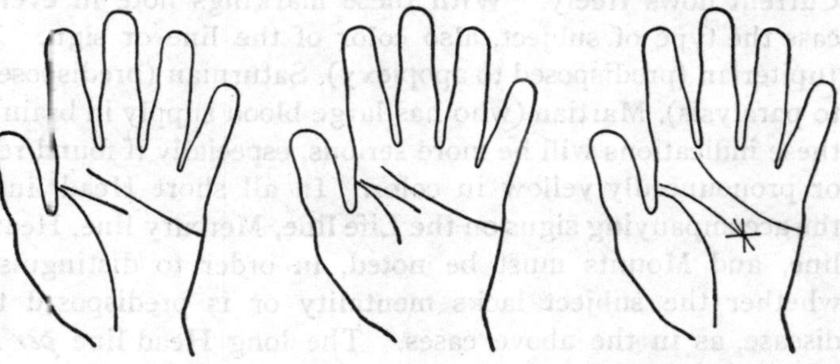

NO. 83 NO. 84 NO. 85

your attention. It should not run to the percussion as does the Heart line, but if the line runs across the hand, as in No. 82, it tells by its length of abundant mentality the *kind* to be estimated by the character and color of the line. If the line is short (83) it indicates that the subject is not so "long headed," or, in other words, has not strong mentality. This latter line must be carefully noted, for it may *also* mean that the life of the subject is short and stops at the point where the Head line ends; for illness and duration of life are to be read on several of the lines and not on the Life line alone.

If with a short Head line is also found a short Life line, corresponding in length with the line of Head (84), the fatality is quite certain. If a star is seen on the end of this short Head line (85) the indication will be sudden death, the star showing the explosion. If a star be seen on the end of both the short lines of Head and Life (86) the fatality may be read confidently if seen in the right hand, or, as *threatened*, if seen in the left hand. The larger and better formed these stars, the more certain the indication.

A cross on the end of a short Head line must be read as stopping the Current, ending the mentality, and producing death, but not so surely by apoplexy or in a sudden manner as if indicated by well-formed stars. A cross on the end of a short Head line, and of a Life line (87) must be read as an indication which is nearly as strong as a star. These defects stop the Current, and life cannot continue unless the Current flows freely. With these markings note in every case the type of subject, also color of the line or sign. If Jupiterian (predisposed to apoplexy), Saturnian (predisposed to paralysis), Martian (who has large blood supply in brain), these indications will be more serious, especially if found red or pronouncedly yellow in color. In all short Head lines the accompanying signs on the Life line, Mercury line, Heart line, and Mounts must be noted, in order to distinguish whether the subject lacks mentality or is predisposed to disease, as in the above cases. The long Head line *per se* shows abundant mentality and the short line less of it.

In this examination for the length of the line, proportion must always be kept in mind. If the Head line extends

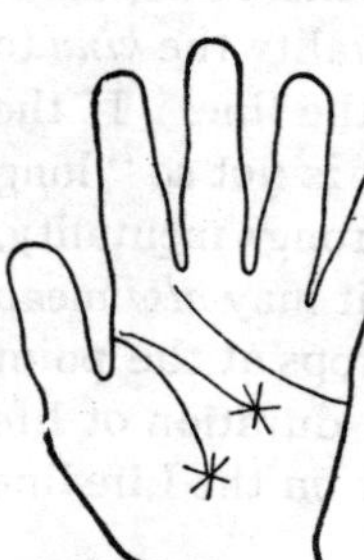

NO. 86

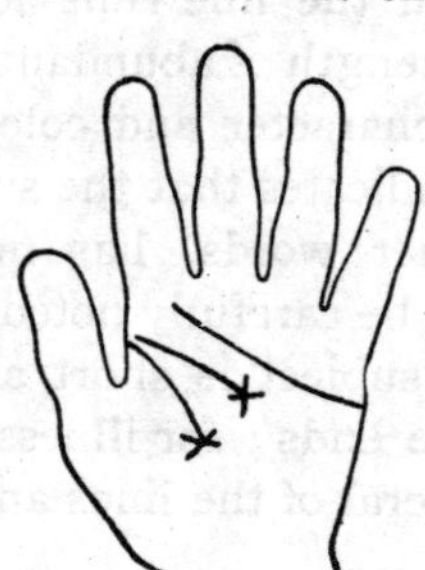

NO. 87

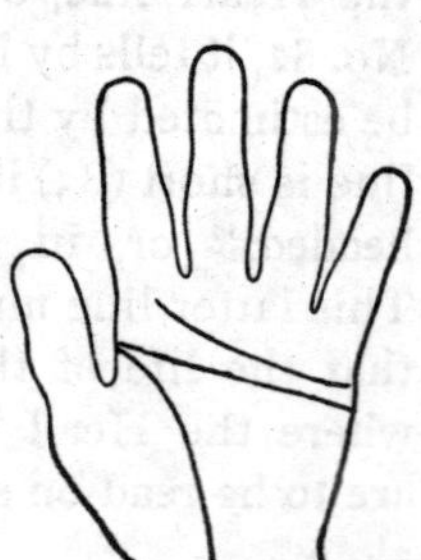

NO. 88

across the entire hand in a straight line (88), with a Heart line normal, it will show the preponderance of head and the subject will be out of balance in this respect. He will be avaricious, will view all things from the mental standpoint, sentiment will be subservient to interest, he will be practical in all things, and more interested in whatever is capable of producing direct results than in beautiful things which please the eye or appeal to the heart. If this long, straight Head line has no accompanying Heart line, the subject will be cold, heartless, merciless, miserly, avaricious, extortionate, and demanding his "pound of flesh." The proportionate depth and character of all the lines must be noted. If the Head line be straight and long and *also deep*, it makes a stronger combination. When the Head line without the Heart line is found also *long* and it is *straight* and *deep*, it makes worldly interests greater and the subject harder and more avaricious. If this line be also red, it makes the subject aggressive in his avarice, and if yellow he will be doubly mean and hard. If the Head line be long, but thinner and smaller than the other lines, the head will be on a constant strain and must not be overworked or the brain will be wrecked. If the line be short, narrow, and shallow, it will be a pronounced indication of small mentality. If all the other lines are deep and well cut, and the Head line short and thin, it shows a person easily led, weak in mentality, the servant and creature of others, never the leader. So, together with the length of the line, must be estimated its size and proportion to the other lines, and the subject must be placed above or below the normal balance in accordance with the proportion found. *In every case* use both hands. If the line be short in the left hand and long in the right, the subject has developed his mentality. If the line be long in the left hand and short in the right, he has retrograded mentally, or else there is danger of fatality from the short line. Examine at once Life line, type, and all health indications to discover which. If the line be narrow and thin in the left hand and deep and well cut in the right, the subject is improving mentally. If this combination is reversed the opposite condition is present. If the line be long and straight in the left hand and shows the same formation in the right, but with the Heart line absent in the right hand, the subject is naturally grasping and self-interested, and these qualities in him have been tremendously increased until he has become intensely selfish and avaricious. By noting in this way the two hands and their changed condition of lines, you will be able to read changes from the past to a present mental attitude, and can tell the subject how he formerly regarded certain matters and how he views them at present.

One of the first things to do in reading the Head line is to distinguish *disease* from *character* of the mentality. To do this it will be necessary to use not only defects in the line arising from breaks, dots, islands, and similar causes, but also the narrowness and thinness of the line, as well as its proportion to other lines. Inasmuch as the Head line indicates both the extent and character of the mentality and also diseases, it will be necessary at times when a defective line is seen, to distinguish between the two and to estimate whether your subject is lacking in character directions, or whether brain illness or insanity are indicated. Any defect seen on the Head line will indicate mental disturbance, which may be the result of illness, or it may be an indication of the unsteady character of the mentality. In making a distinction between character and diseases the Life line should be examined to see if it is also defective at about the same period as the defect appears on the Head line. Anything abnormal found on the Life line will fix the defect on the Head line as an illness. The nails must also be consulted in connection with the Head line, for if badly fluted they tell of great nervous disturbance, which is emanating from the centre of nerve force, the brain. If in addition to a defective Head line, fluted and *brittle* nails are found you are warned that the subject is using up his nervous vitality faster than it can be generated and is in danger of paralysis. This is further confirmed if the subject be either a Saturnian, Mercurian, or Lunarian. The color of the hand and particularly of the lines is exceedingly important in this investigation. If too white, the anæmic condition furnishes little blood, and the operation of the brain will be weakened. On the other hand, extreme redness will show that blood in excessive quantity and in too great strength is being forced to the brain. Either of these indications show an abnormal condition and indicate disease, whiteness predisposing to weakness and insufficiency, and redness indicating liability to fevers or apoplexy. The latter condition is to be read from the presence of stars, crosses, dots, or deep cutting of the line, red color being also present with these markings.

When a defective Head line is noted, use the Life line as indicated above, the Mercury line in the same way as the Life line, together with nails and color, for all these must be

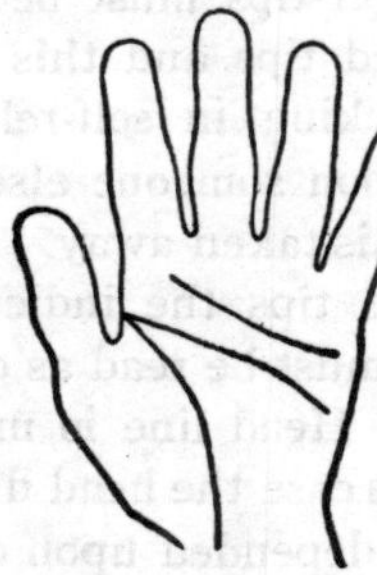

NO. 89

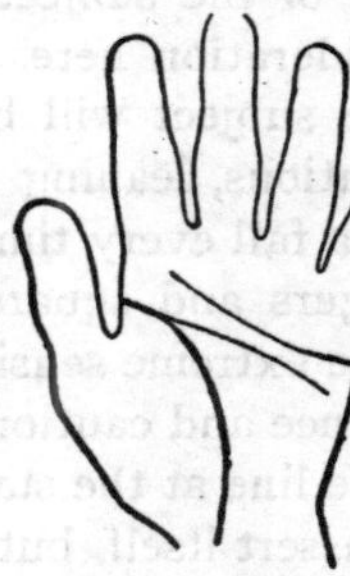

NO. 90

consulted along with the type of the subject, and from this combined point of view you will be able to distinguish health defects from mental defects.

The starting-point or source of the Head line must be noted. In the greater number of hands the line rises from the line of Life, to which it is slightly attached at the start (89), and branches away from the Life line, sometimes near the beginning of that line, sometimes farther along (90). At this point the Head line registers the early years of life, and the sooner the line separates from the Life line, the younger was the subject when he began to think for himself. The longer the Head line is tied to the Life line the less self-confidence has the subject and the more he relies upon the advice of others. The longer the period covered by this union of the two lines, the later in life did the subject begin to rely upon himself. The Head line is not often bound to the Life line longer than the twelfth year, and many Head lines are seen which only touch the Life line at its beginning, showing that as a mere child the subject was self-reliant.

In examining the beginning of the Head line note how

sharp the angle formed by the lines of Head and Life. The more pointed this angle (90), the more sensitive the subject. the easier are his feelings hurt, and if in addition the sensitive pads are found on the ends of the fingers, this sensitive disposition will be extreme. The subject will do almost anything rather than hurt the feelings of others, and the lives of such will be often made unhappy by unintentional slights. The type of the subject and his finger-tips must be taken into consideration here. With pointed tips and this acute angle the subject will be entirely lacking in self-reliance, timid, cautious, leaning constantly upon someone else, and suffering a fall every time the support is taken away. With thick fingers and square or spatulate tips the indications will not be extreme sensitiveness, but must be read as denoting prudence and caution. Often the Head line is merged in the Life line at the start, and in this case the head did not begin to assert itself, but the subject depended upon others until the year when the line breaks away from the line of Life. Sometimes the Head line does not leave the Life line until well along in its course (91). In this case the mental

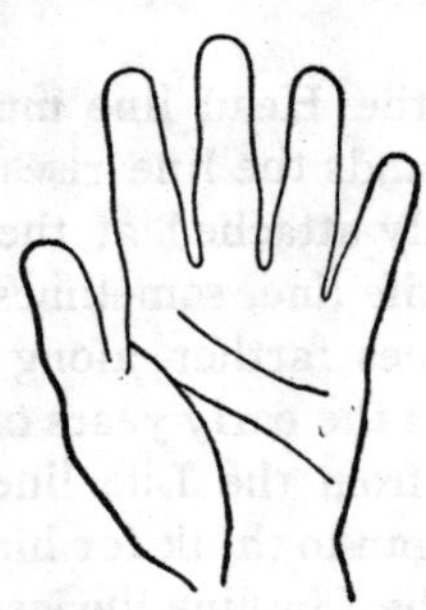

NO. 91

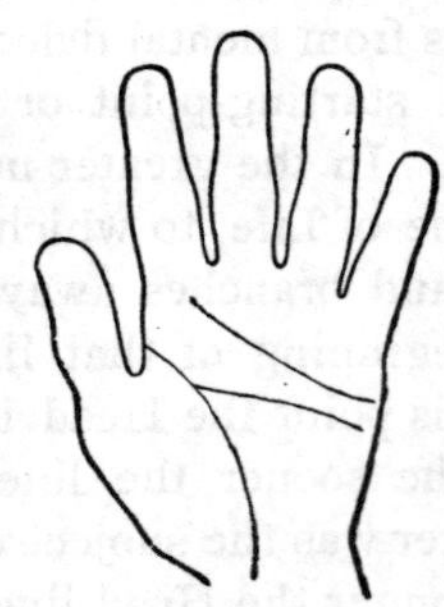

NO. 92

activities began later in life. This even goes so far as to produce in some hands the formation of an obtuse angle (92), which shows the subject to be somewhat callous to slights If, with this latter marking, the finger-tips be square or spatulate and the fingers and palm thick and red, the subject will be very dense, and if only the lines of Head, Heart, and Life are present, it will indicate elementary heaviness of intellect and unimpressionability. These subjects will be cautious, non-committal, dependent on others, lacking ability to command, unoriginal, blunt, and tactless. When the line of Head is distinctly separated from the line of Life (93) it shows primarily self-reliance. The subject is original, is not bound down by the views of others, acts for and depends upon himself, can plan well, is guided by his own judg-

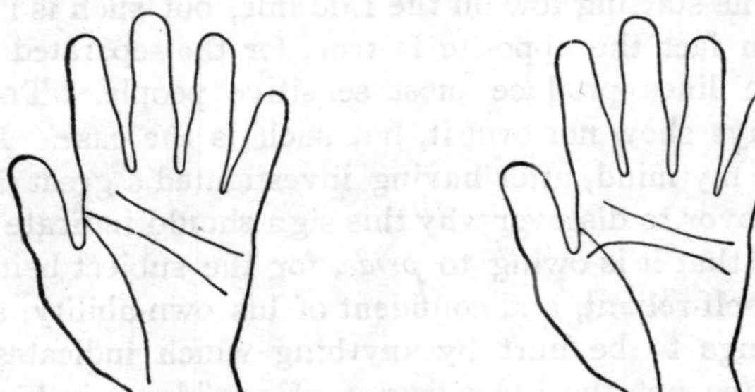

NO. 93 NO. 94

ment, is independent and courageous in his views, and therefore this separation, if not too wide, is a fine marking. The wider the separation the greater the degree of self-reliance, consequently the marking may degenerate into such boldness and self-esteem that the subject becomes foolhardy and not a safe counsellor. With this separated line note the tips, for, if pointed, the self-reliance may run to idealism, if spatulate, to great energy and originality, producing a brain fertile in new schemes, and, as the subject does not ask advice, he is likely to commit grave errors. Square tips are safest, for their good common-sense will be a restraining element. Note the length of the fingers, for, if very short, the quickness in making up the mind, added to the self-reliance of the separated lines, easily leads to impulsive, hasty, and dangerous conclusions. If, in addition, the fingers are smooth, impulsiveness will be intensified. Knots indicate a restraining element that it is good to have present with these separated lines. This marking, in whatever degree of separation it is seen, always indicates a subject with well-defined individuality; the wider the separation the more marked is the self-reliance and the consequent individuality. Always regard this marking as requiring care, for the owner is an unusual subject, and everything must be weighed in order to determine whether the self-reliance and self-esteem shown by the indications run to a danger point.

It might be supposed that these separated lines would indicate lack of sensitiveness, as does an obtuse angle formed by the line starting low on the Life line, but such is not the case. In fact the opposite is true, for the separated Head and Life lines produce most sensitive people. They do not always show nor own it, but such is the case. I have made up my mind, after having investigated a great deal in the endeavor to discover why this sign should indicate sensitiveness, that it is owing to *pride*, for the subject being extremely self-reliant, and confident of his own ability, allows his feelings to be hurt by anything which indicates that others have not the same degree of confidence in him that he has in himself. Sometimes the line of Head rises inside the line of Life on the lower Mount of Mars, and, after crossing the Life line, winds its way across the hand (94). This subject is extremely vacillating. He starts many things with enthusiasm and before he dies will have made innumerable changes. He is a shifter who constantly alters his opinions and does not continue in the same way of thinking long at a time. He is always intense in his views, makes most violent resolutions, and changes his mind with facility, but always with the same vigor. These subjects are rarely successful, for they do not stick to anything long enough to win. They are always aggressive, for the Head line rises from lower Mars, consequently they are frequently in trouble, always picking quarrels, and are avoided by those who do not want contention. The shifting mind and quarrelsome disposition are a poor combination, for one can never tell what tack these people may take next. If the color of the hand and lines be red, this will add to the unpleasantness of the indication, if yellow, the subject will be intolerably mean, in addition. The less mentality the hand indicates, the less will the subject be able to overcome the trouble, but good first phalanges to the fingers, a long second phalanx of thumb, with a long, narrow, or paddle-shaped first phalanx of that member, will give the subject forces with which he can largely counteract the shifting disposition indicated by such a Head line.

Sometimes the Head line rises from the Mount of Jupiter (95). This line shows fine capability for leadership, a person who can handle men with ease and get the most out of them, one who is self-confident ; and this source of the Head line is always an indication of strong mentality. There is diplomacy present which enables the subject to dictate without being harsh, to rule when he seems to be ruled, to appear dependent when he knows all depends on him ; he is brainy, brilliant, and successful. Always note his type ; if of a coarse make-up, the tact and diplomacy will disappear ; he will lead but men will feel his strength. If the hand be fine, he will accomplish all he wishes, and men will not know how he does it. Sometimes the line will rise just at the base of the Mount of Jupiter (96), sometimes it will sweep clear up to the base of the finger, as in No. 95. Between these

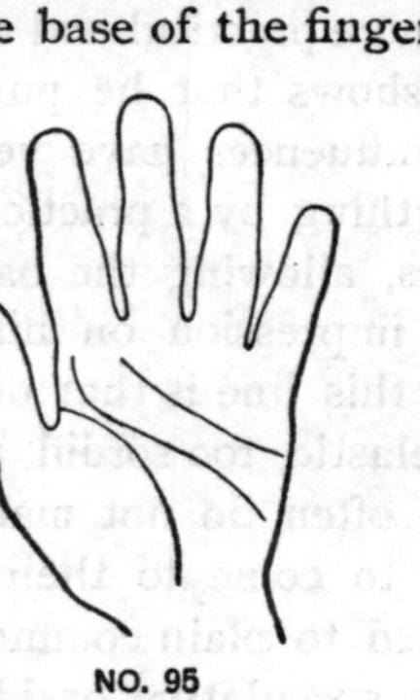

NO. 95

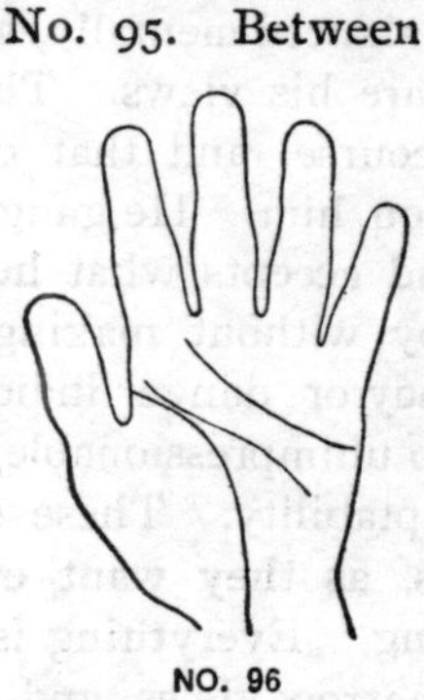

NO. 96

two sources are many degrees, and your estimate of the strength of the indication must be in proportion to its degree of marking on the Mount. Sometimes the line rises from the Life line but a branch rises to the Mount of Jupiter (97). This shows that ambition and the desire to be great or famous rule the subject. If the hand be purely a mental one, the subject's ambitions will be for mental fame. If the hand be purely artistic, his ambitions will be for fame in that direction. If the hand be purely material, his ambition will be for riches. He will always strive to rise, and the life generally follows an upward grade.

The course of the line through the hand is next to be considered. In cutting its way across the hand, the straighter the line runs (98), and the less it is changed in its course,

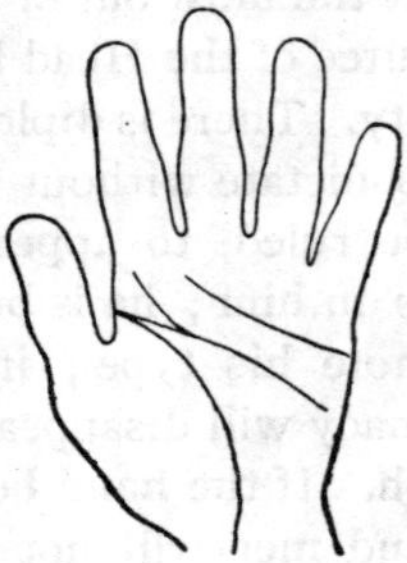

NO. 97

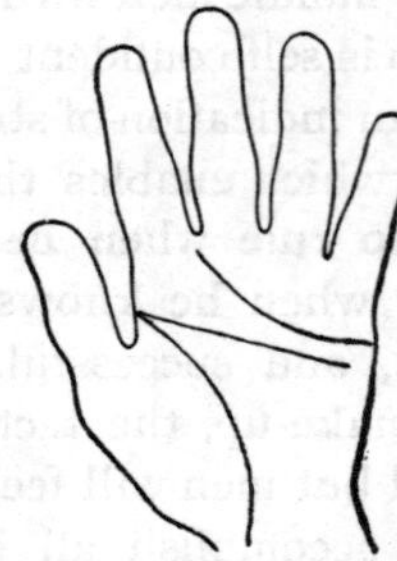

NO. 98

the more fixed are the ideas of the subject, the more evenly is he balanced mentally, and the more practical and common-sense are his views. This line shows that he pursues an even course, and that outside influences have very little effect on him. He gauges everything by a practical standard and accepts what he chooses, allowing the balance to pass by without making much impression on him. The tendency or danger indicated by this line is that of becoming too unimpressionable, too inelastic, too sordid, to allow of adaptability. These subjects often do not make many friends, as they want everyone to come to their way of thinking. Everything is subjected to plain common-sense, often narrow views, and anything speculative or ideal is an abomination. This straight line must be the gauge by which you judge all deflections. When the line of Head rises on or under Jupiter, we have the qualities of that Mount exerting strong influence on the subject, and it is seldom that a line will be so placed that it can be deflected upward toward the Mount of Jupiter, but we do find the line deflected under the other Mounts. The line of Head normally curves upward slightly in the beginning of its course, and in most hands this curve is about midway between Jupiter and Saturn.

When the line so perceptibly curves under Saturn (99) that its course is greatly changed, it shows that the subject is strongly tinged with Saturnian ideas. Often when every other method of classifying your subject into his proper type has failed, the Head line deflected toward a Mount will do it for you. The greater the deflection of the line toward Saturn the more surely will Saturnian ideas be strong in the subject. You must note the character of the hand with this marking; if the mental world rules, then your client will love the study and research for which the Saturnian is famous; if the middle world rules, he will love farming, mining, and horticulture; if the lower world rules, his ideas will run toward the saving of money. If the line is deflected toward Apollo (100), the subject's mind will run in Apollonian channels. If the upper world rules, it will be art, pure and simple; if the middle world is stronger, money-making and love of beauty will be combined; if the lower world domi-

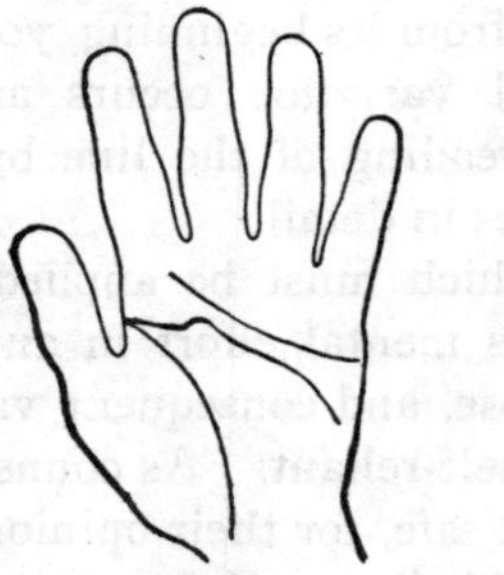

NO. 99

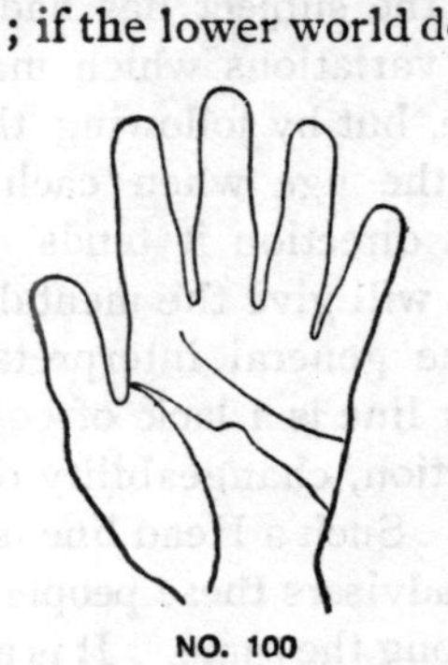

NO. 100

nates, love of display, and a coarser love of the artistic will be indicated. The larger the deflection the greater is the degree of influence exerted by Apollo, and this is true of all deflections. When the line is deflected toward Mercury (101) it shows that Mercurian ideas are strong. If the upper world rules, fine powers of expression, persuasive force, even oratorical power, are indicated. The kind will be shown by the shape of the finger-tips. If the middle world is strongest, the mind will lean toward scientific investigations and the subject will be a good physician, teacher, or lawyer. If the lower world rules, money-making talent is strongly indicated. With a deflection toward this Mount, watch the crooking and twisting of the finger, to determine how much added shrewdness is present, and how near the subject is to roguery. If

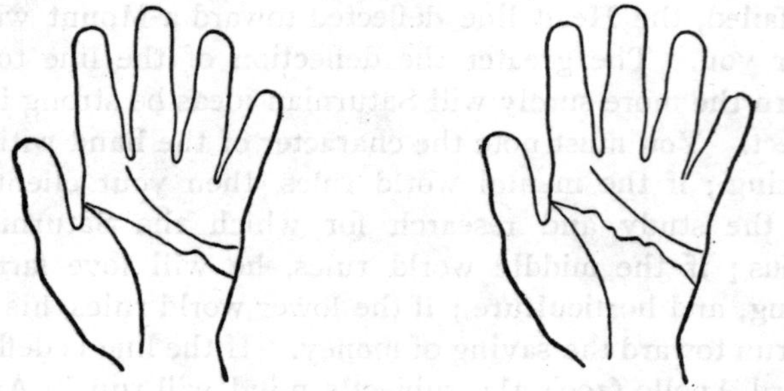

NO. 101 NO. 102

the line is wavy from source to termination (102) it will show that the subject has had no permanent fixedness of ideas. The variations which may occur in this wavy line are infinite, but by following the line from its beginning you can tell the age when each mental variation occurs and in what direction it tends. This reading of the line by sections will give the mental changes in detail.

The general interpretation which must be applied to a wavy line is a lack of continuous mental effort in any one direction, changeability of purpose, and consequent vacillation. Such a Head line is never self-reliant. As counsellors and advisers these people are not safe, for their opinions are not long the same. It is an unstable line, and shows unstable ideas. The line is often seen deflecting upward in a curve which may take it close to the line of Heart (103). This will show that the heart is a stronger factor than the head, and that sentiment will largely influence the subject. If the deflection of the Head toward the Heart line begins early in the line, and continues to the end, it will show that the heart was always the strongest, even from the beginning of life. If the deflection occurs later, this condition began later. If the deflection is slight, the heart will influence but not entirely rule the subject ; if it is very great the heart will largely dictate. It is necessary with this indication to note which line is the deeper and stronger. If the Heart line, then sentiment will guide and reason will give way. If the Head, then reason will assert itself, often producing mental distress because the dictates of the heart cannot be followed. Sometimes the line is found deflecting downward (104). The straight Head line marks the medium or nearest normal condition, and, generally speaking, all rising deflections come from an uplifting force, and conversely all downward deflections come from a downward influence. Consequently when the line of Head is seen to deflect downward, we feel that the mental attitude of the subject has been lowered during the period covered by this deflection. As the straight Head line shows the operation of a practical mentality, the downward deflection shows that a departure from the practical lines of thought occurs during the deflection, at what age can be read on the line. The Mount of Moon, the seat of imagi-

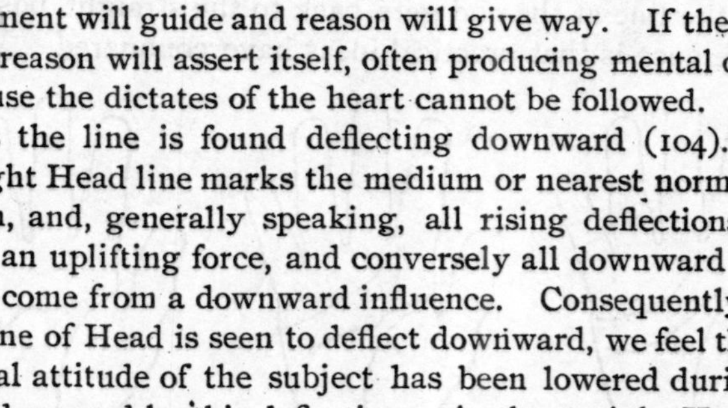

NO. 103 NO. 104

nation, being set at the base of the hand, is considered as the attracting power which causes the Head line to start downward. I have observed in the hands of many spiritists and of persons strongly impressed with psychic phenomena that the period at which these matters began to greatly interest them could be determined by a downward deflection of the Head line. If the deflection is short, the subject is for a time pulled in that direction, but the line coming back to the straight course again shows that the ideas have been drawn back into the practical line again. If the deflection covers the whole line (105), there has been conflict between practical ideas and a desire to indulge in imaginative things, but as the line at the end gets back to the straight position, the inference is that practical ideas have conquered. When

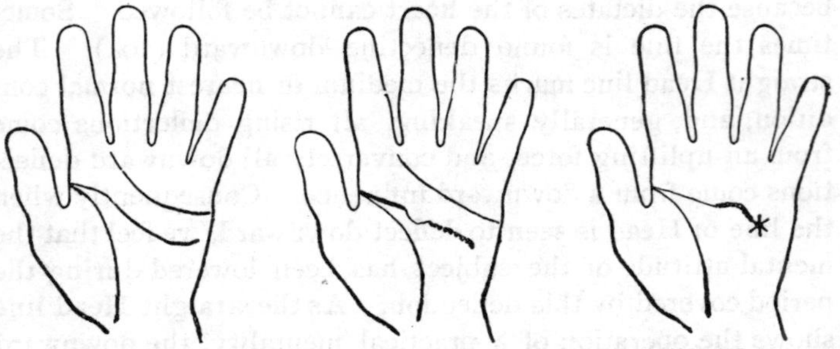

the line is deflected downward under a Mount (as in 104) the qualities of that Mount have impelled the subject to such thoughts as are indicated by the downward deflection. The three worlds will tell which side of the type qualities, mental, money-making, or baser, have caused the mental change.

With all deflections note the character of the line before, during, and after a deflection and this will show the outcome. If a line is found deep and well cut before, thin during, and chained after (106), it will show that a vigorous mind (before) became less vigorous (during) and was impaired (after), the ages to be read from the line. If the line is thin at the start, chained during deflection, and ends in a star (107), the subject has a weak mind to start with, which was impaired by whatever caused the deflection, and ends in an explosion, as shown by the star. This will show either insanity or death; look to Life line, nails, color, type, etc., to determine which. These illustrations are only two out of the infinite number of combinations which may be found, and are given simply in order to show the method of reasoning.

The source of the line shows the starting of the mental

activity, the course through the hand indicates the changes which have affected it, and the termination shows the ultimate outcome. If the line be short, either the mentality is not great, or the termination of it comes early in life, by death or loss of mind. This matter has been treated under the head of "Length of the Line," and will not be reconsidered here. When the line is very short and turns upward toward Saturn (108) the mental attitude of the subject will be Saturnian, and a health defect of Saturn will cause early death. As we are considering the Head line, this health defect must apply to something affecting the head, which is manifestly the brain. Paralysis being a prominent defect of the Saturnian will be the cause to which you may ascribe the end. Nails fluted, turning back, or brittle, yellow color, and many chance lines in the hand, a thin Life line, chained, islanded, broken, or otherwise defective, will enable you to confirm the indication. Older palmists gave to this line the reading "sudden death," the reason for this must be apparent. If this line runs up *on* to the Mount of Saturn (109), the indication is doubly sure. If it ends in a star, a cross, or a dot (110), the sudden termi-

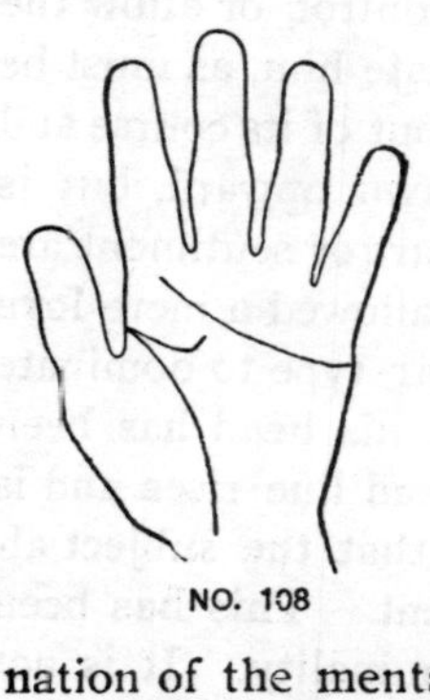

NO. 108

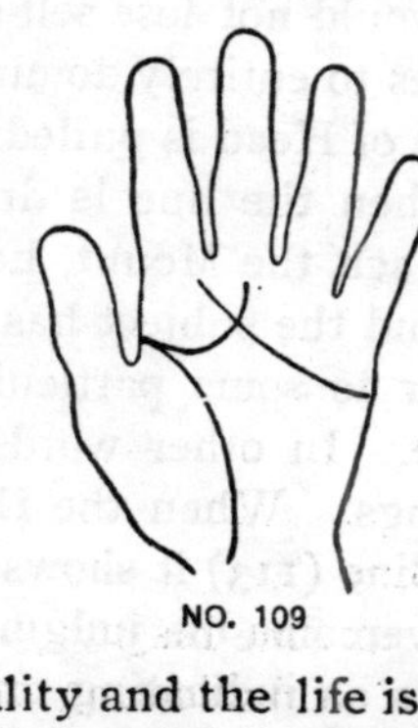

NO. 109

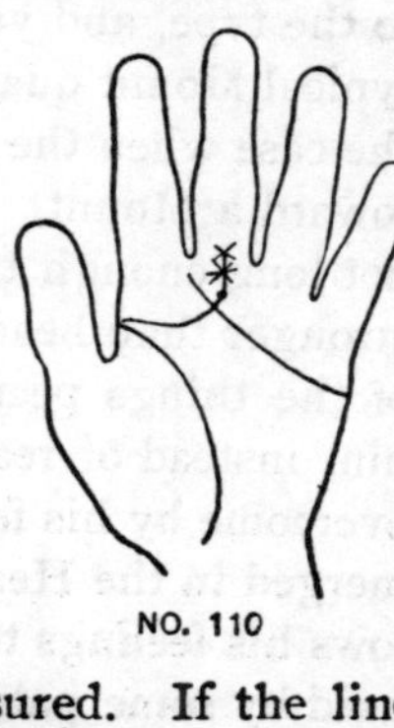

NO. 110

nation of the mentality and the life is assured. If the line ends in a tassel (111), paralysis followed by paresis is indicated, as the tassel shows the gradual dissipation and diffusion of the mental powers and not the sudden shock and catastrophe which the cross, the dot, or the star portend.

The older palmists ascribed grave results to all indications in which Saturn was concerned. This was because of the serious disorders peculiar to the Saturnian. When the line of Head turns up toward Apollo (112) it shows that the subject is strong in Apollonian ideas. The world which rules in each case will determine to which side of the type the ideas lean. In all of these cases where the Head line turns up toward a Mount it is an indication that the mental stamina is not especially strong. If it were, the subject might belong

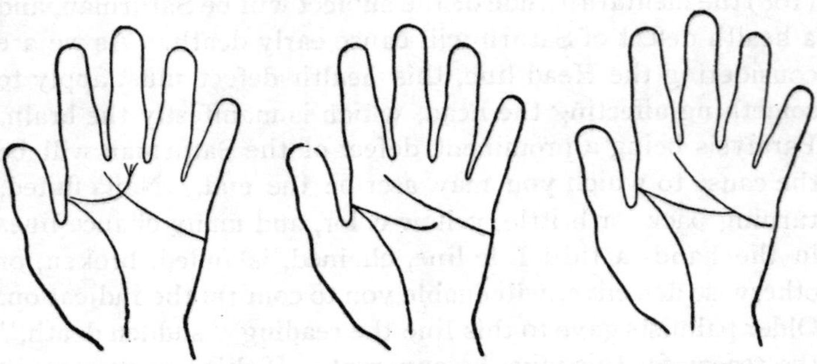

NO. 111 NO. 112 NO. 113

to a type, might be strong in his love of all things peculiar to the type, and yet would not lose self-control, or allow the typical Mount qualities to entirely dominate him, as must be the case when the line of Head is pulled out of its course and toward a Mount. When the line is drawn upward, but is not long enough to reach the Mount, heart or sentiment are stronger than head, and the subject has allowed a mere love of the things peculiar to some particular type to dominate him instead of reason. In other words, his head has been overcome by his feelings. When the Head line rises and is merged in the Heart line (113) it shows that the subject allows his feelings to overcome his judgment. This has been used by some palmists as indicating criminality. It is not *per se* an indication of such tendencies. It *does* show that when the emotions, the sentiments, the feelings, the desires, or whatever it may be are aroused, that the subject will lose self-control and often commit crime in response to the appeal of his passions. He is not necessarily criminal, though he may be weak. Viewed in this light, if the hand be brutal,

Mount of Venus large, full, and red, with Heart line deep and red, nails short, Mounts of Mars large, you will have one, who to satisfy his desires would become criminal and even commit murder. His head will not be strong enough to control the passions which rage within him. If the line cut clear up into Apollo (114), the cutting of the Heart line under Apollo by the Head line, will indicate a complication of the heart difficulty of the Apollonian, and some disorder in the mental health, most probably apoplexy. Note the Mount of Jupiter, color of hands, lines, nails, and all other indications which may throw light on the subject. If at the point where the two lines cross they are deep cut and red, the danger will be serious. If at this point there is a star (115) the danger is very grave, for the explosion is most likely. If this marking is followed by an island (116), the shock will permanently weaken the mind, and at the least brain fever is indicated. If the line of Head turns toward Mercury (117), it will show how strongly the Mercurian qualities attract the subject. No matter what side of the

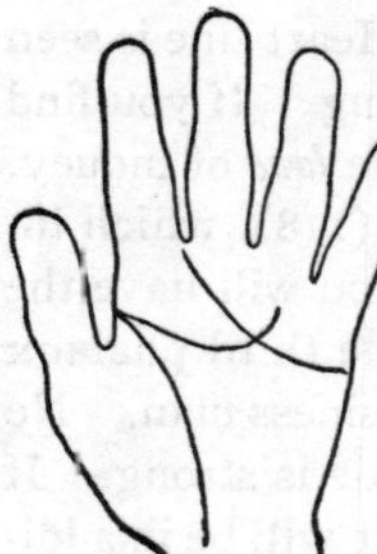

NO. 114

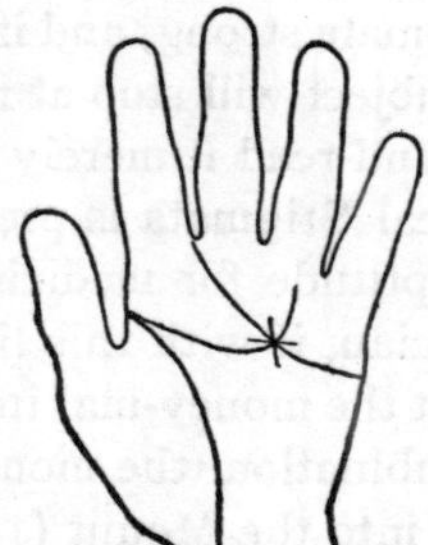

NO. 115

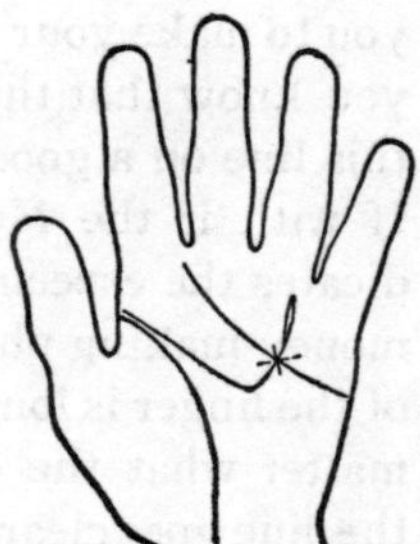

NO. 116

Mercurian is developed, there will be a love of and talent for money-making. So strong is this desire for money that the subject will ruin his health or make any sacrifice to obtain it. As employers these people are tyrannical and exacting, they desire to make "every edge cut" and will work employees just as long as they can, and give them the least possible material with which to do the work. They love bargains, and will go miles to save a few pennies. Everything is measured by its money value.

When this line is seen, note carefully the type of the subject. If he be a bad or mean Saturnian, the combination of this type with the Head line rising to Mercury is distressing. If he be a crooked Mercurian you know that honestly or dishonestly, as may be necessary, he *will* have money. The

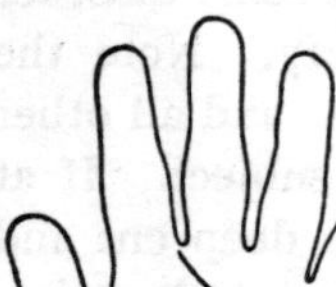

NO. 117

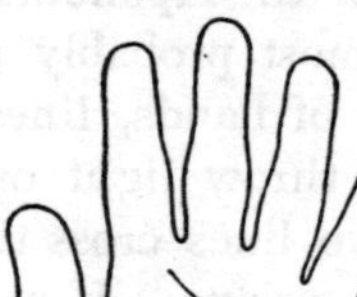

NO. 118

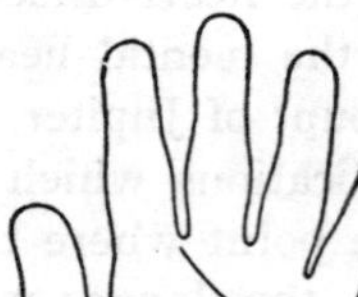

NO. 119

crooked and twisted finger, with short nails should cause you to make your estimate strong, and if no Heart line is seen you know that the subject will stop at nothing. If you find this line on a good hand read it merely as the *love* of money. If with it the Medical Stigmata is present (118), which indicates the especial aptitude for medicine, you will have the money-making physician, if with this line the third phalanx of the finger is longest the money-making business man. No matter what the combination, the money side is strong. If the line goes clear up into the Mount (119), it will be in addition a health warning. The bilious tendency, the stomach disorder, and the nervousness, always present, will affect the head and produce vertigo, though serious results are not often encountered from the indication *per se*. The time period of the line when it has reached this point is about seventy and at that time the end is naturally not far distant. If the line should end in a star (120), sudden death is indicated. When the line runs into the upper Mount of Mars (121) it shows that practical common-sense ideas prevail. It is the medium position and the mental qualities are not pulled out of their balance. If upper Mars be well developed, it will give its qualities to the subject, who will defend himself when attacked, will be cool, calm, brave, and warlike in spirit. If the Mount be deficient, the mentality will partake of these deficiencies in Martian qualities and the subject will be easily discouraged, unable to resist strong attacks, and lacking in confidence. Whatever would be attributed to the Mount, attribute to the line. But whatever these attributes may be, the line ending here always gives practical ideas about everything. In very many hands the Head line slopes more or less toward the Mount of the Moon (122). This sloping of the line shows that the subject is somewhat influenced by imagination and is not practical to the exclusion of everything else.

There is a great misconception prevalent concerning this sloping Head line, which has been used as indicating danger of insanity. Nothing can be farther from the truth, for such a Head line is found on the hands of most sensible, self-con-

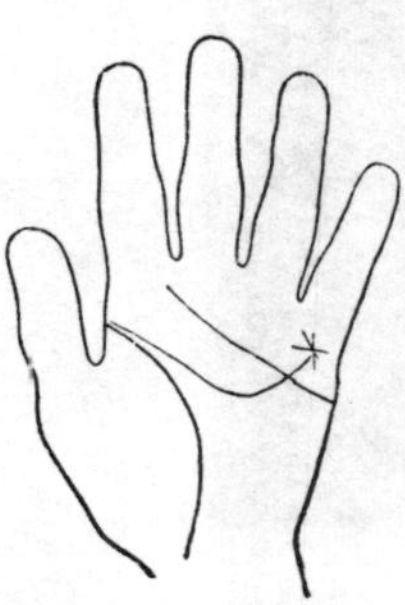
NO. 120

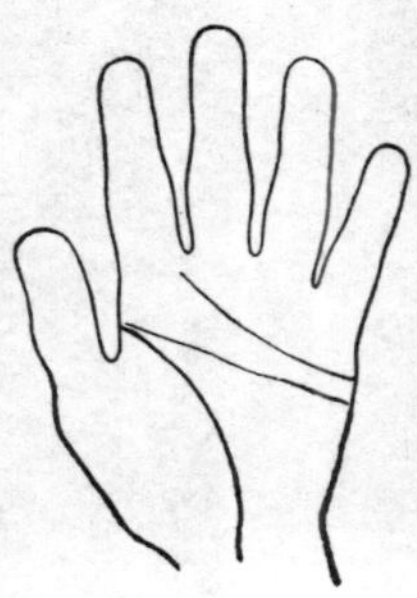
NO. 121

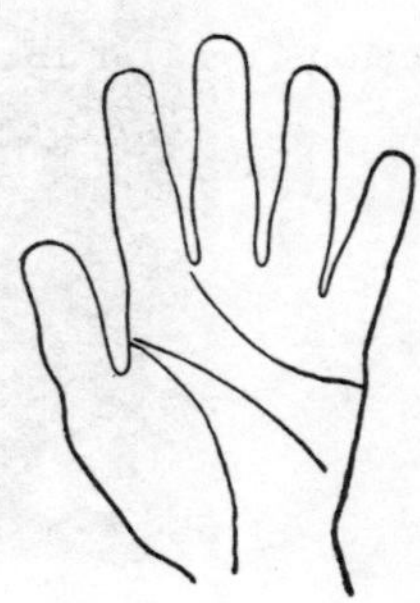
NO. 122

tained, practical persons. Because one has the ability to *imagine* does not mean that he is insane or likely to be, neither does it follow that he is unpractical, so, if the line of Head be good, deep, well cut, and clear, little concern need be felt because it inclines toward the Mount of Moon. With this indication, as with all others, excess may make it bad. Other combinations with the line, or the character of the line itself, may spoil it, but the general proposition is, the line running toward the Moon shows that the subject is not entirely material in his ideas, but has the power of imagination. This is an essential qualification for writers, speakers, and linguists, and in the most successful men of these professions I

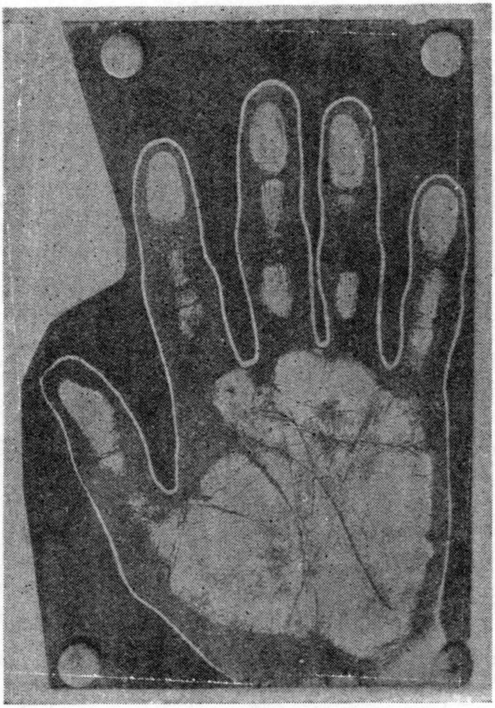

NO. 123. A CELEBRATED AUTHOR

find all degrees of droop to the Head line, some going far down into the Mount, and these persons have ability as writers of fiction and poetry (123). A line to reach the Moon must be a long one, so there is in these cases no lack of mentality. It is only when the drooping line is seen on a poor type of subject or when it is thin or defective that it is unfavorable. As excess of imagination is one species of insanity; the drooping Head line with other unfavorable signs will clearly indicate mental derangement. If the line droops low on the Mount and ends in a star (124), it will indicate insanity. Drooping to the Moon and ending in a chain (125), it will tell of mental impairment. If it droops to the Moon

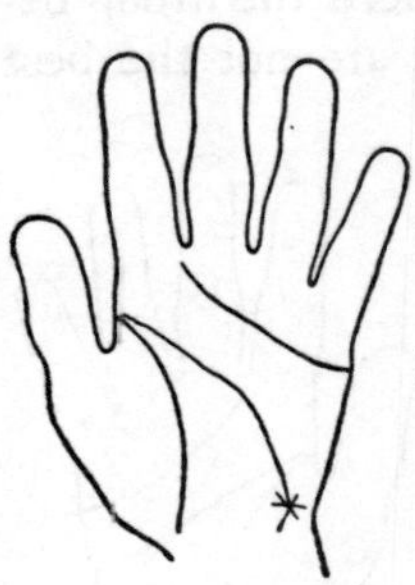

NO. 124

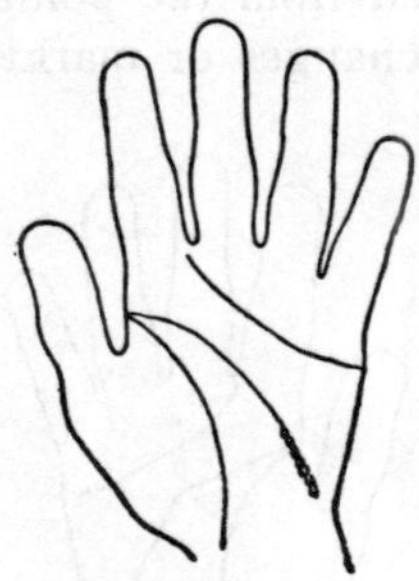

NO. 125

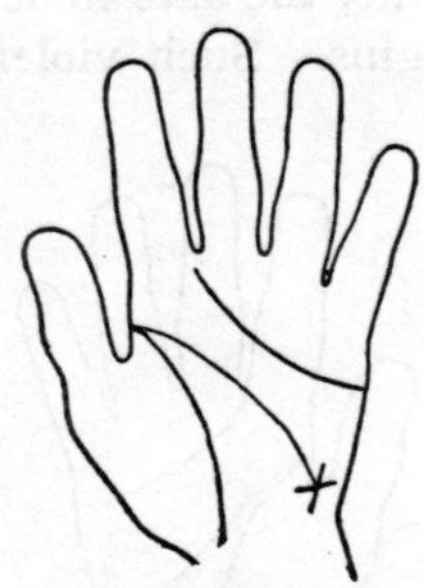

NO. 126

and ends in a cross (126), it will indicate a check to the mentality. If it droops and ends in an island (127) or a dot (128), there is danger of mental disturbance. In these cases the size of the island or dot will tell how serious. If on the Mount of Moon the line is broken (129) and intermittent, it

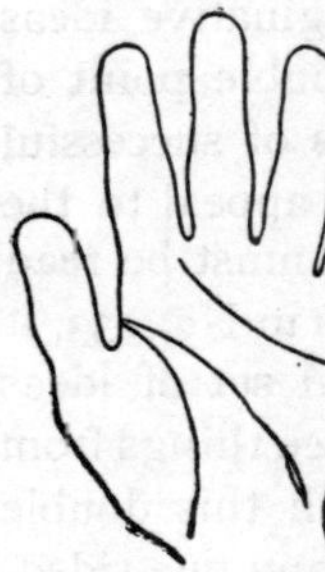

NO. 127

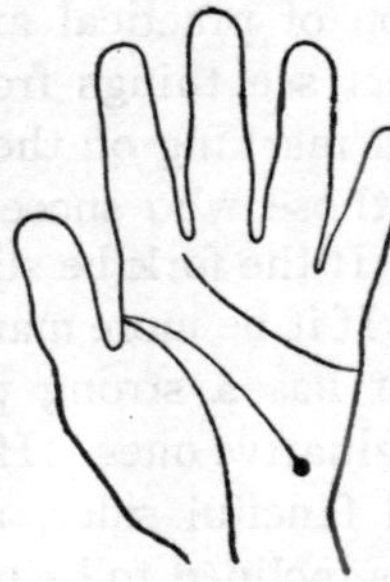

NO. 128

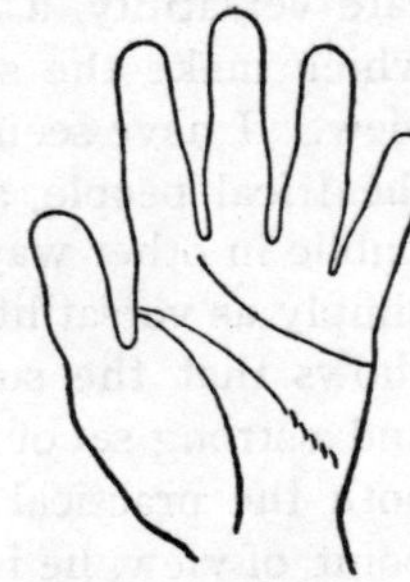

NO. 129

is another indication of mental disturbance. These markings of the line are more dangerous because the line droops to the Moon, the imaginative tendencies of the Mount making it a fertile place for such trouble. In every case the curve toward the Moon must be carefully considered. If it begins to droop from the start of the line (130), the tendency of the ideas have always been in that direction. If the line runs straight during the first part of its course and then slopes downward (131), the practical plane at the beginning is changed to a tendency toward imaginative ideas later in life, the date to be read from the point where the droop begins. Such violent changes or markings are not the best

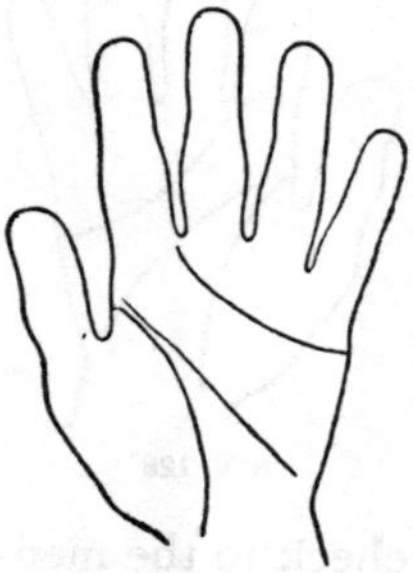

NO. 130

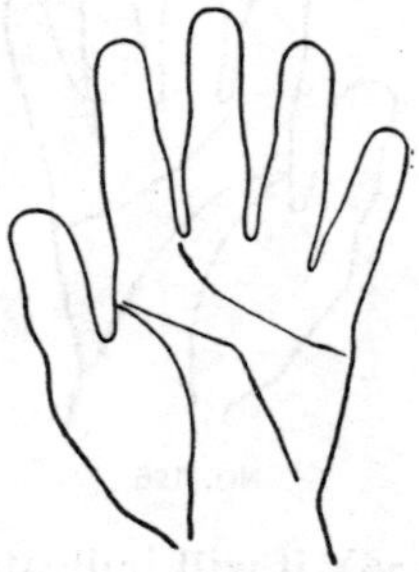

NO. 131

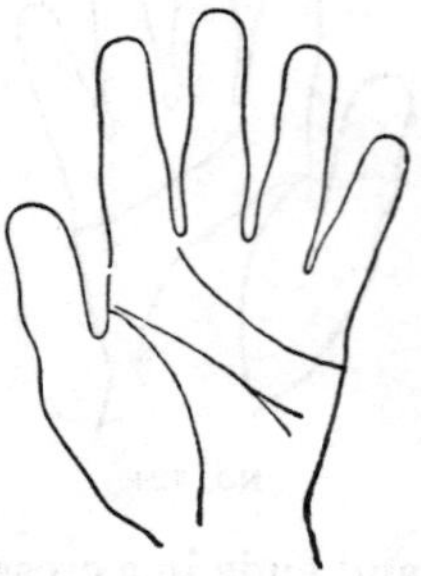

NO. 132

ones with this line; it is when the line forms a graceful curve, and gradually tends downward that no bad results follow. Sometimes the line forks at the end (132). This will indicate versatility, a union of practical and imaginative ideas which make the subject see things from a double point of view. I have seen this marking on the hands of successful theatrical people, and those who successfully appeal to the public in other ways. If the fork be slight, it must be read simply as versatility. If it be more marked, as in No. 133, it shows that the subject has a strong practical set of ideas and a strong set of imaginative ones. He can see things from both the practical and fanciful sides, and with this double point of view, he is less inclined to be narrow and one-sided. By noting which of the two forks is deeper and stronger, you can tell which side (practical or imaginative) will obtain the mastery.

This is a fine marking on a good hand. The double line, however, with its double point of view, often leads a subject into the habit of falsifying. He is not always an intentional liar; often he is not sure whether he is telling the literal story or the imaginative one. His imagination is vivid, and he sometimes makes himself think he is telling the truth when he is not. From the forking Head line is produced the liar, and when seen on an otherwise bad hand, it will make you sure of this interpretation. In habitual liars, I have found the forking Head line always present. Sometimes they lie from pride or vanity, for mercenary or vicious ends, and in each case the forking Head line will be seen. This applies to habitual falsifiers, not mere occasional "story tellers."

If the line has a fork with one line running to upper Mars and one going low on to the Moon, with this fork again forking (134), it will show that the double-pointed imagination, shown by the *forked* FORK on the Moon, will be so vivid that the subject will "stretch" everything and will lie when the truth is better. He possesses such an enlarged imagination that he magnifies everything to double the original size, and all descriptions show this distortion. If the fork

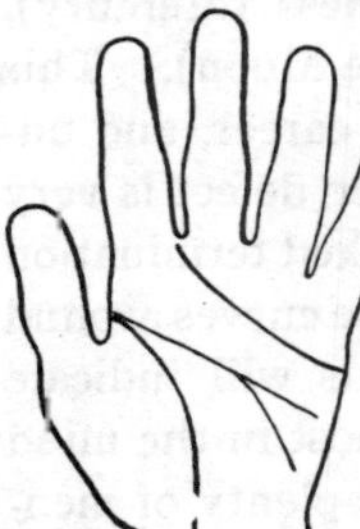

NO. 133

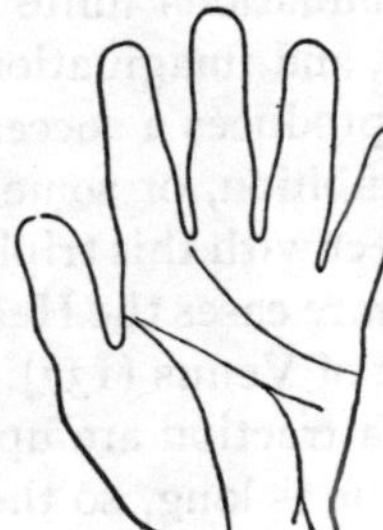

NO. 134

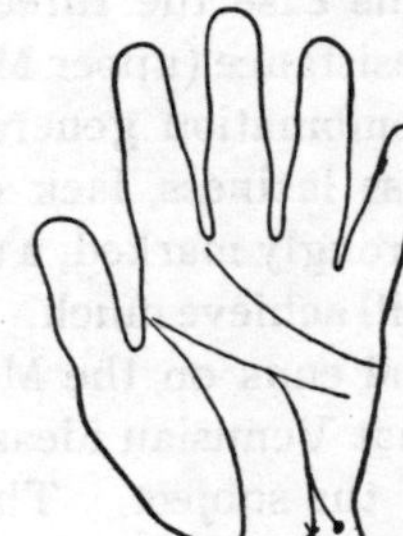

NO. 135

on the Moon ends in a star, a cross, or a dot (135), it will be practically certain that the enlarged imagination will produce insanity from, first, over-imagination; second, mental disease shown by the star, cross, or dot. In the two cases above mentioned, if the Mount of Moon be grilled and much rayed, it will add to the force of the indication all of the restlessness of the Lunarian. It will emphasize every bad indication found on a much drooped and forked line of Head. By

P

keeping constantly in mind what constitutes a clear line of Head and what makes it defective, you can distinguish between a good, healthy imagination and mental disorder, and you will never tell a fine writer that he is going crazy.

Sometimes a line of Head divides into three well-cut forks, one going toward Mercury, one toward Mars, and one toward

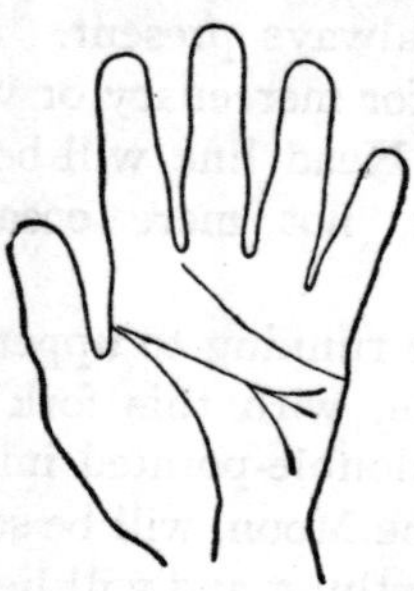

NO. 136

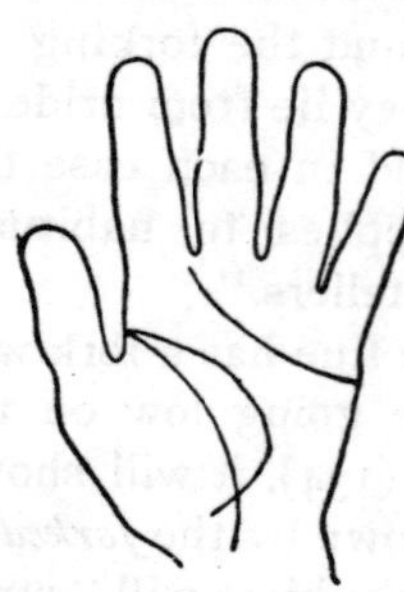

NO. 137

the Moon (136). This is a splendid marking, showing great diversity of intellect, adaptability, and versatility. In this case the three terminations unite business (Mercury), resistance (upper Mars), and imagination (the Moon). This combination generally produces a successful career, and unless laziness, lack of ambition, or some other defect is very strongly marked, a subject with this triple-forked termination will achieve much. In rare cases the Head line curves around and ends on the Mount of Venus (137). This will indicate that Venusian ideas of attraction are uppermost in the mind of the subject. This line is long, so there is plenty of mentality, and if it be deep and clear it is not *per se* an indication of defective mental health, but it shows the drawing, attracting power of Venus.

The *character* of the Head line, which will next be considered, shows what strength there is to the mental qualities, and what ability to concentrate the mind. A deep and well cut line shows great mental power, good self-control, fixedness of purpose, good memory, and general mental health and strength. There is in this case a good clear channel for the Current to flow through, consequently the ideas run evenly and smoothly—no breaks, no jars, but steadiness and strength. The deep and well cut Head line shows one who is self-contained, does not "lose his head," is not flighty or erratic, but is dignified, even-tempered, evenly balanced, and has the ability to make and carry out his determinations. If the long Head line be deep and well cut, its length shows great mentality and its depth shows strength of this quality. Long Head lines are often broken or defective while the subjects are very bright. From this you may think that a deep and well cut line is not necessary to produce mental stamina. But close analysis will show that while your subject is bright and has much mentality it is not the steady, deep, and strong kind, but is unstable. The length of the line shows the *quantity*, the depth and clearness shows the *quality*. Owners of deep, well cut Head lines do not always make up their minds as quickly, but weigh and consider carefully. Once reaching a decision, subjects with such a Head line are firm in execution ; they can concentrate their ideas, pursue a single aim in life, and bring to bear on this aim a fund of strength and information drawn from many sources. They are cool in moments of danger, collected, not easily thrown off their guard, and possess self-control in the greatest degree. A strong thumb added to a deep and well cut Head line will make the subject firm, cool, and irresistible. The large thumb indicates the will which dominates others, the deep and well cut Head line shows the will which can control *self*. Give a subject both a large thumb and deep and well cut Head line, and he can accomplish almost any task if he sets out to do it.

Observe the proportion of the lines to each other and also the size of the hand. If the Head line be deeper and clearer than the other lines, then the subject is a mental specimen of whatever type he belongs to, and his first phalanges will corroborate this. If the hand and the lines in general are small, but the Head line is deep and well cut, it is a grave danger, for it indicates more mental power than the subject has physical strength to carry easily. I have noted a number of incurable cases of insanity with this marking, and also that the Head line was deep red in color. So while the deep and well cut Head line, other things being equal, is the best marking, in excess it is one of the worst. The deep line shows excellent physical health of the brain, and with such a normal line you rarely find headaches, or any trouble from brain disorders. It is only when the line is seen in excessive development and red that you should fear trouble, and then vertigo, fainting spells, and, in extreme cases, apoplexy or insanity are indicated. This is more certain if your subject is a Jupiterian, especially if the third phalanx of the finger of Jupiter be thick. The strong Head line shows the capacity of the brain to think and do work; it shows a healthy brain, consequently one which can stand much exertion, and can also do *better* work than a weak or unhealthy organ. It is less swayed by others, more reliable, and in every way stronger. Take the deep and well cut Head line as the basis for best results in estimating a subject. There are many hands in which the Head line is thin and narrow, and traces itself delicately across the hand. This thin line shows that the brain power is not vigorous, but that the subject is mentally delicate. He may be clever, and will be if the line is long, but will lack mental vigor. He will have good ideas but will be easily talked out of them, nor will he make great mental exertion, for it tires him. He cannot put his brain at work for any length of time, for it becomes weary. He cannot pass through trials without headaches, and, whenever possible, he avoids severe mental tension and great brain effort. He does not like to concentrate his mind, and cannot do so for any length of time. He has little self-control, but gives way to his feelings, either temper, low appetites, laziness, or whatever they may be This thin line shows mental inertia, a lack of desire and ability to operate with vigor, lack of firmness, aggression, and of strong mental concentration. Its owner never does great things requiring continued mental exertion, but he does bright things which come to him by intuition and which do not require much brain exertion. It is dangerous to overcrowd these thin Head lines, for they cannot stand it. The channel is not deep enough to carry a large Current, and if such a Current is forced into it the thin line will give way and break. Here again observe proportion. If the hand and lines are large and the Head line thin, greatest care must be used. No mental over-excitement must be allowed, no loss of sleep, no narcotics, no stimulants, no excess of any kind. The subject must care for the stomach, and when fatigued must rest; any other sort of living will produce mental disorders. With these thin lines on the hands of men who make great mental exertions, you will often see places where the line cuts much more deeply than in others (138). These deep cuts show times at which the pressure has been too great and, at such a time, if the pressure is continued the brain will collapse, producing paralysis or nervous prostration. The age at which these strains occur can be read on the line. Such markings will often be seen on the hands of active business or professional men, and the warning to "ease up" must always be given. By noting these variations in depth of the line, you can tell the years of best brain power, age to be read from the line.

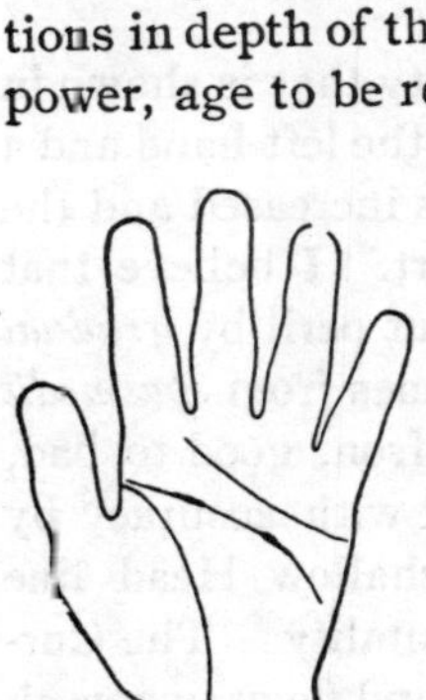
NO. 138

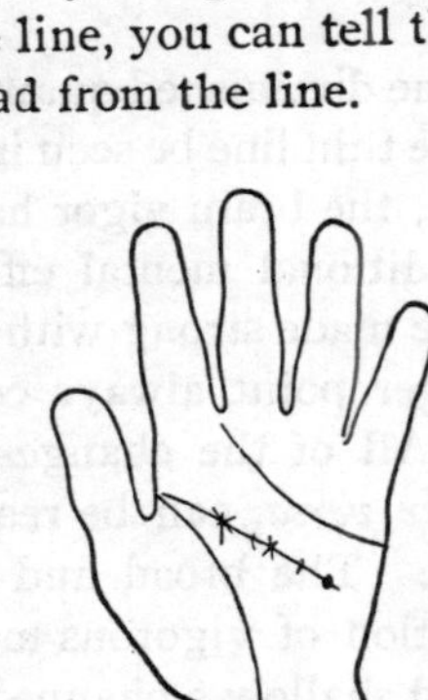
NO. 139

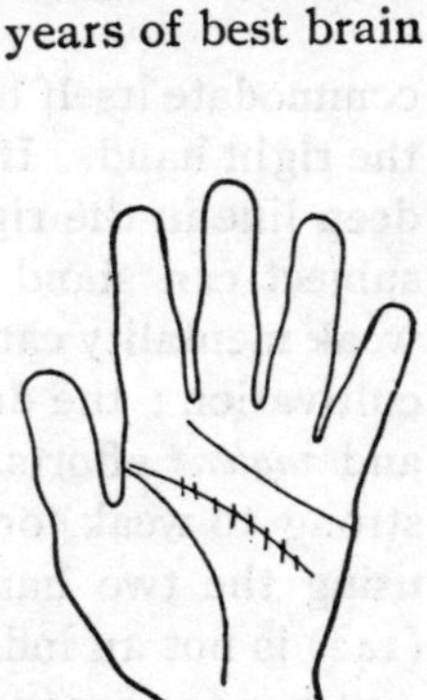
NO. 140

Stars, crosses, and dots (139) on a thin line will show dangers to the mental life that must not go unheeded. They show that explosions or checks will occur unless care be used, as well as the time, by the age at which they are seen. Cuts of the line show danger points. If small and frequent (140) they indicate headaches; if deep, and the

Head line thin (141), they show brain fever, nervous prostration, or paralysis. In all examinations look at both hands. If the Head line be deep in the left hand and thin in the right the natural brain power is strong, but has been weakened and it is dangerous to make great mental exertion. These subjects seldom heed warnings, for the natural brain strength, coming from the deep line in the left hand, cannot easily ac-

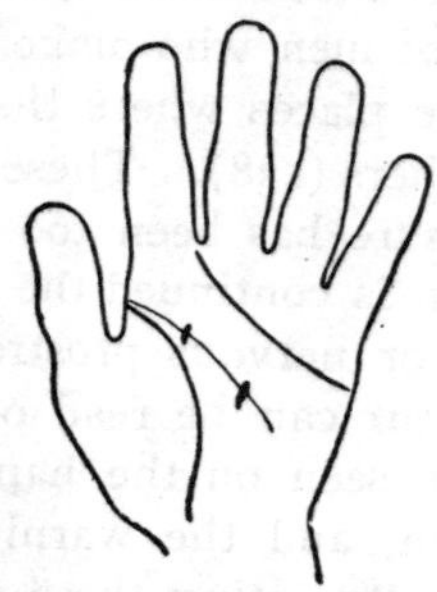

NO. 141

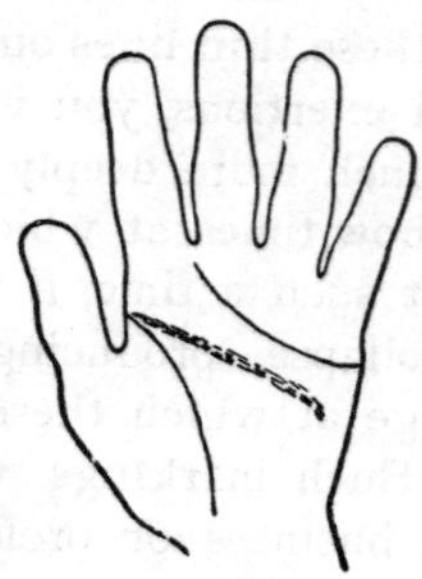

NO. 142

commodate itself to the diminished quantity that is shown in the right hand. If the thin line be seen in the left hand and a deep line in the right, the brain vigor has increased and the subject can stand additional mental effort. I believe that weak mentality can be made strong without peril by *gradual* cultivation : the danger point always comes from *spasmodic* and *violent* efforts. All of the changes from good to bad, strong to weak, or *vice versa*, can be read with accuracy by using the two hands. The broad and shallow Head line (142) is not an indication of vigorous mentality. The Current has too broad and shallow a channel and flows in a weak and shallow stream. It is not a vigorous brain but a weakened one, liable to aches and deterioration. The subject with this Head line is not firm, resolute, and courageous, but is undetermined, vacillating, uncertain, and lacks self-reliance and boldness. He may be bright, if the line is long, but he is weak in mental aggression. The broad and shallow line shows a lack of force or intensity in the mental attitude, the subject is not self-assertive; or, if possessed of a large thumb, he may be this, and yet lack *real* self-assertion ; what he does show being merely a veneer. He has poor control of himself, small power to influence others, little concentration of mind, and poor memory. This subject is easily influenced and yields to temptations. He was not intended for mental occupations and does not often seek them. He is mentally lazy and does but little thinking, is satisfied to have others think for him, so does not create much stir in the world. If broad and shallow lines be seen in both hands your subject will continue in his weak way until the end of life. If the line improves and gets clear in the right hand you are safe in saying that the natural mental inertia will be replaced by as much more strength as the line in the right hand shows itself deeper and clearer cut than the one in the left. If a broad and shallow line be seen in the left hand and splits up and breaks to pieces in the right, the subject is utterly vacillating and hopelessly weak. With any subject a fine Head line may pull him out of the worst places, and subjects whose hands are seen to be wofully lacking in many desirable qualities may overcome their weakness if a strong mental structure is back of them. A broad and shallow line will weaken any hand no matter how strong in other respects, and make the results of what might be an otherwise successful life negative. It reduces the strength of strong Mounts. The Jupiterian ambition is diminished, the Martian vigor is greatly weakened, and every Mount feels the blight of mental laziness. In many hands the line runs broad and shallow during the earlier years of life and then becomes deep and clear (143). The age at which this change occurs will show the time at which the subject energetically took up life's battle, and really began to think for himself. This marking is often seen in the hands of women who have been "spoiled" and who have never had to do anything until suddenly thrown upon their own resources, when they have had to take up life's struggle in earnest, and the Head line changes and grows deeper, clearer and straighter as they rise to the occasion and develop strength.

The chained Head line (144) is a bad indication. The

channel is not only broad and shallow, but is continually obstructed. The mentality is weak and labored, utterly lacking in power of concentration, vacillating, timid, sensitive, and changeable. You can place no reliance on the promises of these subjects; they do not mean to break faith but they do so. They have poor memories, poor judgment, are continually subject to headaches and various mental disorders. They cannot apply themselves continuously to any kind of work, either mental or manual. If the Heart line be strong they will be ruled by sentiment and utterly unpractical. If the thumb be weak they will be unable to think out a plan or to execute it. To such subjects any mental shock is exceedingly dangerous and likely to throw them off their balance. This done they have not the power to recover it. They are prone to delusions and hallucinations, chimerical and impractical in their ideas, and such a Head line drooping to the Moon produces phantasms, over-imagination, or insanity, and the person having such a line cannot be trusted to deal safely with speculative matters. A

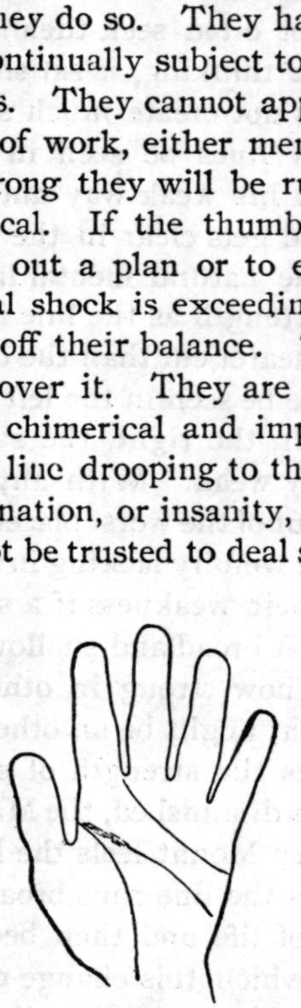

NO. 143

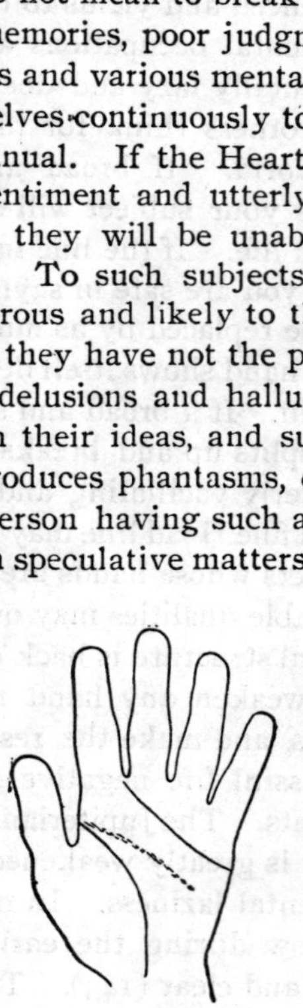

NO. 144

subject with a chained Head line should not attempt mental vocations, should not choose literature, scientific studies, or any brain-exerting occupations, but should take out-of-door positions where labor with the hands or legs is required. He should have a firm master under whom to work, for he will not be able to direct his own efforts, but will rely on being directed. If the chain appears in only a portion of the Head line, its weakening effect will apply only to the portion of the line it covers. If it be replaced by a deep, well cut line (145) the subject will develop mental weakness into mental vigor. It is not frequent that the chained condition is at once replaced by a deep line, for the change from such opposite mental conditions comes slowly, and in most cases the chained line is followed by a thin line which gradually grows

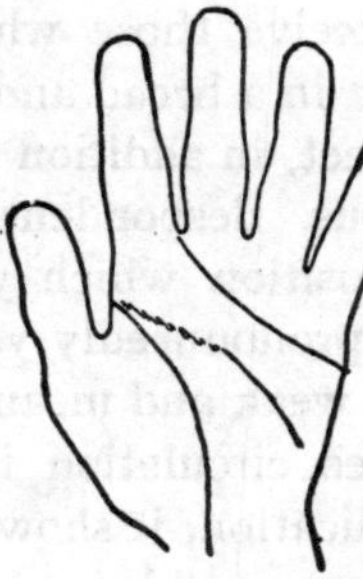

NO. 145

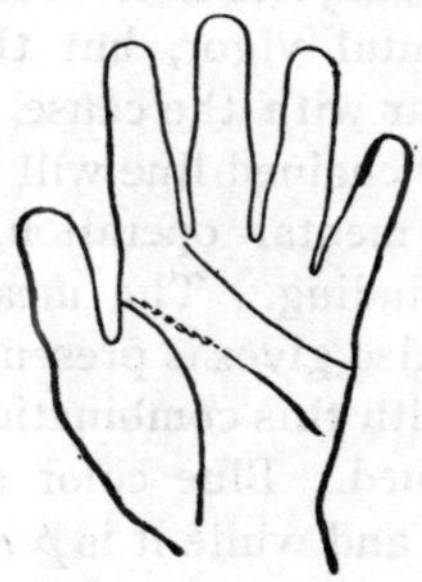

NO. 146

stronger (146), showing the gradual progress from mental weakness to strength. Look to both hands for the outcome when a chained Head line is seen. If it grows clear in the right hand your subject will gain mental strength. If it goes from a deep line in the left to a chained line in the right, the subject is going from a strong condition to a weak one. The Life line will show the effect, and the age at which this deterioration begins can be read from the Head line, and confirmed on the Life line. You will find the different character of lines marked in great variety on Head lines. If you remember the *kind* of mental strength each one indicates, you know that each kind of a line will operate in the manner peculiar to its character during the period it covers on the line, and that when the character of the line changes, the mental view and qualities change at the same time.

The color of the Head line must always be noted. White color will show poor blood supply to the brain and consequent weak operation of that organ. This color is most often seen on the broad and shallow or chained lines, and it adds to the poor indication of these lines, making them weaker. Pink color gives better force and takes away some of the weakness. Red color makes them more intense and less liable to absolute weakness; but red color will make broad and shallow and chained lines violent and spasmodic in their action. Thus for periods they show great force, but the effort is only temporary and has no lasting quality. These subjects often deceive even close observers by displays of mental vigor, but they do not deceive those who are familiar with the cause. Yellow color in a broad and shallow or chained line will make the subject, in addition to the weak mental operation, cross, nervous, despondent, and fault-finding. The meanness of disposition which yellow color also gives is present if the line is pronouncedly yellow, and with this combination you have a weak and mean head combined. Blue color shows congested circulation in the brain, and while it is *per se* a heart indication, it shows that the mentality may be cut off at any moment by a sudden heart failure. In deep and well cut lines, white color is not often seen, but when the line on pressure does not show the red blood flowing along it, but remains white, it is an indication of coldness which must be added to the strong operation of the good line. The owner of this brain is calculating, cold, avaricious, and seeks self-aggrandizement at the expense of others. As this deep line shows great determination and strength of mind, the white coldness also seen in it indicates one who has little sympathy or feeling for others, and such a subject easily becomes the master and the tyrant, whether in home or business. The deep white line shows the strong, cold head. Pink color is often seen in all kinds of lines and gives its added strength to the deep line. The subject with this combination has a vigorous, healthy brain and a strong mentality. His danger is from overwork. Red color often means excess with a deep Head line, and it results in mentally unbalancing the subject. Too much brain and too much blood in it are the indications of this combination, and apoplexy, fainting fits, and insanity follow. Always regard red color in a deep Head line as a menace, and look over all the hand for the place it will make its danger felt. Yellow color adds its baleful qualities to the deep line and makes the subject strong of brain but mean. This will produce the really vicious subject who conspires against his fellow-men. With a thin line, white color makes it weaker than if it were pink, while red color adds much strength. With the latter color the danger is that more force will be exerted than the thin line can stand and the subject will overstrain his brain. Yellow color in a thin line makes the subject narrow, little, mean, nervous, and unstable.

On the Head line we encounter all the defects possible to lines, and have frequent calls made upon us to read these defects correctly. The defects commonly seen on Head lines are uneven lines, splits, cross-bars, islands, dots, and breaks. These constitute *specific defects* or, as commonly known, single signs, which are common to broad and shallow or chained lines, but are not often encountered on deep or even thin lines. These specific defects in the Head line show that the operation of the mental activity is not continuous, regular, and strong, for these defects have intervened, obstructing the flow of the Current and the operation of the brain. They show that periods of health occur, followed by periods of weakness or disease, and consequently that the mental powers have at times been interfered with. How great these interferences are, or have been, may be judged by the size and importance of the defect. When they begin and how long they last may be judged by the duration of the defective condition of the line. The first defective condition which we will consider is the uneven line. This is a line which is thin for awhile, then thick, then thin again, and following a like variation throughout its course (147). These alterations may occur frequently, or only once or twice in the whole line. They show that the mentality of the subject changes, now weak for a period of years, then strong, then weak, then strong, as many changes being indicated as there are uneven places on the line. At the time the deep lines occur there is no doubt that great concentration of thought takes place, and the pressure on the brain is very strong. If the Head line at the beginning be thin, class it as a thin line and the deep places are the periods when great pressures occur. This is a dangerous line, for at these deep places the thin line may be crowded too much. These subjects alternate between enthusiasm and despair, are changeable, and not reliable counsellors or guides. If a star, cross, or dot occurs in the course of this uneven line, paralysis, apoplexy, or insanity will be indicated. The greatest care, plenty of sleep, and no excitement must be the advice given this subject. On the Head line will be seen splits of an infinite variety of sizes, and running in many directions. As a general rule splits which *rise* from the line are better indications than those which *fall* from it. If these rising splits are small and frequent but not large enough to impair the line (148) they show that the subject is aspiring to rise and to improve and that he seeks all avenues for advancement, as is indicated by these splits rising under *all* the Mounts. If these splits are large and long (149) they indicate that the head is influenced by too

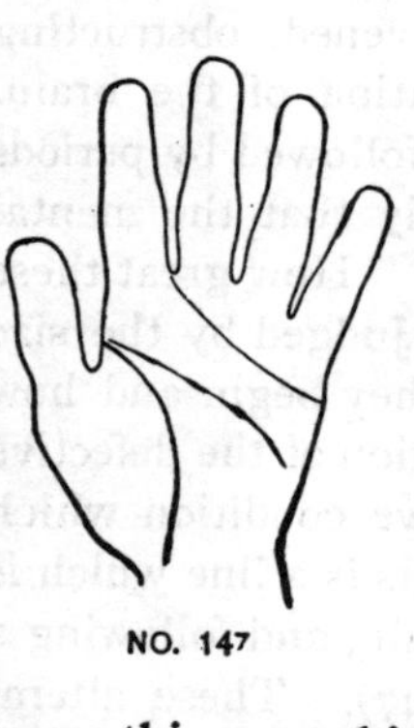

NO. 147

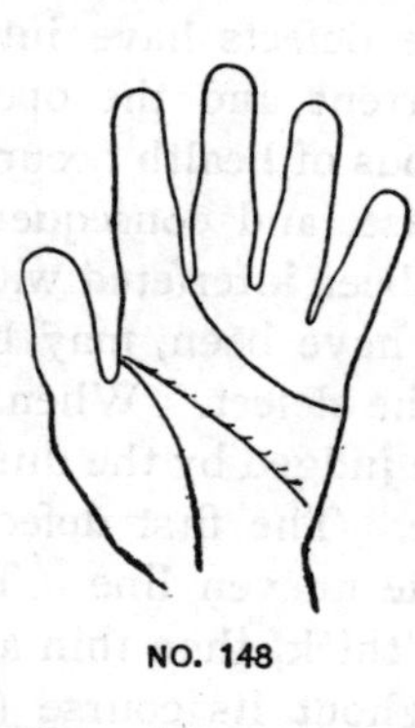

NO. 148

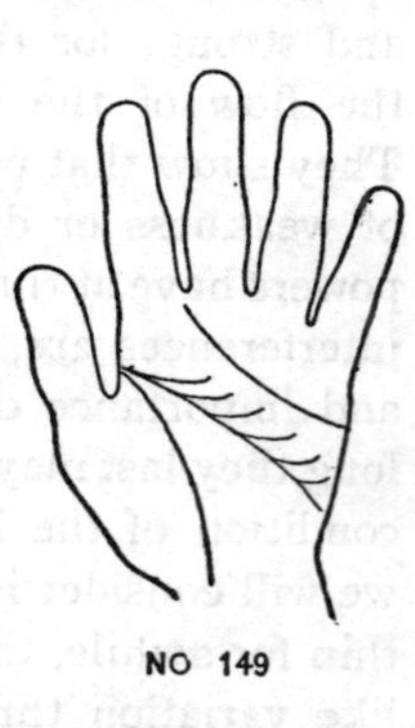

NO 149

many things, making the subject vacillating. Such a subject will never have the concentration of mind that a deep and well cut line gives. The thoughts wander too much, and if the Head line droops toward the Mount of the Moon, these subjects are day dreamers. If the splits drop below the line (150) it shows that the subject is easily discouraged, does not fight the battle of life with vigor, but is prone to say, "I am unlucky." Such subjects start into every enterprise saying they know "it will fail," and as they really believe this, it generally does. Older palmists read this indication as "sorrows and disappointments," which is generally correct, for the reasons above stated. Always give these subjects advice along the line of "resisting more and not giving way so easily." A single split rising under

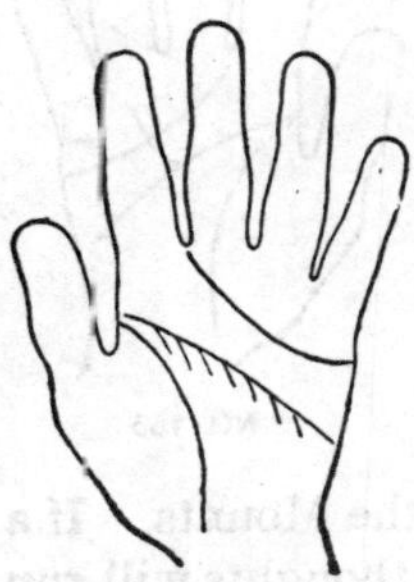

NO. 150

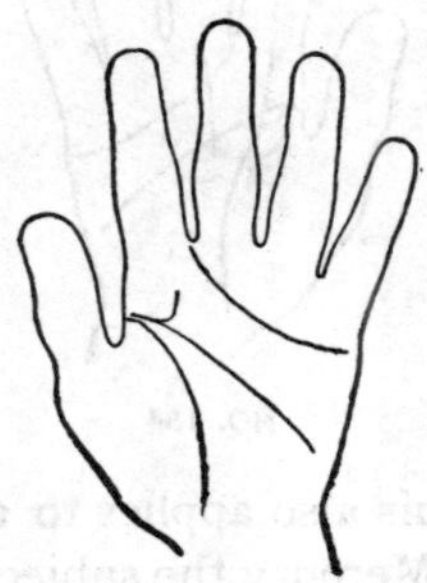

NO. 151

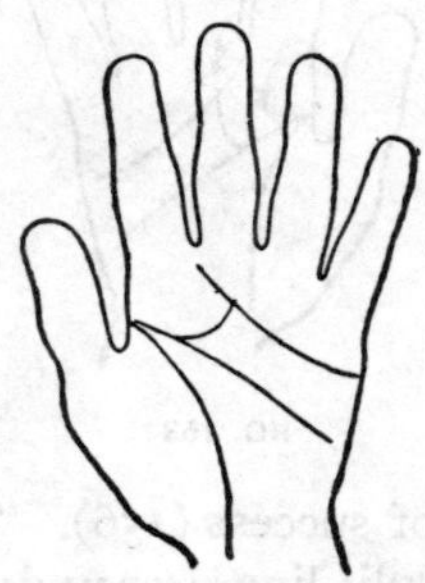

NO. 152

Jupiter (151) shows that ambitious thoughts fill the mind of your subject, and that Jupiterian desires are his. He wishes to rise and to achieve fame and notoriety. This is a mark of great ambition and pride if found with a large Mount of Jupiter. If a split rises under Saturn (152) it shows that the thoughts are Saturnian, and wisdom, soberness, studiousness, and other Saturnian attributes attract your subject. These splits show the pulling force of some attraction which is not strong enough to deflect the entire line, but is powerful enough to split a part from it; thus they show the attracting force of the place to which the split goes. If in either of the above cases the split line should end in a star (153) it will show that success rewards these ambitions or desires. The same construction applies to all the other Mounts. In these cases be certain that the line is a split from the line of Head and not a chance line cutting it as 154. By closely examining the point where the split leaves the Main line you can easily diagnose the indication as a split. If a split line rises from the line of Head and runs to Apollo (155) it shows that

Apollonian pride, love of display, beauty, desire for wealth and fame, art, and celebrity occupy the thoughts of your subject. If the split line ends with a star, the prognosis is favorable, if with a dot, cross, or island, there is small chance

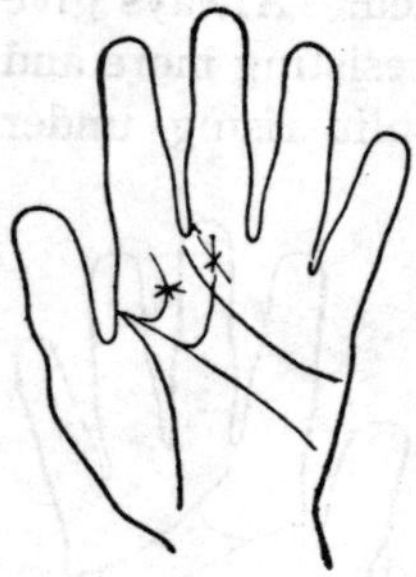

NO. 153

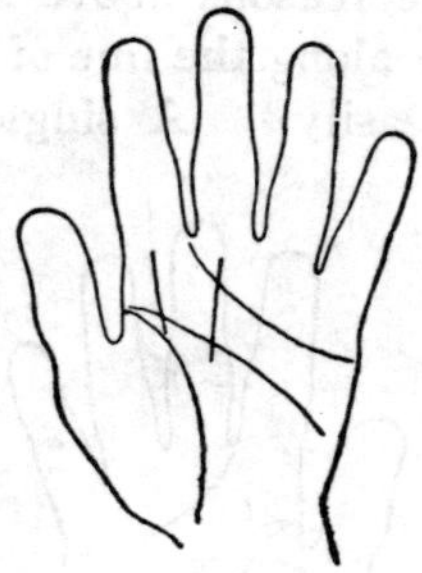

NO. 154

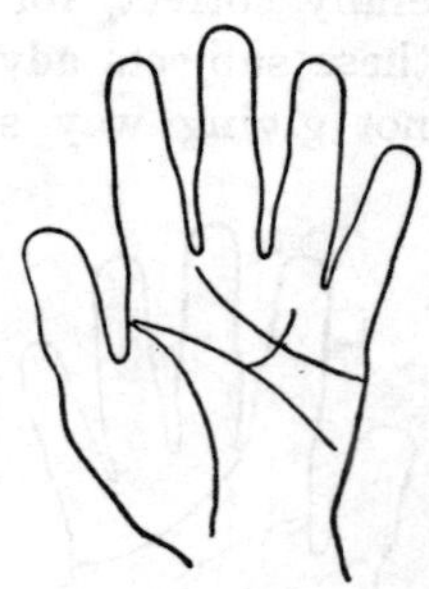

NO. 155

of success (156). This also applies to all the Mounts. If a split line rises under Mercury the subject's thoughts will run in Mercurian channels. Either he will love the scientific side, in which case the second phalanx of the finger will be longest, and the Medical Stigmata will be seen on the Mount

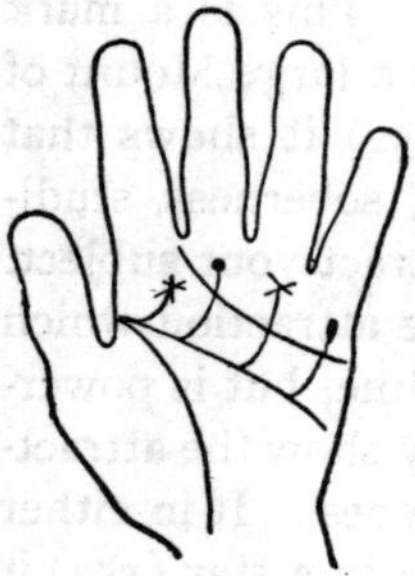

NO. 156

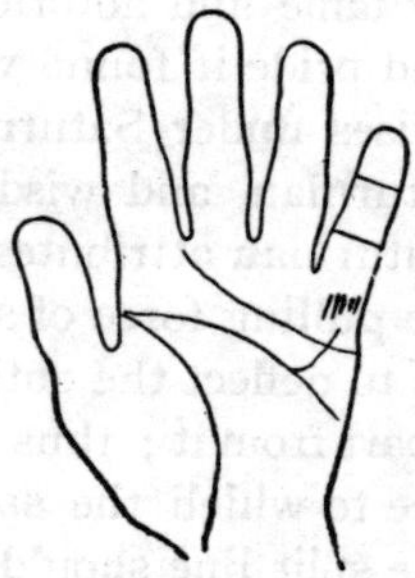

NO. 157

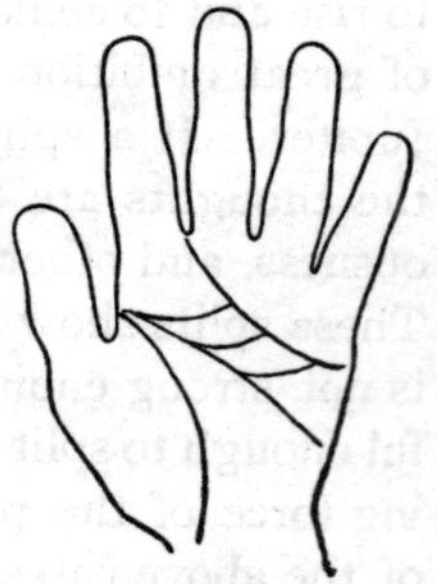

NO. 158

(157), or he will love the business side of Mercury, in which case the third phalanx will be the best developed. All split lines rising and touching the Heart line (158) show that sentiment, love, and affection occupy the thoughts of the subject. Even with a deep and well-cut line he will be less sordid and mercenary and more given to doing for others.

He will also be more sympathetic and humane. If split lines rise from the line of Head and merge into the line of Heart the head has been powerfully guided by heart. Often these lines are seen cutting the line of Saturn (159); in this case sentiment has interfered with business success.

Cross-bars are lines which cut the Head line, sometimes only one being seen, and again the entire line is cut by them (160). They are short lines which have no particular beginning or ending, but are apparently just long enough to cut the line of Head. They cannot be classed as chance lines, but must be distinguished as cross-bars. If these lines are deep, cutting the Head line sharply, and are also red, they indicate a brain disorder, may be fever, may be only

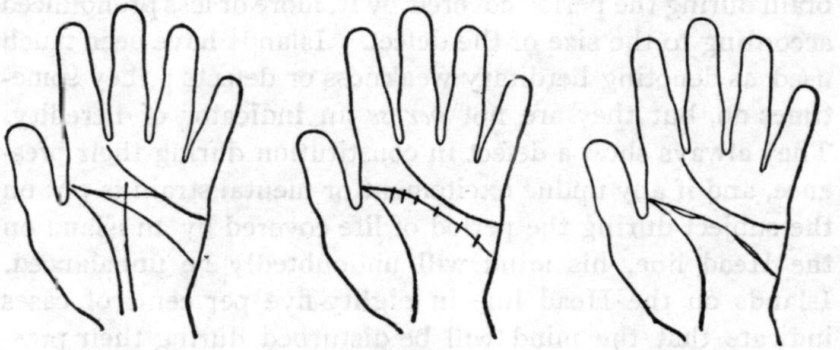

NO. 159 NO. 160 NO. 161

headaches, the severity of the attack being proportionate to their depth and redness. The age can be read from the line. If several of these deep bars cut the Head line there is predisposition to brain trouble, and with a Jupiterian subject this is a serious matter, for apoplexy may result. If these cross-bars are merely little fine lines which cross the Head line they show mental worries and predisposition to severe headaches, but do not go so far as brain fever. They are generally seen on the hands of hyper-nervous persons. Islands on the line (161) show that at the time they occur the mental strength operates with diminished force. I have seen islands on the Head lines of many insane persons whose aberration lasted through the duration of the island. I have seen them on the Head lines of those whose line of thought had been changed, and who confessed that during the period indicated by the island they felt that they were not mentally balanced. I have seen the islands at points on lines where brain fever has occurred, or where delirium has been produced by other fevers. I have seen them also on the hands of many spirit mediums who said they were " developed " into mediums at the age when the island appeared. I have seen them on the hands of women who have suffered from female trouble until their reason has been affected. Many similar instances might be cited, all of which would lead to the statement that during the period covered by an island, the mind is not in full health and power, and that an island shows delicacy of the brain during the period covered by it, more or less pronounced according to the size of the defect. Islands have been much used as denoting herditary weakness or defects ; they sometimes do, but they are not *per se* an indicator of heredity. They always show a defect in constitution during their presence, and if any undue excitement or mental strain is put on the subject during the period of life covered by an island on the Head line, his mind will undoubtedly be unbalanced. Islands on the Head line in eighty-five per cent. of cases indicate that the mind will be disturbed during their presence. If islands are deep cut and red, the trouble will be brain fever, or possibly it may be female trouble, delirium of typhoid or other fevers, hyper-nervousness, or severe mental strain, sometimes the embracing of a new religion, that will produce the loss of mental equilibrium. In hands full of lines crossing in every direction it is safe to read islands as periods of mental unbalance. The subject who has hands free from lines—which shows him to be phlegmatic and without nervous strain—may avoid the danger by his naturally calm, even temper. It is a danger, however, and a grave one, in every case when these islands are seen in the Head line. You can estimate the results by the character of the Head line before and after the island. If after it a star, a cross, a dot, or a severe break in the line be seen the subject will not avoid serious mental disorder. If the line be deep and well cut after an island the results are not likely to be so serious. Always note the color of an island in the Head line, and apply color qualities. Deep red is always an added danger to the indication. With every island watch for a deep cut in the Head line preceding it (162). This will show that the brain was forced too much, and this produced the mental disturbance shown by the island. Note

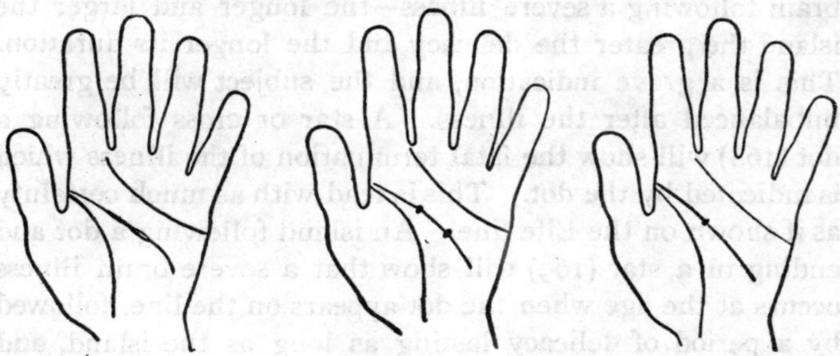

NO. 162. NO. 163 NO. 164

chance lines which connect the island with some other part of the hand; these will often show that diseases peculiar to the Mount types have caused the island. These chance lines are very trustworthy if they run from grilles or crossbars on the Mounts to an island on the Head line. An island on the Head line under Saturn is seen in the hands of ninety per cent. of deaf mutes.

Dots in the Head line (163) are acute brain disorders more or less severe according to the size and color of the dot. If small and white or pink the trouble is an illness, but not *per se* of grave import. If the dot be large and deep red or purple, the brain trouble indicated is severe and great care should be taken by the subject at the age it occurs. The character of the line following dots will tell the effect which the illness has on the head. If the line continues deep and well cut the effect is only temporary. If the line grows thin (164) it shows that mental vigor has decreased. If the dot be followed by a chained line (165) it shows that the brain sickness has much impaired the mind, and unless the chain is very short and replaced by a deep line (166) the mind will never entirely recover from the injury. During the period covered by the dot and chain there will be some mental disturbance, and no attempt should be made to pursue usual vocations. White dots almost always tell of past brain illness, and when the dots are deep red or purple they will generally be found in advance of the present age of the subject. Islands following a dot (167) show great delicacy of brain following a severe illness—the longer and larger the island the greater the delicacy and the longer its duration. This is a grave indication, and the subject will be greatly unbalanced after the illness. A star or cross following a dot (168) will show the fatal termination of the illness which is indicated by the dot. This is read with as much certainty as if shown on the Life line. An island following a dot and ending in a star (169) will show that a severe brain illness occurs at the age when the dot appears on the line, followed by a period of delicacy lasting as long as the island, and ending fatally at the age at which the star appears. If the Head line runs on after the star (170) it will show insanity instead of the termination of life.

Breaks in the line (171) show the interruption of the Cur-

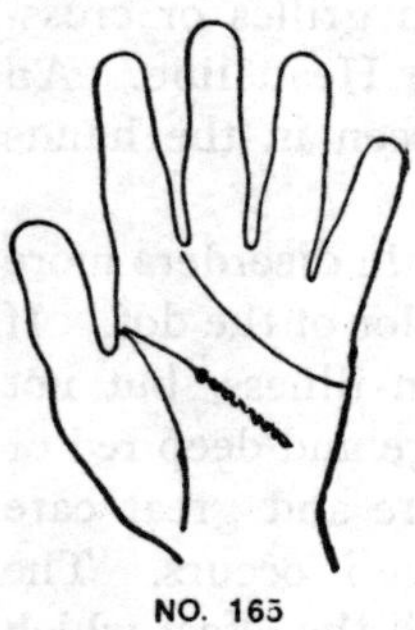

NO. 165

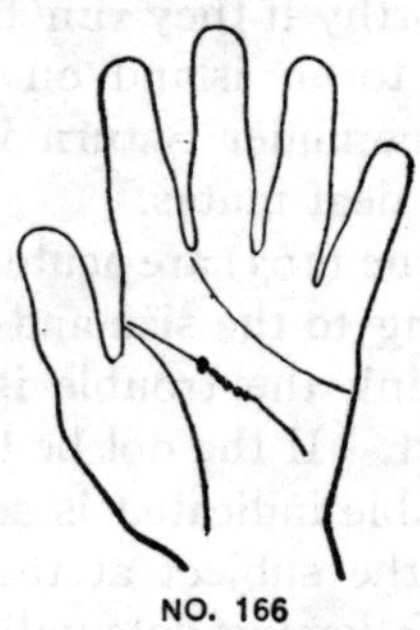

NO. 166

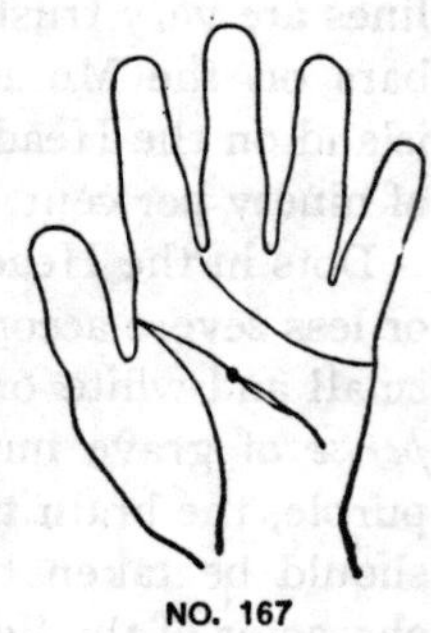

NO. 167

rent, its unsteady flow, producing irregular action and consequent lack of concentration, firmness, and self-control. These breaks may be illnesses ; if so they will be corroborated by nails, Life line, and other indications of disease. They are often seen on the hands of flighty, nervous, changeable subjects, and there is illness present at each time the line breaks. The age at which all of these illnesses occur can be read from the line. If the line is continually broken and ladder-like (172) it shows an utter lack of stability ; the subject is fickle and shifting, has continuous headaches, poor health, visions, phantasms, and unless cared for by

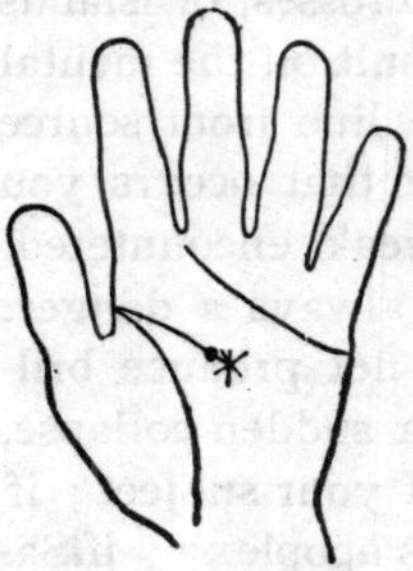
NO. 168

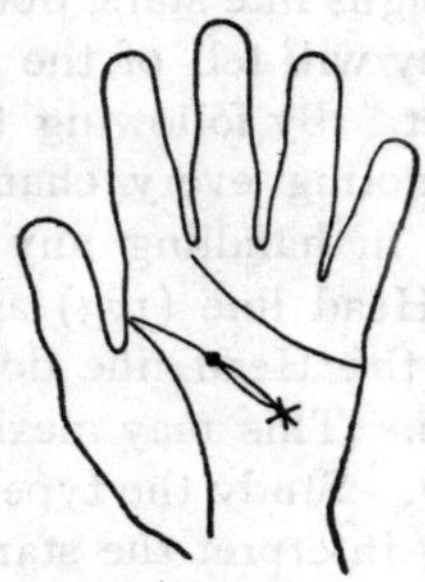
NO. 169

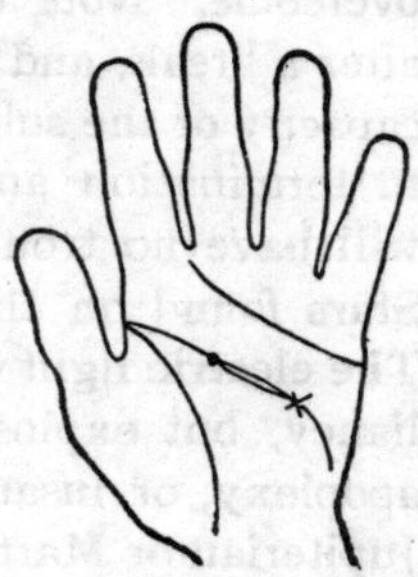
NO. 170

someone else goes insane or borders on it from nervousness. These subjects fly off on tangents, are always seeking for the unrealizable, and if pointed tips are present they are utterly unpractical and unreliable, especially if the Head line goes far into the Mount of Moon. With every break

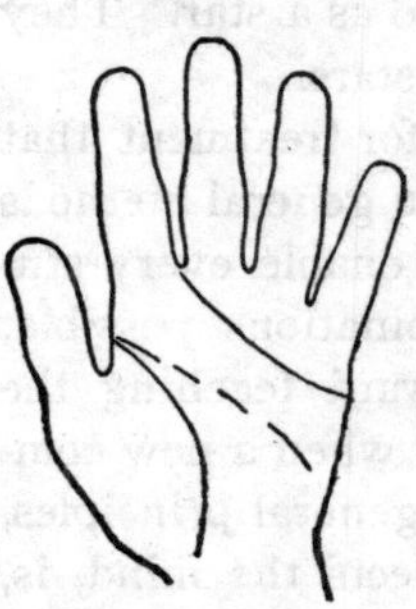
NO. 171

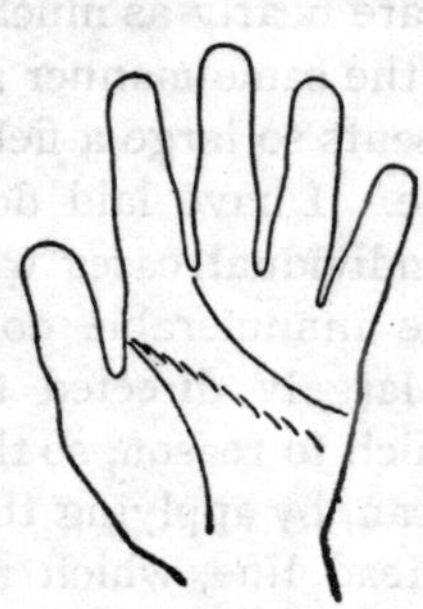
NO. 172

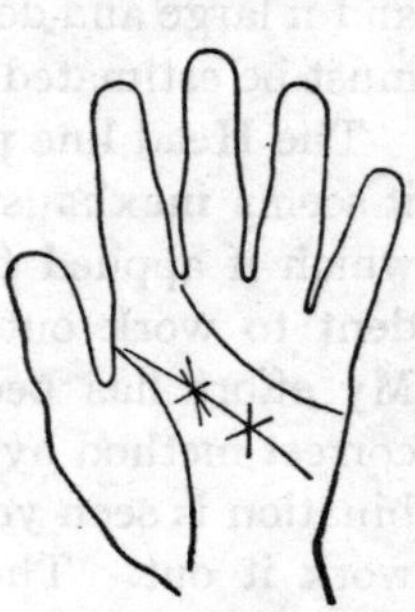
NO. 173

in the Head line note whether it is repaired by sister lines, by the overlapping ends, connecting bars, squares, or any other repair signs. If so the subject will have a mental jar at the time of the break which will be more or less severe according to the size of the break and to how well it is repaired. If the end of the broken line turns toward any

Mount, handle it as in the case of the split running to a Mount. Wherever the broken end goes it will show the force which produced the break. Note the condition of the line after a break, and it will tell whether the break has permanently impaired the mental stamina, or whether it is overcome. Note all signs like stars, dots, crosses, or islands after a break, and they will tell of the result on the mental capacity of the subject. By following the line from source to termination and noting every change that occurs you will have no trouble in handling any break encountered. Stars found on the Head line (173) are always a danger. The electric light on the Head line does not produce brilliancy, but explosion. This may mean a sudden collapse, apoplexy, or insanity. Study the type of your subject; if Jupiterian or Martian interpret the star as apoplexy; if Saturnian or Lunarian, read it as paralysis or insanity. Follow all the instructions given in diagnosing disease, and you will never be at a loss. Watch for chance lines to the star, which will help to tell the cause of it. In every case consider a star on the Head line a danger and seek its explanation. Crosses on the Head line are also dangerous, and if large and deep are nearly as much so as a star. They must be estimated in the same manner as stars.

The Head line presents so large a field for treatment that it seems inexhaustible. I have laid down general methods which if applied to individual cases will enable every student to work out the innumerable combinations possible. My effort has been largely directed toward teaching the correct method by which to reason, so that when a new combination is seen you can, by applying the general principles, work it out. The Head line, which reflects the mind, is, with the thumb, the most important subject to a palmist. This chapter dealing with the line which most directly reflects the workings of the brain is therefore commended to your earnest consideration.

CHAPTER VII

THE LINE OF LIFE

THE line of Life is, according to our hypothesis, the third line which receives the Electric Current upon its entrance through the finger of Jupiter. This line rises at the side of the hand under the finger of Jupiter, encircles the Mounts of Lower Mars and Venus, and in most cases ends under the Mount of Venus at the base of the hand (174). The line of Life indicates the health of the subject during the various periods of life, his physical strength in general, and whether he lives during each period on his nervous force or relies upon muscular robustness. By reason of these facts, it records many detailed events in his life, and forms a basis to fall back upon when seeking confirmations or explanations of indications found elsewhere in the hand. It shows whether the course of the life is upward or downward, and will fix the year when the zenith of the subject's powers are reached. In many cases it also shows the probable termination of the life, and often by what disease or agency. If you ask, "Why does the line of Life show these things?" we must answer, "We do not know, unless our hypothesis that the *lines are the life map* of the subject be correct." But we must add that thousands of recorded cases in the past prove, beyond a doubt, that these facts *can* and *have been* obtained from the line of Life, and, reasoning from past to present, we feel confident that the same information may *still* be secured from the same source. If

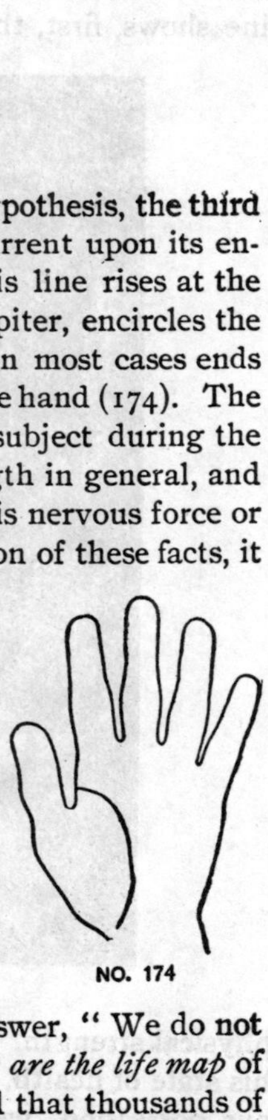

NO. 174

our hypothesis is *not* correct, it works out just the same as if it were, and in the absence of any better explanation of the phenomena of the Life line, we must, for the present at least, rest upon the statement that the *Life line is the map* of the *natural* course of the subject's life. When we think that the line shows, first, the health of the subject, and, second, his

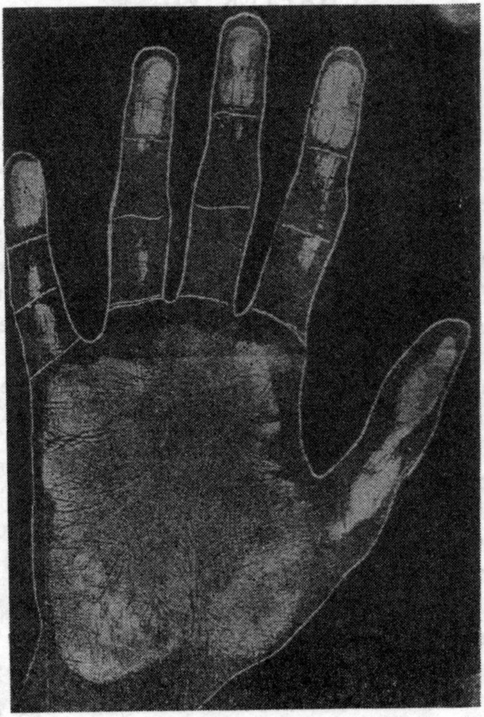

NO. 175

physical strength, we cannot deny that with a knowledge of his state of health, general vitality, and physical strength in our possession, we would be poor reasoners indeed if we could not take such information and from these causes figure out their results. It is from such a basis that the present work upon the Life line has been deduced, and many experiments prove it to be correct.

There is little use in discussing an absence of the Life line, for few cases will be found where none is present. A great variation will be found in the length of lines, but where it seems at first sight to be absent you will in nearly every case discover a remnant of it, showing that the line has existed in some form. I have seen a few cases where no Life line at all was present (175), and in such cases have found that the subject had but little muscular strength and vitality, but has lived on nervous energy. These people were subject to many nervous collapses, and had constantly to husband the strength, sleep much, and avoid excitement. The absence of a Life line simply shows that the life of the subject hangs only by a hair, and for such an one Death is a visitor who may come at any moment. These subjects have never lived in a *robust condition*, but have always been delicate. In the beginning of your study of the Life line, I wish to say that a big thumb and a good Head line indicate qualities that often overcome the poorest Life line, prolonging the life far past its natural ending place. In no case, therefore, should absolute statements be made that death will come at a given time, for, while you may see great danger, will power may be strong enough to wrest life from death. It is far better for your subject's course through life that some kind of a line be present, even though it may be a weak one, for in this case there is some resistance, some vital force, while with the absent line all energy depends upon the nerves, and when these give way collapse ensues. You will sometimes find it difficult to distinguish the Life line from the Saturn line (176) or from strong influence lines found inside of the Life line (177). In 176 the inside line is the Life line, though the second or Saturn line takes up a part of the Life line's function from the time the Life line leaves off. In 177 the outside line is the Life line, and the inner line gives it strength. As a guide in all such cases remember that the Life line should *enclose* the Mount of Venus and not run *on top* of it. By keeping this point in view you can always properly distinguish the Life line from other lines.

The Life line usually rises at the side of the hand under Jupiter (178). This is the normal source, and marks the beginning of the life. Sometimes, however, the line rises *from* the Mount of Jupiter (179). This shows that the life

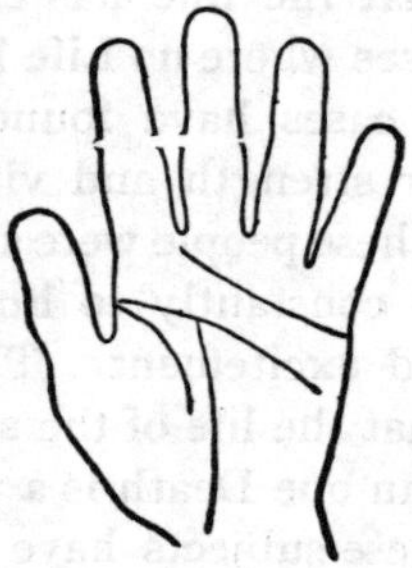

NO. 176

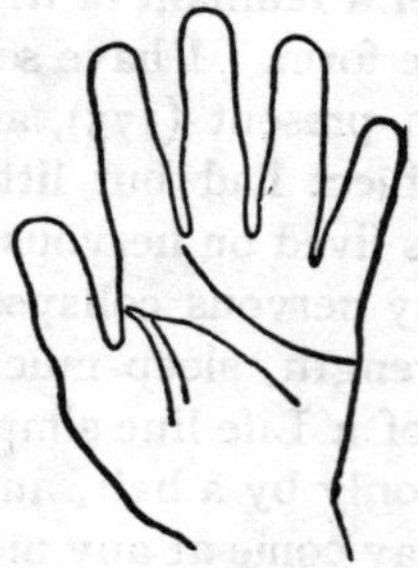

NO. 177

is a most ambitious one, filled with desires for wealth, success, and fame, and that the subject will take every opportunity to become acquainted with people of note. If he be a Saturnian, he is ambitious for success along Saturnian, lines, such as occult studies, physics, chemistry, medicine,

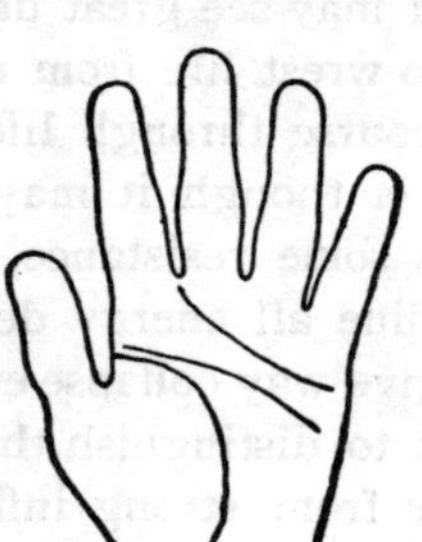

NO. 178

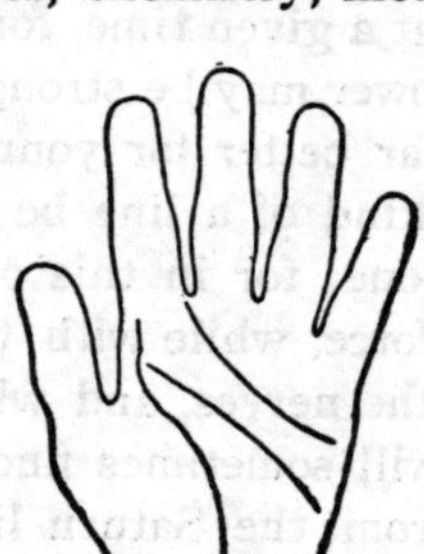

NO. 179

farming, mining, or is greedy for money, according to which phalanx of the Saturn finger rules. If he be an Apollonian, he is ambitious for success and fame as an artist, as a money maker, or as one who makes a display in the world, according to which phalanx of the finger rules. If he be a Mercurian, he is ambitious as an orator, a scientist, or in money matters, according to the ruling phalanx of this finger. The same reasoning applies to the other Mounts. In all cases this subject will be extremely proud. It is seldom that any other source is seen for the Life line than that shown in 178, and if any other combination is encountered it must be reasoned out from the qualities belonging to that part of the hand from which the line rises. In its course through the hand the Life line varies little, the principal deflections being when the line runs close to the thumb (180), in which case it reduces the size of the Mount of Venus, thus checking the operation of that Mount, and the subject is cold, unsympathetic, lacks sexual desire and attraction for or to the opposite sex. This is a most important marking when you desire to estimate the probability of a fruitful marriage, for the less Venusian sexual desire present, the less likely is the subject to have children. It shows one who repels advances from the opposite sex instead of courting them, and for such reasons this line was used by the older palmists as an indication of barrenness. It may for the above reasons produce this condition, but it is not *per se* an indication of sterility.

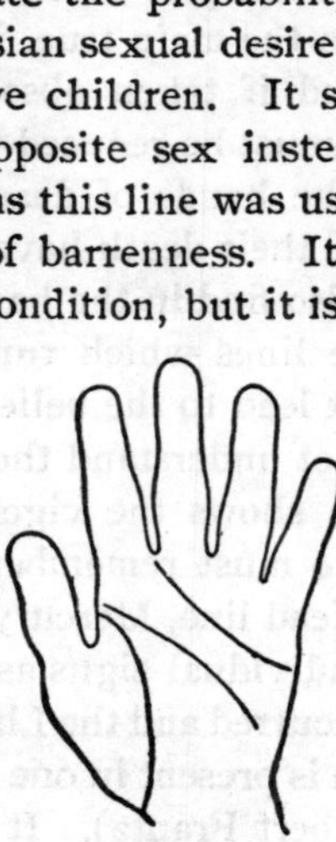

NO. 180

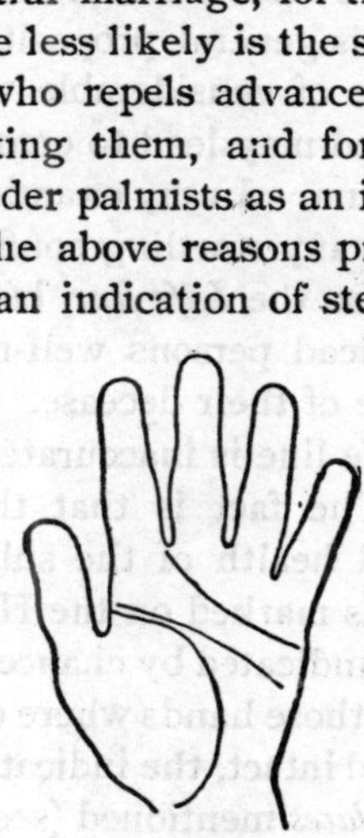

NO. 181

This restriction of the Life line is also an indication of a diminished probability for long life, as it shows an abnormal dryness in the subject, and such conditions do not show the health and vigor that are present in subjects full of desire and warmth. Coldness indicates nearness to death, either of the physical body, or, as in this case, of some necessary emotion. When the line sweeps wide into the palm (181) it increases the boundary and scope of the Mount of Venus. All things which increase the size of the Mount increase its powers and effectiveness. This subject will be ardent, full of desire and warmth, passionate, generous, sympathetic, and will attract others. He will also be strongly attracted, will marry early, and in ninety-nine per cent. of cases the union will be fruitful. This comes from the converse of the reasoning applied to the restricted line. This converging line also indicates long life and a strong vitality and constitution. It is the presence of warmth as opposed to cold.

As a general proposition, the longer the line of Life, the longer will be the life of the subject, and the shorter the line, the shorter will it be. Experience has proven, however, that this general proposition, while in the main true, is still capable of considerable variation, and if taken absolutely as stated may lead to error, and this must be reduced to the minimum. In my examinations of the hands of dead persons, many startling confirmations of their death have been found on the *Life line*, but you will also find in the hands of other dead persons well-marked Life lines which run past the age of their decease. This might lead to the belief that the Life line is inaccurate if we did not understand the matter. The fact is that the Life line shows the vigor and natural health of the subject, but we must remember that death is marked on the Heart line, Head line, Mercury line, and is indicated by chance lines and individual signs as well, and in those hands where death has occurred and the Life line is found intact, the indication of death is present in one of the *other places* mentioned (see hand of Albert Frantz). It is because severe illnesses and death have been looked for on the *Life line* only, that so little proficiency has been attained in palm-reading. The Life line has been expected to perform a greater duty than it was able to do, and received the blame for ill-success that belonged to the practitioner alone. In a study of the hands of those who have died from disease, accident, violence, hanging, or electrocution, these premises have been absolutely verified, for the indications of death were in each hand, if only sought in the proper place. Sometimes that place was in the Life line, sometimes in other lines. This matter I desire to make very clear at this point, for it will prevent your falling into the same mistakes which have overtaken others. When the line is found strong, good, and *long*, we may safely assume that the strong constitution will uphold that life *in its natural course* until old age is reached. The shorter the line, the shorter is the period that this vitality will remain in full operation and the sooner will the subject have to depend upon a careful handling of his forces to ensure the continuance of life. The two hands are most necessary in the examination of the Life line, for a naturally strong constitution shown by a long, deep line in the left hand may be found ruined in the right hand by a chained line. You can, in every case, read the natural condition correctly from the left hand and the present state from the right. These changes will be shown by the character of the line. You will often encounter a short Life line in one hand and a long one in the other; if the *longer* line occur in the right hand, this must be read as prolonging of life and strengthening of constitution; if the *shorter* is in the right hand, it must be read as the shortening of the life. Nowhere is it necessary to use both hands more continually than in examinations of the Life line. In all hands where good, long Life lines are seen, feel sure that the natural vigor will last a long time, and in all hands where a short line is seen, there is a danger point indicated for that subject at the termination of the short line, and this cannot with safety be ignored by him.

The character of the line is most important, for from it you read the muscular strength, robustness, and vigor of your subject. If the line be deep and well cut, the Current is coursing in a good supply through a deep channel, and your subject is strong, vigorous, full of vitality, will resist disease, and have few illnesses. These strong lines are found most often on phlegmatic persons, for these subjects live on muscular strength, not nervous energy. So the deepest lines are in the hands having the least sensitive nerves, and consequently the fewest lines. The lives of these subjects are more even, for they worry little and are not burdened with delicacy and poor health. They are capable of great exertion physically.

In connection with consistency of the hands the deep-cut Life line is important to note. If the line be shallow and broad or chained, the subject, even with elastic consistency, will not possess the energy of one with a deep line. The subject with a deep Life line has more ability to throw off worry and remain calm in moments of excitement. He is endowed with vigor of constitution, is filled with self-confidence, and inspires it in others. He is intense in everything he does, work and play alike. If a Life line be deep and long it will show that the vitality and robustness continues during the entire life, but most Life lines become thin at the lower end, when the vitality naturally wanes. Vigor, strength, health, ardor, self-confidence, intensity, and energy sum up the attributes of the deep-cut Life line, and this line will affect all of the types. The strength and vigor will increase the Jupiterian propensities to "eat, drink, and be merry," and from this Life line and the Jupiterian type we get many drunkards. This is one of the distinguishing combinations which tells of danger in this direction. If the third phalanx of Jupiter be very full and the color of hand and line red, your subject is likely one who has already indulged heavily. He has, however, only the illnesses which are produced by excess, as his strong Life line shows, and he can indulge in a good deal of dissipation before it begins to impair his vitality. This subject lives a life free from disease and generally drops with apoplexy. The same danger is present with a strong Martian type, especially with red color and red hair. The deep Life line makes the Apollonian a strong, healthy fellow, one to make his way through the world with ease. The Venusian is intensely passionate, and so strong in health and vitality that the exercise of natural Venusian passions is much increased. In all cases it is the addition of good health and great vitality to the type, and with this idea in mind you can reason out the various combinations. A narrow and thin line indicates less vitality, less robustness, less resistance to illness, and greater liability of the subject to be overcome by various troubles of health. The thin line does not mean that the subject is necessarily delicate or sickly, but it shows that he cannot endure as much hardship, exposure, or resist disease as well as a subject with a deep Life line. In all character of Life lines observe the proportion to the other lines. If the Life line be deep and all other lines thin or nervous, the subject will go through life with less worry and fewer nervous spells. If the Life line be thin and all other lines deep and well cut, the subject will be continually overstrained and health will surely suffer, for the thin Life line is not of sufficient size to carry the amount of Current which is flowing through the hand. The result of such a combination will be that the health will give way at some point in the line. The thin Life line is not distinctly a nervous line, yet the subject with such a line will be more nervous than one with a deep line. He will be apprehensive of coming evils, he seems instinctively to feel that the tension on health is great, and he fears the day when it will be overstrained. In choosing persons to go through great privations, such as explorers and prospectors, select those with deep and well-cut Life lines, not subjects with thin lines. The thin Life line is summed up when we say that it indicates a lack of robust, muscular vitality and great endurance, and subjects who have such a marking should never go beyond their strength. For a Jupiterian and a Martian this thin line will reduce the tendencies to excess. They will not have the strong impelling force of great vitality to urge them, consequently such subjects do not stand in danger from apoplexy and blood disorders resulting from dissipation, but they suffer from nervous disorders. The Apollonian will run on a lower schedule of speed, and the Venusian will not be impelled toward as great physical gratifications. As strong vitality urges and feeds the desire of all types, so the thin Life line, indicating lack of robustness, minimizes and reduces the operation of every type, and makes each milder. These subjects are often lazy, and thin

Life lines must be noted even with elastic consistency, for sometimes a lack of energy is accounted for by a lack of physical vigor.

A broad and shallow line (182) shows an utter lack of vitality. There is in this case no power to resist disease, no robustness, no strong constitution, no physical vigor, no muscular power. We find these subjects an easy prey to all kinds of disorders. Their system is in a flabby, weak condition, and furnishes a fertile soil in which bacteria germinate. These subjects have no endurance, no stamina, no confidence in themselves. They have weak constitutions, and lack energy and push. This is because they are not physically strong, and must not be taken as an indication of inherent laziness. They are conscious of a labored effort whenever they undertake physical exertion, and from this kind of a Life line we get the chronic complainers and those who never feel well. These subjects are very dependent ; they lean on friends and relatives, and soon fall into the way of being looked after. They do not often achieve great success, for they have not the strength to breast the tide of competition and the "hustle" of the age. They lack aggression and strength, and consequently must be taken care of or they go under. Such Life lines are an indication of great nervousness, and these subjects are carried purely by their nervous force. Often when necessity forces them to make strong efforts they will work when they feel that they can hardly put one foot in front of the other. Only positions where the work is purely routine, easy, and does not require much responsibility are suited to subjects with such Life lines. When they are forced into vocations requiring greater physical exertion and the shouldering of responsibilities they do not hold out a great while. Such a Life line on a flabby hand indicates the extreme of laziness. Even an elastic consistency cannot overcome the lack of vital strength and energy of a broad and shallow Life line.

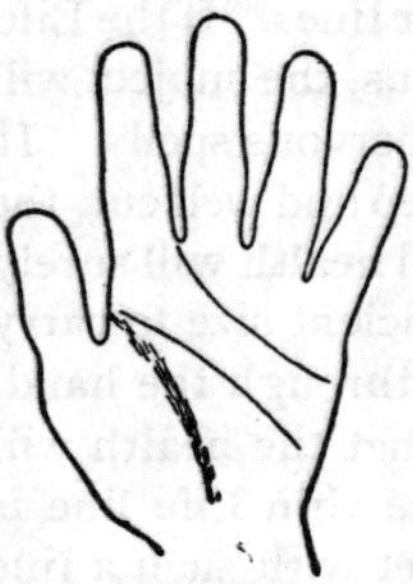

NO. 182

Spatulate tips will be only mentally active with this line; the skill these splendid tips give to a subject in all kinds of sports and games, or in the battle of life, will be only a shadow if accompanied by such a line, for all the type qualities will be lessened in their force and achievement. The Jupiterian will have no strength for excess, the Martian will be too weak to fight. Venusians will lack physical sexual power, no matter how much the thought of sexual relations may attract them. Children are seldom born to or from such subjects. There are many variations in this line; some are very broad and very shallow, and show that the Current has no deep channel through which to flow. Other lines will only approach such a condition. Estimate the intensity of any line by its degree of breadth and shallowness. Note both hands. If the Life line be good in the left hand and broad and shallow in the right, the weak constitution is growing on the subject. If the marking be reversed, the weak constitution is growing stronger.

Note the proportion of the lines. If the Life line alone be broad and shallow, and the other lines are good, the constitution cannot carry its share of the life's effort, and such a subject will be unsuccessful, sickly, despondent, and miserable. With this line study the Mount of Saturn carefully; if it be large or gives in any way a large share of Saturnian quality to the subject, he will be melancholy, gloomy, and wretched. Such subjects commit suicide more frequently than any other. If the lower third of the Mount of Moon in a woman's hand shows female weakness the subject will be much more strongly impelled toward self-destruction. With such a line at once locate the type of your subject and hunt for health defects, either of his primary type or of the secondary or tertiary types, whose qualities will be supplementary; or health defects which may be shown on any other part of the hand. Chance lines will often point you to these defects. No subject with such markings should marry, for it will turn the home into a hospital. Sometimes people are found who are strong enough to make them willing to spend a life in nursing and humoring whims, but these cases are few.

Parents are the safest reliance for such subjects. The Life line running like a ladder (183) has the same general effect as the broad and shallow line. The health will be very unstable and intermittent with this line, and not only is the subject delicate, but he has repeated illnesses, all of more than ordinary severity. When the Life line is composed of several fine lines close together (184), instead of a single deep line, it shows an intensely nervous state of health, great delicacy, and a liability to general debility. All of these lines reduce the vigor of every type, diminish their strength, and render them less likely to be pushing, active persons. Examine the Mounts to locate the health defects present, which will be exaggerated with these poor Life lines. The very thing that is causing your subject to be delicate, and which shows through the poor Life line, is some one of the health defects of the types. You need have no trouble in locating the source of the difficulty. A chained Life line (185) is one which shows great obstruction of the life Current, and the subject with this line will be delicate

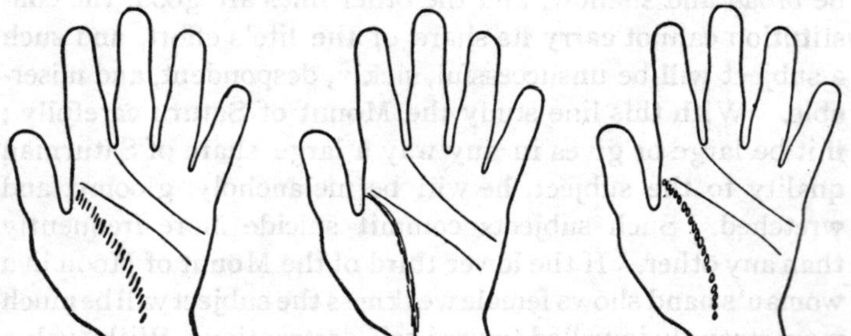

NO. 183 NO. 184 NO. 185

and suffer repeated annoying illnesses. If the chaining run through the entire course of the line, this poor condition of health will be always present, but if it cover only a part of the line, the delicacy will only extend over the part of the life covered by the chain. The chained line is an aggravated addition of delicacy to the broad and shallow line. Conceive the Life Current bumping over the many rocks and shoals in the channel of a badly chained Life line, and you can figure something of the miserable health such a line indicates.

The character of the Life line as we have considered it above is a study of the line in general. The application of these general characteristics must be made in detail to the line from its source to termination. It is by such a method of procedure that we are able to locate from the line the

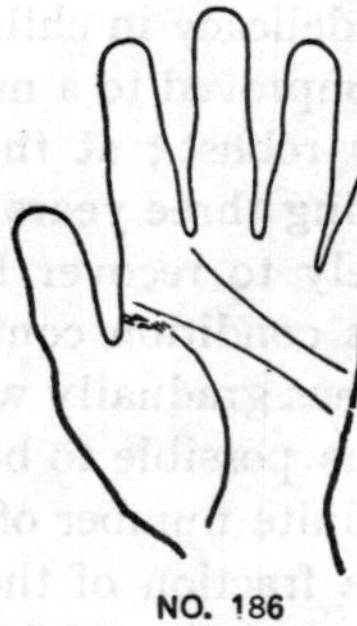

NO. 186

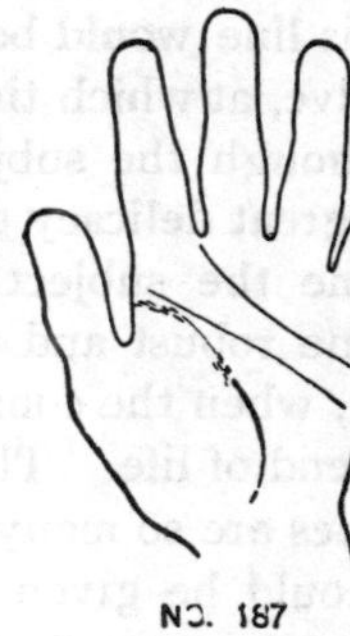

NO. 187

periods of ill-health or delicacy and to read at what ages they occur. It is from the character of the line that we read *constitutional* tendencies to disease or debility, and it is to the signs and chance lines that we look for indications of acute attacks of fever or other diseases which come upon the subject suddenly and not as a result of constitutional deficiency. With nearly every Life line we find the first years chained, or poorly marked in some way (186). This shows the period of life covered by infantile diseases. If this beginning of the line is bad for a long distance, the child did not pass the danger point until late. If this bad beginning runs only a short distance, the period of childish delicacy was soon over. After this period, if the line become deep and well cut, and continue so to its end, the subject will have a strong constitution which asserts itself as soon as the delicacy of infancy is passed, and continues as long as the subject lives. If, after the delicacy natural to the early years, the line be thin and continue so to the end, the subject has not a vigorous constitution to start with, and is never robust. If after the childish delicacy the line continue chained, broad, and shallow, or otherwise poorly marked, the subject will never be strong during life, but will always have a weak constitution. There are periods in almost every one's life when he is stronger than at others. Even a weak constitution will have times of revival. This will be shown by an uneven line in which the combinations of the character of the line may vary infinitely. We may find a line marked like 187. This line would be read : great delicacy in childhood up to twelve, at which time the health improved to a marked degree, though the subject was never robust ; at thirty a period of great delicacy developed, lasting three years, after which time the subject seemed entirely to recover health and become robust and vigorous ; this condition continues until fifty, when the constitution becomes gradually weaker until the end of life. The combinations possible to be seen in Life lines are so many that an indefinite number of illustrations could be given, and yet not a fraction of the possibilities be shown. By handling every variation of the line, however, according to the general rules governing the different characters of lines, and by following the method of reading as given in 187, you can correctly decipher every line. Back of all of these delicacies of constitution there are causes which produce them, and these causes are the health defects of the types, which in most cases are chronic ailments. Having discovered that your subject has a weak constitution, endeavor to discover what has made it weak. In this examination the type of the subject will aid, for it will tell to what he is predisposed. After you have located his type or combination of types, look at the primary Mount for grilles, cross-bars, crosses, or any marking which will enable you to locate a health defect of the type. If one be seen, go over the list and look at nails, color, Mercury line, and from some of these you will be able to locate which one of his type health defects has undermined the constitution. With this information you can tell him not only that he is constitutionally weak, but what is the cause. If you see no health defect of his primary Mount, look to the second, and tertiary, and all the other Mounts for health defects. It is written somewhere, if only looked for in the right place. Sometimes a chance line will point from the delicacy on the Life line to the cause producing it, and generally it will be found on one of the Mounts. The individual signs, or as we have called some of them, "defects," in the line will locate specific points when illnesses occurred or will occur. These defects are cross-bars cutting the line, islands, dots, breaks, and splits.

All lines which cut across the Life line interrupt or cut the Current, and at the time the cutting occurs they produce a defective operation which in the case of the Life line is one of health. In some cases, especially with very nervous persons, the Life line is continually cut by little lines which are fine and do not cut the Life line in two (188). These lines show innumerable worries, the result of an intensely nervous condition, and the subject is prone to numerous small illnesses which have kept him in a continual state of depression or of ill-health. If these cross-bars be fine, the illnesses have not been serious but annoying, and there

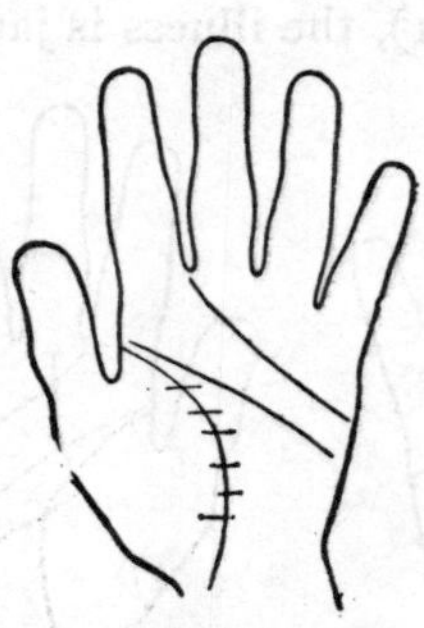

NO. 188

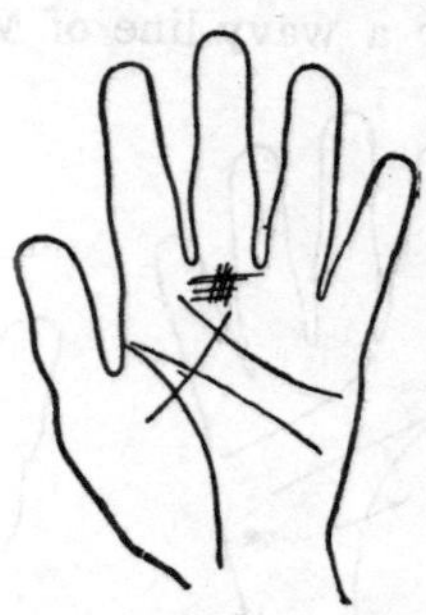

NO. 189

have been as many as there are bars cutting the Life line. If these bars be deep and cut the Life line, there have been severe illnesses. If they be red the illness has been by fever. It is by the depth of these cross-lines that you must estimate their seriousness, and generally they will end somewhere on a Mount or line which will give you the clew to the nature of the trouble. The age at which these illnesses occur can be read from the Life line. If a cross-bar cut the Life line and end in a grille on Saturn (189), the illness will be a health defect of Saturn ; which one you can determine from nails and color. If the cross-bar go to a

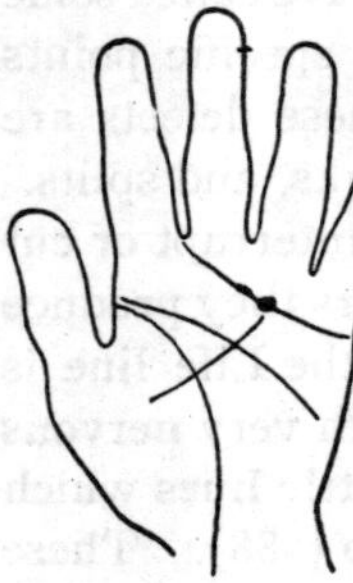
NO. 190

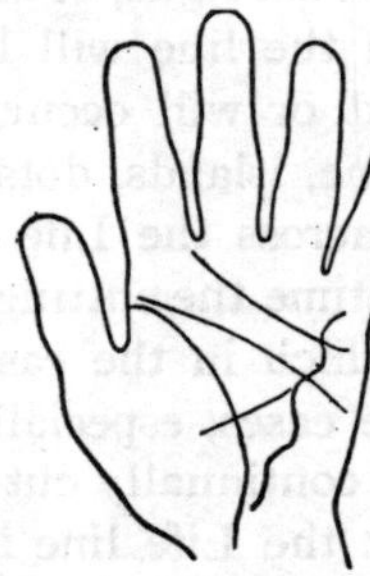
NO. 191

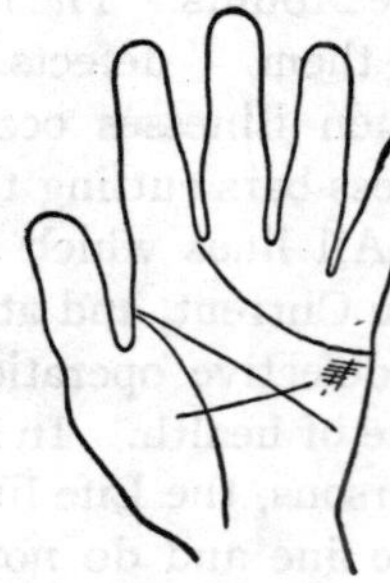
NO. 192

dot, island, or a break in the Heart line under Apollo (190), the illness is heart disease ; the outcome can be read from the Heart line or the termination of the Life line. Nails and color will aid to confirm the diagnosis. If the cross-bar run to a wavy line of Mercury (191), the illness is jaundice

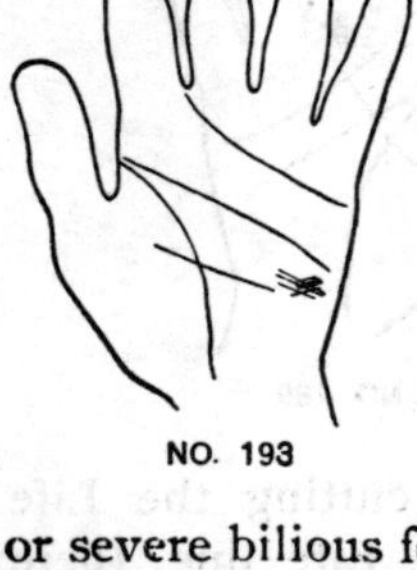
NO. 193

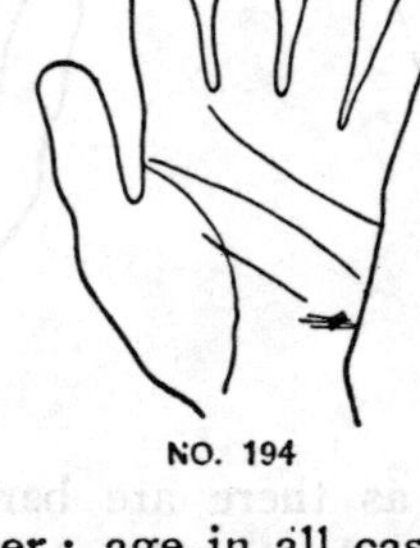
NO. 194

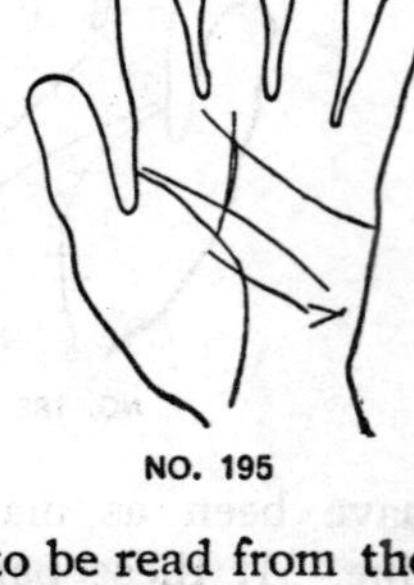
NO. 195

or severe bilious fever ; age in all cases to be read from the point at which the cross-bar cuts the Life line. If the cross-bar run to a grille on Upper Mars (192), with the Martian type strong, the trouble will be either blood disorder or throat and bronchial trouble. Nails will confirm the latter, or islands on the line of Mercury. If the cross-bar go to a grille or cross on the Upper Moon (193), bowel trouble or intestinal inflammation is the difficulty. If the cross-bar run to the middle of the Mount of Moon (194), especially if grilled, gout or rheumatism is the difficulty. This is completely confirmed if a line with an island runs to Saturn (195). This double indication is reliable even though no grille or cross is found on the Mount of Moon. If the

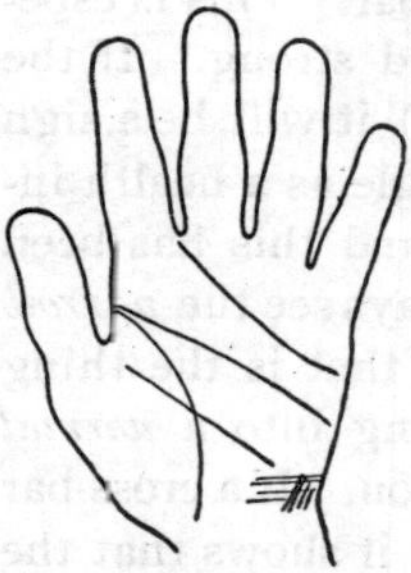

NO. 196

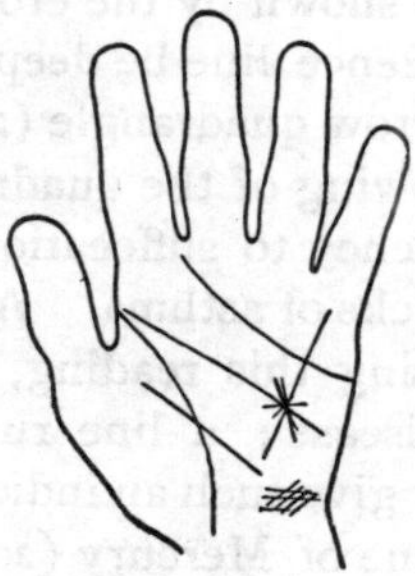

NO. 197

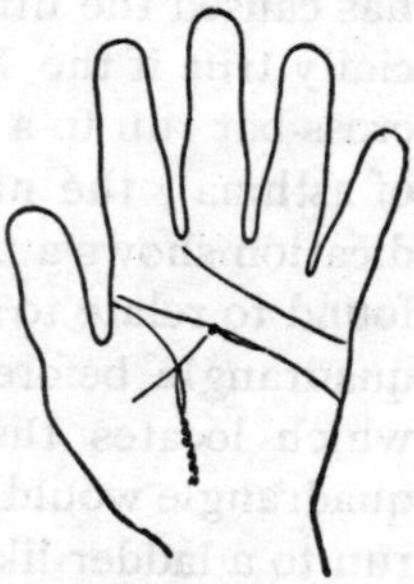

NO. 198

cross-bar goes to a grille, cross-bar, or cross on Lower Moon (196), the trouble is with kidneys or bladder, or from female disease. White color and soft or flabby hands, transparent in appearance, will confirm the former; a star in the Mercury line, especially if at the point where it crosses the line of Head, will confirm the latter (197). If the Life line be good with the above markings, the type defects are natural to the subject, as shown by the grille or other defects on the Mounts. However, the strong Life line shows a vigorous constitution and ability to resist and throw off disease, consequently the chronic trouble only manifests itself in a severe illness, not by a prolonged period of delicacy. If the Life line be thin, chained, or broad and shallow, these cross-bars will be found more frequently, for the constitution is not robust and cannot shake off the type health defects as in the case of the deep line. With all cross-bars note the Life line after it is cut, and it will tell whether recovery is complete or not. If, after a cross-bar cutting a thin Life line and running to an island, dot, cross, or break on the Head line, the Life line has an island and becomes broad and shallow afterward (198), the subject, naturally not robust, has a severe attack of brain trouble which leaves him delicate, and from which he never regains his normal strength. The head is also left delicate as a result of this illness, shown by the island on the Head line. Sometimes the cross-bars cutting the Life line begin on Influence lines on the Mount of Venus (199). In these cases worry concerning the influence has caused the illness shown by the cross-bar. This is especially true if the Influence line be deep and strong. If the cross-bar run to a narrow quadrangle (200), it will be a sign of asthma ; the narrowing of the quadrangle as a health indication shows a tendency to suffocation, and this has been found to relate to attacks of asthma. Always see the *narrow* quadrangle before using this reading, as that is the thing which locates the disease ; a line running into a *normal* quadrangle would not give such an indication. If a cross-bar run to a ladder-like line of Mercury (201), it shows that the illness comes from stomach trouble, as that is the weakness shown by such a Mercury line. If the cross-bar run to an islanded line of Mercury (202), it shows that throat and lung

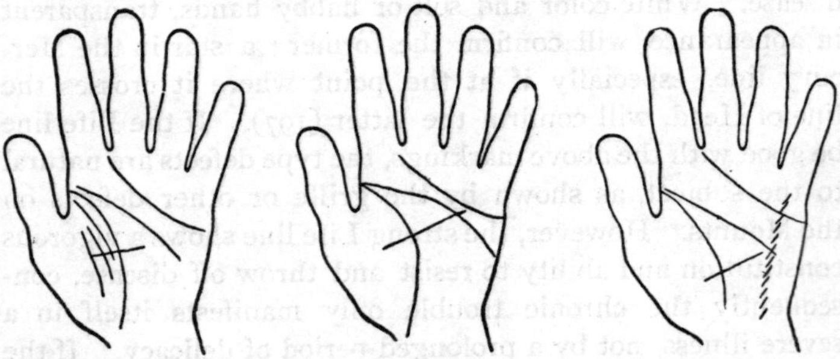

NO. 199 NO. 200 NO. 201

trouble is the difficulty, that being the indication of such a Mercury line.

Islands on the Life line (203) show that the Current is split in two during their continuance, and consequently operates with a diminished force. They are always indications of periods of delicacy. The point where the island begins will mark the commencement of this period of delicacy, and the end of the island will tell when it is over, provided the line is good afterward. If the island be a very small one (204), it will indicate a single illness, and you must proceed by examining Mounts, Head, Heart, Mercury, chance lines,

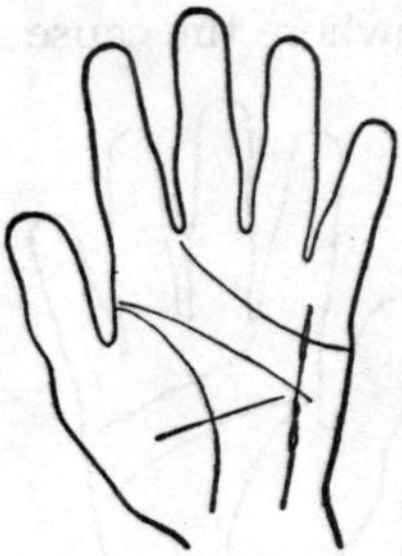

NO. 202

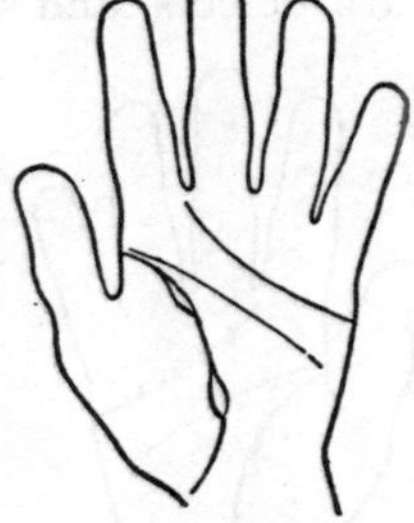

NO. 203

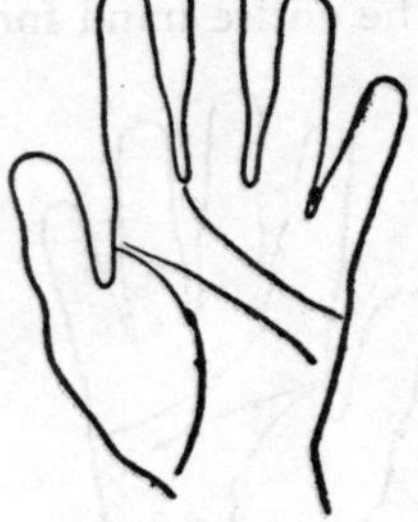

NO. 204

and all other health indications to find out the nature of the illness. If the line contain a series of islands (205), it operates like a chained line, indicating a continuous succession of illnesses and delicacy, and you must locate the cause of trouble from other parts of the hand. If in this case the first

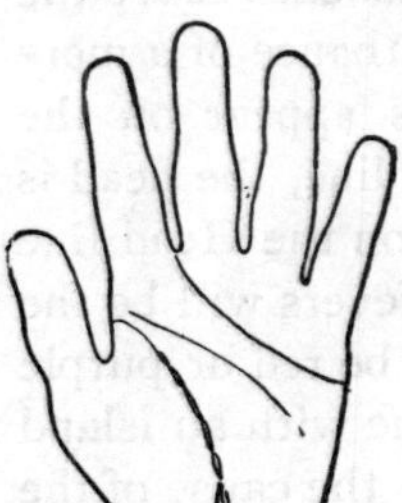

NO. 205

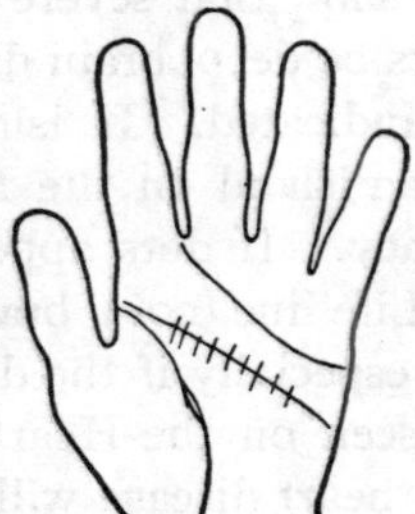

NO. 206

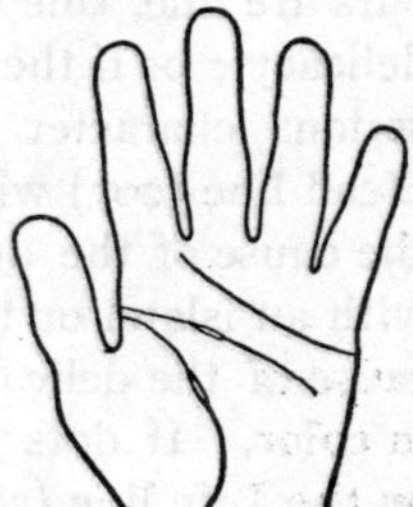

NO. 207

island be small and they grow larger as they continue, the trouble is increasing. If the reverse marking appears, the trouble is diminishing. As most islands appear larger than mere dots, they generally indicate a chronic state of ill-health during their presence rather than acute attacks. Primarily the island indicates delicacy, and gives warning to look out for trouble. Your first duty is to discover what is causing the delicacy. In very many hands islands in the Life line will be seen, and the rest of the hand *filled* with cross-lines. This will indicate great nervousness, and that will likely be the cause of the islands. It will certainly be one cause. On seeing an island, at once begin a search of the entire hand for health defects, and somewhere the cause

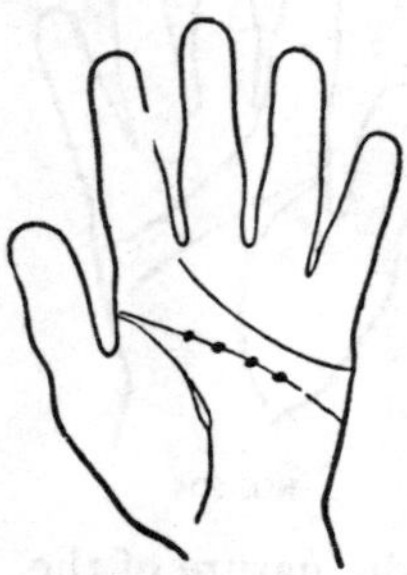

NO. 208

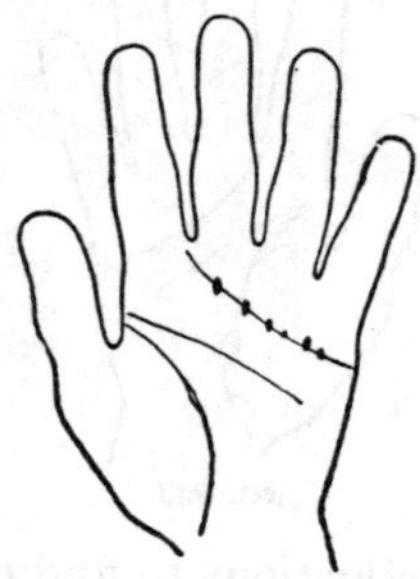

NO. 209

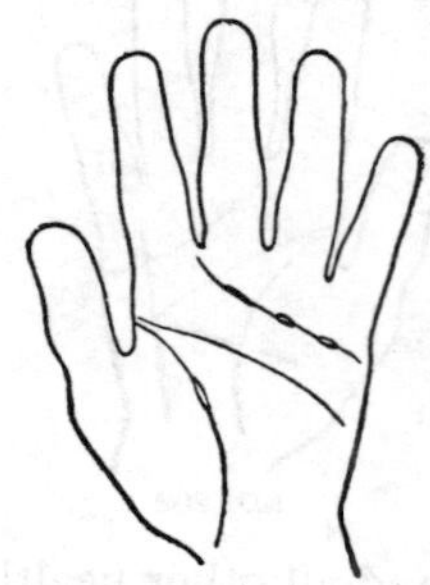

NO. 210

of the island will be found. Sometimes you will find an island in the Life line and the Head line cut by numerous bars (206); if no other health defects be seen and the cutting bars are fine, this will show that severe headaches cause the delicacy; or if the bars be deep, brain disturbance of a more serious character is indicated. If islands appear on the Head line (207) with an island on the Life line, the head is the cause of the delicacy. If dots appear on the Head line with an island on the Life line (208), brain fevers will be the cause of the delicacy, especially if the dots be red or purple in color. If dots be seen on the Heart line with an island on the Life line (209), heart disease will be the cause of the delicacy. Dots on the Heart line will indicate acute attacks, and if many are present these attacks come frequently, producing the continued delicate health shown by the island in the Life line. Nails and color will confirm these indications. If islands appear in the Heart line (210), general heart weakness will cause the delicacy shown by the island in the Life line. Nails and color will confirm this. This will not indicate the acute attacks shown by the dots in the Heart line, but general structural deficiency. If a wavy line of Mercury be seen with an island in the Life line, biliousness will be intense, and will cause the delicacy (211). If the line of Mercury be ladder-like (212), and an island is seen on the Life line, dyspepsia, indigestion, and all forms of stomach trouble will cause the delicacy. Grilles, crosses, cross-bars, and all defective markings on the Mounts will locate the cause of the delicacy as a type defect peculiar to the Mount on which the defect appears. If a dot be seen before the island on the Life line (213), an acute attack will be followed by a period of delicacy ; the nature of the acute trouble to be located from the rest of the hand. Sometimes you will encounter a double set of indications. An island will be seen in the Life line early in life, and some trouble may be shown in the Head line. Later in the Life line another island may appear, and on the Heart line islands may be seen, or a wavy Mercury line, or defect on a Mount (214). This should be read as two periods of delicacy in the life, one early, and as the defect in the Head line also shows

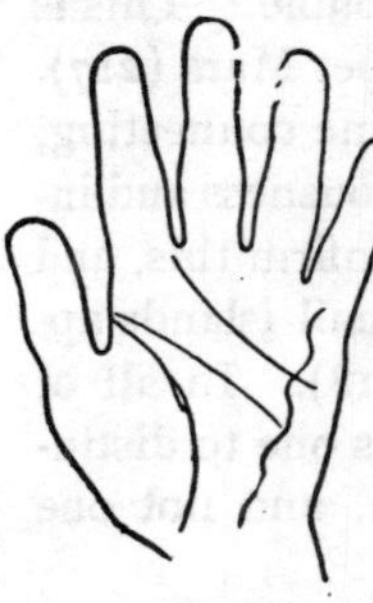

NO. 211

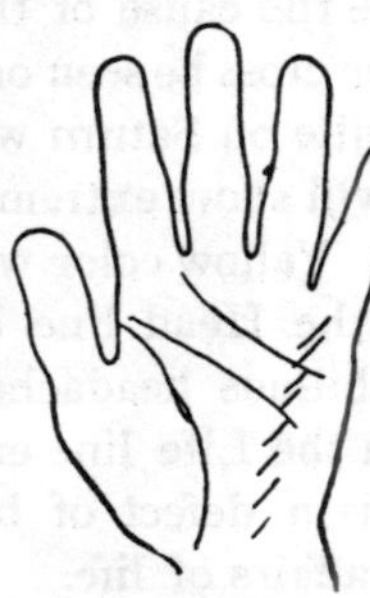

NO. 212

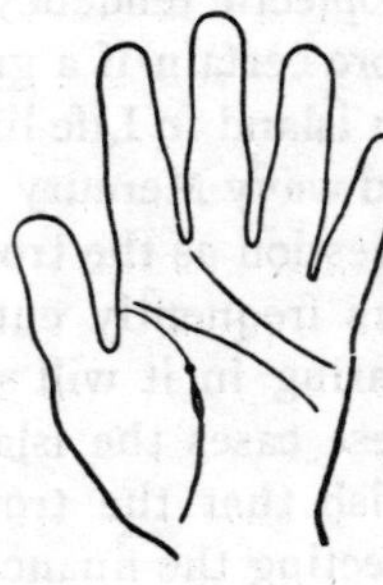

NO. 213

early in that line, this will be the cause of the first island in the Life line. The second island shows a second period of delicacy, and the trouble in the Heart line will explain it. The number of islands seen in the Life line will indicate the number of periods of delicacy in the life of the subject, but each one may be caused by a different disease, and these can be found by following the method employed in 214. An island in the Life line, with an islanded line running to it from Saturn, and a second line from middle third of Moon, will locate gout or rheumatism as the cause of the delicacy (215). An island in the Life line with a grille on Saturn and line connecting it with the island, with dots or islands in the Head line under Saturn, fluted and brittle nails, will locate paralysis as the trouble (216). An island in the Life line, with a line connecting it with a red or purple dot on Jupiter, color of hand and lines red, and thin Head line, will show an

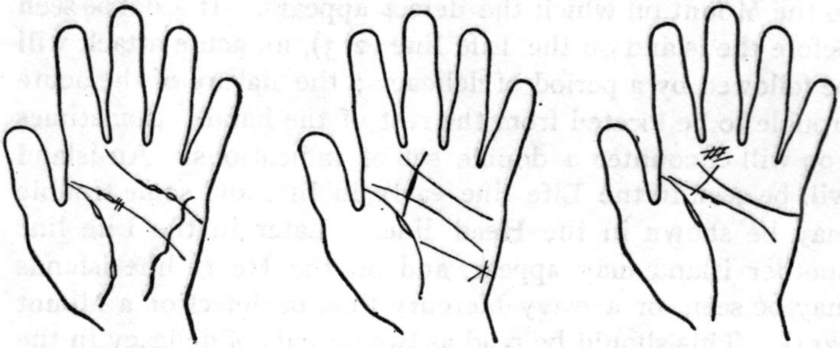

NO. 214 NO. 215 NO. 216

apoplectic tendency to be the cause of the trouble. This is more certain if a grille or cross be seen on Upper Mars (217). An island in Life line, grille on Saturn with line connecting, and wavy Mercury line will show extreme biliousness and indigestion as the trouble. Yellow color will confirm this, and bars frequently cutting the Head line or small islands appearing in it will show bilious headaches (218). In all of these cases the island in the Life line enables one to distinguish that the trouble is a defect of health, and not one affecting the finances or affairs of life.

Disease we read from the Life line, financial affairs from the Saturn and Apollo lines. Poor health may affect these matters, but they are not read from the Life line. It is very common to see an island in the Life line of women at ages forty-two to forty-six. This will indicate the age at which their change of life occurs, and the duration of the island will tell you how long it lasts. Whenever an island is seen in this location (219), it should always be read in the hands of women as change of life. The line after this island will tell you how seriously this change affects the subject. If the island be followed by a deep line, the effect is only a delicacy during the period of the change ; if the line become thin, broad and shallow, or chained, the subject never recovers her full strength and vigor afterwards. If with this island

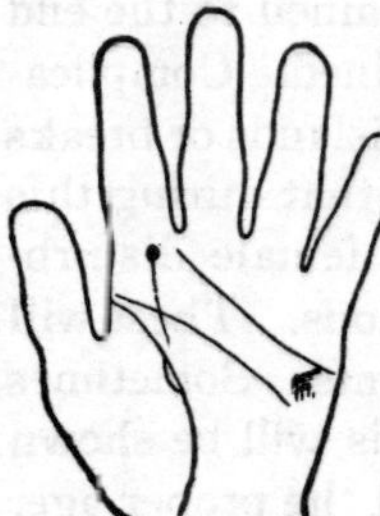

NO. 217

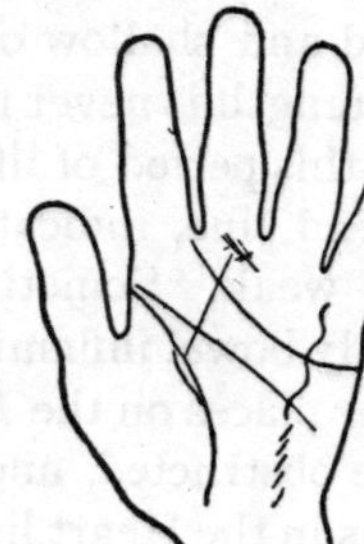

NO. 218

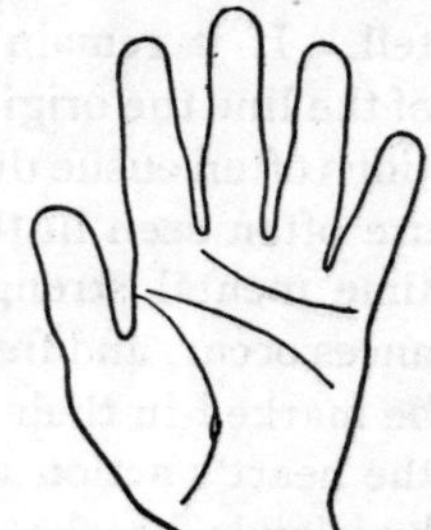

NO. 219

there appears a grille on Lower Moon (220), female weakness will be an added impediment to a successful change. If you read this hand before the change has occurred, it is your duty to advise that the subject take medical treatment in order, as far as possible, to remove this difficulty before the

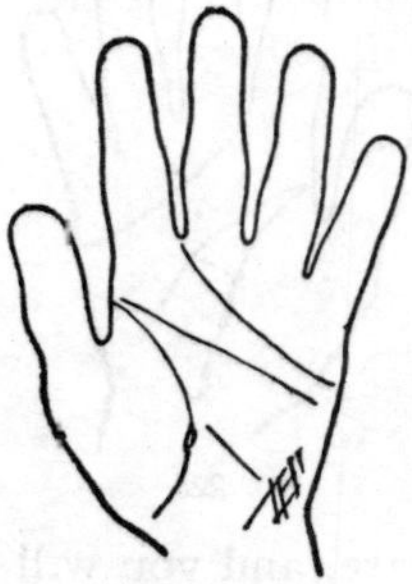

NO. 220

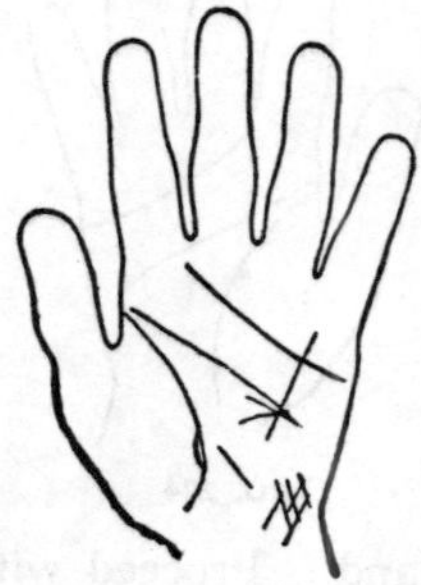

NO. 221

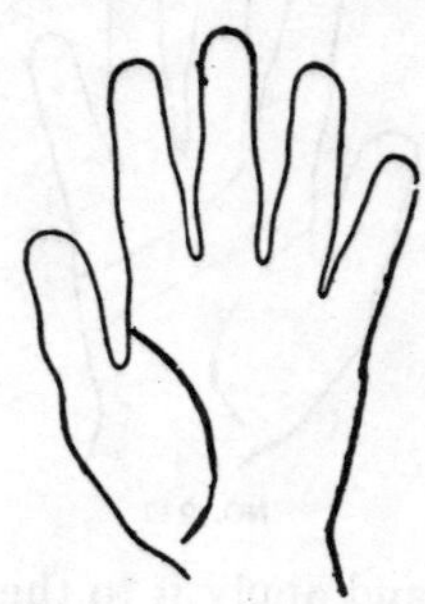

NO. 222

change of life comes on. If, in this indication, a line connects the island and the grille, the indication is more certain, and if a star be seen on the Mercury line at or near the juncture with the line of Head, it is absolutely correct (221). This change of life is shown not only by the island, but by other defective conditions of the Life line at this age. If the line has been deep and strong, and at this age becomes thin (222), it indicates the time and the trouble, but shows that it is less serious. If the line at this age become broad and shallow (223), it shows that the change greatly weakens the constitution, how seriously the remainder of the line will tell. If it remain broad and shallow or chained to the end of the line the original strength is never regained. Complications often ensue during this period of life : islands or breaks are often seen in the Head line, indicating that during this time mental strength is weak. Sometimes female disturbances occur, and frequently bowel inflammations. These will be marked in their proper places on the Mounts. Sometimes the heart's action will be obstructed, and this will be shown by islands, breaks, or dots in the Heart line at the proper age. With the idea in mind that an island in the Life line is a period of delicate health, you will always be warned, and begin the search for its cause. Do not be in a hurry; look the entire hand over, consider everything. This cannot be done hastily. Bring to bear every point relating to health

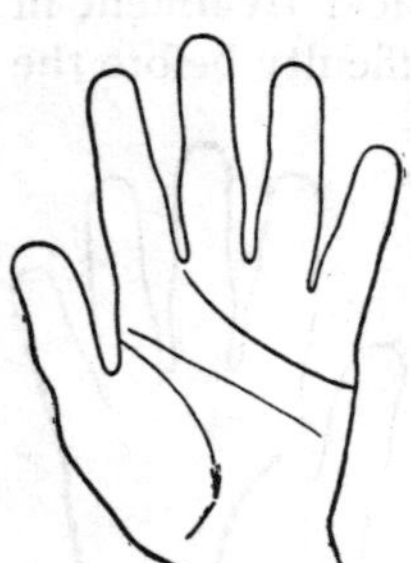

NO. 223

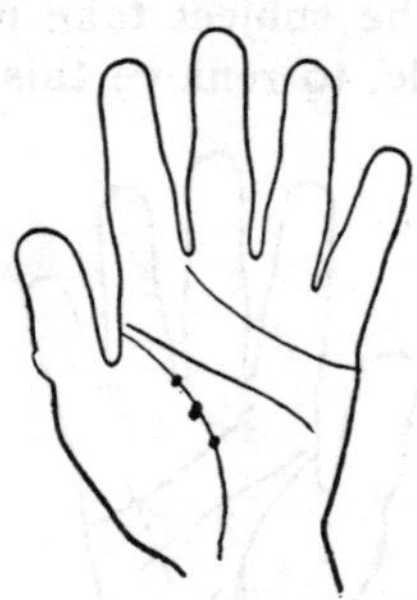

NO. 224

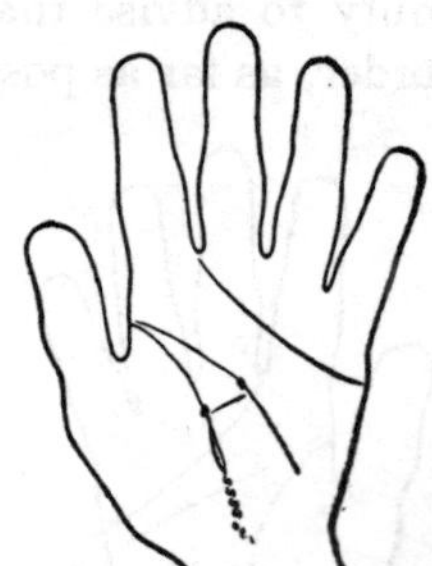

NO. 225

and apply it to the island. Proceed with care, and you will be able to locate the cause and effect of every one.

Dots on the Life line (224) are rare. They are indications of acute illness or of accident. They vary in size from mere pin points, hardly noticeable, to large holes which destroy the line. They are found of all colors, and their importance must be graded by size and color. White dots are the most harmless, and their meaning must be searched for in the hand according to the method of locating disease heretofore explained. Red dots indicate a febrile tendency, and the deeper the color the more accurate is this reading. When of a deep crimson and purplish hue, they portend grave fevers, such as typhoid, typhus, and the like. In all cases they are useful in locating a point of special incident in the life of a subject, and will precede islands, chains, and other

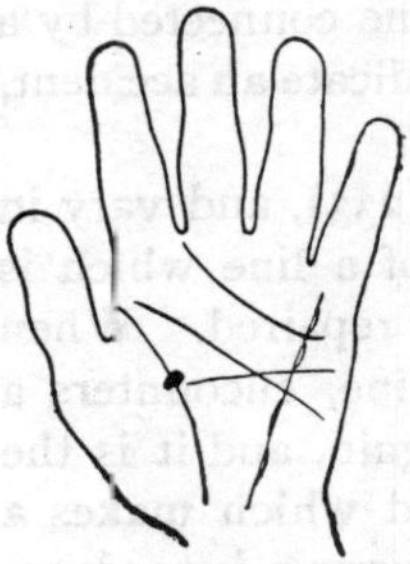

NO. 226

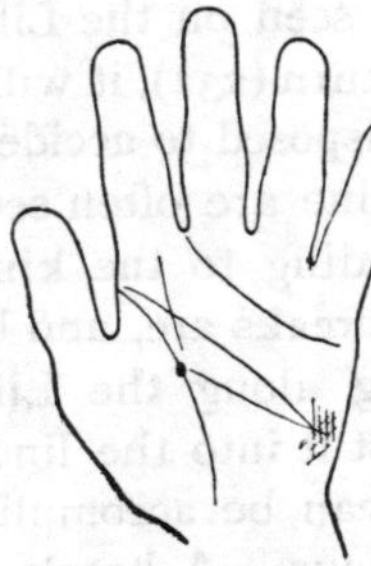

NO. 227

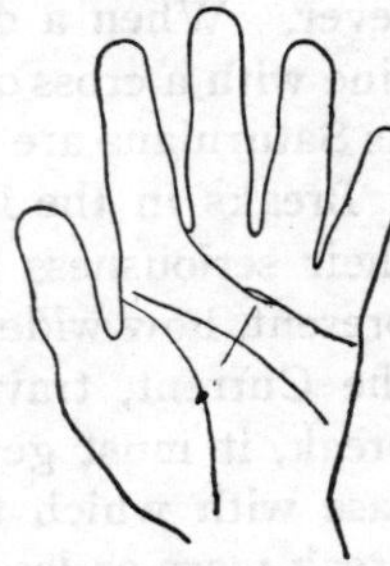

NO. 228

defects, thus showing that the illness recorded was of such severity that the constitution did not again become strong. A dot on Life line followed by an island and a chained line, with a line running to a bar, a dot, a small island, a cross, or a star on the Head line (225), will show that an attack of brain fever undermined the constitution, and complete recovery did not follow. A dot on Life line connected by a line to Upper Mars and an islanded line of Mercury (226) will show that the illness was bronchitis or other throat trouble. A dot on Life line connected by a line to Upper Moon, which has a grille, and a line running to Mount of Jupiter (227), shows the illness to be inflammation of the bowels. A dot on Life line connected by a line with an island, dot, or a cross under Apollo (228) shows the illness to be heart disease. A dot on Life line connected by a line with a dot, a bar, or a cross on a wavy line of Mercury (229) shows the illness to be bilious fever. The dot on the Mercury line indicates the acute attack ; chronic biliousness is shown by the wavy line. A dot on Life line, with cross-bars, a grille, a cross, or a poorly formed star on the Middle of Moon, shows the illness to be gout (230). This is emphasized by a line running from a dot on Saturn. A dot on Life line connected by a line with a grille, cross-bars, a cross, or poorly formed star on Lower Moon (231) shows the attack to be kidney or bladder trouble of an acute nature. If on the Life line a dot be seen which is pronouncedly yellow in color, it will indicate without further confirmations an attack of bilious fever. When a dot is seen on the Life line connected by a line with a cross on Saturn (232), it will indicate an accident, as Saturnians are predisposed to accident.

Breaks in the Life line are often seen (233), and vary in their seriousness according to the kind of a line which is present, how wide the breaks are, and how repaired. When the Current, travelling along the Life line, encounters a break, it must get past it into the line again, and it is the ease with which this can be accomplished which makes a break more or less serious. A break occurring in a deep, strong line is less serious than one which appears in a broad and shallow or chained line. In the deep line the Current is

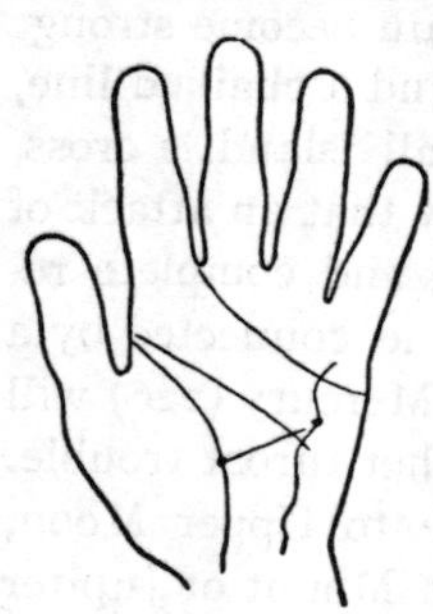

NO. 229

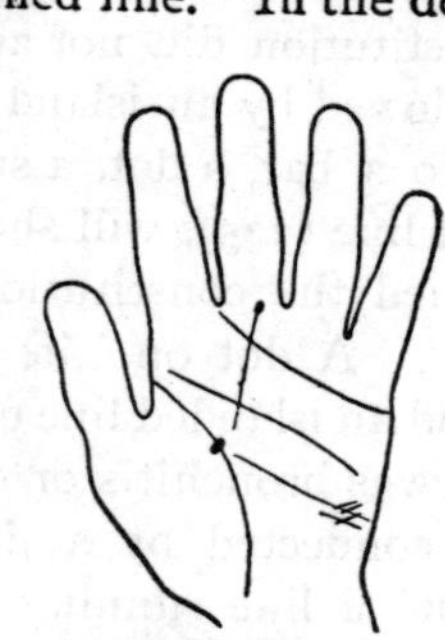

NO. 230

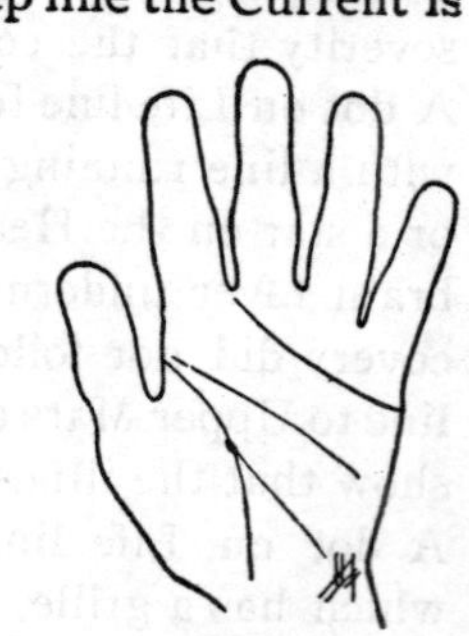

NO. 231

flowing with volume and force at the time it reaches the break, and consequently it has the benefit of its own momentum to carry it past the break and into the line again. I have seen breaks in deep and strong Life lines where the line has subsequently cut its way through the intervening space, forming a good line. With shallow or chained lines, the Current is moving sluggishly when the break occurs, and there is not the momentum to assist in lessening the damage.

All breaks indicate a check or impediment to the health, consequently to the life of the subject, and these impediments come either from illness or accident. The matter of accidents is hard to diagnose, but I follow the rule that in a hand which

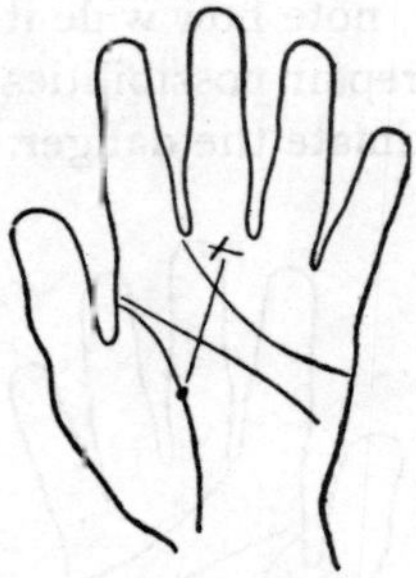

NO. 232

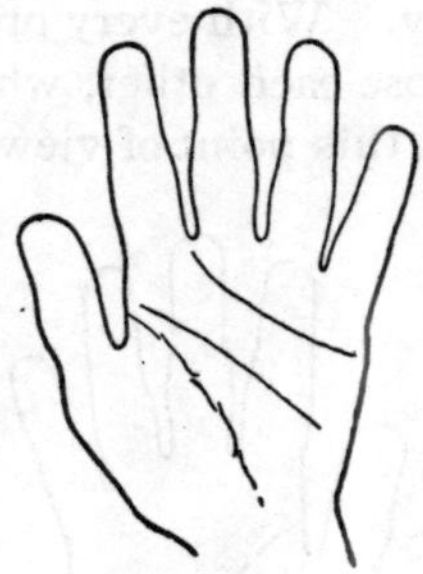

NO. 233

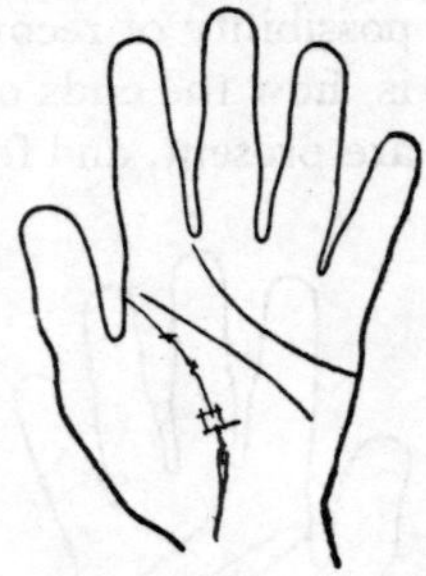

NO. 234

is healthy in every other way, a break in the Life line should be read as an accident. Sickness in such a hand would be shown in some other way than by a break. In a number of hands in which fine Life lines were noted and perfect health otherwise shown, breaks were verified as accidents. There

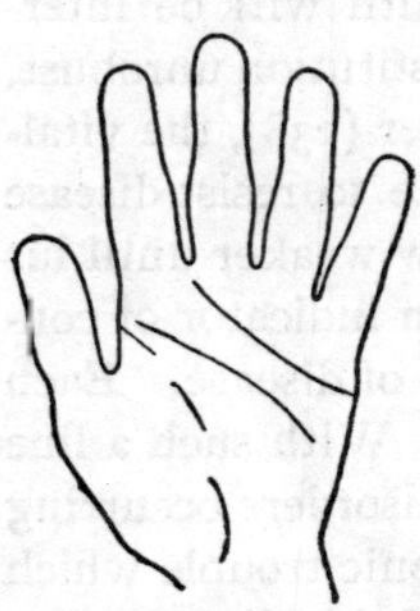

NO. 235

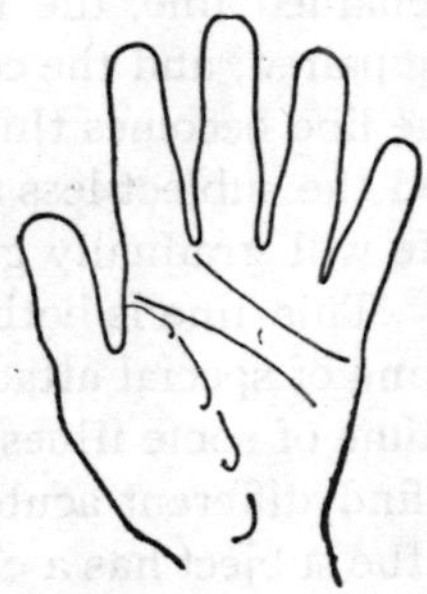

NO. 236

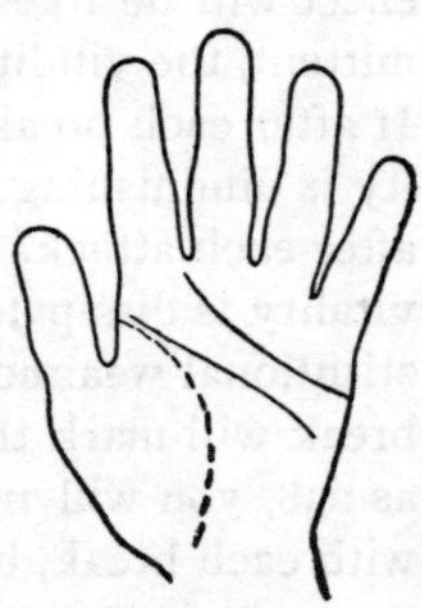

NO. 237

is no question as to their indicating jars to the health whenever seen. Numerous instances are encountered where the cause of the break is easily located by health defects seen on the Mounts, by chance lines, or individual signs. Small breaks which are at once repaired (234) need not be considered as more serious than islands or dots, but wide breaks unrepaired (235) must be considered as a menace to the life. All tendency of the ends of the line to turn back after a break (236) is gravely serious. The wider the separation of the ends and the more the ends hook, the more hopeless is the possibility of recovery. With every break, note how wide it is, how the ends oppose each other, what repair possibilities are present, and from this point of view estimate the danger.

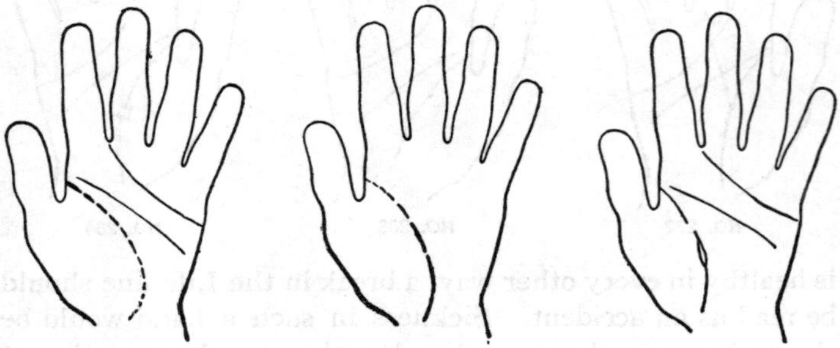

NO. 238 NO. 239 NO. 240

If the line is filled with a series of small breaks (237), the effect will be like a chained line, the health will be intermittent, the vitality impaired, and the constitution unrobust. If after each break the line becomes thinner (238), the vitality is diminishing, and the subject less able to resist disease after each attack. He will gradually grow weaker until his vitality is dissipated. This line is both an indicator of constitutional weakness and of special attacks of disease. Each break will mark the time of some illness. With such a line as 238, you will not find different acute disorders occurring with each break, but the subject has a chronic trouble which recurs at frequent intervals. The nature of this disorder can be located from the Mounts and by other health indications. The line may start thin, and after each break grow deeper (239). In this case after the first few years of life the breaks will not come so close together, and it will show that the subject is gradually overcoming his difficulties.

To diagnose what has occasioned each break in the Life line, the method of procedure is the same as applies to other defects in the line. The Mounts will show defects, chance lines will point to special marks of disease, and in every way the manner of locating the cause of breaks is the same as in the case of islands, dots, and other defects. The character of the line after the break must be noted to determine the extent of damage which has been done. If after a break an island is formed (240), the disease which caused the break creates a period of delicacy, the duration of which is shown by the extent of the island. The same reading will apply if a chained line forms after a break (241). With such a marking as this there will be poor chance of complete recovery. When breaks occur at about fifty years of age (242), with the line growing very thin just before the break, and seeming continually to grow thinner until the break occurs, it shows the gradual waning of vital force until it runs out; that a period of great weakness comes on when there is not enough strength left to resist disease, and an illness recorded by the break occurs. If the line continues after this break it will begin very thin and gradually grow stronger, showing that the health returns by degrees. The breaks in a Life line may

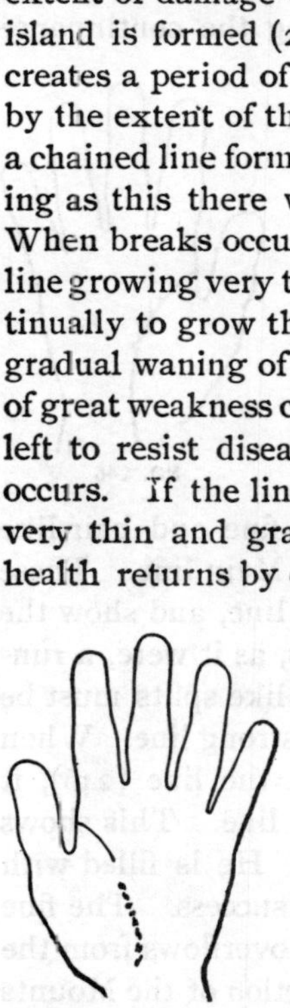

NO. 241

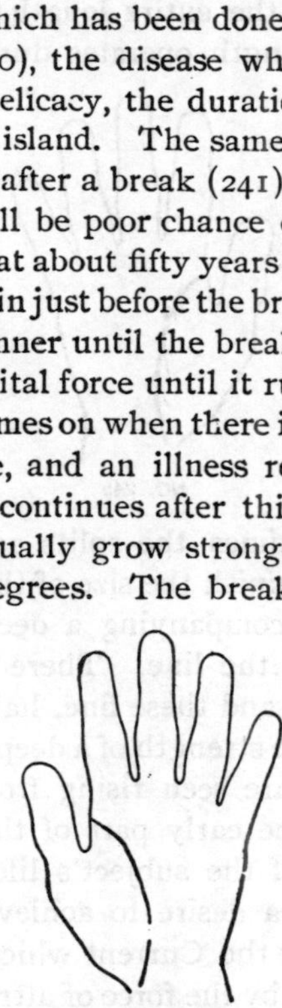

NO. 242

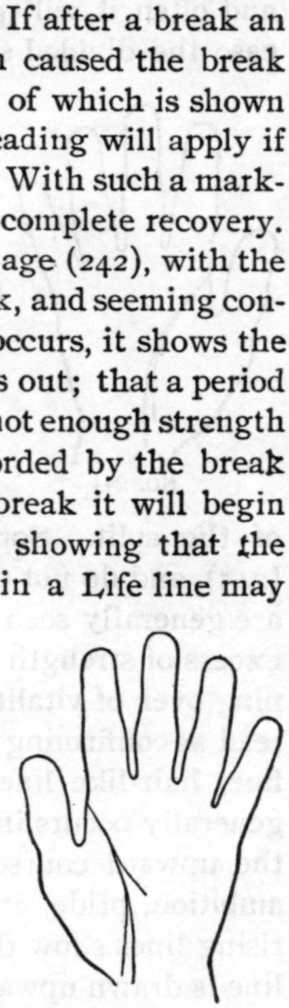

NO. 243

be repaired by overlapping ends of the line, sister lines, squares, and in other ways. These repair signs, in whatever form, will be recognized by their tendency to turn the Current back into the line again, and their repair of the line is complete in proportion as they succeed in doing this. Splits on the Life line (243) divert a portion of the Current from the main channel. Sometimes they only divide it, and the line continues a double line with the splits running close together (244). This reduces the strength of the constitution during the period of the split, and while it may not result in positive delicacy, it will diminish the vitality. Sometimes such a split will extend for only a short space, and often it will go the entire length of the line. In any case the divided strength operates during the continuance

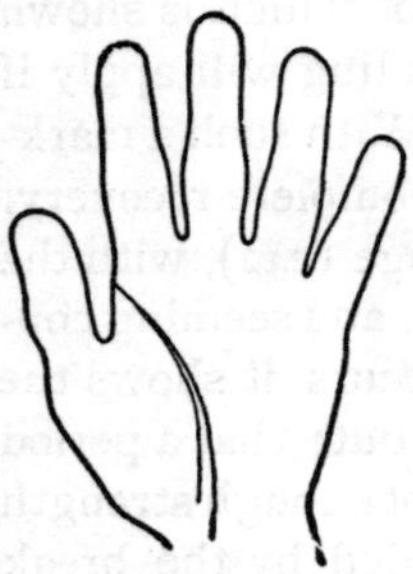

NO. 244

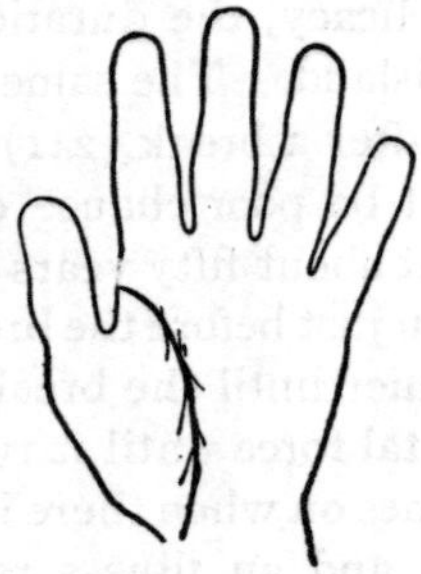

NO. 245

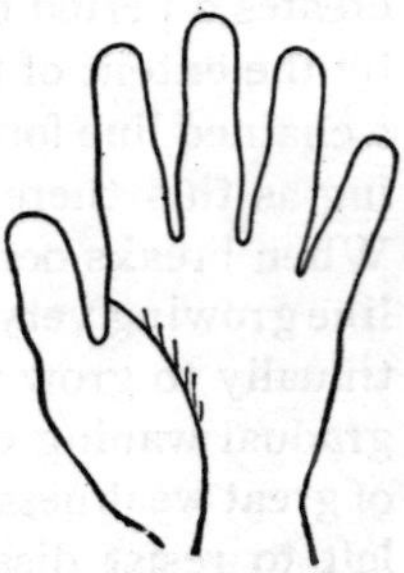

NO. 246

of the split. Sometimes the splits are fine and hair-like (245), and do not diminish the size of the Main line. These are generally seen accompanying a deep line, and show the excess of strength of the line. There is, as it were, a running over of vitality, and these fine, hair-like splits must be read as confirming the strength of a deep, strong line. When fine, hair-like lines are seen rising from the line (246), it generally occurs in the early part of the line. This shows the upward course of the subject's life. He is filled with ambition, pride, and a desire to achieve success. The fine rising lines show that the Current which overflows from the line is drawn upward by the force of attraction of the Mounts under the fingers. The exit of the Current, you remember, is through the fingers of Saturn, Apollo, Mercury, and these rising hair-like lines from the Life line show that the Current is being impelled in its proper direction, with a force strong enough to pull these fine lines upward. The period covered by these rising lines on the Life line is that of the years of greatest power in the life of the subject. He will have his greatest earning capacity and command of his best brain power and strength. During this time he should accomplish the most important part of his life's work. A time will come when the little lines do not rise from the Life line, but fall downward (247). At this time there is no such strength as during the period covered by the rising lines. The Current is not forced upward by the great power of enthusiasm and vital energy, and the life forces, ambition, and the capacity to do, begin to wane from the time of life when these hair lines begin to fall downward. At the point where the rising lines cease to rise and the drooping lines begin (248) is the turning-point in the life of the subject. This point marks the pinnacle of his capabilities, the period of greatest power, the zenith of ability to perform great things, and he will never be able to do afterwards what is possible before this point is reached.

This turning-point in the life was I believe placed before us for our guidance. I have made a great study of this indication, and have verified it in the lives of hundreds of men and women. From it you can tell your client when he must have his house in order and be ready to begin the de-

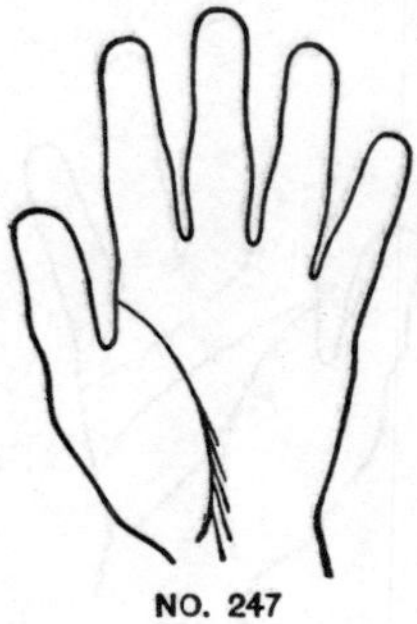

NO. 247

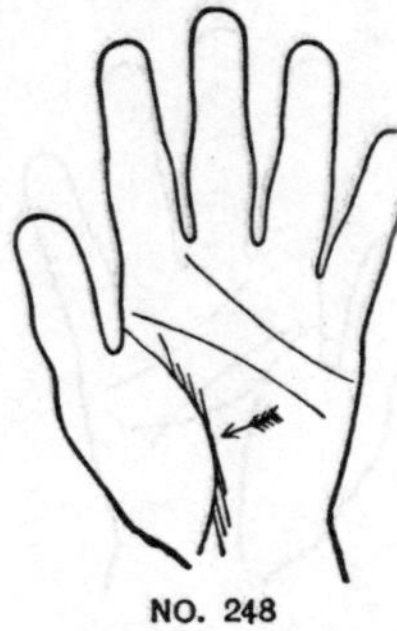

NO. 248

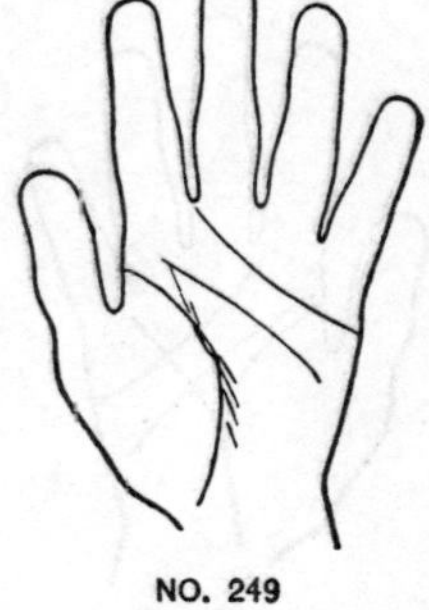

NO. 249

scent of the hill of life. In some hands it is seen early in life, in others later, but whenever it occurs, that year marks the point of greatest power in the subject's life. When seen early in life it is sometimes formed around an island (249), which will show that a delicacy occurring at that time will dissipate the powers so that they will never fully recover. When the turning-point shows at near fifty, it is the natural decline of physical power coming on with age. When rising lines or a single line from the Life line rises to Jupiter (250), it shows the great ambition which leads its possessor constantly to struggle to win. You can tell in which world by

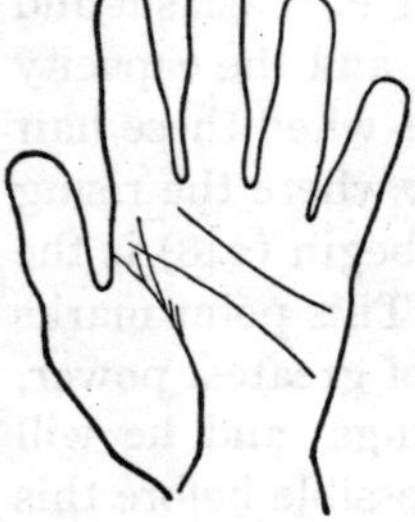

NO. 250

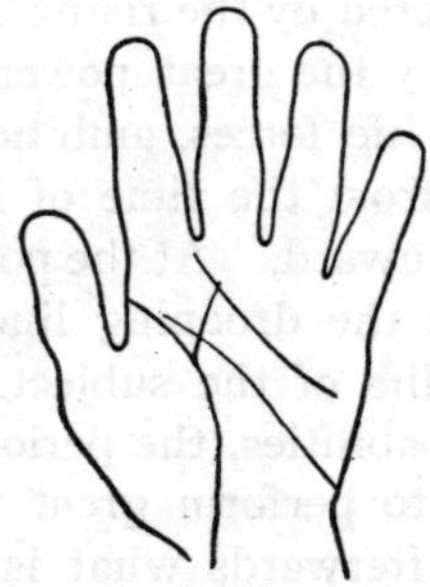

NO. 251

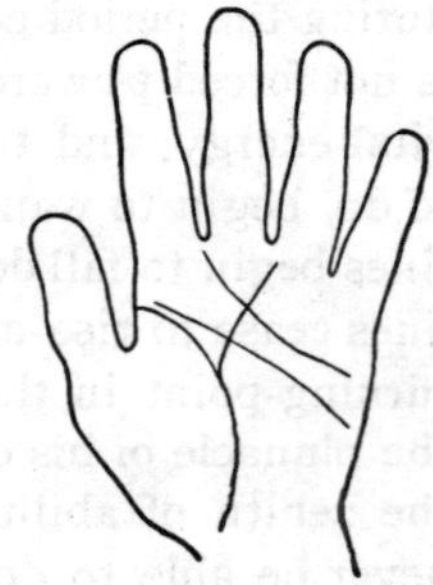

NO. 252

the phalanx of the finger which rules. If a rising line runs to Saturn (251), it will indicate a great desire of the subject to succeed along Saturnian lines. In which world will be indicated by the phalanx of the finger which rules. If a line rises to Apollo (252), the subject will have great desires in

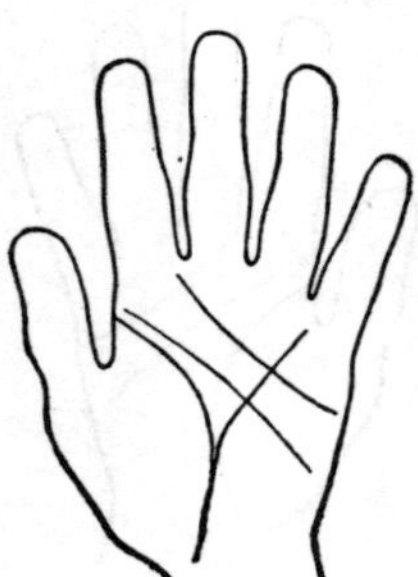

NO. 253

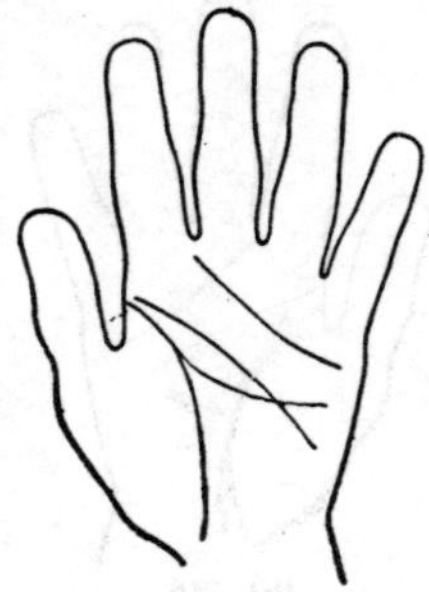

NO. 254

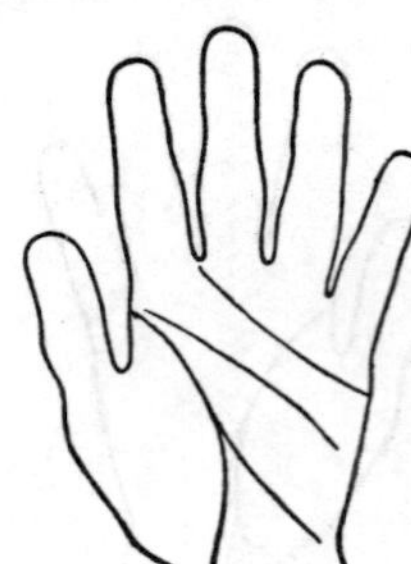

NO. 255

Apollonian directions, the particular world being read from the phalanx of the finger. If a line rises to Mercury (253), the subject will have great desire to succeed in some Mercurian direction, indicated in more detail by the ruling phalanx of finger. This line must not be confused with the line of Mercury. If a line runs from the Life line to Upper

Mars (254), the subject will be strongly ambitious in Martian directions; and Lunar qualities will strongly influence the life if a split line is seen running to the Moon (255). All of these lines must be fine lines rising *off* of the Life line, and not chance lines crossing or cutting the line.

In an estimate of the Life line the termination is most important, for it shows how the life ends. In all of the changes

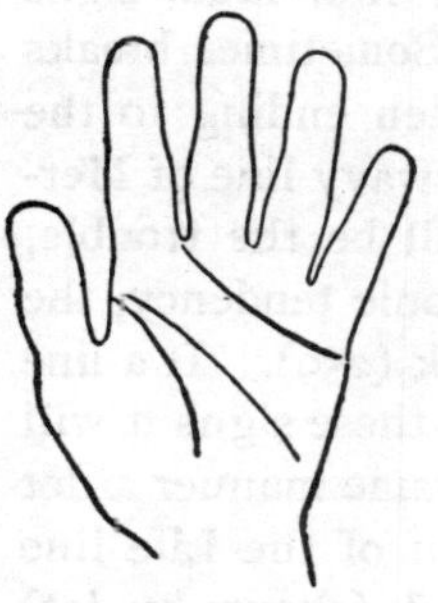

NO. 256

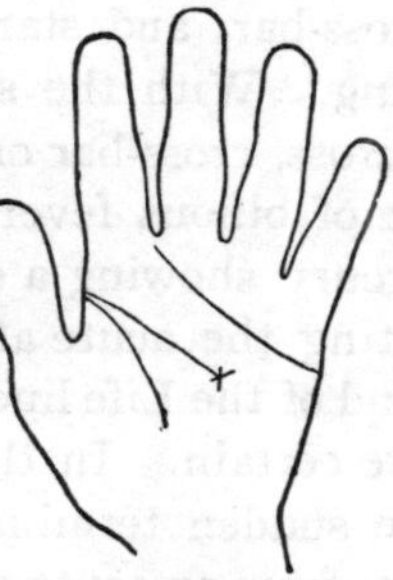

NO. 257

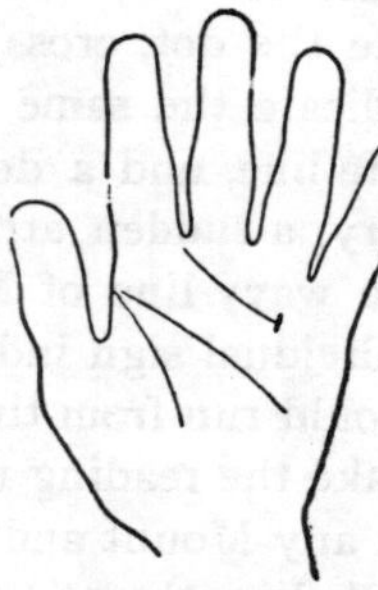

NO. 258

on the line we find that they have shown the strength of the constitution during life, various states of health, strength, delicacy, and numerous diseases. When we come to the *termination* of the line, we learn the outcome of these various conditions. The Life line will be found ending in different hands at all periods of life. It will be found ending in different manners, and that is what we consider under the general heading of "Termination of the line." If a line is deep and strong it may end as strong as is its course through the hand. This line simply stops short, ending in no sign or special marking (256). This indicates that the subject will remain strong till the end of life, will die of no lingering or wasting disease. With such a termination examine the Head line, the Heart line, and study the type of the subject carefully. If a Jupiterian or Martian, it will make his quick ending more certain. While no sign is seen on the Life line, a deep cut or cross, a dot or a star, may be discerned on the Head line corresponding to the age at which the Life line ends, and this will be the sign of the demise (257). In this case the abrupt termination of the Life line will give the clue to a quick end, and the sign on the Head line will tell that some affection of the head will be the cause. In the same manner an impairment of the Heart line by some individual sign, such as a cut, a cross, dot, or star, will show that heart failure will be the end (258). With sudden terminations of the Life line you should not look for chronic diseases but for acute attacks, and these are indicated by individual signs like the dot, cross, cross-bar, and star. Sometimes breaks indicate the same thing. With the sudden ending to the Life line, and a dot, cross, cross-bar on a wavy line of Mercury, a sudden attack of bilious fever will be the trouble, the wavy line of Mercury showing a chronic tendency, the individual sign indicating the acute attack (259). If a line should run from the end of the Life line to these signs it will make the reading more certain. In the same manner a dot on any Mount and the sudden termination of the Life line will show the end to be from an acute attack (shown by dot) of the health defect of the Mount. If a line runs from the

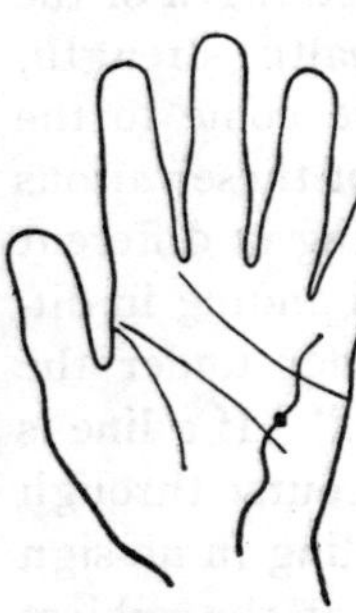

NO. 259

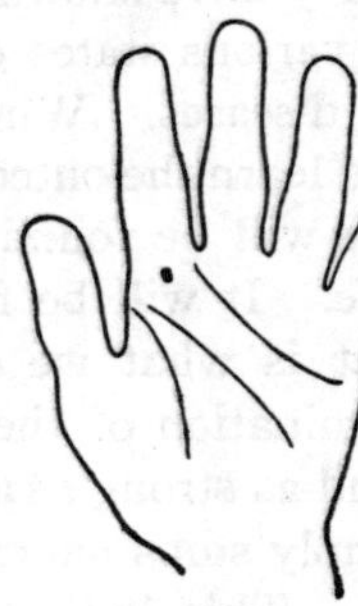

NO. 260

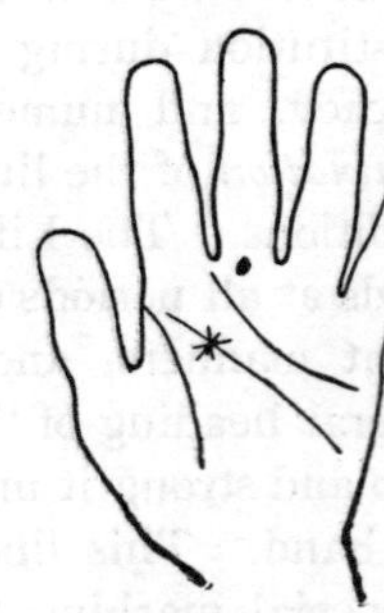

NO. 261

end of Life line to the dot, it will make the indication unmistakable. Thus while the termination of the life may not always be read from the Life line, it is read from the other lines and Mounts. If the Life line end suddenly and a dot is seen on Jupiter (260), apoplexy will be the trouble ; if a dot is seen on Saturn, paralysis, and if in this case a star, cross, or dot is seen on the Head line under Saturn, the reading is absolute (261). All of the other Mounts must be handled in the same way when searching for a sudden termination to life. With each Mount disease the one which would kill quickly is the probable one, and a chronic trouble will not be the cause. When a deep Life line ends abruptly there is always a chance that it may continue. Even though the line be short, it is not as serious as if it ended in a cross, star, tassel,

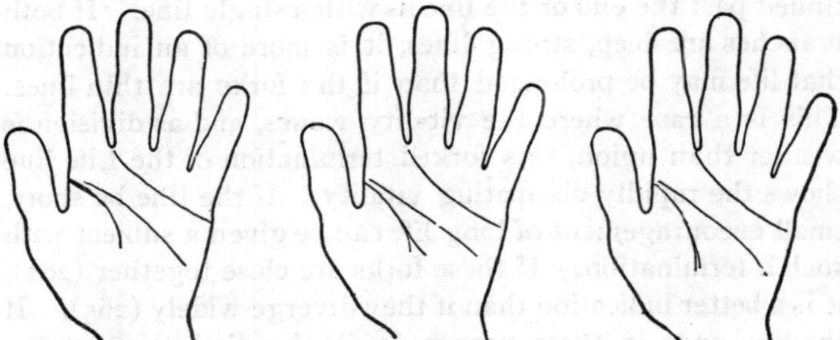

NO. 262 NO. 263 NO. 264

dot, or like sign. Life lines which are deep and strong but short, and sometimes even short thin ones, often cut their way through the hand, forming new channels; for a strong will and determination to live, often prolong the life of many persons with such markings. When the line ends clear, without a defect or tassel, it shows that there is no great impediment at the time, and that care and determination can keep the life going. If a line which begins deep and strong begins to taper as it cuts through the hand, gradually growing thinner as the line advances until it fades away and disappears in the capillary lines (262), it shows that the vitality grows less powerful as age comes on until it almost disappears, leaving the subject weak, nerveless, and feeble. These subjects will not die from sudden diseases, but death will come from exhaustion. They are liable to develop some chronic ailment as the line decreases, and any defect of their type will be almost certain to develop. By making a thorough examination, you can discover the difficulty. This fading Life line does not stand so good a chance to continue the life past the age indicated by its length. If it be a short line, the subject will begin to decline early and will not live past the end of the line, as he has not enough vitality to create great determination to live. A good Head line is a fine possession with such a disappearing line. If the Life line forks at the termination (263), it shows that the Current separates, and, going in two directions, there is only one half as much chance that the life may be continued past the end of the line as with a single line. If both branches are deep, strong lines, it is more of an indication that life may be prolonged than if the forks are thin lines. This is a case where the vitality wanes, and as division is weaker than union, this forked termination of the Life line shows the rapidly dissipating vitality. If the line be short, small encouragement of long life can be given a subject with such a termination. If these forks are close together (264), it is a better indication than if they diverge widely (265). If the line ends in three prongs (266), the dissipation of the vitality is more complete, and this is more certain if all three

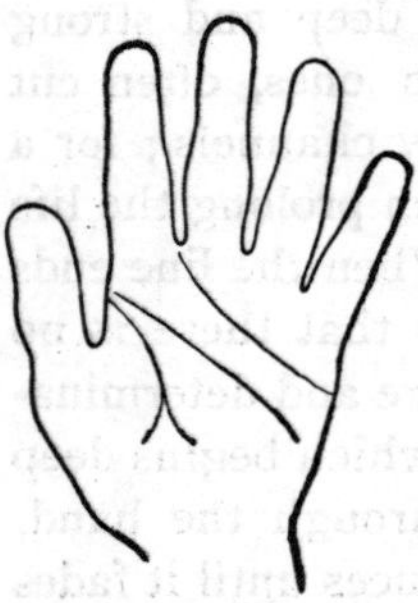

NO. 265

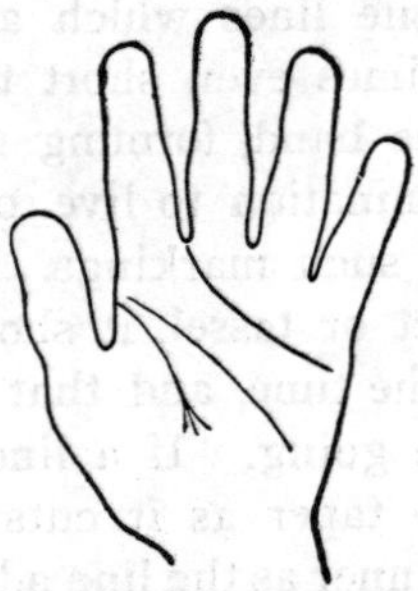

NO. 266

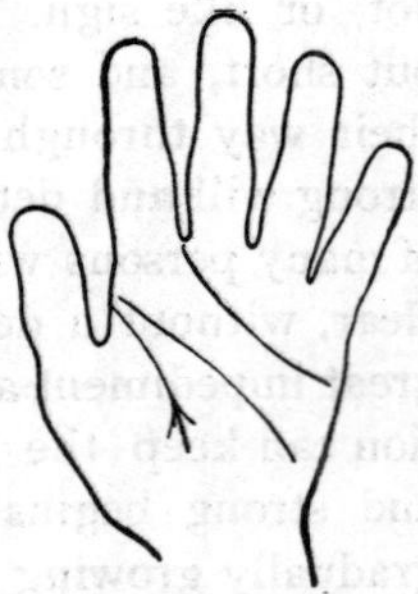

NO. 267

of the forks be thin. In this case the vitality will be dissipated when this point is reached. If the middle fork is strong and deep (267), it may be a new lease of life beginning to manifest itself, and hope may be given that the subject will live past the end of the line. If the line ends in a tassel (268), it shows entire dissipation of the vitality and end of the life. Such tassels are frequently seen from sixty to sixty-five years of age. In those cases it is the natural end of the life. If the tassel appears early in the line it shows premature dissipation of vitality, and death of the subject at the age at which the tassel is seen. In many works on Palmistry this tassel has been given the meaning "Poverty in old age." This is incorrect. I have seen it in the hands of old men who were rich. The vitality was

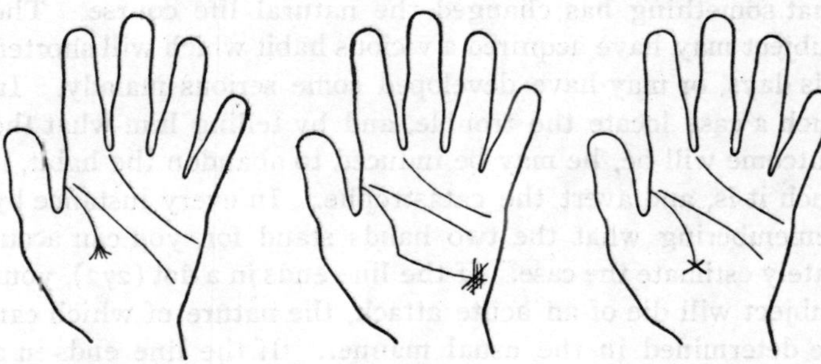

NO. 268 NO. 269 NO. 270

fast diminishing, however, as the age neared the point of the tassel. Sometimes the Life line runs to a certain age and then crosses the hand to a Mount. If there is no health defect on the Mount it will show that the quality of the Mount largely influences the life course of the subject. If a grille, cross, dot, cross-bars, or any defect on the Mount is present, the indications are that the disease peculiar to that Mount took hold of the subject at the age the line deflected from its regular course. For instance, if at thirty the line be so deflected and runs to the middle of Mount of Moon to a grille, gout or rheumatism will be the disease which afflicted the subject (269). Whenever the line runs to a defect, the disease peculiar to the point where it stops is the one to look for. This marking running to Lower Moon is most frequent in the hands of women, and indicates female weakness. If the line ends in a cross (270), the life will terminate at that age, and the disease can be determined by the usual search through the hand. This is a sudden ending of life, and there will be no lingering illness. The more perfectly the cross be marked, and the deeper its lines the more certain is the indication. If a cross-bar cuts the end of the Life line (271), it is the sudden ending of the life. In all these cases the usual methods of examination will disclose the cause. It is absolutely necessary with every termination of the Life line to examine both hands. If the line and termination in the left hand be good and strong, and one of the defective terminations is seen in the right, it is certain that something has changed the natural life course. The subject may have acquired a vicious habit which will shorten his days, or may have developed some serious malady. In such a case locate the trouble, and by telling him what the outcome will be, he may be induced to abandon the habit, if such it is, and avert the catastrophe. In every instance by remembering what the two hands stand for, you can accurately estimate the case. If the line ends in a dot (272), your subject will die of an acute attack, the nature of which can be determined in the usual manner. If the line ends in a star (273), the subject will die suddenly ; the cause can be located from the rest of the hand. You will encounter many

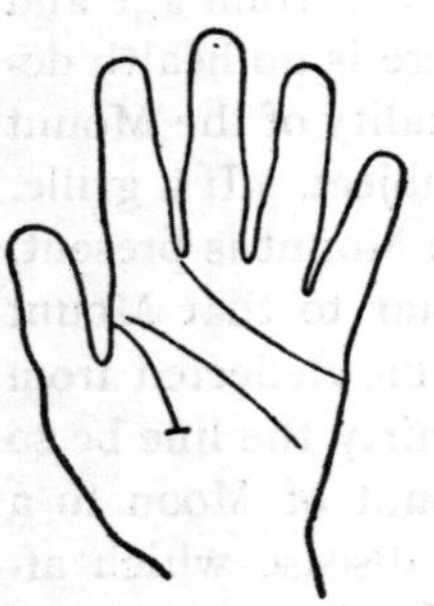

NO. 271

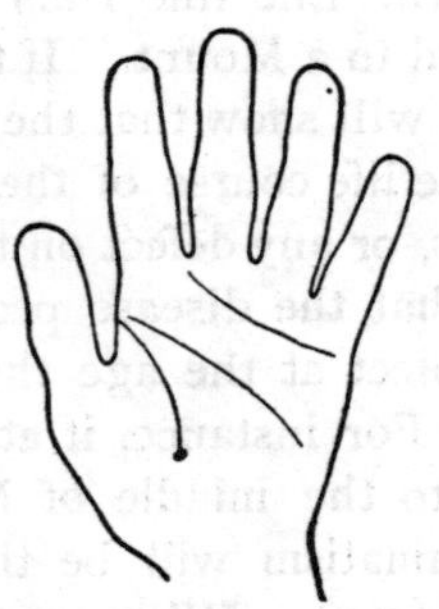

NO. 272

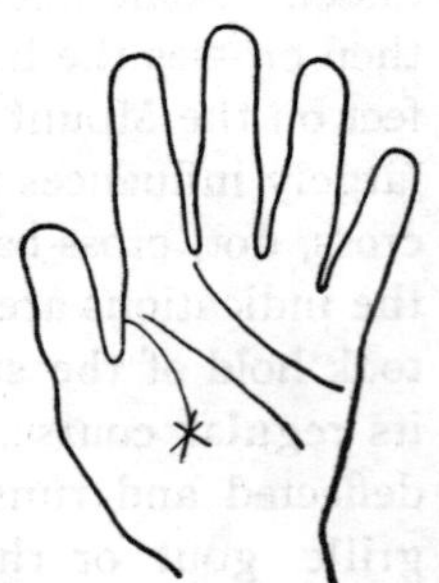

NO. 273

combinations of all these signs in the termination of Life lines. By this time you have doubtless learned how to use them in combination, and can properly estimate them.

Crosses will be found appearing in the Life line (274). These will be impediments to the life Current, and generally you will find on the Saturn line or the Apollo line some marking occurring at the same age. This change is generally the result of illness or accident. Crosses quite frequently indicate accidents.

Stars on the Life line are a menace to the life (275). They have been verified many times as indicating sudden death. The type of the subject will have much to do with these signs. A fine line leaving the Life line and ending in a star near it (276) is also a dangerous sign, indicating sudden

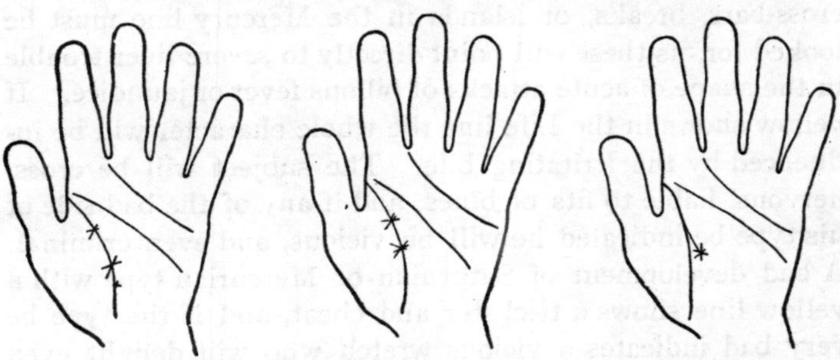

NO. 274 NO. 275 NO. 276

death. The star representing the explosion in the Life line, or at least an intense illumination, is not a safe indication to be found.

The color of the line will be useful as a further confirmation of the strength or weakness of the constitution. White color diminishes the power of a deep and well-cut line, and the subject will not have as much robustness and vitality as if the line were pink. A deep and well-cut line, pink in color, will be the best for a Life line. Then neither deficiency nor excess of vitality is indicated, but a normal balance. Red color, with a deep line, is too intense, and the subject will be liable to febrile diseases, and also very ardent in everything, and will have strong appetites. If stars, crosses, dots, or cross-bars are seen on a line which is very red in color, the subject will have some violent attack at the age indicated by the sign. Such a combination is most dangerous to the life. All markings which indicate febrile troubles or inflammations will be made more serious by a very red Life line. Yellow color in the Life line will indicate chronic biliousness, and all the defects of health and character which are induced by bile will be aggravated. With such a subject the Mounts of Saturn and Mercury should be carefully studied, as well as all matters pertaining to those Mounts, for being of the bilious type, yellow color in the Life line will increase any health defect which these Mounts show. A wavy line or a ladder-like line of Mercury will be sure to indicate severe bilious complications and indigestion. Dots, crosses, cross-bars, breaks, or islands in the Mercury line must be looked for, as these will point directly to severe liver trouble in the shape of acute attacks of bilious fever or jaundice. If yellow shows in the Life line the whole character will be influenced by the irritating bile. The subject will be cross, nervous, liable to fits of blues, and if any of the bad side of his type be indicated he will be vicious, and even criminal. A bad development of Saturnian or Mercurian type with a yellow line shows a trickster and cheat, and if the type be very bad indicates a vicious wretch who will delight even in murder. Blue color shows poor circulation and consequent heart weakness. This color present with a defective and badly colored Heart line and blue nails will indicate an advanced state of heart trouble. The bluer the Life line and the more indications of defective heart action, the more serious the estimate. With a blue Life line, stars on the line will be accurate as indication of sudden death by heart disease. Crosses, dots, and cross-bars are bad indications with blue color, but the star is the worst. Stars which are not directly on the line but near it, will have almost as much force as if on the line. All of the above observations in regard to color apply to thin Life lines as well as to deep and well-cut lines. A thin line which is exceedingly red is most dangerous, for the line is not strong enough to support the vitality shown by very red color. Yellow thin lines will make the subject small, petty, and mean. With chained lines or broad and shallow lines, white color makes them weaker. They have none of the strength which follows the presence of pink color. Subjects with thin lines are cold, sickly, complaining, and vacillating. They lack energy, and are not persons to be relied upon. Pink color makes a broad and shallow or a chained line stronger. The subject will have more vitality, and will not be despondent as frequently as with white color. Red will add more strength, but this combination is rare. When found, however, it should be regarded as no menace to these lines, for they need all the strength which can be given them. Yellow color with broad or chained lines is a distressing combination. It will show inertia, intense nervousness, and an ugly streak of meanness in the subject. This combination produces a weak, sickly, nervous, petty person who will have a hard time to get along in the world.

The line of Life is an intensely interesting study, and one which will amply repay any effort expended upon it. A mastery of the general principles which govern the various changes in the line, and its infinite combinations with other lines and Mounts, will enable you with practice to read it accurately. At first the combinations may come slowly, but this should be no cause for discouragement. Patience and labor will enable any student to master it.

CHAPTER VIII

LINES OF INFLUENCE

ON the Mount of Venus and inside the Life line are a set of lines, some of which run parallel to the Life line and others which run across the Mount (277). These are called Lines of Influence, and are the first introduction in this book to any factors outside of the subject himself, forming a part of what is called his "environment." Only those indications which my own experience as well as that of other careful investigators has fully verified are here considered, and all matters which are traditional or hypothetical have been left out. The Hindus have an elaborate system of using these lines of Influence, and depend upon them for a large part of their work. Only the lines which run *inside* the Life line are properly lines of Influence, and I have found that they indicate persons who have strongly influenced the life either for good or ill, and that they generally represent members of one's own family or the closest of friends. If the latter class, and blood relationship is not present, they are those who have grown into the life and have become a part of it. In all cases they have strong *influence*, hence their name. In some hands few of these lines are seen, in others there are many, and the more there are the greater the number of persons who have exerted strong influence. The less the number the more self-contained is the subject; he makes few close friendships, and even blood relations do not greatly influence him. The reason these lines are seen

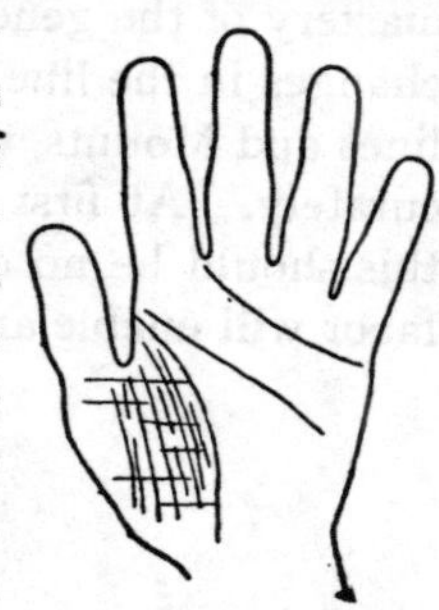

NO. 277

is because the influences have made strong impressions on the mind of the subject, and these mental impressions have shown themselves in the hand. The Lines of Influence, both vertical and horizontal, form what is commonly called the Grille on the Mount of Venus. This generally indicates an increase of Venusian qualities, particularly the sexual appetites. This *general* reading of a large number of Influence

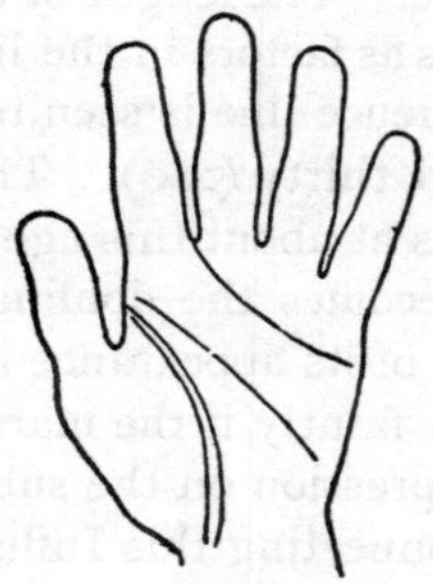

NO. 278

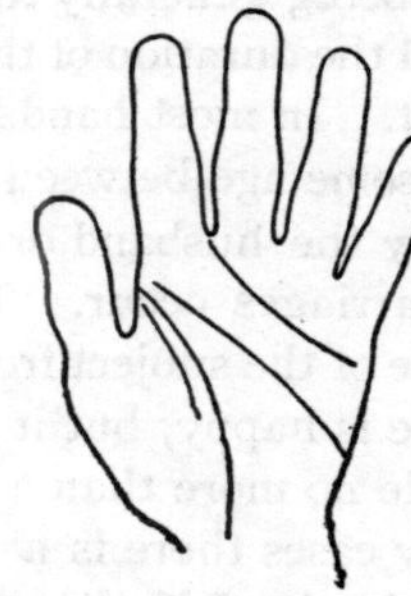

NO. 279

lines on the Mount of Venus is correct, as has been clearly demonstrated in the hands of subjects known to have strong sexual appetites. Every line of the Grille represents an influence which has affected the life, and the more of these there are, the more the Mount will have Currents which excite it, and consequently fire its qualities. The absence of lines on the Mount of Venus shows an absence of electrifying Currents, and this calm Mount expends its energy in a love of beauty, gayety, color, art, and dress, instead of in sexual desires.

The line of Mars is a sister to the line of Life, running inside of that line and parallel to it (278). This is really an Influence line, but it is an influence upon the health of the subject, sustaining and strengthening it, and does not relate to the influence of other persons. The line of Mars is comparatively a rare marking, and the greater number of lines seen alongside the Life line are simply Influence lines. The Influence line which runs closest to the line of Life is the closest influence. This may be mother, father, a brother or a sister. I have noted that a line starting near the beginning of the Life line and running close to it is generally the mother (279), as a mother's influence begins earlier in life than that of any one else. Next to this line, counting from the Life line, comes a line representing the father, and the line which represents this parent is usually found to be deeper than the others. Next follow other relatives, grandparents being generally the fourth line. The length of these lines tell the duration of the influences as factors in the life of a subject. In most hands a new Influence line is seen to appear at some age between twenty and thirty (280). This is generally the husband or wife, as it is at about this age that most marriages occur. This line becomes the dominating influence of the subject from the time of its appearance if the marriage is happy, but it only shows faintly if the marriage has made no more than a passing impression on the subject. In many cases there is a fine line connecting this Influence line with the Life line, showing that the influence has merged into the life of the subject. On the Mount of Venus, then, are congregated the close influences of a subject's life.

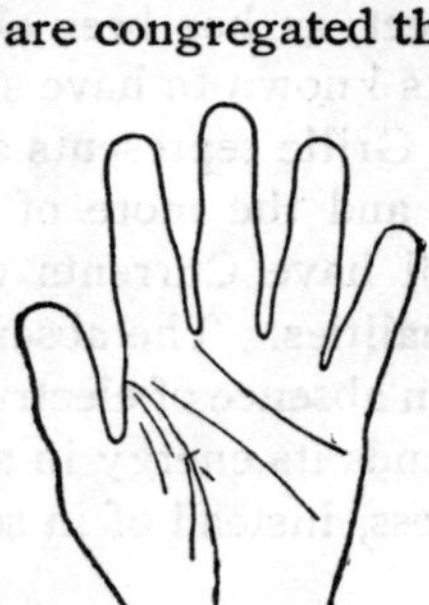
NO. 280

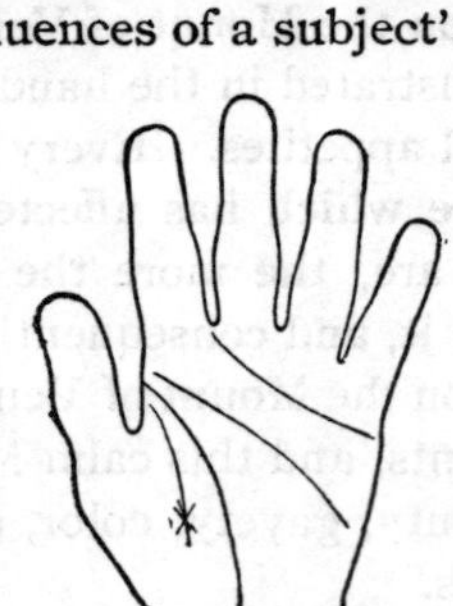
NO. 281

Many things which happen to the persons who influence the subject are also shown on the lines of Influence, but they are events which have made a considerable impression on his mind. A star on the end of a line of Influence (281) will indicate the ceasing of that influence, whatever it may be; and, while you cannot state definitely who the person is, yet by noting the distance between this Influence line and the line of Life, you can determine whether the line represents one closely connected with the subject or a more distant relative. This is an important indication to master thoroughly, for the death of a relative will often change the course of a life, and

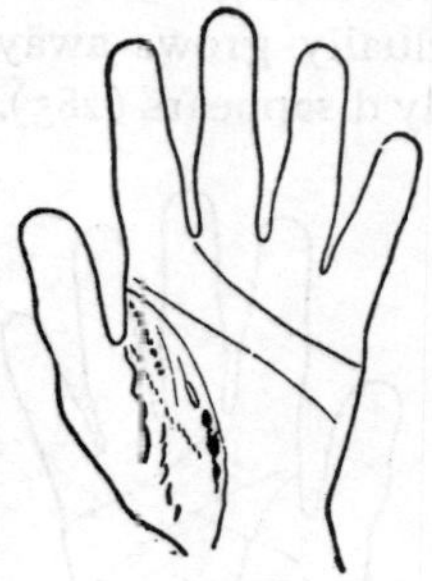

NO. 282

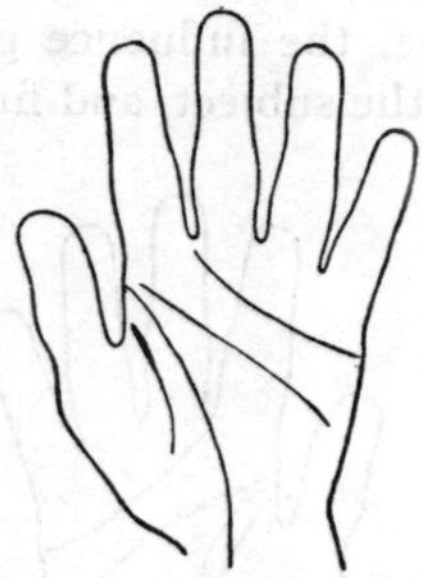

NO. 283

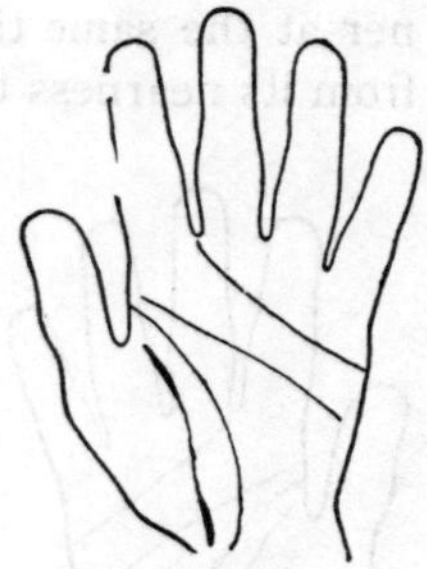

NO. 284

if some indication be encountered which cannot be explained in any other way, a line of Influence with a star on it may give the clew. In connection with the lines of Saturn and Apollo it is of constant service. The death of relatives also seriously impairs the health of some subjects, and thus in all directions Influence lines are valuable indications.

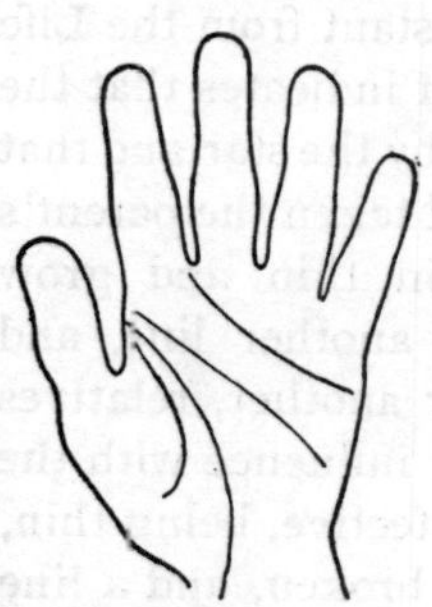

NO. 285

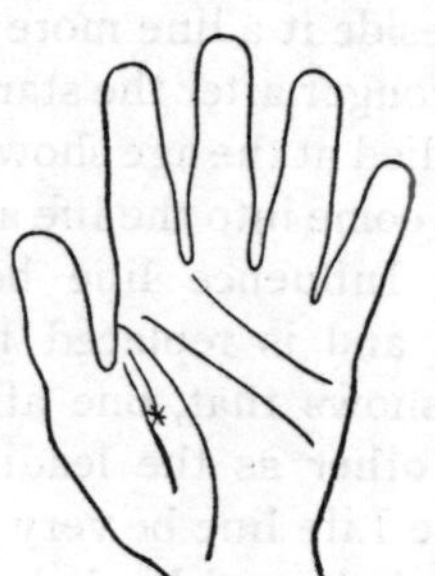

NO. 286

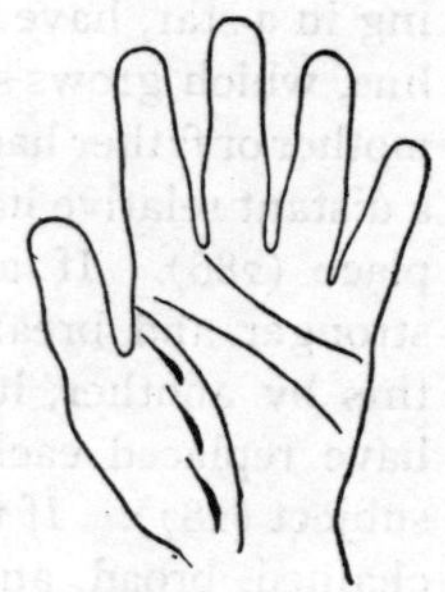

NO. 287

When lines of Influence are deep, strong, and well colored, the influence is powerful; when they are thin, shallow, chained, uneven, or broken in any way (282), the influence is not strong. When an Influence line begins deep and then grows thin, until it gradually fades away, the influence was strong in the beginning, but has gradually grown weaker until it has no effect (283). If this line should be revived and gradually grow stronger, the influence will return into the life of the subject and grow in power (284). If an Influence line draw away from the Life line and grow thinner at the same time, the influence gradually grows away from its nearness to the subject, and finally disappears (285).

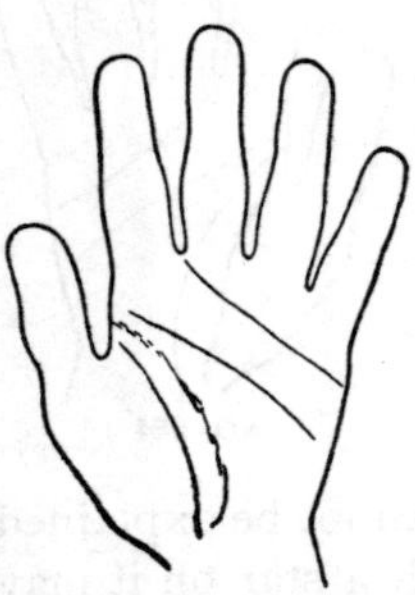

NO. 288

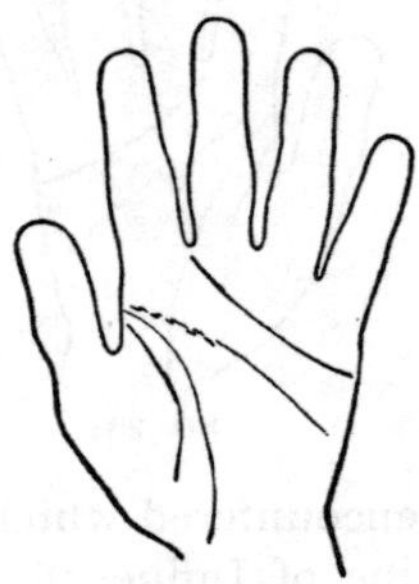

NO. 289

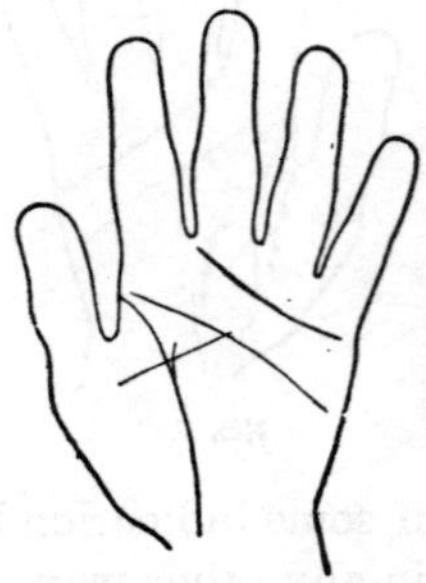

NO. 290

This is an indication of the estrangement of some near one. The ages of each one of these occurrences can be read from the Life line. If an Influence line, beginning early and ending in a star, have beside it a line more distant from the Life line, which grows stronger after the star, it indicates that the mother or father has died at the age shown by the star, and that a distant relative has come into the life and taken the parent's place (286). If an Influence line begin thin and grow stronger and break, and is replaced by another line, and this by another, it shows that, one after another, relatives have replaced each other as the leading influence with the subject (287). If the Life line be very defective, being thin, chained, broad, and shallow, islanded or broken, and a line of Influence be strong (288), it indicates that while the subject's health has been delicate, some relative has been his mainstay in life. This line just described has the same effect on the subject as a line of Mars, and the influence may, by constant nursing, have kept the subject alive. I incline to this opinion rather than to the idea of the line being a line of Mars. If the Head line be poor early in life, and gradually grow stronger, and an Influence line be strong in the beginning and grow farther away from the Life line or become thinner, the weak mental condition of the subject in early life is sustained by the strong influence of some-one during the time such help was needed, and, as the head grew stronger, the influence was no longer needed and faded away (289). The rising branches from the Life line indicating an upward tendency in the life of the subject are sometimes cut by Worry lines (290). This marking shows an impediment to the career of the subject, a check to the upward tendency. These Worry lines frequently start from an Influence line (291), and this will indicate that the influence has caused the check. In a large number of cases these Worry lines cutting an upward branch from the Life line have been verified as indicating a legal difficulty. Older palmists used this marking as an indication of divorce. The single indication must not be given this reading, but with this marking and other confirmatory signs it can be so interpreted, viz., if the line cutting the rising branch from the Life

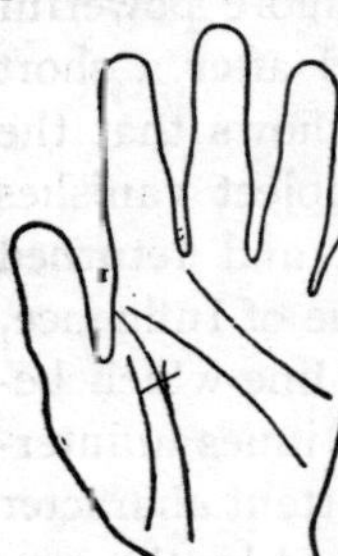

NO. 291

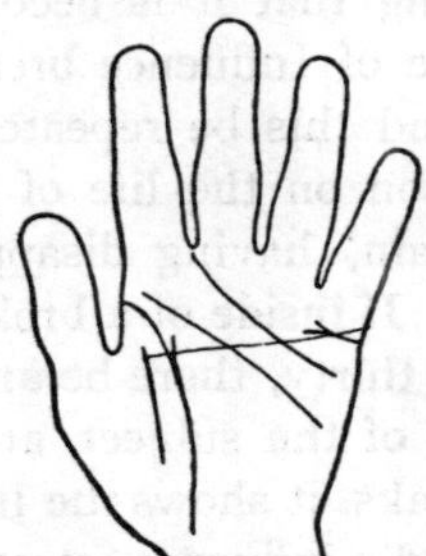

NO. 292

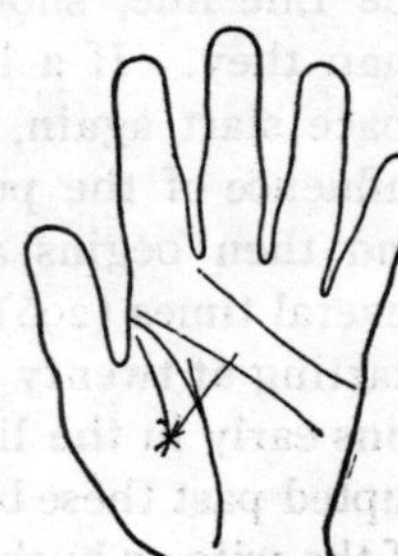

NO. 293

line cross the hand and cut a line of union which is forked (292), this reading will be found correct. If the Worry line start from an Influence line, the influence has made the trouble. By itself the marking indicates a check to the upward career. If a Worry line start from a star on the end of an Influence line and cut a rising line from the Life line (293), it indicates that the death of a relative caused the trouble. If the Influence line be deep, then thin, and alternates in this way, the influence is strong, then weak, and only exerts its power spasmodically (294). If an Influence line begin away from the Life line and gradually come toward it, growing stronger as it progresses (295), it indicates that the influence of some distant relative is gradually coming nearer to the life of the subject and growing stronger. This

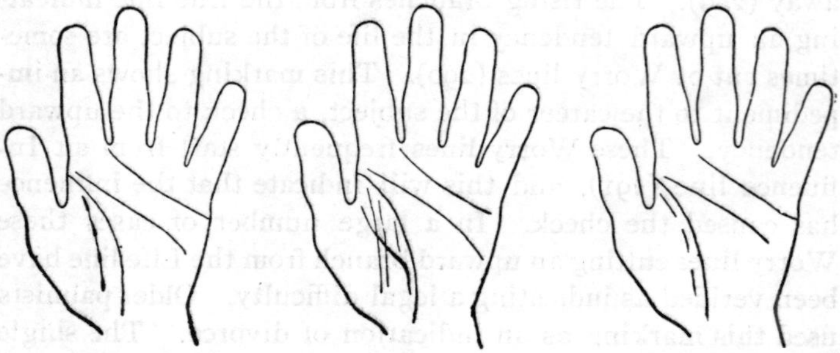

NO. 294 NO. 295 NO. 296

line may cut through other Influence lines lying closer to the Life line, showing that it is becoming more powerful than they. If a line of Influence break and after a short space start again, and this be repeated, it shows that the influence of the person on the life of the subject vanishes and then begins again, having disappeared and returned several times (296). If inside of a broken line of Influence, starting at twenty to thirty, there be another line which begins early in the life of the subject, and continues uninterrupted past these breaks, it shows the intermittent character of the wife or husband's influence, strengthened by the constant influence of the mother or father. Often such a marking will heal and correct a poor marriage (297).

Islands on Influence lines parallel to the Life line indicate a delicate condition of the influence, and such a line ending in a star, cross, dot, or cross-bar (298) will indicate that the delicate influence dies, the age to be read from the line of Life. Horizontal lines on the Mount of Venus (299) are persons or events which have crossed our lives and impeded them. Parallel lines are not impediments, and while they may be weak or defective, they are not influences strongly hostile to our best development. Cross-lines both impede our influences and worry and harass us. This is why these cross lines cutting the Life line have been called Worry lines. If deep and red, they are serious impediments ; if thin and puny lines, they are only annoyances. These Worry lines which continually cross the Life line must be regarded as more or less serious, according to their depth and extent. When deep, they indicate illness of a serious nature. If these horizontal lines cross the entire Mount of Venus and Life line, from top to bottom, they are continuous worries. If only short lines, they are temporary annoyances. If they cut some particular Influence line repeatedly (300), that influence will have a continual life of worry and impediment. If a line of Influence, cut by a strong cross-line, show after this cut an island and end in a star (301), some disaster has happened to the influence which has brought on delicacy and ended in death. If the cutting line be a *deep* one, and

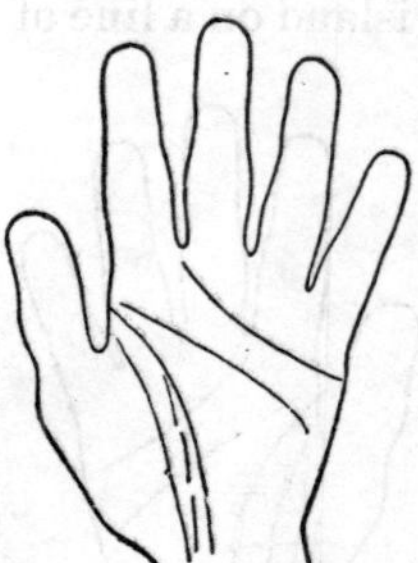

NO. 297

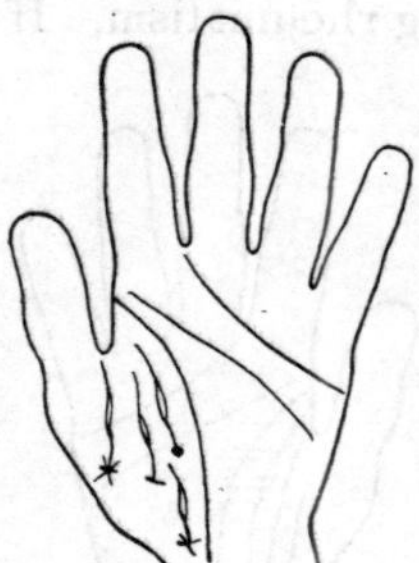

NO. 298

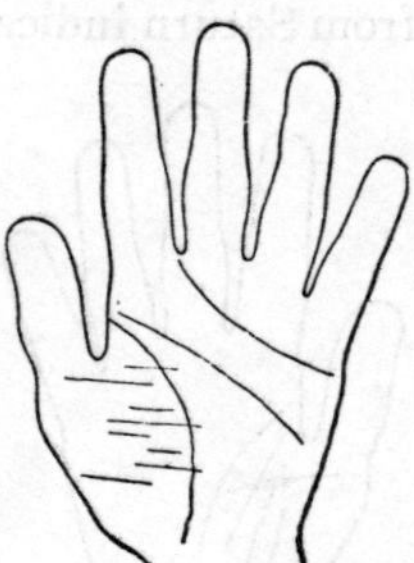

NO. 299

the cut line begin so early that you judge it to be a parent, the cause of the cut has often been verified as the father. I have seen several cases of this kind ; the father having died, or been injured, has so shocked the mother that she never recovered. If a number of Influence lines run parallel to the Life line, and these are cut by numerous small lines, the family life of the subject has in many cases been found to suffer constant interruption and be unhappy (302). If a cross-line have an island in it, there will be something most unpleasant connected with this impediment. It will be a bar to the subject's life owing to

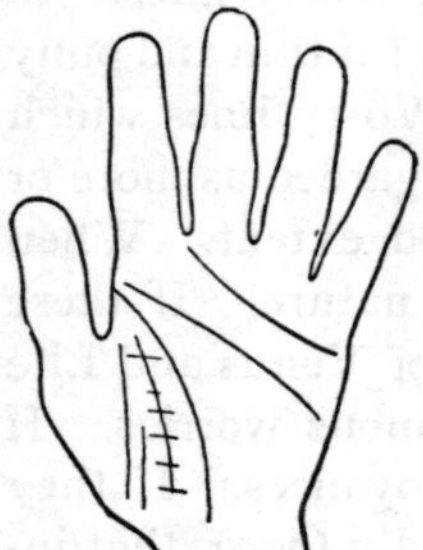

NO. 300

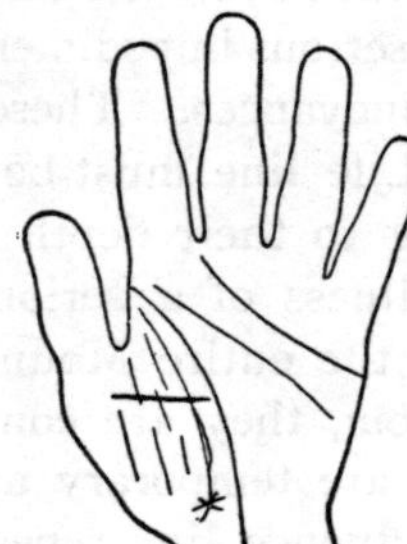

NO. 301

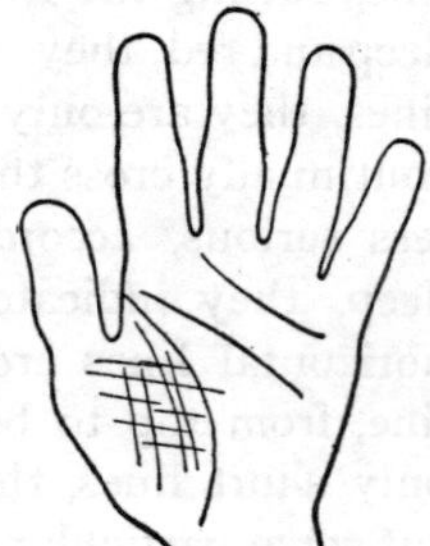

NO. 302

some fault not his own (303). If this line only cut the lines of Influence inside the Life line, it will be expended on the relatives, but if it cut the Life line it will affect the life of the subject. Do not confound this marking with the island from Saturn indicating rheumatism. If an island on a line of

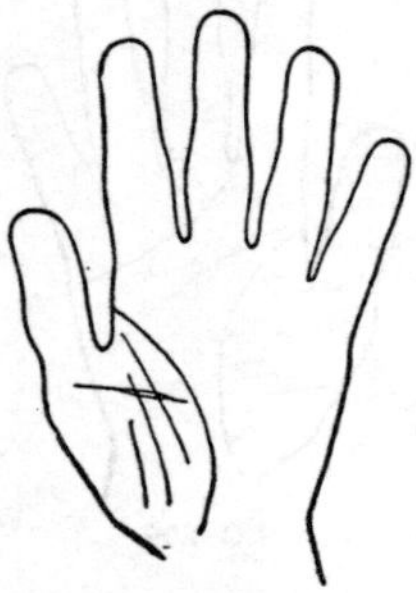

NO. 303

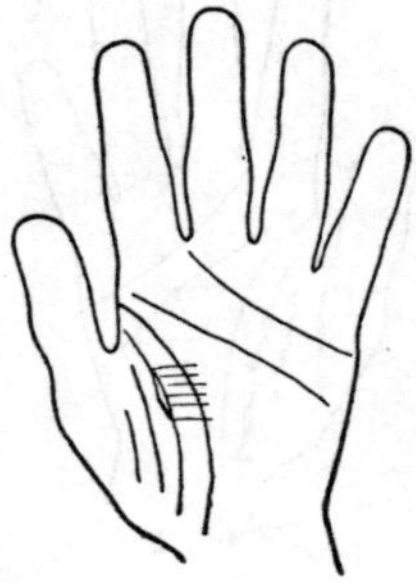

NO. 304

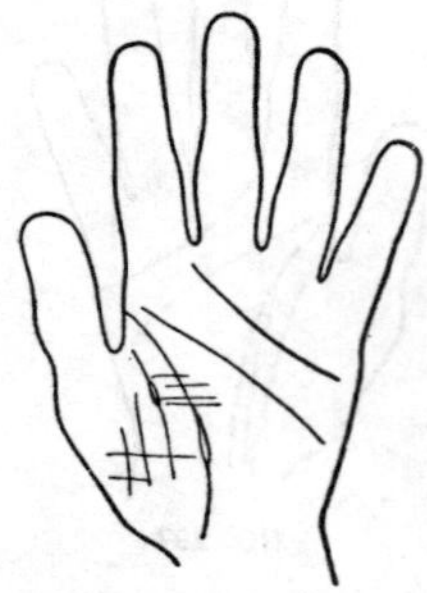

NO. 305

Influence have running from it numerous small bars cutting the Life line, the delicacy of some relative will prove a constant worry to the subject (304). If on the Life line an island appear after this point in life, these cares or worries will seriously affect the health of the subject. Probably close nursing of some invalid relative breaks the health (305).

If an Influence line deep at the beginning gradually grow thinner and end in a star, and Worry lines cross from it to the Life line, which grows thin and has a dot on it, the increasing delicacy of a relative ends in death, and the worry over this case brings on delicacy of the subject ending in a severe illness (306). If the Life line end on this dot, the subject will not recover; if it go on, he will regain

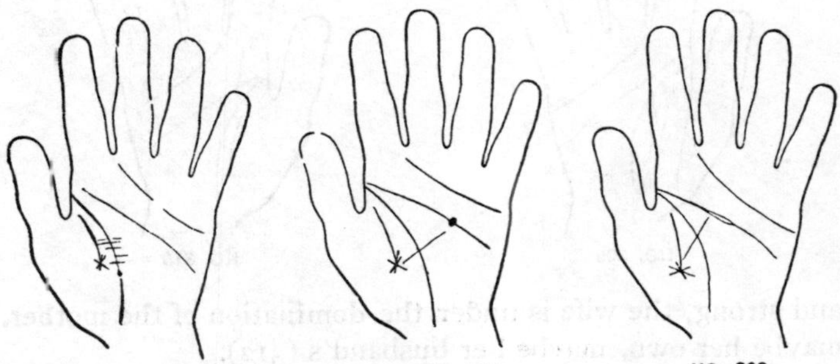

NO. 306 NO. 307 NO. 308

his strength. If an Influence line end in a star, and a Worry line connect this with a dot on the Head line, the death of a relative will bring on a severe illness of the brain (307). If a line of Influence end in a star, and this be connected by a Worry line with an island on the Head line (308), the delicacy and death of a relative produce a weakened mental condition of the subject. In each one of these cases it is understood that you are to try and discover how near a relative has died by the closeness of the Influence line to the Life line. If lines rise from the lines of Influence and run to, but do not cut, the Life line, it shows that relatives will uplift the subject, but if lines droop from the Influence lines to the Life line, the subject will be continually pulled down by his kin (309). If a line of Influence which has been diagnosed as the wife or husband have a line rising from it to the Mount of Jupiter, it indicates that this relative is most ambitious (310). If the Saturn line be more than usually good after this period, it indicates that this ambitious partner has spurred the subject on and increased his success. If a line of Influence rising early be supported by one which rises at about the time of marriage, the wife or husband has supplanted the mother completely (311). If the marriage influence be thin and the mother influence deep

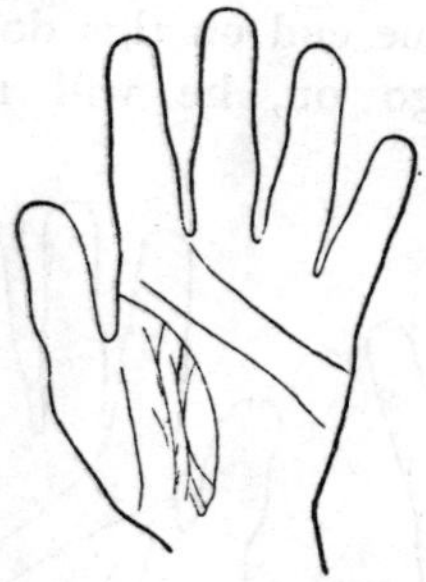

NO. 309

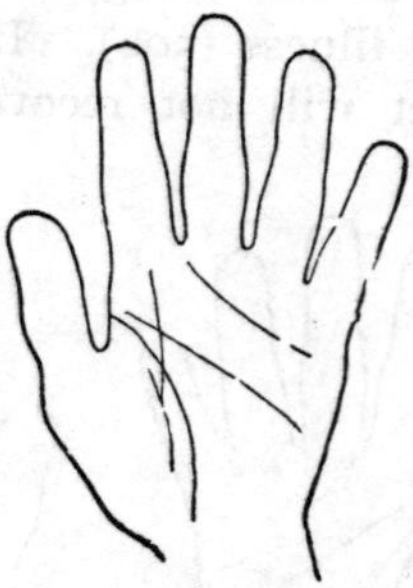

NO. 310

and strong, the wife is under the domination of the mother, maybe her own, maybe her husband's (312).

The general principles which must be applied to lines of Influence are the same in all cases as those which apply to other lines. Remembering that these lines represent other

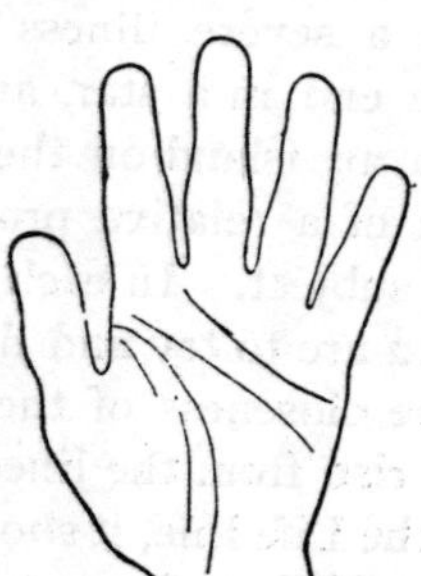

NO. 311

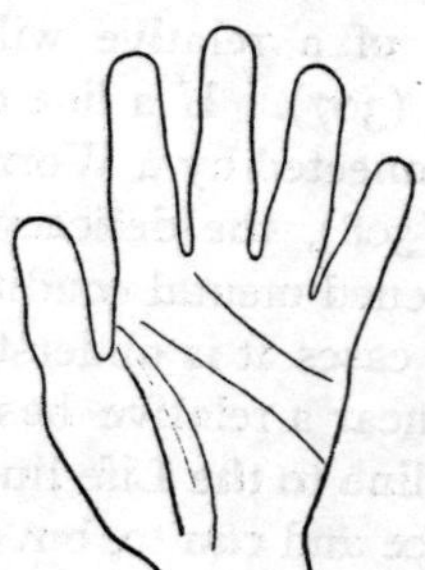

NO. 312

people, and by discovering who these persons are in relation to the subject, you can estimate very closely what effect they have on his life. Defects on Influence lines, connected by Worry lines with defects on other lines, will show that the influence has caused the defect. Changes in the Life line, following defects or changes in Influence lines, show that the influences have affected the life in a harmful manner. In all such cases the character of the Life line will tell what this bad effect has been. In estimating the Influence line which represents the husband or wife, it should be borne in mind that in women's hands it will begin at from eighteen to twenty-five, and in men from twenty-five to thirty, these years representing the average years when marriages occur. In reading Influence lines always proceed slowly until you have gained practice enough to work out the combinations. As students, do not hesitate to ask questions, and find out where you have made mistakes. Acquire the general principles, and apply them with good methods of reasoning to the Influence lines, and they will prove to be an increasing source of benefit.

CHAPTER IX

THE LINES OF AFFECTION

THE lines of Affection or Marriage, as they are commonly called, lie on the Mount of Mercury, and run from the percussion toward the inside of the palm (313). In some hands there are none of these lines and in others many are seen. From time immemorial they have been used by older palmists as indications of marriage or unions of the sexes. Their value in practice is considerable if used up to their limit, and in combination, but used by themselves, as a hard-and-fast indication of marriage, they will lead to constant error. Marriage does not affect every subject in the same way. Some people are no more impressed on entering into this relation than if they were performing any ordinary routine of daily life. Such persons will have no Marriage lines. Others sink their whole life and soul into a union, and these will have deep Marriage lines. To use the word "marriage" in connection with the lines of Affection is misleading, for it is in no sense to be taken as always indicating a legal marriage contract. These lines are often seen when no such contract has ever been entered into, but when the subject has loved as fondly as if he had been joined in wedlock. In such subjects a line of union will appear the same as though the ceremony had been performed. More properly speaking, these are lines of deep affection rather than lines of marriage or union, and, viewed from this standpoint, they are remarkably accurate. In every case there must have

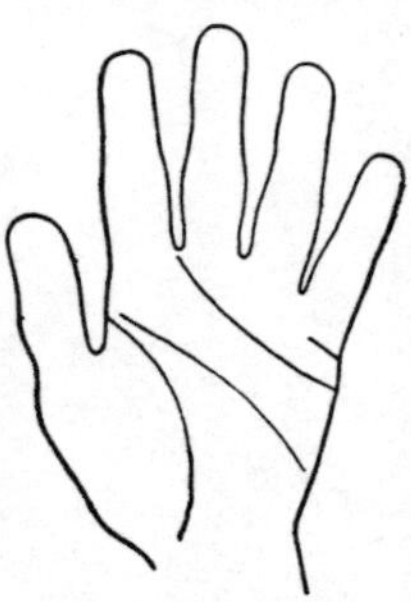

NO. 313

been a profound impression made upon the subject by an affection before these lines will be strong, and the more impressions and affections which have existed, the more of these lines of Affection will be seen in the hand.

The type of the subject will always be a great aid in reading the lines of Affection, as each type has distinct views on the marriage question. The Jupiterian is inclined to marriage and to marry young. So in the hand of a Jupiterian a line of Affection early in life will most often be correctly read as marriage. The Saturnian dislikes marriage ; if he be of a very pronounced or at all bad development, and even in good specimens of the type, a Saturnian does not rush into the marriage state. This type does not naturally love his fellow-creatures, and a most profound impression must be made on him by someone before he will enter the marriage relation. Consequently in the hand of a Saturnian a line of Affection should be very strong, and occur well toward middle life, before you are justified in reading it as marriage. Even when the combination of a Mount of Venus shows a Saturnian to be possessed of sexual desire, he will prefer to gratify these appetites outside of the marriage state rather than to tie himself permanently to anyone. Apollonians desire to marry, and do so when young, but they often make unhappy marriages because while they like brilliant partners they do not always get them. Lines of Affection on Apollonians will be quite safely read as marriages. Mercurians are great matchmakers ; they also marry quite young. On this type, lines of Affection will very often mean marriage. Martians are prone to marry, so with this type lines of Affection also have full meaning. Lunarians are very peculiar about marriage, sometimes despising it, and sometimes making odd matches, and the line of Affection on this type must be excessively strong to be read as marriage. Venusians cannot keep from marrying, even if they cared to, for they will not be allowed to remain single, because other persons are so attracted to them. On the Venusian type it requires only a small line to mean marriage, though on this type you will generally find strong lines. The practice of looking at the Mount of Mercury, and predicting one, two, or as many marriages as there are lines of Affection on the Mount, is a most inaccurate and unscientific thing to do, constantly leading to error, and making our science ridiculous. No practitioner should say in advance, as is the custom with many professionals, that he can tell about marriage. Many professionals in their printed circulars claim to tell a client "everything concerning love, marriage, divorce, etc.," and such professionals are kept continually in hot water by their mistakes. If they did not promise what they could not perform, there would be no trouble. The only honest way is to make no promises, for you cannot tell what a hand will show until it has been seen. It may be asked, "Why is it necessary to deal with marriage at all?" The answer to this question is, that marriages do so much to make or to mar the career that all the information possible should be had for use in its general bearing upon the life of a subject. My only object in introducing the lines of Affection at this point is that we may be able to bring them to bear upon the lines of Saturn and Apollo, which they often powerfully influence.

The first thing to determine is whether lines of Affection be present or absent. If none be seen, your subject is not likely to be powerfully impressed by anyone. If the subject be robust, and belong to an ardent type, he may have strong desires toward the opposite sex, but when these are satisfied, he relapses into a state of indifference, until the superabundance of vitality again turns his thoughts in the same direction. These subjects are undemonstrative, and a defective Heart line in a hand which has no line of Affection will indicate heart disease and not affection. If many lines of Affection be present (314) the subject is susceptible in affairs of the heart, more or less seriously so as the lines are strong or weak. These lines of Affection are always cross-lines, and start from the outside of the hand, sometimes at the back cutting around into the Mount of Mercury. If only a single line be seen, there will be but one deep affection, and it must be stated here that the lines of Affection relate only to persons of the opposite sex, and those who are in no way related to us by blood. They are never an indication of the love a subject may have for his family. If a line of Affection begin with a fork (315) it shows that the affection is of unusual strength, the two lines of the fork having united to form a single line, producing the effect of two Currents turned into one, which thus takes on double strength. To read the

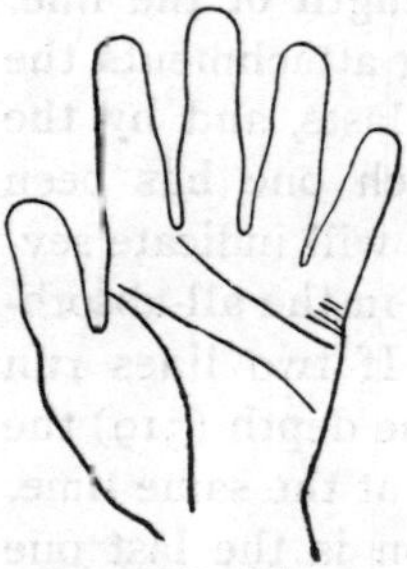

NO. 314

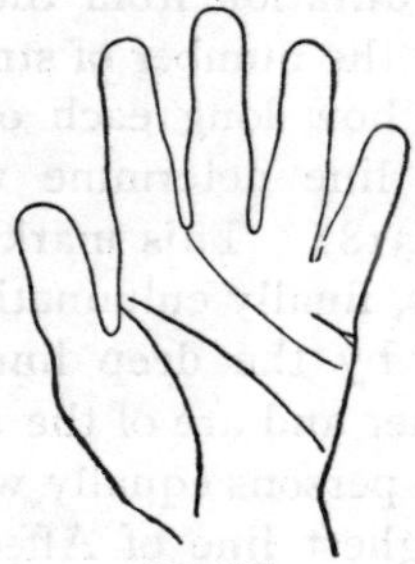

NO. 315

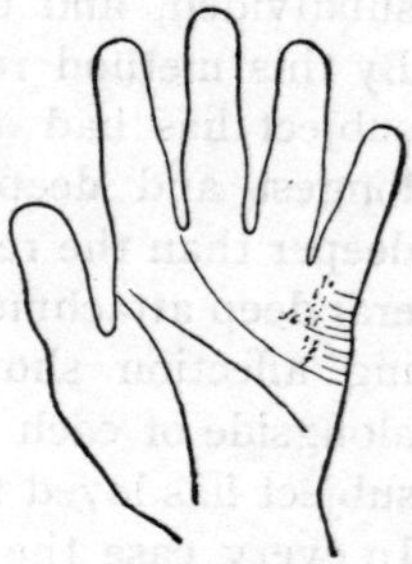

NO. 316

age on lines of Affection, two methods are employed. One is to determine at what age the affection occurs, and the other to tell how long it lasts. In order to determine the age at which an affection occurs, take the Heart line as a lower mark, and the top of the Mount of Mercury as the upper. This space must be subdivided into the average years of life, bringing the middle of the Mount at thirty-six, and the top at seventy years. Thus all lines of Affection appearing before the middle of the Mount occur before the age of thirty-six, and those appearing beyond the centre of the Mount occur after thirty-six. The scale (316) will be found approximating the correct ages and accurate enough for all general purposes. It can, however, be still further subdivided if more exact dates are desired. To determine the length an affection endures, the line itself must be measured from its beginning to its termination. In this way also events in the course of an affection are often recorded. The scale of measurement for such readings begins with the starting of the line and ends with its termination, the line to be divided in the middle as age thirty-six, and seventy to be recorded at the end. The intervening years can be subdivided as minutely as is necessary in order to reach the age of any markings on the line which is desired (317). The longer the line of Affection, the longer the affection continues, and when a number of lines are seen the duration of each affair may be estimated by the length of the several lines. The age at which each occurs is read from the Mount subdivided, and the duration from the length of the line. By this method read the number of strong attachments the subject has had and how long each one lasts, and by the longest and deepest line determine which one has been deeper than the rest (318). This marking will indicate several deep attachments, finally culminating in the all-absorbing affection shown by the deep line. If two lines run alongside of each other and are of the same depth (319) the subject has loved two persons equally well at the same time. In every case the highest line of Affection is the last one which has occurred, and any lines lower than it will record former affections. If a number of lines be seen, the upper

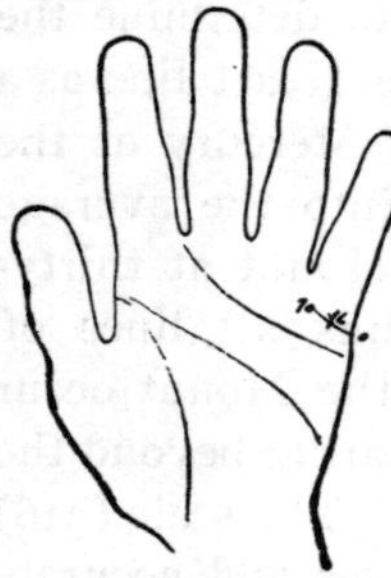

NO. 317

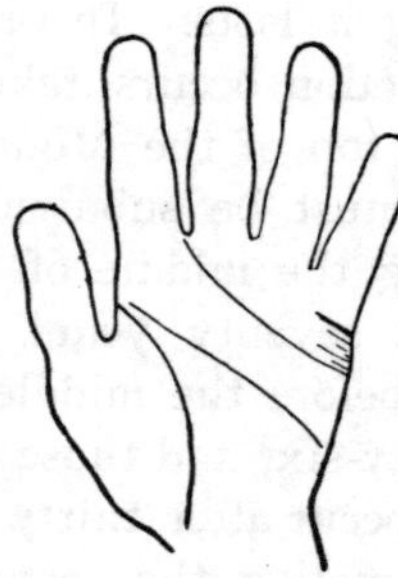

NO. 318

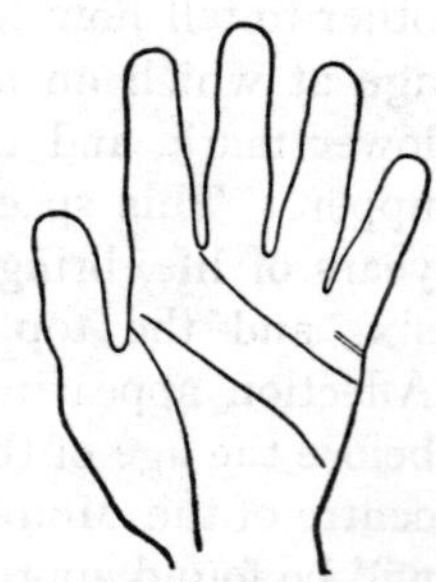

NO. 319

one a dcep line, but one of the early lines deep at the end, it indicates that the early love has never entirely disappeared (320). From every combination of lines select the strongest attachments from the deepest lines, and also determine by the character of the lines how completely this attachment has passed away. If the last line be a thin one, and yet by its length and confirmatory signs proves to be the Marriage line, and if a stronger line lie close under it (321) the subject has married for convenience, or money, but not from strongest love.

If the lines of Affection be thin in proportion to other lines in the hand, the subject has no real strong affections. He has a brotherly or sisterly affection for the one he marries, but *love* will not be the absorbing passion. These sub-

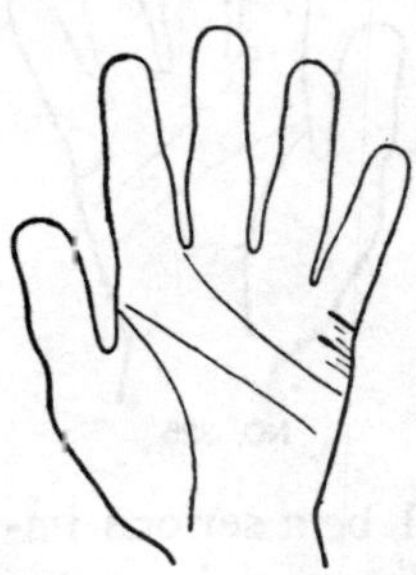

NO. 320

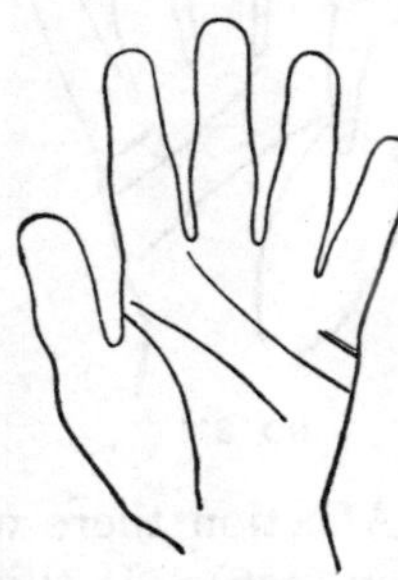

NO. 321

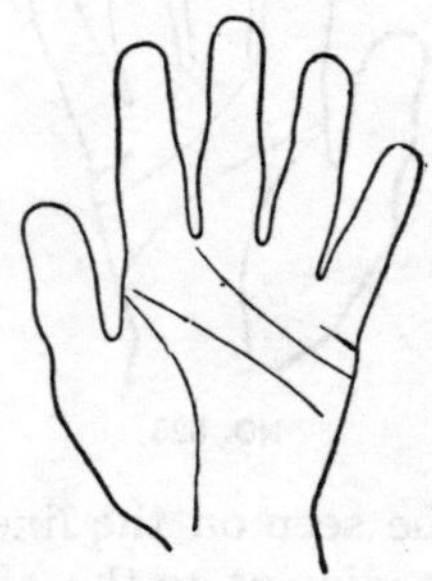

NO. 322

jects giving little demonstration of affection are indifferent, cold, and, if they have many lines of Affection, are apt to be flirts. If such subjects be handsome and attractive they break many hearts. If in a woman's hand the lines of Affection are broad and shallow, or chained, the subject is still more indifferent. She will lead suitors on for the pleasure of disappointing them. These subjects have no real affection, and are selfish, cold, and cruel. White color will add to the coldness of both of these latter lines. The lines which show deep, lasting affection, are the deep and well-cut ones. These are strengthened if they be also pink or red in color. Such subjects love ardently, constantly, and make sacrifices for those they love. It is their pleasure and pride to be constant and true. If such a deep line run to its end without fault or break, the subject will pursue a life of ardent attachment, of reliability and steadfastness, from beginning to end. If the line start deep and gradually grow thin the subject will gradually lose the strength of his attachment (322). If the line start thin and gradually become stronger the subject will grow stronger in his attachment (323). If an island appear on the line of Affection, there will be some unhappiness during the course of the affection (324). If the line of Affection be composed of islands, the subject will never have affection enough for anyone to marry him (325). If a cross

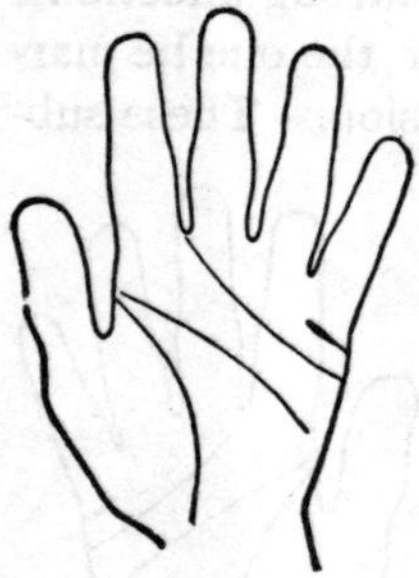

NO. 323

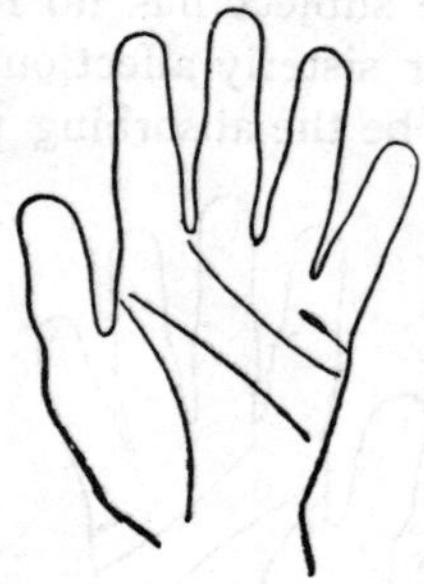

NO. 324

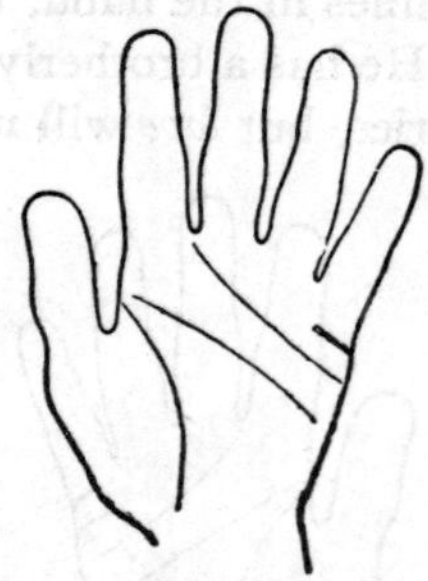

NO. 325

be seen on the line of Affection there will be a serious impediment to the affection (326). If this line end in a star the affection will terminate in an explosion (327). If a line of Affection send a branch into the Mount of Apollo which ends in a star, the subject will have an affection for some-

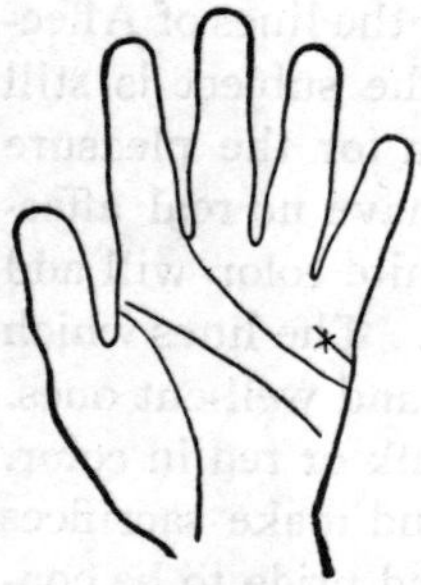

NO. 326

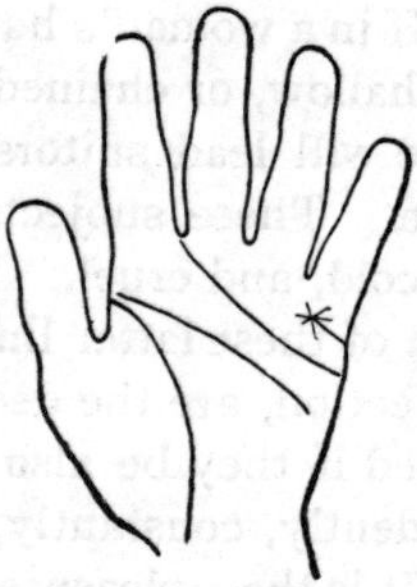

NO. 327

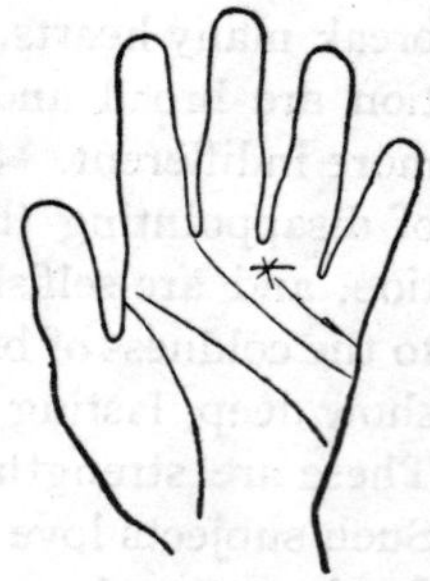

NO. 328

one brilliant and famous (328). If the line of Affection fork at its termination (329), the affection will separate and become less strong. This has been used by the older palmists as an indication of divorce. It is a likelihood of interference in the married life, but not always divorce. It shows the beginning of the dissipation of the affections. If the fork be not wide (330) the estrangement is not so serious as if it diverge greatly, as in No. 329. If the line end in a trident or a tassel, it shows the utter dissipation and scattering of the affection (331). If branches droop from the line of Affection

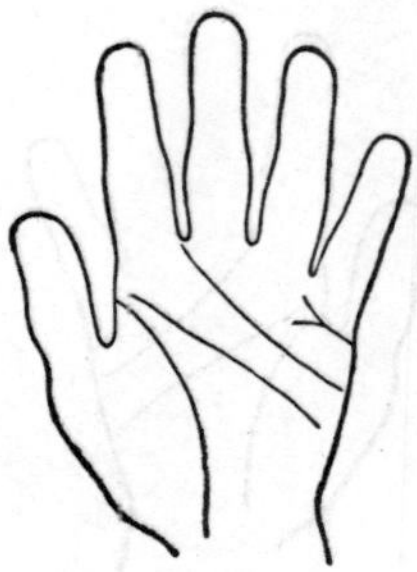

NO. 329

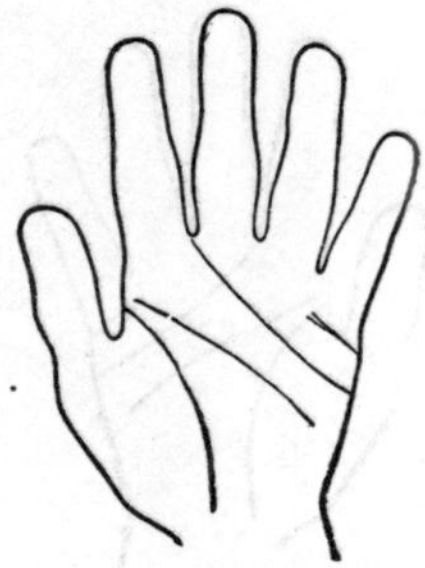

NO. 330

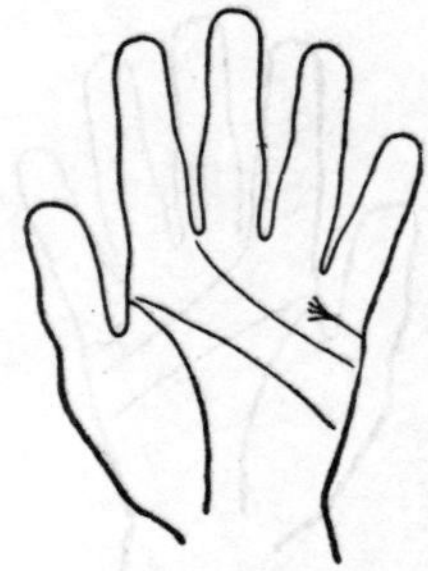

NO. 331

the married life will be full of sorrows and disappointments (332). If branches rise from the line of Affection, the subject will be uplifted and the affection will be a benefit to him (333). If the line be broken it will indicate that the affection is interfered with or broken in some way (334).

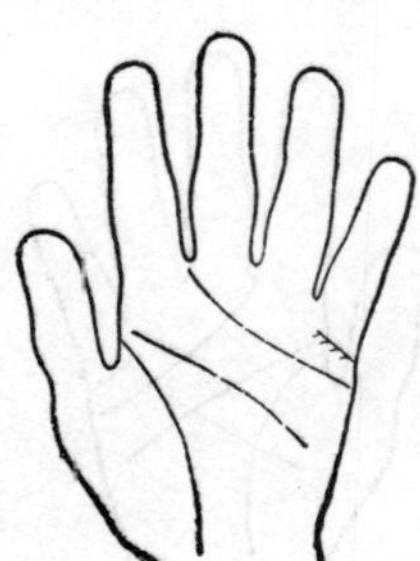

NO. 332

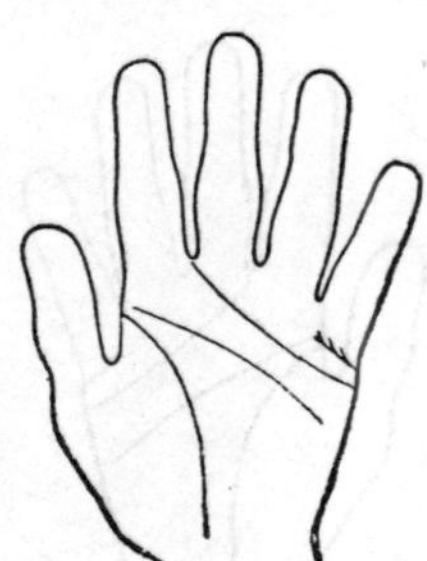

NO. 333

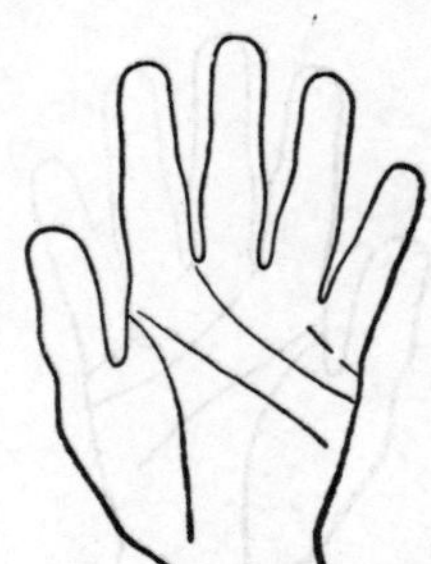

NO. 334

Look for repair signs. If the break be enclosed in a square the subject will recover the disturbed affection (335). If the line make a hook on the Mount, the subject will lose his affection, which will not be regained (336). If a dot be seen on a line of Affection, it indicates an impediment to the course of the affections (337), the termination of the line showing the outcome, for if the line end in a fork, trident, or tassel the affection will be dissipated (338). If after the dot the line grows thin, the affection disappears gradually (339). If Worry lines run from the Mount of Venus to the

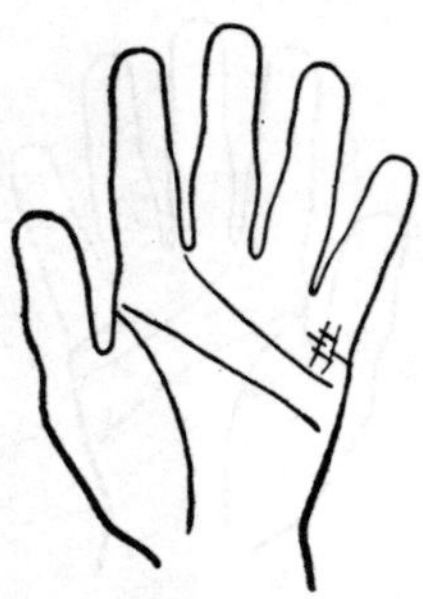
NO. 335

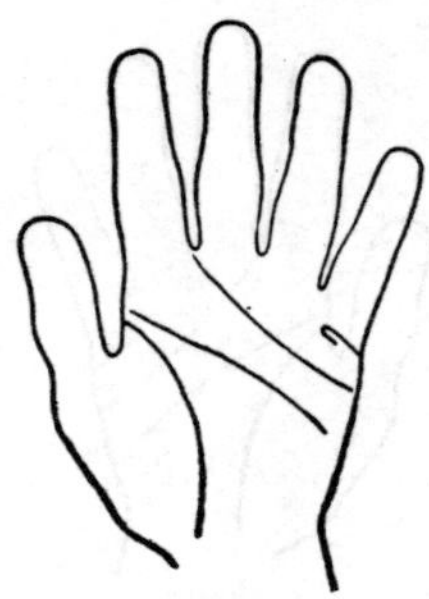
NO. 336

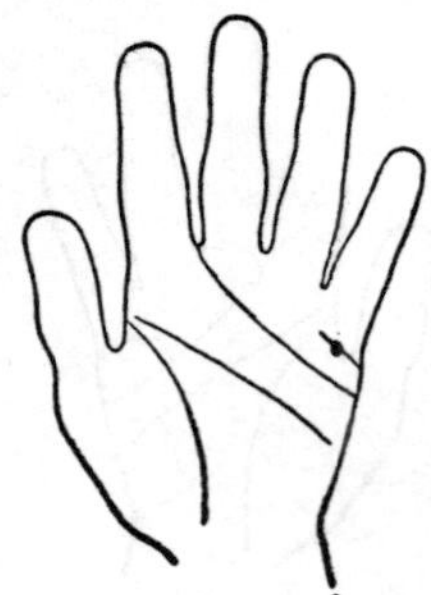
NO. 337

lines of Affection, and cut these lines, it shows that relatives are interfering with the married life of the subject (340). If the cutting line run from Influence lines on the Mount of Venus, it can be determined how close is the kinship of the relative who is causing the difficulty. If a line from a close

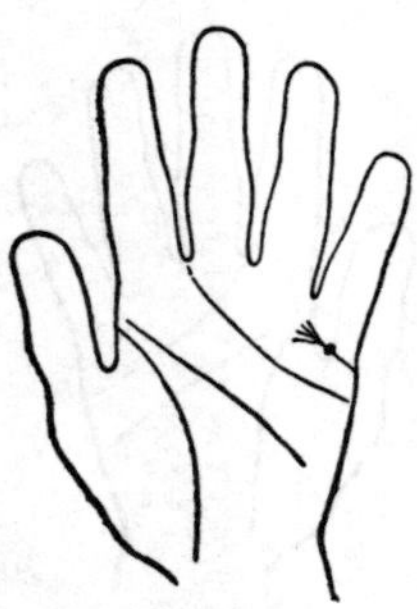
NO. 338

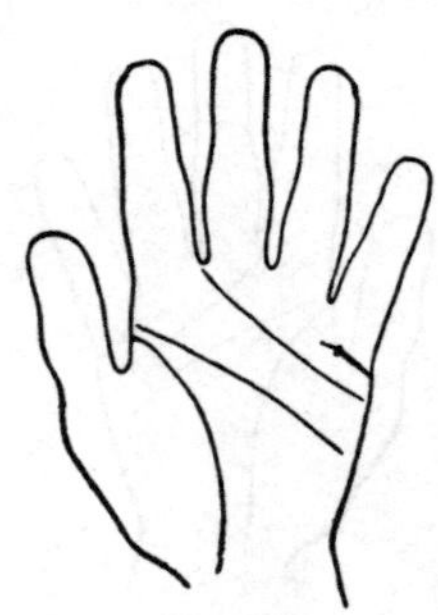
NO. 339

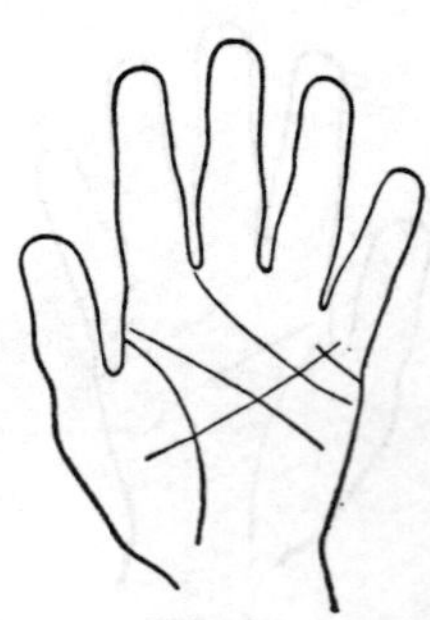
NO. 340

line of Influence cut a forked line of Affection, the married life of the subject will be interfered with by a near relative (341). The forked line shows that the subject loses some enjoyment of the marriage relation through this interference. If the line of Affection end in a tassel, the reading is intensified (342). If a line of Affection cut by a bar have a chance line running to an island, a cross, a bar, or a dot in the Head line, an interference with the married life of the subject will result in some form of brain disturbance (343). In this manner chance lines will be seen running from obstructions in the line of Affection to various parts of the hand, sometimes to defective Life lines, or health defects of the Mounts. In all these cases the trouble pointed to will be brought on by an interference or blemish seen in the line of Affection. Each one of these defects in the line of Affection will indicate an event in the life of the subject. In all cases the lines of Affection should be read in combination with Influence lines on the Mount of Venus. As both relate to the

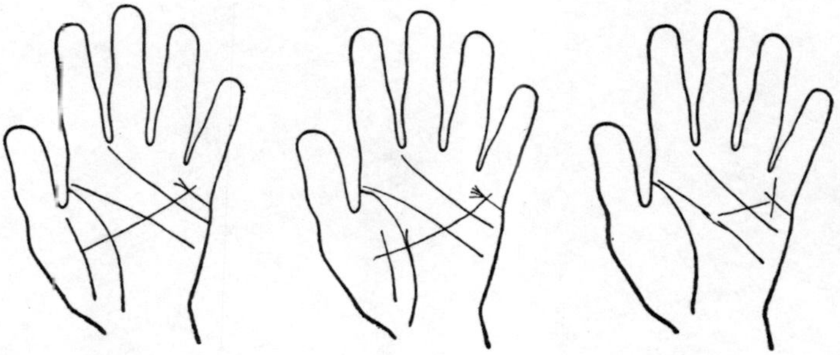

NO. 341 NO. 342 NO. 343

coming into the life of a new factor, viz., someone outside of the subject himself, they are interdependent.

My advice to every practitioner is to use great care in all matters relating to marriage and home life. The real object of an examination of the hand is to give a client a better knowledge of himself. Unless the matter of marriage is so interwoven with his existence that the two seem inseparable, it is only gratifying curiosity to deal with it, and does no real good. When his career is being ruined or interfered with by adverse influences, these matters should be pointed out. Merely to tell about them in order to show whether you can do it or not, is lowering the standard of the profession. A surgeon would not amputate a limb to show that he knew how, but he would do so if the limb needed amputating and the operation would help the patient. All palmists should proceed upon that idea. Do what is necessary for the help or guidance of the client, but nothing merely to exhibit skill. A strict adherence to this principle will win in the long run, and nowhere more surely than in the matter of the lines of Affection.

CHAPTER X

THE LINE OF SATURN

"We make our fortunes and we call them fate."—B. DISRAELI.

THE line of Saturn is the fourth Main line which receives the Current, and is frequently called the "line of Fate." Upon first thought, it may not be apparent why fatality, good or bad, has been ascribed to this line, but the claim is justified in various ways. The line of Saturn rises at the base of the hand and runs upward toward the fingers; and, according to our hypothesis, the Current which passes into it does so on its return from the brain where it has been sent from the end of the Life line. The line of Saturn thus reads from the bottom upward and the scale indicating the various years of life will be found in Chapter IV. According to this scale the period of childhood is the extreme lower part of the line, and old age is recorded by it on the Mount of Saturn. From the line of Saturn health difficulties are not read, nor is anything shown concerning the general make-up or constitution of a subject such as is indicated in other lines that we have considered. It does indicate the course of the subject through life from a standpoint of material success, and shows whether he must make his own way, whether he will have a hard time, or whether things will apparently come easy to him. It will also locate his most productive periods. This is what the older palmists had in mind when they named the line of Saturn "Fate or Destiny," as it is generally taken for granted that one whose life runs smoothly must have luck in his favor. In these cases it has not always been remembered that such a subject may have had every qualification which would enable him to *merit* success, and that he has achieved it because he has worked, and because success has been deserved. Combined with a good line of Saturn, there may be health, brains, determination, ambition, and similar qualities, and in that case the presence of these qualities accounts for the good line of Saturn, which consequently indicates that the subject will get through the world comfortably and successfully. A combination of such forces as the above, if wisely and faithfully *used*, produces so-called *luck*, and most of the persons who are pointed out as particularly fortunate, or lucky, attribute their success primarily to brains, health, energy, ambition, and kindred allies, and not to blind chance, luck, or fate. There is, however, some magic glamour around the words "fate" and "luck," which seems to speak of results achieved without effort, and this has always been the goal toward which the eyes of lazy folk are turned. Such people are ever ready to account for their failures by saying, "Others are lucky, I am not," but this should be followed by the further explanation that most often the "lucky" subject is a *worker* and the "unlucky" one is not. Day dreamers expect luck to reach down and touch them with a magic wand. Those who are called lucky say that the magic wand is *industry*. In many cases luck consists in having the foresight to seize opportunities. "Unlucky" persons tell of chances they have passed, and console themselves by saying that luck was not on their side. In the majority of cases, it would be more proper to say that *foresight* and *perseverance* were not. This much moralizing I beg to introduce here, because I wish it distinctly understood that I do not believe in blind fate or chance.

In the beginning of a study of the line of Saturn, or line of Fate, I wish to give my definition of that word and to assure you that we are not to plunge from a treatment of the hand which has thus far proceeded entirely under laws of cause and effect into one which deals with chance. The line of Saturn is a wonderful line, its revelations are accurate and important, but we shall find causes for all the effects we see upon it. On every line of Saturn, we note periods when everything is propitious for the subject. These are the harvest periods of his life. At such times we find good health, the presence of mental powers such as discernment, will, ambition, and various good companions which he may turn to his account, or which he may leave unused. During these periods, life *is* easier for the subject. He is well and in possession of his full powers. He works with less effort, and, in superstitious parlance, he is "lucky" and "fate" is on his side. Many persons take advantage of these periods of greatest possibilities and "make hay while the sun shines." Others pass such times in enjoyment and laziness, confident that "luck is with them," and will never leave. When the powers begin to wane luck is not so constant in attendance; it takes more effort to accomplish the same results, and finally all kinds of effort fail to produce anything considerable. At this time the cry is raised, "luck has gone." The truth is that the subject has passed his harvest period and has slept his golden moments away. The opportunities placed before him have not been seized; he has taken his pleasure during the time when he should have worked hardest, and by the law of compensation he must toil to make up for it. "You cannot eat your cake and have it too"; you cannot waste your harvest days and be "lucky." He who has *worked* through his productive time may rest when powers fail. The laws of cause and effect are present in the line of Saturn, or Fate, as everywhere else. It is only after much observation of this line that it is possible to state what can actually be told from it. The superficiality which has been shown in its treatment has served principally to disgust sensible persons. Why the line shows these matters, which are so obviously beyond the consciousness of the individual, can only be explained on the already stated hypothesis, that the lines are the life map of every person, placed before him in order that he may be guided to the achievement of his best results.

The line of Saturn, when strong, emphasizes the Saturnian traits, especially if the line be deep on the Mount, and these traits are wisdom, soberness, and the faculty of seeing life from its serious side. The fact that these balancing qualities are present in some degree with a good line may account for the success in old age which comes to one with a strong line on the Mount. Saturnian traits are energy and frugality, as well as studiousness and the ability to think, and these qualities will do much to make a life successful. The Saturnian has a penchant for explorations in the earth, and has from this natural love been led to discovering gold, silver, coal, and other mine treasures. He has found gas and oil wells, and thus, through following his natural inclinations, "fate" has been said to be with him, and the Saturnian has for these reasons been called the "child of fate." The greatest part that fate or luck plays with humanity is to give one person more brains and a better type than another, and this has been sometimes called the "accident of birth." In these cases the subject will also have the best Saturn line. The Apollonian and Venusian, or a good Jupiterian, or Mercurian, are much greater examples to my mind of a kind fate than is the Saturnian.

The line of Saturn is not found in every hand. Older palmists gave to a hand without a Saturn line the interpretation of a "negative existence." Observation will show that the line is absent in the hands of many successful people, and in other prosperous subjects it is present only in rudimentary form. These persons have not led negative lives, so this interpretation cannot be correct. In a great many cases of this kind coming under my observation, I have found that the subjects are what are commonly called "self-made men," that they began life in humble positions, and only by dint of energy and application have they made their way in the world. These "self-made" people are not always brilliant to start with, but they have determination and energy and will educate themselves, even if it must be done at night after the day's work is over, and they will not fail to seize every opportunity for progress. They seem to feel that *everything depends upon their own efforts* and no amount of labor is allowed to stand between them and ultimate success. They are the kind of men who can "carry the message to Garcia."

As the result of my observation, I read hands in which no Saturn line is seen as belonging to a subject who must depend upon himself entirely; who should not trust to luck or fortunate circumstances, but if he would accomplish much in the world, it must be the result of his own efforts.

The line of Saturn may start from one of many places. These are always at the base of the hand (344) but may be

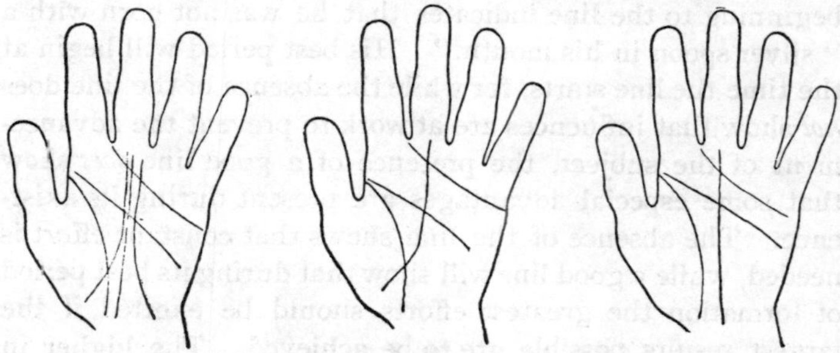

NO. 344 NO. 345 NO. 346

any point between the end of the Life line and the Mount of Moon. Sometimes the line rises inside the Life line, and sometimes as high as the upper Mount of Moon. The course of the Saturn line is always *toward* the Mount of Saturn, sometimes reaching the Mount, and sometimes falling far short. It always runs through the centre of the palm. When the Saturn line rises inside the Life line and runs on to the Mount of Saturn (345) it indicates that the subject will have material success in life, and that near relatives will assist him greatly. When the line rises from the centre of the palm (346) and runs into the Mount of Saturn, the subject will achieve success in life largely by his own efforts. When the line rises from the Mount of Moon and runs on to the Mount of Saturn (347) the subject's success in life will be materially assisted by one of the opposite sex. This may either be by good advice or by rendering financial aid. I have noted this marking on many hands where the wives have been of great assistance in the career of the subject. In most instances the sources of the line will be in one of these three positions, all other beginnings being a modification of one or the other of them, and all readings should be modified in proportion as the source of the line is from these three pronounced centres. Sometimes the line does not rise low in the hand, but starts higher up (348). In this case the subject will have a more negative existence for the first part of the life, as this point is the time when he is so young that he can accomplish little by his own efforts, and such a beginning to the line indicates that he was not born with a "silver spoon in his mouth." His best period will begin at the time the line starts, for while the absence of the line does *not* show that influences are at work to prevent the advancement of the subject, the presence of a good line *does* show that some especial advantages are present during its existence. The absence of the line shows that constant effort is needed, while a good line will show that during its best period of formation the greatest efforts should be exerted if the largest results possible are to be achieved. The higher in the hand the line starts, the later in life will be the period of easiest sailing. Whenever a deficiency is noted in the Saturn line you will find an explanation in some of the other lines

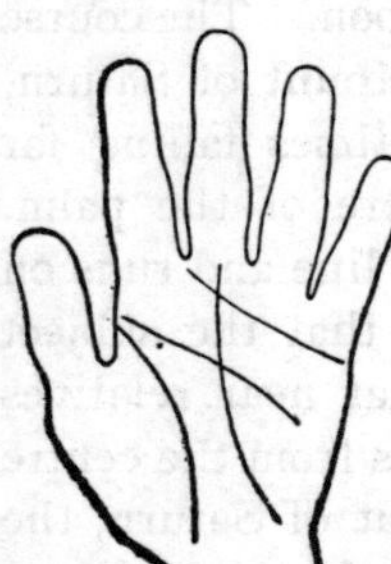
NO. 347

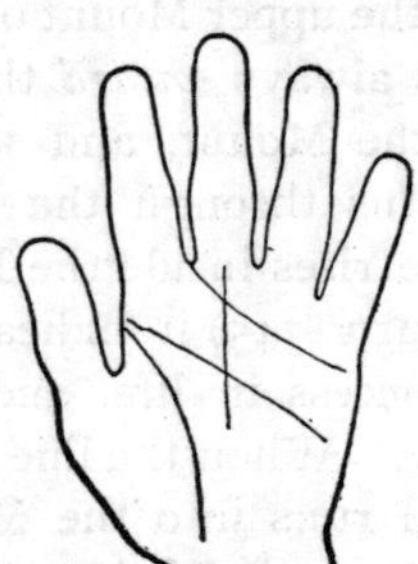
NO. 348

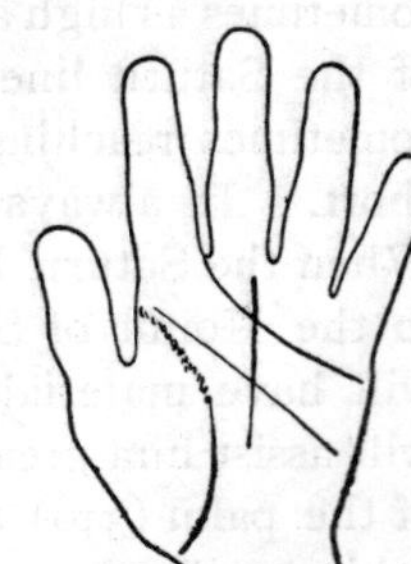
NO. 349

or signs. With the line absent at the beginning, it may be found that the Life line will show great delicacy for the same period of years that is covered by the absence of the Saturn line (349). Thus you will know that the subject did little during the earlier years because he was delicate. As the Saturn line *begins* at the time this delicacy *ends* on the Life line, he will at that time begin a period which he may make productive. If the Life line be thin when it begins to recover, and grows thicker as it progresses, and if the Saturn line does the same, the subject will continue to do better in a business way as his strength increases. It will be noted that it is necessary to read the beginning of the Saturn line from the bottom and the Life line from the top. If with the line rising late we find a defective Head line at the start (350)

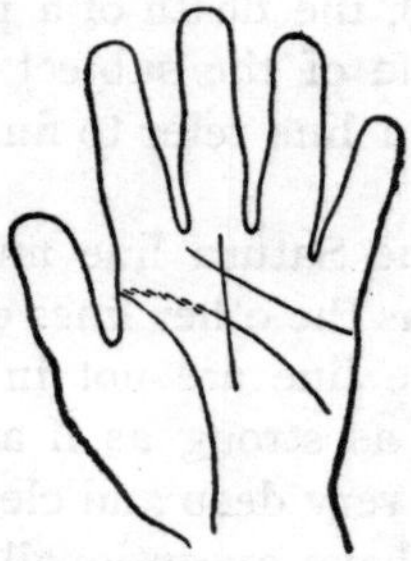

NO. 350

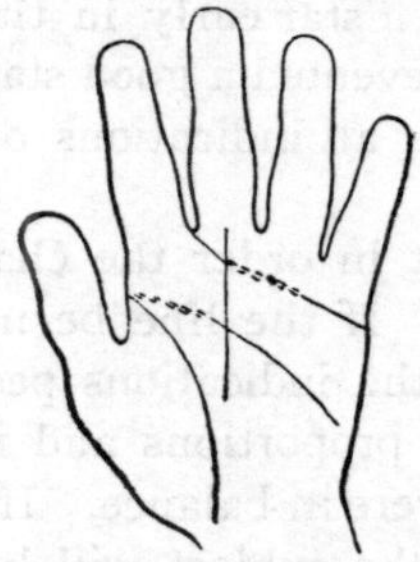

NO. 351

the subject will have his start in life impeded by brain weakness, and the Saturn line will not grow good until the Head line does. If the Head line be weak at the start, and as soon as it recovers the Heart line become weak, the Life line being thin all of this time (351), the career of the subject will be hindered first by head trouble, and then by heart weakness, and he does not begin to do his best until these have passed away. If the line rise high in the hand and the lines of Head or Heart are not defective, you must look for health defects in other parts of the hand, on lines and Mounts, and somewhere you will discover the cause of the absence of the Saturn line. Use both hands with the Saturn line. If the line begin low in the left hand and rise high in the right, you will know that the natural course of the line was favorable, but as it shows its defects in the right hand, something has occurred to alter the original plan. This may be health, laziness, or influences from family, friends, or outsiders, and inasmuch as we do not believe that mere chance has produced the alteration we must look somewhere for the unfavorable condition which has prevented the rising of the Saturn line low in the right hand. The absence of a Saturn line where it should normally begin will often be explained by some accident to the parents. As this early period of the line covers the childhood of the subject, it will not be through his own fault that the start in life is not as good as it should be. If a line of Saturn rise high in the hand, and a line of parental influence on the Mount of Venus end in a star early in the line (352), the death of a parent has prevented a good start in the life of the subject. Remember all indications on the Saturn line refer to financial affairs.

Next in order the character of the Saturn line must be noted. If the line be not so deep as the other lines on the hand, the indications peculiar to the line are not in their proper proportions and will not be as strong as if all the lines were in balance. If the line be very deep and clear cut (353), the subject will be found to have exceptionally fine qualities, with a proper use of which he should be enabled to achieve great success. If this deep line extend up on to the

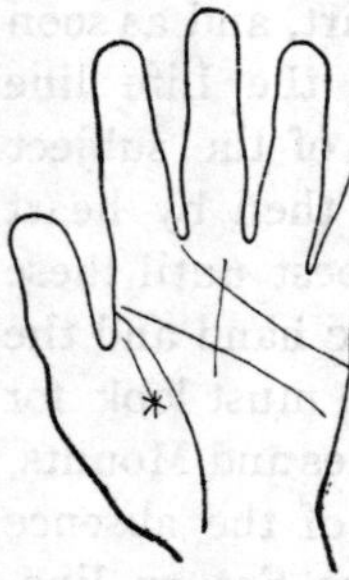

NO. 352

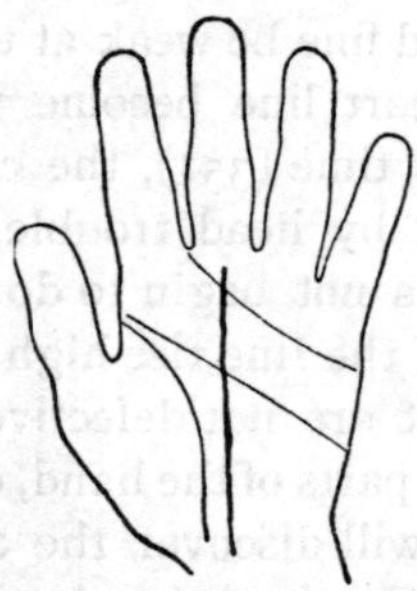

NO. 353

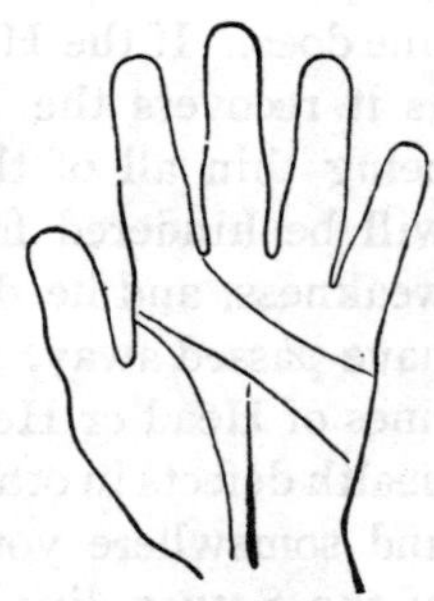

NO. 354

Mount of Saturn, these favorable conditions will continue during the entire life. If the line be short, they will be present only during the length of the line, the age to be read from the line. If this deepness of the line be early in life, the subject will have his best period during childhood (354). This is an unfortunate marking, for at this age the subject is seldom old enough to take advantage of opportunities.

The deep line of Saturn is the most favorable line to possess. A thin line (355) will show that the subject has much in his favor in the way of natural advantages, and while he will have to exert himself more to bring forth great results than a subject with a deep line, he will still have an easier time to succeed than one with a defective line or with no line at all. A broad and shallow line (356) indicates a condition little

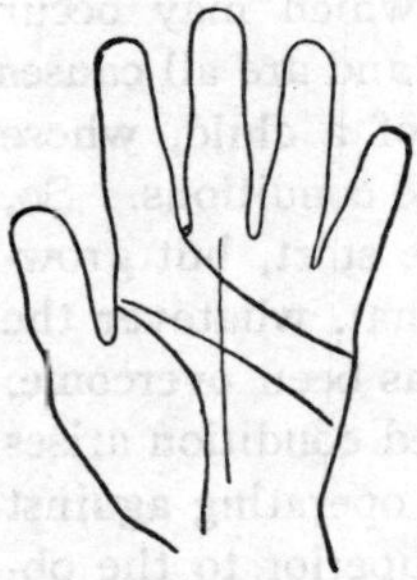

NO. 355

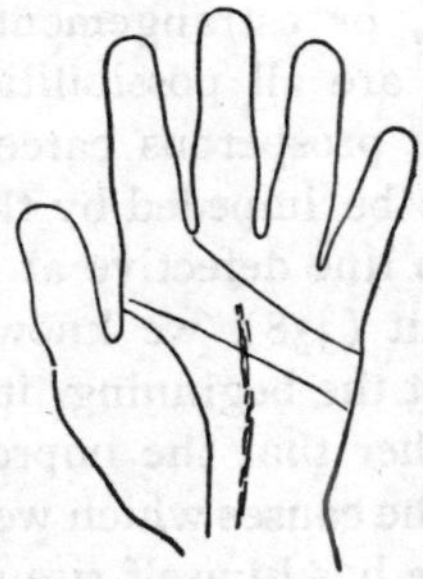

NO. 356

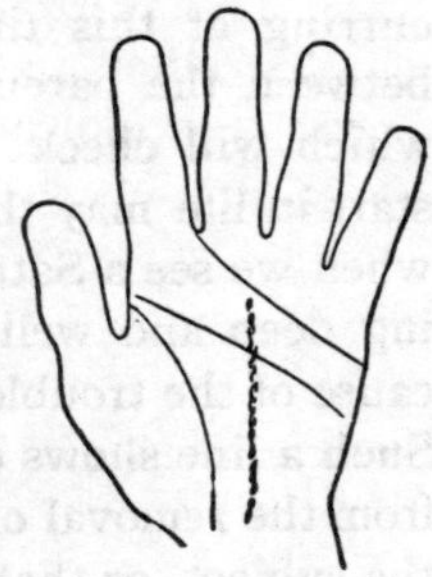

NO. 357

better than no line at all, and if the Saturn line alone be of such a character, while the other lines are well marked, the subject will have continual struggles. A chained line of Saturn indicates that the career will be a hard one. If the line be chained, during its entire length, the subject will have continuous obstructions and the life will be a labored one, full of disappointments (357). If chained only part of the way, the difficulties will last during this condition.

Color, being an indication of the strength and condition of the Blood Current, does not affect the line of Saturn, as it does other lines, for this line is in no manner an index of the health or the disease of the subject, and thus the line of Saturn will be the first line to which it is unnecessary to apply the color test.

All defects in the Saturn line are important, for they show how many and what kind of impediments will occur in the subject's life, how serious they will be, and as the cause producing most of these checks can be located in various parts of the hand it is quite possible to remedy or avoid a good many of them. All defects found in the beginning of the line refer to the childhood of the subject, and during this period the child is too young to do much by himself, either toward improving or hindering his condition. Consequently, all defects or impediments to childhood are either the result of ill-health, or come from paternal influences, both of which are beyond the power of the child to control. The death of parents, their financial difficulty occurring at this time, or estrangements which may occur between the parents, are all possibilities and are all causes which will check the prosperous career of a child, whose start in life may thus be impeded by these conditions. So, when we see a Saturn line defective at the start, but growing deep and well cut (358), we know that, whatever the cause of the trouble at the beginning, it has been overcome. Such a line shows either that the improved condition arises from the removal of the causes which were operating against the subject, or that he has himself risen superior to the obstacles. It makes no difference as to the character of the

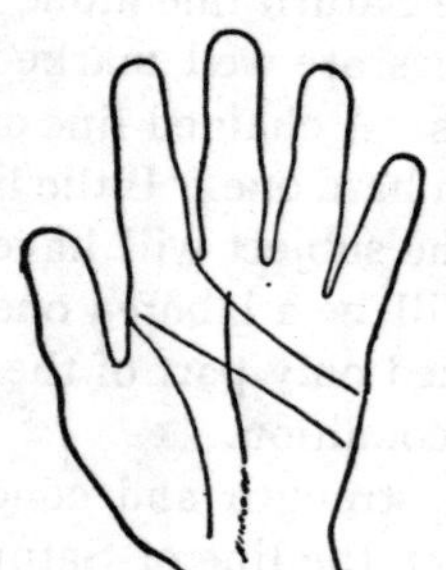

NO. 358

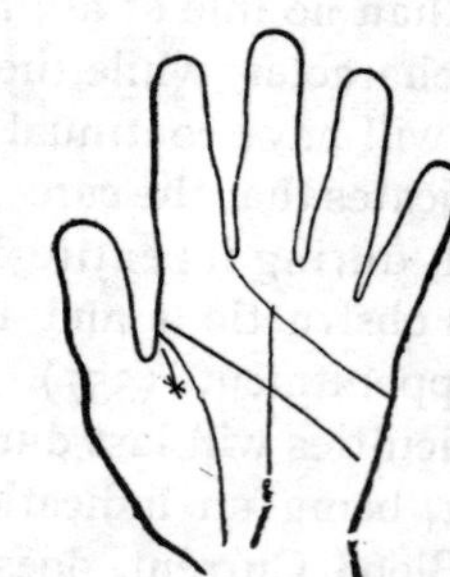

NO. 359

defect which appears in the beginning of a Saturn line, the general rule is the same. It indicates an impediment to the early years of the subject. If a short Influence line on the Mount of Venus end in a star, and the Saturn line be chained at the beginning, the death of a parent has clouded the early career of the subject (359). The age at which this parent died can be read from the distance the star reaches on the Life line. The date at which the improvement in the affairs of the subject occurred can be read from the line of Saturn. If a short line of Influence end in a star and a Worry line run from it and cut a rising branch on the Life line ending in an island on the line of Head (360), the death of a parent has brought on a check to the upward course of

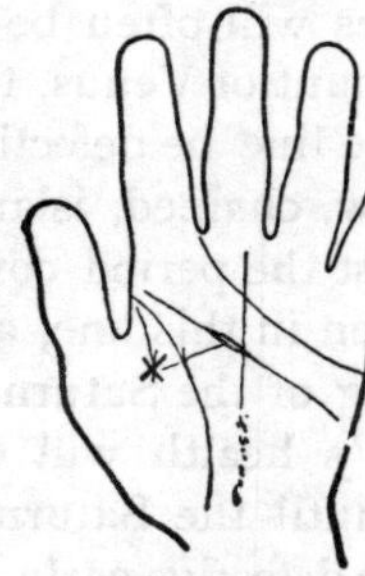

NO. 360

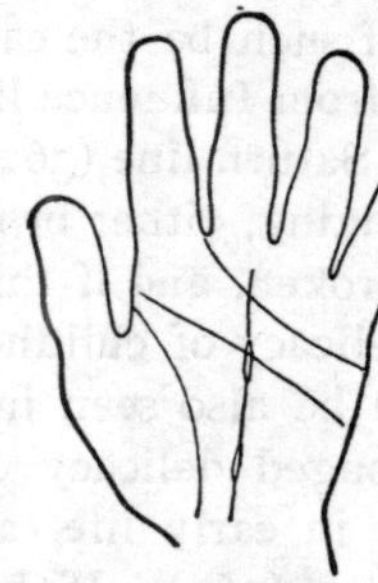

NO. 361

the subject's life which has affected his mental strength, and thus checked and retarded his career.

Islands in the Saturn line (361) have very generally received the interpretation of a check to the career, arising from the marital infidelity or moral depravity of the subject. It was recognized by older palmists that islands always indicated trouble, and as the above reading of immorality originated in lands where virtue among women was rarer than in this country, it was seen on the hands of many women who had bad reputations and ruined and checkered careers. These women being known to be profligate, this interpretation of immorality was given the island in the line of Saturn. This indication has caused much discussion among palmists, and much confusion and error among practitioners. After careful study of the subject, I can say that an island in the Saturn line indicates a period of financial difficulty, lasting the length of the island, and that the marking is not *per se* an indication of infidelity. This conclusion has been reached after the examination of hundreds of hands having such a marking, in which financial trouble or losses have been completely verified, and in which only a few cases of infidelity were found accompanying it. In these latter cases I am sure that the infidelity caused the financial trouble. An island, if found at the beginning of the Saturn line, could not indicate infidelity of the subject, for he is then too young to make such a thing possible. Financial difficulty might be present in his life through a difficulty of his parents. If such be the case, Worry lines will often be seen running from Influence lines on the Mount of Venus, to the island in Saturn line (362). If the Life line be defective at the beginning, either broad and shallow, chained, islanded, split or broken, and if this continue past the period covered by the delicacy of childhood usually seen in this line, and if an island be also seen in the beginning of the Saturn line, the prolonged delicacy of the subject's health will cause difficulty in early life, and will last until the Saturn line grows better (363). If the Head line be defective early in its course, with an island at the beginning of the line of Saturn (364), poor mentality will be the impediment which is caus-

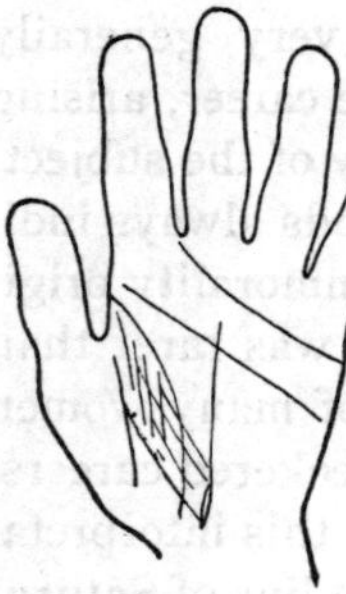

NO. 362

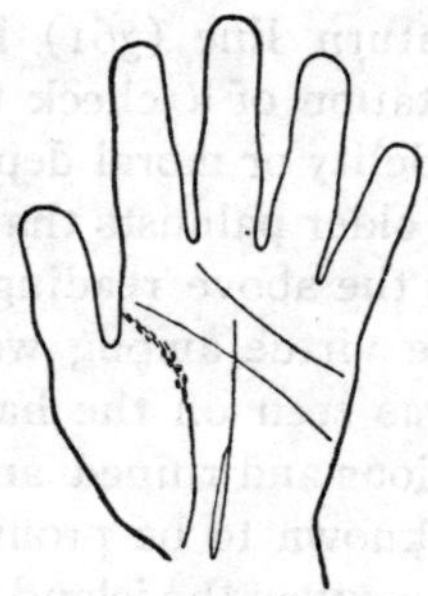

NO. 363

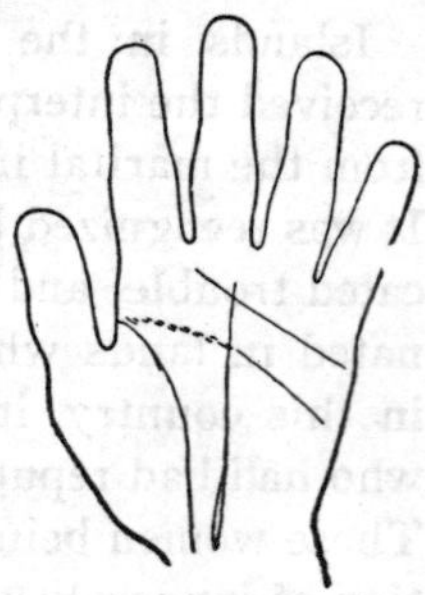

NC. 364

ing the check to the career of the subject. In these cases of ill health the Life line and other parts of the hand will be weak in sympathy. If a short Influence line on the Mount of Venus end with a star, with an island in the line of Saturn at its beginning, the death of a parent will cause financial difficulty during early life (365). This indication is intensified if Worry lines run to the island from this star.

If Worry lines run from Influence lines on Mount of Venus to an island at the beginning of the Saturn line, constant annoyances in the early life of the subject bring about a check to his career (366). This shows quite plainly, for these Worry lines cut the Life line and point to the effect they produce by the island on the Saturn line. With all islands at the beginning of the Saturn line, there is an explanation some-

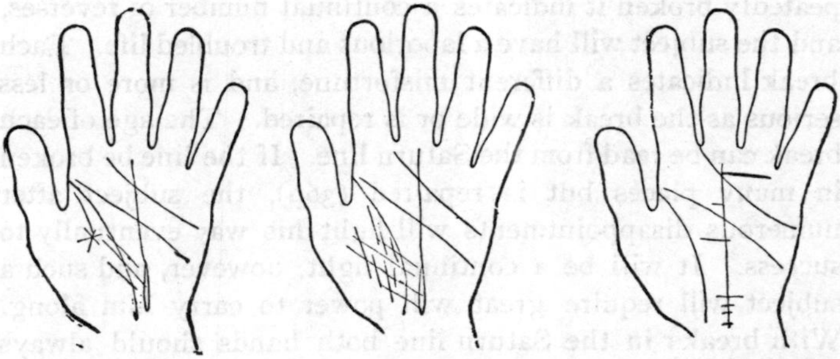

NO. 365 NO. 366 NO. 367

where in the hand as to the cause which produces them. There is no element of chance in this indication other than health or heredity, and the cause can be found if you apply diligence and good reasoning. When an island in this location is seen, go over every line in the hand and hunt for defects. Go over the Influence lines on Mount of Venus to discover what part relatives may play ; look to the Mounts for health defects of all the types, and for chance lines pointing from these defects to the island. In this way the cause of trouble can be found.

Cross-bars cutting the Saturn line (367) are obstructions to the career of the subject. Each one of the bars is a separate obstruction, and by noting the depth of each you can tell how serious it is. If only faint lines which do not cut through the Saturn line but pass over it, they indicate continual annoying interferences and impediments. If they cut the line in two, they are serious checks which threaten to destroy the success of the subject. The age at which each of these interferences occurs can be read from the Saturn line, their seriousness by the depth of the cutting line, their cause from other lines and signs, and their outcome by the termination of the Saturn line. Breaks in the line (368) are most serious. At the time they occur some force has been sufficiently strong to check the career entirely, and if the line takes a new character, starts in a new direction, or does not start at all, these breaks indicate an entire change in the course of a subject's life-work. If the Saturn line be repeatedly broken it indicates a continual number of reverses, and the subject will have a laborious and troubled life. Each break indicates a different misfortune, and is more or less serious as the break is wide or is repaired. The age of each break can be read from the Saturn line. If the line be broken in many places but is repaired (369), the subject after numerous disappointments will fight his way eventually to success. It will be a continual fight, however, and such a subject will require great will power to carry him along. With breaks in the Saturn line both hands should always be examined, for from them you will read whether all of the

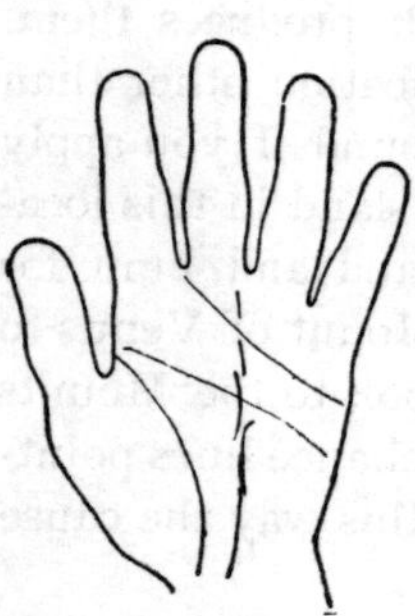

NO. 368

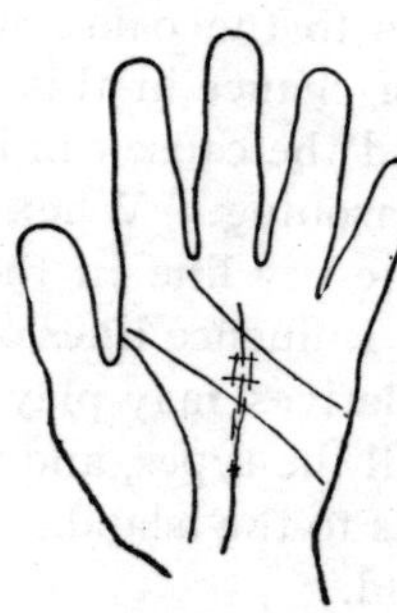

NO. 369

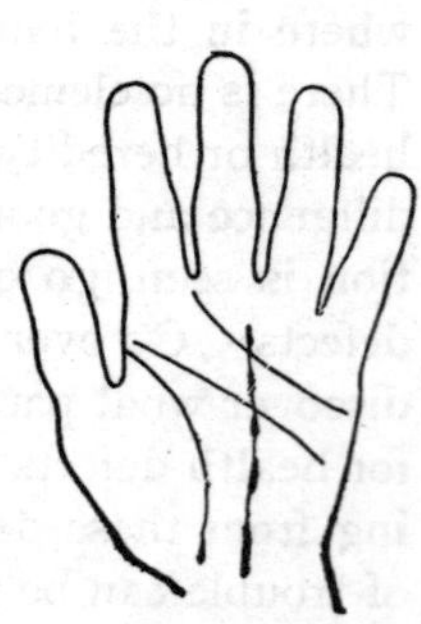

NO. 370

impediments in the line are a part of the natural plan or are the result of acquired habits, mistakes of calculation, ill health, or other causes. In a large majority of cases, the Saturn line is much better in the left than in the right hand, showing that a great many of our trials are brought on by ourselves. If a line of Saturn be uneven (370), alternately deep and thin in character, the subject will have intermittent periods of prosperity, and one with such a line must use continual watchfulness in order that, during the periods indicated by the thinness of the line, all which was gained while the line was deep may not be lost. This line indicates an unreliable and varying state of affairs. If the line of Saturn be wavy (371), it indicates that the subject will follow a constantly changing course. If, in addition to its

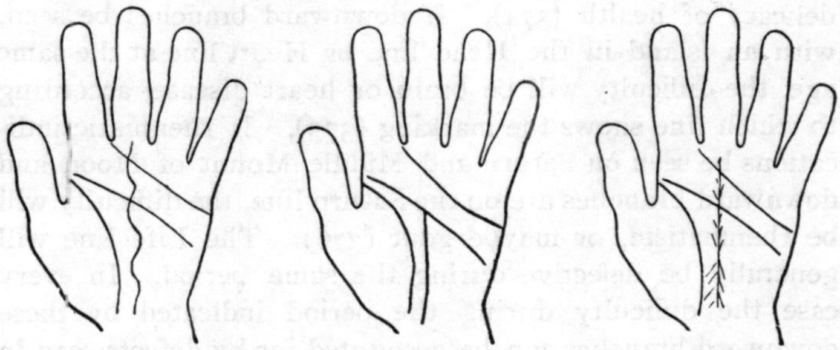

NO. 371 NO. 372 NO. 373

wavy course, this line be uneven or defective in other ways, the subject will have increased difficulty in his journey through life. If a line of Saturn begins deep at the base, and runs to the line of Head and there stops (372), the career of the subject will be favorable up to thirty, when errors of judgment will interfere, and from that time he will have a harder time to get along; he must rely entirely upon effort, not chance, and do the best he can to force his way. His period of greatest production has passed. After the age at which a line of Saturn stops, the subject will have to exert great effort in order to accomplish much, as it is during the life of the line that he must achieve the greater part of his results.

Many Saturn lines will be seen which have little fine lines rising from them, or falling in a downward direction (373). Rising lines will indicate the upward tendency of the life, and will add strength to the line on which they are seen. During whatever portion of the line these branches appear, that part of the line will be filled with hope and ambition and will be more successful than any other period. During the time when downward branches are seen, the life will be harder, more filled with discouragements, and progress will be difficult. The appearance of these upward and downward branches I have found to follow the health of the subject closely. When upward branches are seen, the physical powers will be found good. With downward branches on the Saturn line and an island in the Life line, the unfavorable condition of the Saturn line is to be accounted for by delicacy of health (374). If downward branches be seen, with an island in the Head line or Heart line at the same age, the difficulty will be brain or heart disease, according to which line shows the marking (375). If rheumatic indications be seen on Saturn and Middle Mount of Moon and downward branches are on the Saturn line, the difficulty will be rheumatism, or maybe gout (376). The Life line will generally be defective during the same period. In every case the difficulty during the period indicated by these downward branches can be accounted for by defects seen in some other part of the hand. The downward branches are the warning to look for trouble, and the task of the palmist

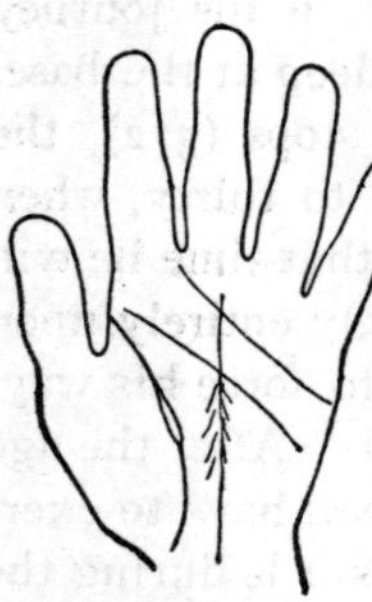

NO. 374

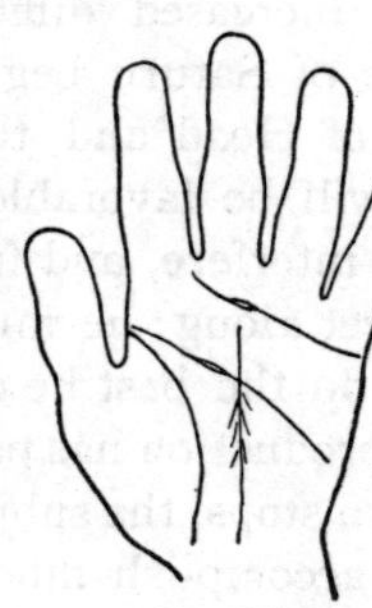

NO. 375

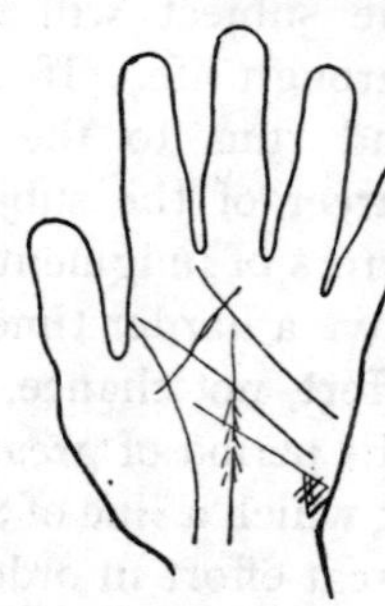

NO. 376

must be to find out what will cause it. Upward branches on the Saturn line, being favorable, do not need this care, for during favorable times people get along well enough ; it is the periods of trouble that need to be guarded against. There is one marking of the upward branches, however, which is useful. With upward branches from the Saturn line, if Worry lines from Mount of Venus cut the Life line and in turn cut these upward branches, the course of the subject, which is upward, will be constantly interfered with (377). While these interferences may not be able to destroy the effect of his favorable period, they will materially hamper and annoy him. In many hands Worry lines from the Mount of Venus, lines from the Mount of Moon, and chance lines from all parts of the hand will be

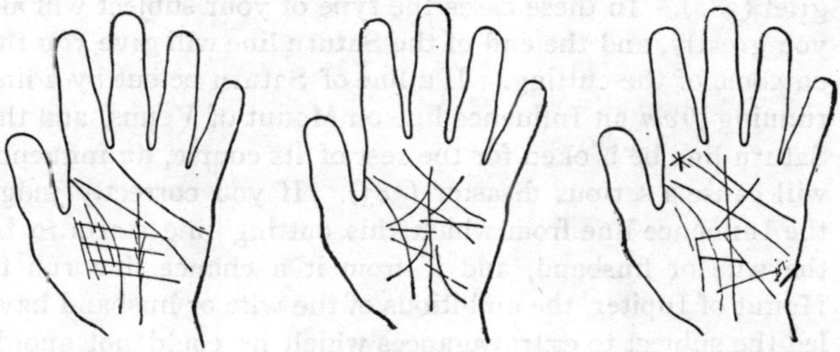

NO. 377 NO. 378 NO. 379

found crossing and joining themselves to the line of Saturn (378). This is particularly the case with nervous persons, who have much lined and rayed hands. Each one of these events, persons, illnesses, or whatever may be the interpretation of the several lines, will in some way affect the career of the subject. Some of these will be a positive detriment, others will strengthen and aid in the advancement of the subject.

As a general proposition, all lines which cut the Saturn line weaken it, and impede the progress of the subject at the age indicated by the cut (379). And all lines which merge into or run alongside the line strengthen it. These lines will rise from all parts of the hand, and will represent different factors which are a detriment and a check to the subject's progress, or which aid him. In all cases, the place from which these lines start will give you the clew to the influence. If a chance line from a star on Mount of Jupiter cuts the Saturn line, the subject will suffer a severe check from too much ambition. His endeavor to know distinguished people will lead him to do foolish things which injure his prospects (380). If this chance line runs to an island in the Saturn line, his ambition to move in the front rank will cause him to be extravagant, and financial difficulties will result (381). If with a bad Mercurian hand, grilled Mount, twisted finger, and large third phalanx of Mercury, a chance line from the Mount of Mercury cut the Saturn line, the dishonesty of the subject will bring him to grief (382). In these cases the type of your subject will aid you greatly, and the end of the Saturn line will give you the outcome of the cutting. If a line of Saturn be cut by a line running *from* an Influence line on Mount of Venus, and the Saturn line be broken for the rest of its course, an influence will cause a serious disaster (383). If you correctly judge the Influence line from which this cutting line starts to be the wife or husband, and if from it a chance line run to Mount of Jupiter, the ambitions of the wife or husband have led the subject to extravagances which he could not afford, and if the Saturn line be defective for the balance of its course, he will never recover from the reverses (384). If the Saturn line be cut by Worry lines from the Life line which is defec-

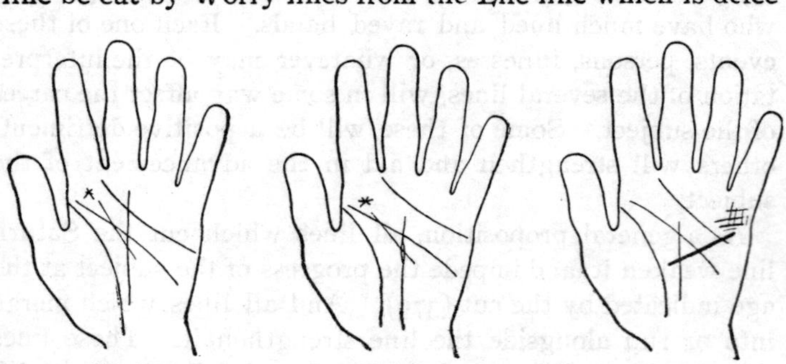

NC. 380 NO. 381 NO. 382

tive, ill health will be a bar to the prospects of the subject, and if the Saturn line be defective after the cut, the subject will never be able to get over it (385). The combinations of these cutting chance lines are infinite ; in some hands several will be seen, each one of which indicates a check from a different source. In these cases every cutting line is an object of special inquiry. Many chance lines run toward the Saturn line but do not touch it (386). These lines are events or influences, according to their source, but are abortive attempts to influence the career, and, while they exist as possible menaces, for the lines may grow until they cut the Saturn line,

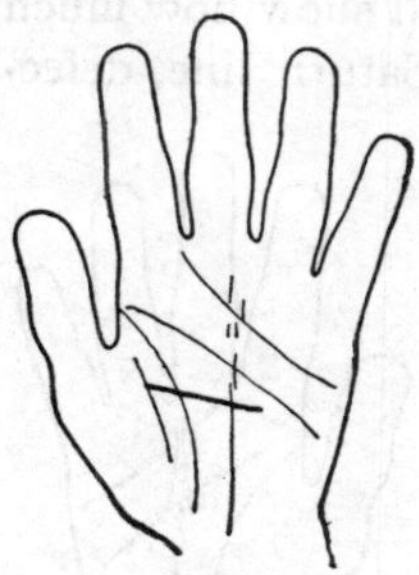
NO. 383

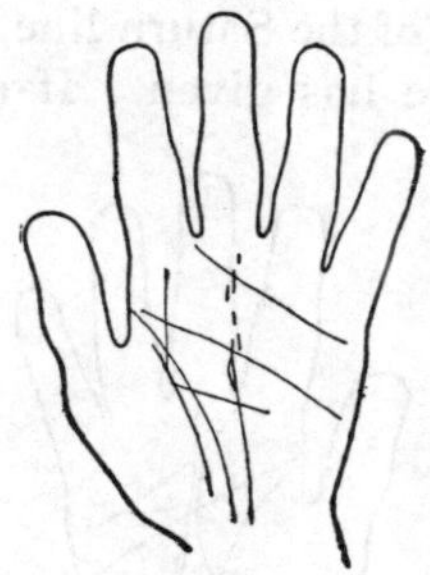
NO. 384

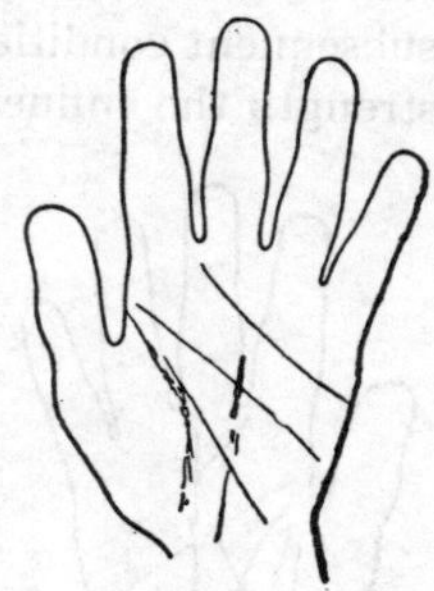
NO. 385

they are not immediate dangers. Some chance lines merge into the Saturn line (387). These lines represent events or influences which have come into and become a part of the life of the subject, but as they do not cut the line the career is not checked. If the Saturn line be thin or defective in any

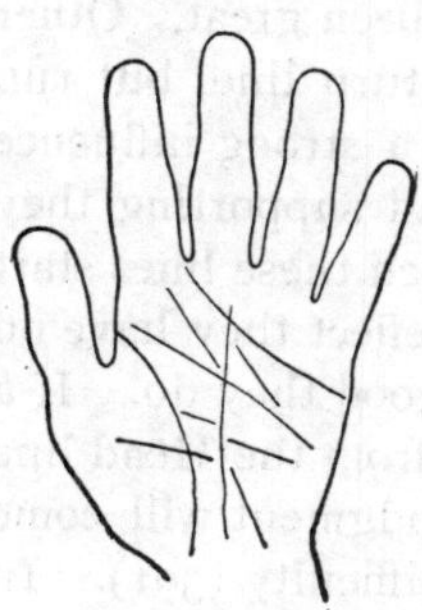
NO. 386

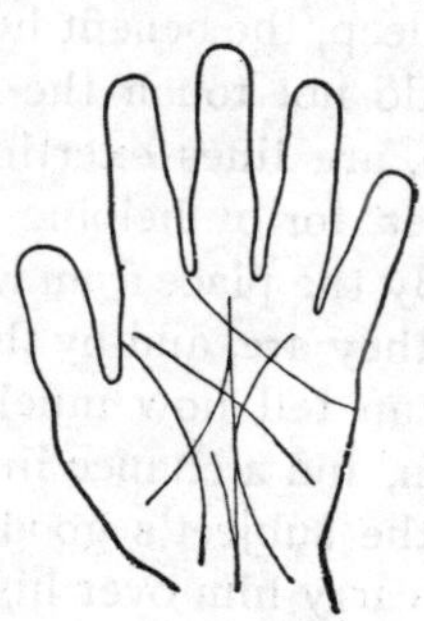
NO. 387

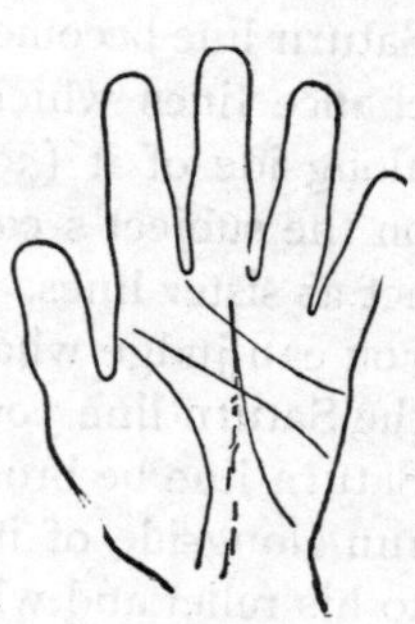
NO. 388

way, and these influencing lines are deep and strong, they will add to the prosperity of the subject and assist to overcome his difficulties. If, in the beginning, a Saturn line be chained or otherwise defective, and a chance line merges into it, after which it becomes deep, the influence which has come into the life has improved the subject's condition. If this chance line comes from the Mount of Moon it will be some outside influence (388), if it comes from Mount of Venus it will be the influence of close relatives (389). At whatever point these chance lines merge into the Saturn line, the good effect of the influence will be exerted at the age indicated, and the subsequent condition of the Saturn line will show how much strength the influence has given. If a Saturn line, defec-

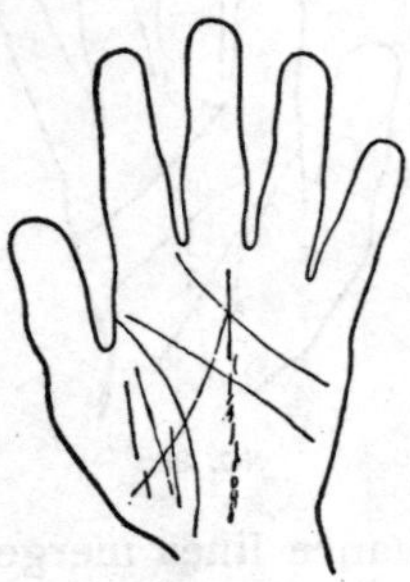
NO. 389

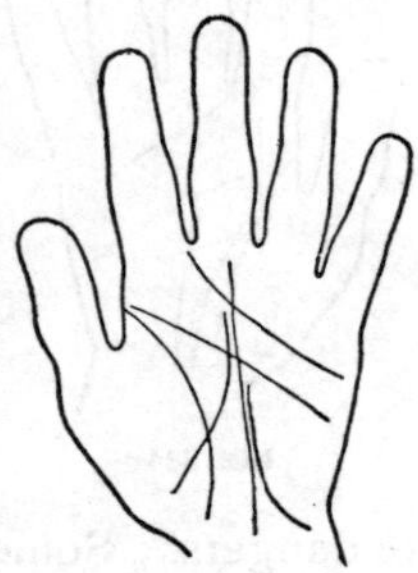
NO. 390

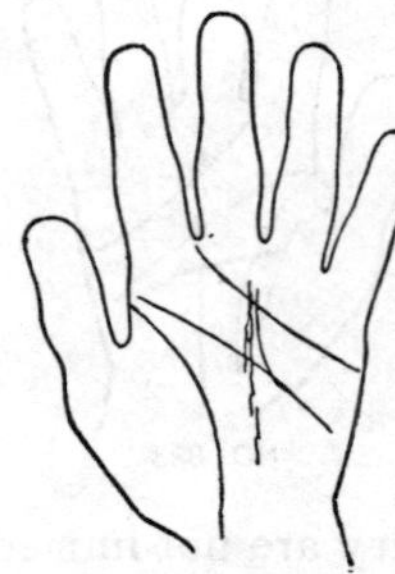
NO. 391

tive at the start, has a chance line merging into it, and if the Saturn line becomes only *thin* afterwards, or *not quite so defective*, the influence has not been very beneficial. If the Saturn line becomes deep, the benefit has been great. Other chance lines which do not touch the Saturn line, but run alongside of it (390), are lines exerting a strong influence on the subject's career, for by helping and supporting they act as sister lines. By the place from which these lines start you can judge what they are, and by the effect they have on the Saturn line you can tell how much good they do. If a Saturn line be broken, and a chance line from the Head line run alongside of it, the subject's good judgment will come to his relief and will carry him over his difficulty (391). In all cases where defects in the line are seen, look first for their cause and then to the repair indications. If a defective Saturn line have a chance line from a smooth and good Upper Mars running by its side, the resistance of the Mount will not permit discouragements to overthrow the subject, and this determination will save him from trouble (392).

In most hands there are two places where the Saturn line

shows the greatest number of defects. The first is at the start of the line, which period covers events brought into the child's life by his parents, and which show the manner in which he is started in life. If the Saturn line at this period be deep and strong, he will have little difficulty in getting started in life. It is a noticeable fact that those subjects who have the best kind of a start often fall into trouble later on, because, never having experienced it, they do not know how to act under adversity and how to take its consequent hard knocks. There seems to be a given amount of experience necessary to each individual, and if he does not receive this at one time he does at another. Those hands on which the Saturn line is defective at the start, generally improve, for the subject having adversity when young, early learns to avoid the dangers that beset him and becomes able to do for himself. The second period which is so often filled with difficulties is from thirty to forty-five, in most hands filling the period or space between the Head and Heart lines. This is the critical time in most business careers, and is the

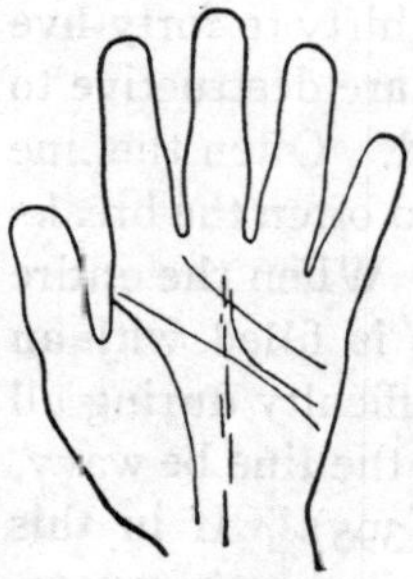

NO. 392

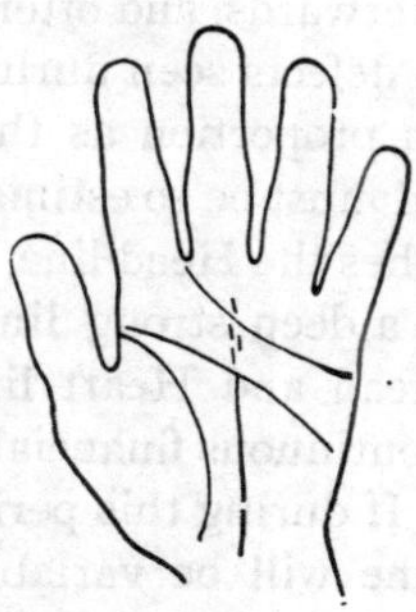

NO. 393

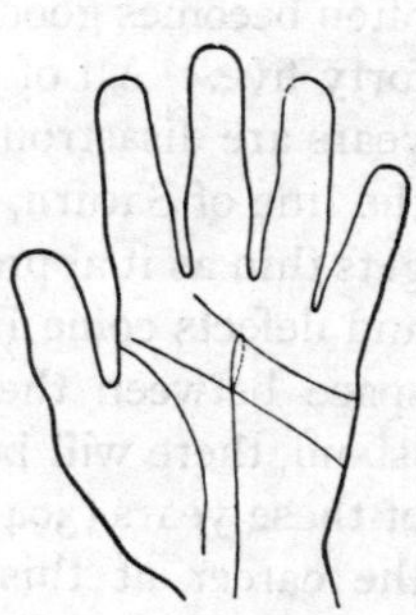

NO. 394

formative financial period in life. In most hands before this age the subject has been cared for and guided by parents or relatives. As the time approaches when these aids are no longer so closely depended upon, the subject begins to be guided by his own ideas. If these be good, he gets along all right, but if he believes that the experience of others will not apply to him, he will have disappointments, and will have to " pay for his experience." During the period of life indicated by the space between the Head and Heart lines, sometimes beginning earlier than this, the greatest number of defects are generally seen in the Saturn line. Between childhood and the age of twenty-five, most Saturn lines are deep. It is most interesting to note the number of hands in which the line is defective at thirty to forty-five (393). It

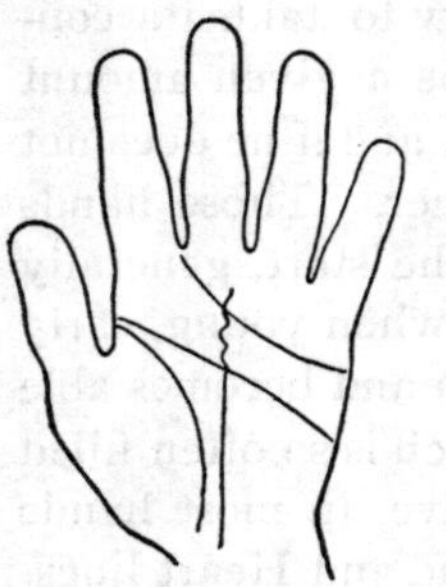

NO. 395

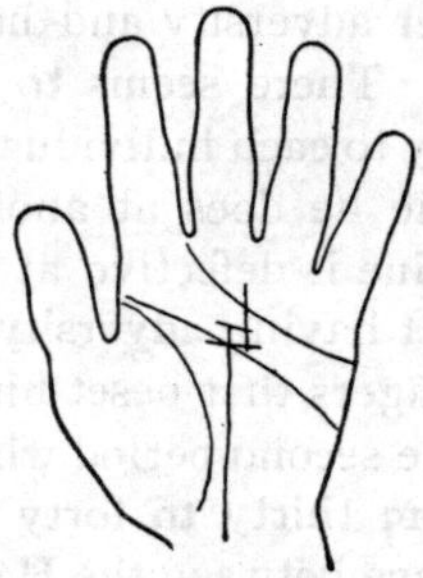

NO. 396

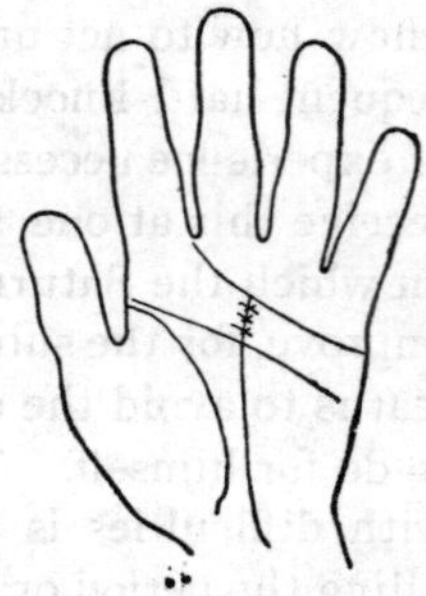

NO. 397

often becomes good afterwards, and often no line is seen after forty-five. All of the defects seen during thirty to forty-five years are disastrous in proportion as they are destructive to the line of Saturn, and must be so estimated. Often the line gets thin as it approaches the Head line, and often the breaks and defects come into a deep strong line. When the entire space between the Head and Heart lines is filled with an island, there will be continuous financial difficulty during all of these years (394). If during this period the line be wavy, the career at this time will be variable (395). If in this portion of the line a break should be repaired by a square, one side of which continues, the subject will have a serious reverse at the age indicated, but will be able to get through it (396). If the Saturn lines between Head and Heart line be covered with crosses, the subject will have repeated reverses which he will withstand if the line continues after this period, but which will overcome him if it does not (397). If this portion of the Saturn line be cut with cross-bars, the subject will meet with obstacles to his career (398). If the line cuts through these bars and severs them, the subject will overcome the difficulties ; but if these bars cut the Saturn line he will have great difficulty in doing so. If this portion of the Saturn line be cut by chance lines from the Head line, the

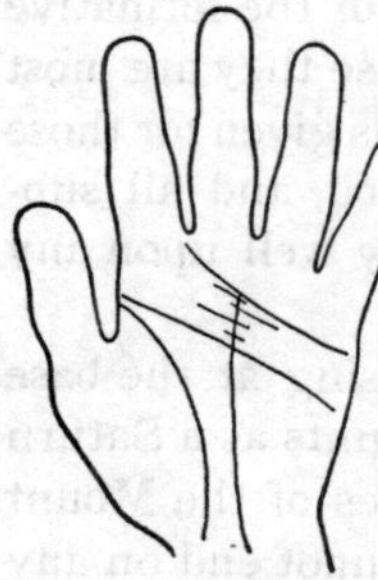
NO. 398

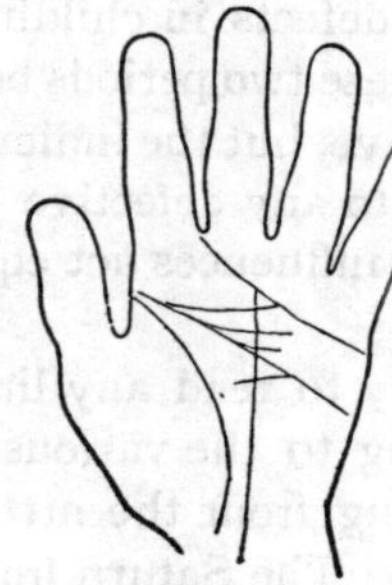
NO. 399

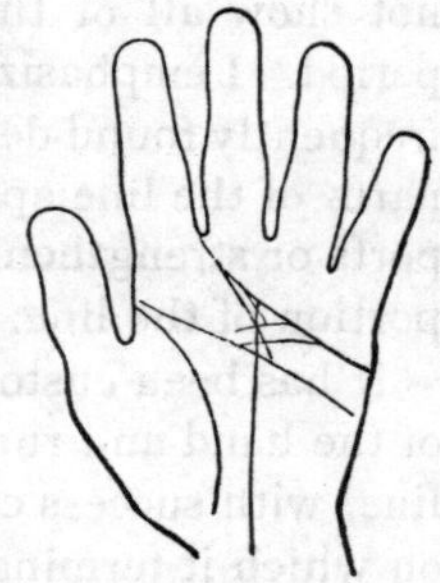
NO. 400

difficulties will arise from errors of judgment (399). If the Saturn line during this period be cut by chance lines from the Heart line, the subject permits his affections to get the better of him, and sentiment in business is disastrous (400). If the Life line be defective, and chance lines from it

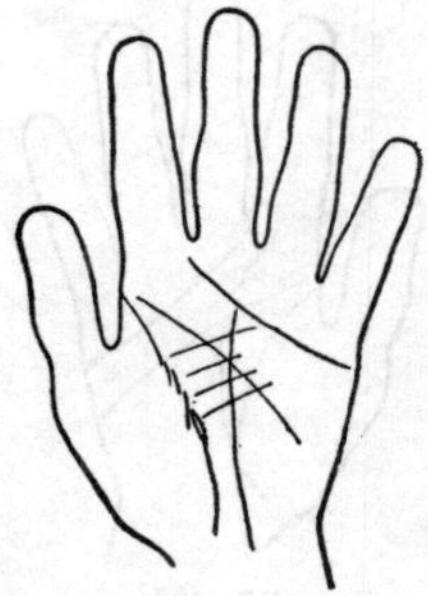
NO. 401

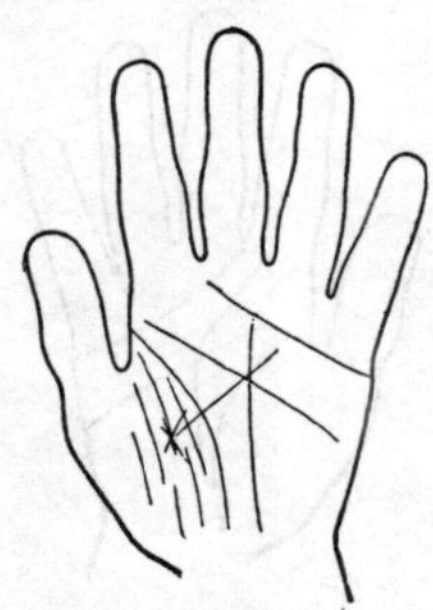
NO. 402

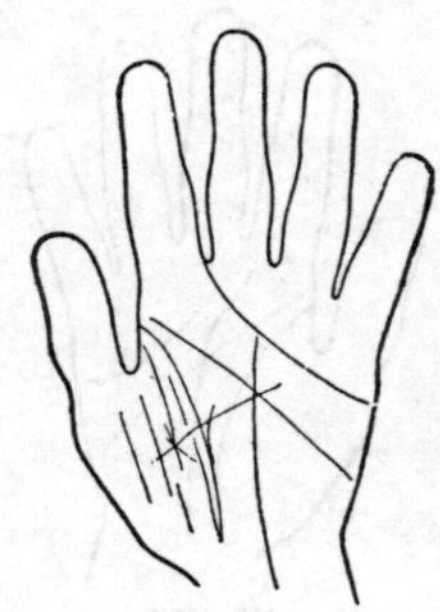
NO. 403

cut the Saturn line at the period between thirty and forty-five, ill health has obstructed the career during the financial formative period (401). If an Influence line on Mount of Venus ends in a star, and a Worry line from it cuts the Saturn line between the lines of Head and Life, the death of a relative will obstruct the career at this period (402). If this

Worry line cuts a rising line from the Life line, the death of a relative will bring on a check to the upward career of the subject (403). It must be understood that defects in any part of the line must be read at the age they occur. All lines do not show all of their defects in childhood or the formative period. I emphasize these two periods because they are most frequently found defective, but the indications given for those parts of the line apply to any defective period, and all supports or strengthening influences act equally well upon any portion of the line.

It has been customary to read any line rising at the base of the hand and running to the various Mounts as a Saturn line, with success coming from the attributes of the Mount on which it terminates. The Saturn line cannot end on any Mount but Saturn, with the one exception that it may run to Jupiter. If the Saturn line runs through its usual course in the centre of the hand and ends on the Mount of Jupiter, the success of the subject will be the result of great ambition (404). If the Saturn line be deep and rises from inside the Life line ending on the Mount of Jupiter, the influence of

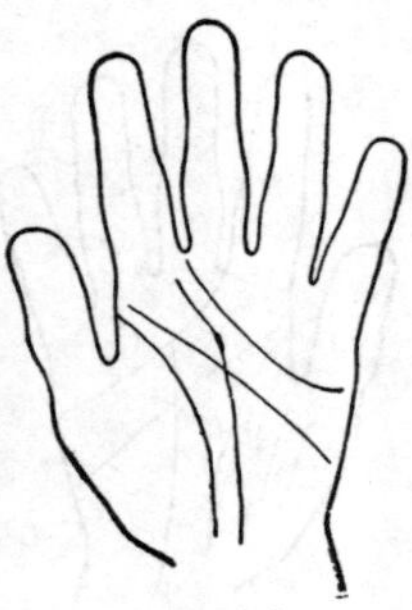

NO. 404

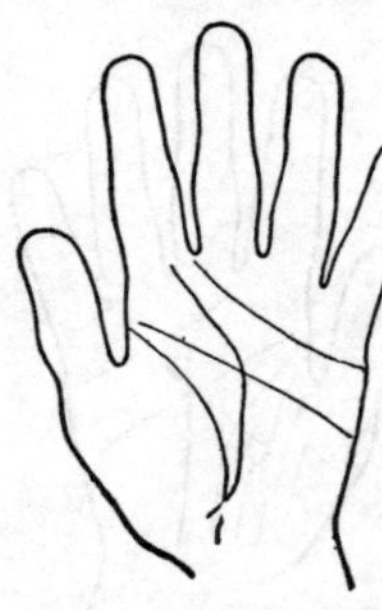

NO 405

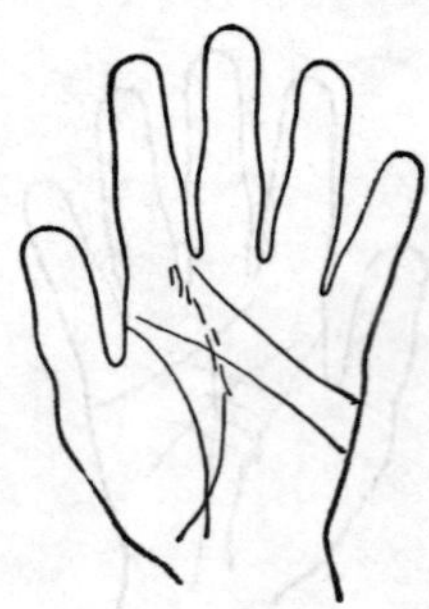

NO. 403

relatives and great ambition unite to make the career of the subject a success (405). If the Saturn line rises inside the Life line runs deep for a while and then becomes defective, the assistance of relatives and ambition help for a while, but do not bring ultimate success (406). At the point where the ill success begins, look for a cause. This may be ill health, loss of mental power, unhappy environment, or some special disease. If such a Saturn line be seen, and a Worry line, cutting a rising line from the Life line, crosses the hand and cuts a forked line of Affection, an unhappy marriage has injured the prospects of the subject (407). In the same manner the death of a relative, outside influences, ill health, will be shown by chance lines running from the cause of the trouble and cutting the Saturn line. Sometimes bad

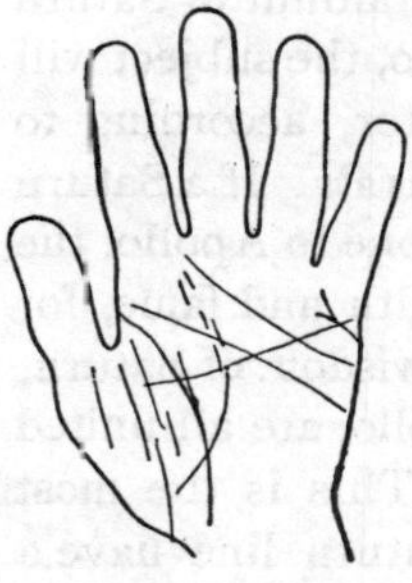

NO. 407

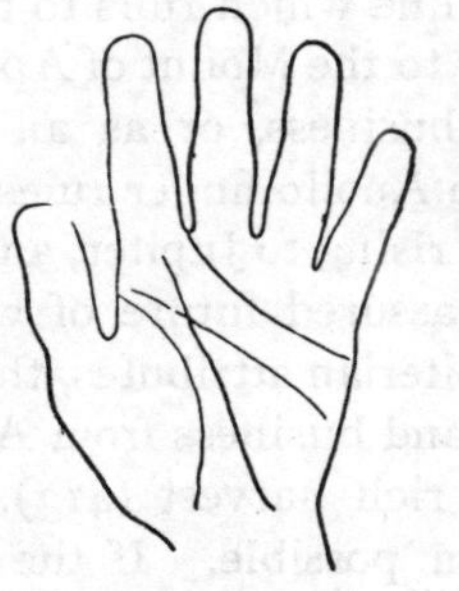

NO. 408

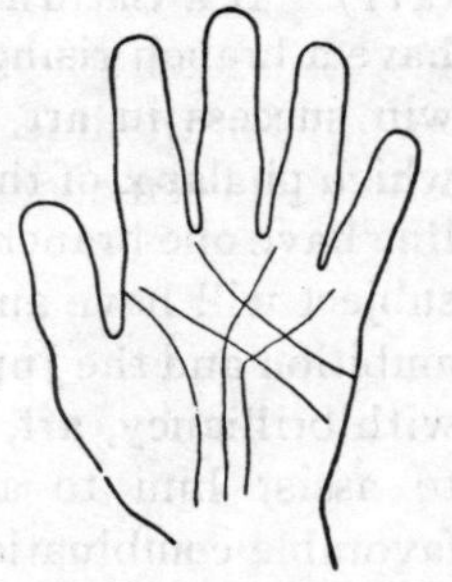

NO. 409

defects are seen, but chance lines do not connect them with the Saturn line. These defects are, however, the cause of the trouble. If a Saturn line rises on the Mount of the Moon and runs deep and strong to the Mount of Jupiter, the influence of one of the opposite sex together with the great ambition of the subject cause his prosperity (408). If the confirmations of marriage be present, the influence will be husband or wife. If a Saturn line running in this manner be defective in any part, the combination of influences has not been sufficient to prevent trouble. When a line rises at the base of the hand and runs to the Mount of Apollo or Mercury, I regard it as the line belonging to the Mount toward which it runs, and not the Saturn line. A line running toward Upper Mars is also likely to be the Mercury line, consequently in practice it is best to consider as a line of Saturn, only lines which *run through the centre of the hand*. If such lines are *then* deflected toward the Mounts, it is proper to read them as Saturn lines, strongly influenced by the Mount to which they run (409). If such a Saturn line ends on Upper Mars, the subject will achieve success from his leadership, power of resistance, and because he does not become discouraged (410). All of these indications will be accented if the Mounts be large and well developed. If the Saturn line runs in its usual course, but a line *branches* from it to Mount of Jupiter, the subject's success will be largely their due to ambition and ability to command men and obtain support. Such a line is a fine one for a politician (411). If a Saturn line which runs to the Mount of Saturn have a branch rising to the Mount of Apollo, the subject will win success in art, business, or as an actor, according to which phalanx of the Apollo finger rules (412). If a Saturn line have one branch rising to Jupiter, and one to Apollo, the subject will have an assured future of wealth and fame, for ambition and the Jupiterian attributes, the wisdom of Saturn, with brilliancy, art, and business from Apollo, are all united to assist him to a rich harvest (413). This is the most favorable combination possible. If the Saturn line have a branch rising to Mercury, the subject will have the assist-

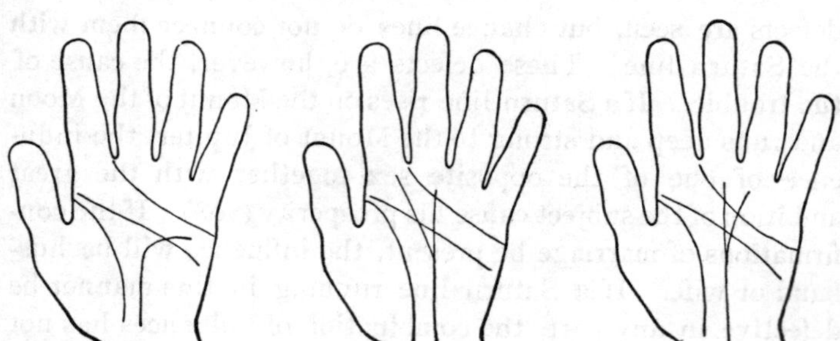

NO. 410 NO. 411 NO. 412

ance of shrewdness, business ability, good power of expression, and a scientific turn of mind to assist in his success (414). If a Saturn line have a branch rising and joining but not cutting the Head line, the subject will have the assistance of a good head in the shaping of his career (415).

The termination of the line will show the outcome of the career. In a large number of hands the line does not reach the Mount of Saturn but ends somewhere below it. Indicating as it does the periods of productive capacity, it is not strange that it should be absent in old age, for at this time disease or delicacy generally makes the career negative. The presence of a Mount without a line shows at least that no forces are working *against* the subject, and if the line be good in its early course it shows that a productive life is behind

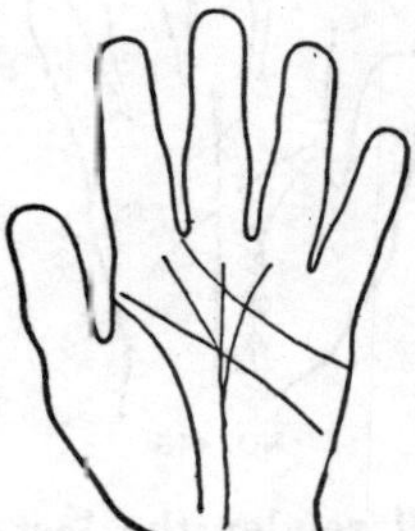

NO. 413

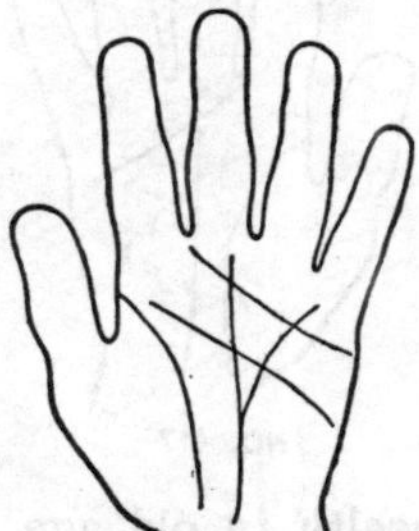

NO. 414

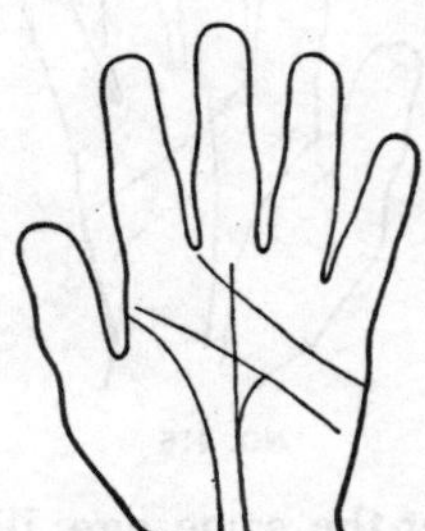

NO. 415

him, and it will be found that he is enjoying in old age the result of his early labors. On some Mounts a deep line is seen, and this is a strong indication of well-to-do old age. In any event the point at which the line ceases, be it in youth or old age, terminates our work with it, except that we can say to those whose line has stopped and no other has taken its place, that the future is as they make it. If a deep line runs only for twenty years, the subject can be promised a productive period only during that time; the period after it, is as he makes it by effort. If the line runs deep for part of the way and terminates in a wavy line (416), the career during the latter years will be uncertain, and there will be worries in old age.

So these defective terminations on the Mount may not mean poverty or money losses in old age, but they may mean financial checks to the career from disappointments in children, or similar troubles. I mention this in order to warn against reading defective terminations as necessarily meaning poverty when the Saturn line has previously been deep for its entire course. Breaks in the line, bars cutting it, crosses or dots following a hitherto deep line, will indicate trials and crosses in old age. If the Saturn line breaks on the Mount, and the Life, Head, and Heart lines be defective

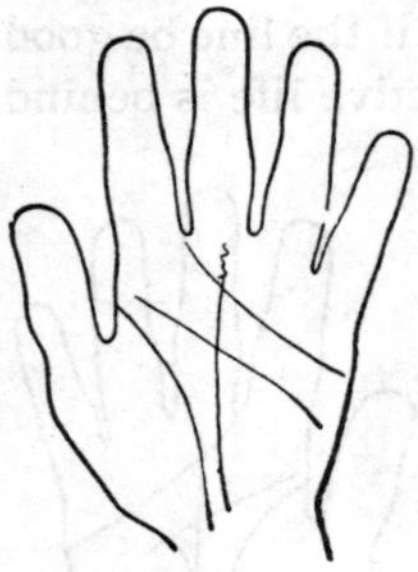

NO. 416

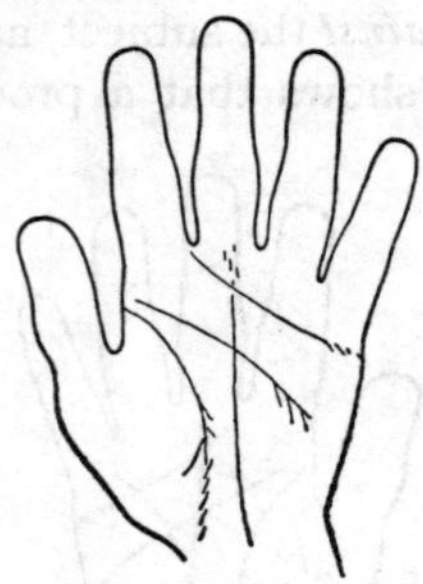

NO. 417

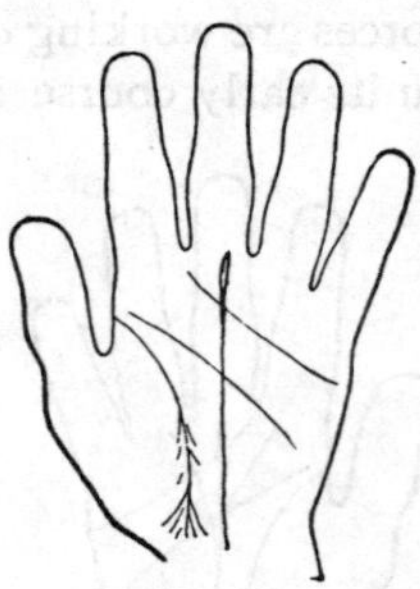

NO. 418

at the same age, ill health in old age will render the last days ones of trouble (417). If the Saturn line end in an island and downward branches be seen on the Life line with a long tassel, financial difficulties due to ill health will cloud the last days of the subject (418). If the line be crossed by

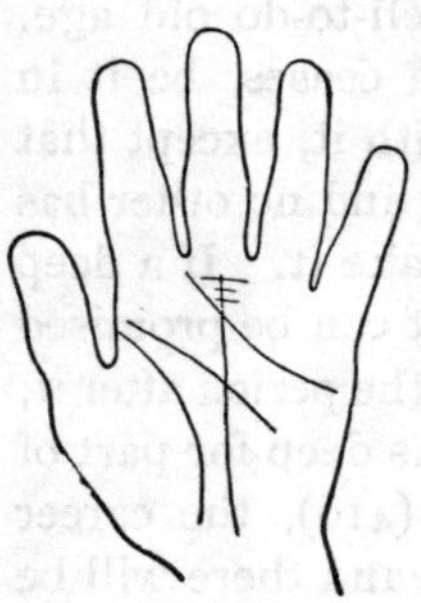

NO 419

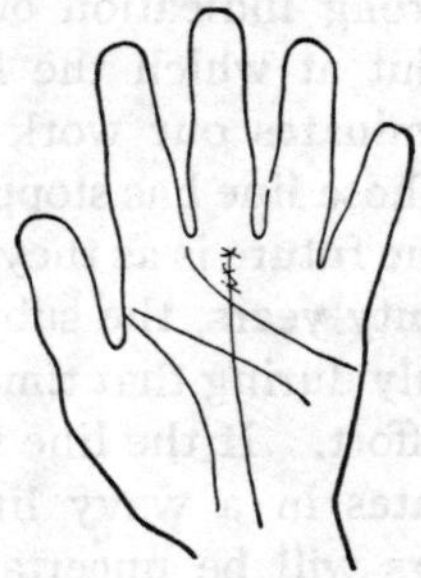

NO. 420

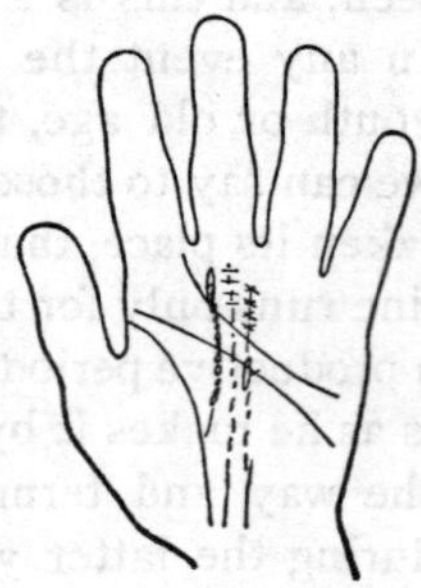

NO. 421

bars which cut it on the Mount, the subject will suffer losses and trials in old age (419). If the bars be faint and do not cut the line they are troubles and worries. If the line has crosses on the Mount, great trials and misfortunes will harass the latter years of the subject (420). All of these terminations apply to the line *on* the Mount of Saturn, and have their various indications in old age. If the line terminate in these signs at *any* age the reading will be the same, except that it applies to the age indicated on the line at the time at which it occurs. If the line be defective during its entire course and terminates in any of these signs, the indication will be worse than when these markings terminate a deep line, for in the first instance the subject will not have a prosperous life behind him, during which he might have provided for old age. No. 421 will give various examples of such defective lines.

We have now followed the Saturn line from babyhood to extreme old age, and have seen how it records success and failure, as well as the causes which have produced them. It is poor consolation for one to look back upon a life of meagre fruitage and say, "If I had only known the productive periods, the end might have been different." This oft-repeated exclamation is sadly true, for in only few lives are productive periods taken advantage of in their fullest measure. If by a careful application of the rules laid down in this chapter you are enabled to help struggling humanity to make use of the harvest portion of their lives, and thus provide for the days when vital forces wane and labor can no longer be done, you will have wasted no time which has been spent in a study of the line of Saturn.

CHAPTER XI

THE LINE OF APOLLO

THE line of Apollo is a vertical line rising, if long, from the upper part of the Mount of Moon, if short, higher in the hand, and running toward the Mount of Apollo, sometimes ending high on that Mount, and sometimes not reaching to it (422). It has been variously called the line of the Sun, and the line of Brilliancy, and to it has been ascribed the gift of great artistic talents, wealth, and fame. It is one of the most thoroughly misunderstood of all the lines, and the mistaken reading of it has caused practitioners many mortifications. Whenever a good line of Apollo was seen, it has been customary to "gush" about the wonderful talent the subject possessed for art, music, the stage, and various other artistic callings, of which perhaps no idea had previously entered his mind. Often a subject especially well fitted to be a good housewife has been made to feel indignant towards her parents by some well meaning palmist because alleged latent talents were not discovered and developed. Many such have been told that the world was the loser because they have never entered their proper sphere. Sometimes these great talents have been ascribed to people who were color blind or musically deaf, and both palmist and client have wondered at the failure of a good line of Apollo to give the proper indication. This has not been entirely the fault of practitioners, for such interpretations have been sanctioned by the best authors. In many cases conscientious students have

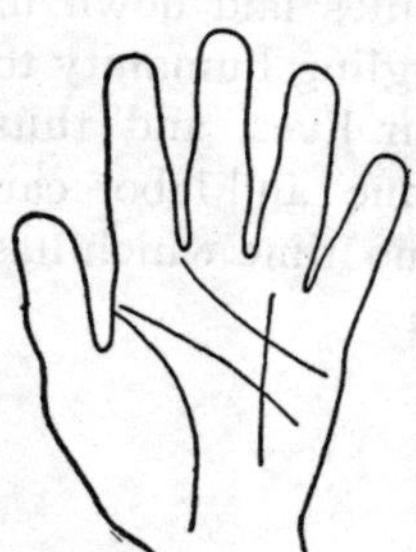

NO. 422

dropped the use of the line entirely, deeming it unreliable and misleading. This is certainly true of it according to its present understanding, and it had much better be dropped than used as extravagantly as it has been in the past.

"The line of Apollo, running as it does to the Mount of that name, emphasizes the Apollonian traits and qualifications. The Apollonian is brilliant, consequently the line of Apollo indicates brilliancy, and the subject who has it should shine in art and artistic callings." Such is the reasoning from which the present interpretation of the line was derived, and it would be good reasoning if one factor had not been forgotten. The Apollonian has many sides to his character; there are good, bad, and indifferent subjects of this type. He also moves in one of the three worlds, the mental, practical, or material, in any of which he may be brilliant and successful, and in any of which he may secure fame or wealth. But if an Apollonian who is built to shine in the *material world* has a good line of Apollo, and you tell him he is a *great artist*, you have placed him *out of his sphere*, and made an error which counts against the accuracy of the science of Palmistry. If this same subject had been told that he was brilliant in the world of *material matters*, perhaps a successful gamester, an owner of racehorses, a leading butcher, or foremost in other callings in which some Apollonians engage with success, the estimate would have been correct. It is the reading of a line of Apollo as always indicating wealth and fame derived from *artistic pursuits* that has impaired its usefulness and successful application. It is the attempt to make the line of Brilliancy always indicate brilliancy in *art*, which is only *one* of the directions it may take, and the disregard for the fact that a subject may be brilliant in *many directions*, that has made the reading of the line of Apollo so inaccurate. The line of Apollo, like all other lines, can only be successfully used when it is made to fit the subject. It is only accurate when the subject has first been understood and the line has been applied *to him*, and it never has been and never will be accurate when the attempt is made to force every subject to fit the line. No better name has ever been given this line than the *Line of Capability*. This name expresses in a nutshell the *idea* which should be applied to the line. It indicates a *capability* or *possibility* of accomplishing a great deal, the *field* in which the capability will best operate to be shown by Chirognomy, indicating the forces *behind*, which will direct the ability into some calling which produces results. A good line of Apollo is undoubtedly an indication of the possession of the characteristics of the Apollonian, who makes friends, money, and reputation more easily than any other type. But in reading the qualities of the line be sure that you have placed the subject in his proper world, after which you can successfully apply the brilliancy indicated by the line to the affairs of that world. You will not find a great number of really fine Apollo lines, though you will see a good many of *some* value; but by far the greatest number of hands examined will have no Apollo line at all.

The presence of a fine line of Apollo is an indication that the subject has been endowed with exceptional talents for getting on in the world, and if other parts of the hand be good, he most surely will do so. The line of Apollo must be estimated continually in the light of the Chirognomic development of the subject. A fine line of Apollo is ruined by a flabby hand, a weak thumb, a poor Head line, poor Mounts of Mars, Jupiter, Mercury, and Venus, or other deficiencies which may be seen in the hand. In making a final estimate of the worth of any lines, these factors must all be taken into account.

The absence of a line of Apollo does not necessarily indicate that a subject will be unsuccessful, for, as in the case of an absent line of Saturn, the qualities that make "self-made men" may exert themselves, and produce even greater results than come from the brilliant talents which a fine line of Apollo indicates. In my examination of hands during the study of this line, I find that in most cases the subjects having good Apollo lines rely too much upon their *talents*, and not enough on the industry and perseverance that should be expended in developing them. For this reason less talented plodders often produce greater results in life than their far more talented brethren. If only the talents of a fine line of Apollo are coupled with *energy*, almost unlimited success is possible. It is absolutely incorrect to say that the absence of a line of Apollo indicates ill success in life, but it *is* true that the *presence* of this line makes success easier. It must be understood then that in the treatment of this line, when

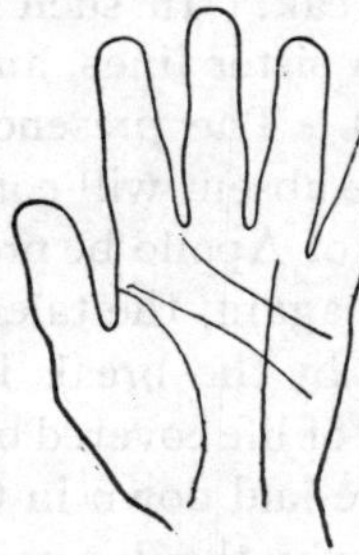

NO. 423

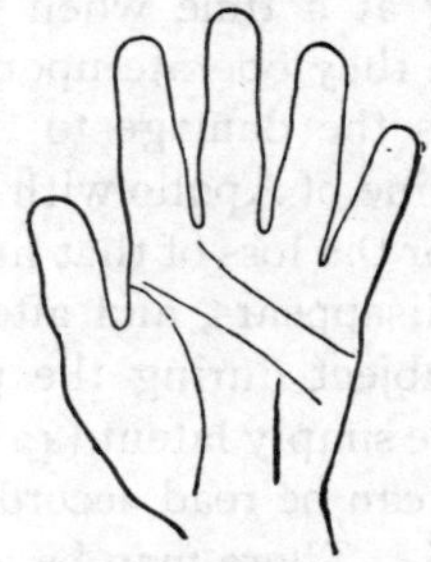

NO. 424

we use the word *success*, it applies to effort in *the world in which the subject moves*. Remember that the proper world to which the line must be applied is determined by examination of the three worlds of the hand as a whole, and as shown by the three phalanges of the fingers.

The line of Apollo is like the Saturn line in that it does not give any health indications. The effect of ill health may be seen as *affecting* the line, but the line itself will not give these indications.

The length of the line determines the extent of its influence ; the longer the line the more it will sway the subject, and the shorter, the less important is it found to be. A line of Apollo reaching from the wrist to the Mount indicates the possession of great talent, so great that it will continue to develop during the life of the subject, and he will achieve much (423). If the line begins low and runs only a short distance, the subject has talents, but they will not be productive of great results (424). If the line rises higher and covers the space between the Head and Heart lines, the special brilliancy of the subject will operate during the formative period of life, and will be of assistance in aiding him to pass this critical period with greater ease (425). If the line runs on to the Mount, the subject will be well endowed with Apollonian characteristics, and in whichever world he moves will be brilliant and acquire reputation (426). Frequently the lines of Saturn and Apollo are interdependent, and in many cases one will be strong at a time when the other is weak. In such an instance they operate upon each other as sister lines, and one repairs the damage to the other (427). The presence of a good line of Apollo with the Saturn line absent will compensate for the loss of that line. If the line of Apollo be present then disappears, and afterwards begins again, the talents of the subject during the period covered by the break in the line are simply latent (428). The period of life covered by this break can be read according to the scale laid down in Chapter IV. There may be a special cause why the line vanishes for a time, as ill health may render inoperative even the most brilliant talents. With such a break look for defects in the other lines and Mounts which may account for it.

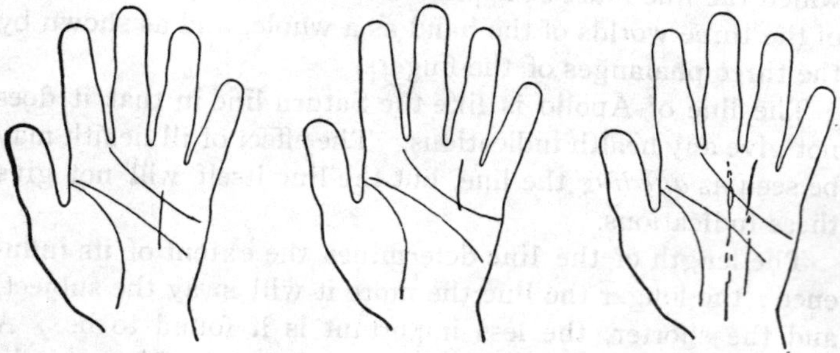

NO. 425 NO. 426 NO. 427

If during this period the Life line be in any way defective, delicate health is against the operation of the subject's talents (429). If at the age indicated by this space in the Apollo line, the Head line be defective, the mental power of the subject is weakened, and he cannot give the attention necessary to make his affairs successful (430). Similar defects seen in other portions of the hand, whether connected by chance lines to the space in the Apollo line or not, show something which has for the time being impeded the career of the subject, by suspending the operation of his strongest talents.

To be regarded as a true line of Apollo, the line must begin more or less low in the hand, directly under the Mount and finger of Apollo. A line coming from the Life line and

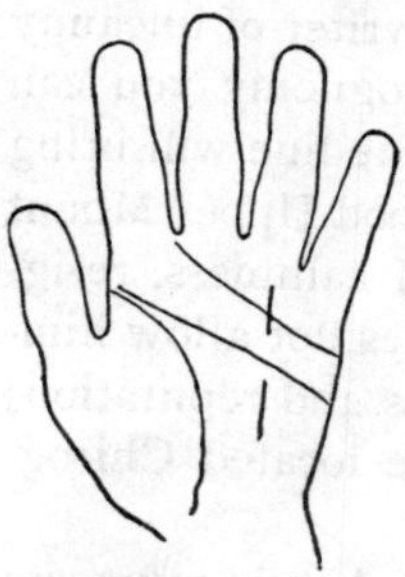

NO. 428

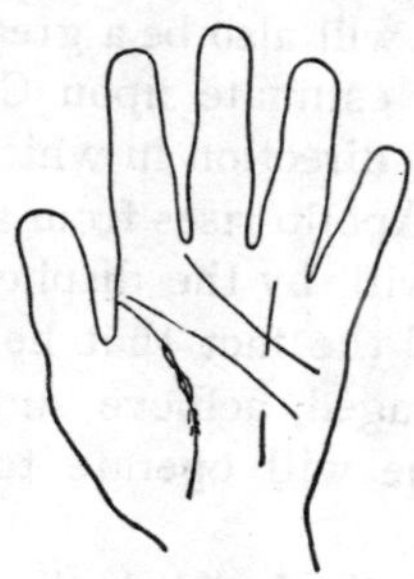

NO. 429

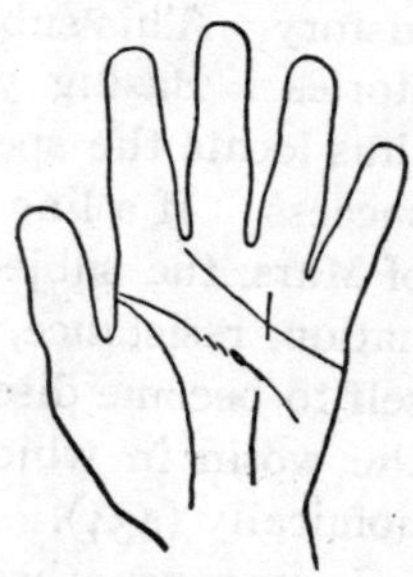

NO. 430

ending on the Mount of Apollo, while it will largely have the effect of the Apollo line, is still not, properly speaking, that line, but is a chance line, showing success of the subject arising from the same set of qualities which makes the Apollo line indicate fortunate conditions (431). To avoid possible confusion, it is best to limit the Apollo line to a line wholly under the Mount, and if necessity arises to read such a line as is indicated in No. 431, read it as a chance line from the Life line to the Mount of Apollo, and not as the Apollo line. Use everything for what it really is, and do not get into the habit of calling all sorts of chance lines, Apollo lines. In like manner read a line rising from the Saturn line and ending on the Mount of Apollo as a branch of the Saturn line, adding greatly to the success of the career, rather than call it the Apollo line (432). When the line of Apollo rises from the top of the Mount of Moon near the percussion (433), it indicates imagination and the power of language; to a line so rising we should, if the mental world be strongest, say that the subject will achieve success as an author. If the tips be conic and fingers smooth, he will love poetry.

If his fingers be knotty or square, he will write history, epic poems, historical novels, or works of that nature. If the Mount of Mars be large, he will write of battles and heroes. If Venus be large, he will move the heart and bring tears to the eye, so near to nature and human sympathy will be his productions. If Saturn be high, he will write on chemistry, physics, or scientific subjects, and often on history. This subject will also be a great writer of uncanny stories. Basing your estimate upon Chirognomy you can thus locate the special direction in which the line will bring success. If a line of Apollo rises from a good Upper Mount of Mars, the subject will, by the display of calmness, resignation, resistance, and the fact that he does not allow himself to become discouraged, achieve success and reputation; the world in which he will operate to be located Chirognomically (434).

In its course through the hand the line of Apollo must run toward the Mount of Apollo, for it is the effect of the qualities of this type which give to the line its meaning and its name. There is a constant danger of reading chance lines

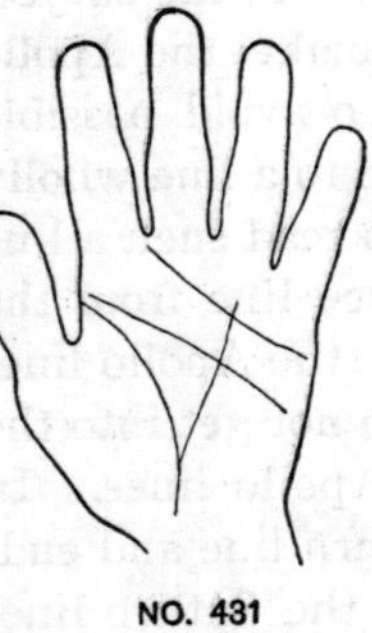
NO. 431

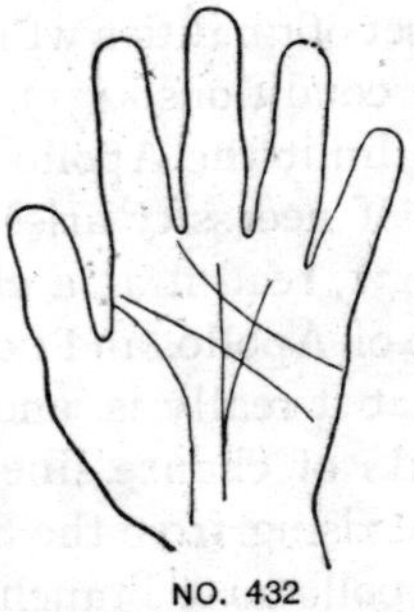
NO. 432

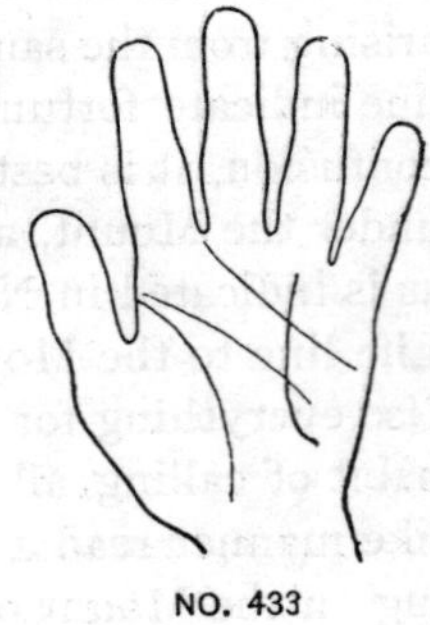
NO. 433

as the Apollo line, and to avoid doing this the rule must be fixed that while in its course through the hand the Apollo line may *slightly* deflect, may stop at any point, throw out branches, or be met, strengthened, or crossed by chance lines, the general direction of the line itself must be from the Mount of Moon to the Mount of Apollo. Any line which cannot possibly be thus specifically classed as the line of Apollo, must be read as another line. This will increase accuracy; for only thus can a line have its proper meaning, and the erroneous readings which are constantly given to supposed Apollo lines will be avoided. Most mistakes with the line come from an enthusiasm due to the fact that the influence of an Apollo line is known to be so beneficial, that practitioners are tempted to overestimate the success of their clients. This

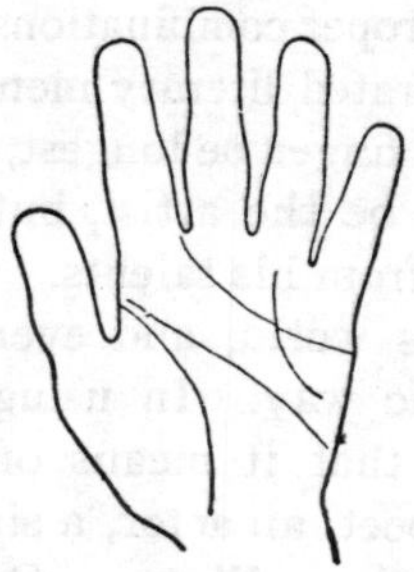

NO. 434

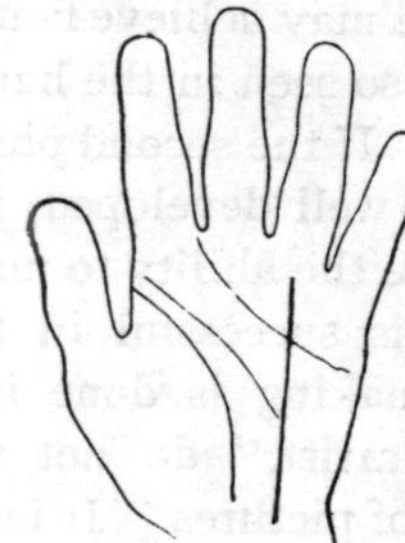

NO. 435

is especially true because praise is what gives greatest satisfaction and is what clients are most anxious to hear. It is easier and more profitable for the palmist, for it is remarkable how clients agree with the reader when told of brilliancy, wonderful perception, latent talents, etc., and each one will say he has always thought this was the case, but was never quite sure of it before. Palmists who have a pleasant story to tell, get the most clients, and this being known to professionals, leads to a system of flattery totally out of proportion to the subject. Most of this is referred to supposed lines of Apollo for corroboration. Our effort here is to reach the facts only, that we may deal with the line just as it deserves, and in order to do this we must limit ourselves to the consideration of the lines whose course between the Mounts of the Moon and Apollo mark them unmistakably as Apollo lines.

The character of the Apollo line indicates the intensity and power of the qualities it represents. The best line is that which is deep and well cut (435). This gives in the highest degree the beneficial qualities of the line, indicates success and reputation, and gives to a subject creative power in whatever world he operates. He is not one who is merely *fond* of color, painting, and art, but has the creative power which will enable him to produce work of merit. It distinguishes the real artist from the lover of, or dabbler in art, and when the first phalanges of the fingers, especially if that of Apollo, be longest, and a long deep Apollo line cuts the hand, your client is entitled to be told that in the artistic world he may achieve fame. With proper combinations this line is also seen in the hands of celebrated literary men and women. If the second phalanx of the finger be longest, with the first well developed, he will still be the artist, but will also have the ability to make money from his talents. This subject is successful in the business world, and even his money-making is done in an artistic way. In using the word "artist," do not understand that it means only a painter of pictures. It may mean a poet, an actor, a singer, or refer to any other of the artistic callings. On all sides of his character, the Apollonian loves beauty, and

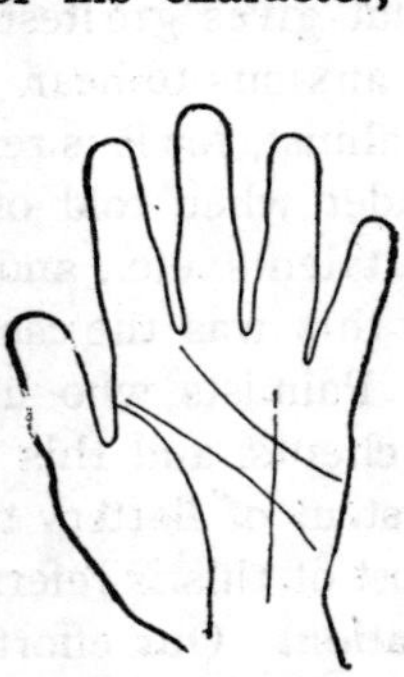
NO. 436

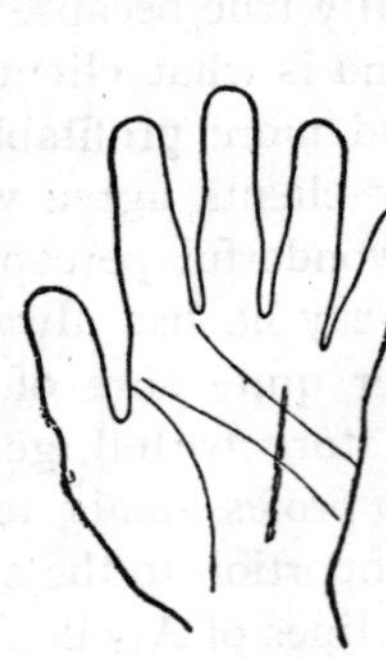
NO. 437

whatever is pleasing to the eye or sense. If the third phalanx be longest, especially if it be thick, and a deep line of Apollo is seen, the subject is not an artist, for he will like chromos better than the old masterpieces, will love high colors, flashy dressing, and will seek to display his taste on all occasions, much to the amusement of people of true artistic feelings, whose society he affects. Such subjects are always money-makers. These three illustrations show the method of applying a deep line to the three worlds of the finger, by giving an intense interpretation to the line, *based* upon the quality of the subject. A thin line of Apollo (436) will decrease the intensity of the reading. The subject will not have the great creative power of the deep line. If an artist, he will be more guided by the effects produced by other ar-

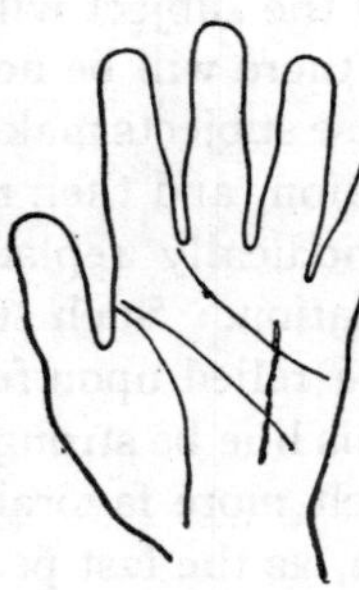

NO. 438

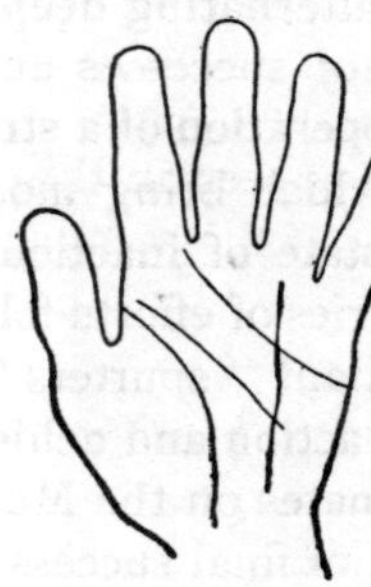

NO. 439

tists, and, whether the mental, business, or material worlds rule, he will achieve less celebrity and make less money. If a line be broad and shallow (437) it will show that little of the Apollonian power is left. The subject will like pretty things, will be fond of artists, will affect a little bohemianism, but will avoid attempting any productions himself. If the hand be coarse in its development, the taste will be for showy things, and little refinement will be indicated. If the hand be refined, the subject will dress in taste, will have an eye for harmony in colorings, his home will be tastefully furnished, and he may do a little dabbling in writing or painting. From this class come the army of literary and art copyists. A chained line of Apollo (438) will indicate an utter lack of artistic talent, although the subject may be impressed with his own knowledge on matters of art, most of which is incorrect. These subjects do not realize their shallowness and most of their effort is expended in talk. In dealing with these lines, apply each one to the subject according to the world in which he moves, and give its defective operation to the affairs of that world. Color in the line of Apollo is not an important consideration, for this line does not bear upon the health of the subject. To a pink colored line give a better estimate of strength than one which is white or yellow. This is as far as color will be considered as affecting the line of Apollo.

Defects in the line which form special signs, or which destroy its continuity, will impede its best operation. If the line be alternating deep and thin (439) the subject will have a series of successes and failures, but there will be no even, steady operation of a strong line. These subjects make some efforts which bring money and reputation, and then relapse into a state of inaction, which is periodically replaced by other series of efforts followed by stagnation. Such subjects are brilliant "spurters," but cannot be relied upon for continuous action and achievement. If this line be strong when it terminates on the Mount, it is a much more favorable indication of final success and reputation, as the last period of the life will be one of its better efforts. If the line be wavy (440) it indicates that the subject will have a vacillating

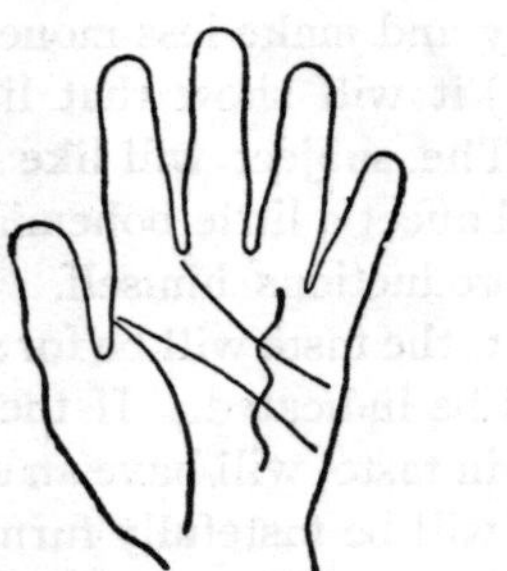

NO. 440

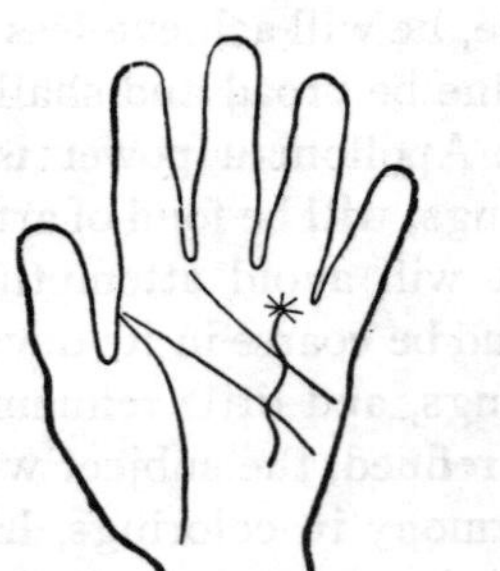

NO. 441

career. He will be clever and able to do much in his particular world of effort, but will be erratic, unstable, unreliable, and bohemian. These people are versatile, but go off at a tangent, and waste their brilliancy and talents in "chasing butterflies" instead of pushing forward steadily in one direction. The outcome of such a line is uncertain.

The subject may do something wonderful, or may pass everything by and accomplish nothing. If this line becomes strong on the Mount of Apollo, the subject will finally round up with force in some direction. It may be that he becomes a great wanderer, very erratic, or a crank, but he will earn reputation for something. If this line should end in a star (441) the life will end brilliantly, the subject will have

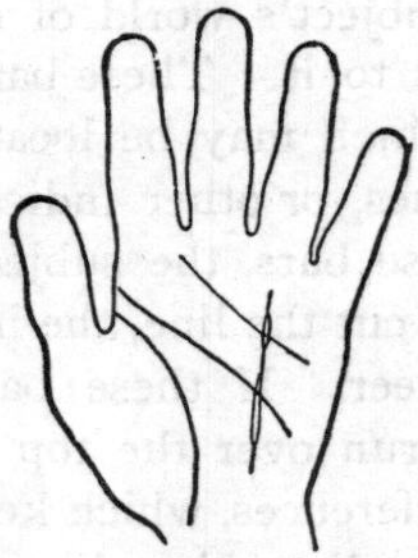

NO. 442

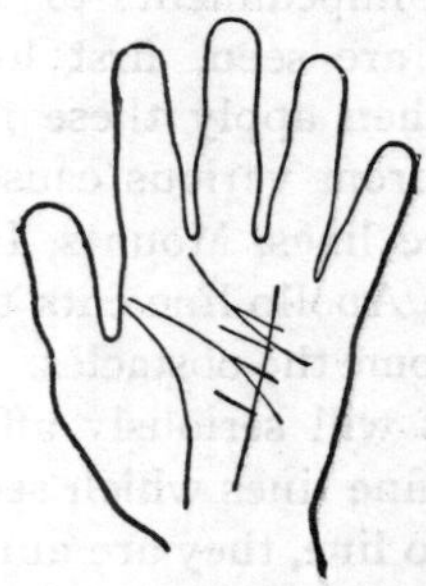

NO. 443

achieved wide reputation, and an unsteady though talented subject will have his work finally crowned with success. The direction from which this success will come must be estimated Chirognomically. If islands be seen in the line (442) they will prove serious obstructions. Islands appearing in a deep line will show that the realization of wealth and fame will be impeded, and the subject stands in danger of a positive loss of reputation and of money. In whatever world the subject moves, he will attempt things which promise reward, but the failure of which will bring him loss. If the Apollo finger be as long or longer than Saturn, the subject will be a "plunger," he will dazzle the stock market with his daring, and will take desperate chances to win. If his Head and Life lines be widely separated this plunging disposition will be increased by his extreme self confidence. But with the island in the Apollo line he is in constant danger of a loss of money, and of his reputation as well. If the third phalanx of the Apollo finger be long and thick, with the above combination, this subject will be the common gambler. If the Mercury finger be crooked and twisted, the Heart line thin or absent, and the hand otherwise bad, he will be the card sharper and trickster, who resorts to cheating, and uses the brilliancy afforded by the Apollo line to further the basest ends. Such a line in any hand, no matter how good, should be a constant warning to the subject. Bars cutting the line of Apollo (443) will show constant impediments to the success of the subject. When these are seen, first locate the subject's world of action, and then apply these impediments to it. These bars may arise from various causes, all of which may be located by chance lines, Mounts, Influence lines, or other indications. If the Apollo line cuts through these bars, the subject will overcome the obstacles. If the bars cut the line, the impediments will seriously affect the career. If these bars are little fine lines which seem only to run over the top of the Apollo line, they are annoying interferences, which keep the subject constantly worried and by disturbing his mental peace impede his progress. Dots on the Apollo line (444)

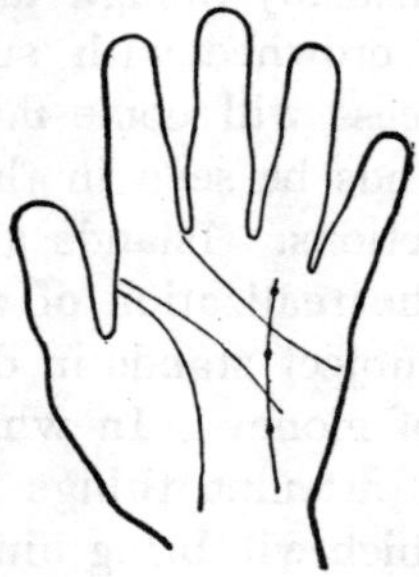

NO. 444

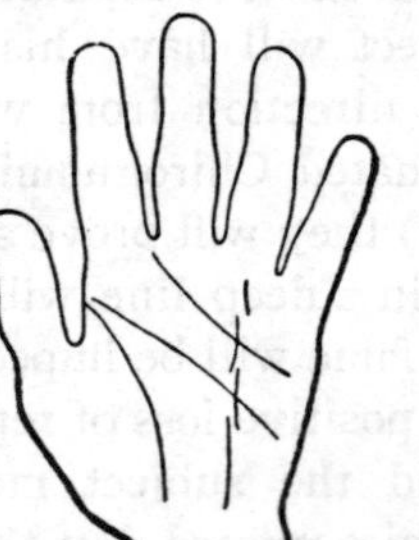

NO. 445

are a menace to the reputation of the subject. If they be small they only indicate the whisperings of enemies, but if they be large and deep, they indicate the actual loss of good name. Chance lines and the usual indications will locate the causes.

Breaks in the Apollo line (445) indicate setbacks to the ambition and upward course of the subject, and are impediments which destroy the usefulness of the line and render inoperative all of its beneficial influences. Such a line shows that the subject may have a strong liking for art, if that world rules, but that he will never be a producer or a creator of it; he is, if wealthy, the art patron. If the business world be strong, these people will be only partially successful, and even with some of the beneficial effects of the line present, will make many costly mistakes. With breaks in the line,

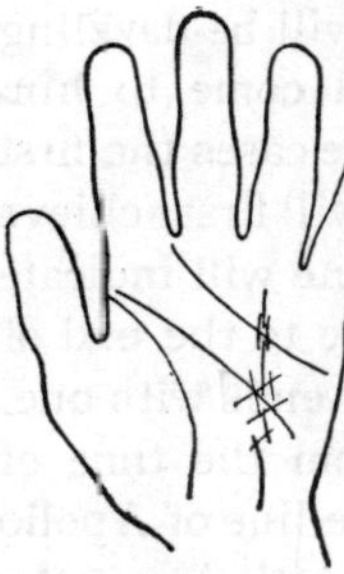
NO. 446

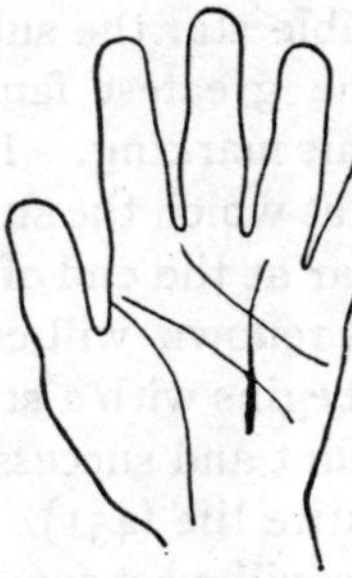
NO. 447

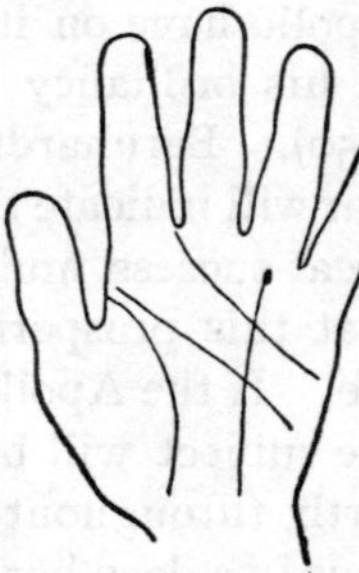
NO. 448

one cannot see more than ordinary success for the subject, and many failures. With all breaks seen in the line, look for repair signs which will tend to overcome the obstacles and bring about better conditions. The usual repair signs will be found in a variety of combinations (446). Such a repaired line is not better in grade than a broad and shallow one.

The termination of the Apollo line will tell the outcome of the line. If it be a deep line at the start and grows thin until it gradually fades away, the best period of the life will be during the time when the line is deep, and the wealth-producing capacity will diminish as the life progresses. In this case the final success of the subject will only be ordinary (447). If a line of Apollo ends in a dot (448) the subject will after a life of prosperity lose his reputation in the end. If the line of Apollo ends in a star (449) it will be an indication of brilliant success. A star on the Mount of Apollo is an electric light ending a good line, and intensifies the entire combination. If the subject be mental he will win great fame and renown as a poet, writer, painter, sculptor, actor, or in other artistic callings. Bernhardt, Nordica, Modjeska, Kathryn Kidder, and many brilliant actresses, vocalists, or instrumentalists have this marking. If the subject belongs to the practical world he will make money fast and easily. His ventures will be uniformly profitable, and he will be celebrated for his success. If the third phalanx of his finger predominates he may not have a high grade of refinement, but will make a great deal of money. If the line of Apollo have on it a double star the subject will be dazzling in his brilliancy and the greatest fame will come to him (450). Bernhardt has this marking. In these cases the first star will indicate the age at which the subject will first achieve great success, and the star at the end of the line will indicate that this prosperity and renown will continue to the end of life. If the Apollo line begins with a star and ends with one, the subject will be brilliant and successful from the time of birth, throughout the entire life (451). If the line of Apollo ends in a deep bar the life will meet some obstruction near the

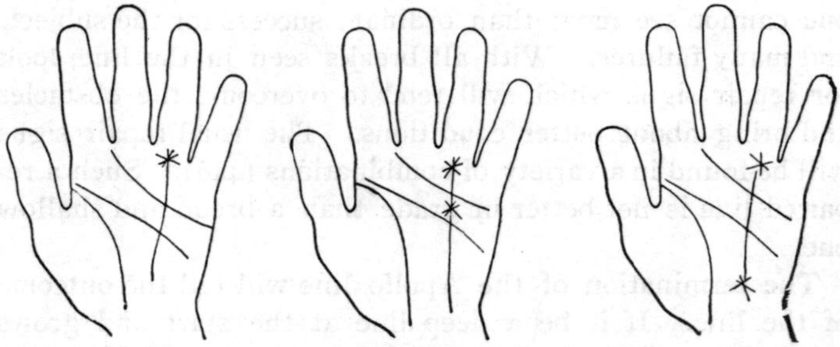

NO. 449 NO. 450 NO. 451

close which will be insurmountable (452). This will be a decided check to the career and with this sign the Saturn line should be closely examined, as well as all other indications which may locate the cause. If with this marking the Life line be defective at near fifty years, and continue so, ending in a tassel, fork, island, star, cross, or other defect, the subject will have ill health and delicacy at that age, from which he never recovers, and which ruins his prospects in life (453). If an island and a star or either be seen in the Head line at age fifty, the subject will fail in mental powers, which will check his career and put a stop to his success (454). If a rising split from the Head line runs to a bar on the Mount, an error in calculation will cause a check to the subject's career

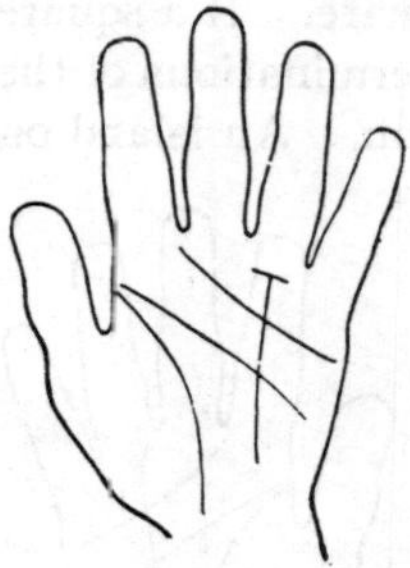

NO. 452

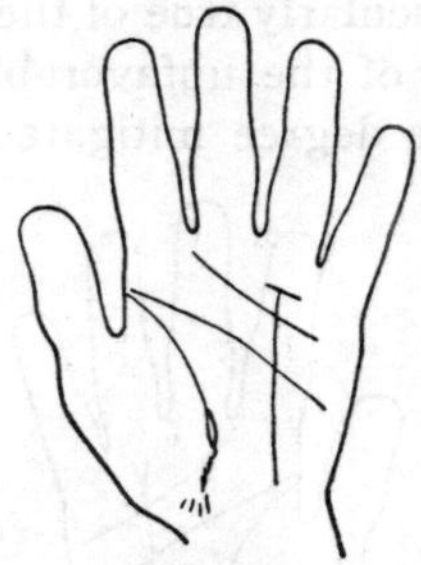

NO 453

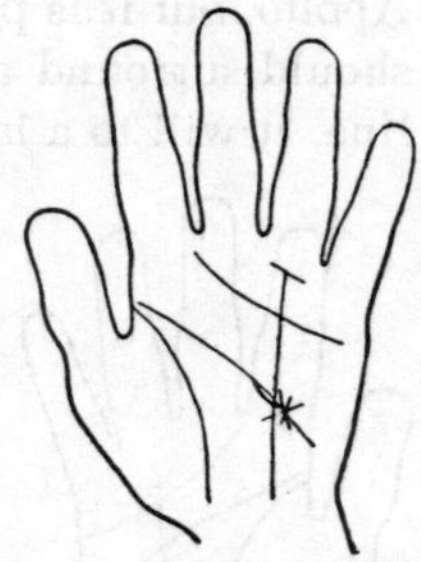

NO. 454

from which he does not recover (455). Often this refers to investments made early in life, and which turn out badly. A cross on the end of the line of Apollo (456) is a worse obstruction than a bar. It means an absolute blemish to the reputation of the subject. It also indicates poor judgment,

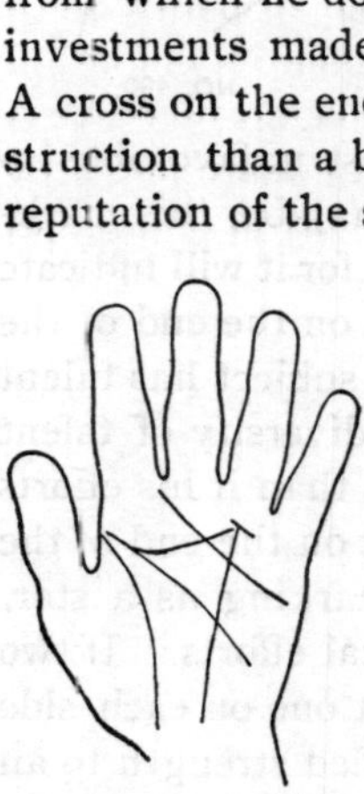

NO. 455

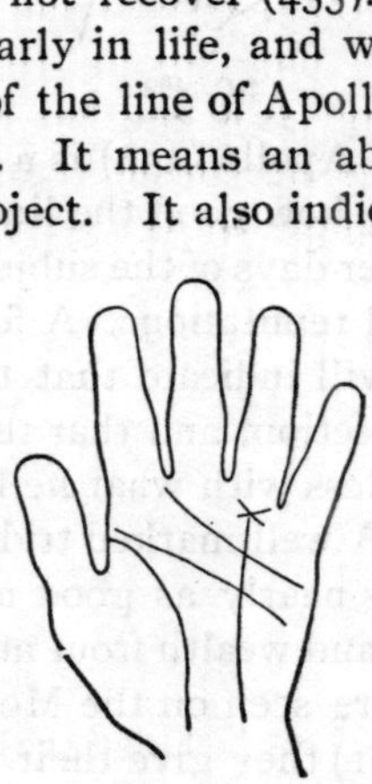

NO. 456

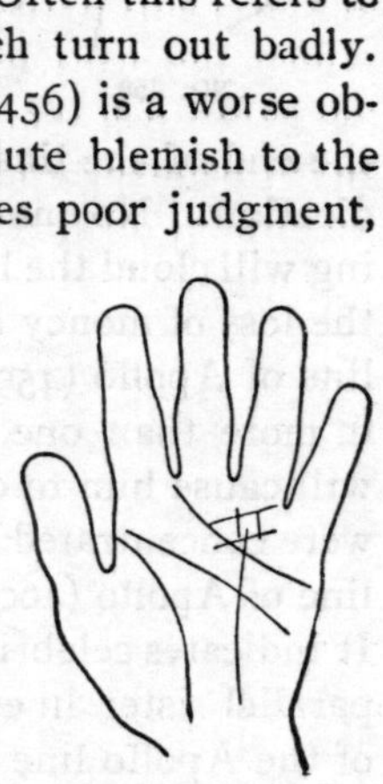

NO. 457

and the subject will make many mistakes in the course of his life, which consequently terminates unfavorably. All of these terminations we are presuming to happen on *good* lines of Apollo. If they should occur on poorly marked, defective lines, their reading must be intensified, and made to agree proportionately with the poorness in quality of the line.

A square on the end of a line of Apollo (457) will indicate protection from evils of all sorts. It will exert its influence not only on the end of the life, but during the whole of it. This is largely true of all signs that terminate a line of Apollo, but it is particularly true of the square. If a square should surround any of the unfavorable terminations of the line, it will to a large degree mitigate them. An island on

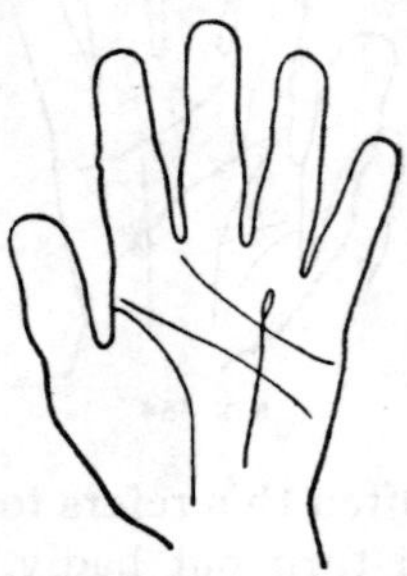

NO. 458

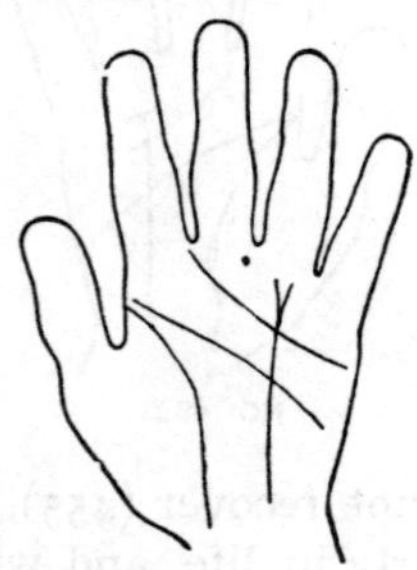

NO. 459

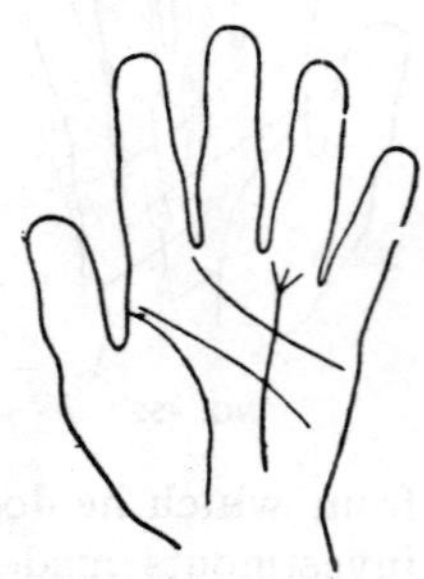

NO. 460

the end of the line of Apollo (458) is a most unfavorable indication. No matter how good the line may be, this marking will cloud the latter days of the subject, for it will indicate the loss of money and reputation. A fork on the end of the line of Apollo (459) will indicate that the subject has talent in more than one direction, and that this diversity of talent will cause him to do less with what he has than if his efforts were concentrated. A well marked trident on the end of the line of Apollo (460) is nearly as good a marking as a star. It indicates celebrity and wealth from mental efforts. If two parallel sister lines are seen on the Mount one on each side of the Apollo line (461) they give their added strength to an already fine indication. The line of Apollo is intensely favorable by itself, but when supported on both sides by strong sister lines, the subject will have the greatest success. These were named by older palmists lines of reputation. If the Apollo line runs to the Mount, and on the Mount there are several or many vertical lines (462), the subject will have *some* talent in many directions, and because of this diversity will accomplish little. If the Apollo line ends in a tassel (463) the subject will scatter his efforts in so many directions that he will accomplish little. Talent he has, but too diversified. If on the end of the Apollo line, one branch goes to the Mount of Saturn, and one to the Mount of Mercury (464),

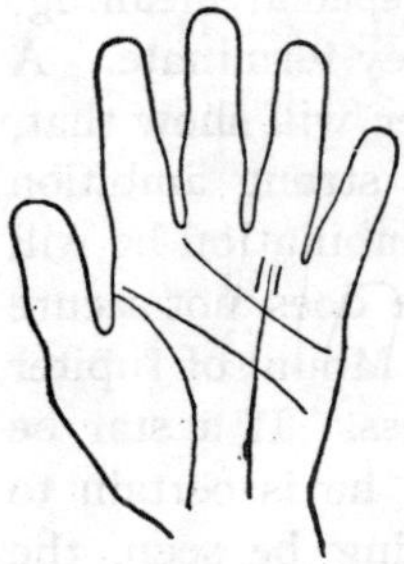
NO. 461

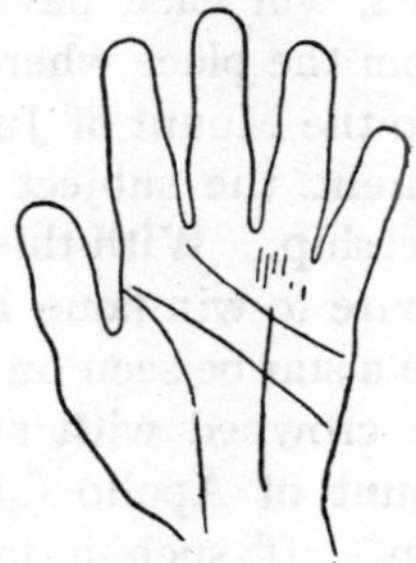
NO. 462

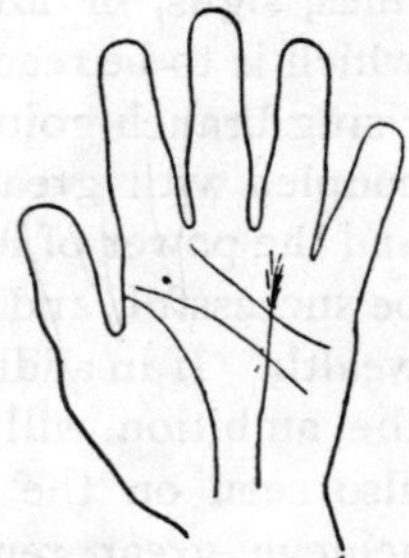
NO. 463

the subject will have combined wisdom (Saturn), brilliancy (Apollo), and shrewdness (Mercury), and with this combination he will reap wealth and renown. Branches or fine lines *rising* from the line of Apollo (465) will increase the good effect of the line, and when seen on a good line will make

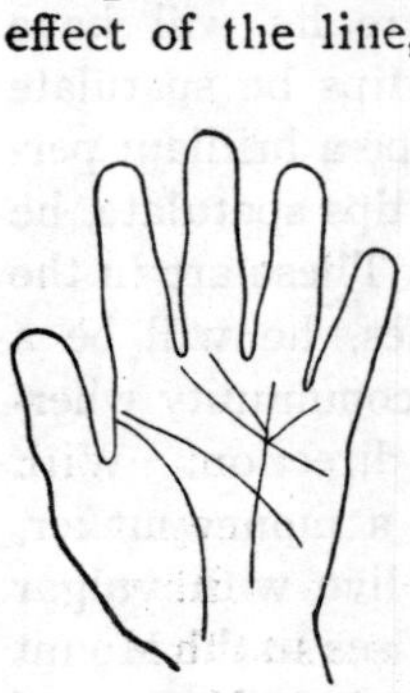
NO. 464

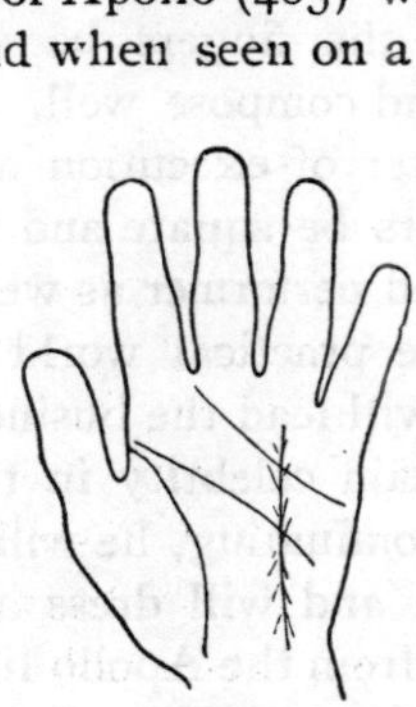
NO. 465

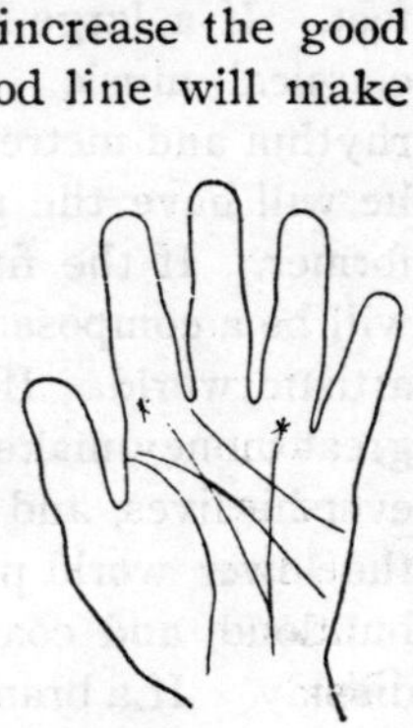
NO. 466

the success of the subject more certain. His life seems buoyant enough to rise over obstacles that may get in its way, and thus he floats over the top of difficulty instead of being dragged under by it. Fine lines *falling* from the line indicate that the subject will need greater and more constant effort to achieve success. He will have an up-hill pull, and there will be times when the load gets very heavy. He does not overcome obstacles easily, and such a line bears no such promise of a brilliant life as when the branches rise.

Branches which leave the Apollo line and run to other lines, signs, or Mounts, will each have a special meaning, which is to be read from the place where they terminate. A rising branch going to the Mount of Jupiter will show that, coupled with great talent, the subject has strong ambition and the power of leadership. With this combination he will be successful, and is sure to win fame if he does not secure wealth. If in addition a star be seen on the Mount of Jupiter the ambition will be crowned with success. If a star be also seen on the Mount of Apollo (466), he is certain to achieve great renown. If such a marking be seen, the Chirognomic indications should at once be studied. A soft hand, large Mount of Venus, and conic tips will make him a musician. He will love melody best and those gay, tuneful compositions which appeal to the heart and move the feet. If a large Mount of Moon be added he will also love classical music. If the fingers be square he will have rhythm and metre, and compose well. If tips be spatulate he will have the power of execution and be a brilliant performer. If the fingers be square and the tips spatulate, he will be a composer and performer as well. These are in the artistic world. If the practical world rules, he will be a great money-maker, will lead the business community wherever he lives, and attain celebrity in this direction. With the lower world predominating, he will be a money-maker, but loud, and coarse, and will dress and live with vulgar display. If a branch from the Apollo line rises to the Mount of Saturn, wisdom, soberness, frugality, a scientific turn of mind, and the balancing qualities of Saturn will increase the success of the subject. With this combination, if his mental world predominates, he will excel in occult sciences, chemistry, physics, or mathematics. If his fingers be smooth he will be guided by inspiration in these matters ; if with knotty joints he will be the reasoner and calculator ; square fingers will give him great exactness, and spatulate tips originality. This Apollonian-Saturnian will not be led by traditions, but will think for himself. All of these faculties will increase the certainty of his success and fame. If a star be seen on the branch to Saturn, the qualities of that Mount will bring great success. If in addition one be seen on the Mount of Apollo (467), the success of the subject is more certain. If the practical world rules, the subject will gain wealth

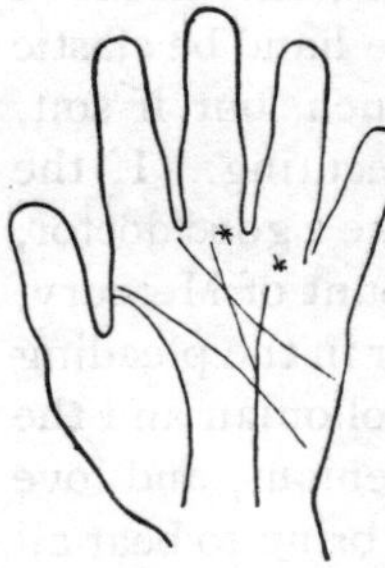

NO. 467

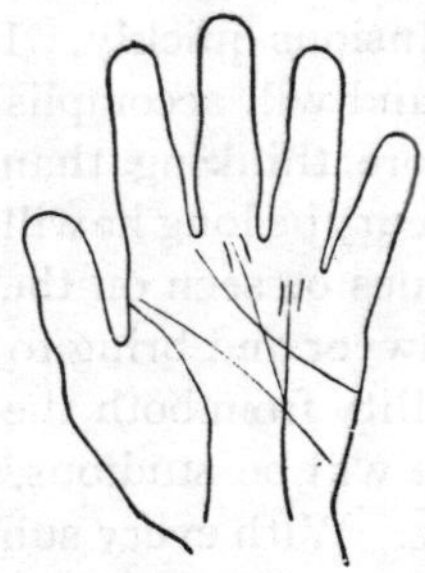

NO. 468

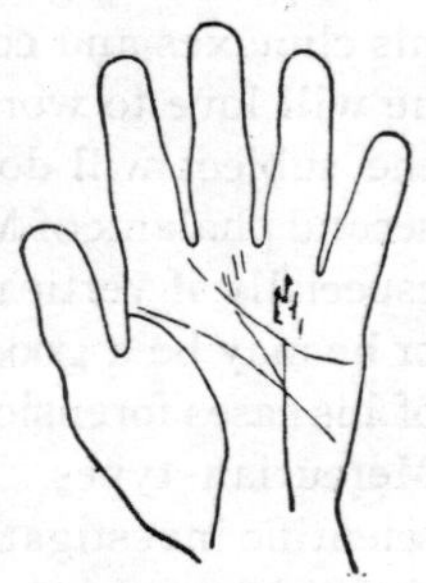

NO. 469

as well as fame from his efforts, and if the lower world be strong, he will be economical, frugal, and even stingy. If the thumb be stiff this will be more certain. If with this marking the hand be bad, the subject will be most successful in his meanness. If crosses, bars, dots, or other defects terminate the lines, the subject will be unsuccessful and will lose instead of gaining reputation. If the lines have sister lines on the Mounts, he will have the greatest success (468). If the lines should not reach the Mounts, and on the Mounts are seen many vertical lines, the subject will fail of ultimate success by reason of too great a diversity of effort (469). If a branch from the line of Apollo rises to the Mount of Mercury the qualities of that Mount will come to the assistance of the subject. He will have shrewdness, business ability, a scientific turn of mind, and great powers of expression, in addition to all the train of Apollonian brilliancies, and will achieve distinguished success in some direction. If the mental world rules, this Apollonian-Mercurian will have fluency of expression, and make a successful author, writer, or speaker on any subject which he may study. If his fingers and tips be square he will choose common-sense, practical subjects. If conic or pointed, artistic or idealistic matters will be chosen. If spatulate he will be original in his ideas and methods of expression, and if the fingers be smooth will depend upon inspiration. If his fingers be knotty he will have everything cut and dried, prepared in advance, and a reason for everything on the end of his tongue. If his fingers be long he will go into the detail, but if short, he will reach his climaxes and conclusions quickly. If the hand be elastic he will love to work, and will accomplish much, but if soft, the subject will do more thinking than executing. If the second phalanx of Mercury be long he will make a good doctor, especially if vertical lines be seen on the Mount of Mercury, or he may be a good lawyer and bring to bear in the pleading of his cases forensic ability from both the Apollonian and the Mercurian types. He will be studious, ingenious, and love scientific investigations. With every subject bring to bear all the Chirognomic indications in such cases; thus you can tell from what standpoint every act will be executed. If with the subject marked as No. 470, the third phalanx of the Mercury finger is longest, he will be devoted to business, shrewd, calculating, keen, and hard to beat. He knows men thoroughly, reads character easily, and understands a good business proposition when it is presented. Spatulate tips will make him original, square give great regularity and system, elastic consistency will give him the power to do and to accomplish, and a large thumb the determination to use his powers. Such a combination is an indication of great success and wealth.

If stars be seen on the Mounts of Apollo and Mercury (470), the success is intensified; if crosses, dots, bars, or other defects, the subject will make costly mistakes. If with this marking the Mercury finger be crooked or twisted, or both, the subject may use his brilliant talents to get the best of people. If a branch from the Apollo line rises to the Mount of Mars (471), the subject will have added to his Apollonian character the sterling qualities of Mars. Thus he will be self-reliant, able to defend himself, not easily discouraged, and if necessary will force his way through the world. If he be a mental type of subject, he will use these physical qualities to strengthen his mental ability. If a material subject he will use his talents in the business world or he will be a soldier. If the latter he will win renown. If crosses, dots, bars, or other defects be seen on the Mounts of Apollo and Mars, the subject will have trials hard to overcome. If sister

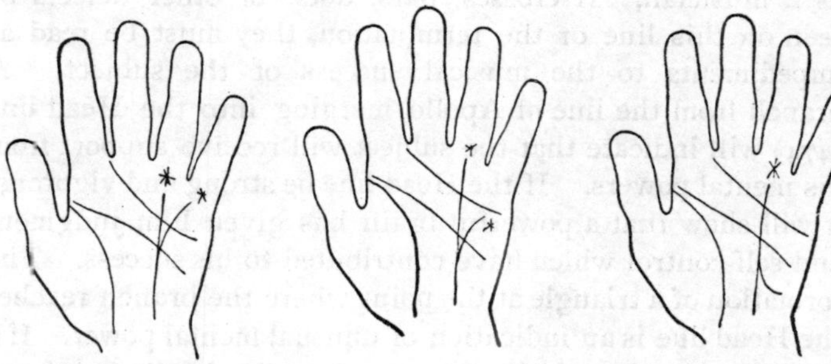

NO. 470 NO. 471 NO. 472

lines run beside the line on the Mount of Mars, the subject will have added renown. If a branch from the Apollo line comes from the Mount of Moon (472) the subject will have the power of imagination, the ability to paint word pictures, and a good power of expression. As an author he will be successful. If the hand be a musical one he will love only the classic form. If the fingers be smooth and tips conic, he will be an inspired writer and will deal in romance and poetry of a romantic character. If the fingers be knotty, he will write prose, and if at all poetic will incline to the epic form. If a star be seen on the end of the Apollo line the subject will achieve great renown from these spheres of action. If crosses, bars, dots, or other defects end the line, he will make errors which will interfere with his reputation. If a line runs from the Apollo line to a strong Mount of Venus (473) the subject will be passionately fond of music of a melodious character. This will be accented if the fingers be smooth and tips conic or pointed. If this subject be an instrumentalist, he will excel in expression and feeling.

If the fingers be square, he will excel in rhythm and metre, and if spatulate in technique. If he has square fingers and spatulate tips he will have both rhythm and technique. If with such a hand the consistency be soft or flabby, the subject will love to hear music, but will never have the energy to acquire proficiency in it. If a star be seen on the Mount of Apollo, the subject will achieve great distinction as a musician. If crosses, bars, dots, or other defects be seen on this line or the termination, they must be read as impediments to the musical success of the subject. A branch from the line of Apollo merging into the Head line (474) will indicate that the subject will receive support from his mental powers. If the Head line be strong and vigorous, it will show that a powerful brain has given him judgment and self-control which have contributed to his success. The formation of a triangle at the point where the branch reaches the Head line is an indication of unusual mental power. If a line from the line of Heart merges into the Apollo line (475) the subject will be much assisted by goodness of heart. Warmth of heart, sympathy, and an affectionate disposi-

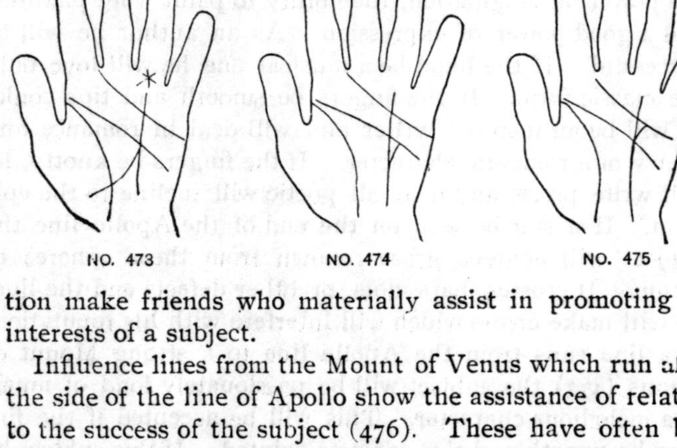

NO. 473 NO. 474 NO. 475

tion make friends who materially assist in promoting the interests of a subject.

Influence lines from the Mount of Venus which run along the side of the line of Apollo show the assistance of relatives to the success of the subject (476). These have often been read as legacies from relatives, but they do not necessarily indicate this particular form of help. They are sympathy, counsel, and support, as well as financial aid. If a line branching from the Heart line cuts the line of Apollo, the affections will stand in the way of the subject's success (477).

The line of Apollo, when based upon and fitted to the subject, can thus in many ways be made of wonderful value in the complete delineation of the hand. Standing as it does,

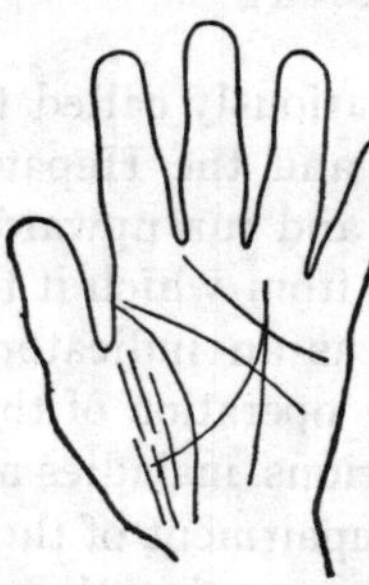

NO. 476

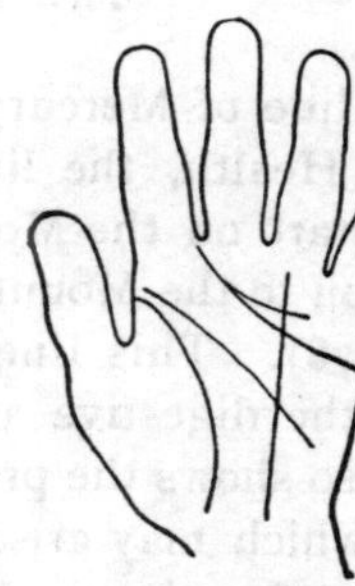

NO. 477

when good, for a brilliant career, we cannot afford to pass it by because of errors that have crept into its treatment in the past. By keeping constantly in mind the fact that it does not always apply to art, but to *every form* of daily occupation, we can divest it of the inaccuracies that have grown around it when estimated only as relating to an artistic career. Remembering that it is the "Line of Capability," and that it indicates the possibility of a vast amount which can be accomplished in *some* direction, we may by the aid of Chirognomy tell in what direction the capability exists. By following the line from source to termination and by noting each variation in its character, each defect which may appear, all chance lines which merge into, cut, or run alongside of it, by noting the source of each of these chance lines, and by applying the qualities of this source as a help or hindrance to the line, you can reason out any formation or combination of the Apollo line which can possibly occur.

CHAPTER XII

THE LINE OF MERCURY

THE line of Mercury has been variously called the line of Health, the line of Liver, and the Hepatica. It should start on the Mount of Moon and run upward on the percussion to the Mount of Mercury, from which it takes its name (478). This line is valuable as an indicator of the state of the digestive apparatus, the operation of the liver, and it also shows the presence of various maladies and conditions which may arise from the impairment of these most important functions. Bad conditions seen in other parts of the hand can often be referred to a poor Mercury line for explanation, and some of the most accurate work possible in the entire range of hand-reading can be done with the aid of the Mercury line. In connection with the lines of Life, Saturn, and Apollo, it is an important adjunct, and in all combinations any indication seen on the Mercury line should be given great weight. When we remember what an important part in the human economy is played by the digestive apparatus and by the proper secretion and discharge of bile, we see that the line of Mercury has influence upon many parts of our lives, and that it is an ever-present factor in our success or failure. Physicians say that with a good digestion and a normal flow of bile, disease would be unknown to the human race. In a large percentage of illnesses, without doubt the correction of derangement of the digestive apparatus and a control of the bile supply cures the patient. It is also a

NO. 478

fact that the bilious types are the only ones which are really criminal, other types doing bad things under a stress of some exciting cause. Bad types of Saturnians and Mercurians prefer the criminal way of doing things to the honest one. All through the study of human nature and character, we see the ill effect and plague of bile when not properly regulated. The Mercury line is exceedingly useful as a guide to business success, as no factor more surely enables one to cope with the affairs of the world than a clear brain, and nothing more surely keeps the brain from clogging than a good digestion and an active liver. Added to good health, no set of qualities will more surely aid in obtaining the best results from business than those peculiar to the Mercurian type. As the Mercury line indicates both the condition of the digestive organs and the state of the liver, and accents the strength of the Mercurian type, it is manifestly of unusual assistance when estimating the outcome of a business career.

The Mercury line in its relation to health must always be used in connection with the type of the subject. If we see indigestion or biliousness in the hand of a Jupiterian subject, a type naturally predisposed to overeating, we consider that to him it means an increased danger. And as certain disorders of the stomach cause vertigo, we know that if the case be very pronounced the subject is likely to be stricken with one of his type diseases, apoplexy. In a similar manner, the Mercury line will aid in estimating the degree of danger indicated by health defects of all the types. In connection with defects in the Head line, the Mercury line is a valuable assistant, for it is well known that the stomach and liver largely influence the condition of the physical brain. Functional disturbances of the heart are also brought on by indigestion, consequently a defective Heart line may find its disturbing cause indicated in the Mercury line. Poor health may wreck a brilliant career, and the Mercury line may explain defects seen in the Saturn or Apollo lines. All over the hand the influence of the defects it indicates may be felt and in any perplexing case do not forget to examine the

Mercury line before completing the estimate. The Mercury line will not be found in all hands. Without being able to state the exact percentage, I should say that at least one half the hands will be without it. In few cases is it a perfectly marked line, and this is not hard to explain, when perfect health is the possession of so few. I do not regard the absence of the Mercury line as necessarily a detriment, for on many hands which I have examined while making a study of this line, the health of those who have no line was found to be uniformly good. If there is to be a choice between no line or a defective one, it is preferable that none be seen. The absence of the Saturn line leaves a subject free to carve his way through the world, and in a similar manner the absence of the Mercury line shows that in its health directions there are no disturbances which *must* cause a subject trouble, and if he takes care of his stomach and liver he has open to him the possibility of no trouble from them. His health in these directions will be largely "self-made," and proportionate to the care he takes of himself. One other condition is generally present when the Mercury line is absent: the hand is not usually much lined and rayed, for if it were, a Mercury line would surely be present. Such a hand, having few lines, is consequently less nervous, and as nervousness greatly increases the improper action of the liver, a lack of nervousness increases the subject's favorable condition. In making the final estimate for a subject, consider that, with the Mercury line absent he has to face at least no inevitable disease of digestion, and no disorder of the liver that he cannot control by caring for himself.

The Mercury line *should* rise from the Mount of Moon, but in practice it rarely does. In the largest number of cases it rises toward the Saturn or Life line, and from the centre or base of the hand, often in the Plain of Mars. It is much better that the line should rise between the Saturn line and the percussion (479) than between the Saturn line and the Life line (480); rising from the Life line (481) is one of the most unfavorable markings. To give the most favorable health indications, as well as the best promise of business success, the Mercury line should at no time touch the Life line, but branches from the Life line may go to it, or *vice versa*, or chance lines may connect the two, without bad results. The source of the Mercury line, outside of its unfavorable connection with the Life line, has no special meaning. Unless it rises from or touches the Life line it may be considered a normal line.

The character of the line is important. A deep line of Mer-

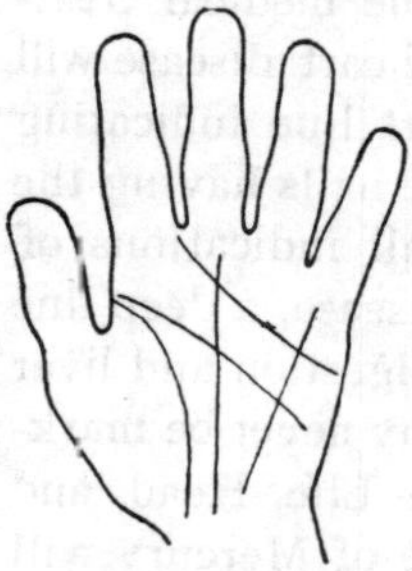

NO. 479

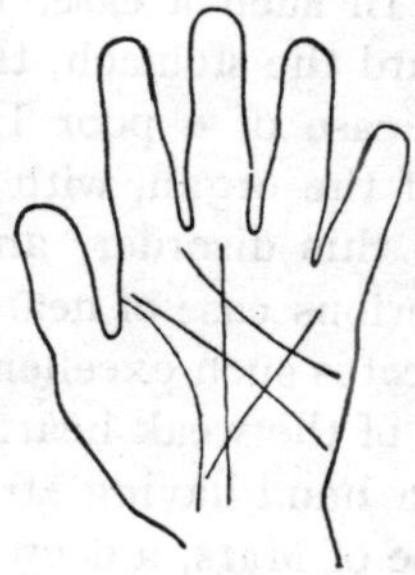

NO. 480

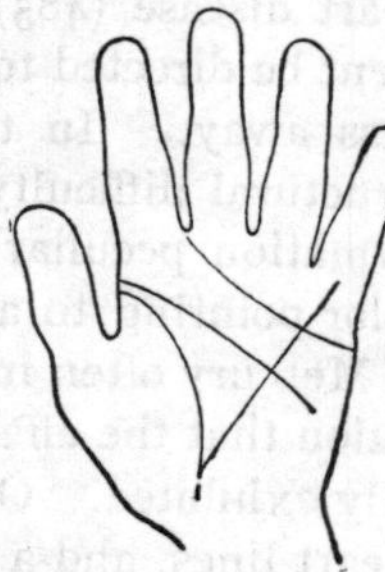

NO. 481

cury indicates a good digestion, a healthy action of the liver, good vitality, strong constitution, a clear brain, and good memory. Whatever the type of your subject or whatever his occupation, he will have the assistance of these powerful allies. If the Life line be thin, chained, or otherwise defective, and the Mercury line deep and strong (482), its effect upon the Life line will be fully as favorable as a strong line of Mars, to build up and strengthen whatever delicacy exists; and such a Mercury line will many times replace the functions of the Life line. This will often account for the health of a person with a defective Life line.

There are no more potent factors in the healthy and vigorous operation of the brain than a good digestion and the proper action of the bile secretion. The first effect of dyspepsia is to produce intense depression. The subject becomes morbid, and sees everything through a glass colored by a disordered stomach. When the attack of dyspepsia has passed, his brain clears up and he sees things in their proper light. Thus the Mercury line will be invaluable in conjunction with the Head line in estimating mental strength and balance. A good Head line will be much disturbed by a poor Mercury line (483), and a defective condition of the head may be accounted for by a bad Mercury line (484). Disturbed action of the stomach sometimes produces functional derangement of the heart, and a poor Heart line with a defective Mercury line will often entirely account for a condition of so-called chronic heart disease (485). In such a case, if the medical treatment be directed toward the stomach, the heart disease will pass away. In the case of a poor Heart line indicating structural difficulty of the organ, with the nails having the formation peculiar to this disorder, and all indications of color pointing to a serious case of heart disease, a deep line of Mercury often indicates such excellent digestion and liver action that the effects of the weak heart may never be markedly exhibited. On a hand having strong Life, Head, and Heart lines, and a line of Mars, a deep line of Mercury will indicate a subject who will virtually never know a day's sickness. If such a combination be seen on a hand which is ani-

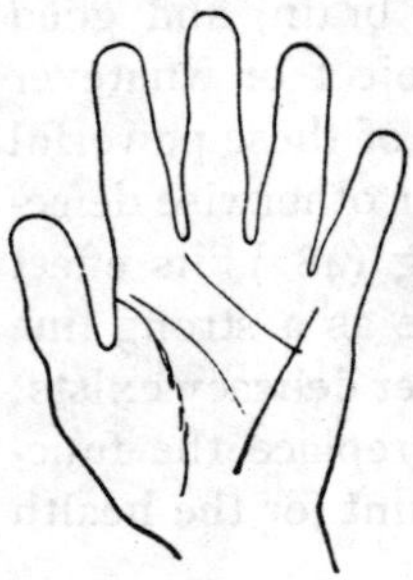
NO. 482

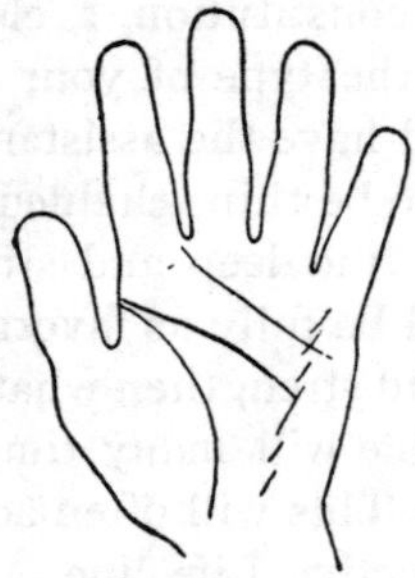
NO. 483

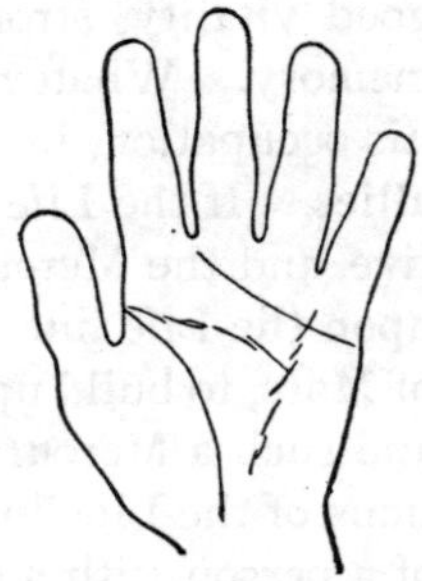
NO. 484

mal in its Chirognomic aspect, the intense good health and strength of vitality will render the subject fierce in his passions, inordinate in his appetites, and from this class often come rapists and drunkards. Such persons should never choose indoor occupations. They need fresh air and plenty of exercise to work off the animal vitality. If with this combination there be the addition of red hair, the indications of great excesses will be intensified, and quick, fiery temper will be added. Black hair shows an abundance of volatile qualities and needs no addition from red. If the Mercury line be thin it shows that the subject may still have good digestion, proper action of the liver, and that his health and Mercurian attributes will act in conjunction to produce success in business. The mere thinness of a Mercury line

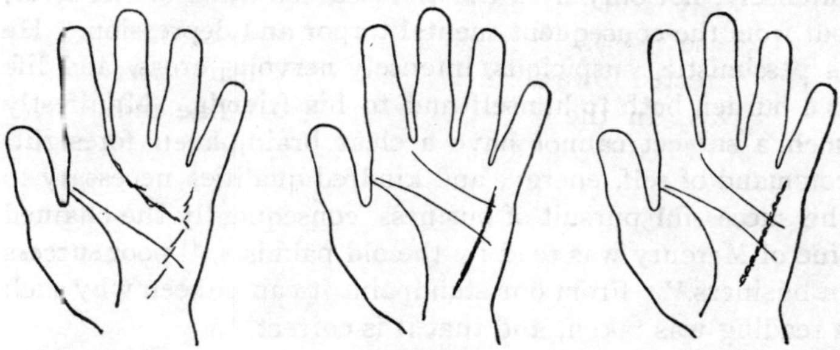

NO. 485 NO. 486 NO. 487

does not lessen its influence, for it shows that the subject is receiving support from good operation of the liver, though not in such a degree as with a deep line. If the type of the subject be refined, and shows good but not excessive vitality, the thin line is better for him. In all estimates of the Mercury line, the proportion of the lines must be kept in mind, for here as everywhere else the normal balance is best. A broad, shallow Mercury line (486) shows that the subject is not vitally strong, and any severe tax upon his stomach will result in its derangement. The liver is unsteady in its operation and secretes its bile in unequal quantities. As a consequence the subject is frequently despondent, is predisposed to sudden and violent headaches, heartburn, sour stomach, and dyspepsia. During the intervals when the functions are properly performed, the subject gets along all right, but with such a Mercury line, constant care is necessary as to diet and hygiene, for while such subjects cannot be said to be sickly, they are not over healthy, and this weakened condition of vitality tells upon the energies, the ambitions, and the business life. A chained line of Mercury (487) indicates a positive condition of diseased liver and stomach. This must not be confounded with islands in the line, but the chains must be short loops. With this marking the subject will be predisposed to inflammation of the gall duct, gall stones, cirrhosis, and numerous structural liver troubles which are always serious and often fatal. The chained line is one of the worst formations, and the subject who has it suffers intensely, not only from the diseased condition of the liver, but from the consequent mental torpor and depression. He is pessimistic, suspicious, intensely nervous, cross, and life is a burden both to himself and to his friends. Manifestly such a subject cannot have a clear brain, keen foresight, command of self, energy, and kindred qualities necessary to the successful pursuit of business, consequently the chained line of Mercury was read by the old palmists, "poor success in business." From our standpoint it can be seen why such a reading was taken, and that it is correct.

The length of the Mercury line adds to the power of the line and its usefulness. If the line be long, running from the base of the hand to the Mount of Mercury, its influence will be

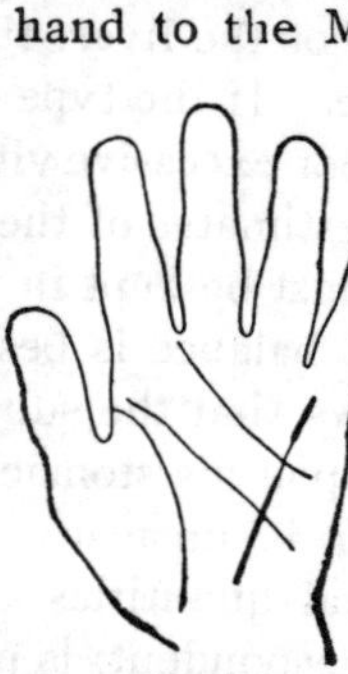

NO 488

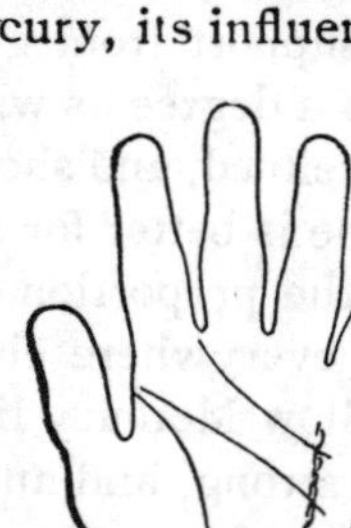

NO. 489

felt during the subject's entire life. If the long line be also a good one its influence means good health and success during the entire life. If this long line be a defective one, it will indicate ill health and attendant indifferent business success during the entire life. By the length of the line and its character during the different periods of life, you can tell what years will be blessed with the greatest strength, best action of the liver, good digestion, and consequently the most productive periods in a business way. If the line starts deep, then grows thin, and then is deep again (488), there is a period covered by the thinness of the line when the health is impaired, and at such a time the subject must use great care, take much sleep, and avoid dissipation. If this be done, with the good ending of the line, trouble may be

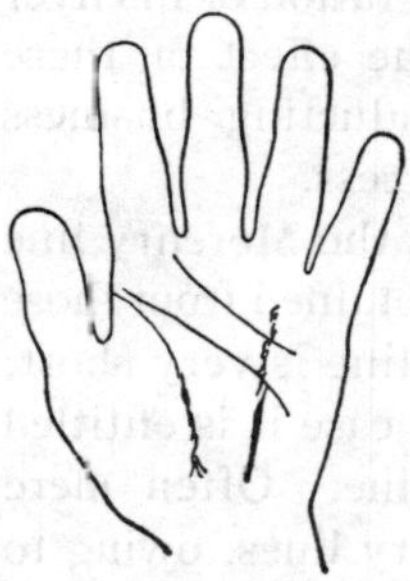

NO. 490

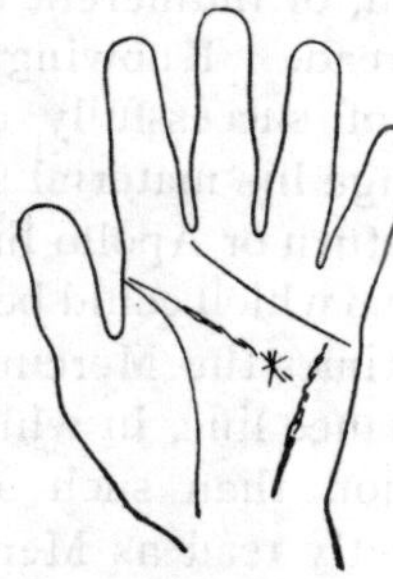

NO. 491

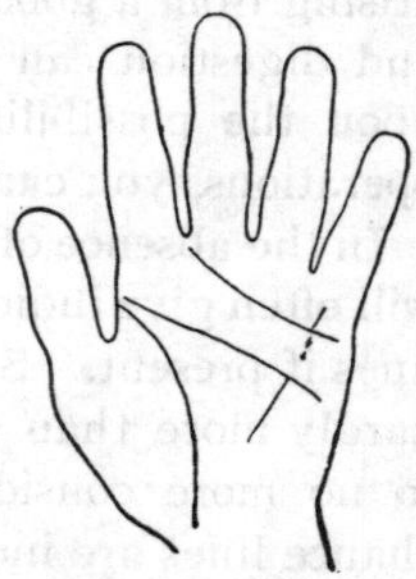

NO. 492

avoided. If (reading, of course, from its source upward) the line begins deep and grows chained (489) the good health of the first years on the line is followed by some serious affection of the liver and consequent stomach derangement will impair the health and success of the subject ; the age of all periods to be read from the line, reading, of course, always from its source upward. If with this marking the Life line be defective after the chaining begins, the case is serious (490). If after the chaining of the Mercury line begins the Head line shows islands or other defects, the liver trouble will affect the mental strength of the subject. This will often account for sudden attacks of temporary insanity, especially if a star be seen in or near the Head line (491). If the Mercury line runs to the Head line and is absent or defective during the space between Head and Heart lines, but runs again *on* the Mount of Mercury (492), the subject will need to do as much as possible before the age of thirty, for at that time the powerful allies of the good Mercury line will for a time desert him, and as the years between Head and Heart lines are among the most important in his life, he will lose these supports at a critical period. The line running again on the Mount will show that he *may* recover himself if care be used. If bars, crosses, dots, islands, or other defects terminate or are near the ending of the line, he is not likely to recover. By following the line from its source, noting its length, any changes in its character, during which parts it is good or deficient, all the changes in the conditions of the subject arising from a good, bad, or indifferent operation of his liver and digestion can be read. Knowing the effect of these upon the possibilities of successfully conducting business operations, you can gauge his material success.

In the absence of a Saturn or Apollo line, the Mercury line will often give indications which could be obtained from those lines if present. Sometimes the Mercury line is very short, hardly more than a chance line, in which case it is entitled to no more consideration than such a line. Often mere chance lines are incorrectly read as Mercury lines, owing to the large number of hands in which this line is either absent or wofully deficient. In this part of the work great caution should be used lest mere chance lines be mistaken for and read as *Main lines*. A line of *Mercury* cannot run to the Mount of Apollo, or anywhere but to the Mount of Mercury, and to be diagnosed as this line must at least show that it is *heading* in that direction, even though it may not be quite long enough to reach the Mount. Before any line is called a Mercury line it must be *enough* of a line to entitle it to be classed among the Main lines.

Color in the Mercury line should increase or diminish the estimate of the strength of the qualities it indicates. If the line shows biliousness and defective liver conditions, yellow color will generally be present as a strong confirmatory indication. The type of the subject will, however, greatly affect color, and you should not fall into the way of expecting yellow color with all bad Mercury lines. A Jupiterian, Apollonian, Martian, or Venusian subject, even with pronounced biliousness, rarely has any color but pink or red, though blue is sometimes seen. These warmer types have bad Mercury lines occasionally, but they take more exercise, are more cheerful, and consequently throw off many of the ill effects arising from improper action of bile. The Saturnian first, Mercurian second, and Lunarian third, will show yellow color easily. On a Saturnian subject we expect yellow, for he is always more or less impregnated with bile, while the Mercurian has bile enough to give him an olive complexion. The Lunarian may be yellow, but white more often. A Saturnian who has a bad Mercury line will be doubly sure to be gloomy, pessimistic, and disagreeable, and with such a subject all defects in a Mercury line must be given their full interpretation, for a bad Mercury line on a Saturnian is an exceedingly unfortunate combination. If yellow color be seen with the warmer types, it shows that the defects in the Mercury line are most pronounced, for when the natural red or pink of these types has been overcome by yellow, the poison has taken serious hold. In all estimates of color with the Mercury line, take full account of the type of the subject, and the natural color he should show, from which it can be judged how seriously he is affected. If the Mercury line shows indigestion, and yellow color be likewise present, the latter indicates that the subject has also *liver disorder*, even though it is not marked in the Mercury line.

If perfect health were always possible, we should find perfect Mercury lines, but as a large part of the human family have bodily ills more or less in evidence, we find a very large proportion of these lines defective. A wavy line (493) indicates chronic biliousness. This subject will have attacks of bilious fever, malaria, and various liver complications, often ending in enlargement of the liver and jaundice. There is a very frequent complication of rheumatism with biliousness, and with wavy Mercury lines the indications of rheumatic difficulty should be looked for. If the subject be a Saturnian with a wavy Mercury line he will have serious bilious attacks. When this is seen on other types, the liver trouble often brings out those health defects of the type that are influenced by an excess of bile. The Jupiterian will have gout; the Saturnian bilious fevers, gout, rheumatism, and nerve disorders; the Apollonian functional heart derangement ; the Mercurian indigestion, nerve difficulty, and grave liver disorders ; the Martian intestinal inflammations ; the Lunarian gout or rheumatism ; and the Venusian acute attacks of bilious fever.

With a wavy Mercury line the business career of the subject will be unsteady and subject to many vicissitudes. An uneven line of Mercury (494) indicates a fitful condition of the stomach and liver. There will be periods when the subject has excellent health, and at such times will do well. These will be followed by periods when the liver does not properly perform its functions, the digestion will be poor, and life becomes a drag. These alternating intervals of good health and weakness mar life's steadiness and prevent the accomplishing of much result. When the line of Mercury rises in the form of a ladder composed of broken fragments (495) it indicates the worst form of stomach trouble. Dyspepsia, with its train of ills, gastric fever, catarrh of the stomach or intestines, or inflammation of the bowels are among the acute disorders which are likely to attack the

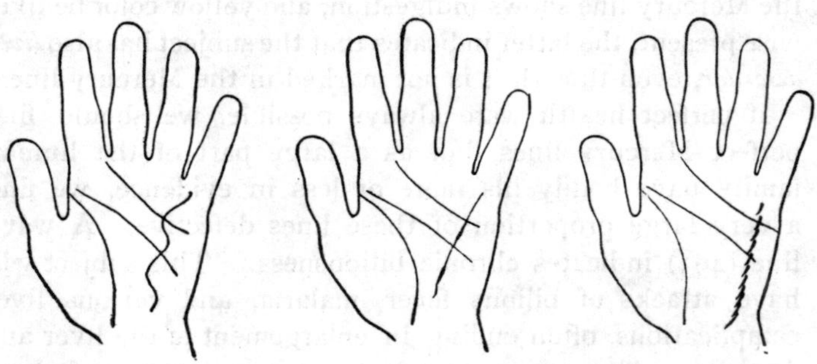

NO. 493 NO. 494 NO. 495

subject. If in the course of such a line there be a highly colored dot (496) an attack of severe stomach disorder has occurred at the age indicated by its position. If this dot be highly colored, red or purple, it has been very severe. Dots on the Mercury line (497), wherever seen or on whatever kind of a line, indicate *acute* attacks of bilious or stomach trouble at the age at which they occur on the line. If red they indicate fevers, if white some disorder arising from a chronic disease. When a dot is seen on the Mercury line note whether a chance line from it points to a health defect on some line or Mount. If none be seen, the lines and Mounts should be scanned for markings indicating chronic or acute attacks that may be referred to the dot on the Mercury line for an explanation. Health defects on the Mount of Jupiter (498) will

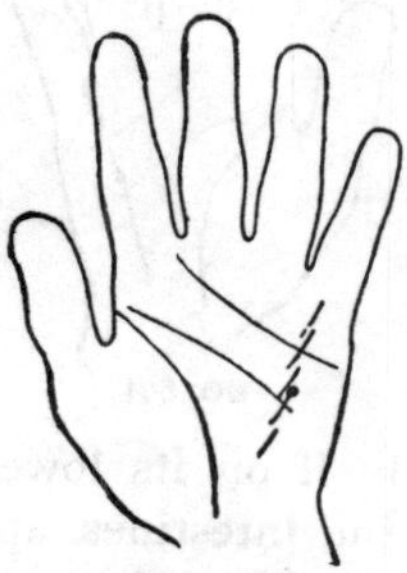

NO. 496

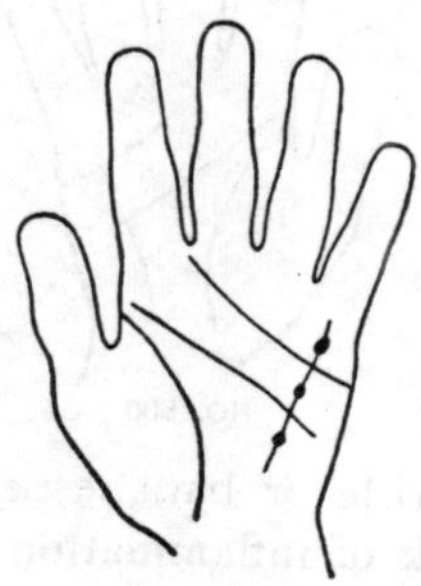

NO. 497

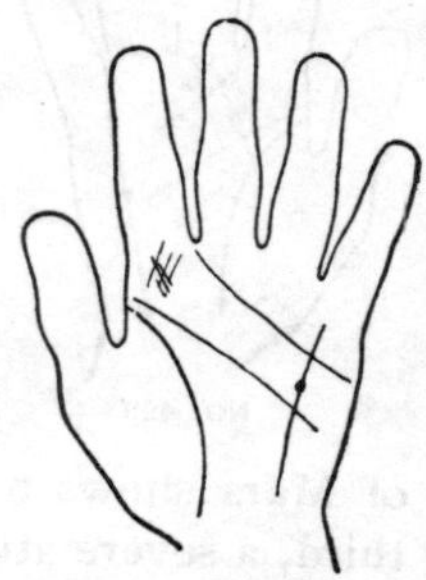

NO. 498

mean the natural stomach delicacy of the Jupiterian which has caused this trouble. If the third phalanx of the Jupiter finger be large and full, this is certain, for this subject will abuse his stomach. If the third phalanx of the Jupiter finger shows that it has been full, but has become flabby, the subject's stomach has become so delicate that he has had to limit his diet to the simplest kind of food, and a chronic state of dyspepsia is probably present. A health defect on Saturn with a dot in the Mercury line will indicate an acute attack of bilious fever if the dot be red ; if it be pale or yellow an attack of gout or rheumatism. This will be more certain if a chance line runs from Saturn toward the Life line, and one from the middle of the Mount of Moon to the Life line (499). If the Heart line under Apollo shows an island, break, or dot, and a dot appears on the Mercury line, a severe attack of heart trouble, brought on by derangement of the digestive organs, will occur at the age indicated by the dot on the Mercury line. A grille on Apollo with blue color and heart-disease nails will intensify this reading and indicate that the trouble is chronic (500). If, with a dot on the Mercury line, the line be broken or otherwise defective on the Mount of Mercury, a severe attack of bilious or gastric fever has occurred at the age indicated by the dot in the Mercury line (501). If, with a dot in the Mercury line, the Upper Mount

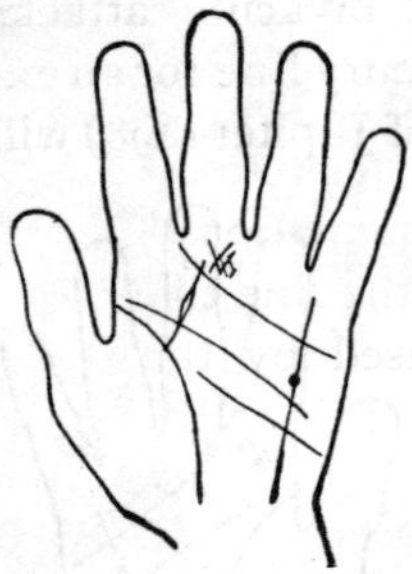

NO. 499

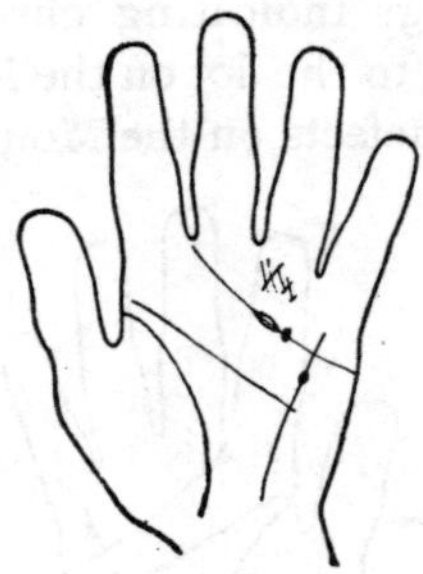

NO. 500

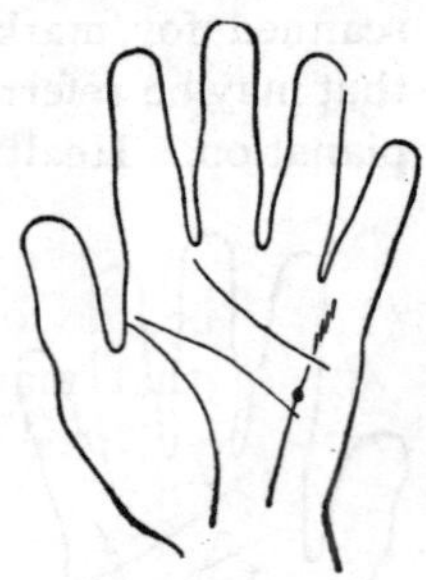

NO. 501

of Mars shows a grille or bars, especially if on its lower third, a severe attack of inflammation of the intestines, appendicitis, peritonitis, or some other acute intestinal disorder has occurred at the age denoted by the position of the dot on the Mercury line (502). If, with a dot in the Mercury

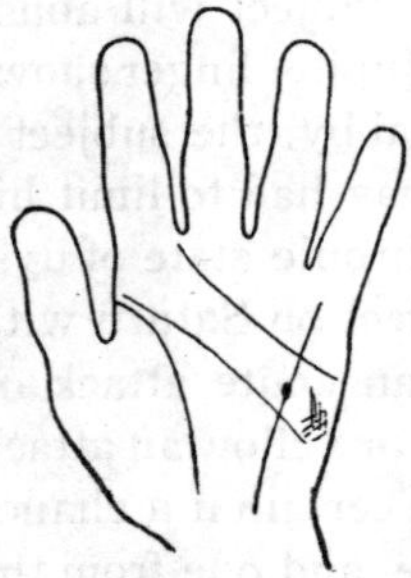

NO. 502

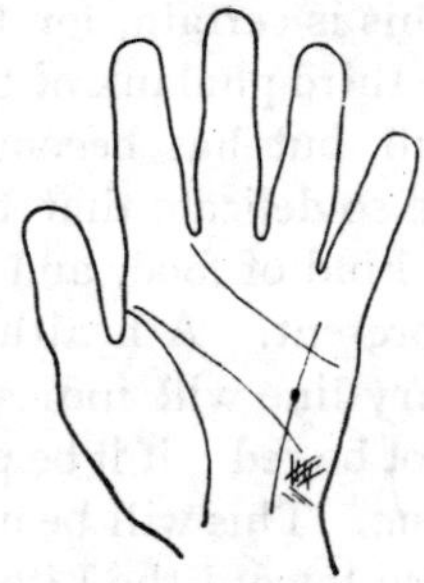

NO. 503

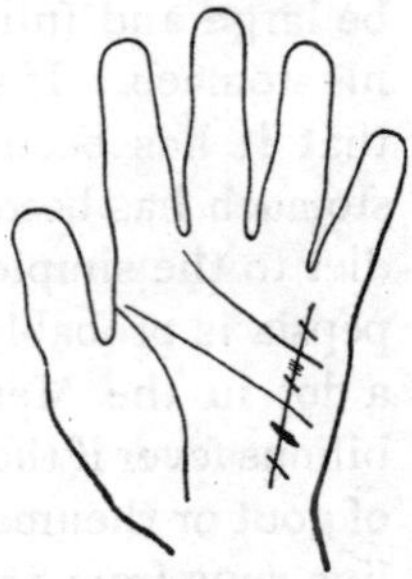

NO. 504

line, the middle third of the Mount of Moon be grilled, gout or, more likely, rheumatic fever has occurred at the age shown by the dot in the Mercury line. If the upper third of the Mount of Moon be grilled the same character of intestinal disorders which are peculiar to the lower part of Upper Mars are indicated (503). Cross-bars cutting the Mercury line (504) indicate illnesses at the age at which they are seen. These bars will vary from the finest little lines which seem to run over the top of the Mercury line and only fret it, to deep bars which cut the line in two. The extent to which they cut the line must indicate the severity of the attacks. If they be only fine fretting lines, they indicate bilious or sick headaches. If they are deep-cutting bars they are severe illnesses, and you should look to the lines and Mounts in the usual manner for an explanation of them. If there be only one or two bars crossing the line there will only be that many serious illnesses caused by the peculiarities indicated by the line, but if they continually cut the line during its entire length, they will indicate continuous sickness if deep, or headaches if fine. There are often seen a series of fine bars crossing the Mercury line, and also fine bars crossing the Head line (505). This indicates great suffering from nervous, bilious, or sick headaches, but they all arise from imperfect action of the stomach and liver. Such a marking often results in an impairment of the Head line after the bars are seen, showing that the headaches have weakened it. With every form and variation, and every

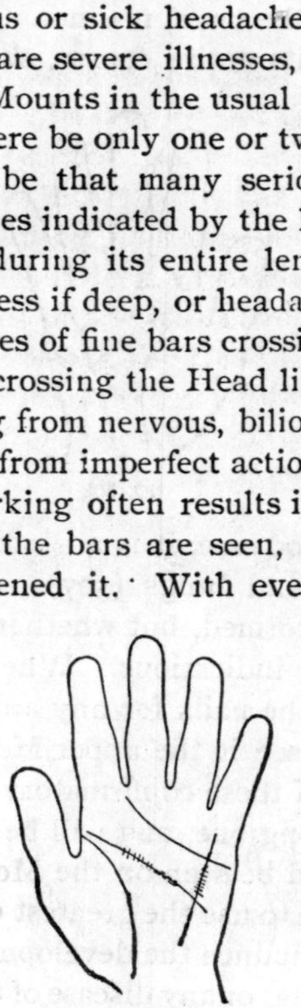

NO. 505

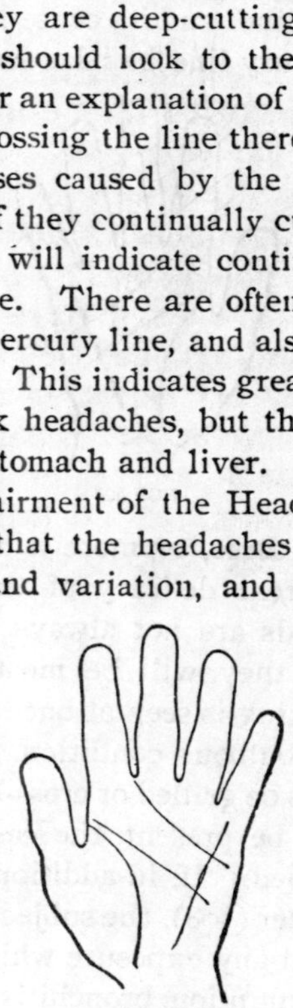

NO. 506

defect in the Mercury line, the Head line should be at once consulted.

An island in the Mercury line (506) indicates a delicacy of health during its presence. This may arise from the liver and stomach, or from appendicitis inflammation of the intestines, or it may be a difficulty of head, heart, or any other organ, which one, can be located by the examination of Mounts and lines. The peculiarity of the island in the Mercury line is that its detrimental effect upon the health is not always confined to stomach and liver disorders, but relates equally to other kinds of illnesses or delicacy. A single island must be read as a delicacy to health just as is done in the Life line, and its cause located in the usual manner. If the Mercury line be islanded during its entire course, showing

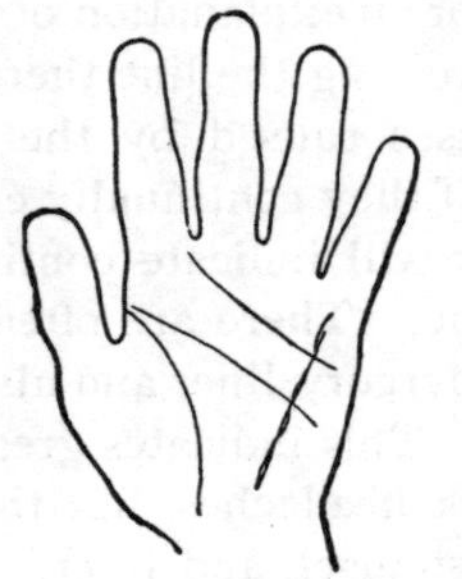

NO. 507

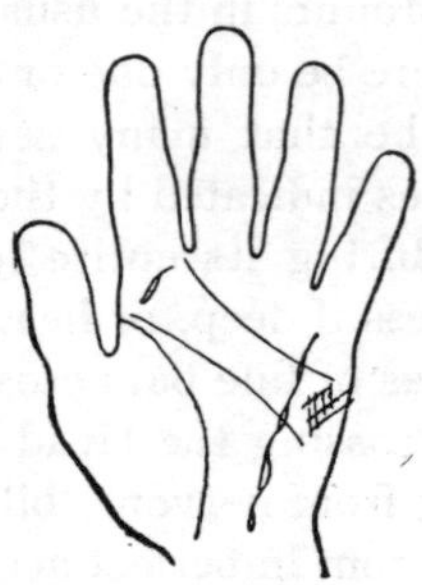

NO. 508

two, three, or more islands of good size, it is an indication of great delicacy of the throat and lungs (507). These islands are not always perfectly formed, but whether so or not, they will be most accurate indications. When this marking is seen at once examine the nails for any approach to a bulbous condition, and also see if the upper Mount of Mars be grilled or cross-barred. If these confirmatory markings be present, the case is a strong one, and will be easily verified. If, in addition, an island be seen on the Mount of Jupiter (508), the subject will need to use the greatest care to avoid any exposure which might induce the development of consumption, bronchitis, pneumonia, or any disease of throat, bronchia, or lungs. I have recently seen this marking on a patient suffering from cancer of the throat. An old reading of the Mercury line when islanded was as an indication of "Bankruptcy." This came from the fact that the health of those with such a marking was precarious and precluded the likelihood of enough effort to produce success in business. This old reading, while it has a strong foundation, will not be accurate if applied to your clients. You will find many islanded lines of Mercury in the hands of those who are by no means financially Bankrupt, but who *are* Bankrupt in health. Such subjects, if in business, must spend so much time in the care of their health that business will probably be neglected. Certain it is a delicate subject cannot push business with the vigor of one who is well, and these reasons led to the interpretation of "Bankruptcy" by older palmists. When the Mercury line is broken (509) it indicates that the subject's health will be impaired, at the time of the break, and, consequent upon this, his business career will suffer. If the line have only one or two breaks and is good the rest of the way, find the cause of the breaks in the usual manner. If the line be continuously broken, it shows extreme delicacy of the stomach, and has the same effect as a laddered line. The more the line be broken, the more continuous will be the succession of illnesses, and such a line will show a subject to be in a continual state of dyspepsia. Such a subject will have many headaches, and will have to use constant care not to disturb his digestion. With broken lines repair signs may be seen and squares will be most beneficial. If a

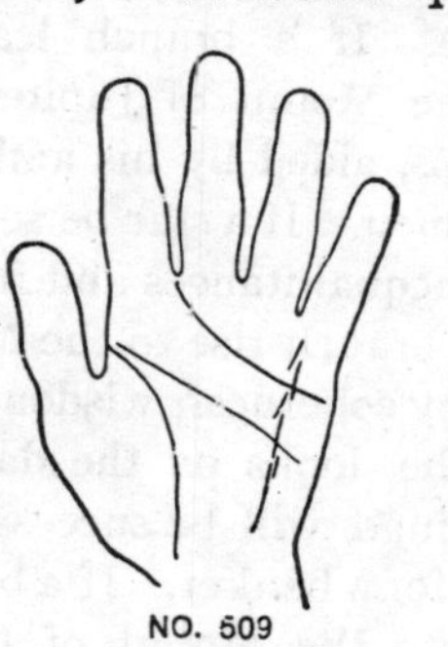

NO. 509

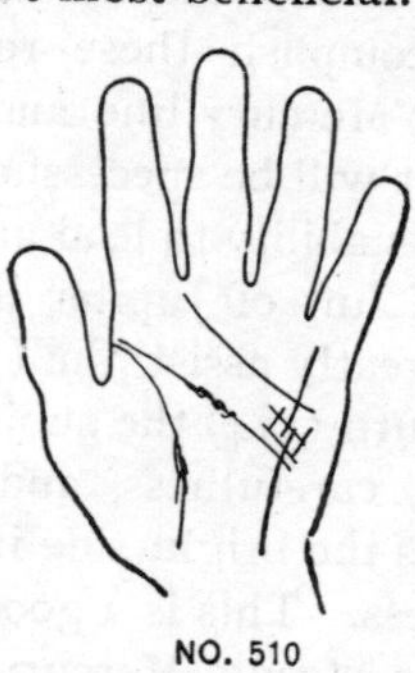

NO. 510

serious break be seen in the Mercury line surrounded by a square (510), a danger to the life of the subject has been averted. The cause of the trouble may come from several directions. You may be able to locate it by a defect in the Head line, or find health defects on the Mounts, or serious delicacy or danger to life in the Life line, all of which should be brought to bear upon the repaired break as a location of the cause for it. Sister lines are useful in repairing breaks, and all markings which help to continue the Current in the line must be considered as benefiting the broken condition just that much. If the Mercury line runs deep onto the Mount of Mercury and branches rise from it (511), the subject will have excellent health and great success in business. If from a deep line branches droop down-

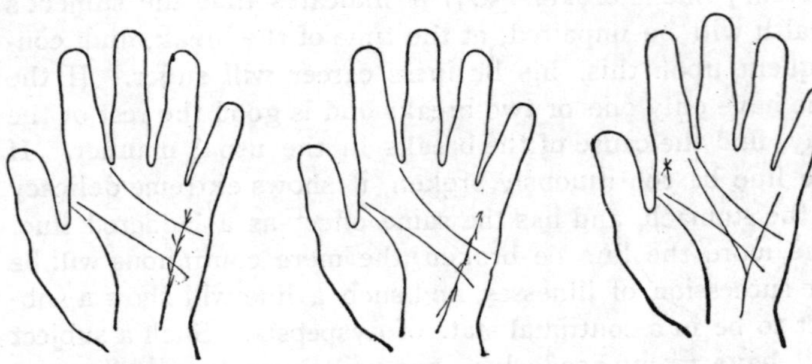

NO. 511 NO. 512 NO. 513

ward, the subject will succeed, but will have to work harder to accomplish these results (512). If a branch leave a strong Mercury line and run to the Mount of Jupiter, the subject will be successful in business, aided by his ambition and his ability to lead and control men. If a star be seen on the Mount of Jupiter influential acquaintances and friends will greatly assist him (513). If a branch rise to the Mount of Saturn (514) the subject, aided by soberness, wisdom, frugality, carefulness, and because he looks on the dark as well as the bright side in undertakings, will be successful in business. This is a good marking for a banker. If a branch from a strong Mercury line rise to the Mount of Apollo (515) the subject, owing to great shrewdness and business ability, aided by brilliant mind and agreeable manners, will be most successful. This is an ideal marking for a merchant. The long Mercury line in these cases will show that this type will lead and the branch lines show which type will aid him.

In all these instances place the subject in his proper world by the phalanges of his Mercury finger. If he have the third world strongest he will have business success. If the second be strongest he will have success in the scientific or professional world. If the first phalanx be strongest he will succeed as an orator or writer, and this latter indication will be increased if a branch from the upper third of the Mount of Moon merges into the Mercury line (516). A branch from the Mercury line rising and merging into the Head line (517) will indicate success due to the subject's mental powers. Such persons will be best adapted to literary or scientific careers, especially if the Head line be deep and strong. Note here the formation of a triangle, which, in this position, always indicates mental brilliancy and power. The termination of the Mercury line will indicate the general outcome of the career of the subject, as regards the health qualities of the line and the success of the subject in the directions peculiar to the Mercurian type. The Mount of Mercury has so many markings that some of them may be confused with the termination of the Mercury line if care be not observed. If the line ends on the Mount,

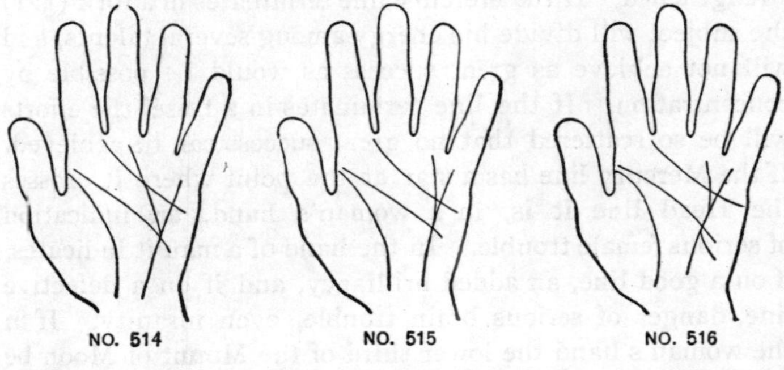

NO. 514 NO. 515 NO. 516

the lines of Affection may cross it (518). If there are a number of these lines, one of which is deep and cuts the Mercury line sharply, there will be one affection which will be a bar to the best interests of the subject. If the Mercury line ends in a bar or a cross (519) the career of the subject will be hampered, and if the type of hand be bad, with crooked fingers, and the Heart line thin or absent, the deceitful or tricky qualities of a bad Mercurian will cause the lack of success. If a grille terminates the line, even worse ill-success is indicated, resulting from either poor health or dishonesty. If with this marking a dot be seen on the Mount of Apollo, the subject will lose his reputation. If the line terminates in a star (520) the career will be successful in the world indicated by the phalanges of the fingers, and if the lines of Apollo

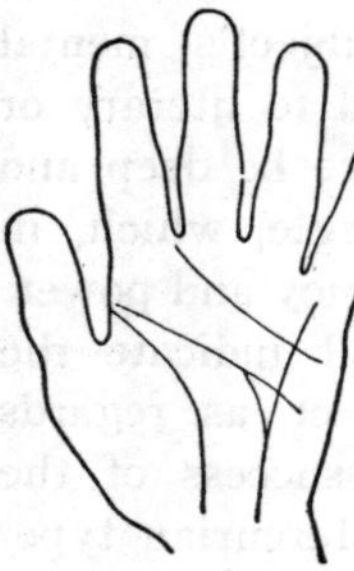

NO. 517

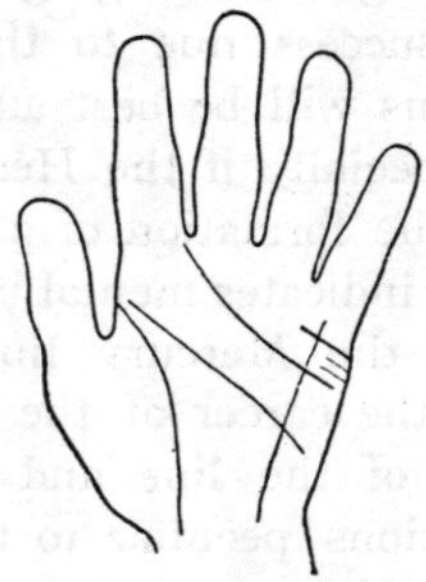

NO. 518

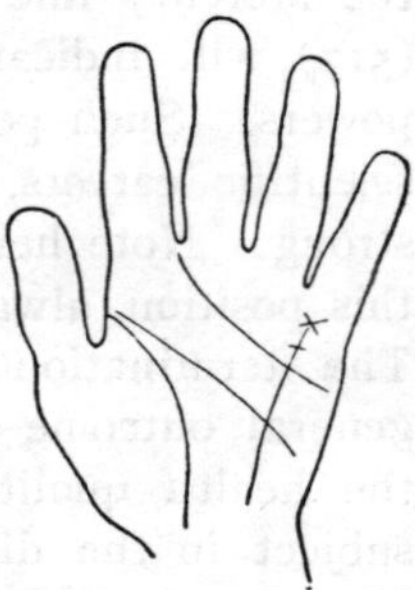

NO. 519

and Saturn be present and good, this indication will be strengthened. If the Mercury line terminates in a fork (521) the subject will divide his energy among several talents, and will not achieve as great success as would be possible by concentration. If the line terminates in a tassel the efforts will be so scattered that no great success can be achieved. If the Mercury line has a star at the point where it crosses the Head line it is, in a woman's hand, an indication of serious female trouble. In the hand of a man it indicates, if on a good line, an added brilliancy, and if on a defective line, danger of serious brain trouble, even insanity. If in the woman's hand the lower third of the Mount of Moon be grilled or cross-barred (522), the female weakness will be very serious. Such subjects will have great difficulty in child-bearing, and with a Life line which runs close to the thumb and restricts the Mount of Venus, they will probably be childless. This is valuable as a pre-marriage indication. Whenever this marking is found the woman is nervous and highly strung. She will at times become depressed, and then recover her cheerfulness, alternating between exaltation and despair. These subjects should receive the greatest care, and ought always to be the recipients of very tender treatment. They often magnify or even imagine ills, but they suffer just as much as if these were real. Hysteria and hypochondria are often thus indicated, and pronounced mental unbalancing frequently occurs. If the star should not be exactly *on* the line it still gives the same indication.

The combinations of the indications contained in this chapter are innumerable, but the general principles governing them are always the same. If a good Mercury line shows defects it is not so bad an indication as when a *defective* line has these same flaws. If a wavy line be *also* full of islands it is a worse condition than when a straight deep line has them. Often there are two different defects seen in a line, and each will refer to a different cause. These can both be found in the usual manner. The Mercury line should be used continually in connection with the Life, Head, Heart, and Apollo lines, and the type of each subject should never be overlooked.

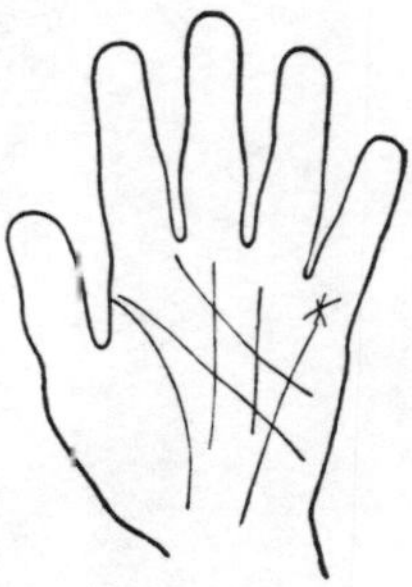

NO. 520

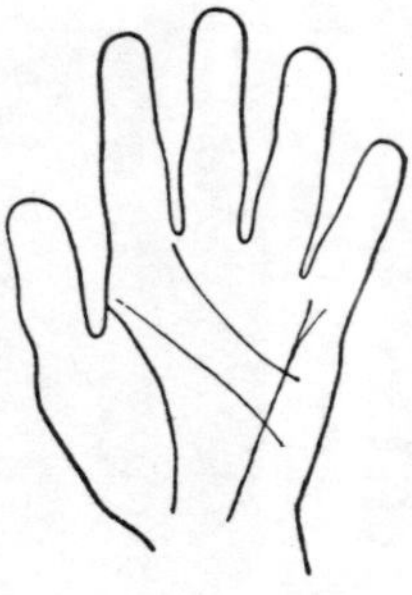

NO. 521

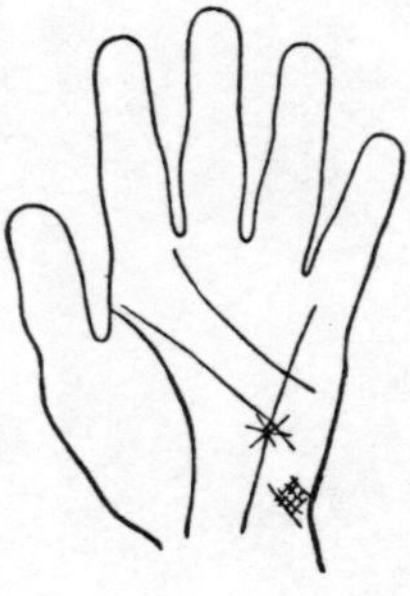

NO. 522

The value of the line is largely its use in *combination*, and especially is this true with the Life and Head lines. Health and brains are essential to successful lives, and the Mercury line, in connection with the Life and Head lines, will always enable one absolutely to estimate these elements. By keeping in mind for what the line stands, what each change in its character and each defect means, and by following the line from source to termination, noting every change and working out its meaning, the Mercury line will yield a fund of confirmatory evidence which will sustain the testimony given by other lines and signs, and enable you more completely to understand your client.

CHAPTER XIII

THE GIRDLE OF VENUS

THERE is a group of small lines, known as Minor lines, which do not appear in every hand, but which occur often enough in the same locations to take them out of the class called chance lines, and to form them into a division by themselves. As a rule these Minor lines are not of great importance, often having only a single interpretation, but they are reliable as far as they go. The first of the Minor lines is the Girdle of Venus, which rises between the fingers of Jupiter and Saturn and runs across the Mounts of Saturn and Apollo, ending between the fingers of Apollo and Mercury (523).

The Girdle of Venus does not always run exactly over this path, but sometimes rises on the Mount of Jupiter and runs over onto the Mount of Mercury, sometimes ending on the percussion. It is, in part, a sister line to the Heart line, and in some hands, when the Heart line is absent, takes the place of that line. Older palmists conceived the idea that when they saw this line in a hand which had also a strong Heart line, that being virtually a sister line to the Heart line, it indicated a double supply of heart qualities. This was not meant in a physical sense, but as regards the affections, and for this reason the line was named by them the Girdle of Venus, meaning the Girdle of Love. As this reading of the line was first made in the days when love meant license, the interpretation was attached to it that anyone with such an

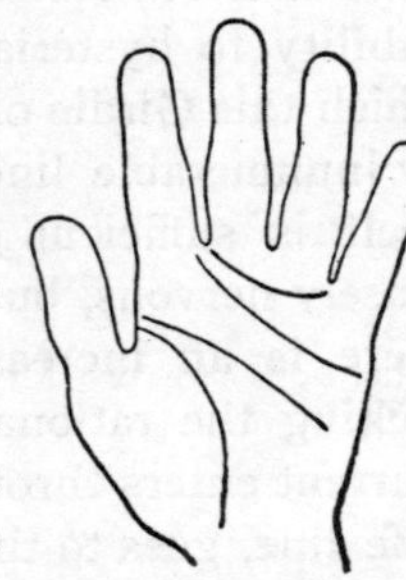

NO. 523

abundant supply of affections would seek occasion to lavish them, and the Girdle of Venus became the synonym of license, profligacy, debauchery, and was considered the mark of unchastity and abandonment. Through all the writings or Palmistry this interpretation has been largely adhered to, often with evident misgivings on the part of some writers, who have frankly stated that they were at a loss for an explanation of this line. Some few have doubted its accuracy, and many practitioners have abandoned its use entirely, because they could not reconcile its accepted interpretation to the lives of the subjects they encountered, and many embarrassing errors were occasioned by the use of the line. To arrive at a correct solution of this much vexed question, we have only to apply our general hypothesis, and to *adapt the line to the subject*, not the subject to the line. Also to remember that this is the twentieth century, instead of 400 B.C., when the original reading was given, and that conditions to-day are different from those prevailing at that time.

From an exhaustive study of the Girdle of Venus, I have found that it does not as a rule indicate debauchery and license, but that it nearly always *does* indicate an intense state of nervousness, and in a large majority of cases great liability to hysteria. In a large percentage of hands in which this Girdle of Venus is found, the palm will be crossed by innumerable lines running in every direction. This by itself is sufficient ground for pronouncing the subject intensely nervous, but with the addition of a Girdle of Venus there is an increased degree of nervous excitability. In seeking the rationale of the line remember that the vital Current enters through the finger of Jupiter, runs down the Life line, goes to the brain, and, returning, transfers itself to the lines of Saturn, Apollo, and Mercury, which are its natural channels of egress from the body. When this course is pursued without interruption, the action of the fluid is normal. But the Girdle of Venus being an abnormal line, by virtue of its location, deflects part of the Current from its usual course immediately upon its entrance into us, and the balance of the Current seeking egress from the body through the lines of Saturn, Apollo, and Mercury on its return from the brain flows *against* the *barrier formed by the Girdle of Venus*, and cannot easily flow *out* through the finger-ends, but, being obstructed by the Girdle, *overflows* into the palm of the hand. As the *entire* Current is seeking egress through the fingers of Saturn, Apollo, and Mercury, the *entire* Current is thus obstructed or deflected by the Girdle and overflows, cutting new channels for itself, in many directions, and thus producing the multiplicity of lines that we see. The large amount of vital Current thus turned loose to zigzag its way out of the hand as best it can acts upon every nerve, electrifies it, intensifies its action, and from this excitation of the nerves we have the production of a highly nervous person. Thus as a first result of a Girdle of Venus we often have intense nervous activity.

Having this much information to begin with, we have reached the point where we must apply the line to the subject. In the greater number of instances the Girdle of Venus is found in the hands of women, though in some types of subjects men's hands show it. If the subject be naturally a delicate, nervous, finely constituted person, the nervousness produced by the Girdle will be greater than if he be phlegmatic and heavy in construction. In the first case the nervous force will electrify his organization to a great degree. Such an one will suffer from any slight or inattention, will be easily depressed, and in the world of to-day, when even people with the best intentions have not time to humor the eccentricities of nervous humanity, he will soon come to think that he has no place in the world, and that no one cares for him. This brooding once begun, grows instead of decreases, until every act of even his best friends is distorted, every grief is magnified, pain is imagined where there is none, and we have a fully developed case of hysteria. On a hand with few lines and a phlegmatic temperament, the Girdle of Venus is never of so great importance as an indication of *hysteria* and *great nervousness* as in the highly strung subject, but it may turn to the other horn of the dilemma, and if the hand be coarse or sensual, have a swollen Mount of Venus, and be red and animal in its general make-up, there will likely be present the lasciviousness which has always been the accepted reading of the line. It is from the type and Chirognomic make-up of a subject that you must determine which interpretation should be given. In every case the Girdle will indicate *some* degree of nervousness and *some* degree of ardor, but to reach a correct estimate of the extent of either, your subject must first be correctly estimated, and then the line *applied* to *him*. If the Mount of Venus be flat and flabby, the Life line running close to the thumb, the color white, the third phalanges of the fingers waist-like, and the Heart line thin, a Girdle of Venus will not indicate lasciviousness, for the physical make-up and conditions of the subject preclude the possibility of such a thing. This subject will, however, undoubtedly be a prey to intense nervousness and dejection, and hysteria has a fertile soil in which to develop. On the other hand, if with a Girdle of Venus the Mount of Venus be large, swollen, and grilled, the third phalanges of the fingers thick, the first phalanges short, the Life line running wide into the palm, Heart line deep and red, the Mounts of Mars full, and the color of the hand red, with black or any approach to auburn or red hair on the hands, it should never be read as indicating nervousness and hysteria, but as the greatest lasciviousness possible, added to a taste for drink and general debauchery. A Girdle of Venus on such a hand must be given the full strength of its old traditional interpretation. All of the nervousness in such a subject will become nervous energy which will be expended in gratifying animal appetites. So impress it upon your mind at once that the form of interpretation which you give to the Girdle of Venus must depend entirely upon the kind of subject on which it is seen.

There is another danger from the Girdle of Venus, which comes to all types of hands which have it. This may only be a transitory danger, or it may result in the formation of a permanent habit if not checked early in life. At the age of puberty, when the youth passes from the child to the adult, subjects with the Girdle of Venus are liable to indulge in self-abuse. In the subject with animal hands this arises from the heat of his passionate nature, which finds its outlet in this way. But with such subjects the danger of a continuance of the habit is only slight, for they quickly have relations with the opposite sex, and do not continue self-abuse. In the very nervous hand puberty brings a sense of desire,

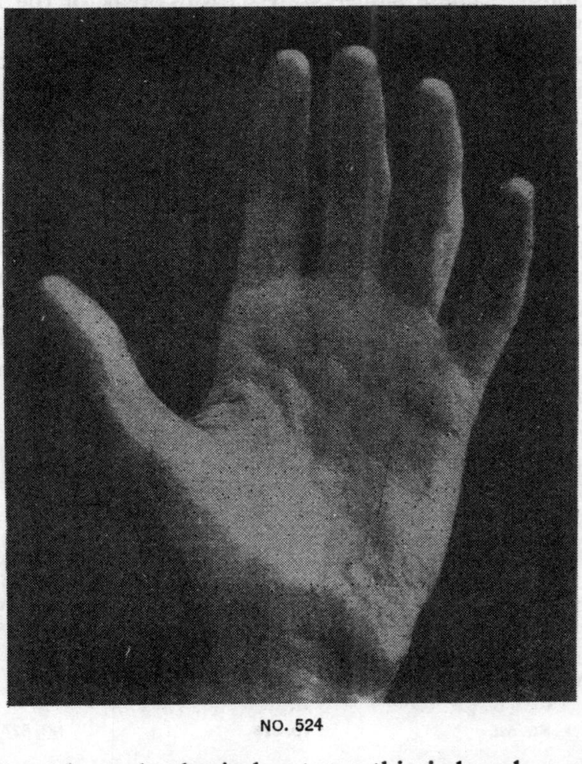

NO. 524

but in such weak physical natures this is largely a *mental* condition. There is no real heat or warmth of physical passion, but the mind becomes inflamed and has lascivious dreams. Such subjects are full of imagination but weak in physical heat. It gives them greater delight to think of intercourse than the actual experience would bring them. With such subjects, when the age of puberty gives them a knowledge of desire, they easily fall victims to the habit of self-abuse. If the lower third of the Mount of Moon be largely developed, with a thin, bony hand, flat Mount of Venus, Girdle of Venus, waisted third phalanges of the fingers, deficient Mounts of Mars, and thin Heart line (524), the subject will, because of his imaginings, commit the act of self-abuse. These subjects are hard to break of the habit, for their lack of real physical heat makes them prefer self-abuse to actual intercourse. They are shy, diffident, and retiring by nature, and neither court nor love the society of people in general, or of the opposite sex in particular. Many such subjects are found in the Saturnian type. When such a hand is seen, if you look into the upturned palm intently, then at the subject without saying a word, an oozy perspiration will soon begin to form in the palm. This will become more plentiful the longer you continue the experiment, and such subjects will not often deny the charge of self-abuse. If these indications are seen in the hands of children, good wholesome advice and plain talks from the parents will often prevent the formation of this vicious habit.

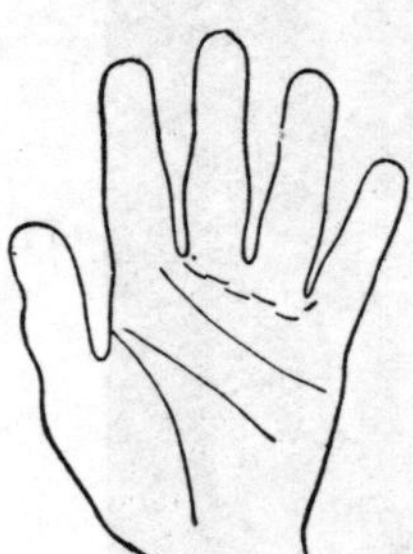
NO. 525

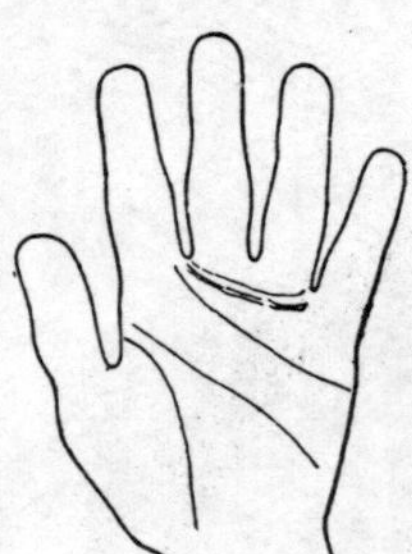
NO. 526

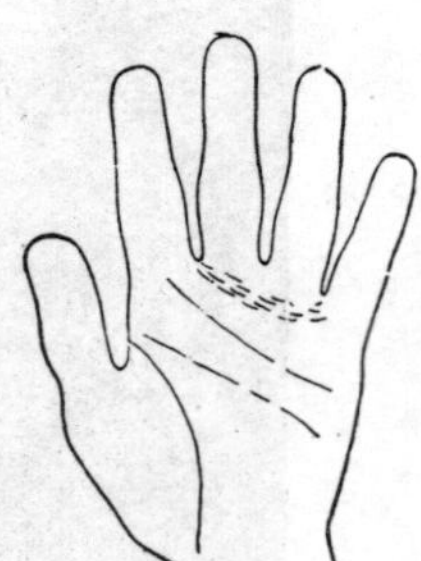
NO. 527

The Girdle of Venus is usually a single deep line. This is most often seen on the least nervous hands, and is for this reason not so frequently an indication of hysteria as of increase of animal appetites. Often the Girdle is composed of broken fragments (525). This will increase the nervousness, the danger of hysteria, and also the retiring disposition. If such subjects fall into bad practices, the habits are very hard to overcome. If the Girdle of Venus be composed of double or triple lines, which is often the case (526), it will make its indication, whether of health or temperament, doubly strong. If the Girdle be composed of a number of broken lines (527) and the rest of the hand be a nervous one, the danger from hysteria is great and all nervous symptoms will be intensified. If with such a marking there are indications of female

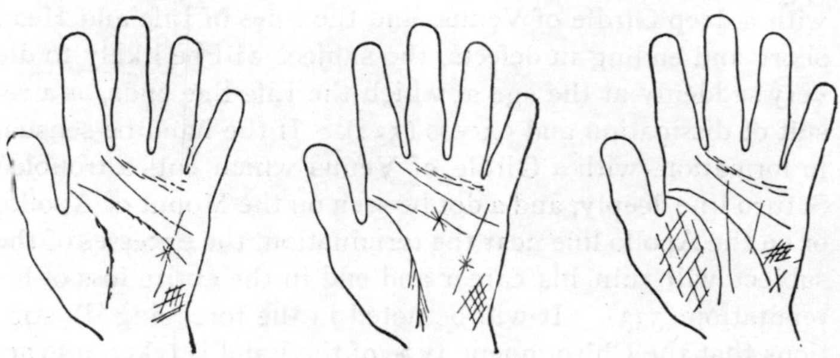

NO. 528 NO. 529 NO. 530

trouble (528) the subject will be a great sufferer, and nervous depression, ill-health, and constant discontent and unhappiness will surround her. These subjects should be taken to a specialist, who may relieve them, but often the real trouble is not known. With such a marking you will frequently find very defective Life and Head lines. If the Head line in this case should have islands, dots, crosses, or a star on it, there will be grave danger of insanity (529). The ultra-nervous condition shown by a bad Girdle of Venus will have its effect upon every phase of life. Defects in the Saturn or Apollo lines may be accounted for by a bad Girdle of Venus. They may come from either lasciviousness or ill-health; which one may be indicated by a Chirognomic examination and by the Main lines. With the Girdle of Venus, a factor which may be so potent in its operation, there will be many combinations in which it will play an important part. If the Head line slopes low into the Mount of Moon, and on it or near its termination a star, dot, cross, or island be seen, with a broken Girdle of Venus, and many lines in the hand (530), the subject is in grave danger of insanity, as a result of intense nervousness and excessive imagination. This subject will be erratic, cranky, and hard to get along with. If a cross be seen on the Mount of Saturn, a broken Girdle of Venus, dots or islands in the Head line *under* Saturn, a grille on the Mount of the Moon, with brittle or fluted nails, the subject will be in grave danger from paralysis (531). If the hand be thick at the base, fingers thick, color red, lines deep and red, with a deep Girdle of Venus, and the lines of Life and Head short and ending in defects, the subject will be likely to die very suddenly at the age at which the Life line ends, as a result of dissipation and excess (532). If the hand be sensual in formation, with a Girdle of Venus which cuts a troubled Saturn line deeply, and a dot be seen on the Mount of Apollo, or on the Apollo line near the termination, the excesses of the subject will ruin his career and end in the entire loss of his reputation (533). It will be noted in the foregoing illustrations that the Chirognomic type of the hand is taken into account, and that a *broken* Girdle of Venus indicates the *nervous* condition and a *deep* Girdle indicates its *excessive* side. If a

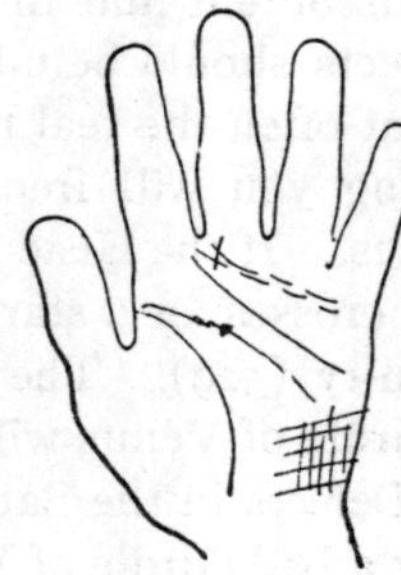

NO. 531

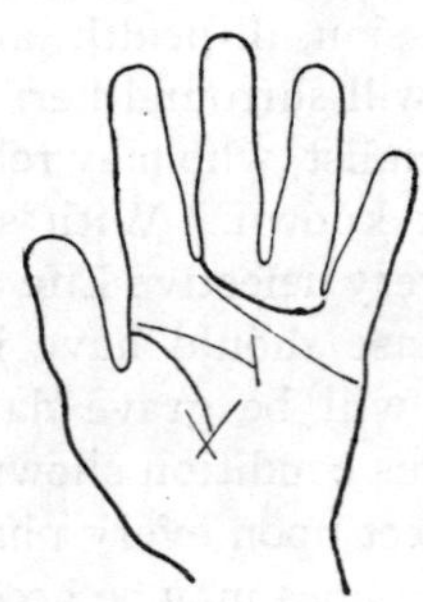

NO. 532

deep Girdle of Venus cuts a line of Affection, the Heart line has drooping lines from it, the Head line becomes defective toward the end and terminates in a star, and the Saturn line is cut by a bar which stops it, the excesses of the subject will ruin his married life and cause great sorrow, finally ending in an impairment of the mental faculties, insanity, and the ruining of his career (534). You will meet the Girdle of Venus in all kinds of hands. Some of the best men and women have had it, and their careers have never suffered. It has been argued that the added warmth imparted by the Girdle of Venus gives a greater richness to the character that can hold it within bounds. From this standpoint it would be considered as an absolute blessing. But its presence may produce unpleasant results and in many ways. The diffi-

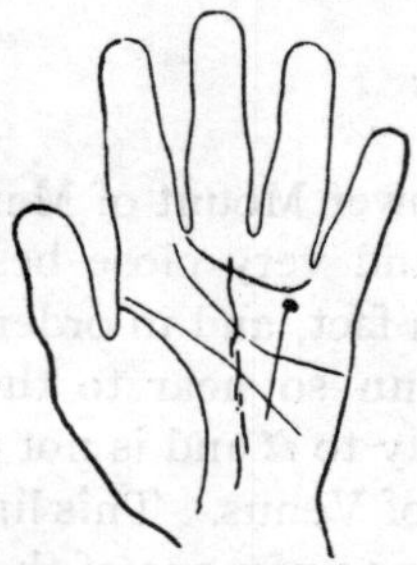

NO. 533

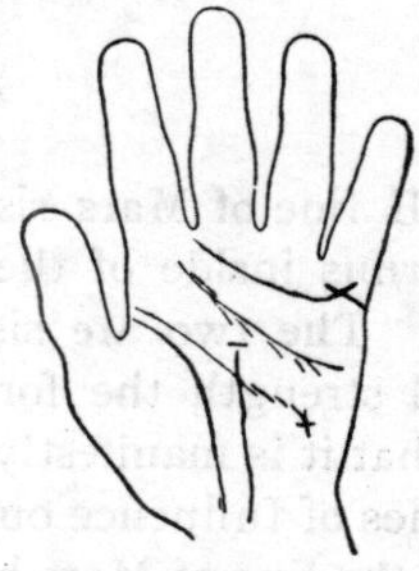

NO. 534

culty of telling which meaning to give the Girdle is made easy when you fit the line to the type of hand which has it, and do not try to fit lasciviousness to every person on whom the Girdle is seen. A poor, trembling, nervous, cold-handed subject with a Girdle of Venus should not be told that he indulges in great excesses, for to such an one an extra cup of coffee or tea would mean great dissipation, and yet it is on such subjects that you will find a large percentage of Girdles. Good judgment and a clean way of looking at things must be displayed in handling the Girdle of Venus, which, used with *discrimination*, will produce only good results for the practitioner. There are those who seek unpleasant sides to every character, and for such the Girdle has peculiar charms, but in the largest number of cases, pity and tenderness should be the feeling it inspires.

CHAPTER XIV

THE MINOR LINES

Line of Mars

THE line of Mars rises on the lower Mount of Mars and runs inside of the Life line and very close beside it (535). The two are sister lines, in fact, and in order to be in full strength the former must run so near to the Life line that it is manifestly related only to *it* and is not one of the lines of Influence on the Mount of Venus. This line was called the line of Mars because it rises upon one of the Martian Mounts, and its effect is to strengthen its sister line and to indicate a stronger constitution than is shown by even a deep Life line.

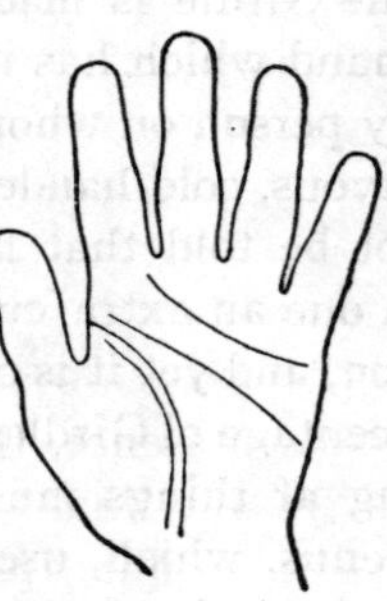

NO. 535

The line of Mars must always be used in connection with the Life line and with the type of the subject. If the Life line be thin, broad and shallow, or chained, and a line of Mars be present, the subject will be inherently delicate, but there will be an underlying vital strength which will prevent the delicacy from taking any serious form. If the Life line be deep, and a strong line of Mars be also present, the subject will have tremendous vitality, great endurance, and much aggression. These subjects are intense and their danger lies in overdoing. The great vital force which they possess is constantly impelling them to action, and they never do anything by halves. They have vitality to spare. and are constantly seeking a source of outlet. If Jupiterians, they are great feasters and drinkers, and if red color be present will indulge in carousals in which only those as strong as themselves can keep the pace. Martians with this marking are also great eaters and drinkers, and in addition are natural fighters. They can endure more physical strain than any other type, consequently they make good soldiers and campaigners. The danger to such a subject is that when he is not kept under the strain of physical exertion, he will

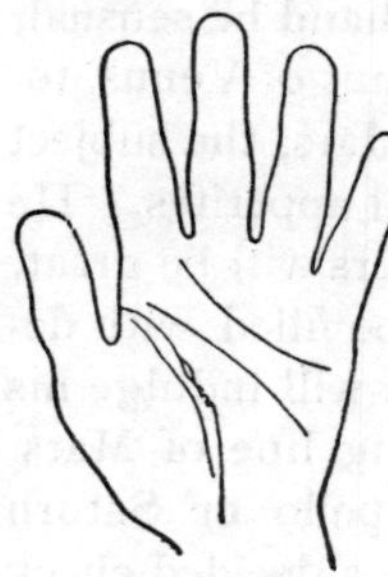

NO. 536

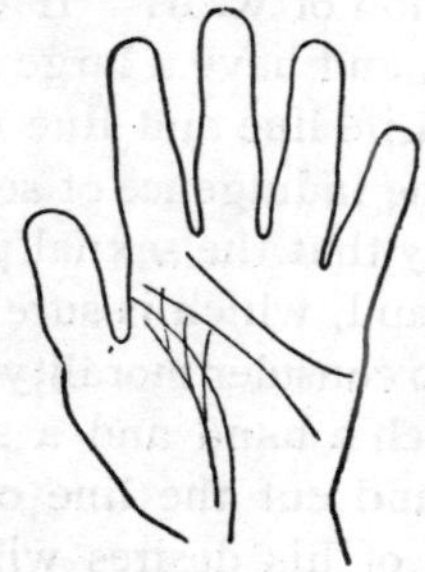

NO. 537

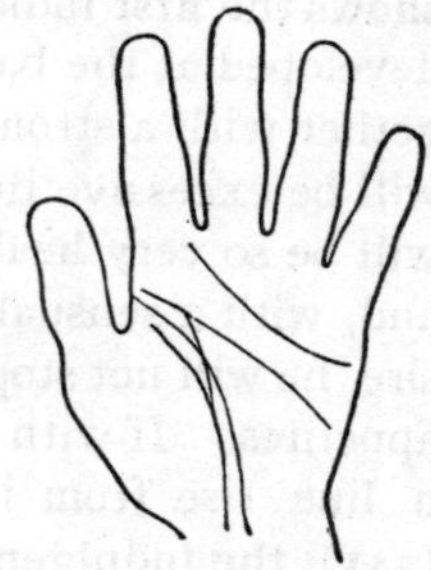

NO. 538

work off his surplus energy in rioting and drinking. Many confirmed drunkards have this marking, their trouble having originated in an excess of vital force, without hard work enough to use it up. Black or red hair on the hands adds to these indications. If the line of Mars extends the full length of the Life line, its strengthening power will be present during the entire life of the subject. If it runs but part of the way it will be exerted only during its presence, the age at which it disappears to be read from the Life line. If any defects be seen in the Life line, and a line of Mars runs past this point (536), the delicacy or danger shown by the defects will not prove fatal, owing to the underlying vitality indicated by the line of Mars. If lines rise from the Line of Mars and cross the Life line (537), they show a constant tendency of the subject to rise in life, owing to the strengthening of the constitution indicated by the line of Mars. If a line or lines rise from the line of Mars and merge into the Head line (538), the subject will have increased mental strength, owing to the overflow into mental channels of some of the vitality of the line of Mars. If a line rises from the line of Mars and *merges* into the Saturn line (539), the upward career of the subject will be more certain, owing to the strong vitality behind him. If rising lines from the line of Mars *cut* the Head line (540), the great vitality will be too strong for the brain, and it will be injured by constant straining. In this case the subject is so strong that he does not know when he has overtaxed his strength, and the brain shows the first indication of wear. If the hand be sensual, developed at the base, and have a large Mount of Venus, together with a strong Life line and line of Mars, the subject will be excessive in the indulgence of sexual appetites. He will be so very healthy that the sexual powers will be great, and, with a sensual hand, which is sure to be filled with desire, he will not stop to consider morality but will indulge his appetites. If with such a hand and a strong line of Mars, a line rise from it and cut the line of Apollo or Saturn (541), the indulgence of his desires will be a decided check to the career. If the Line of Apollo ends in a dot, cross, or bar, the reputation of the subject will be lost. If with such a hand a rising line from a strong line of Mars cuts the

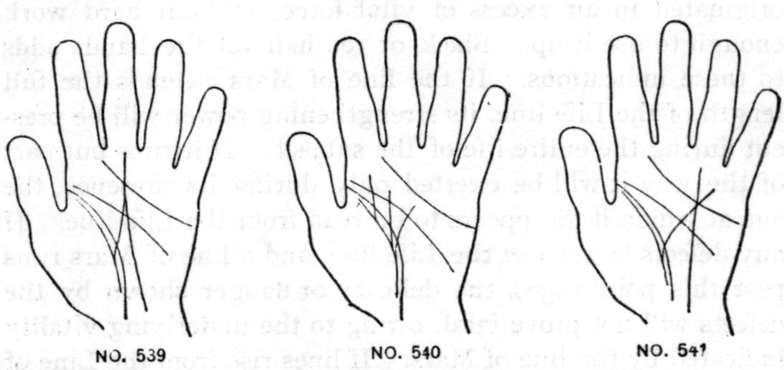

NO. 539 NO. 540 NO. 541

line of Affection, the unfaithfulness of the subject will ruin the happiness of the married life. This will be intensified if the line of Affection ends in a fork (542). If the line of Mars sweeps across the hand at its base and ends upon the Mount of the Moon (543), it will show so much vitality that the ordinary length of life is not sufficient to expend it. This is a frequent marking on the hands of drunkards, who have all of the restlessness of the Lunar subjects. They will be great travellers, and expend a good deal of energy in this way. The rest will be used in "wine, women, and song." If this line ends in a cross, dot, bar, or star, the subject will die very suddenly after a life of great excess. If the Life line ends in a cross or star, this reading will be intensified. If the Head line about midway becomes defective it will show

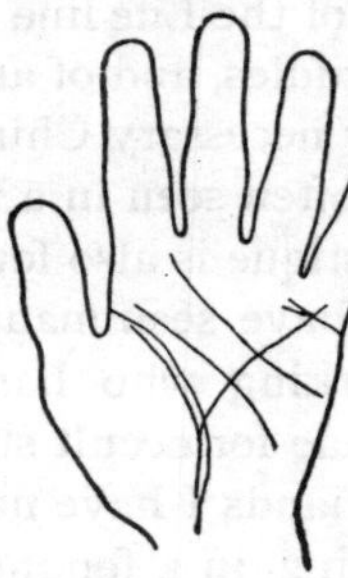

NO. 542

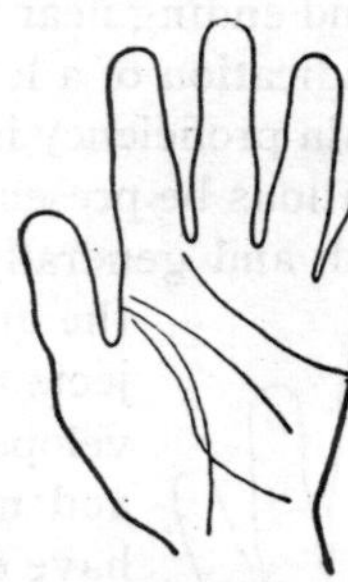

NO. 543

that the pace is too rapid and the brain is being exhausted. If the Head line ends in a star, the subject will at that age become insane. If the line of Mars be deeper than the Life line it shows that the underlying strength is more powerful than the natural constitution. With such a marking this secondary force will be a stronger factor than the Life line, and the line of Mars must be read most carefully by applying to it the same methods used with the Life line. If the line of Mars be thinner than the Life line, it shows that it is simply acting as a sister line, and its effort will be to strengthen the constitution and improve the condition of life for the subject. The line of Mars, of itself a good indication, may, by running to excess, prove disastrous. There will be no trouble, however, to accurately gauge its effect, if good judgment be used and the line be made to fit the type of subject having it. If the Life line runs an even course to the end of the life, and is supported by a line of Mars proportionate to it in strength, the subject will have a smooth career, unclouded by ill-health, with vital force enough to meet all the necessities of life; he will live well, peacefully, and long, and die beloved and respected. Gladstone had such a Martian line as this.

The Ring of Solomon

The line which has received the title of the Ring of Solomon is a small line rising between the fingers of Jupiter and Saturn, running downward and encircling the Mount of Jupiter, and ending near the beginning of the Life line (544). It is an indication of a love for occult studies, and of an ability to obtain proficiency in them if other necessary Chirognomic indications be present. It is most often seen in a much-lined hand, and generally a Croix Mistique is also found in the quadrangle. I have seen many subjects with this marking who have developed great aptitude for occult studies, and none in whose hands I have noted it have ever been lacking in a fondness for Psychology. The great raying and lining present in most of the hands in which I have seen it would of itself indicate great impressionability and numerous emotions, and such subjects are always interested in new things. The Ring of Solomon by itself, however, must not be taken as a sign manual of proficiency in the realm of occult thought. It is only an *indication* which should draw your attention in this direction. Before committing yourself to any extent on the occult powers of the subject, see if a good brain and other necessary adjuncts be present. See if energy, ability to study, and perseverance are indicated. Dreamy idlers who rely upon inspiration or revelations from on high, and not upon good reasoning, compose only the cranks in the field of occult studies. Even a good Ring of Solomon will not rescue such from the multitude of those who have done nothing but talk. People who have accomplished much in the psychic world have square or spatulate tips with knotty joints, and their success has been largely due to hard study and the application of good reasoning.

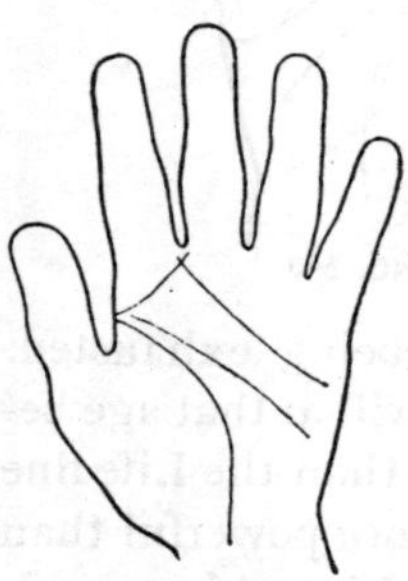

NO. 544

The presence of a Ring of Solomon will help all of these students. The kind of subject on which it is seen must, however, be the guide in reading this line.

The Ring of Saturn

The Ring of Saturn is a line which rises between the fingers of Jupiter and Saturn, encircles the finger of Saturn, and terminates between the finger of Saturn and Apollo, thus crossing the Mount of Saturn completely (545). Sometimes it makes a perfect circle, and often it is composed of a couple of lines which cross on the Mount of Saturn. In many cases the circle is not entirely completed, but the ends will show that they form part of an imperfect Ring of Saturn (546). The presence of this line shows a disposition to jump from one occupation to another, and not to stick to any one long enough to make it successful. There is a lack of continuity of purpose in a subject having this marking, and poor success in his undertakings is the usual result. While this line, *per se*, does not make failure in life a necessity, it

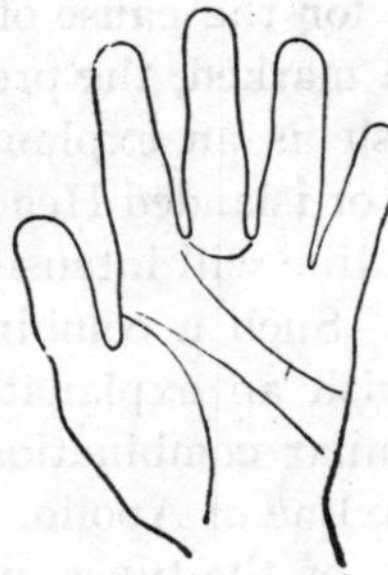

NO. 545

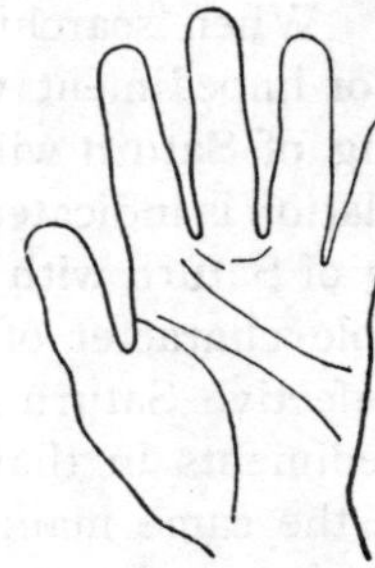

NO. 546

is to be seen on a great many hands where the lives have been unsuccessful. I have observed it on the hands of prisoners in penitentiaries, some of them the most desperate of their class. I have seen it also on the hands of a number of suicides. As the Ring of Saturn cuts completely across the Mount of Saturn, it forms a barrier to the Current at that point. This makes the Mount of Saturn defective, shuts out its wisdom, seriousness, and balancing qualities, and turns them into defects. These subjects will either develop into bad Saturnians, often reaching the stage where they stop at no crime, or else, as the balance-wheel is gone, they shift from one thing to another, with no continuity in any direction, until their lives are total failures. If in such cases the upper Mount of Mars be d ficient, thumb small, and Mercury line defective, especially if showing islands or a star, the subject will give way to discouragement, and become either insane or commit suicide. Soft or flabby hands, vacillating Head line, weak thumbs, poor Mounts of Mars, or a large Mount of Moon are all poor companions for the Ring of Saturn. If with a Ring of Saturn the Head line slopes low on to a Mount of Moon which is large or grilled, or both, the subject will be imaginative in the extreme, flighty, restless, changeable, and will make nothing of himself. Often defects and obstructions in the line of Saturn, with the Ring of Saturn present, will show that the career of the subject has been ruined because of his lack of continuity of purpose. The Apollo line will frequently be similarly affected. When searching the hand for the cause of some disaster or impediment which we see marked, the presence of a Ring of Saturn will often furnish us an explanation. As vacillation is indicated by a broken or islanded Head line, the Ring of Saturn with such a Head line will intensify the changeable character of the subject. Such a combination with a defective Saturn-line will furnish an explanation of the impediments in that line. A similar combination will affect in the same manner a defective line of Apollo. The Lunarian, being the most changeable of the types, will be made much more so by a Ring of Saturn. It is hardly possible fcr such a subject to obtain enduring success. If the Ring of Saturn does not completely circle the Mount but is broken, it is not as unfavorable a marking as if it completed its course. In this case some outlet will be left for the Current, and the Mount of Saturn will not be made so defective. Even with this imperfect ring, however, there is a degree of its defect present, the subject having at least a tendency in that direction, and in a final estimate this fact must not be lost sight of. When the Ring of Saturn is composed of two lines which cross each other on the Mount of Saturn (547), it must be read in the same manner as a large cross on that Mount. This marking I have seen on several suicides.

Whenever the Ring of Saturn is seen in a hand, it should warn you of a grave danger to the subject. Knowing its meaning, be ready to search for all indications that may help him to overcome the vacillation which may ruin him. Apply Chirognomy, study his type and everything the lines can tell bearing on the subject of changeability of temperament. A strong will phalanx on the thumb with a good Head line are the best companions for a Ring of Saturn. With all the facts in your possession, you should be able to tell just how much influence the Ring of Saturn will exert upon any subject.

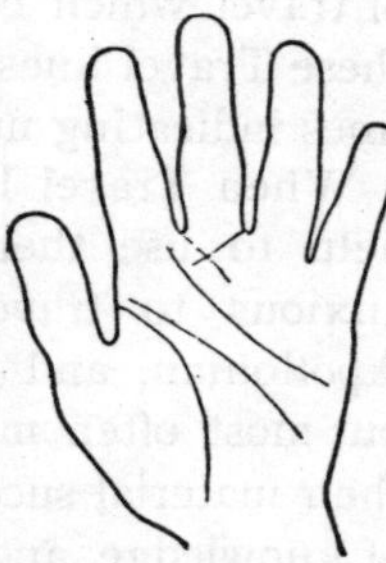

NO. 547

The Rascettes, and Lines of Travel

The Rascettes, or Bracelets, are the lines which cross the wrist at the base of the hand (548). Sometimes there are three, and there may be only one. In practice I have found them of little use, especially any save the first one. There are traditional indications, handed down from the older palmists, ascribing the addition of thirty years to the life of a subject for each Bracelet seen. I have failed to find any confirmations of such indications, and never use them as bearing upon longevity. There are other traditions concerning signs found on the Bracelets which experience has proven fallacious, and which I will not enumerate. The first Bracelet, if deep, adds an additional confirmation to other indications of a strong constitution. With a deep Life line, a deeply cut Rascette will prove an added strength. If the Rascette be poorly marked, chained, or broad and shallow, the constitution of the subject is not so strong. If short branches rise from the Rascettes, it indicates a rising tendency in the life of the subject, ambitious efforts, and a desire to im prove. Long branches which rise high into the Mount of the Moon have been called "Travel lines," and read to indicate journeys. These lines increase the restlessness and desire to travel which belongs to a Lunarian subject, and there is no doubt that such a subject will improve every opportunity of travel which comes to him. From such a point of view these Travel lines can often be quite successfully used, long lines indicating more restlessness and longer journeys.

When Travel lines are seen, the type of the subject will help to use them correctly. The Lunarian is the most anxious to travel, the Mercurian next. The Martian, Apollonian, and Jupiterian all like travel to some extent, but most often make journeys with the idea of improving their material success. The Saturnian will travel in search of knowledge, and the Venusian purely for pleasure. Spatulate tips with Travel lines are the strongest possible confirmatory companions. If the hand be very soft, however, the travels will often be mental ones. I have seen a branch from the Life line to a Travel line (549) indicate the

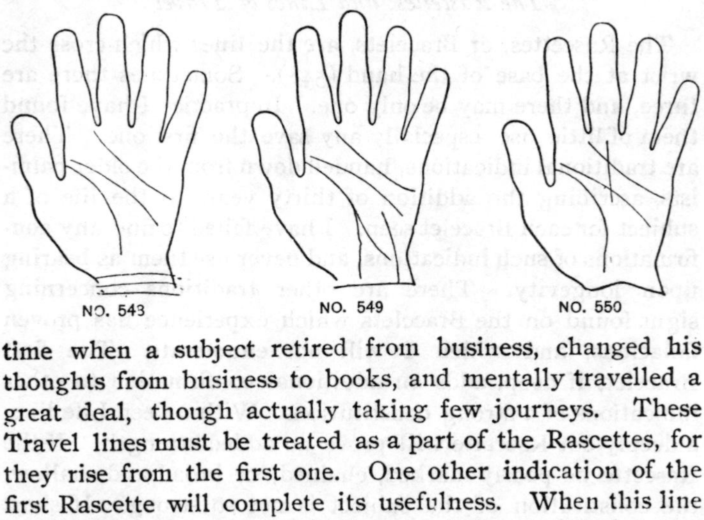

NO. 543 NO. 549 NO. 550

time when a subject retired from business, changed his thoughts from business to books, and mentally travelled a great deal, though actually taking few journeys. These Travel lines must be treated as a part of the Rascettes, for they rise from the first one. One other indication of the first Rascette will complete its usefulness. When this line rises in the centre (550) it indicates a delicacy of the internal organs contained in the abdomen ; in women most often the procreative organs, and constitutes a danger to them in maternity. If evidence of female weakness appears on the lower Mount of Moon, or in the Mercury line, the bulging Bracelet will add a strong confirmatory indication. These are valuable as premarriage indications, denoting the probability of a fruitful marriage. While these markings do not show absolute sterility they show a defective condition of the parts which will produce the same results.

The Line of Intuition

The line of Intuition lies at the side of the hand near the percussion. It rises on the Mount of Moon, and after describing a curve toward the Plain of Mars, ends on or near the Mount of Mercury (551). It occupies the same position as the line of Mercury, but is distinguished from it by its curved formation, though I consider it practically a Mercury line. The presence of this line, if well marked, adds greatly to the intuitive faculty of a subject, though this may be only another name for Mercurian shrewdness. These subjects seem to receive impressions for which they cannot account, and to form opinions which are accurate, and yet if asked the reason for these opinions they are unable to give any. There seems to be an added faculty of sensitiveness, of keenness in estimating people, and of adroit shrewdness in arriving at correct opinions concerning many of their fellows. Some subjects having this marking are not conscious of these faculties, and upon being asked to give a reason for some statement will tell you that they "feel it in their bones." This faculty of receiving correct impressions from those you meet can be cultivated. If a subject be unconscious of such powers and does not use them, he goes along *feeling* many things concerning other people, but dismisses the impressions

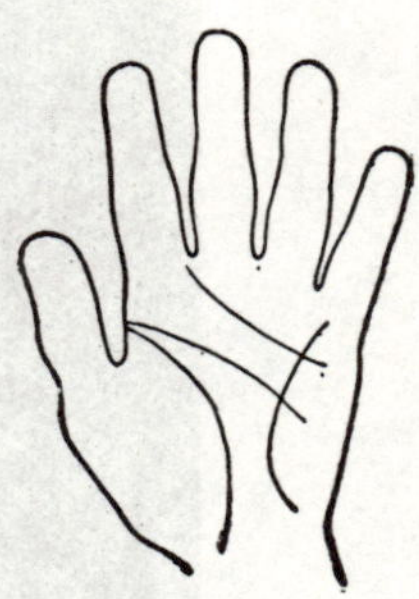

NO. 551

from his mind as vain fancies. By allowing the impressions to take some definite form, for instance, by thinking of each person, "he impresses me favorably, or unfavorably," as the case may be, gradually the impressions will increase. At first a subject may impress him unfavorably; the next impression may be that the subject is not honest or truthful, or that he is playing some part and not showing his real character. As he begins to put the impressions into words and give them

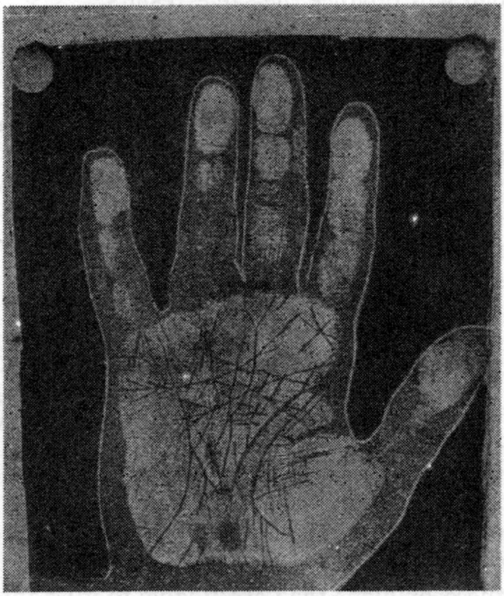

NO. 552

form, they increase, and the ability to receive and classify them increases. I have noted this mark in the hands of celebrated spirit mediums (552), who tell me that their inspirations seem to "come to them"; that impressions about their visitors form in their minds, they often have mental pictures, and, as they come to rely upon these intuitions, they find them increasing in number and accuracy. Whatever intuition is, it operates to give a mental impression from one person to another. and those who have the line of Intuition in their hands seem to be endowed in the highest degree with the faculty of receiving these impressions.

If with a line of Intuition the hand be square, hard, and few lines be seen, the subject will dismiss his intuitions as foolishness. If the fingers be long, tips pointed, Mount of Moon full, Head line sloping, tip of thumb pointed, and a line of Intuition be seen, the subject will be a "Psychic." He will have visions, dreams, strong impressions of impending danger, and will see signs and believe in omens. He is dreamy, nervous, highly strung, and wears out easily. From this class genuine "Psychics" are recruited. They have been supposed to be those who can obtain the greatest proficiency in occult studies. They do not, however, for they do not want to study or work, but wish to rely entirely upon their impressions and visions, and, except in rare cases, never accomplish as much in any line as do those who use industrious effort thoughtfully expended. A deep line of Intuition will indicate the greatest amount of intuition, and broken or defective lines will show only a limited amount.

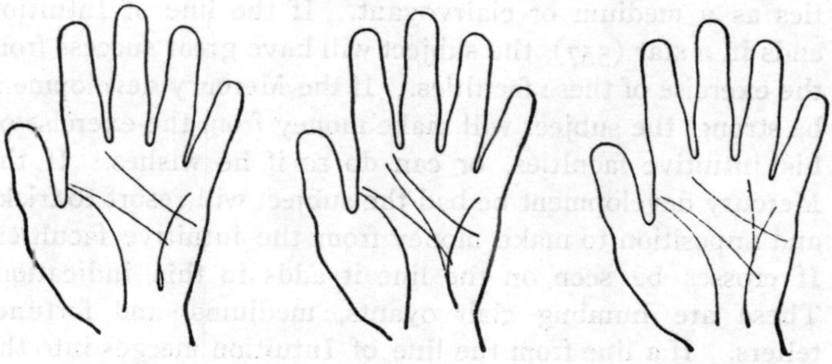

NO. 553 NO. 554 NO. 555

Islands in the line will show that the faculty will bring poor success, and islands in the beginning of a line of Intuition indicate a tendency toward somnambulism (553). If the line of Head sinks low on the Mount of Moon and the line of Intuition cuts it, the mental forces will be injured by allowing too much imagination and intuition to have play. If a branch rises from a line of Intuition and runs to the Mount of Jupiter, the subject will be ambitious to accomplish something with his intuitive faculties ; these are successful occultists (554). If a line rises from the line of Intuition to the Mount of Apollo (555), the subject will achieve renown through the exercise of his intuitive faculties. If a line from the line of Intuition cuts the Saturn line (556), the exercise of the intuitive faculties will impair the career of the subject.

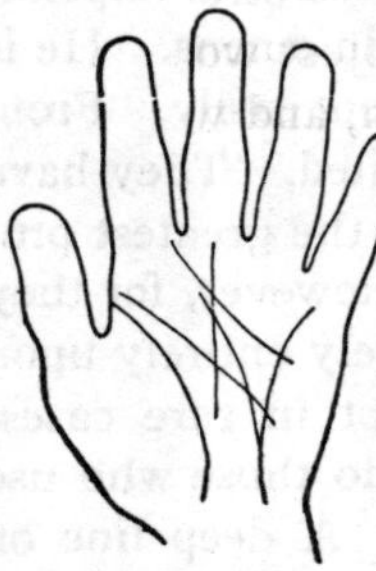
NC. 556

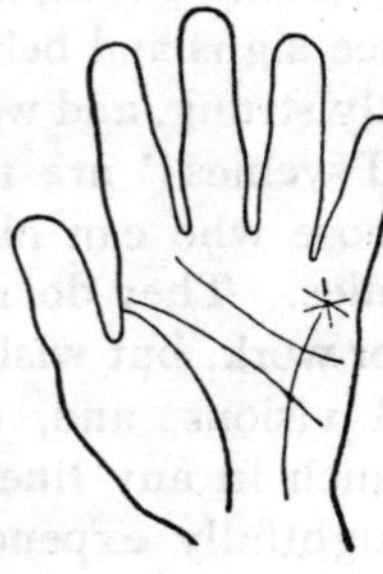
NO. 557

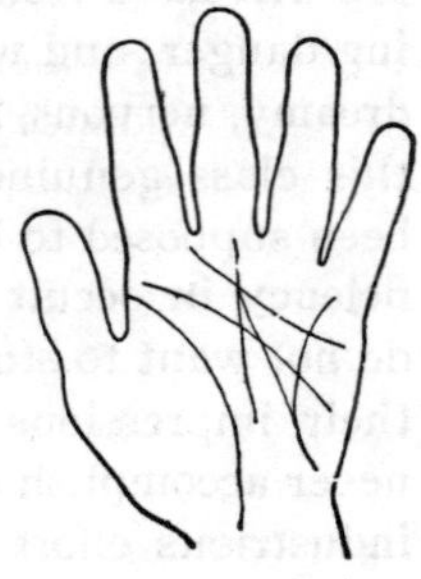
NO. 558

In all of these cases the subject will probably use these faculties as a medium or clairvoyant. If the line of Intuition ends in a star (557), the subject will have great success from the exercise of these faculties. If the Mercury development be strong, the subject will make money from the exercise of his intuitive faculties, or can do so if he wishes. If the Mercury development be bad the subject will resort to tricks and imposition to make money from the intuitive faculties. If crosses be seen on the line it adds to this indication. These are humbug clairvoyants, mediums, and fortune-tellers. If a line from the line of Intuition merges into the Saturn line (558), the exercise of the intuitive faculties will assist the career of the subject. With good common-sense to back it, this line is a help to any hand. If the subject be so constituted that he is likely to become unbalanced from believing he is a medium or clairvoyant, a line of Intuition is a poor possession. With a careful estimate of the Chirognomic indications you can apply the line and tell what its effect will be on any subject, and this is the proper use to make of it.

The Via Lascivia

The line which has received the name of Via Lascivia is seldom seen, but should run so as to form itself into a sister line to the line of Mercury (559). It is generally supposed to occupy a slanting position rising from the inside of the base of the Mount of Moon and terminating on the lower part of the upper Mount of Moon near the percussion. The cause for its name was the fact that with a strong line of Mercury and a sister line beside it, the subject would have a superabundance of vitality and good health, and would work off a good part of it in lascivious practices. This might be the case if the type of the subject's hands were sensual, but if they were not, he could just as easily, and would be much more likely to expend his surplus energy in the sphere of activity in which the type of his hands placed him. Because it occupies a slanting position, and does not rise to the top of the hand was another reason why the line was taken as indicating an operation in the lower world located at the base of the hand. If a Via Lascivia be deep and clearly marked,

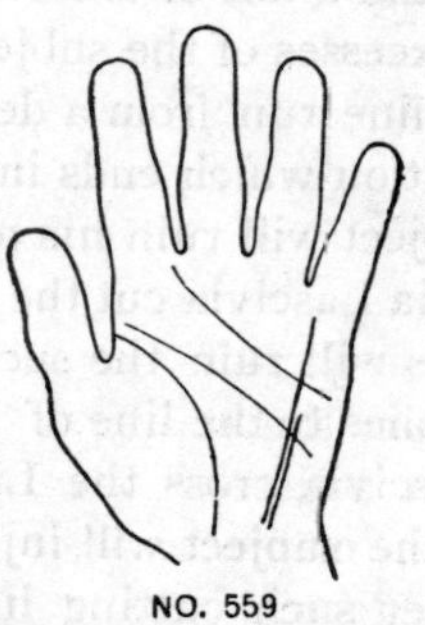

NO. 559

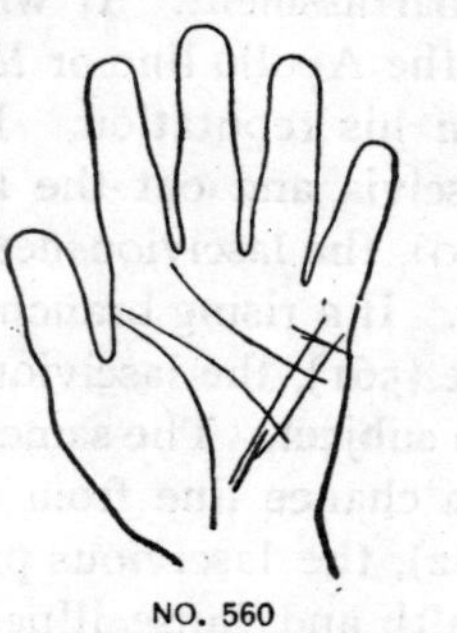

NO. 560

it will undoubtedly have a strong tendency to lower the subject in some directions. He will be more apt to think evil, even if he does not practise it, and temptation will more surely cause him to fall than if the marking were not in his hand. With a soft, pleasure-loving hand, full Mount of Venus, and a well-marked Via Lascivia, the subject will devote himself to pleasure, and will pursue it regardless of the cost in dollars and cents or in consequences.

If the Via Lascivia be seen, estimate carefully and at once the appetites of the subject, and the likelihood that he will be led where pleasure calls, and if any indication be seen that he is a voluptuary, the line will be a menace to his career. If with such a line the Head line becomes defective, the excesses are affecting the brain. If with such a hand the Saturn line have islands, pleasure seeking will cause financial

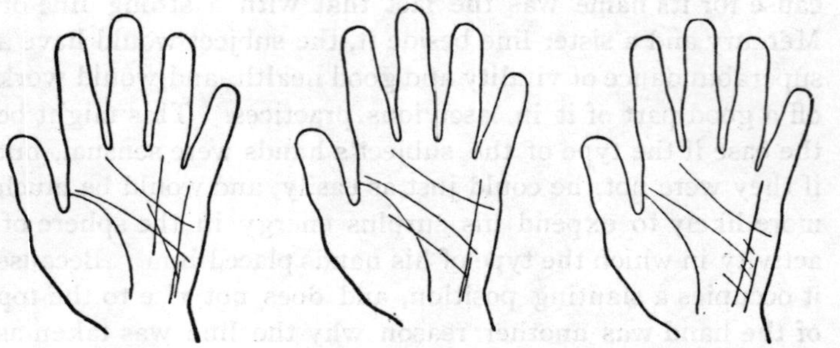

NO. 561 NO. 562 NO. 563

embarrassment. If with such a hand a dot or cross be seen on the Apollo line or Mount, the excesses of the subject will ruin his reputation. If a chance line run from a deep Via Lascivia and cut the line of Affection which ends in a fork (560), the lasciviousness of the subject will ruin his married life. If a rising branch from the Via Lascivia cut the Apollo line (561), the lascivious tendencies will ruin the success of the subject. The same reading applies to the line of Saturn. If a chance line from the Via Lascivia cross the Life line (562), the lascivious practices of the subject will injure his health and cause illnesses. If after such cutting lines the Life line becomes defective or in any way impaired, the excesses will permanently injure the subject's health. If bars from the Via Lascivia cut the Mercury line (563), the excesses will injure the health and prospects of the subject. If a chance line from the Via Lascivia run to a dot in the Life line (564), the excesses will cause a severe illness at the age which the dot indicates. If numerous lines from the Via Lascivia run across the Head line (565), the excesses will weaken and impair the brain, the subject will have many headaches, and if a dot, deep bar, break, or cross occurs in the Head line after these cutting lines, the subject will have an attack of brain fever. If with such a combination a star be seen in the Head line he may become insane as the result of excesses. If a well-marked Via Lascivia be seen, with a strong line of Mars, all the lines deep and red, big Mount of Venus, thick third phalanges and short first phalanges, the subject will debauch himself continually, and if a thick or a clubbed thumb be added, will commit rape, brutal murder, arson, or any crime to accomplish his desires or to hide their commission. If the hand be not so animal, but the line of Mars sweeps across to the Mount of the Moon, and the Via Lascivia is present (566), the subject will drink heavily and commit intolerable excesses. If the Via Lascivia is present as a sister line to the Mercury line, it will repair that line wherever defective. A wavy line of Mercury with a Via Lascivia will not indicate the bad results from biliousness that would occur without it. A broken line of Mercury with a Via Lascivia will not indicate such serious stomach

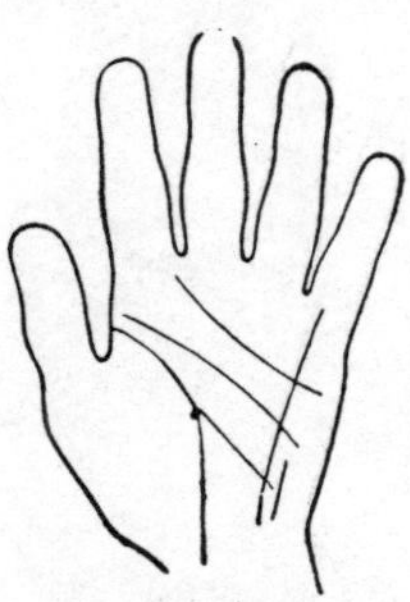

NO. 564

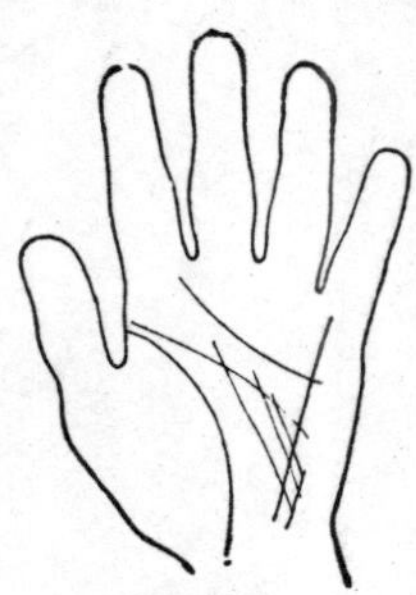

NO. 565

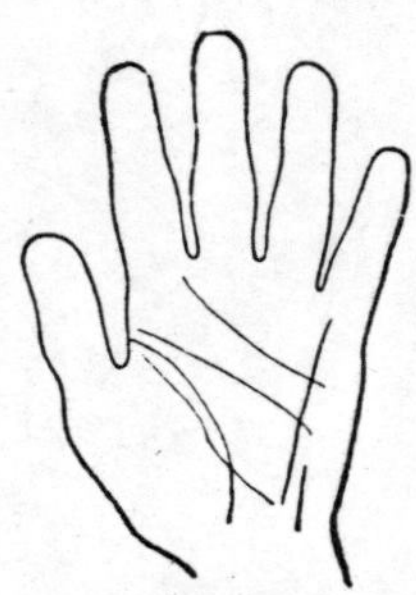

NO. 566

trouble. If the Via Lascivia only runs part of the way alongside the Mercury line its strength will be exerted during the time it continues. Whatever period the Via Lascivia covers on the Mercury line will be correspondingly stronger as a result of the companionship. If a Mercury line runs to the Mount of Mercury, the subject will have good health and success. If the Via Lascivia runs beside this line this reading will be doubly certain. The Via Lascivia, it will thus appear, has a good side as well as a bad one. To determine which to attribute to a client, estimate him thoroughly Chirognomically. A strong Via Lascivia in a low, animal hand will be read as a menace, and danger of excess. The same line in a fine, high-minded type of hand should be read to indicate fine results. Thus Chirognomy and good judgment must again form the foundation upon which the reading of the line will rest, and with these guides you need never fail in accuracy.

APPENDIX

FOR the benefit of the antiquarian I here reproduce the chapter on Palmistry written by Aristotle about 350 B.C., which, translated into English, was embodied in a copy of *Aristotle's Masterpiece*, published in 1738 in London. This being the oldest treatise on the subject known, and having been written by so celebrated a philosopher as the tutor of Alexander the Great, it will, I am sure, prove interesting to my readers. There has been progress made in the study since the days of Aristotle, which the philosopher would doubtless enjoy were he alive to-day.

OF PALMISTRY, SHOWING THE VARIOUS JUDGMENTS DRAWN FROM THE HAND

Being engaged in this third Part to shew what Judgments may be drawn according to Physiognomy, from the several Parts of the Body, and coming in Order to speak of the Hands, it has put me under a Necessity of saying something about Palmestry, which is a Judgment made of the Conditions, Inclinations, and Fortunes of Men and Women, from their various Lines and Characters which Nature has imprinted in the Hands, which are almost as various as the Hands that have 'em. And to render what I shall say the more plain, I will in the first place present the scheme or Figure of a Hand, and explain the various Lines therein.

By this Figure the Reader may well see that one of the Lines, and which indeed is reckoned the Principal, is called the Line of Life ; this Line encloses the Thumb, separating it from the Hallow of the Hand. The next to it, which is called the Natural Line, takes its beginning from the Turning of the Fore-finger, near the Line of Life, and reaches the

Table-Line, and generally makes a Triangle thus; △ The Table-Line, commonly called the Line of Fortune, begins under the little Finger and Ends near the middle Finger. The Girdle of *Venus*, which is another Line so called, begins near the Joint of the little Finger, and Ends between the Fore-Finger and the middle Finger. The Line of Death is that which plainly appears in a Counter Line to that of Life ; and is by some called the Sister-Line ending usually as the other Ends : for when the Line of Life is ended, Death comes, and it can go no further. There are also Lines in the fleshy Parts, as in the Ball of the Thumb, which is called the Mount of *Venus;* under each of the Fingers are also Mounts, which are each one govern'd by a several Planet ; and the Hallow of the Hand is called the *Plane of Mars;* Thus,

The Thumb we to Dame *Venus* Rules commit;
Jove the fore Finger rules as he thinks fit;
Old *Saturn* does the middle Finger guide,
And o'er the Ring Finger *Sol* does still preside;
The outside Brawn pale *Cynthia* does direct,
And into the Hallow *Mars* does most inspect:
The little Finger does to *Merc'ry* fall,
Which is the nimblest Planet of 'em all.

I now proceed to give Judgment from these several Lines : And in the first place take notice that in *Palmestry* the left Hand is chiefly to be regarded ; because therein the Lines are most visible, and have the strictest Communication with the Heart and Brains. Now having premised this, in the next place observe the Line of Life, and if it be fair, extended to its full length, and not broken with an intermixture of Cross Lines, it shews long Life and Health ; and it is the same if a double Line of Life appears, as there sometimes does. When the Stars appear in this Line it is a Significator of great Losses and Calamities : If on it there be the Figure of two O's or a Y, it threatens the Person with Blindness : If it wraps itself about the Table-line, then does it promise Wealth and Honor to be attained by Prudence and Industry. If the Line be cut or jagged at the upper-End, it denotes much Sickness. If this Line be cut by any Lines coming from the Mount of *Venus*, it declares the Person to be unfortunate in Love and Business also, and threatens him with sudden Death : a Cross between the Line of Life and the Table Line, shews the Person to be very liberal and charitable and of a noble Spirit. Let us now see the Significations of the Table-line.

The *Table-line*, when broad, and of a lovely Colour shews a healthful *Constitution*, and a quiet and contented Mind, and of a couragious Spirit ; but if it have Crosses towards the little Finger, it threatens the Party with much Affliction by Sickness. If the Line be double, or divided into three Parts in any of the Extremities, it shews the Person to be of a generous Temper, and of a good Fortune to support it : but if this Line be forked at the End, it threatens the Person shall suffer by Jealousies, and Doubts, and with the Loss of Riches got by Deceit. If three Points such as these . . . are found in it, they denote the Person prudent and liberal, a lover of Learnin, and of a good Temper. If it spreads itself towards the fore and middle Finger, and Ends blunt, it denotes Preferment. Let us now see what is signify'd by

The *Middle-line*. This Line has in it oftentimes (for there is scarce one Hand in which it varies not) divers very significant Characters ; many small Lines, between this and the Table-line, threaten the Party with Sickness, but also give him hopes of Recovery. A half cross branching into this Line, declares the Person shall have Honour, Riches, and good Success in all his Undertakings. A half Moon denotes cold and watery Distempers ; but a Sun or Star upon this Line, promises Prosperity and Riches ; This Line double in a Woman, shews she will have several husbands, but without any Children by them.

The *Line* of *Venus*, if it happens to be cut or divided near the Fore-finger, threatens Ruin to the party, and that it shall befal him by means of lacivious Women, and bad Company : Two crosses upon this Line, one being on the Fore-finger, and the other bending towards the little Finger, shews the Party to be weak, and inclin'd to Modesty and

Virtue ; indeed it generally denotes Modesty in Women, and therefore those who desire such Wives, usually choose them by this Standard.

The *Liver-line*, if it be strait, and cross'd by other Lines, shews the Person to be of a sound Judgment, and a piercing Understanding : But if it be winding, crooked, and bending outward, it shews Deceit and Flattery, and that the Person is not to be trusted. If it makes a Triangle △, or Quadrangle ▭, it shews the Person to be of noble Descent, and ambitious of Honour and Promotion. If it happens that this Line and the middle Line begin near each other, it denotes the Person to be weak in his Judgment, if a man ; but if a Woman danger by hard Labour.

The *Plane of Mars* being in the hallow of the Hand, most of the Lines pass through it, which render it very significant. This *Plane* being hallow, and the Lines being crooked and distorted, threaten the Party to fall by his Enemies. When the Lines beginning at the Wrist, are long within the Plane, reaching the Brawn of the Hand, they shew the Person to be one giving to Quarrelling, often in Broils, and of a hot and fiery Spirit, by which he shall suffer much Damage. If deep large Crosses be in the middle of the *Plane*, it shews the Party shall obtain Honour by Martial Exploits ; but if it be a Woman, that she shall have several Husbands, and easy Labour with her Children.

The *Line of Death* is fatal, when any Crosses or broken Lines appear in it; for they threaten the Person with Sickness and a short Life. A clouded Moon appearing therein, threatens a Child-bed Woman with Death. A bloody Spot in the Line, denotes a violent Death. A Star like a Comet threatens Ruin by War, and Death by Pestilence. But if a bright Sun appears therein, it promises long Life and Prosperity.

As for the *Lines of the Wrist*, being fair, they denote good Fortune ; but if crost and broken, the contrary.

Thus much with respect to the several Lines in the Hand. Now as to the Judgment to be made from the Hand itself ; if the Hand be soft and long, and lean withal, it denotes the Person of a good Understanding, a Lover of Peace and Honesty, discreet, serviceable, a good Neighbour, a Lover of Learning. He whose Hands are very thick, and very short, is thereby signified to be faithful, strong and laborious, and one that cannot long retain his Anger. He whose Hands are full of Hairs, and those Hairs thick, and great ones, if his Fingers withal be crooked, is thereby denoted to be luxourious, vain, false, of a dull Understanding and Disposition, and more foolish than wise. He whose Hands and Fingers do bend upwards, is commonly a Man liberal, serviceable, a Keeper of Secrets, and apt to his Power (for he is seldom fortunate) to do any Man a Courtesie. He whose Hands are stiff, and will not bend at the upper Joynts near to his Finger is always a wretched, miserable Person, covetous, obstinate, incredulous, and one that will believe nothing that contradicts his own private Interest.

And thus much shall suffice to be said of Judgments in Physiognomy concerning the Hands.

Thus he that Nature rightly understands,
May from each Line imprinted in his Hands,
His future Fate and Fortune come to know,
And what Path it is his Feet shall go:
His secret Inclinations he may see,
And to what Vice he shall addicted be:
To th' End that when he looks into his Hand,
He may upon his Guard the better stand;
And turn his wandering Steps another way,
Whene'er he finds he does from Virtue stray.

APPENDIX II

VOCATIONAL HAND ANALYSIS is not to be confused with fortune telling. The shape and formation of the hands are more important than the lines. If one has a good type and test combination in the hands he can, through the proper mental attitude, change the lines in his hands. IT IS POSSIBLE TO CHANGE ANYTHING IN THE HANDS INCLUDING THEIR SHAPE. It is much easier to change the lines and the tests than it is to change the types and the thumb. Changes are brought about over periods of time through environment, influences in the life, intellectual and spiritual development and most important of all the mental attitude of the individual. One must first have the desire to change in order to bring it about.

Through the analysis of the hands, it can be determined what changes are necessary and would be beneficial in order to improve the character and disposition and thus make for a complete and more successful way of life. A person must recognize a weakness in order, by effort, to overcome it.

Illustrations #1 and #2 show the changes which took place in the formation of the hands of this subject in one year and eight months. Print #1, made 8/30/43, shows the third world of the entire hand to be the strongest and in primary place. In print #2, made 4/17/45, twenty months later, after intensive study on the part of the subject, the fingers are longer and held in a more open and alert manner. The longer fingers give him more mental capacity and interest in mental subjects indicating that this subject has become more of a student and has gained in

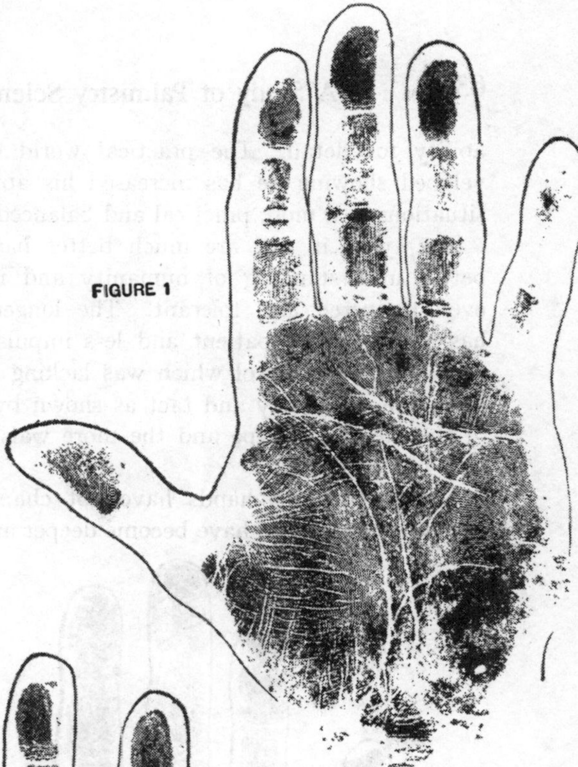

FIGURE 1

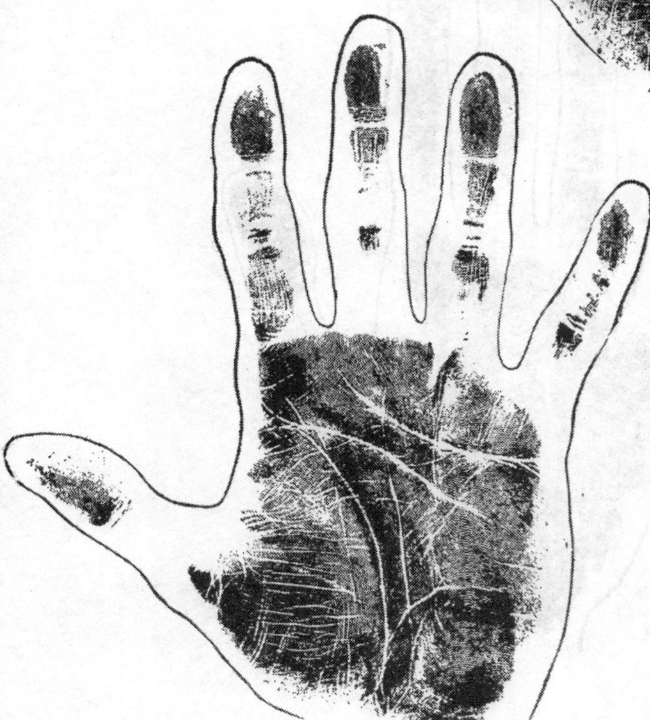

FIGURE 2

ability for detail. The practical world is also better developed showing he has increased his ability to cope with situations in a more practical and balanced manner.

The types in #2 are much better balanced giving him better understanding of humanity and making him more even tempered and tolerant. The longer fingers show he has become more patient and less impulsive. He has also developed self control which was lacking in print #1. He has more diplomacy and tact as shown by the development of the Mercurian type and the more waist like second phalanx of the thumb.

The lines in his hands have not changed to any great degree other than to have become deeper and clearer, indicat-

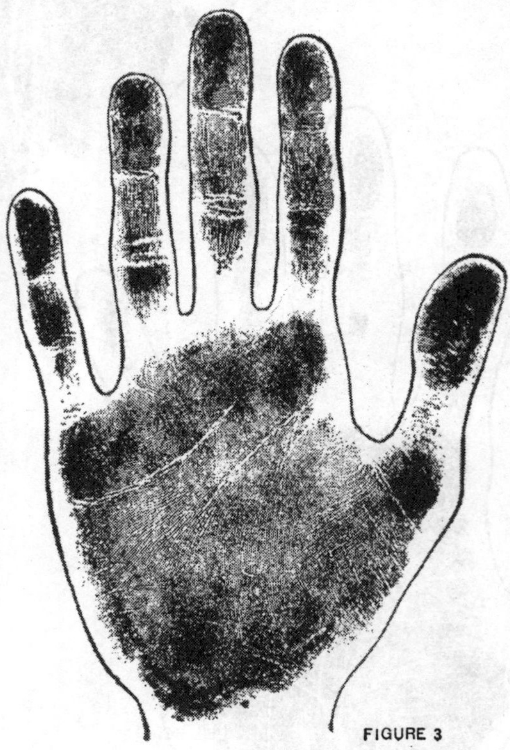

FIGURE 3

ing a more even temper and better balance. The deeper lines also give him greater physical resistance and better health.

Illustrations #3, 4, 5 show the possibility of changing, through effort, the lines of the hand. In these plates, which are a verified case, it will be noted that the lines are very fine and indefinite. This is especially shown in plate #3, which is the left hand, and in plate #4 of the right hand, both having been taken August 19, 1932. The lines in the left hand are not so apt to change as those in the right hand, though through the re-education of the subconscious mind the lines in the left hand change also. In plate #5 which is the right hand taken July 11, 1943, thirteen years later, is shown how lines can be changed by effort. The lines in #5 are generally much deeper and clearer, THE LIFE LINE HAS DEVELOPED, AND CONTINUES AROUND THE MOUNT OF VENUS TO THE BASE OF THE HAND, while in #4, the 1932 print, the life line is weak and TERMINATES HALFWAY DOWN its course through the hand. In these hands, all through the years, the mount and finger of Jupiter are very well developed. Jupiter being the primary type gives her ambition and self confidence, while the thumb gives her determination and strength of character. These qualities have enabled her, by effort, to change the lines in her hands. While the lines are still on the fine side for the size of the land, indicating that she still needs plenty of rest, she is physically much better qualified than she originally was to cope with life, and better able to enjoy a full life of service which her type combination and thumb indicates she will do. It is the strength of the types and tests in these hands which enabled her to accomplish what she has, and us to determine that she could strengthen and lengthen her lines, and consequently give her better health and greater strength.

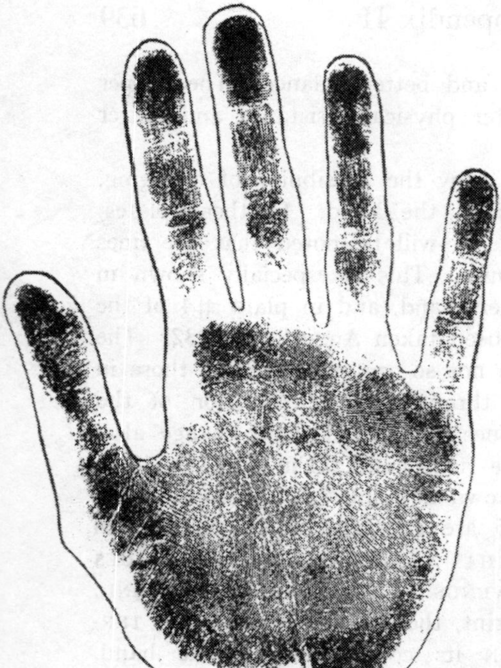

FIGURE 4

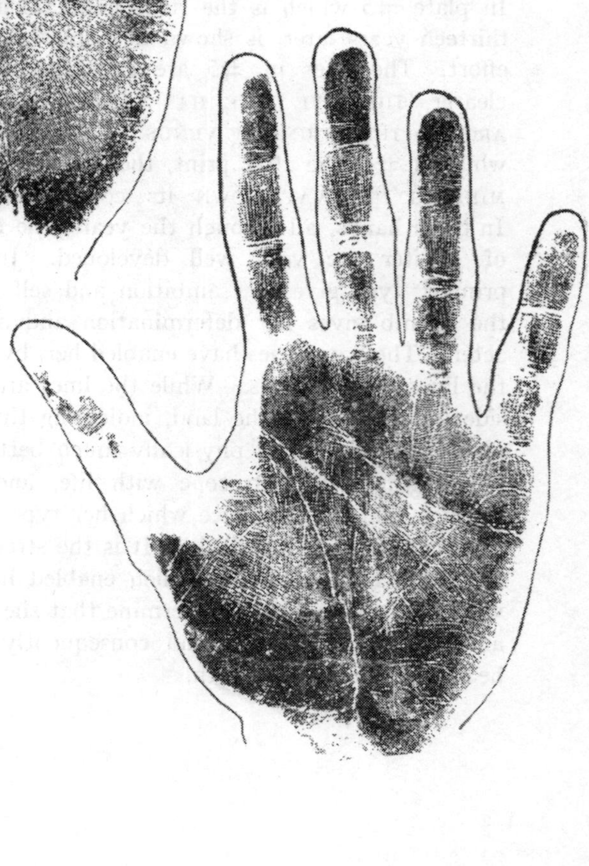

FIGURE 5

Medical Indications

There are many medical indications in the hands which our experience has shown to be very accurate. Many of these are health defects peculiar to the types and are shown in the original text. In the course of an extensive practice we have discovered NEW HEALTH INDICATIONS not peculiar to any type nor mentioned in the original text. When these have been seen we have advised clients to consult their physician and many excellent results have been obtained.

A series of small islands, illustration #6, at the end of the heart line indicate low blood pressure. This applies to the

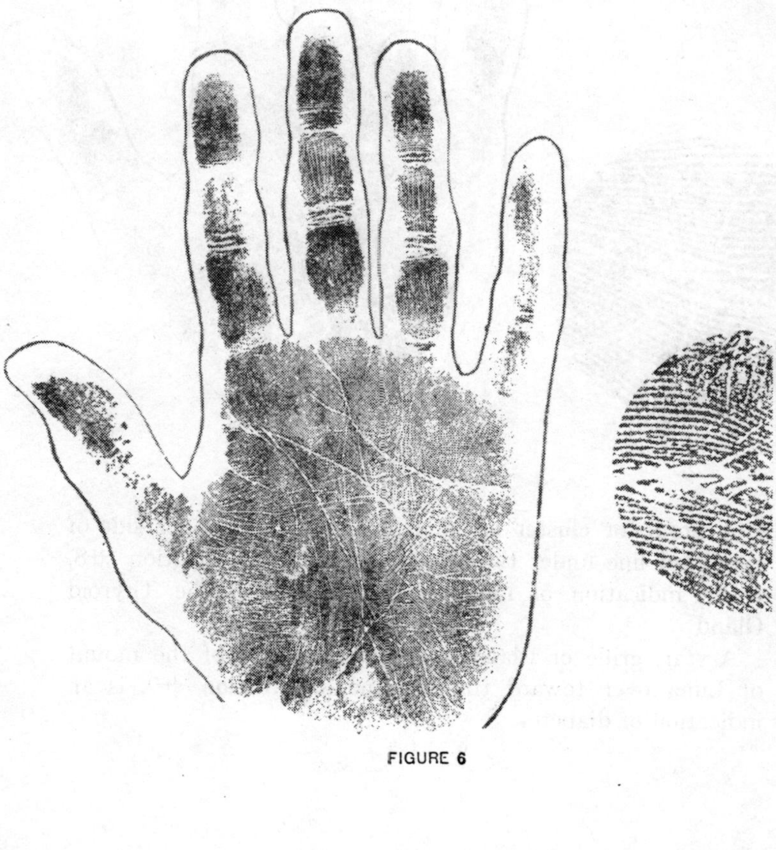

FIGURE 6

individual at any time of life. One large island at the end of the heart line, illustration #7, is an indication of high blood pressure.

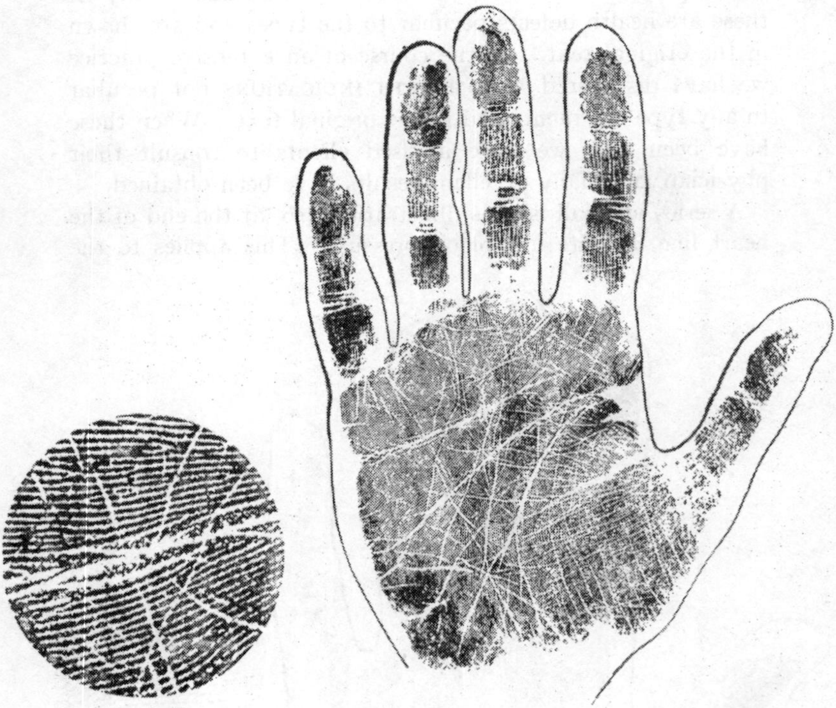

FIGURE 7

A group or cluster of small circles on the under side of the head line under the mount of Saturn, illustration #8, is an indication of improper functioning of the Thyroid Gland.

A star, grille or island on the lower third of the mount of Luna over toward the life line, illustration #9, is an indication of diabetes.

FIGURE 8

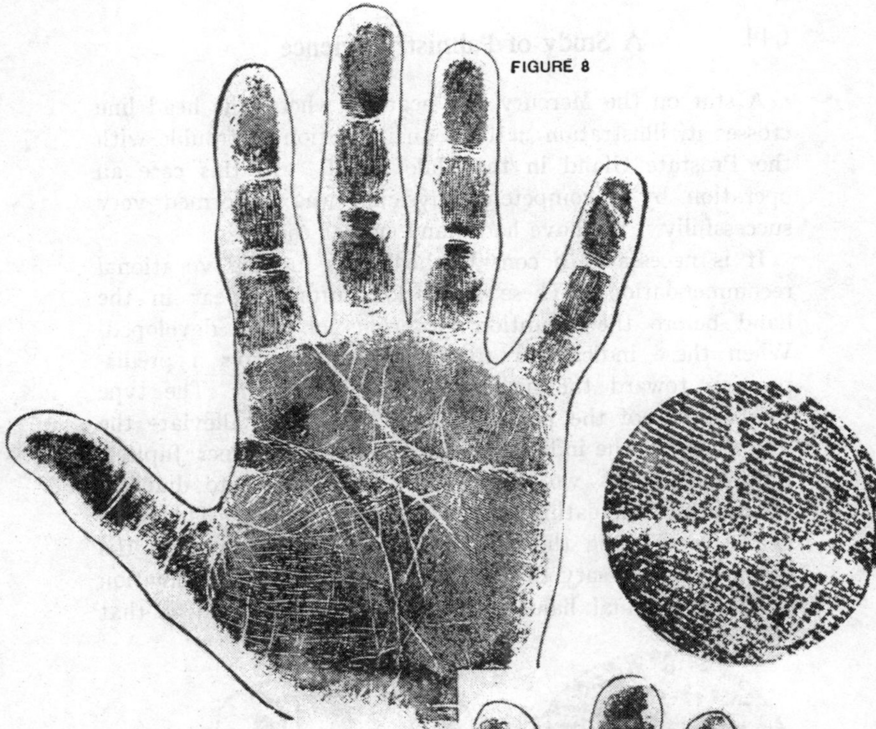

FIGURE 9

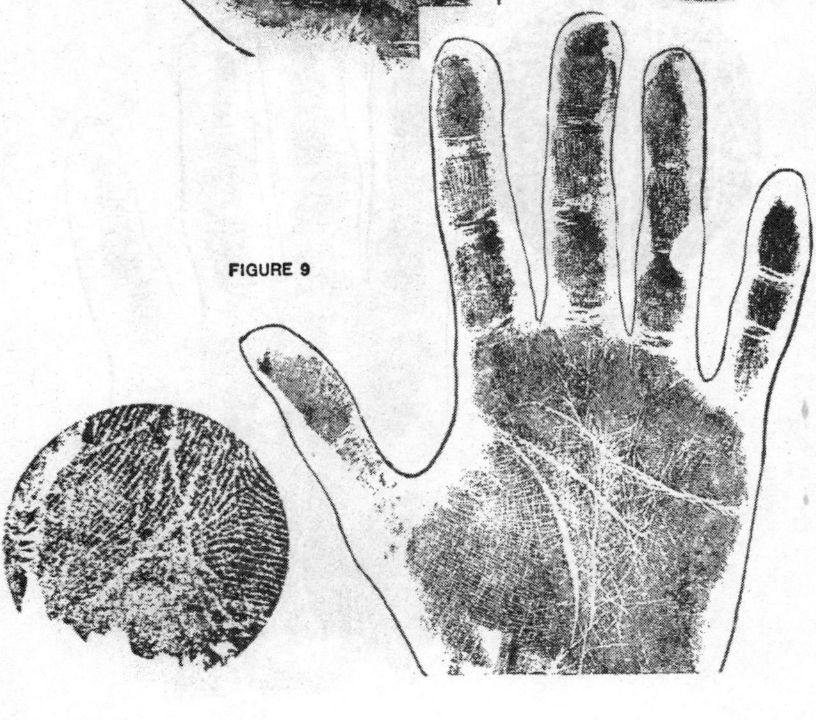

A star on the Mercury line near, or where, the head line crosses it, illustration #10, is an indication of trouble with the Prostate Gland in the Male Hand. In this case an operation by a competent physician was performed very successfully. We have had many similar cases.

It is necessary to consider health in making vocational recommendations. These indications often appear in the hand before the condition is serious or even developed. When these indications appear there is always a predisposition toward the health deficiencies shown. The type combination of the person will accentuate or alleviate the seriousness of the indication, for example; the types Jupiter, Luna and Mars wo ld be more predisposed to diabetes because of their eating habits and love of food. Therefore, before considering the lines or individual markings on the hand, it is necessary to know the type and test combination of the individual hand in order to properly analyze that hand.

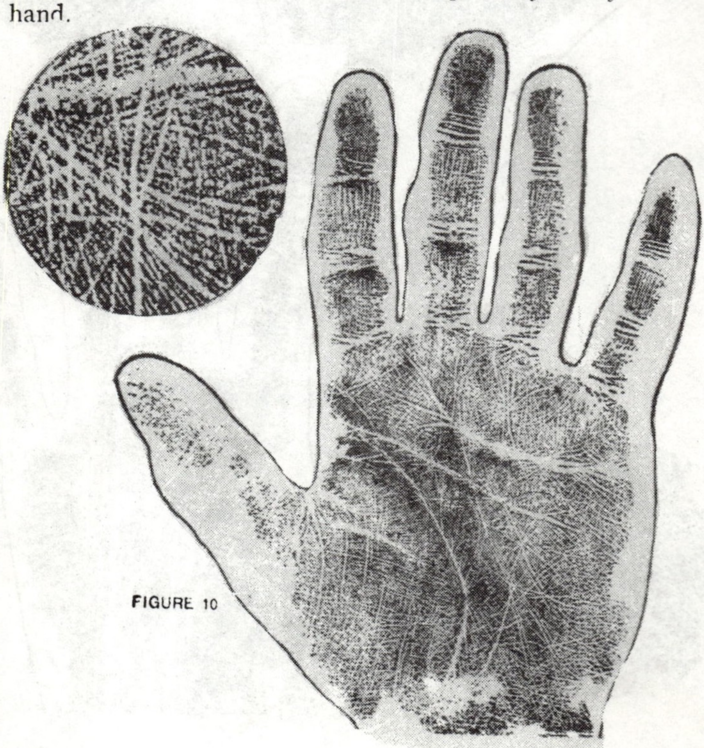

FIGURE 10